A Commentary to Hegel's *Science of Logic*

Also by David Gray Carlson

HEGEL'S THEORY OF THE SUBJECT

A Commentary to Hegel's *Science of Logic*

David Gray Carlson

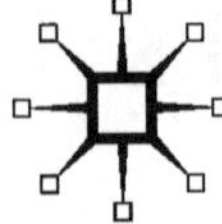

First published 2007 by
PALGRAVE MACMILLAN
Houndmills, Basingstoke, Hampshire RG21 6XS and
175 Fifth Avenue, New York, N. Y. 10010
Companies and representatives throughout the world

PALGRAVE MACMILLAN is the global academic imprint of the Palgrave Macmillan division of St. Martin's Press, LLC and of Palgrave Macmillan Ltd. Macmillan® is a registered trademark in the United States, United Kingdom and other countries. Palgrave is a registered trademark in the European Union and other countries.

ISBN-13: 978–1–4039–8628–3
ISBN-10: 1–4039–8628–2

This book is printed on paper suitable for recycling and made from fully managed and sustained forest sources.

A catalogue record for this book is available from the British Library.

Library of Congress Cataloging-in-Publication Data
Carlson, David (David Gray)
A commentary to Hegel's Science of logic / David Gray Carlson.
p. cm.
Includes bibliographical references and index.
ISBN-13: 978-1-4039-8628-3 (cloth)
ISBN-10: 1-4039-8628-2 (cloth)
1. Hegel, Georg Wilhelm Friedrich, 1770-1831. Wissenschaft der Logik.
2. Logic. I. Title.

B2942.Z7C37 2006
160—dc22

2006046893

10 9 8 7 6 5 4 3 2 1
16 15 14 13 12 11 10 09 08 07

Printed and bound in Great Britain by
Antony Rowe Ltd, Chippenham and Eastbourne

For Jeanne, my inspiration.

Contents

Acknowledgements

I have incurred countless debts in producing this work. I owe much to eight years worth of students at the Benjamin N. Cardozo School of Law in New York who have suffered through a seminar on the *Science of Logic* and who never failed to teach me something about the subject. I also owe a debt of gratitude to the Cardozo Law School itself for allowing the course to be taught in the first place and for a research professorship that helped me finish this work in 2005. Thanks go to the editors of the *Cardozo Law Review*, who worked diligently to improve the preliminary versions of first nine chapters of this book, to my beloved partner Jeanne Schroeder, whose expertise in Hegel and Jacques Lacan (Hegel's modern disciple) have been a *sine qua non* of this project, to Arthur Jacobson, without whose patience and prodigious knowledge of Hegel and mathematics I could never have fathomed Hegel's seemingly endless commentary on the calculus, to Jon Heiner, who skeptically read this manuscript from an empiricist perspective, to Drucilla Cornell, who first convinced me that Hegel was worth the considerable investment in learning his vocabulary, to Cyn Gabriel, who worked diligently and faithfully for years on the artwork for this project, to John Burbidge, Stephen Houlgate, Jean Hyppolyte, Herbert Marcuse, Robert Pippen, Stanley Rosen, Richard Dien Winfield, and Slavoj Žižek (to mention just a few), whose works have been essential in expanding my understanding of the *Science of Logic*.

Introduction

> The system of logic is the realm of shadows [*Reich der Schatten*], the world of simple essentialities freed from all sensuous concreteness.[1]

This book explains in pictographic terms precisely how Hegel's monumental *Science of Logic* (*SL*) functions – one step at a time. As it now stands, few have ever mastered the *SL* since it was published between 1812 and 1816[2] and revised in 1831.[3] In the anglophone world, that number is small indeed. Yet it is Hegel's major work against which all his other, more accessible work must be read.[4] Unfortunately, the *SL* is the *single densest book ever published*. No one who has peeked under its covers would dare dispute this claim. Yet, thanks to the pictures I will draw, the secrets of the *SL* will yield themselves forth.

Experienced Hegelians will not miss the paradox of pictifying Hegel, the outspoken opponent of "picture thinking." I am unabashed by the paradox. The pictures I present eerily replicate Hegel's logical moves,

---

[1] G.W.F. HEGEL, HEGEL'S SCIENCE OF LOGIC 58 (A.V. Miller trans. 1969).

[2] The first edition was published in three parts: Being (1812), Essence (1813) (these two parts comprising the Objective Logic) and the Subjective Logic (1816). GIACOMO RINALDI, A HISTORY AND INTERPRETATION OF THE LOGIC OF HEGEL 103 (1992).

[3] The "second preface" was finished only one week before Hegel died in 1831. JOHN W. BURBIDGE, HEGEL ON LOGIC AND RELIGION: THE REASONABLENESS OF CHRISTIANITY 11 (1992).

[4] QUENTIN LAUER, ESSAYS IN HEGELIAN DIALECTIC 114 (1977) ("unquestionably the keystone of the entire Hegelian system").

sometimes quite expressly. They will prove a most useful tool by which to interpret Hegel's sibylline text.[5]

In portraying the system pictorially, I try to intrude upon the logical progress as little as possible, as is only right, since, according to Hegel, the Logic travels a strictly necessary path; anything *I* might add would be "contingent" material.[6] Peter Goodrich has written, "The systematizer is always a follower and in a sense a moderate who defers to the author of the system itself."[7] This describes my task. I try to follow Hegel as closely as I can, giving him the benefit of the doubt wherever possible, untangling his dense yet precise prose[8] so that ordinary mortals can follow it,[9] and defending him from his critics whenever they trouble to address Hegel's exact logical analysis.[10]

Alas, the work before you is scarcely shorter than Hegel's seemingly interminable work. This is because *Hegel wrote too quickly*. His work is too compact. No one took the principle of "writing for the experts" to a higher plateau than Hegel. For this reason, when approaching the *SL*, "the reader has to develop an intellectual slow-motion procedure, to slow down the tempo at the cloudy places in such a way that they

---

[5] *See* WALTER KAUFMANN, HEGEL: A REINTERPRETATION 143 (1978) ("Almost like Shakespeare, Hegel often thinks in pictures . . . .").

[6] "Hegel himself, indeed, was opposed on principle to any such preliminary exposition of principles. Learning to philosophize, he thought, is like learning to swim: you cannot do it on dry land. Truth is the whole as result, and for the student it lies ahead. He must watch it develop itself . . . " G.R.G. MURE, THE PHILOSOPHY OF HEGEL ix (1965). Mure alludes to a famous Hegelian dictum: "But to seek to know before we know is as absurd as the wise resolution of Scholasticus, not to venture into the water until he had learned to swim." G.W.F. HEGEL, HEGEL'S LOGIC § 80 (William Wallace trans., 1975).

[7] Peter Goodrich, *Anti-Teubner: Autopoiesis, Paradox, and the Theory of Law*, 13 SOC. EPIST. 197, 203 (1999).

[8] Hegel's prose "turns out to have a startling precision of its own." TERRY PINKARD, HEGEL'S DIALECTIC 3 (1988).

[9] Clark Butler has called this an "arid approach to Hegel." CLARK BUTLER, HEGEL'S LOGIC: BETWEEN DIALECTIC AND HISTORY 6 (1996). Nevertheless, it is the one I embrace here.

[10] In this endeavor I hazard what Karl Marx had no time to do. In a letter to Engels, he wrote: "In the *method* of treatment the fact that by mere accident I again glanced through Hegel's *Logic* has been of great service to me . . . If there should ever be time for such work again, I would greatly like to make accessible to the ordinary human intelligence, in two or three printer's sheets, what is *rational* in the method which Hegel discovered but at the same time enveloped in mysticism . . . " Peter Singer, *Hegel*, in GERMAN PHILOSOPHERS 109, 196 (1997).

do not evaporate and their motion can be seen."[11] I hope my diagrams slow the progress down so that every step can be isolated and evaluated.

Who was Hegel? I will say the minimum.[12] Born in 1770, Hegel was an extraordinary (*i.e.*, "adjunct") professor, a pro-French newspaper editor, a high school principal, and eventually (after a stopoff at Heidelberg) a chaired professor of philosophy at the University of Berlin, where he was generally acknowledged to be the greatest living philosopher.[13] Yet, soon after he died, his work lapsed into obscurity – perhaps because it was so difficult. If he was remembered at all, it was because Karl Marx famously turned him on his head.[14]

In modern times, Hegel's reputation had fallen so precipitately low that it became a term of contempt to call a theory Hegelian.[15] Yet by the turn of the millennium, it has dawned on many that Hegel had foreseen virtually all philosophical developments that followed him – and had successfully critiqued them.[16] Today, when it is fashionable to style oneself "post-modern," it is foolish indeed (though very common) to undertake a philosophical project without a thorough grounding in the Hegelian method.[17]

---

[11] THEODOR W. ADORNO, HEGEL: THREE STUDIES 123 (1999).

[12] "One might venture to say that few philosophers have been subjected to so minute a documentation, ranging from close analysis of his schoolboy notebooks to every draft of his unpublished university lectures." STANLEY ROSEN, G.W.F. HEGEL: AN INTRODUCTION TO THE SCIENCE OF WISDOM 3 (1974). A monumental biography of Hegel has recently appeared. *See* TERRY PINKARD, HEGEL: A BIOGRAPHY (2000); *see also* JACQUES D'HONDT, HEGEL IN HIS TIME: BERLIN, 1818-1831 (John Burbidge trans., 1988). An excellent history of the *SL* itself and its relations to the abundant drafts and unpublished manuscripts that survive is RINALDI, *supra* note 2.

[13] KAUFMANN, *supra* note 5, at 143 ("Since Hegel's death there has probably never been a time when there was any widespread agreement that some one individual was unquestionably the greatest living philosopher").

[14] 1 KARL MARX, CAPITAL 20 (Samuel Moore & Edward Aveling trans. 1967) ("With [Hegel] it is standing on its head. It must be turned right side up again, if you would discover the rational kernel within the mystical shell.").

[15] "Hegel's writings have so long been shunned and despised, and his theories so commonly ridiculed as mere fantasy and paradox, that few are likely to approach with tolerance any attempt to rehabilitate him. The term "Hegelian" applied to any philosophical essay has become one of opprobrium and almost of abuse in some philosophical circles, and many academic philosophers would shrink from research into, or serious criticism of, Hegel's philosophy, as endangering their professional reputations." ERROL E. HARRIS, AN INTERPRETATION OF THE LOGIC OF HEGEL xi (1983).

[16] *See id.* at 61 ("astonishingly prophetic").

[17] "Hegel's *Logic* is not some relic from a bygone age of naive metaphysical

A word of warning: the *SL* is not to be confused with a later, much shorter work often called the *Encyclopedia Logic* (*EL*).[18] The *EL*[19] is part of the so-called Encyclopedia, Hegel's attempt to describe all knowledge. The two books are quite different. I refer to the *EL* from time to time, where useful. The book now in the reader's hands, however, is strictly an explication of the *SL*.

The major contribution of the current book, if any, is that it reduces every move in Hegel's logic to a discrete diagram. In all, there are precisely 79 official logical progressions, organized in groups of three.[20] Each official move is diagrammed in a "Figure." Thus, Figure 1(c) (Becoming) is the third sub-step of the first step of the Logic. Figure 2(a) (Determinate Being as Such) would be the first sub-step of the second stage. Other drawings will be offered, but, if they are not labeled a "Figure," they are not official steps of the Logic. Rather they represent some digression by Hegel or perhaps by myself.

Hegel usually memorializes each official move with a distinct name. To help remind you when I refer to the official steps, I shall capitalize the term. However, if I am quoting from Hegel's English translator, I will reproduce the language exactly as he sets it forth. Nothing very significant, however, is intended in my capitalization policy. It is just a reminder that certain terms have won official status in the logical progression, while certain others (*e.g.*, concrete, rationality, or "being-within-self") have not. Certain commonly used terms ("determinateness") win official status, but given the very commonness of such terms, I capitalize them only when there is some specific reference to their place in the logical system.

Where quotations are followed by a parenthesized number, I am

---

speculation or grandiose system-building but *the* quintessentially modern philosophy and the model for all post-Hegelian thinkers." STEPHEN HOULGATE, THE OPENING OF HEGEL'S *LOGIC* 39 (2006).

[18] *Supra* note 6. It is occasionally maintained that the *EL* is the more authoritative statement of Hegel's philosophy because it is published later in time. TOM ROCKMORE, ON HEGEL'S EPISTEMOLOGY AND CONTEMPORARY PHILOSOPHY 30 (1996). But the *SL* is the definitive work. The *EL* should be taken for what it is – a guide to students. Much of the intricacy in the *SL* is omitted, and often the results of the *EL* are merely announced. *See* ROBERT B. PIPPIN, HEGEL'S IDEALISM: THE SATISFACTIONS OF SELF-CONSCIOUSNESS 213 (1989); John W. Burbidge, *Hegel's Conception of Logic*, in THE CAMBRIDGE COMPANION TO HEGEL 93 (Frederick C. Beiser ed. 1993).

[19] All citations are to the Wallace translation, *supra* note 6.

[20] Others count differently. BUTLER, *supra* note 10, at 287 (twelve definitions of the absolute); G.R.G. MURE, A STUDY OF HEGEL'S LOGIC 371-2 (1950) (72 categories).

citing to Arnold Vincent Miller's excellent translation[21] of the *SL*.[22] Where quotation marks are not followed by any such citation, I am either using "scare quotes" for ironic purposes, or perhaps I am referring to some snippet from a longer passage from Hegel that I have just quoted in full. Perhaps I am indulging in anthropomorphism,[23] allowing the concepts themselves, like the stones of Rome, to rise and speak. I trust the reader will be able to tell the difference.

Hegel himself warned that the Logic could not be described in mere introductory material. (43)[24] Therefore, I largely resist the temptation. Let's proceed, then, to watch how Hegel's *SL* unfolds.

---

[21] Miller recounts the history of his translation in *Defending Hegel's Philosophy of Nature*, in HEGEL AND NEWTONIANISM 103 (Michael John Petry ed., 1993).

[22] I cite occasionally, where useful, to a German edition of the *SL*. G.W.F. HEGEL, WISSENSCHAFT DER LOGIK 41 (Georg Lasson ed., 1975) (two volumes). These citations will appear in brackets.

[23] Anthropomorphism is peculiarly suited to the explication of Hegelian philosophy. John Findlay has remarked, "My images will antagonize many, and seem anthropomorphic, but what they picture is the varied forms of that distinction-without-separation which analytic thought hates, and which is the central feature of Hegelianism." John N. Findlay, *The Hegelian Treatment of Biology and Life*, in HEGEL IN THE SCIENCES 87, 90 (Robert S. Cohen & Marx W. Wartofsky 1984).

[24] According to the opening words of the *Phenomenology*:

> It is customary to preface a work with an explanation of the author's aim, why he wrote the book, and the relationship in which he believes it to stand to other earlier or contemporary treatises on the same subject. In the case of a philosophical work, however, such an explanation seems not only superfluous but, in view of the nature of the subject-matter, even inappropriate and misleading.

G.W.F. HEGEL, PHENOMENOLOGY OF SPIRIT ¶ 1 (A.V. Miller trans. 1977).

PART I
QUALITY

1
Being-Nothing-Becoming

A. Pure Being

Our journey begins with the simplest of simples – Pure Being. Hegel's opening words are: "*Being, pure being*, without any further determination." (82) This anacoluthon "lacks a verb – for Hegel cannot even say that being *is*."[1] Too simple for something so active as a verb, Pure Being is immediacy *as such*, taken on its own terms without reference to anything else.[2]

This radical "immediacy" (*unmittelbarkeit*)[3] must be compared to the immediacy on display in Hegel's *Phenomenology of Spirit*.[4] Indeed, in his introduction, Hegel refers to the *Phenomenology* as a necessary

---

[1] ANDREW HAAS, HEGEL AND THE PROBLEM OF MULTIPLICITY xxiii (2000). An anacoluthon is a sentence lacking grammatical sequence. According to Adorno, Hegel's opening anacoluthon "tries with Hegelian cunning to find a way out of the predicament that 'indeterminate immediacy' . . . would thereby receive a definition through which the sentence would contradict itself." THEODOR W. ADORNO, HEGEL: THREE STUDIES 120 (1999).

[2] *See* Arnold Vincent Miller, *Defending Hegel's Philosophy of Nature*, in HEGEL AND NEWTONIANISM 103 (Michael John Petry ed., 1993) ("it is particularly important to note that in Hegel's vocabulary *being* nearly always implies immediacy").

[3] *Unmittelbar* is a word Hegel uses "lavishly." ADORNO, THREE STUDIES, *supra* note 1, at 114.

[4] G.W.F. HEGEL, PHENOMENOLOGY OF SPIRIT (A.V. Miller trans. 1977). Arguably Hegel only wrote two books: the *Phenomenology* and the *SL*. Everything else is an essay, lecture, or student guide. HANS-GEORG GADAMER, HEGEL'S DIALECTIC: FIVE HERMENEUTICAL STUDIES 75 (Christopher Smith trans., 1976).

presupposition to Logic.

The *Phenomenology* starts with consciousness "immediately" perceiving an object. Immediacy means that consciousness is aware of nothing that comes between the object and *knowledge* of the object. The object and knowledge of it are taken to be the same thing. Such an immediacy, however, is *not* purely immediate but rather is covertly mediated by its parts. By the end of the *Phenomenology*, however, consciousness abolishes itself in favor of absolute or pure knowing.

> Absolute knowing is the *truth* of every mode of consciousness because, as the course of the *Phenomenology* showed, it is only in absolute knowing that the separation of the *object* from the *certainty of itself* is completely eliminated: truth is now equated with certainty and this certainty with truth. (49)

Consciousness, then, reveals itself to be nothing else but *impure* knowing and therefore no adequate foundation for philosophy.[5] Pure knowing, in contrast, "ceases itself to be knowledge," (69) because knowledge insists on a distinction between the *knower* and the *known*.

The *SL* takes up where the *Phenomenology* left off – with a purer immediacy than consciousness comprehends.[6] "[P]ure science presupposes liberation from the opposition of consciousness." (49) Pure Being is no *unity* of distinguishable parts. It is immediacy before there *are* any parts to break it up.[7]

---

[5] Marx, Kierkegaard *et al.* therefore miss the punchline of the *Phenomenology*. "Instead of properly regarding absolute knowing as the collapse of the posited structure of consciousness, they have commonly interpreted it as a determinate cognition that somehow unites subject and object such that its knowing both comprehends and constitutes things as they are in themselves . . ." RICHARD DIEN WINFIELD, OVERCOMING FOUNDATIONS: STUDIES IN SYSTEMATIC PHILOSOPHY 26 (1989).

[6] *See* JEAN HYPPOLITE, GENESIS AND STRUCTURE OF HEGEL'S *PHENOMENOLOGY OF SPIRIT* 588 (Samuel Cherniak & John Heckman trans., 1974) ("in the *Logic* the identity of being and self is implicit or presupposed at the beginning and progressively becomes explicit, whereas in the *Phenomenology*, this identity is the problem which must be resolved . . . ").

[7] William Maker notes Dieter Henrich's criticism that immediacy is not immediate because it is the negation of mediation. Negations are never immediate. WILLIAM MAKER, PHILOSOPHY WITHOUT FOUNDATIONS: RETHINKING HEGEL 94 (1994), quoting Dieter Henrich, *Anfang und Methode der Logike*, in HEGEL IM CONTEXT 85 (1971). This is wrong, Maker claims; it was the function of the *Phenomenology* to refute the givenness of objects as presented to consciousness. Yet Hegel confesses to Henrich's point when he writes, "Simple immediacy is itself an expression of reflection and contains a reference to its distinction from what is mediated." (69) In my view, Hegel understands well that Pure Being is a failure and is ultimately a reference to determinacy. Hegel argues that

We can draw this elementary move in an elementary way. Figure 1(a) shows the beginning in Pure Being. In all the Figures that follow, the left side of the diagram represents "being." The right side of the diagram will represent "nothing." The fact that Pure Being is represented by a simple circle leaning to the left signifies that Pure Being is an immediacy.

Figure 1(a)
Pure Being

In the pure light of Being, nothing can be distinguished. We need some shade, some lines, to make anything out. As Hegel puts it:

> Pure light and pure darkness are two voids which are the same thing. Something can be distinguished only in determinate light or darkness . . . [F]or this reason, it is only darkened light and illuminated darkness which have within themselves the moment of difference and are, therefore, *determinate* being. (93)

Just as one needs a *contrast* between light and dark to see anything, so it is with Pure Being. Pure Being will require the darkness of Pure Nothing before it can be thought at all. So far, everything is indeterminate. In fact Pure Being is *indeterminacy as such*.

In Pure Being, we think nothing. But this is what we would perceive in a world of pure nothing. Hence, we might as well say that Pure Being *is* Pure Nothing. They are *identical*. "Being, the indeterminate immediate, is in fact *nothing*." (82)

If Pure Being and Nothing are the same, where does their *difference* come from? Certainly there is a *belief* that Being and Nothing are different, but belief counts for naught in logic. Difference must be *inferred* if it is to count.[8] Does Pure Being – the starting point – create difference? The answer is, certainly not. Pure Being "has no diversity within itself . . . It would not be held fast in its purity if it contained any determination." (82) The origin of difference precedes Pure Being, but this is best discussed in the context of Hegel's introductory essay, *With What Must Science Begin?*[9]

---

beginnings are by their nature failures; otherwise they would be *results*, not beginnings.

[8] As Gadamer (or his translator) puts it, *belief* "is not in the sequence of this exposition." GADAMER, *supra* note 5, at 88. Here, the translator reworks Miller's translation, which states: "Opinion, however, is a form of subjectivity which is not proper to an exposition of this kind." (92) ("Aber das Meinen ist eine Form des Subjektiven, das nicht in diese Reihe der Darstellung gehört" [I:78])

[9] *Infra* at 26-39.

Self-equality. Pure Being is "equal only to itself." (82) It is not equal *to another*. This should make sense. So far, there is nothing *but* Pure Being. Nothing else is allowed to be distinguished.[10] Otherwise, we have smuggled in foreign "determinateness," which is not yet permitted.

To the ear of common sense, this is a strange phrase. To be equal to oneself: is that not always true by definition, as in $A = A$? Here A is *not* equal to itself. Rather, it is equal to another A, with different time-space coordinates than the first A. One cannot even express true self-equality using an equal sign, because an equal sign is a mediating term between two other terms. So far we have only one term – Pure Being, which is "self-identical."[11] Self-identity is usually an insult in Hegel's Logic, yet, eventually, it is spirit's triumph that it becomes authentically self-identical.[12]

"*For us.*" Before moving on to Pure Nothing, I would like to raise an objection that may have occurred to some readers. Hegel implies that Pure Being cannot be thought by concrete human intellect. "*Being* is simple as *immediate* being; for that reason it is only something *meant* or *intended* and we cannot say of it what it is." (601)[13] "Whatever is conceivable is complex."[14] But you may object, "I am sitting here *thinking* about Pure Being. How can Hegel claim these things cannot be thought?"[15]

Hegel would respond that here you *are* thinking, but this is inconsistent with the rules of Pure Being. Absolute knowing "has sublated [*i.e.*, erased] all reference to an other." (69)[16] Since it is without distinction, it has ceased to be knowledge. "[W]hat is present is only *simple immediacy* . . . being and nothing else, without any

---

[10] Hegel says that Pure Being "is also not unequal relatively to another." (82) This double negative should be read to mean that *there is no other*, not that there *is* an other to which Pure Being is "not unequal."

[11] *See* EL § 193, at 257 ("being is nothing more than simple self-relation").

[12] Spirit is Hegel's name for the entire system of thought thinking itself. On spirit, see R.C. Solomon, *Hegel's Concept of "Geist,"* in HEGEL: A COLLECTION OF CRITICAL ESSAYS 237 (Alasdair MacIntyre, ed., 1972).

[13] *See also* EL at § 86 (Pure Being "is not to be felt, or perceived by sense, or pictured in the imagination.").

[14] ERROL E. HARRIS, AN INTERPRETATION OF THE LOGIC OF HEGEL 78 (1983).

[15] This is a poignant question because Hegel vigorously criticizes Kant's discovery that we can know nothing of the thing in itself – the object beyond phenomenal experience of it. Hegel's point is that Kant knows *all* about the thing in itself because he is naming it and describing its properties. Since we can think the *thing-in-itself*, we are entitled to know why we can't think *Pure Being*.

[16] On sublation, see *infra* at 29-31.

further specification and filling." (69) Pure Being precludes an other that thinks. This means *you*, among other things.[17]

If Pure Being were really here before us (and not just in our thoughts) we would be obliterated – sucked into a very black hole. Indeed, the very fact that we are thinking at all is proof that Pure Being is not before us. Rather, it is apparent that Pure Being *has already* passed away. Pure Being is never before us. "Hegel says explicitly that not being but having been (*Gewordensein*) is to be grasped as a becoming."[18]

To sound a Cartesian note, we think, therefore Pure Being/Nothing has long since passed on. This is a good thing, given our aversion to obliteration. Self-conscious entities are much further down the road than Pure Being. Yet, inevitably, we are the audience that witnesses the unfolding of Logic. Naturally, we have to admit that *we* are advanced, thinking beings, engaged in the archeology of our own being.[19]

Hegel reserves the phrase "for us" to indicate that he is breaking faith with the strict logical progression in order to speak to his audience. What is "for us" is like a prologue in a Shakespeare play, suited in like condition to the argument. The audience can hear the prologue, but the players are oblivious. Similarly, "for us," Pure Being can be thought – here we are doing it! But "for itself," Pure Being will not suffer us to contemplate it.

Several of the "remarks" following "The Unity of Being and Nothing" are designed precisely to warn readers of the rules of Pure Being. In the presence of Pure Being, there can be no determinate thing that thinks. Any attempt to smuggle in thought (or any other "determinate being") is, so far, illegitimate.

---

[17] *See* William Maker, *Beginning*, in ESSAYS ON HEGEL'S LOGIC 36 (George di Giovanni ed., 1990) ("given what consciousness instantiates, we can see that its suspension is specifically, indeed, preeminently relevant to the beginning of presuppositionless science").

[18] HERBERT MARCUSE, HEGEL'S ONTOLOGY AND THE THEORY OF HISTORICITY 15 (Seyla Benhabib trans. 1987).

[19] This is Henrich's objection: by negating mediation, Hegel implicitly appeals to the logic of consciousness (*i.e.*, Reflection). *See* Henrich, *supra* note 7, at 80. Such criticisms apparently date back to 1812, when the *SL* first appeared. Of such critiques, Clark Butler writes, "hermeneutic self-alienation into a transcended definition of the absolute does not require that we abstract from all we know. It requires only that we project ourselves out of our own definition (or nondefinition) of the absolute . . . and that we allow that definition to analyze and critique itself . . . ." CLARK BUTLER, HEGEL'S LOGIC: BETWEEN DIALECTIC AND HISTORY 28 (1996).

B. Pure Nothing

> The proposition that Being and Nothing is [sic] the same seems so paradoxical to the imagination . . . that it is perhaps taken for a joke . . . No great expenditure of wit is needed to make fun of the maxim that Being and Nothing are the same . . . If Being and
>
> Nothing are identical . . . it follows that it makes no difference whether my home, my property, the air I breathe, this city, the sun, the law, mind, God, are or are not . . .[20]

Pure Being is Pure Nothing. Since Pure Being is self-identical, so is Pure Nothing. To illustrate it, we place a second circle to the right side of Figure 1(b). Rightward leaning represents nothingness, just as the leftward leaning represents being.

Figure 1(b)
Pure Nothing

Of Pure Nothing, Hegel remarks, "In so far as intuiting or thinking can be mentioned here, it counts as a distinction whether something or *nothing* is intuited." (82) But thinking *cannot* be mentioned here. Thinking stands opposed both to Pure Being and Nothing. If you have a thought, you have already trafficked in distinction, contrary to the premises of Pure Being.[21]

Nevertheless, Hegel breaks character and speaks "for us," to remind us that we probably *believe* that "something" is different from nothing. Indeed, what could be more radically different from *Pure* Being than *Pure* Nothing? Yet, paradoxically, they are the same!

Still speaking "for us," Hegel sounds the note of an important maxim: *nothing is, after all, something*. Nothing *is* – a paradox! According to Hegel, "To intuit or think nothing has, therefore, a meaning; both [being and nothing] are distinguished and thus nothing *is* (exists) in our intuiting or thinking." (82) That Nothing *is* – this paradox reflects the claim that there is no difference between Pure Being and Nothing.

---

[20] EL § 88.

[21] How we can proceed beyond Pure Being, if, in it, we are obliterated? Undoubtedly, our relation to Pure Being is ambiguous. We are thinking the unthinkable. Furthermore, we can only borrow on advanced concepts – such as human beings who think and who stand over against Pure Being in violation of Pure Being's rules – to move the process along. Hegel admits this, from time to time, as we shall see.

C. Becoming

(a) The Unity of Being and Nothing

"*Pure being* and *pure nothing* are, therefore, the same," (82) Hegel writes.[22] We started with Pure Being but it was Pure Nothing. The two moments[23] would seem to be the most opposite of opposites. They are "absolutely distinct, and yet . . . they are unseparated and inseparable and . . . each immediately *vanishes in its opposite*." (83) That is to say, we – the audience for whom the Logic performs – contemplate the first two steps and we notice that, being *two* steps, they are distinct from each other. But this is "a merely fancied or imagined difference." (92) In fact, the two steps are one. Yet change is apparent. What is changing into what? It is *not* the case that Pure Being *changes* into Pure Nothing, if these are the *same* – not different. Change requires difference.

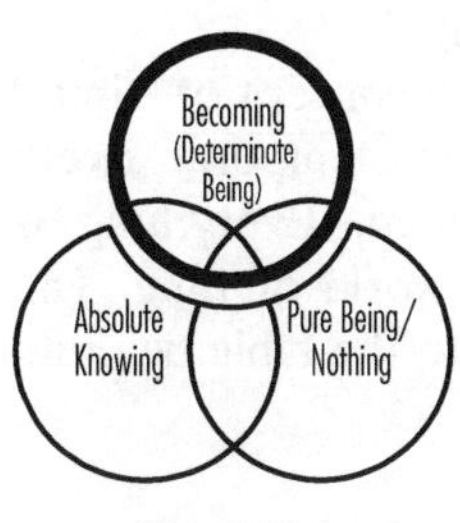

Figure 1(c)
Becoming

Pure Being fails to materialize when we try to fix it in thought. What modulates is the resolve to think Pure Being and the failure to have a thought at all. The fact that we notice movement allows us to produce Figure 1(c).[24] In this diagram, the concept of change as such can be "distinguished" from its predecessor. Change is a complex entity. It mediates Being/Nothing and what

---

[22] This sentence could be translated as: Pure Being and Pure Nothing *is* the same ("Das reine Sein und das reine Nichts ist also dasselbe" [I:67]). Some read Hegel as making a deliberate grammatical mistake to emphasize the inability of ordinary grammar to account for speculative philosophy, which requires *simultaneous* immediacy and mediation. JOHN W. BURBIDGE, HEGEL ON LOGIC AND RELIGION: THE REASONABLENESS OF CHRISTIANITY 14 (1992) ("The singular verb reinforces the content of the sentence to suggest that there is not movement [between Pure Being and Nothing] at all, but simply a single identity"); HAAS, *supra* note 1, at 97.

[23] Strictly speaking, "[t]he indeterminate moments of becoming are not true moments: they cannot be concretely specified, since such moments 'are always changing into each other, and reciprocally cancelling each other.'" ROBERT B. PIPPIN, HEGEL'S IDEALISM: THE SATISFACTIONS OF SELF-CONSCIOUSNESS 189 (1989). Hegel, however, calls them moments. (105)

[24] According to Terry Pinkard, "The opposite of nothing turns out not to be being, but determinate being (a such and such). Only as determinate being is being not nothing." TERRY PINKARD, HEGEL'S DIALECTIC 31 (1988). It is true that Being is not Nothing when Being is Determinate, but it is wrong to say that Nothing and Determinate Being are *opposites*. Nothing *has* no opposite. It is the *same* as Being.

precedes it, and is simultaneously different from them.[25] In Figure 1(c), we encounter *distinction*.

From the beginning, then, Hegel's logic is a play between (a) *stasis*, (b) *movement*, and, in addition, (c) the unity of stasis and movement.[26] Becoming is the first name of that unity.

Time. Of this failure to hold the poles of Being and Nothing apart, Hegel says: "What is the truth is neither being nor nothing, but that being – does not pass over but has passed over – into nothing." (82-3) This remark has a temporal flavor to it. Since logic moves of its own accord, it already moved into Pure Being/Nothing. We can never observe it *now* because it "always already" happened.

Here is a good "time" to warn readers about the concept of "time." Logic does not occur in time. Logical relations are atemporal. Every step occurs simultaneously with every other step. Everything is "present." Human beings, however, do live in a world of time. The "time" it takes to accomplish the steps is brought to the table by finite thinking beings.[27]

---

[25] *See* Thomas J. Bole, III, *The Cogency of the* Logic's *Argumentation: Securing the Dialectic's Claim to Justify Categories*, in HEGEL RECONSIDERED: BEYOND METAPHYSICS AND THE AUTHORITARIAN STATE 111 (H. Tristram Engelhardt, Jr., & Terry Pinkard eds., 1994) (becoming reflects "both the indistinguishability and the intended distinction of being and nothing").

[26] JOHN W. BURBIDGE, ON HEGEL'S LOGIC: FRAGMENTS OF A COMMENTARY 41 (1981). ("the double process by which *being* vanishes into *nothing* and *nothing* vanishes into *being* itself vanishes and leaves a tranquil but comprehensive result") (footnote omitted); HARRIS, LOGIC, *supra* note 14, at 95 ("Their unity is thus a perpetual oscillation, a perpetual timeless activity or discursus, which requires the self-identity of each, their mutual opposition and their mutual identity, all at once"); JEAN HYPPOLITE, LOGIC AND EXISTENCE 61 (Leonard Lawlor and Amit Sen trans., 1997) (truth is "simple rest as well as bacchanalian revel. This very duality is constitutive of the dialectic."). It is no surprise that Hegel showers "deep-thinking Heraclitus" (83) with praise:

> The advance requisite and made by Heraclitus is the progression from being as the first immediate thought, to the category of becoming as the second. This is the first concrete, the absolute, as in it the unity of opposites [exists]. Thus with Heraclitus the philosophic Idea is to be met with in its speculative form . . . Heraclitus was thus universally esteemed a deep philosopher and even was decried as such . . . there is no proposition of Heraclitus which I have not adopted in my Logic.

1 HEGEL'S LECTURES ON THE HISTORY OF PHILOSOPHY 279 (E.S. Haldane & Frances H. Simson trans., 1892).

[27] Errol Harris considers the accusation of Adolph Trendelenburg, a 19th century critic: Hegel smuggled "time" into the system along with Becoming. Harris acquits Hegel

Nevertheless, the very idea of negation refers to a past. If I say that Being is *not*, I am also saying Being *once was*, because negation always works on some positive entity that preceded it. As we shall soon discover, Dialectical Reason *remembers*, and so Logic entails *sequence*, a kind of fantasy time – not to be confused with chronological time.

Movement. We have before us Becoming, a *middle term*. Becoming represents *movement*. (83)[28] Movement can be perceived only because it has as background the static, passive non-movement of Pure Being and Nothing. Yet as we contemplate movement, we "freeze" it in a thought. Becoming therefore has a dual nature. It arises as the relation between Being/ Nothing and Absolute Knowing, which precedes it. As a relation, it is *composed* of simpler parts. It is a complex entity. In its complexity, Becoming moves. But when we think of Becoming as such, we freeze it, so that it does not move.

This paradox of rendering movement static is a necessity of which modern physics is much aware.[29] Two examples must suffice. Suppose a pen is dropped. A photograph is taken of the fall. According to classical mechanics, the photograph freezes, destroys and yet is part of the motion. In quantum mechanics, the collapse of the wave function is a well-known example of the incompatibility of stasis and movement. These examples show that a phenomenon cannot "be" and be perceived or measured at the same time.[30] Such a principle is present in

---

and writes, "Time presupposes becoming; becoming does not presuppose time. Time does not become, and in pure time there is neither change nor movement, for it is change that generates time and not *vice versa* . . . [T]ime is but the measure of change." HARRIS, LOGIC, *supra* note 14, at 96. It may be noted that "time" is not an official category of the *SL*. Hegel theorizes time in his *Philosophy of Nature*, the second part to his *Encyclopedia*. In the *Philosophy of Nature*, Hegel remarks: "The Notion [is] free from the power of time, but is neither within time, nor something temporal. It can be said on the contrary that it is the *Notion* which constitutes the power of time, for time is nothing but this negation as externality." HEGEL'S PHILOSOPHY OF NATURE § 258 Remark (M.J. Petry trans., 1970).

[28] The use of the term "movement" has been criticized. JUSTUS HARTNACK, AN INTRODUCTION TO HEGEL'S LOGIC 14, 18 (Lars Aagaard-Mogensen trans., 1998). Undoubtedly the term is unfortunate if it is taken to imply the dislocation of tangible objects over time. "Movement" must somehow be understood in a nontemporal sense. It stands for *instability* of a concept. (Hartnack prefers "process" to movement.)

[29] On the connections between Hegelian philosophy and quantum theory in physics, see ARKADY PLOTNITSKY, IN THE SHADOW OF HEGEL: COMPLEMENTARITY, HISTORY, AND THE UNCONSCIOUS (1993).

[30] Though, as Andrew Haas points out, "being is a result of measurement; that is, 'to be' means 'to already have a measure' – for being is merely an abstraction from

Becoming. It moves and yet it does not move.[31] We cannot focus on these moments simultaneously. Each side of Becoming is inadequate to the whole. The concept of Becoming is in a deep state of contradiction.

Conventions. At this point, I would like to return to my expository conventions, some of which I have already introduced. These conventions will serve to provide some much needed visual aids for the explication to follow.

All middle terms (such as Becoming) are made up of three circles. The first of these will emphasize the positive, qualitative side. It leans to the left side of the diagram. The second emphasizes the negative side. It leans to the right side of the diagram. Since negation always presupposes something to negate, the negative moment is always a double, "dialectical" pairing. Finally, the two dialectically opposed entities are reconciled by a middle circle, which contains a surplus (*i.e.*, the whole is always greater than the parts). The middle term contains material that exceeds what is provided by the two extremes. This excess guarantees that the dialectic progress grows in complexity and sophistication with each step.[32]

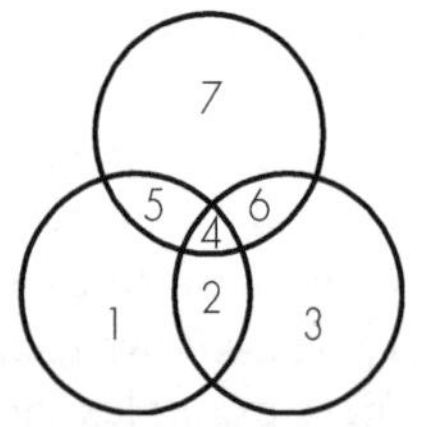

The Borromean Knot

The three circles together form a *Borromean Knot*. These three overlapping circles produce seven distinct areas. The areas marked [1], [3], and [7] are static.[33] These portions do not suffer from overlap. The areas marked [2, 4, 5, 6] are dynamic. These areas have at least two natures – they are subject to more than one jurisdiction. The area marked [4] is subject to all three jurisdictions. Only [4] is present in every single step of the *SL*. Later, we will see that [4] is what Hegel calls "being-within-self."

---

concrete measurement, or a reduction and fixing of immeasurable singularity." HAAS, *supra* note 1, at 139.

31 Michael Kosok, *The Formalization of Hegel's Dialectical Logic: Its Formal Structure, Logical Interpretation and Intuitive Foundation*, in HEGEL: A COLLECTION OF CRITICAL ESSAYS 256-7 (Alasdair MacIntyre, ed., 1972); Pippin, *supra* note 23, at 188 ("Becoming is Being's "continuing instability . . . captured by [a] category").

32 See BURBIDGE, LOGIC, *supra* note 26, at 44 ("As a synthesis something new is added; the new conception does not follow analytically from the preceding terms."); WINFIELD, *supra* note 5, at 50 ("self-thinking thought is synthetic in that each new category is not contained in those that precede it.").

33 From now on, numbers in brackets – *e.g.*, [7] – refer to the spaces set forth in the Borromean Knot.

The Understanding. Logic progresses via propositions about the middle term. In the first step, we depose the middle term from its central position by "abstracting" the "immediate" part of it [7], suppressing the mediated part, and shifting this mutilated entity over to the left of the diagram to create the category "*Coming-to-be*."[34] This first move belongs to the Understanding – the intuition that perceives a concept as an immediate, uncomplicated entity. On the left, the accent is on being [1].[35] Becoming "becomes" Coming-to-Be (*Entstehen*) – one of the two terms that make up Becoming. So conceived, Becoming is taken according to common sense. It has started from nothing and has "come into being."

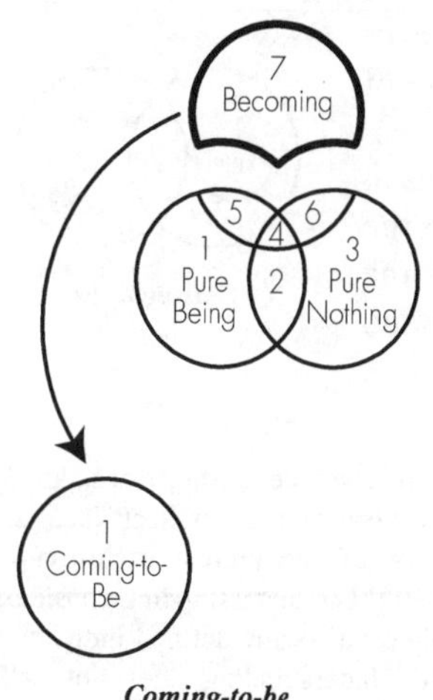

Coming-to-be

In the *EL*, Hegel psychoanalyzes the Understanding and its initial leftwing anxiety in favor of Being:

> If the opposition in thought is stated in this immediacy as Being and Nothing, the shock of its nullity is too great not to stimulate the attempt to fix Being and secure it against the transition into Nothing. With this intent, reflection has recourse to the plan of discovering some fixed predicate for Being, to mark it off from Nothing. Thus we find Being identified with what persists amid all change . . . But every additional . . . characterization causes Being to lose that integrity and simplicity it has in the beginning. Only in, and by virtue of this mere generality is it Nothing, something inexpressible, whereof the distinction from Nothing is a mere intention or *meaning*.[36]

---

[34] I do not interpret Hegel's distinction of coming-to-be and ceasing-to-be as official steps in the Logic. Rather, Hegel is simply discussing aspects of Becoming without moving the process along. Thus, Hegel later announces that Something (Figure 2(c)) is the *first* negation of the negation. If "ceasing-to-be" were an official step, Figure 2(c) would be the *second* negation of the negation. *See* BURBIDGE, LOGIC, *supra* note 26, at 41 (coming-to-be and ceasing-to-be "define the process of *becoming* more precisely").

[35] The idea of "accent" comes from Hegel himself: "Both [being and nothing] are determinate being, but in *reality* as quality with the accent on *being*, the fact is concealed that it contains determinateness and therefore also negation. Consequently, reality is given the value only of something positive from which negation, limitation and deficiency are excluded." (111)

[36] EL § 87.

In short, the Understanding, fearing its own death, wishes to fix its preservation in a unified proposition about the past truths it has been compelled to accept.

In its shift to the left, the Understanding – what passes as "common sense" (45) (*Menschenverstand*) – is, at first, oblivious to the mediatedness of concepts.[37] "The understanding *determines* and holds the determinations fixed." (28)[38] Accordingly, the unmediated portion of the Borromean Knot [7] becomes a self-identical entity [1] like that in Figure 1(a), because the immediacy of the concept is taken as the whole truth of it. The Understanding therefore "abstracts" a part and calls it the whole. Abstraction "means to select from the concrete object for our subjective purposes this or that mark without thereby detracting from the worth and status of the many other features left out of account." (587)

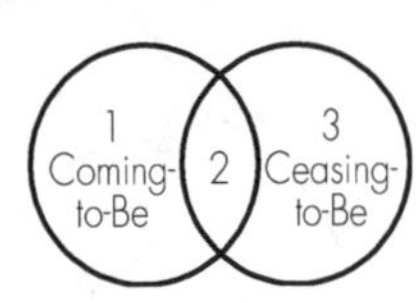

Ceasing-to-be

Dialectical Reason. Dialectical Reason embarrasses the Understanding by recalling the history of the concept. It remembers[39] that the supposedly immediate concept was mediated

---

[37] *See* LUCIO COLLETTI, MARXISM AND HEGEL 9 (Lawrence Garner trans., 1973) ("Philosophy has adopted, Hegel states, the point of view of the 'intellect' [*i.e.*, the Understanding], the principle of non-contradiction or of the mutual exclusion of opposites"); MARCUSE, ONTOLOGY, *supra* note 18, at 10 ("The understanding considers all encountered beings . . . to be at peace, fixed, limited univocally defined individual, and positive"). John Burbidge emphasizes that the Understanding does not self-consciously "abstract" a part from the whole. It thinks it has grasped the whole as a self-identity. BURBIDGE, LOGIC, *supra* note 26, at 42.

[38] *See also* EL § 80 ("The logic of mere understanding is involved in speculative logic, and can at will be elicited from it, by the simple process of omitting the dialectical and 'reasonable' element"). Burbidge and Harris think that the Understanding distinguishes as well as abstracts. BURBIDGE, LOGIC, *supra* note 26, at 39 ("Understanding is to define [a new category] more clearly and distinguish it from other concepts"); *see also id*. at 44; HARRIS, LOGIC, *supra* note 14, at 37 ("it has two main characteristics, which are intimately connected with each other, abstraction and sharp, rigid distinction"). I do not see Understanding's initial function as connected with *distinction*. Understanding is the move that accepts self-identity. Difference is the hallmark of Dialectical Reason. The Understanding, after all, proposes a self-identical theory of the Absolute. But it will develop as the *SL* progresses. Eventually, the Understanding will resemble Dialectical Reason, which *does* makes distinctions.

[39] "[F]or Hegel, thinking – and especially philosophical thinking – is basically a highly sophisticated way of remembering – or, as Hegel puts it, intelligence is cognitive only insofar as it is recognitive." JOHN MCCUMBER, THE COMPANY OF WORDS: HEGEL, LANGUAGE AND SYSTEMATIC PHILOSOPHY 123 (1993).

after all. It accuses the Understanding of ignoring the negative component that dialectic reasoning is able to comprehend.[40]

According to Dialectical Reason, Becoming has a second aspect. It is *ceasing-to-be* (*Verstehen*), which starts from Being and ends at Nothing. It concedes the Understanding's point that Nothing turns into Being. But it embarrasses the Understanding by pointing out that the opposite is just as true: Being turns into Nothing. It has "ceased to be." So we place "ceasing to be" over on the right and consider it together with "coming to be." This is the step of Dialectical Reason. "[R]eason is negative and *dialectical*, because it resolves the determinations of the understanding into nothing." (28) It "negates what is simple." (28) As its name suggests, Dia-lectic Reason reads double. A positive concept always leaves out (and thereby always implies) its opposite, which Dialectical Reason makes explicit. "[W]hat is at first *immediate* now appears as *mediated*, related to an other . . . Hence the second term that has thereby come into being is the *negative* of the first, and if we anticipate the subsequent progress, the *first negative*." (834) Dialectic Reason introduces dynamism – a modulation between the two sides.[41] In it, one side is always becoming the other. What is true of one side is always true of its opposite side.

Dialectical reasoning, however, is too clever by half. In creating duality and modulation between the extremes, it actually replicates the error of the Understanding. Dialectical Reason sees double, but to see double it must "posit" a second abstract entity [3] as opposite to the first. This second extreme is quite the same thing as the "understood" entity [1] that Dialectical Reason thinks it is criticizing.[42]

---

[40] HERBERT MARCUSE, REASON AND REVOLUTION 46 (1999) (Dialectical Reason "criticizes and supersedes the fixed oppositions created by the [Understanding]"). It has been suggested that Dialectical Reason equates with *experience*. The Understanding has made a proposition about the universe. By remembering the past Dialectical Reason inverts it and reveals it to be the opposite of what it was supposed to be. Dialectical Reason is like experience in that "theory" is shown to be inconsistent with the "real" world known to exist beyond theory. KENNETH R. WESTPHAL, HEGEL'S EPISTEMOLOGICAL REALISM: A STUDY OF THE AIM AND METHOD OF HEGEL'S *Phenomenology of Spirit* 130 (1989); *see also* G.W.F. HEGEL, THE JENA SYSTEM, 1804-5: LOGIC AND METAPHYSICS 53 (John W. Burbidge & George di Giovanni trans. 1986) (experience is "the conjoining of concept and appearance – that is, the setting in motion of indifferent substances, sensations, or whatever you will, whereby they become determinate, existing only in the antithesis").

[41] EL § 81 Addition ("Wherever there is movement, wherever there is life, wherever anything is carried into effect in the actual world, there Dialectic is at work.").

[42] *See* STANLEY ROSEN, G.W.F. HEGEL: AN INTRODUCTION TO THE SCIENCE OF

This deserves emphasis, because we have before us the quintessential move from Essence, the midpoint of the Logic. Dialectic Reason has in effect *posited* itself. Speaking from [2] it has said, "I'm *not*. I concede that [1] is. But I [2, 3] am *not*." Dialectical Reason [2] is the voice of the Understanding itself – its negative, suppressed voice.[43] When it speaks up against [1], [2] claims autonomy from [1]. This autonomy is represented by [3]. In its negativity, [3] has created or posited itself by distinguishing itself [3] from itself [1]. The motor of the distinction was [2].[44]

Dialectical Reason produces an autistic modulation between two identical extremes that gets us nowhere; drawing attention to the lack in the Understanding merely replicates the Understanding's own error.

WISDOM 118 (1974) ("the affirmation of -*A* already affirms *A* in order to deny it"). Slavoj Žižek calls this "oppositional determination" – when the universal, common ground of the two opposites "encounters itself" in its oppositional determination. SLAVOJ ŽIŽEK, TARRYING WITH THE NEGATIVE: KANT, HEGEL, AND THE CRITIQUE OF IDEOLOGY 132 (1993). Žižek's example is the political party that criticizes the other party for acting out of partisanship. In this critique, the critic meets itself in its criticism and is doing the very thing it criticizes. Likewise, Dialectical Reasoning accuses the Understanding of resting on abstraction when it too rests on abstraction.

Oppositional determination means that Hegel's entire system could be viewed as a triad (Understanding, Dialectical Reason, speculative unity) or as a quadrad. In the triadic case, Dialectical Reason is taken according to its self-perception – singular and self-identical. In the quadratic case, Dialectical Reason is counted twice from the perspective of Speculative Reason, which sees Dialectical Reason as self-alienated. SLAVOJ ŽIŽEK, THE TICKLISH SUBJECT: THE ABSENT CENTRE OF POLITICAL ONTOLOGY 79-80 (1999). Tetrachotomy is a major concern in Hegel's theory of Judgment, presented in chapter 20.

For Adorno, the double nature of Dialectical Reason is an error that delegitimates the *SL*. THEODOR W. ADORNO, NEGATIVE DIALECTICS 162 (E.B. Ashton trans. 2000) ("At each new dialectical step, Hegel goes against the intermittent insight of his own logic, forgets the rights of the preceding step, and thus prepares to copy what he chided as abstract negation: an abstract – to wit, a subjectively and arbitrarily confirmed – positivity"). In truth, this fault in dialectic reason is an integral part of the system.

[43] As Burbidge characterizes the process, we start with the Understanding in its contemplation of Pure Being. It changes to Pure Nothing. Pure Nothing is likewise the product of the Understanding. The modulation between them is thus the "sequential" work of the Understanding. BURBIDGE, LOGIC, *supra* note 26, at 42. Perhaps a better way of putting it: in the double aspect of Dialectical Reason, a second act of Understanding is always present. Dialectical Reason must "understand" the nothingness it has produced.

[44] In the *EL*, Hegel complains that Dialectical Reason is wrongly seen as "an adventitious [i.e., added from the outside] art which for very wantonness introduces confusion and a mere semblance of contradiction." EL § 81(2).

The Understanding's error was the claim to self-identity [1]. Now Dialectical Reason makes the same error [3]. For this reason, "[t]he first two moments of the triciplity are *abstract*, untrue moments which for that very reason are dialectical." (837)

Determinate Being According to Speculative Reason

Speculative Reason. Speculative Reason[45] wisely intervenes to stop the modulating nonsense. Speculative Reason is like a parent mediating between squabbling siblings. The Understanding fell into error by suppressing or expelling the negative aspect of itself. Its younger brother, Dialectical Reason, exploited this fault, but it only replicated a negative version of the Understanding's own fault.[46] This other extreme [3] shares an identity with the Understanding's extreme [1]. [3] likewise suppresses its own negative [2]. Neither side can account for its lack by itself. Speculative Reason is able to bring forth this lack into the light of day, showing

---

[45] For a history of "speculation," see RODOLPHE GASCHÉ, THE TAIN OF THE MIRROR: DERRIDA AND THE PHILOSOPHY OF REFLECTION 42-3 (1986). Non-Hegelians will recognize in Understanding, Dialectical Reason, and Speculative Reason the triad of thesis, antithesis, and synthesis. Of this notorious triad, Allen Wood writes:

> The regrettable tradition of expounding this theme in the Hegelian dialectic through the grotesque jargon of "thesis," "antithesis," and "synthesis" began in 1837 with Heinrich Moritz Chalybäus, a bowdlerizer of German idealist philosophy, whose ridiculous expository devices should have been forgotten along with his name. [T]o my knowledge, it is never used by Hegel, not even once, for this purpose or for any other. The use of Chalybäus's terminology to expound the Hegelian dialectic is nearly always an unwitting confession that the expositor has little or no firsthand knowledge of Hegel.

ALLEN W. WOOD, HEGEL'S ETHICAL THOUGHT 3-4 (1990). Fichte and Schelling, however, used these terms. WALTER KAUFMANN, HEGEL: A REINTERPRETATION 154 (1978). Hegel himself, at least at one point, renounces the use of the word synthesis: "*Becoming* is this immanent synthesis of being and nothing; but because synthesis suggests more than anything else the sense of an external bringing together of mutually external things already there, the name synthesis, synthetic unity, has rightly been dropped." (96) But, as Michael Inwood points out, an endorsement of thesis-antithesis-synthesis occurs in Hegel's *Lectures on the History of Philosophy*. M.J. INWOOD, HEGEL 550 n. 100 (1983), citing 3 HISTORY OF PHILOSOPHY, *supra* note 26, at 477.

[46] HYPPOLITE, LOGIC, *supra* note 26, at 169 ("This second term is the pivot of the dialectical movement; it is *doubly negative*. It is at first the other, the negation of the first; but, taken by itself, it re-establishes the first").

that each side has a surplus – its own lack [2], which is beyond itself and hence indeed a surplus. In short, the surplus [7] is the positivized version of the negative material [2] expelled by [1] and [3].[47]

Speculative Reason emphasizes that, between the two extremes – [1] and [3] – there is difference [2].[48] This difference is expressed as [7]. It is the surplus and constitutes extra content – a static addition to the dynamic opposition.[49] Speculative Reason, working only with the materials implied by the extremes, produces a new middle term. Its name is *Determinate Being* – Being that is distinguishable from Nothing.[50] This dualism is the subject matter of Chapter 2.

In terms of our Borromean Knot, the middle term is both dynamic [4, 5, 6] and static [7]. When we consider the parts [4, 5, 6], it is dynamic – a ceaseless modulation of birth and death. When we consider the dynamic modulation as such, we "name" the activity and thereby add a static dimension to the dynamic parts. This static equilibrium [7] in turn will be "understood" when it is shifted to the left and made into a new self-identical concept in Figure 2(a).

Speculative Reason yields a surplus [7]. This is why we call it *speculative*. [7] is reason's "return on investment" – the beyond of what was invested in the earlier steps. Speculative Reason is the act of *synthesis*[51] – the process of joining different representations to each other, and of comprehending them in one cognition. Synthesis does not affirm the *identity* of the extremes. It affirms their *difference* (which,

---

[47] *See* WINFIELD, *supra* note 5, at 68 (coming-to-be and ceasing-to-be "collapse of themselves, leaving a unity in which being and nothing are contained not sequentially but in an abiding relation to one another"). In terms of my conventions, coming-to-be [1] denies that its own being [2]. Yet if coming-to-be [1] insists on abstracting itself from [2], it cannot claim to be a sequence of nothing and being. "The movement of becoming comes to a halt because the being that follows from nothing is indistinguishable from the latter just as the nothing that follows from being is indistinguishable from it." *Id*. Coming-to-be therefore ceases to be. Ceasing-to-be does the same; [1] self-destructs. What is left is [2]. Yet [2] is properly part of both coming-to-be and ceasing-to-be "Having lost its dual sequential movements, this whole [2] now simply consists in a unity of being and nothing that contains them as component terms mediated by their identity." *Id*.

[48] Burbidge sees Speculative Reason as containing three separate steps. It develops the relation that unifies the extremes (synthesis). Then it names (or positivizes) the relation (mediation). Then it integrates the whole in a simple unity. BURBIDGE, LOGIC, *supra* note 26, at 44.

[49] *See* ŽIŽEK, TARRYING, *supra* note 42, at 122-3.

[50] I am not here drawing an official step of the Logic. Determinate Being is simply another name for Becoming. *Supra* note 34.

[51] With the proviso that Hegel disfavors the term. *Supra* note 45.

paradoxically, is the *same identical* lack [2] in each of the subordinate terms). The Logic proceeds, then, by a series of *withdrawals* from [2]: "Each new stage of *forth-going*, that is, of *further determination*, is a withdrawal inwards, and the greater *extension* is equally a *higher intensity*." (840-1)[52] Ironically, the Logic grows richer and more concrete as it withdraws deeper and deeper into itself.[53] "The highest, most concentrated point" (841) is subjectivity – the most concrete of things. Absolute Idea – the end of the Logic – will be "*pure personality* which, solely through the absolute dialectic which is its nature, no less *embraces and holds everything within itself*." (841)

The convention we have developed of moving the middle term to the left, generating its opposite and then deriving a new middle term,[54] is designed to represent the movement of spirit in expelling its dependence on otherness – something that it will not achieve until the end of the book. By moving the middle term to the left, the bias, for the moment, is in favor of "being" over negation or death. This is the bias of intuition, which takes things in their immediacy and wishes not to think about the finite nature of its ideas. This bias, however, will change when we reach Essence in chapter 10.[55]

---

[52] *See* MICHAEL ROSEN, HEGEL'S DIALECTIC AND ITS CRITICISM 87 (1982) ("the word determination (*Bestimmung*) can mean either the *act* of determining or the *outcome* of such an act. Hegel is making use of this ambiguity to emphasize that the act of determining and what is determined are parts (or moments, as he calls them) of a single process.").

[53] *See* SLAVOJ ŽIŽEK, THE PUPPET AND THE DWARF: THE PERVERSE CORE OF CHRISTIANITY 3 (2003) ("sometimes in [Hegel's] work we find something I am tempted to call a 'downward synthesis': after the two opposed positions, the third one, the *Aufhebung* of the two, is not a higher synthesis but a kind of negative synthesis, the lowest point"). In truth, since the middle term is always what is *lacking* from [1] and [3], it is possible to view the *entire* path of Speculative Reason as a downward *collapse*.

[54] This movement has been called "the lumpy, bumpy triangular wheel." BURBIDGE, RELIGION, *supra* note 22, at 36. Walter Kaufmann dissents from the notion that Hegel's Logic proceeds in this triadic form. He concedes "a very decided preference for triadic arrangements." KAUFMANN, *supra* note 45, at 154. But these are not deductive relations, Kaufmann alleges. "[H]is dialectic never became the ritualistic three-step it is so widely supposed to be." *Id.* at 158; *see also* 188, 198. Instead, the *SL* is supposed to be organized by "a sidelong glance at the history of philosophy." *Id.* at 284. Such a position denies that Hegel has written a Logic. In my view, Hegel intended the very "ritualistic three-step" that Kaufmann denies.

[55] In the penultimate paragraph in the Doctrine of Being, Hegel remarks, "The being of the determinations is no longer simply *affirmative* as in the entire sphere of being." (384) At this point Hegel signals a fundamental shift in the attitude of the Understanding. Starting with chapter 10, the Understanding contemplates what is *not*.

To summarize, the Borromean knot represents Logic as a circle comprised of circles, in accord with Hegel's comment from the *EL*:

> Each of the parts of philosophy is a philosophical whole, a circle rounded and complete in itself. In each of these parts, however, the philosophical Idea is found in a particular specificality or medium. The single circle, because it is a real totality, bursts through the limits imposed by its special medium, and gives rise to a wider circle. The whole of philosophy in this way resembles a circle of circles. The Idea appears in each single circle, but, at the same time, the whole Idea is constituted by the system of these peculiar phases, and each is a necessary member of the organization.[56]

With What Must Science Begin?

Here is a good place to regress and discuss the essay that precedes Pure Being. Hegel's goal is to develop a presupposition-free philosophy that provides its *own foundations*. Starting with an unproved "given" is precisely a surrender to superstition. Ever the enemy of philosophy, stipulation is "stupid."[57] Every other science distinguishes its subject matter and scientific method. The subordinate sciences are permitted premises that are taken for granted. But Logic may not presuppose any forms, "for these constitute part of its own content and have first to be established within the science." (43)

Yet Hegel *begins* – with Pure Being. Isn't choosing to begin a contingency and a presupposition? Hegel admits this. "All that is present is simply the resolve, which can be regarded as arbitrary, to consider thought as such." (70)[58]

Hegel remarks: "What philosophy begins with must be either *mediated* or *immediate*." (67) But which beginning shall we stipulate? He chooses immediacy, but on what basis?[59] Hegel justifies the choice

---

[56] EL § 15.

[57] Hegel names presupposition "stupid – I can find no other word for it." (41-2)

[58] EL § 17 ("To speak of a beginning of philosophy has a meaning only in relation to a person who proposes to commence the study, and not in relation to the science as science"); *see also* BUTLER, LOGIC, *supra* note 19, at 1 ("the project of defining the absolute . . . is certainly presupposed"); ADORNO, THREE STUDIES, *supra* note 1, at 12 ("the choice of a starting point . . . is a matter of indifference in Hegel's philosophy; his philosophy does not recognize a first something of this kind as a fixed principle . . .").

[59] Maker answers this question for Hegel: A mediated thing has a given, external ground. "[T]he justification for beginning with this given determination rather than another will require either an infinite regress or vicious circularity . . . Only a beginning which is absolutely free, because devoid of any presupposed given determination, can

because what is here presupposed is (much later) proven. By "proven" he means that the very last step of the Logic (Absolute Idea, which is the same as Absolute Knowledge)[60] mediates the first step. His philosophy will take us in a circle. If the beginning is also the end, then the beginning is justified.[61] At this point, the end and the beginning will be a "mediated cognition," which is what Hegel says proof is. (481)

Absolute Knowing (or Method)[62] is the unity of mediation – all the mediations there are – and pure immediacy. It is the final step in the Logic. At that point, the absolutely immediate is also the absolutely mediated. The ultimate step, Hegel says, "is the immediate, but the immediate *resulting from sublation of mediation* . . . This *result* is therefore the *truth*. It is equally immediacy and mediation." (837) Pure Being, then, is merely a one-sided view of Absolute Knowing – the side of immediacy. In order to begin, Absolute Knowing breaks itself apart in a gesture of abstraction[63] (since Pure Being will not suffer being merely a "part" in a greater whole).[64] Absolute Knowing, "in its absolute self-assurance and inner poise," (843) stands back from its content, "allowing it to have free play." (73)

The first move belongs to the Understanding. Hegel warns that it is essential to start in this one-sided way. Any other start provides a *result*, not a beginning. (72)[65] "[T]he immediate of the beginning must

---

make the radical justification of a self-grounding possible." William Maker, *Hegel's Logic of Freedom*, in HEGEL'S THEORY OF THE SUBJECT 6 (David Gray Carlson ed., 2005).

[60] HYPPOLITE, GENESIS, *supra* note 6, at 586 (in terms of result, "there is a perfect correlation between the *Phenomenology of Spirit* and the *Logic*").

[61] "The essential requirement for the science of logic is not so much that the beginning be a pure immediacy, but rather that the whole of the science be within itself a circle in which the first is also the last and the last is also the first." (71) *See also* G.W.F. HEGEL, ELEMENTS OF THE PHILOSOPHY OF RIGHT § 2 (Allen W. Wood trans. 1993) ("Philosophy forms a circle. It has an initial or immediate point – for it must begin somewhere – a point which is not demonstrated and is not a result. But the starting point of philosophy is immediately relative, for it must appear at another end-point as a result. Philosophy is a sequence which is not suspended in mid-air; it does not begin immediately, but is rounded off within itself.").

[62] Hegel sometimes calls this "pure knowledge." (69)

[63] Robert van Roden Allen, *Hegelian Beginning and Resolve: A View of the Relationship Between the* Phenomenology *and the* Logic, 13 IDEALISTIC STUDIES 249 (1983) ("For is not thought the explicit breakup of the notion?").

[64] *See* ADORNO, THREE STUDIES, *supra* note 1, at 133 ("The concept breaks up when it insists on its identity, and yet it is only the catastrophe of such tenacity that gives rise to the movement that makes it immanently other than itself"). Hegel calls this breakup the "diremption" of spirit into the world. PHENOMENOLOGY, *supra* note 4, 357; G.R.G. MURE, THE PHILOSOPHY OF HEGEL 10 (1965).

[65] HAAS, *supra* note 1, at 91 (*not* Pure Being, but the decision of the Understanding

be *in its own self* deficient and endowed with the *urge* to carry itself further." (829) Hegel's "famous and irritating beginning"[66] is therefore a failure – an attempt to conceive of an unmediated self-identity. Immediacy and mediation are "*unseparated* and inseparable and the opposition between them . . . a nullity." (68) And because the beginning is a failure, "advance is not a kind of *superfluity*; this it would be if that which the beginning is made were in truth already the absolute." (829) As Hegel emphasizes throughout the *SL*, the fate of a self-identical (or "diverse") entity is to disappear and render itself into nothing. This is already foretold in Figure 1(b). Pure Being is the first diversity to show its own nothingness.[67]

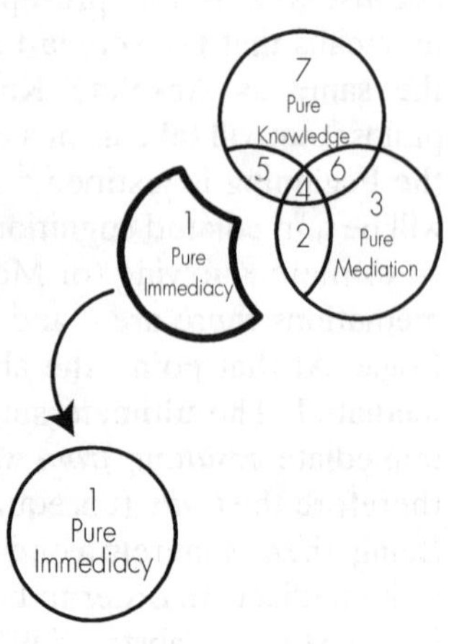

The Beginning

It is often said that Hegel intends the last step of the Logic to be the first. This needs refinement. The first step comprehends immediacy as such – Pure Being. It may be said that Pure Being is the *antepenultimate* step – the third from last. In effect, the Understanding falls back two steps and produces an abstraction.[68] From this retrogressive move, progress is necessitated.

Immanence. If I may interrupt our discussion of scientific beginning,

---

to abstract Pure Being from Pure Knowing constitutes the true first step of the Logic). Hartnack suggests that "[t]he beginning point, that is, the necessary presupposition, is our commonsense view: the world of identifiable and reidentifiable objects." HARTNACK, *supra* note 28, at 20. I disagree. The Understanding that abstracts from Pure Knowledge at the beginning seems quite divorced from anything recognizable as common sense.

[66] Kenley Royce Dove, *Hegel's "Deduction of the Concept of Science"*, in HEGEL IN THE SCIENCES 272 (Robert S. Cohen & Marx W. Wartofsky eds. 1984).

[67] Nevertheless, pure immediacy is a genuine moment. "It would be wrong . . . to understand Hegel as claiming just that whatever *seems* to be immediate will turn out, in fact, to be mediated. Although there can be no such thing as *pure* immediacy, immediacy itself is no more illusory than is mediation. Hegel's point is that mediation and immediacy go together." ROSEN, *supra* note 52, at 87.

[68] *See* David Gray Carlson, *The Antepenultimacy of the Beginning in Hegel's* Science of Logic, in HEGEL'S THEORY OF THE SUBJECT, *supra* note 59, at 206. Walter Kaufmann notes, with justification, that the Logic does not really start from Pure Being. Rather, the Logic starts with the privileging of the immediate over what is mediated. KAUFMANN, *supra* note 45, at 190.

it is now convenient to discuss two key ideas that, for Hegel, are vital. The first of these is *immanence*, which means "derived from within." The only steps permitted in the Logic are those immanent in the earlier step. In the circular journey of the *SL*, no step is authorized unless completely derived from the ones before. "[A]t no stage . . . should any thought-determination or reflection occur which does not *immediately* emerge . . . and that has not entered this stage from the one preceding it." (40) In terms of our conventions, [2] is the voice of Dialectical Reason. It is the suppressed voice of [1] and hence immanent or implicit within [1]. Dialectical Reason merely expresses what was previously hidden. Likewise, Speculative Reason is the voice of [4], which is immanent to both [1] and [3].

From the requirement of immanence, it follows that the earlier steps imply the later ones and the later steps imply the earlier ones. Recall what was said earlier about *time*. In the Logic, time does not unfold what pleated cunning hides. Everything is omnipresent. Hence, the Logic can go forward or it can go backward *instantaneously*. In any case, since the Logic is a circle, going forward is the *same* as going backward. In either direction, we reach Absolute Knowing. "[A]dvance is a *retreat into the ground* . . . from which originates that with which the beginning is made." (71)[69]

Hegel tends to write sentences like: "[N]either being nor nothing truly *is*, but their truth is only becoming." (94) What he means by this sentence is that Pure Being and Nothing are inadequate and one-sided. The later step of Becoming is already implied – is immanent – in the transition to Pure Being/Nothing.

Sublation. The second important concept I would like to introduce is "sublation" – a word not usually encountered by non-Hegelians.

Every step in the circular path of Logic is already "immanent" in every other. Logic "not only does not lose anything or leave anything behind, but carries along with it all it has gained, and inwardly enriches and consolidates itself." (840) As we advance, we never destroy a prior step. Rather, we preserve it. "The whole *Logic* presents nothing other than 'the absolute truth and necessity' of this insight."[70] Every step contains [4], which implies that the prior steps have never been entirely destroyed. Yet the very idea of taking a step means that we have

---

[69] *See* WILLIAM DESMOND, BEYOND HEGEL AND DIALECTIC: SPECULATION, CULT, AND COMEDY 181 (1992) ("Difference of directionality will not count dialectically, since the two directions are different articulations of the one process of total self-mediation").

[70] MARCUSE, ONTOLOGY, *supra* note 19, at 175.

negated its predecessor. Thus, [1], [2], and [3] are expelled from the middle term. Yet the middle term always implies [1], [2], and [3] in the guise of [4], [5], and [6].

German has a marvelous word: *Aufhebung*.[71] It means simultaneously to preserve *and* to destroy (rather like the English word *sanction* means to permit *and* to punish). *Aufhebung* is a word that delights Hegel,[72] and it is key to everything that follows. As we proceed, every step constitutes the creation of a new moment and destruction of the old. Yet, because of immanence, the new step implies (or contains) the old step.[73] The old step's implied truth is the new step. Every step is both destroyed and preserved. It is, *and* it is not – stuff by which we shall make many a paradox. Hegel nowhere says this more clearly than at the end of the *SL*:

> The immediate [1] from this negative side, has been *extinguished* in the other, but the other [3] is essentially not the *empty negative*, the *nothing*, that is taken to be the usual result of dialectic; rather it is the *other of the first*, the *negative* of the *immediate*; it is therefore determined as the *mediated* – *contains* in general the *determination of the first* within itself. Consequently the first is essentially *preserved* and *retained* even in the other. (834)[74]

---

71 Hegel praises German for its phrases of opposite meaning, "so that one cannot fail to recognize a speculative spirit of the language in them." (32) Ordinary speakers use these ambiguous terms, Hegel says, without fully understanding their speculative content. "It must suffice therefore if pictorial thinking, in the use of its expressions that are employed for philosophical determinations, has before it some vague idea of their distinctive meaning." (708) It is the privilege of philosophy to consider such terms for themselves – not as mere tools. "Philosophy has the right to select from the language of common life which is made for the world of pictorial thinking, such expressions as *seem to approximate* to the determinations of the Notion." (708) For use of these passages to acquit Hegel of Derridean logocentrism, see KATHLEEN DOW MAGNUS, HEGEL AND THE SYMBOLIC MEDIATION OF SPIRIT 99 (2001).

It has been suggested that Hegel proceeds by paronymity – investiture of common words with speculative meaning. "Paronymic shifts in meaning are an important and widespread aid in all scientific and philosophical artificial languages . . . As is well known, words such as 'warmth,' 'mass,' 'force,' 'weight,' or 'water' – words that are also used outside of physics and chemistry and are older than these sciences – gain through physics and chemistry entirely new meanings that nevertheless, have content in common with prescientific usage and as such relate paronymically to them." Michael Wolff, *On Hegel's Doctrine of Contradiction*, 31 OWL OF MINERVA 1, 7 (1999).

72 "It is a delight to speculative thought to find in the language words which have in themselves a speculative meaning; the German language has a number of such." (107)

73 It is quite the opposite in the *Phenomenology*. There, as consciousness wends its path from sense certainty to Absolute Knowing, it stupidly forgets everything that went before. HYPPOLITE, GENESIS, *supra* note 5, at 227-8.

74 Here is a concise reproach to those who require the negative to stay negative.

In English, *aufheben* is awkwardly translated into "to sublate"[75] – a term taken from chemistry. According to the *Shorter Oxford Dictionary*, sublation is "[a] precipitate suspended in a liquid, especially urine." Thanks to Hegel's English translators, it also denotes the destruction and preservation of Logical moments by the more progressive moment which it generates.

Notice how sublation fits with Becoming. Abstraction turns Pure Being into Pure Nothing. The modulation itself was Becoming. Thanks to sublation, "this strange autosuppressive category,"[76] Becoming is contained in every moment that follows:

> [T]he *progress* from . . . the beginning is to be regarded as only a further determination of it . . . [T]he starting point . . . remains at the base of all that follows . . . Thus the beginning . . . is the foundation which is present and preserved throughout the entire subsequent development, remaining completely immanent in its further determinations. (71)

Thinking versus Being. Beginning is grounded in a contingent decision to begin. The groundedness of the beginning is an embarrassment that Hegel must overcome, if he is to produce a philosophy without ground.

Hegel refers to Absolute Knowing as both "absolute immediacy" *and* "something absolutely mediated." (72) But mediation is a *result* and therefore *cannot* be the beginning. Thus, "it is equally essential that [Absolute Knowing] be taken only in the one-sided character in which it is pure immediacy, *precisely because* here it is the beginning." (72) In other words, *beginning* implies abstracting an element from the *end*. It is the Understanding that sets the Logic in motion.

With regard to this act of abstracting the beginning from the end, Hegel implies a subtle point. If, by beginning, we wrench pure immediacy from Absolute Knowing,[77] then Pure Being is the positive *content* of Absolute Knowing. The leftovers of Absolute Knowing (after

---

ADORNO, NEGATIVE DIALECTICS, *supra* note 42, at 119; JACQUES DERRIDA, POSITIONS 42-3 (Alan Bass trans. 1971). Although Adorno and Derrida rail against self-identity, they are guilty of it when they insist that the negative must be sustained in *its* self-identity.

[75] Harris traces this translation to the Oxford philosopher Geoffrey Mure (1893-1979). HARRIS, LOGIC, *supra* note 14, at 30; *see* MURE, *supra* note 64, at 35 ("'Sublated' will serve as a translation").

[76] JEAN-LUC NANCY, HEGEL: THE RESTLESSNESS OF THE NEGATIVE 52 (Jason Smith & Steven Miller eds. 1997).

[77] This act of wrenching (or abstracting) being from Absolute Knowing Hegel calls "determination of being." (73)

content is wrenched from it) are purely negative.[78] In other words, to know some *thing* is a highly negative enterprise. The subject who "knows" is very negative toward the content of his thought.[79] This dichotomy between knowing (consciousness) and being is precisely what drives the *Phenomenology* along its path.

Difference. Pure Being suffers no distinctions. It is the *same* as Pure Nothing. Yet Pure Being is *distinguished* from Pure Nothing (in Becoming). Whence came the ability to distinguish Pure Being and Nothing from each other? If distinction is not permitted, then concededly the Logic never gets started.

Difference must precede Pure Being in origin.[80] Hegel's beginning – Pure Being – is the Understanding's abstraction of immediacy from the last step of the Logic. Hegel writes: "Simple immediacy is itself an expression of reflection and contains a reference to its distinction from what is mediated." (69) So *reflection* notices the difference between Pure Being/Nothing and Absolute Knowing – an overarching perspective that comprehends origin and pre-origin at the same time.[81]

---

[78] One could also observe about the leftovers that they are mediation as such. We could also say that the leftovers are "immediate," because it can only mediate if it has content. Yet "content" has just been taken away.

[79] This is especially paradoxical when applied to self-knowledge, or self-consciousness. HYPPOLITE, LOGIC, *supra* note 26, at 75 ("*to know oneself is to contradict oneself*, since this is simultaneously to alienate oneself, to direct oneself towards the Other and to be reflected into, or more exactly, to be reflected into oneself in the Other").

[80] Charles Taylor, whose book did much to reverse the eclipse of Hegel's work in the twentieth century, finds this point a fatal flaw in the Logic:

> The derivation of Becoming here is not as solid as that of *Dasein*. This is the first but not the last place in the *Logic* where Hegel will go beyond what is directly established by his argument, because he sees in the relation of concepts a suggestion of his ontology . . . But of course as probative arguments these passages are unconvincing. They fail, as strict conceptual proof, however persuasive they are as *interpretations* for those who hold Hegel's view of things on other grounds. Thus, in this case, the notion of becoming imposes itself supposedly because of the passage from Being to Nothing and back; but this is a passage which our thought is forced to when we contemplate either . . . [W]e cannot trade on this principle at this stage.

CHARLES TAYLOR, HEGEL 233 (1975) Taylor's plaint is that the movement between Being and Nothing can only be "for us" and must exceed the bounds of the sparse logical development available at the end of the first chapter.

[81] GIACOMO RINALDI, A HISTORY AND INTERPRETATION OF THE LOGIC OF HEGEL 179 n. 2 (1992) (any abstract thought-content "*necessarily* presupposes the activity of the 'abstracting' subject").

The Understanding wrenches Immediacy from its unity with Absolute Knowing. It knows "nothing" but Pure Being/Nothing. But an overarching intelligence can see that Pure Being/Nothing is different from its origin. "Here the beginning is made with being which is represented as having come to be through mediation, a mediation which is also a sublating of itself; and there is presupposed pure knowing as the outcome of finite knowing, of consciousness." (69-70) The Understanding supposes that it accurately summarizes Absolute Knowing in its ultra-simple proposition. But Speculative Reason sees that the proposition is inadequate to (and different from) Absolute Knowing. It knows that mediation comes along with immediacy on the law of sublation. That is to say, the history of Pure Being is steeped in mediation. Speculative Reason merely recovers this history when it summarizes the failed attempt to think of Pure Being as a modulation between thought and non-thought – between Absolute Knowing and Being/Nothing.[82] With Hegel, "everything has already begun."[83]

Beginning with Becoming. This largely accords with what Gadamer suggests in his acute discussion of Hegel's beginning.[84] Gadamer names Becoming the first *true* thought in the Logic, and he has a quotation from Hegel to back it up. "One has acquired great insight when one realizes that being and not-being are abstractions without truth and that the first truth is Becoming alone."[85]

Why is Becoming the true beginning? According to Gadamer, Pure Being and Nothing are retroactively created presuppositions arising from the analysis of Becoming. They are not "things" in themselves. We first *think* of Becoming – we cannot think the unthinkable Pure

---

[82] *Id.* at 314 (to some early commentators, "the essential logical difference between Being and Nothing is just that which subsists between Being and the Act of thinking").

[83] NANCY, *supra* note 76, at 8; *see also id.* at 9 ("Hegel . . . does not begin with a principle or with a foundation. Such a beginning would still remain foreign to the movement and passage of truth."); BURBIDGE, RELIGION, *supra* note 22, at 22 ("The difference that 'reality' introduces is not the result of a simple transition, but has been *posited* by *reflection* when it added to the immediate content . . . its remembered parentage. The move came from outside the immediate concept."). A dissenter on this score is Stephen Houlgate, who insists (without explanation) that difference is already implicit within Pure Being. STEPHEN HOULGATE, THE OPENING OF HEGEL'S *LOGIC* 265 (2006). This must be disallowed for introducing distinction into that which *excludes* distinction.

[84] GADAMER, *supra* note 5, at 75-99.

[85] *Id.* at 91, quoting XIII *Werke* 306 (1832). *See* 1 HISTORY OF PHILOSOPHY, *supra* note 26, at 283 ("The recognition of the fact that being and non-being are abstractions devoid of truth, that the first truth is to be found in Becoming, forms a great advance").

Being/Nothing. Then we reason that, if Becoming stands for change or transition, it must have changed *from* something. Gadamer finds it convincing that one cannot think of Becoming without thinking Being and Nothing.[86] In Becoming, Being and Nothing are differentiated for the first time. Yet, Gadamer says, the converse is not convincing. Why should we think of Becoming when we light upon Pure Being or Pure Nothing? (Of course, these are unthinkable, so we are never in a position to derive Becoming from them.)

Gadamer thinks Hegel is conscious of this problem and that he treats the transition from Pure Being/Nothing to Becoming as a special case – a transition like no other in the *SL*. On their own, Pure Being and Nothing are so little different that they can generate no proper synthesis. Any difference assigned to them is merely a matter of subjective belief, not Logic. For this reason, Hegel says that Pure Nothing "bursts forth immediately" from Pure Being. "Clearly, the expression, 'bursts forth,' is one carefully chosen to exclude any idea of mediation and transition."[87]

Yet Gadamer seems to be criticizing Hegel's claim that Pure Being is the beginning. The modulation between Pure Being and Nothing which Hegel emphasizes is, for Gadamer, "an untenable way of putting the matter."[88] In fact, what precedes Becoming is the very *failure* of the Understanding to form the thought of Pure Being. This dissolution into failure, Gadamer thinks, is not properly dialectical (which requires recollection). For this reason, Gadamer attacks the very question, How

---

[86] Feuerbach also saw that Pure Being was only *retroactively* constructed from the determinacy of Becoming. "But given that the starting point is indeterminate, then moving on must mean determining. Only during the course of the movement of presentation does that from which I start come to determine and manifest itself. Hence, progression is at the same time retrogression . . . But the first principle to which I return is no longer the initial, indeterminate, and unproved first principle; it is now mediated and therefore no longer the same or, even granting that it is the same, no longer in the same form." Ludwig Feuerbach, *Towards a Critique of Hegel's Philosophy*, in THE FIERY BROOK: SELECTED WRITINGS OF LUDWIG FEUERBACH 61 (Zawar Hanfi trans., 1972).

[87] GADAMER, *supra* note 4, at 87. In Miller's translation, the sentence Gadamer refers to is: "In the pure reflection of the beginning as it is made in this logic with being as such, the transition is still concealed; because *being* is posited only as immediate, therefore *nothing* emerges in it only immediately. (99) ("In der reinen Reflexion des Anfangs, wie er in dieser Logik mit dem Sein als solchem gemacht wird, ist der Übergang noch verbogen; weil das Sein nur als unmittelbar gesetzt ist, bricht das Nichts an ihm nur unmittelbar hervor" [I:85]) Gadamer's translator justifiably renders "emerges" into "bursts forth" (*hervorbrechen*).

[88] GADAMER, *supra* note 4, at 89.

does Becoming emerge from Pure Being? The question presupposes that recollection is possible. But Pure Being and Nothing cannot be recalled; they are unthinkable! Indeed, Hegel refers to Pure Being is "only an empty word," an emptiness which "is therefore simply as such the beginning of philosophy." (78) Accordingly, the transition from Pure Being/Nothing to Becoming should not be viewed as a transition at all. Hegel was aware of this when he referred to the fact that "being does not pass over but has passed over – into nothing." (82-3) Pure Being and Nothing are simply what Becoming implies.

Becoming, for Gadamer, is the true beginning, because the thought of Pure Being is a failure.[89] What I have suggested, however, is different. In my view, Becoming *does* recall Absolute Knowing and sees that Pure Being/Nothing is different from it. Pure Being was supposed to be Absolute Knowing but instead is Pure Nothing. Modulation (Becoming) therefore does occur – between Absolute Knowledge and Being/Nothing. The attempt to render Absolute Knowledge immediate means that it *becomes* nothing.

Beginning at the Beginning. Hegel begins by wrenching Pure Being (or Immediacy) from Absolute Knowing. He now addresses various other candidates for beginning and finds them wanting.

First, instead of pulling Absolute Knowing apart and starting with the piece called Pure Immediacy, why not let it stay together as a whole? Hegel calls this possibility the collapse of Absolute Knowing (a complex) into Pure Being (a simplex). (73) In this move, Absolute Knowing disappears. It is obliterated by Pure Being. Indeed, obliteration is what Pure Being specializes in.

Such a view is rejected by Hegel because it is now impossible to begin. Pure Being obliterates all distinctions – including the very idea of beginning at all:

> [I]f pure being is . . . the unity into which knowing has collapsed . . . then knowing itself has vanished in that unity, leaving behind no difference from the unity and hence nothing by which the latter could be determined. Nor is there anything else present, any content which could be used to make the beginning more determinate.

---

[89] Adorno agrees: when Hegel deals with Becoming, "he waits until Being and Nothingness have been equated as wholly empty and indefinite before he pays attention to the difference indicated by the fact that the two concepts' literal linguistic meanings are absolutely contrary. . . . [I]t is not until their synthesis identifies them with each other that the moment will be nonidentical. This is where the claim of their identity obtains that restlessness, that inward shudder, which Hegel calls Becoming." ADORNO, NEGATIVE DIALECTICS, *supra* note 74, at 157.

> [¶] But the determination of *being* . . . for the beginning could also be omitted, so that the only demand would be that a pure beginning be made. (73)

In other words, suppose we collapse Absolute Knowing (the master unity) into Pure Being. "Collapse" is used in a non-sublation sense. The collapse is total, so that distinction as such goes out of existence. In the case of non-sublationary collapse, we do not wrench Being out of its place in Absolute Knowing. This step can be omitted. All we are left with is "demand" for a beginning. Whose demand? Ours, the fully formed beings in the audience, who want the show to begin![90]

Taking up the audience's impatient demand for a beginning ("our" presupposition that there must be a start), Hegel suggests that the audience is "without a particular object." (73) The beginning is no object. The beginning must bring *nothing* to the table (if the system is truly to be "groundless"). The beginning is supposed to be "wholly form without any content; thus we should have nothing at all beyond the general idea of a mere beginning as such." (73)

Granted that "beginning" is pure form and no content, can we at last begin? No. To say beginning is pure form is to say that it is nothing. It has no content – or rather has only itself for its content. And yet it will progress and become something. This means the nothingness of beginning – its purely formal nature – is a cheat. We *have begun*; ergo the hat of pure beginning had the rabbit of "being" in it all along. That

---

[90] EL at § 17 ("the beginning has relation only to the subject who decides to philosophize"). Some take the above passage to be a *legitimate* move of the Logic – in effect, simply a restatement of the principle that one should start with Pure Immediacy. MAKER, *supra* note 7, at 73-4; WINFIELD, *supra* note 5, at 31. Rather than viewing the true commencement of the Logic as the one-sided proposition of the Understanding, Winfield thinks that determinacy arises for *no reason*:

> One could thus say that the proper answer to the question "Why is there determinacy? is that there is and can be no reason, for any attempt to assign one presupposes determinacy by treating indeterminacy as if it were a definite determiner. All that can be offered in answer is an account of *how* indeterminacy gives rise to something else. What is clear from the start is that what follows from indeterminacy must do so immediately, which is to say, without reason, and without being determined by anything.

Id. at 50. But if this is so, one cannot account for how Speculative Reason finds the tools to differentiate stasis from movement.

I think Hegel is presenting a straw man here. The passage rejects the non-sublationary collapse and sets the stage for admitting that the Understanding elects to begin the Logic by abstracting Pure Being from Absolute Knowing.

is the only reason it could "become" something: "therefore being, too, is already contained in the beginning. The beginning . . . is the unity of being and nothing." (73) In slightly different words, if we do not wrench Pure Being from Absolute Knowing and if we rely on the bare thought of a beginning, we imply that we begin from *nothing*, because we cannot introduce content. But if we actually go anywhere, then we didn't really isolate Pure Nothing after all.[91] We smuggled in some content (some "being"), and *that* is what really got us started.[92]

With regard to beginning with the pure idea of beginning, one gets the impression that Hegel is responding to some philosopher who thought he knew better how to begin than Hegel. It is not clear with whom Hegel is debating,[93] but against this opponent Hegel defends his choice by noting that commencement with Pure Being reaches the same result as commencement with the pure idea of a beginning:

> But let those who are dissatisfied with *being* as a beginning because it passes over into nothing and so gives rise to the unity of being and nothing, let them see whether they find this beginning which begins with the general idea of a *beginning* and with its analysis (which, though of course correct, likewise leads to the unity of being and nothing), more satisfactory than the beginning with being. (74)

Thus, both Hegel and the unidentified "beginner" produce the same unity of being and nothing.

The ego. In exploring possible beginnings, Hegel considers a Car-

---

[91] Hegel suggests that beginning at Pure Nothing is impossible, because nothing comes of nothing. Later, he states that, if there is such a thing as Becoming, if we now are *something*, then obviously we did *not* begin at Pure Nothing. (84) Cynthia Willett argues that Hegel *could* have begun with Pure Nothing instead of Pure Being. Cynthia Willett, *The Shadow of Hegel's* Science of Logic, in ESSAYS ON HEGEL'S LOGIC, *supra* note 17, at 88; *see also* HOULGATE, *supra* note 84, at 269, 289. Willett is able to quote this passage: "[T]hat the beginning should be made with nothing (as in Chinese philosophy) need not cause us to lift a finger, for before we could do so this nothing would no less have converted itself into being." (99-100) Here, however, Hegel is arguing *against* starting at Pure Nothing. The claim against which he is arguing is that one should begin by abstracting everything away. The result would then be Pure Nothing. Hegel disagrees; the result would be Pure Being – exactly the beginning that he proposes.

[92] "If being had a determinateness, then it would not be the absolute beginning at all; it would then depend on an other . . . But if it is indeterminate and hence a genuine beginning, then, too, it has nothing with which it could bridge the gap between itself and an other; it is at the same time the *end*." (94)

[93] Hegel's erstwhile friend Schelling would be a good guess. GADAMER, *supra* note 4, at 85. Another might be Reinhold. Tom Rockmore, *Foundationalism and Hegelian Logic*, 21 OWL OF MINERVA 40, 48-9 (1989).

tesian possibility: begin with the ego that is certain of itself. (75-6)[94] The ego, however, is the most concrete of concrete things, according to Hegel. (76) By "concrete," Hegel means *that which is constructed of many complex parts.*[95] When a thing is concrete, "it is *differentiated within itself.*" (830) The opposite of "concrete" is "abstract." Abstraction is dead. It "strays from the highway of the Notion and forsakes the truth." (619) "When [concepts] are taken as fixed determinations and consequently in their separation from each other and not as held together in an organic unity, then they are dead forms and the spirit which is their living, concrete unity does not dwell in them." (48) Concrete things are alive with spirit. They have content and are in the process of filling themselves with yet more content.[96]

The ego is concrete. The beginning cannot be concrete; it must be abstract. To serve as a beginning of a groundless logic, the ego would have to purge itself of all content. But if ego did undergo such a purge, it wouldn't be the "familiar ego" of which we are "certain." So purged, the abstract ego reduces to Pure Being after all. But the process of abstraction would not be a logical progression. Rather, it would be driven by the arbitrary will to create a beginning of a groundless philosophy. Meanwhile, the whole reason for beginning with the ego was that it is "familiar." Only the concrete ego (our empirical experience of our selves) is familiar. Abstract ego is utterly strange and not a suitable beginning.

The ego is unsuitable for another reason. It develops in opposition to an object. In the *Phenomenology*, consciousness discovers that the object is its own self, and so the consciousness becomes self-consciousness. In this story, the ego shows that in its development

> the object has and retains the perennial character of an other for the ego, and that the ego which formed the starting-point is, therefore, still entangled in the world of appearance and is not the pure knowing which has . . . overcome the opposition of consciousness. (77)

---

[94] Feuerbach, *supra* note 86, at 61 ("Fichte's clamorous 'I'").

[95] In the *EL*, Hegel writes that Becoming is the first concrete thought. EL at § 88 Addition. "Concrete" and "abstract" are not official steps of the Logic but "belong, as it were, to the metalanguage of logic." ERROL E. HARRIS, THE SPIRIT OF HEGEL 78 (1993). On the various uses of the terms "abstract" and "concrete," see DARREL E. CHRISTENSEN, THE SEARCH FOR CONCRETENESS (1986); Philip T. Grier, *Abstract and Concrete in Hegel's Logic*, in ESSAYS ON HEGEL'S LOGIC, *supra* note 17, at 59.

[96] *See* DESMOND, *supra* note 69, at 122 ("thought not concrete is not thought at all").

The ego always faces an *other*. Because it is always correlative to some object, it cannot serve as a beginning. It is not simple enough.

To conclude, the essay *With What Must Science Begin?* yields three lessons worth remembering. (1) The *SL* is to be a groundless logic, utterly free of presupposition. (2) Deciding to begin at all is a contingent fact. (3) Given that we have chosen to begin, Pure Being is the best starting place, because it develops into the ultimate result – Absolute Knowing – which then mediates the beginning.

I have argued that the Logic's true beginning is the Understanding's one-sided attempt to summarize the very last step of the Logic – Absolute Knowing. It cannot fix this thought. Its attempt fails. The collapse of thought is the modulation Hegel writes of. The beginning of the Logic is failure, and that is what makes it a success.

The Opposition of Being and Nothing in Ordinary Thinking

Having finished with Hegel's essay on beginning, we advance to the remarks Hegel appends to his analysis of Becoming. In the first of these, Hegel bids his readers to follow the rules of Pure Being and Nothing. These are *indeterminate*. Do not smuggle in *determinateness*, the stuff of chapter 2.

This gives occasion for the first instance of "Hegel's severe and sometimes almost violent critique of Kant."[97] The assault concerns Kant's own attack on St. Anselm's "ontological proof of God." Hegel accuses Kant of using illegitimate moves against St. Anselm (with whom Hegel, in any event, disagreed).

---

[97] QUENTIN LAUER, ESSAYS IN HEGELIAN DIALECTIC 114 (1977). Hegel draws attention to his special focus on Kantian philosophy in his introduction, where Hegel writes, "whatever may be said . . . about the precise character of this philosophy . . . it constitutes the base and the starting-point of recent German philosophy and this its merit remains unaffected by whatever faults may be found in it." (61 n.1) Hegel credits Kant with paying attention to "*more specific* aspects of logic, whereas later philosophical works have paid little attention to these and in some instances have only displayed a crude – not unavenged – contempt for them." (61 n.1) Hegel finds that "[t]he philosophizing which is most widespread among us does *not* go beyond the Kantian results, that Reason cannot acquire knowledge of any true content . . . and in regard to absolute truth must be directed to faith." (62 n.1) This may have been Kant's result, but, Hegel complains, it is the *starting point* for *genuine* philosophy.

Hegel viewed Kantianism as a huge advance over the empiricists whom Kant sought to refute. Yet Kant's critical philosophy only went half-way. Because of this, and because of Kant's extreme prominence, "Hegel felt acutely the need to point out and to overcome Kant's shortcomings." HARRIS, LOGIC, *supra* note 14, at 63.

Here is Hegel's rendition of St. Anselm's ontological proof of God:

> Certainly that, than which nothing greater can be thought, cannot be in the intellect alone. For even if it is . . . , it can also be thought to exist in fact: and that is greater. If then that, than which nothing greater can be thought, is in the intellect alone, then the very thing, which is greater than anything which can be thought, can be exceeded in thought. But certainly this is impossible.[98]

Or, to paraphrase this, God ("that than which nothing greater can be thought") cannot be merely a figment of our imagination. If so, then I can think of something greater than the merely imagined God: God that exists both in and out of the imagination. If this greater God (God+) can be thought, then God+, which already exceeds thought, can be captured *in* thought. This is impossible – thought cannot exceed itself. Hence, we are somehow left with God+, which is both thinkable *and* existent in a realm beyond mere thought.

Hegel held that such a proof merely presupposes "a being possessing all realities, including . . . *existence*." (86)[99] Hegel's real purpose in invoking Anselm is to attack Kant's refutation of him, which Hegel takes as a threat to the triad of being-nothing-becoming.

According to Kant, all that the ontological proof accomplishes is to add existence (+) to the *thought* of God. Yet existence is not an independent predicate to any object. In other words, + = 0, and nothing is achieved in the proof.[100] Thus, if I have 100 real dollars and I add the predicate "existence" to them, my fortune has not increased. I still have only $100. Or, if I have 100 imaginary dollars in mind, my imaginary fortune is likewise not increased if I think "existence" in connection with the concept.[101]

---

[98] EL § 193, at 258.

[99] *See id.* at 259 ("The real fault in the argumentation of Anselm is [that the] unity which is enunciated as the supreme perfection . . . is presupposed, i.e. it is assumed only as potential. This identity . . . between the two categories may be at once met and opposed by their diversity; and this was the very answer given to Anselm long ago.").

[100] For the view that this misinterprets Kant, see S. Morris Engel, *Kant's 'Refutation' of the Ontological Argument*, in KANT: A COLLECTION OF CRITICAL ESSAYS 189 (Robert Paul Wolff ed., 1968). According to Engel, what Kant meant to say was that existence *is* a predicate, but not a logical or real one. Rather, it is a third kind. As a nonreal predicate, existence *posits*, rather than amplifies or explicates, a thing.

[101] IMMANUEL KANT, CRITIQUE OF PURE REASON A599/B627 (Paul Guyer & Allen W. Wood trans., 1990). Kant's ultimate point is that "any attempt to *prove* that God exists is ultimately reducible to the 'ontological argument,' which involves an illegitimate leap from the order of concept to the order of being." LAUER, ESSAYS, *supra* note 97, at 114.

Hegel protests that, in the chapter on Pure Being, consciousness is supposed to think in a *very* abstract manner. But consciousness will be tempted to focus on something concrete – not allowed at this stage of the Logic.[102] If this happens, consciousness will ridicule the proposition that Being turns into Nothing. Hegel fears that people will interpret him as saying that it is a matter of indifference whether $100 are imaginary or real. Obviously, even the most ardent idealist sees that $100 in the mind is empirically different from $100 in the wallet. But $100, in either form, are *concrete entities*. Pure Being/Nothing, as it exists in chapter 1, is the ultimate *abstract* concept – so abstract that it cannot properly be called a "concept." "Having" or "not having" is a matter of consequence. But "having" is *complex*. "Being" and "not being" operate at a quite lower level. They are perfectly *simple*.[103] If Pure Being is Pure Nothing, this does not mean that, in real life, you can dream up $100 and use it to buy dinner.[104]

---

[102] "Nothing is usually opposed to *something*; but the being of *something* is already determinate and is distinguished from another *something*; and so therefore the nothing which is opposed to the something is also the nothing of a particular something, a determinate nothing." (83)

[103] On the distinction between "being" and "having," Hegel writes:

> As a term of relation, "to have" takes the place of "to be". True, some[thing] has qualities on its part too: but this transference of 'having' into the sphere of Being is inexact . . . [T]he character as quality is directly one with the some[thing], and the some[thing] ceases to be when it loses its quality. But the thing is reflection-into-self: for it is an identity which is also distinct from the difference, i.e. from its attributes. In many languages 'have' is employed to denote past time. And with reason: for the past is absorbed or suspended being, and the mind is its reflection-into-self; in the mind only it continues to subsist – the mind . . . distinguishing from itself this being in it which has been absorbed or suspended.

EL § 125.

[104] Later, Hegel returns to the hundred thalers:

> attention was drawn to the confusion that arises when, in the case of a particular determinate being, what is fixed on is not the *being* of that determinate being but its *determinate content*; then, comparing *this determinate content*, for example a hundred dollars, with another *determinate content*, for example, with the content of my perception or the state of my finances, it is found that it makes a difference whether the former content is added to the latter or not – and it is imagined that what has been discussed is the difference between being and non-being, or even the difference between being and the Notion. (705)

In other words, what concerns Kant about the hundred thalers is not being as such, but

Hegel also takes Kant to task for suggesting that an actual $100 is indifferent to my thought of them. This presupposes that the $100 has "self-identity" – a position that Hegel strongly opposes.[105] Hegel will argue that all concepts contain "being-for-other."[106] Hence, the $100 is not indifferent to what I think, because part of its constitution is to be *thought*. The $100's being-for-other is what I think of them. But perhaps these issues are presented by Hegel far too early for a full appreciation of their import.

Finally, Hegel criticizes Kant for comparing God to dollars. Dollars are finite things. With regard to finite things, our thought of them is different from the reality of them. In contrast, God is infinite (*i.e.*, self-determining). Kant is accused of borrowing the attributes of finite things and applying them to infinite things – a category mistake.

Defectiveness of the Expression: Unity, Identity of Being and Nothing

Consider the phrase, "the relation of *A* and *B*." On the one hand, the remark refers to parts – *A* and *B*. On the other hand, the relation is a thing unto itself. The "relation" is just as separate a thing as *A* and *B* are. Is the aforementioned relation complex or simple? Obviously, it is both. Becoming in Figure 1(c) is just such a "relation" between Pure Being and Nothing. [7] is simple; [4, 5, 6] is complex.

In Remark 2, Hegel analyzes the paradox of relations in the proposition "being and nothing are one and the same" (91)[107] – the proposition depicted as [4] in Figure 1(c). On the one hand, the proposition asserts a relation – the identity or "sameness" of being and nothing. On the other hand, the proposition refers to being and nothing as if they are different. The proposition is thus contradictory. One could not refer to being and nothing as the same unless they were sufficiently different so as to be named "being" and "nothing."

---

the determinate concept of one hundred thalers. Given the difference found between the one hundred real and imaginary thalers, what *is* is distinguished from what is *not*. But this cannot count as contributing any insight about being.

[105] LAUER, ESSAYS, *supra* note 97, at 123 ("The point is that the concept of the 100 Talers simply is not a true concept, precisely because it is isolated, abstract, and, therefore, unreal"). In effect, Hegel accuses Kant of empiricism – reliance on sense-certainty of perceived objects as the ultimate criterion of truth. HARRIS, LOGIC, *supra* note 14, at 63. Ironically, Kant himself thought he was *refuting* the empiricists. *Id*. at 48.

[106] *Infra* at 74-75.

[107] "Sein und Nichts ist Eins und dasselbe." [I:75] This is better translated as "being and nothing *is* one and the same." ROSEN, *supra* note 52, at 151.

What is the significance of *contradiction*, such as the one we have just identified? Contradiction – the "motor of things"[108] – destroys proposition. Vanishing is immanent in the proposition. Vanishing is the proposition's "result." (90) This vanishing is Becoming, "ceasing-to-be" what it is and "coming-to-be" something else.

The result, however, is not expressed in proposition. The proposition at hand ("being and nothing are the same") should, but does not manage to, say "being and nothing are the same *and* the truth of this has already vanished." Thus, we have this important dictum from Hegel: "the proposition in the *form of a judgement* is not suited to express speculative truths." (90) Any given proposition expresses a *moment* of truth, but it is also a lie because it fails to add: *and the truth of this proposition is about to and already has vanished.*

Where is the truth, then? It is in the *movement* of the sequence of Understanding, Dialectical and Speculative Reason. Truth is in *motion*. Propositions only capture a one-sided view of it.

Hegel, for the moment, calls propositions *judgments*.[109] "Judgment is an *identical* relation between subject and predicate." (90) For example, "the rose is red," or "being/nothing is identical." These judgments fail to capture the whole truth:

> [T]he subject has a number of determinatenesses other than that of the predicate, and also that the predicate is more extensive than the subject. Now if the content is speculative, the *non-identical* aspect of subject and predicate is also an essential moment, but in the judgement this is not expressed. (90-1)

In other words, the rose is many things other than red, yet this "speculative content" is not expressed. In addition, many things are red besides roses. This too is not expressed.

To fill out the inadequacy of the judgment, the opposite judgment should be added: "being and nothing are not the same." (91) Between the stated and speculative content, there is ceaseless movement. The moment of identity is legitimate but incomplete. The moment of difference is likewise legitimate but incomplete.

With regard to "that unfortunate word 'unity'" (91), it is usually discovered by "mere comparison," (52) (*Vergleichung*) – a mediocre technique, in Hegel's view. Comparison is accomplished by *external*

---

[108] TAYLOR, *supra* note 82, at 243.

[109] Later, Hegel warns against equating these two, since Judgment *guarantees* that subject is predicate, whereas proposition does not. *Infra* at 465.

reflection – a reflection quite divorced from the things compared.[110]

> When this reflection finds the same thing in two *different objects*, the resultant unity is such that there is presupposed the complete *indifference* to it of the objects themselves which are compared, so that this comparing and unity does not concern the objects themselves . . . Unity, therefore, expresses wholly *abstract* sameness and sounds all the more blatantly paradoxical the more the terms of which it is asserted show themselves to be sheer opposites. (91)

The abstract sameness of *A* and *B*, toward which they are indifferent, is not the unity which Pure Being and Nothing enjoy. Pure Being and Nothing are simultaneously the same and different. Sameness is constantly disappearing into difference. And vice versa, difference is vanishing into sameness. Identity and difference are constantly coming-to-be and ceasing-to-be. The isolation of one of these as the predominant moment is the work of external reflection – mere "subjective *opinion* [*Meinen*]." (92)

Suppose the moments of being and nothing could endure. Then they would be *determinate* being and *determinate* nothing. These concepts are too advanced. So far we have *indeterminate* Being and Nothing. These moments are not yet in the least way self-subsistent. Indeed, they are *less than moments*.[111]

Incomprehensibility of the Beginning

In Remark 4, Hegel addresses Kant's first antinomy of reason. According to this antinomy: (a) The world has a beginning in time and a limit in space. Or (b) the world has *no* beginning in time and is spatially unlimited.[112] In proving (b), Kant argued that, if time began, there must have been a void before time. Yet a void cannot be a beginning. Nothing can come of nothing.

Hegel responds that the claim of "nothing from nothing" does not describe his own theory of Becoming as the unity of Being and Nothing. Kant's claim of "nothing from nothing" works only if Being and Nothing can be kept apart and isolated. If they cannot be isolated, then Hegel is acquitted of this charge.

---

[110] External reflection is an important category in Essence. For now, think of external reflection as ordinary consciousness perceiving supposedly self-identical objects (*i.e.*, naive metaphysics).

[111] Pippin, *supra* note 23, at 189.

[112] CRITIQUE OF PURE REASON, *supra* note 101, at A426-7/B454-5.

Hegel accuses Kant of sophistry: "This style of reasoning which makes and clings to . . . absolute separateness of being and non-being is to be named not dialectic but sophistry. For sophistry is an argument proceeding from a baseless presupposition which is uncritically and unthinkingly adopted." (105) Dialectics are opposed to argument from baseless presupposition. "[W]e call dialectic the higher movement of reason in which such seemingly utterly separate terms pass over into each other spontaneously . . . a movement in which the presupposition sublates itself. (105) Notice, in this formulation, that sublation is *spontaneous*, the Kantian term for freedom.[113] Similarly, in Dialectical Reason, an isolated moment *freely* and spontaneously sublates itself. It destroys itself and becomes its opposite. Hegel is the philosopher of *positive freedom*. Spirit has a program. In most merely "liberal" philosophies, only *negative* freedom is produced – freedom from outside compulsion. Nothing positive is generated.

We also find in Remark 4 a reference to differential calculus, a concept that endlessly pleased Hegel.[114] In differential calculus, we imagine the effect of a small change on a mathematical expression. For example, take $y = 5x$. Differential calculus asks, "if we change x by a small amount (δx), what is the effect on y?" Obviously, the answer is: no matter how small the change, it will be visited five-fold on y. Or $\delta y / \delta x = 5$. Notice that, in this expression, as δx approaches zero, we approach dividing by zero – an impossibility. The differential is in the process of vanishing. It is an example of Hegel's "determinate nothing," and a mathematical illustration of his dictum that *nothing is, after all, something*. Of deeply spiritual entities like δx, Hegel writes:

> These magnitudes . . . *are* in their vanishing, not *before* their vanishing, for then they are finite magnitudes, or *after* their vanishing, for then they are nothing. Against this pure notion it is objected and reiterated that such magnitudes are *either* something *or* nothing; that there is no *intermediate state* between being and non-being . . . Here too, the absolute separation of being and nothing is assumed. (104)

Thus, δx is *in between* something and nothing.[115] Those who argue

---

[113] HENRY E. ALLISON, KANT'S TRANSCENDENTAL IDEALISM: AN INTERPRETATION AND DEFENSE 317 (1983) ("In the Dialectic, transcendental freedom is defined as absolute spontaneity, and this is understood as a causal power that is itself independent of determination by antecedent causes").

[114] Hegel dedicates almost 80 pages to calculus in his second chapter on Quantity.

[115] Later, Hegel says that $\delta x / \delta y$ is a determinateness. It is "not nothing" but is "an intermediate state . . . between being and nothing." (254) According to one commentator:

like Kant that nothing is nothing (and not something) therefore place themselves in opposition to the prestige of differential calculus.

(b) Moments of Becoming: Coming-to-Be and Ceasing-to-Be

Becoming – middle term between Being and Nothing – is concrete. It has difference within it [4, 5, 6] but it is a unity [7]. Pure Being/Nothing, however, is the *same*. Difference precedes this identity. How does Being/Nothing move if difference is outside it? I have said that what is different is Absolute Knowing and the nothingness of Pure Being/Nothing. The beginning is a failure to begin. Yet Hegel speaks of the modulation as being from *Being* to *Nothing* and back again: "nothing passes over into nothing, but nothing is equally . . . transition into being, coming-to-be." (106) This transition requires that Pure Being first be *distinguishable* from Pure Nothing, then *undistinguishable*.

To make sense of this modulation, we must associate Absolute Knowing with Being and Pure Being/Nothing with Nothing. After all, Absolute Knowing is what Being becomes across the entire *SL*. Absolute Knowing is what the Understanding *intends* Pure Being to be. So conceived, Being becomes Nothing when the Understanding attempts to begin. Yet Being *is* Nothing. So Nothing likewise ceases to be and yields to Being. As such, it is *coming*-to-be. This is the retrospective conclusion of Speculative Reason from the perspective of Becoming.

In Becoming, each extreme, Being and Nothing, becomes the other. Movement characterizes *both* of the extremes. In fact, the extremes *are* movement – two sub-Becomings. "Becoming therefore contains being and nothing as *two* such unities, *each* of which is itself a unity of being and nothing." (105) Each extreme changes into the other, and, in this transition, brings along its properties as it becomes the other. The

---

The objection was raised against the differential calculus, that an intermediate position between being and nothing is an impossibility. The calculus . . . is based on this assumption, however, for it derives from the notion that the determinations of quantum are vanishing quantities, that is, that they are neither a quantum nor a nothing, but a mutual determination in respect of other quantities. The objection raised was therefore rejected by Hegel, who maintained that the unity of being and nothing is not a state but a disappearing as well as a becoming, only the middle or the unity itself constituting the truth of the matter.

Host-Heino Von Borzeszkowski, *Hegel's Interpretation of Classical Mechanics*, in HEGEL AND NEWTONIANISM, *supra* note 2, at 75.

extremes are in a state of perfect communication. This idea of the extremes investing the other with its properties, Hegel's "most distinctive move,"[116] has been called the "chiasmic exchange of properties."[117] This chiasmic exchange is sublation itself.

(c) Sublation of Becoming

Coming-to-be and ceasing-to-be are in motion. In Figure 1(c), [7] constitutes the equilibrium – the unity at rest. "The resultant equilibrium of coming-to-be and ceasing-to-be is in the first place *becoming* itself. But this equally settles into a stable unity. Being and nothing are in this unity only as vanishing moments . . . Becoming is an unstable unrest which settles into a stable result." (106) One can say, in a double sense, that, if being and nothing are a contradiction, then Becoming "contains" the contradiction: Becoming has contradiction inside it (and hence "contains" it). Becoming, so long as it stays a fixed moment, prevents contradiction from blowing apart.

But we have said that Becoming has active parts and static wholeness. This contradictory state of affairs means that Becoming must disintegrate. How can something move and stay put simultaneously? This contradiction implies "the vanishedness of becoming." (106)

Becoming must go.[118] We can focus on only one of the two features

---

[116] John W. Burbidge, *Hegel's Logic*, in HANDBOOK OF THE HISTORY OF LOGIC 131, 137 (2004).

[117] SLAVOJ ŽIŽEK, FOR THEY KNOW NOT WHAT THEY DO: ENJOYMENT AS A POLITICAL FACTOR 39-41 (1991). A chiasmus is the inversion of the order of syntactical elements in the second of two juxtaposed and syntactically parallel phrases or clauses. An example: "All professors are clever men, but clever men aren't all professors." WALTER NASH, RHETORIC: THE WIT OF PERSUASION 114 (1989).

[118] Clark Butler distinguishes between basic and nonbasic logical moves. The basic moves name the absolute directly. Pure Being and the Determinate Being of Figure 2(a) qualify as "basic" moves. The "nonbasic" moves – Figures 1(b) and 1(c), for instance – do not purport to name the absolute, but merely comment on any such definition. BUTLER, LOGIC, *supra* note 19, at 35. Butler specifically announces that "Becoming is not necessary to the dialectical development." *Id*. at 36. Indeed, it is a positive impediment because, as the modulation between the extremes in Figure 1(c), it prevents an advance to [7] – the step of Speculative Reason. I disagree. Becoming is, first of all, *named* in Figure 1(c) for the first time. By the time we are conscious of the modulation, we have already overcome it. The modulation was therefore no dead end. In the very naming of the activity we have progressed. Becoming – and Speculative Reason generally – is essential to the process and *is* a proposed version of the absolute, which, in Figure 2(a), the Understanding will proceed to misunderstand.

of Becoming – stasis or movement. We have to choose. Shall we view Becoming as active or passive? Hegel advises: choose passive. The passive is the initial position of the Understanding. It is the side of being. Hence, in the fourth official move of the *SL*, we take the static part of Becoming [7], and move it to the left of the diagram (where the Understanding resides).[119]

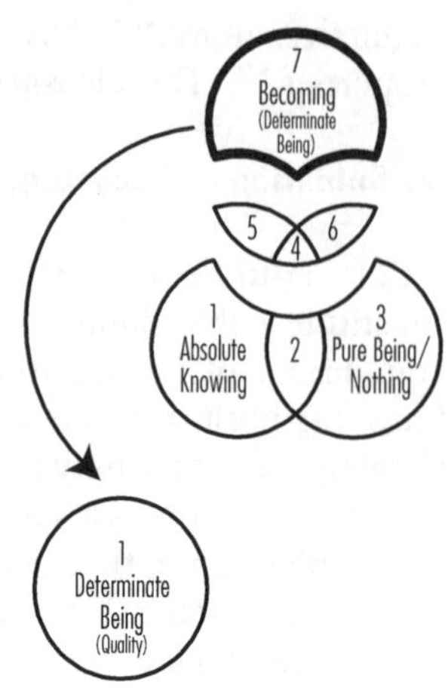

Figure 2(a)
Determinate Being

Had we made the opposite choice – had we moved the active part over to the right side of dialectical reasoning – we would "relapse into one of the already sublated determinations." (106) In effect we would drop back to the alternation of Figure 1(b) and 1(a). Of course, we could do this. Being a circle, Logic works forwards and backwards. But we will learn more if we insist on pressing forward to chapter 2. This is the "progressive" move (for us).

In Figure 2(a), we take misshapen [7] and round it out to [1]. This represents the fundamental error of the Understanding, which sees simplicity in lieu of complexity. We contemplate Becoming *as if* it were a whole. In describing [1], Hegel writes: "But this stable oneness is being, yet no longer as a determination on its own but as a determination of the whole. Becoming . . . , a unity which is in the form of being or has the form of the one-sided *immediate* unity of these moments, is *determinate being*." (106) Figure 2(a) shows the transition to Determinate Being. In the transition from middle term to a new one-sided term, Becoming is now Determinate Being.

The Nature of Hegel's Logic

Hegel's introductory materials emphasize that Logic is metaphysics, "purely speculative philosophy." (27) Modernity, he complains, has lost

119 *See* BURBIDGE, RELIGION, *supra* note 22, at 22 (Determinate Being "is an immediate concept whose mediating 'becoming' has disappeared from view").

its interest in metaphysics. He blames Kant's "exoteric"[120] philosophy, which teaches "that the understanding ought not to go beyond experience, else the cognitive faculty will become a theoretical reason which by itself generates nothing but fantasies of the brain." (25)

Kantianism conceives of thought as a relation (or syllogism) in which subject and object are the two extremes. So conceived, thought cuts us off from the object. Thinking is reduced to *form*. The *content* of the cognition remains beyond thought. The object "is taken as something complete and finished on its own account, something which can entirely dispense with thought for its actuality." (44) Thought, on this view, contains no real truth and is taken as defective. "Knowing has lapsed into opinion." (46)

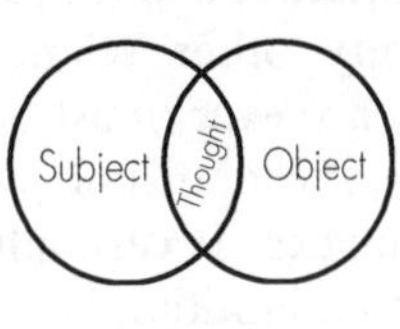

Thought

Hegel says of the view that we know only phenomena [2] (not things-in-themselves [3]): "This is like attributing to someone a correct perception, with the rider that nevertheless he is incapable of perceiving what is true but only what is false." (47) Such contradictory ideas "bar the entrance to philosophy [and] must be discarded at its portals." (45)

The Kantian view "can be countered by the simple observation that these very things which are supposed to stand . . . beyond the thoughts referring to them, are themselves figments of subjective thought." (36) Here we have Hegel's famous critique of Kant's thing-in-itself: it is supposed to be beyond thought, but in fact it is itself *just a thought*, on the same level as the phenomena it supposedly grounds.[121] Thoughts are taken to be *forms*, referring to a content (*i.e.*, the object) that is beyond thought. But the truth of the object is its *Notion* – the *thought* of it. Notion therefore *is* the content of the object. "The great joke, Hegel wrote in a personal note, is that things are what they are. There is no reason to go beyond them."[122]

If we can draw the Notion from the object, then thinking becomes free. *Free* thought is that which is "performed with an awareness of what is being done." (37) When thinking is merely instinctive (unaware of itself), "spirit is enmeshed in the bonds of its categories and is

---

[120] The opposite of "esoteric."

[121] Sally S. Sedgwick, *Hegel's Treatment of Transcendental Apperception in Kant*, 23 OWL OF MINERVA 151, 158-9 (1992) ("Since the idea of a content outside thought is itself a product of thought, the distinctions between appearances and things in themselves . . . can only be drawn, as Hegel says, 'on *this side* in consciousness'").

[122] HYPPOLITE, GENESIS, *supra* note 6, at 125.

broken up into an infinitely varied material." (37) Instinctive thinking cannot fathom the unity in diverse things.

Free thought follows a necessary development. In this development, the steps must *necessarily* follow one another. Even the very idea of necessity must itself be derived *necessarily*. Logic must therefore be self-referential: it has its own self as its subject matter. It is both (a) method and (b) the derivation of method. Every other science distinguishes subject matter and method. Method, however, must be Logic's own final result. If logic would be a *science*, it cannot borrow methods from "subordinate" fields such as mathematics. It certainly cannot be satisfied with "categorical assurances of inner intuition." (27) Hence, "what logic is cannot be stated beforehand." (43) Its method must emerge as the final outcome. For this reason, no "introduction" can establish Logic's notion. It can only make Logic "more accessible to ordinary thinking." (43)

Common sense (*i.e.*, unfree thought, or the Understanding) leaves truth and content to one side and considers only form. Nevertheless, the Understanding actually achieves something profound. By separating form and content (*i.e.*, thought from the object), the Understanding's eye, glazed with blinding tears, divides the object.[123] "But *equally* it must transcend . . . its *separating* determinations and straightway *connect* them." (46) This connecting activity (Speculative Reason) is the great "negative step" that leads to the true Notion of reason.

From what point of view must Logic be considered? Hegel's answer is, from mind's own view. In Logic, mind learns what it is. In the *Phenomenology*, a thinking subject faced an object. The end result was the unity of subject and object – Absolute Knowing. The *Phenomenology's* result was the elimination of consciousness as a valid philosophical standpoint. It is also the beginning point of the *SL*: "Thus pure science presupposes liberation from the opposition of consciousness. It contains *thought in so far as this is just as much the object in its own self, or the object in its own self in so far as it is equally pure thought*." (49) In other words, thought thinks itself. Logic's point of view is strictly its own – not ours. The *SL* is no phenomenology.

> Consequently, far from it being formal, far from it standing in need of a matter to constitute an actual and true cognition, it is its content alone which has absolute truth . . . Accordingly, logic is to be understood as the system of pure reason, as the

---

[123] "Understanding has a bad press amongst Hegelians." BURBIDGE, RELIGION, *supra* note 22, at 29. But it is a necessary (though one-sided) part of the process.

> realm of pure thought. This realm is truth as it is without veil and in its own absolute nature. (49-50)

The *SL* is nothing short of "the exposition of God as he is in his eternal essence before the creation of nature and a finite mind." (50) "[S]trong stuff from a relatively unknown writer who was at the time still only a *Gymnasium* professor with unfulfilled aspirations for university employment."[124]

Ordinary logic, Hegel observes, has fallen into contempt. It is dealt with out of habit rather than conviction. Such a logic accepts its determinations "in their unmoved fixity." (52)[125] It brings together its

---

[124] TERRY PINKARD, HEGEL: A BIOGRAPHY 342 (2000); *see* KAUFMANN, *supra* note 45, at 174 (the *SL* "is not as mad as these words may seem; in any case, it is still the labor of an utterly lonely genius"). Was Hegel a blasphemer, claiming divine powers for himself and for those who comprehend his Logic? HARRIS, SPIRIT, *supra* note 30, at 226 (Hegel's remark "has offended . . . many professing Christians, to whom it has seemed to be a palpable blasphemy"). Maker argues not. Absolute knowing obliterates consciousness. Therefore, no merely conscious individual can attain the position of absolute knowing. MAKER, *supra* note 7, at 130. Maker interprets Hegel as *emphasizing* man's finitude, but without the problems inherent to antifoundationalism, which insists on the contradictory dogma, "there *are* no universal truths." "Therefore, rather than being the ultimate philosophical blasphemy, Hegel's presentation of absolute knowing is the consummate critique of it." *Id.* at 131. Hegel is guilty of blasphemy "only so long as we see consciousness' mode of knowing as the only possible one." *Id.* at 134.

[125] Miller's translation includes at this point a notorious footnote from the first edition of the *SL* (deleted in the subsequent edition):

> The latest treatment of this science which has recently appeared, *System of Logic by Fries*, returns to the anthropological foundations. The idea or opinion on which it is based is so shallow, both in itself and in its execution, that I am spared the trouble of taking any notice of this insignificant publication. (52 n.1)

This footnote created a scandal at the time it was printed. J.F. Fries, Hegel's lifelong enemy, was a popularizer of philosophy and considered a liberal (though a virulent anti-semite). Irritatingly, Fries obtained jobs at the universities at Jena and Heidelberg before Hegel did and Fries's book on logic appeared in 1811, one year before Hegel's publication. Hegel apparently looked forward to royalties on the *SL* and felt that Fries's book would eat into his income. Publication of the above-quoted footnote caused comment in the philosophical community and contributed to Hegel's failure to receive a professorship at Heidelberg until Fries himself vacated his position for a chair in Geneva. JACQUES D'HONDT, HEGEL IN HIS TIME: BERLIN, 1818-1831 83-98 (John Burbidge trans., 1988). In private, Hegel could be even more scathing of Fries. In a letter to a friend, Hegel referred to Fries' volume as "utterly disorganized dirty linen that only a fool sitting on his toilet could possibly produce." HORST ALTHAUS, HEGEL: AN INTELLECTUAL BIOGRAPHY 123 (Michael Tarsh trans. 2000). Fries would later write a

concepts by external (not immanent) relation. It is mere *analytical* philosophy. Ordinary logic "is not much better than a manipulation of rods of unequal lengths in order to sort and group them according to size," or "a childish game of fitting together the pieces of a coloured picture puzzle." (52-3) It is mere reckoning, vulgar mathematics, base empirical science, bearing no trace of scientific method.

"Before these dead bones of logic can be quickened by spirit" (53), Hegel writes, a "quite *simple* insight" (54) must be grasped:

> the negative is just as much positive, or that what is self-contradictory does not resolve itself into a nullity . . . but essentially only into the negation of its *particular* content, in other words, that such a negation is not all and every negation but the negation of a specific subject matter which resolves itself, and consequently is a specific negation, and therefore the result essentially contains that from which it results; which strictly speaking is a tautology, for otherwise it would be an immediacy and not a result. Because the result, the negation, is a *specific* negation it has a content. It is a fresh Notion but higher and richer than its predecessor; for it is richer by the negation . . . of the latter, therefore contains it, but also something more, and is the unity of itself and its opposite. It is in this way that the system of Notions as such has to be formed – and has to complete itself in a purely continuous course in which nothing extraneous is introduced. (54)

Here is the very nerve and bone of the *SL*: *nothing is, after all, something*. Negation contains and preserves what it cancels. It adds content (itself) to what it cancels.[126]

The negativity embedded within the positive entity enables the Logic to advance. Its recovery is the function of dialectics. In Hegel's

---

critical review of the *SL*. *Id*. at 126.

[126] This passage draws criticism from Michael Rosen, who sees Hegel as making two claims: (1) Negation is not *all* negation but is the negation of a determinate matter. (2) The *result* of negation contains that *from which* it resulted. Hegel connects these with a "so that," as if the first claim entails the latter. According to Rosen, "this is certainly wrong." Hegel assumes negation is an activity, or operation on a thing. ROSEN, *supra* note 52, at 32. "But why should we make this assumption?" he asks. *Id*. If we refuse to make it, the second proposition above does not follow from the first.

If Rosen were correct, Hegel's Logic would be utterly destroyed. Fortunately for Hegel, it is Rosen who is wrong; he confounds negation (a more advanced point in the logic) with Pure Nothing. Negation is not nothing. Negation is *cancellation*. It is an *act*, not a fact. It is therefore always a correlative term; it can *never* stand alone but must refer to (and therefore is constituted by) what it cancels. By the time negation appears in chapter 2, Determinate Being has also appeared. Determinate Being *was*, after Negation is through. In Negation, there is the *memory* of Determinate Being. Once Determinate Being is on the scene, it is impossible to return to Pure Nothing, which admits of no distinction and no memory.

philosophy, Dialectical Reason has a different connotation than in the old philosophies. Plato took dialectics to be "mere conceit" or "a subjective itch for unsettling and destroying what is fixed and substantial." (56) Kant rated dialectics higher. In the *Critique of Pure Reason*, it becomes a necessary function of reason. Nevertheless Kant held it to be "merely the art of practicing deceptions and producing illusions." (56) It was

> only a spurious game, the whole of its power resting on concealment of the deceit . . . Kant's expositions in the antinomies of pure reason . . . do not indeed deserve any great praise; but the general idea on which he based his expositions . . . is the *objectivity of the illusion and the necessity of the contradiction* . . . primarily, it is true, with the significance that these determinations are applied by reason to *things-in-themselves* but their nature is precisely . . . intrinsic or in itself. This result, grasped in its positive aspect, is nothing else but the inner negativity of the determinations as their self-moving soul. (56)

In Hegel's view, where Kant found four antinomies in pure reason, he should have seen that *every* concept has antinomy within it. There are infinite, not four, antinomies. (190)

Hegel says that he cannot pretend that the *SL* is incapable of greater completeness. (54) But he knows that the method is the only true one.[127] "This is self-evident simply from the fact that [method] is not something distinct from its object and content." (54) As we shall discover, Absolute Knowing *is* method – the unity of the Understanding, Dialectic and Speculative Reason.

---

[127] Gadamer sees Hegel's posture toward the *SL* as one of modesty, presumably on the basis of this passage:

> The ideal of a science of logic . . . does not imply that . . . perfection might ever be completely attained by any individual. Hegel himself fully acknowledges that his own logic is a first attempt which lacks ultimate perfection. What he means, obviously, is that by pursuing multiple paths of derivation, one could work out . . . the fine distinctions of what had only been given in outline form in the *Logic*. Indeed, one can discern, not only in the second printing of the first volume of the *Logic* as contrasted with the first, but also within one and the same text, that Hegel corrects himself even in his publications. He can say, for instance, that he wishes to present the same subject matter form another point of view, that one can arrive at the same result in another way, etc. Thus Hegel's point is not only that in his *Logic* he did not complete the enormous task before him, but beyond that, in an absolute sense, that it cannot be completed.

GADAMER, *supra* note 4, at 82.

2 Determinate Being

A major goal of the Logic is to account for *determinateness*.[1] Determinateness denotes a unity of being and nothing – a *presence* and an *absence*.[2] Determinateness arises because Dialectical Reason invokes *history* against the Understanding. This history *was* present, but now is *not*. The sublated *past* is the determinate nothing to which present Being refers.

Becoming was a determinateness – a two-sided entity in a state of contradiction. Determinateness contradicts the idea of immediacy. Yet the Understanding sees immediacy before it and so does violence to the principle of determinateness.

In Figure 2(a), the Understanding makes a one-sided Being of determinate Becoming. Accordingly, Determinate Being or Quality is shown as an immediate entity [1], the same as Pure Being. Yet special care should be taken in interpreting Figure 2(a). Thanks to the law of sublation, we know that Determinate Being contains all past steps. It has a history and is *covertly* a determinateness. Determinate Being is a *determinateness* with the *accent on being*. It "corresponds to *being* in the previous sphere, but being is indeterminate and therefore no

---

1 ROBERT B. PIPPIN, HEGEL'S IDEALISM: THE SATISFACTIONS OF SELF-CONSCIOUSNESS 204 (1989).

2 *See* RICHARD DIEN WINFIELD, OVERCOMING FOUNDATIONS: STUDIES IN SYSTEMATIC PHILOSOPHY 69 (1989) ("Without referring to any other properties, determinacy seems to be defined simply by what it is and what it is not").

determinations issue from it. *Determinate* being, however, is *concrete*; consequently a number of determinations, distinct relations of its moments, make their appearance in it." (110)

Hegel also asserts that Quality is *alterable* and *finite*. Why alterable? This becomes comprehensible only later, but it has to do with the fact that Determinate Being is in a state of Becoming – a movement that is present on the logic of sublation. Why finite? Quality is a one-sided view of determinateness and is therefore *limited by its other*, as Figure 2(b) will show.

Hegel trifurcates his second chapter into (A) Determinate Being as Such; (B) Something and its Other (or Finitude); and (C) Qualitative Infinity. Roughly, (A) is the move of the Understanding. (B) entails the modulating doubleness of Dialectical Reason. (C) is Speculative Reason's conciliatory move.

A. Determinate Being as Such

(a) Determinate Being in General

Hegel describes the transition from [7] to [1] in Figure 2(a): "From becoming [7] there issues determinate being [1], which is the simple oneness of being and nothing. Because of this oneness it has the form of *immediacy*. Its mediation, becoming, lies behind it; it has sublated itself." (109) Becoming is a oneness by virtue of [7]. The *whole* of Becoming [4-7] is certainly not a oneness. Only from [7] does Determinate Being spring forth. In this form it is immediacy. Its mediated history is suppressed.

The German word for Being is *Sein*; the word for *Determinate* Being is *Dasein* – being *there*.[3] Determinate Being is *being* in a certain *place*. Yet, Hegel warns, "space" is too advanced for chapter 2. *Dasein* does, however, hint at negation. If a thing is *there*, it is not *here*.[4]

---

[3] John Burbidge prefers "*a* being: "The indefinite article suggests that it is not absolutely indeterminate but is in some way limited by a nothing out of which it comes and to which it may return." JOHN W. BURBIDGE, ON HEGEL'S LOGIC: FRAGMENTS OF A COMMENTARY 42 (1981).

[4] Clark Butler suggests that the significance of Something – more advanced than Determinate Being – is that a determination is *this* as opposed to *that*. CLARK BUTLER, HEGEL'S LOGIC: BETWEEN DIALECTIC AND HISTORY 47 (1996). But Determinate Being already incorporates this notion of "this, not that." As Butler puts it somewhat earlier, the significance of Determinate Being is that things become "determinable." *Id*. at 41. What is present – a *this* – is distinguishable from what is absent – a *that*.

"Determinate being as the result of its becoming is, in general, being with a non-being such that this non-being is taken up into simple unity with being." (110)

Determinate Being – heir to the "being" portion of Becoming [7] – is to be viewed as "a sublated, negatively determined being." (110) That is to say, [1] in Figure 2(a) is the negation of the earlier history of Becoming. [7] is simply what [4, 5, 6] are *not* – the static moment of the unity. But, if Being is negatively determined, it is only so "for us." For itself, the negative nature of this activity is "not yet posited."

The silent fourth. In this subsection, Hegel hints at something interesting about the Understanding: "That the whole, the unity of being and nothing, is in the one-sided determinateness of being [1] is an external reflection; but in the negation, in *something* and *other* and so on, it will come to be *posited*." (110) The move of Understanding – abstracting [7] and making it [1] – is an *external reflection* not strictly necessitated as a matter of logic. It comes from the outside.[5]

This point should be understood as follows. The Logic is a circle. We can go forward or backward. If we go forward, through the move of Understanding, this is *our choice*. We do this because *we* have an interest in watching the Logic unfold in that particular direction.[6] What follows automatically, however, is Dialectical and Speculative Reason. These, at least, are "immanent" to the Logic itself. In short, Logic needs the Understanding to move forward. Without it, Logic lies fallow. Hence, the abstracting move of the Understanding represents a necessary *contingent* moment in the Logic.[7] But once the Understanding makes its move, Dialectical and Speculative Reason follow necessarily.

---

5 The 1812 edition of the *SL* commenced "Determinate Being" with: "A being as such determines itself." But in the 1831 edition, a passive beginning is substituted: "From becoming [7] there issues determinate being." (109) *See* JOHN W. BURBIDGE, HEGEL ON LOGIC AND RELIGION: THE REASONABLENESS OF CHRISTIANITY 21 (1992). Stephen Houlgate would strongly disagree with the conclusion of the text and tries to account for logical development without any intervention of external reflection in the progress of Being. For example, Houlgate thinks that Determinate Being is a "speculative unity" in which the purity and difference of Being and Nothing have vanished. STEPHEN HOULGATE, THE OPENING OF HEGEL'S *LOGIC* 301 (2006). If so, Determinate Being is not the position of the Understanding toward Becoming.

6 *See generally* Cynthia Willett, *The Shadow of Hegel's* Science of Logic, in ESSAYS ON HEGEL'S LOGIC 85 (George di Giovanni ed., 1990).

7 George di Giovanni, *The Category of Contingency in the Hegelian Logic*, in SELECTED ESSAYS ON G.W.F. HEGEL 41, 45 (Lawrence Stepelevich ed., 1993).

Slavoj Žižek suggests that there is always a "fourth" in addition to the triad of Understanding, Dialectic, and Speculative Reason.[8] He compares it to the dummy in a game of bridge – the silent spectator that actually controls the game – a "Master Signifier" or vanishing mediator that makes sense of all the other signifiers. Hegel's remark equating the Understanding with "external reflection" vindicates Žižek's observation. The silent fourth is in charge of the game at this point.[9]

The Understanding's intervention is a *contingent* event. It is necessary if the Logic is to progress, but it is not necessary that Logic progress *for us* unless an external reflection – not yet part of the logical system – prods it into action. Logic is, after all, still only in the primitive stage of being. We have not yet reached subjectivity, which moves of its own accord.

This point is important in refuting the canard that Hegel is some sort of totalitarian.[10] Here we see the implication that *contingency* is a *necessity* within the system. This unity of contingency and necessity will prove the key to the last part of the Doctrine of Essence.

(b) Quality

Figure 2(a) isolates Determinate Being in [1] as the "immediacy of the oneness of being and nothing." (111) At this stage, Being and Nothing "do not extend beyond each other." (111) "[A]s yet no differentiation . . . is posited." (111) But we know from its history that Determinate Being is a determinateness. In transforming [7] into [1], the Understanding suppressed active mediation [4, 5, 6]. Mediation is now resurrected as [2] in Figure 2(a).

Quality is immediate;[11] it appears only when [2], the negative voice

---

[8] SLAVOJ ŽIŽEK, FOR THEY KNOW NOT WHAT THEY DO: ENJOYMENT AS A POLITICAL FACTOR 179 (1991).

[9] Burbidge likewise suggests that the progress of the Logic is infected with contingency: "Transitions are essential, and comprehensive wholes are essential. But this can be acknowledged only because understanding can isolate and fix each of them, and hold them together in a disjunction . . . In other words, dialectical transitions will introduce contingencies; reflection will integrate this new subject matter into a comprehensive perspective; understanding will fix its terms and relations." BURBIDGE, RELIGION, *supra* note 5, at 36.

[10] Most notoriously propounded by Karl Popper. *See* KARL POPPER, THE OPEN SOCIETY AND ITS ENEMIES (1971). For the Hegelian response, see Walter Kaufmann, *The Hegel Myth and Its Method*, in HEGEL: A COLLECTION OF CRITICAL ESSAYS 21 (Alasdair MacIntyre, ed., 1972).

[11] What is the difference between Determinate Being in Figure 2(a) and Quality in

of [1], is suppressed. But Dialectical Reason brings forth [2] expressly and names it *Negation*. In Figure 2(b), Negation [2] is internal to [1, 2]. The isolation of [2] always implies [3], an *immediacy*. [3] is just as much a one-sided Determinate Being as [1]. Determinate Being is "equally to be posited in the determination of nothing [3], when it will be posited as a differentiated, reflected determinateness, no longer as immediate or in the form of being." (111)

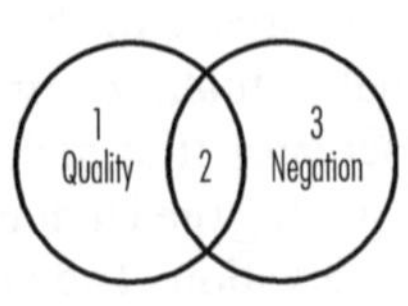

Figure 2(b)
Quality and Negation

Negation was supposed to be *different* from Determinate Being but ends up being the *same*. It is therefore a *reflected determinateness*. Reflection involves the statement, "I am not *that*." It entails the shedding of *inessential* Being so that Essence can reveal itself. Hence, [2] is a reflective voice because it distinguishes itself from [1] and thereby becomes [2, 3]. Yet [2, 3] is *just another Determinate Being*. In *distinguishing* itself from [1], [2, 3] proves to be the *same* as [1]. Accordingly, Negation is a "determinate element of a determinateness." (111)[12]

Quality and Negation. Reality, for Hegel, is "quality with the accent on *being*." (111) This same reality is *negation* when "burdened with a

---

Figure 2(b)? Each occupies the space of [1], yet the name changes. Why? Hegel hints that Quality more clearly implies its opposite, while Determinate Being declines to make any such reference: "Determinate being, however, in which nothing no less than being is contained [1], is itself the criterion for the one-sidedness of quality – which is only *immediate* or only in the form of *being*." (111) In Quality, "there *is* distinction – of reality and negation." (114) Quality (as compared to Determinate Being) emphasizes a dialectical relation between Quality and Negation.

Burbidge analyzes this step differently. He would rewrite Figure 2(b) so that [1] = Determinate Being (which he calls "*a being*") and [3] = Quality. BURBIDGE, LOGIC, *supra* note 3, at 47-8. As this leaves out Negation altogether, it cannot be sustained.

12 Terry Pinkard denies that Negation is produced by Quality's reflective voice and thinks the move from Determinate Being to Negation is not *necessary*. "To speak of a conception as a negation of another conception would require . . . that the two conceptions be determinate. That is, it might be argued that negation is no less external than a number of other relations. Indeed, a negation is always a negation of something, hence, negation must assume the prior determinateness of that of which it is the negation. Therefore, Hegel's use of negation would be just as arbitrary as the use of any other means." TERRY PINKARD, HEGEL'S DIALECTIC 28 (1988) This criticism must be rejected. Negation is *not* external to Quality. Negation represents the recovery of something internal to the constitution of Determinate Being that the Understanding suppressed. Furthermore, at this early stage, there *are* no other means to use except that which is negative to the positive Determinate Being.

negative." (111) In other words, Negation is just as "real" as reality. Negation is a "quality but one which counts as a deficiency."[13]

Hegel compares this definition to common usage. Ordinary speakers claim realities are perfections, containing no negation. In the ontological proof of God,[14] God was defined as the sum total of all realities. In this totality no contradiction exists. No "reality" cancels any other. Without negation, realities do not oppose one another, but exist perfectly indifferent to each other.[15] Such realities abolish determinateness itself. Reality regresses to Pure Being. It is "expanded into indeterminateness and loses its meaning." (112)[16]

Suppose reality is a determinateness. Then the sum total of all realities is also the sum total of all negations and hence of all contradictions. Since contradiction is power and force, such a view makes of God "absolute *power* in which everything determinate is absorbed." (113) This absolute power destroys reality, once again reducing God to nothing: "reality itself *is*, only in so far as it is still confronted by a being which it has not sublated; consequently, when it is thought as expanded into realized, limitless power, it becomes the abstract nothing." (113) The subsistence of a force requires the presence of a counterforce against which it can act.[17]

Property. Hegel also compares Quality to the *property* of a thing. Quality is property when it manifests itself immanently to another in an "*external* relation." (114) By this, Hegel signals (rather mysteriously, at this stage) that we speak of properties only when "things" have great resilience. A "thing" potentially remains the same thing, even if it loses one or more of its properties. A thing "exists" as a negative unity of all

---

[13] Charles Taylor calls *Dasein* a "marriage . . . of reality and negation." CHARLES TAYLOR, HEGEL 233 (1975). This is slightly inaccurate. "Reality" is *already* the unity of being and negation (with the accent on being). Reality is married to a negation that is just as much a reality as the reality it negates.

[14] *Supra* at 39-42.

[15] Hegel described this view as "pantheism." (84)

[16] Hegel warns against making Negation (the mirror view of reality) into an abstract Nothing, as Spinoza did. Nothing can stand before Pure Nothing, which obliterates everything. Rather, we must always take Nothing as *determinate Negation*. Spinozist substance is abstract nothingness. It is supposed to be the unity of thought and being (*i.e.*, extension). But substance's abstractness reduces thought and extension to mere *moments* – "[o]r rather, since substance in its own self lacks any determination whatever, they are for him not even moments." (113) Individuals cannot persist in the face of Spinoza's substance. Everything is obliterated.

[17] *Infra* at 129-32.

its properties. This resiliency Hegel will call Existence.[18] Such resilience is far too advanced for chapter 2. Quality has no resilience.

Hegel offers this example of property:

> By properties of herbs, for instance, we understand determinations which are not only are *proper* to something, but are the means whereby this something in its relations with other somethings *maintains* itself in its own peculiar way, counteracting the alien influences posited in it and making its own determinations *effective* in the other – although it does not keep this at a distance. (114)

Using a term Hegel has not yet introduced, a thing's properties partake of "being-for-self." The observer is capable of imposing its own view on the herb, introducing "alien influences." Property counteracts such influences that the observer *posits* into the herb. Properties are, in short, the authentic statements of the thing to the outside world. Thus, Hegel agrees with Friar Lawrence: "Oh mickle is the powerful grace that lies in herbs, plants, stones and their true qualities."

These "proleptic" remarks about properties have misled many into misinterpreting the entire status of Determinate Being. In chapter 2, the Understanding attempts to describe the *totality of all existence* in terms of Determinate Being. We have before us *one single, indivisible thing*. The universe is not yet an aggregate of discrete things. Taking to heart a point by G.R.G. Mure, we must realize that, throughout the first two chapters, we have before us *quale* only – quality lacking any quantitative determination.[19] "[W]e are in a world prior to the thought of a thing, and the dialectic will be a sort of fluent instability, an impotent shifting rather than an active self-determining of spirit."[20]

There is but *one thing* before us – Determinate Being as such. Ironically, in describing this *one* totality, Dialectical Reason shows that there are in fact *two* totalities – one that is and one that is *not*. These two totalities are two sides of the same totality.[21] There is no reference in chapter 2 to some *other* thing that is "diverse" from the

---

[18] See chapter 13.

[19] G.R.G. MURE, THE PHILOSOPHY OF HEGEL 116 (1965).

[20] *Id.*; *see also* JUSTUS HARTNACK, AN INTRODUCTION TO HEGEL'S LOGIC 17 (Lars Aagaard-Mogensen trans., 1998) ("Hegel does not apply Becoming to the world of objects; for Hegel, this concept is applicable to the behavior of categories").

[21] *See* HERBERT MARCUSE, HEGEL'S ONTOLOGY AND THE THEORY OF HISTORICITY 42 (Seyla Benhabib trans. 1987) ("Being has the fundamental character of being 'split' into two: it *is* in being *other*, as equality-with-self in transformation. It carries its negativity within itself, and is negativity in its innermost essence").

one "double-sided" totality of Being.[22] Several authors have not attended to this important aspect of Determinate Being.[23]

Under the impression that Hegel is concerned with self-identical properties, Charles Taylor complains of a disjunction between the "contrast" of properties and negation as the substance of Determinate Being.[24] Of course, there *is* a disjunction,[25] but Hegel does not, at this stage, concern himself with properties. Taylor takes Hegel as making the common sense point that the property of some thing can be discerned only in contrast to some other property, We cannot have the shape "square" without the shape "round."[26] Taylor concludes:

> Although the quality by which we can characterize a given *Dasein* may be defined in contrast to imaginary properties, that is, properties which are not instantiated, some of the contrasts on which we base our descriptions must be instantiated. In

---

[22] "That which is initially given can be *referred to* positively as that which *is present* . . . and negatively as that which is *lacking* (called 'negative presence,' since the given makes *itself* evident as a *lack*). The concept of negation viewed dialectically as a type of 'negative presence' is therefore qualitatively different from the standard notion of logical negation. Given a term A, its negation not-A is usually interpreted to be a positive presence of something other than A, '-A,' called, e.g., 'B,' such that A and B are not only distinct but *separable* 'truth values.' However the form 'other than' is actually a referral *to A* since no *content* different from A has been posited: to simply *deny* A is *not to assert* anything *else* in its place." Michael Kosok, *The Formalization of Hegel's Dialectical Logic: Its Formal Structure, Logical Interpretation and Intuitive Foundation*, in HEGEL: A COLLECTION OF CRITICAL ESSAYS 237, 241 (Alasdair MacIntyre ed., 1972).

[23] Walter Kaufmann, for one, misinterprets chapter 2 in the course of claiming that Hegel did not intend a triune logical progression in the *SL*. One piece of evidence Kaufmann presents is that chapter 2 is not the "antithesis" of chapter 1: "finitude is certainly not the antithesis of existence [*i.e.*, *Dasein*] as such, and infinity cannot well be construed as their synthesis." WALTER KAUFMANN, HEGEL: A REINTERPRETATION 198 (1978). Kaufmann, however, errs in focusing on "nothing" as the sole allowable antithesis of "being." If chapter 1 is seen as standing for *immediacy*, then chapter 2 stands for mediatedness and *is* the antithesis of chapter 1. Furthermore, chapter 3 (which takes up the status of the True Infinite) is indeed the "synthesis" of the first two chapters.

[24] TAYLOR, *supra* note 13, at 234 ("What may worry us is that Hegel seems to move from this unexceptionable point that all reality must be characterized contrastively . . . to the notion of determinate beings in a kind of struggle to maintain themselves in face of others, and hence, as 'negating' each other in an active sense.").

[25] Errol Harris sees a conjunction: Alteration always involves contrast. Suppose *A* becomes *B*. Before this change, *A* is "contrasted" with *B*. Change occurs. *A*, altered, is now *B*. *B* is to be contrasted from what it was – *A*. Hence, alteration and contrast go hand in hand. ERROL E. HARRIS, AN INTERPRETATION OF THE LOGIC OF HEGEL 107, 109 (1983). But more to the point, the contrast of *A* and *B* is not yet admissible. At this early point, we can speak only of *A* and not-*A*.

[26] TAYLOR, *supra* note 13, at 234.

> these cases, the contrast between *Daseine* as qualities is a contrast between distinct things: Hegel uses the word "something" here (*Etwas*) . . . [27]

This interpretation of Determinate Being seriously misses the point. Hegel would surely say that such comparisons presuppose the self-identity of the property perceived.[28] Indeed, self-identity of realities is precisely the position Hegel attacks. In short, Taylor criticizes Hegel for making properties into things, when this is the very position that Hegel is criticizing.[29] To be sure, Hegel discusses the properties of herbs, but this discussion is strictly "for us." Property is too advanced for the realm of Determinate Being, which concerns only *quale*.[30]

Taylor goes on to complain that the properties of a "thing" *causally* maintain the thing in its integrity (as Hegel recognized in his analysis of herbs). He judges Hegel's argument to be "a bit loose" and "embarrassing," as "cause and effect" are relations developed only in the Doctrine of Essence.[31] These objections disappear if Mure's observation concerning *quale* is honored. Contrary to Taylor's point, it is far too early for the doctrine of the "thing," which appears only in

---

[27] *Id*. "Something" will appear in Figure 2(c) as the unity of Quality and Negation.

[28] In chapter 1, we saw Hegel's low opinion of "comparison." Later, Hegel will analyze Negative Judgments – "the rose is not red." Hegel thinks a Negative Judgment not only negates a specific universal of the rose ("red") but also implies that the subject (rose) has universality (a color which, however, happens not to be red). Hegel warns against the point that a given property is simply *not* all the other properties, because this presupposes that a property is self-identical. "If we stop at white and red as *sensuous* images, we are giving, as is commonly done, the name of Notion to what is only a determination of pictorial thinking . . . But this kind of sensuous content, like *not-being* itself, must be *conceptually grasped* and must lose that indifference and abstract immediacy which it has in blind, static, pictorial thinking." (639) This passage indicates that Hegel would disagree with Taylor that not-square means round or triangular, etc., or that this proposition is at all relevant to the second chapter of the *SL*. Such equations, Hegel would say, are merely subjective and uncritical. Rather, what is at stake at the beginning of the Logic is the fact that non-being in general is in a state of Becoming – a simple proposition compared to the world of things and their properties.

[29] "Commentators are apt to attribute to Hegel, as the position he is advocating, the 'false' abstractions that he is in fact criticizing." HARRIS. LOGIC, *supra* note 25, at 78.

[30] Taylor is far from alone in misinterpreting Hegel's second chapter. The ordinarily astute Marcuse writes: "Moreover, every quality is what it is only in relation to other qualities, and these relations determine the very nature of a quality." HERBERT MARCUSE, REASON AND REVOLUTION 132 (1999). Such a view reduces qualities into metonymic "things" – far too advanced for this early stage. In fact, Quality is determinable by virtue of the Negation it implies, without any reference to multiple qualities.

[31] TAYLOR, *supra* note 13, at 234.

the Doctrine of Essence.[32]

How, Taylor asks, does the common sense notion of comparison lead to "the notion of Determinate Beings in a kind of struggle to maintain themselves in the face of others, and hence as 'negating' each other in an active sense"?[33] The question is falsely put. Determinate Being is not derived from the comparison of "things." Nevertheless, the balance of the question is a good one. How does it follow that Being struggles to "be" in the face of negativity? The answer is that external reflection intervenes into the realm of Determinate Being to insist on affirmativity. With this assistance, Being is in motion. It is in the process of Becoming. The act of Becoming (as opposed to ceasing-to-be) is the act of the Understanding that accents being at the expense of nothing. Of course, it falls to Dialectical Reason to do the opposite – to emphasize the negative.

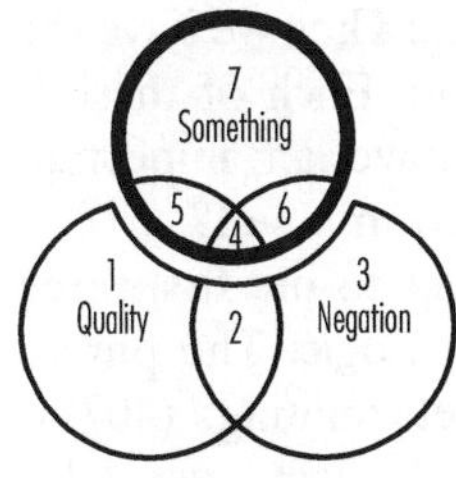

Figure 2(c)
Something

(c) Something

In Figure 2(b), Dialectical Reason accused the Understanding of ignoring its own negative voice [2]. But Dialectical Reason [3] is equally guilty of ignoring its *own* positive voice [2] – the same mischievous foul sin for which the Understanding was chided. According to Speculative Reason, "negation is determinate being, not the supposedly abstract nothing but posited here . . . as affirmatively present." (115) So [1] = [3]. The *distinction* between Quality and Negation is now sublated. But this sublating "is more than a mere taking back [of Figure 2(b)] and external omission of it again." (115) We can't retreat to Figure 2(a). The distinction between [1] and [3] "cannot be omitted, for it *is*." (115) Hence, we have Determinate Being [1], the distinction from Determinate Being [2, 3], and sublation of the distinction [7]. This return into self of the Determinate Beings – the return of [1] and [3] into [2] – represents an enhancement [7]. Speculative Reason is a *synthesis*. It always produces a surplus. We now have, not Determinate

32 HARRIS, LOGIC, *supra* note 25, at 106. "And always when a concrete existence is disguised under the name of Being and not-Being, empty headedness makes its usual mistake of speaking about, and having in mind an image of, something else than what is in question." EL § 88.

33 TAYLOR, *supra* note 13, at 234.

Being in General, but "*a determinate being*, a something." (115)

We are, however, still in "a world prior to the thought of a thing."[34] "The universe and all in it is here just an undifferentiated somewhat."[35] Something names the stage at which Determinate Being and Determinate Nothing are recognized as the *same thing*. The Something emphasizes how ephemeral Being is. This was certainly evident from chapter 1, where Pure Being "always already" *was* Pure Nothing. It is still so in chapter 2. The resilience of "things" does not appear until midway through the Doctrine of Essence, when things *have* (but are distinguishable *from*) their properties.[36]

Reflection-into-self. Of Something, Hegel writes that we must take Quality "in the one determination of determinate being as in the other – as reality and negation. But in these determinatenesses determinate being is equally reflected into itself; and posited as such it is (c) *something*, a determinate being." (109) In other words, first we have Quality, a determinateness with the accent on being. Then we have the same determinateness with the accent on negation. Each of these is *reflected into self*. Here for the first time we have an important Hegelian trope. What does it mean to be reflected into self?

"Reflection Within Itself" is the name Hegel gives to the first three chapters on Essence – the middle portion of the Logic. The phrase denotes immanence. Reflection is an "immanent determining." (407) It also denotes thought digging deeper. When we "reflect," we delve

---

[34] MURE, PHILOSOPHY, *supra* note 19, at 116.

[35] *Id*. at 117. Mure invokes William Wallace's translation of *Etwas* – the somewhat, which better captures the world prior to the thing. EL § 90.

[36] On the unbearable lightness of being, Hegel writes: "In our ordinary way of thinking, *something* is rightly credited with reality. However, something is still a very superficial determination; just as reality and negation, determinate being and its determinateness, although no longer blank being and nothing, are still quite abstract determinations. It is for this reason that they are the most current expressions and the intellect which is philosophically untrained uses them most, casts its distinctions in their mould and fancies that in them it has something really well and truly determined." (115)

Terry Pinkard views the function of Something as designed "to introduce the conception of a *plurality* of individual entities. Without this conception of plurality, Hegel would not really have escaped Parmenides [*i.e.*, Pure Being] after all." PINKARD, DIALECTIC, *supra* note 12, at 33. Pinkard finds this introduction of plural things unnecessary. Why individual entities? Why not a plurality of Qualities (where "qualities" would count for less than "entity")? In fact the Something does *not* introduce a world of things. It merely stands for the proposition that Negation is as much Determinate Being as Determinate Being is (and vice versa). In the Something, negativity is in the process of smuggling itself over from the right side to the left side of the page.

beyond the appearances in order to get at a deeper truth. We do this by *shedding* the inessentials. What we shed are the appearances – mere being – and we discover the deeper non-being behind the veil. Reflection-into-self is therefore the very negative enterprise of shedding one-sided being to find negative essence. So whatever Quality and its Negation become, they become it through their own negative force. They *negate* their superficial appearance and reveal their deeper character. In terms of our Borromean Knot, [1] and [3] shed [2], which turns out to be the essence of both [1, 2] and [2, 3]. Difference from [2] is what [1] and [3] have in common. [2] is then raised above its station to [4-7] – the middle term.

In truth, reflection is too advanced for the Doctrine of Being, which is "the sphere of the immediate, the unreflective . . . the simply presented."[37] Nevertheless, as everything in Logic is implied from the start, it is not surprising that we should find activity which "for us" is reflective.

"Posited" and "in itself." We also have in the above-quoted sentence an early use of the important word "posit." When you "posit" a proposition, you put it forth into existence. Positing – "the appeal to ground"[38] – is the work you do. Hence, "positive law" is the law put forth by human beings (as opposed to natural law, which is produced by God or nature).[39] "Positing" is the activity that is shown in Figure 2(a). There, Becoming [7] "is posited" as Determinate Being. It sheds [4,5,6] and becomes [1]. In this activity, [1] *reflects into itself*. [1] says, "I am not [4, 5, 6].

The opposite of "posited" is to be merely "in itself" and "for us."[40] We the audience may intuit some truths in advance of their derivation, but Logic's job is to make express – to posit – what is merely implicit. In positing, the *in itself* becomes *for itself*. "[O]nly that which is *posited* in a Notion belongs in the dialectical development of that Notion to its content; whereas the determinateness that is not yet posited in the

---

[37] HARRIS, LOGIC, *supra* note 25, at 111.

[38] Richard Dien Winfield, *From Concept to Judgement: Rethinking Hegel's Overcoming of Formal Logic*, 50 DIALOGUE 53, 55-6 (2001).

[39] "[W]e take natural law to consist just in this, that nothing happens without a cause sufficiently determined *a priori*, which cause therefore must contain an absolute spontaneity within itself . . . " (738)

[40] The "in itself" can also be viewed as that which is "for us." SLAVOJ ŽIŽEK, THE PUPPET AND THE DWARF: THE PERVERSE CORE OF CHRISTIANITY 38 (2003); *see also* MARCUSE, ONTOLOGY, *supra* note 21, at 166 ("For the uncomprehended object is mere in-itselfness").

Notion itself belongs to our reflection." (110)

At first, positing occurs by placing the emphasis on "being." Each move by the Understanding occurs by shifting [7] (or some other part of the middle term) over into [1]. But in the middle part of the Logic – the Doctrine of Essence – "positing" changes character. In Essence, the paradigmatic move of the Understanding constitutes a shift to the right. Essence posits what it is by announcing what it is *not*. This is the quintessential move of human freedom in the negative sense, and so, at the end of essence, subjectivity is derived. The subject is simply *not an object*, and nothing more than this. Finally, in the Subjective Logic "positing" occurs simultaneously on the left, the right and the middle.[41] Both subject (on the negative right) and object (on the positive left) posit what they are. What they eventually posit is their unity with the middle term of Idea.

In his discussion of Something, Hegel for the first time overtly refers to the "in-itself." (116) By definition, a thing cannot perceive what it is in-itself: "This mediation with itself which something is *in itself*, taken only as negation of the negation, has no concrete determinations for its sides; it thus collapses into the simple oneness which is *being*. (116) Self-mediation of Something is only "for us," not yet "for itself." Indeed, self-mediation is the hallmark of Essence – far too advanced for our present position.[42]

Yet Hegel also says, "In *something*, mediation with self is *posited*, in so far as something is determined as a simple identity." (116) In other words, if, within Something, we focus on [7], we have Something's simple identity. Given [7], mediation is supposedly "posited." But "posited" means made manifest. How can self-mediation be simultaneously posited and "in itself"?

The answer lies in the ephemerality of being. At this stage, the move of the Understanding is to wrench [7] from the middle term and shift it to the left so that it becomes [1] – as Figure 2(a) showed. When this occurs, the middle term "collapses into the simple oneness which is *being*." The Understanding gets away with this distortion because [7] "has no concrete determinations for its sides." (116) Concrete

---

[41] Or, to be more precise, the Notion is *beyond* positing, which implies a reference to otherness. In the Notion, there is no other as such but only an otherness encompassed within a totality. *Infra* at 436.

[42] *See* KAUFMANN, *supra* note 23, at 110 ("*An sich*, always rendered 'in itself,' does not mean in German that a feature is hidden from view and literally inside, but rather that the feature is 'on' the thing, visible 'for us' (*für uns*) though not 'for it' (*für sich*).").

determinations will build themselves up later. When that occurs, the Understanding cannot do such violence to the middle term. For now, the middle term "collapses" into mere being. The self-mediation, "posited" in Something [4, 5, 6, 7], is merely "in itself" once the Understanding has its way ([7] → [1]). After this operation is accomplished, Being does not manifestly recognize its self-mediation. Self-mediation is merely "in itself" and will not be "for itself" until being becomes self-consciousness at the end of Essence.

Being-within-self. It is said that eskimos have a hundred words for "snow," because snow is so important to their way of life. Apparently this is a canard.[43] What they have is a series of simple expressions which can be translated into "wet snow," or "powdered snow." English has precisely the same phrases.

"Being" is to Hegel what "snow" is to the eskimos. Hegel has many different compound expressions for it. Accordingly, we have in "Something" the first appearance of the expression "being-within-self" (*Insichsein*). Hegel says of Something: "This sublatedness of the distinction is determinate being's *own* determinateness; it is thus *being-within-self*: determinate being is *a determinate being*, a *something*. (115) In this passage, being-within-self is "sublatedness." Sublatedness designates negative immanent activity. It is in the nature of Being to turn into Nothing and then into Something. This development represents being *within* the self. Nothing external is required.[44]

We can also say preliminarily that being-within-self [4] *is the silent fourth*. In the Objective Logic, [4] represents the alien substrate that is not part of Being. It is the *subject*, which is needed to *complete the object*. Later, in the Subjective Logic, the silent fourth [4] becomes the *sublated object* that the subject cannot digest. In the very last chapter, [4] is the empty hole in Absolute Knowing that guarantees the Logic is never complete. This disturbing absence is why the Logic does not conclude the system – why Logic is a never-ending circle forever replaying its own sequence, and why Logic needs nature to supplement its lack. This claim is a very complicated one indeed, and it will take the whole of this volume to explicate it.

Negation of the negation. Negation of the negation is the step of Speculative Reason in creating the middle term. It is the creation of

---

43 GEOFFREY K. PULLAM, THE GREAT ESKIMO VOCABULARY HOAX 166 (1991).

44 Though, earlier in the chapter, Hegel warned that the Understanding entails an external reflection, which *does* indicate something from the outside is required. *Supra* at 57-9. Being is therefore never *entirely* "within self."

something [7] out of a double negative. Hegel now tells us, "Something is the *first negation of negation*." (115)

Figure 2(c) bears the form of the negation of the negation. But did we not see the same configuration in Figure 1(c)? Why wasn't *Becoming* in Figure 1(c) the *first* negation of the negation? The answer is that negation is a *determinate* nothing. In Figure 2(c), Negation canceled Quality, and Something in turn canceled Negation. Figure 1(c) was *not* a negation of the negation. Pure Nothing was an *indeterminate* nothing. Properly speaking, Pure Nothing did not emanate from Pure Being in the same way that Negation emanated from Quality. Becoming "has not yet opposed and developed its moments." (526) For that reason, Figure 1(b) portrays Pure Nothing as non-dialectic. In Figure 2(b), however, Quality's own voice [2] demanded that Negation posit itself. [2] was inherently within Determinate Being under the law of sublation. This internal voice is the birth of Dialectical Reason. For this reason, Quality confesses its being-within-self for the first time, and Hegel can rightly say that Something is the first negation of the negation.[45]

Hegel emphasizes the distinction between the *first* negation in Figure 2(b) and the negation of the negation in Figure 2(c). The first negation is *abstract*. In Figure 2(b), the overlap between Quality and Negation is designated by [2] only. In contrast, the negation of the negation is *concrete*. In Figure 2(c), the overlap between Something and its constituent parts is described by [4, 5, 6]. Furthermore, [2] in Figure 2(b) – an abstraction – itself becomes a "concreteness" [2, 4] in Figure 2(c).

---

[45] "The distinction between Being and Nothing is . . . only implicit and not yet actually made: they only *ought* to be distinguished. A distinction of course implies two things, and that one of them possesses an attribute which is not found in the other. Being however is an absolute absence of attributes, and so is Nought. Hence the distinction between the two is only meant to be . . . . In all other cases of difference there is some common point [2] which comprehends both things. Suppose e.g. we speak of two different species: the genus [2] forms a common ground for both. But in the case of mere Being and Nothing, distinction is without a bottom to stand upon: hence there can be no distinction, both determinations being the same bottomlessness. If it be replied that Being and Nothing are both of them thoughts, so that thought may be reckoned common ground, the objector forgets that Being is not a particular or definite thought, and hence, being quite indeterminate, is a thought not to be distinguished from Nothing." EL § 87 Remark. In effect, when species are compared, genus is the being-within-self of the species [2]. But, because Figure 1(b) lacks any common ground between Pure Being and Nothing, Becoming does not qualify as a negation of the negation.

Alteration. In the preamble to chapter 2, Hegel warned that Quality was *alterable*. In his discussion of Something, Hegel makes good on this claim. Invoking the law of sublation, Something is a more complex form of Becoming: "Something as a *becoming* is a transition, the moments of which are themselves somethings, so that the transition is *alteration* – a becoming which has already become *concrete*." (116) Quality is *on the move*. It is *alterable* – courtesy of its own being-within-self, which is sublation itself. "[S]omething alters only in its Notion." (116)

Can we affirm that the *moments* of Something are themselves Somethings? Hegel stretches his terminology here to make a point. Quality and Negation (the moments of Something) are too crude to warrant the honorable name of Something. But Hegel wishes to emphasize that Quality and Negation are both Qualities. Yet since the Understanding recognizes only [7] at this early stage, Something, which "alters only in its Notion," nevertheless "is not yet *posited* as mediating and mediated, but at first only as simply maintaining itself in its self-relation." (116) Thus, because the Understanding in Figure 2(a) only grasped [7], not [4, 5, 6], it does not yet grasp the double nature of middle terms, which is still "in itself."

B. Finitude

Chapter 2's Structure

In this all-important middle section of Determinate Being, reality sublates itself and becomes ideality. Being "ceases to be." But, before we pass through the looking glass into objective idealism, it is time to reveal a structural feature of chapter 2. In Determinate Being, we experienced the sequence of the Understanding, Dialectical Reason, and Speculative Reason. What now must be revealed is that this development was "left-leaning" within a tripartite structure. Its bias was in favor of "being" and against "nothing." In its journey, Determinate Being stayed relatively leftward, and movement occurred within it.

Finitude is the mirror opposite. Its activity will be "right-leaning." It stays relatively negative vis-à-vis Infinity. In effect, the work is being done in the extremes; for the moment, the middle term of Infinity is still implicit. As Hegel puts it:

> In the first section, in which *determinate being* in general was considered, this . . .

had the determination of *being*. Consequently, the moments of its development, quality and something equally have an affirmative determination. In [Finitude], the negative determination contained in determinate being is developed, and whereas in [Determinate Being, Negation] was at first only negation in general, the *first* negation, it is now determined to the point of the *being-with-itself* or the *inwardness* of the something, to the negation of the negation. (117)

We left off Something as unaware of its own mediated-mediating nature. Now its nature as negation of the negation will be expressed. Accordingly, the first sub-moment of Finitude is itself double: (a) Something and an Other. So is the second step: (b) Constitution and Limit. The doubled nature of the steps reflects their negativity. Negation always requires a positivity to negate.

(a) Something and an Other[46]

Nothing is something after all. This is the truth of [2] in Figure 2(b). The Understanding now sees [4, 5, 6] as the *unity* of Something [5] and Other [6]. In Figure 3(a), we take [4, 5, 6] and represent it in an affirmative guise: [4, 5, 6] → [1]. Figure 3(a) illustrates *positing*, or manifestation of what the thing *is*. So we find that the negative *mediated nature* of Something [4, 5, 6] shifts to the left – not the *immediate* Something [7]. Yet, the modulation between [4, 5, 6] is presented as a static unity [1].

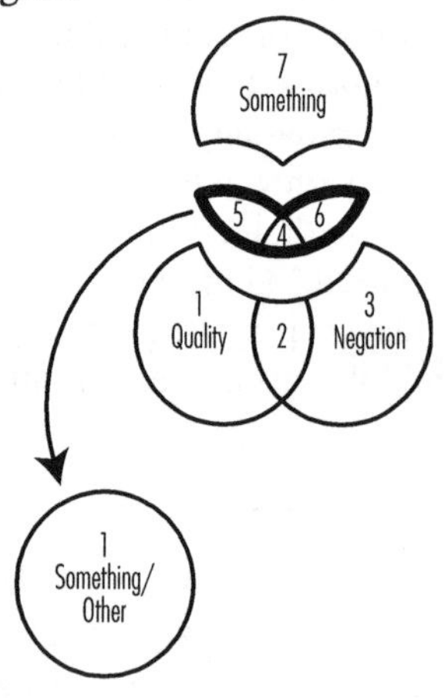

Figure 3(a)
Something/Other

Hegel has emphasized that the constituent parts of Something were each Qualities (or Somethings). Hegel now repeats that Something/ Other in Figure 3(a) are "both determinate beings or somethings." (117) Likewise, Something/Other are each nothings – or "Others." But one of them must be Something and one must be Other. "It is immaterial which is first named and solely for that reason called *something*." (117) The word "this" serves to decide the matter.[47]

---

[46] In the 1812 edition of the *SL*, this section preceded the Something. BURBIDGE, RELIGION, *supra* note 5, at 19-20.

[47] In the *Phenomenology*, the subjective moment of "this" (indexicality) disrupted the unity of sense-certainty. GEORG W.F. HEGEL, PHENOMENOLOGY OF SPIRIT (A.V. Miller trans. 1977). It is likewise disruptive here, in the *SL*.

Accordingly, the choice of Something and Other is a subjective designation that falls outside Something and Other. The designation of one as affirmative and the other as negative is not an *immanent* move. External reflection – the silent fourth – decides which is which. Once again, contingency makes itself manifest.

Yet the meaning of Figure 3(a) is that Determinate Being is determined as itself, but also as *an Other*. "[T]here is no determinate being which is determined only as [a Determinate Being]" (118). What Determinate Being is *not*, however, is expressly a determinateness. At the level of Figure 3(a), Being is *either* Something *or* Other, but not both at the same time. "Determinateness" will denote the contradiction of being and nothing present at the same time. "Determinateness as Such" (or Limit) only appears in Figure 4(c).[48]

So far, Something/Other has no way of distinguishing whether it is Something *or* Other. It is one of them, but not both. Something/Other must posit what it is immanently. This will be done in Figure 3(b), but first Hegel digresses to contemplate nature.[49]

Otherness in Itself (Nature)

Nature. From Figure 3(a), Hegel derives physical nature. Suppose we take Something/ Other as Other *only*, as we are entitled to do. So far, there is no concrete *relation* between Something and Other: "The other is to be taken as isolated." (118)

Because Other is isolated, it is "the other in

---

[48] Burbidge describes Figure 3(a) differently: "When speculative reason synthetically combines two concepts it may find on examination that the relation is one of integration and that the two collapse into a simple unity. On the other hand, however, the relation may not be integration, but something else, which still leaves the moment of thought incomplete." BURBIDGE, LOGIC, *supra* note 3, at 48. In other words, he sees Figure 3(a) as being Speculative Reason's move. I have described it as Understanding's move. We agree, however, that integration fails. Figure 3(a) isolates *non-integration*. Of Figure 3(a), Burbidge writes, "Thought no longer has a simple concept, but wavers between [Something/Other]. The negative moment, implicit in [Determinate Being] has now become explicit." *Id*. at 48. Burbidge is close to the truth of the matter, but I would not say that *negativity* has become explicit. Rather, the *movement* between Something and Other has manifested itself in [1]. *See also* BURBIDGE, RELIGION, *supra* note 5, at 20 ("Here, although with 'something' 'another' is posited, they do not posit each other").

[49] This is not to be taken as an empirical causal claim. "Logos and nature mutually presuppose each other; one cannot be posed without the other. It is absurd to imagine a causality of any kind in logos which would produce nature." JEAN HYPPOLITE, GENESIS AND STRUCTURE OF HEGEL'S *PHENOMENOLOGY OF SPIRIT* 602 (Samuel Cherniak & John Heckman trans., 1974). Rather, logic "is the whole which negates itself as nature." *Id*.

its own self" but also "the other of itself." (118) If the Other is the Other of itself, it is not itself. Otherness is self-alienated. A single entity has now doubled itself. There is Other, and there is the original self to which Other is Other. The original self (Absolute Knowing, on the law of sublation) implies it has an Other (nature).

Was this a legitimate move? The answer is yes. "Other" is a *correlative* term. If Other is taken as isolated, no Other to the Other is supplied. Otherness must therefore turn back on itself and make *itself* its Other.[50] This self-alienation, Hegel says, is physical nature – the *other* of spirit. This definition of nature as Other[51] to spirit is parsimonious. Nature is determined as "not spiritual." Nothing more is established here. Spirit's determination "is thus at first a mere relativity by which is expressed, not a quality of nature itself, but only a relation external to [spirit]." (118) Whatever qualities nature has are not yet posited.

Nature is "other" to spirit. Yet, on the law of sublation, nature is just as much spirit. Hence, nature is self-alienated spirit.[52] The implicit presence of spirit in nature makes reconciliation possible. Nature is spirit's self-inflicted wound. Spirit must heal this wound and make itself whole again.[53]

---

[50] Butler calls this move "nonintentional reference." BUTLER, *supra* note 4, at 29. Burbidge puts it this way: "As *other* it refers to something which is not. Yet because it is isolated by understanding there is nothing else to which it can be related. It can only *be* other in itself by *becoming* other than itself." BURBIDGE, LOGIC, *supra* note 3, at 48.

[51] I do not take nature to be a move in the Logic as such. Therefore, I do not label it as Figure 3(b). Nevertheless, this drawing resembles and is an implication of the official Figure 3(b).

[52] DARREL E. CHRISTENSEN, THE SEARCH FOR CONCRETENESS 155 (1986) (nature contains Notion "not as something explicit, to be sure, but as implicit"); Philip T. Grier, *Abstract and Concrete in Hegel's Logic*, in ESSAYS ON HEGEL'S LOGIC, *supra* note 6, at 64 (nature is "the sphere of the externality of space and time into which [Spirit] 'freely releases itself'"). As Hegel puts it: "the Idea is the *process* of sundering itself into individuality and its inorganic nature, and again of bringing this inorganic nature under the power of the subject and returning to the first simple universality." (759)

[53] *See* HARRIS, LOGIC, *supra* note 25, at 26 ("Nature is rediscovered as the self-external embodiment of the Idea developing itself through the natural process"); William Maker, *The Very Idea of Nature, or Why Hegel is Not an Idealist*, in HEGEL AND THE PHILOSOPHY OF NATURE 18 (Stephen Houlgate ed., 1998) ("Just as logically self-determining thought required thinking *its* other, conceiving nature will require thinking an other to its initial determinacy"). John Burbidge presents a lucid discussion of Hegel's attitude toward nature. According to Burbidge, Hegel saw nature as

> the sphere of contingency and external relations. Things and events are separated

It is possible to make the following grand claim about Hegel's system, as it is spelled out in the *Encyclopedia*. This work commences with logic, proceeds to nature and culminates in the *Philosophy of Mind*. Logic can be equated to Being. As such, it cannot help but become "other" to itself – or nature. Nature corresponds to the Negation of Logic. But on the law of sublation, nature contains logic (*i.e.*, spirit), even as it cancels spirit. The *Philosophy of Mind* chronicles spirit emerging from nature, culminating in the absolute cancellation of the radical difference between spirit and nature.[54] Logic is therefore prior to, or above, nature and is therefore truly *meta*physical in its quality.

Being-for-other and Being-in-itself. The Understanding has proposed that the universe is either Something *or* a shadow "Other" Something. It is one or the other but not both. It draws this conclusion by gazing back on Figure 2(c) and seizing upon [4, 5, 6], which is the mediated portion of Something. [7] – affirmative Being – has been suppressed by the Understanding in Figure 3(a).

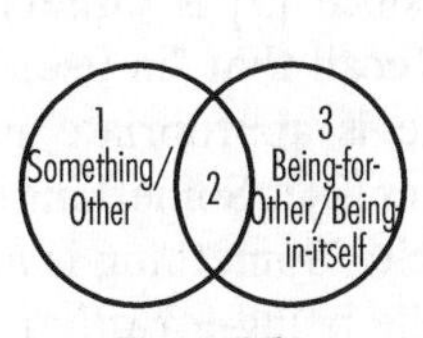

Figure 3(b)
Being-for-other/ Being-in-itself

Always emphasizing what has been suppressed, Dialectical Reason responds, "You may think the universe is something or Other [4, 5, 6], but history shows that it is just as much affirmative immediate Being [7]." [1] is therefore legitimately Some-thing/Other – a double. But if this is true of [1], it likewise must be true of Being [2], which is also a double. Being is therefore a Being for Something, or it is a Being-for-other. It is one or the other of these things, but either way it is affirmative

---

in space and time even though space and time are themselves continuous. If a theory is to explain natural phenomena, it must therefore perform two interrelated tasks. It must show why isolated entities are separated in the way they are; that is, it has in some way to dissolve the contingency of appearances . . .

John W. Burbidge, *Chemistry and Hegel's Logic*, in HEGEL AND NEWTONIANISM 609 (Michael John Petry ed., 1993).

54 JOHN MCCUMBER, THE COMPANY OF WORDS: HEGEL, LANGUAGE AND SYSTEMATIC PHILOSOPHY 42 (1993) (Logic is "the philosophical comprehension of thought taken purely for itself; Philosophy of Nature . . . examines thought in the meaningless spatio-temporal dispersal which is the ultimate 'other' to thought; and Philosophy of Mind . . . considers thought insofar as, in human history, it gathers itself together out of this dispersal") (footnote omitted). Michael Inwood suggests that Logic is the father, Nature is the son, and Mind is the holy ghost. M.J. INWOOD, HEGEL 2, 246-8 (1983).

Being.

Suppose Something/Other [1] is *Something* (not Other). Then [2] is Other and [2]'s Being is Being-for-other [2, 3]. Yet [2] is actually part of [1, 2]. Something therefore negates its own being when it negates [2]. Accordingly:

> Something [1, 2] *preserves* itself in the negative of its determinate being [2] . . . ; it is essentially *one* with it and essentially *not one* with it. [Something] stands, therefore, in a *relation* to its otherness and is not simply its otherness. Its otherness is at once contained in it and also still *separate* from it; it is a *being-for-other*. (119)[55]

Something [1], then, cancels *and preserves* its own being [2]. [1] is therefore with *and* not with [2]. Something is connected *and* disconnected with its Other.

When paired with [3], [2] is Being-for-other (since [3] is Other). When [2] is paired with [1], it is Being-in-itself. Recall that "in itself" means what is implicit – not express. This usage is appropriate in Being-in-itself; Something [1] *denies* that it is [2]. Yet [2] is Something's own self. The identity of [1] and [2] is only implicit: "Something is *in itself* in so far as it has returned into itself out of the being-for-other." (120)[56]

So [2] is *both* Being-for-other *and* Being-in-self, when we conceive of [1] as Something. But what if [1] is Other and [3] is Something? How does [2] fare when [1] is Other? In this case, [2] in [1, 2] is Being-for-other. [2] in [2, 3] is part of Something. But this is precisely what Something denies. From its own negative perspective, the identity of [2] with [3] is merely implicit. The same result is therefore reached. [2] is both Being-for-other and Being-in-itself. But which is it? All we know for the moment is that it is one or the Other, not both.

What is not to be missed here is that [2] serves as the Khyber Pass into the India of Being. Through [2] negativity on the right side of the diagram infiltrates into Being on the left. What was formerly affirmative starts to turn negative. As Hegel puts it, "non-being [2] [is] a moment of something [1, 2]." (119) This coincidence of for-other and in-itself lays open the possibility that *things* are intrinsically related.

---

[55] *See* JEAN-LUC NANCY, HEGEL: THE RESTLESSNESS OF THE NEGATIVE 34 (Jason Smith & Steven Miller eds. 1997) ("Sensible representation is being-for-another").

[56] Houlgate disagrees with this interpretation: "a thing enjoys its ownmost being in itself only insofar as this is explicitly distinguished from the thing's relation to other things." HOULGATE, *supra* note 5, at 336.

The thing-in-itself. According to Hegel, [2] stands for *both* Being-in-itself *and* Being-for-other. This portends that the inner *is* outer. The in-itself as isolated, however, is Kant's noumenal thing-in-itself, of which Hegel is a sharp critic. "[T]he proposition that we do not know what things are in themselves," Hegel complains, "ranked as a profound piece of wisdom." (121)[57] Things are "in themselves" if all Being-for-other is purged. We perceive in a given thing *only* its Being-for-other, "the indeterminate, affirmative community of something with its other." (126) Therefore, Kant insisted, we can have no idea what the thing-in-itself is. Hegel strongly disagrees.

> Things are called "in themselves" in so far as abstraction is made from all being-for-other, which means simply, in so far as they are thought devoid of all determination, as nothings. In this sense, it is of course impossible to know *what* the *thing in itself* is. For the question: *what?* demands that *determinations* be assigned; but since the things of which they are to be assigned are at the same time supposed to be *things in themselves*, which means, in effect, to be without any determination, the question is made thoughtlessly impossible to answer, or else only an absurd answer is given. (121)

The thing-in-itself is the absolute, and, furthermore, it is *one*. That is, once appearance is abolished, there is but *one* thing-in-itself in its indeterminacy – not many: "What is *in* these things in themselves, therefore we know quite well; they are as such nothing but truthless, empty abstractions." (121) In contrast, Hegel's analysis has shown the thing-in-itself [2] is concrete.[58] It is *the same* as being-for-other.

For Hegel, what a thing is in itself is also what it is "for other." *Appearance* has a strong unity with *essence*, and we *can*, through the Logic, glimpse the thing-in-itself. Hegel's logic, then, "extends Kant's transcendental logic by exorcising the phantom of a thing-in-itself, which would always haunt our reflection and would limit knowledge in favor of faith and non-knowledge."[59] This is the strong implication of

---

[57] Even the Kantians complain of this aspect of Kant's philosophy.*See* HENRY E. ALLISON, KANT'S TRANSCENDENTAL IDEALISM: AN INTERPRETATION AND DEFENSE 111 (1983) ("Surely to know that things-[in-themselves] are not spatial (or temporal) is to know a good deal about them").

[58] Hegel's observation that there is but *one* Kantian thing-in-itself is emphasized later, in Existence, where Hegel examines the concept of the "thing." Hegel remarks: "if essence is defined as the *sum total of all realities*, then . . . this sum total reduces to empty oneness." (389-90)

[59] JEAN HYPPOLITE, LOGIC AND EXISTENCE 3 (1997) (Leonard Lawlor & Amit Sen trans., 1997).

considering [2] as the unity of Being-in-itself and Being-for-other.[60]

Positedness. Hegel contrasts Being-in-itself with Being-for-other – both contained (indeterminately) within [2]. He also pauses to contrast Being-in-itself with positedness. "Positedness" must not be confused with the act of positing.[61] Positedness belongs to the realm of Essence and is a passive state of being. Positing, in contrast, is an activity:

> *positing*, properly speaking, first occurs in the sphere of *essence* . . . In the sphere of being, determinate being only *proceeds* from *becoming*, or, with the something an other is posited, with the finite, the infinite [is posited]; but the finite does not bring forth the infinite, does not *posit* it. In the sphere of being, the *self-determining* even of the Notion is at first only *in itself or implicit* – as such it is called a transition. (121)

Roughly, positedness is to Essence what determinateness is to the Doctrine of Being. Both denote a unity of opposites. Positedness results when reflection-into-self retreats and drags into its lair the very

---

[60] Michael Inwood tries to defend the Kantian thing-in-itself.

> It need not involve the assertion that there are things . . . which lie beyond those limits [of knowledge], but only the supposition that there might be. The limits could be assigned not by saying "There are things-in-themselves and they are unknowable to us," but rather "If there are any, then they are unknowable by us." Even if the latter claim is difficult to justify, it does not look self-refuting in the way that the former does.

INWOOD, *supra* note 54, at 119. Inwood's book consists in *ad hoc* potshots at Hegel's system, which seldom or perhaps never ventures near the target. The above claim is particularly weak. In effect, Inwood states, "Assume without deciding that there are things-in-themselves beyond our knowledge. It would then follow that there are things-in-themselves beyond our knowledge." This kind of arguing leaves Hegel's system unscathed.

Inwood also complains that, even if Hegel is right that we know a *little bit* about the thing-in-itself, perhaps we don't know *everything* – there might be more to know. *Id.* at 119-20. Space aliens with cognitive power to perceive the thing-in-itself might exist. These aliens are what Kant would call God's marionette or automaton. IMMANUEL KANT, CRITIQUE OF PRACTICAL REASON 123-4 (T.K. Abbott trans., 1996). If so, such aliens would prove there are things *we* don't (for the moment) know about the thing-in-itself. "[T]he mere possibility of alternative, but equally coherent sets of belief, some of them perhaps inconceivable to us, is sufficient to induce scepticism about our cognitive powers." *Id.* at 122. But doesn't this just mean that the proof of *un*knowability will be revealed when we finally *know* the thing-in-itself? I think the aliens side with Hegel, not Kant.

[61] Stephen Houlgate, *Why Hegel's Concept is not the Essence of Things*, in HEGEL'S THEORY OF THE SUBJECT 21 (David Gray Carlson ed., 2005) ("positing is different from positedness").

inessential Being it seeks to shed.

Hegel says of positedness that it is opposed to being-in-itself. It *includes* Being-for-other (as its etymology would suggest). But "it specifically contains the already accomplished bending back of that which is not *in itself* into that which is being-in-itself." (121) A positedness is an entity that shows what it is by announcing what it is *not*. What it renounces "bends back" upon the announcing entity. By way of a political analogy, when Richard Nixon announced, "I am not a crook," he in effect revealed himself to be a positedness. The American public understood Nixon's remark in just this way.

"Being posited" requires the silent fourth to *do the positing*. "Being posited" is all we have at this early stage. Hegel uses the verb "to posit" but always in its passive tense. Positing is, so far, only passive. Active positing is merely "in itself." Thus, Determinate Being "is posited" out from Becoming. But Becoming does not *posit*. *Self*-determination arrives only later.[62]

Properly, "positing" implies a correlate. For this reason, everything in Essence comes in pairs.[63] Here, in the Doctrine of Being, things are *qualitative*; they simply *are*: "the other *is*, the finite ranks equally with the infinite as an immediate, affirmative being, standing fast on its own account; the meaning of each appears to be complete even without its other." (122) In the realm of Being, self-identity seems possible, for the moment. But it will be otherwise in Essence, where the Positive correlates with the Negative, and has no meaning on its own.

(b) Determination, Constitution and Limit

In Something/Other, "*Being-for-other* is, in the unity of something with itself, identical with its *in-itself*." (122) [2] stands for *both* Being-for-other *and* being-in-itself. This implies that "Being-for-other" [2] is *in* Something [1, 2]. Determinateness is thus reflected back into Something/Other. It *was* an either/or. Now it is also a both/and.

Of this new development, Hegel writes:

The *in-itself* into which something is reflected into itself out of its being-for-other

---

62 Harris correctly identifies the positing of Being-in-itself/Being-for-other as "for us as reflecting philosophers." HARRIS, LOGIC, *supra* note 25, at 108.

63 EL § 112 ("The terms in *Essence* are always mere pairs of correlatives, and not yet absolutely reflected in themselves: hence in essence the actual unity of the notion is not realized, but only postulated by reflection").

> is no longer an abstract in-itself, but as negation of its being-for-other is mediated by the latter . . . It is not only the immediate identity of the something with itself, but the identity through which there is present *in* the something that which it is *in itself*; being-for-other is present *in it* because the *in-itself* is the sublation of the being-for-other, has returned *out* of the being-for-other into itself; but equally, too, simply because it is abstract and therefore essentially burdened with negation, with being-for-other. (122)

This passage says, basically, that the In-itself *is* the Other.

The "in-itself," then, finds itself concretely *determined* in Figure 3(c). Determination is *affirmative determinateness* – precisely what Something was *not*. Something was either/or. "Determination implies that what something is *in itself*, is also *present in* it." (123)

Hegel describes Determination as an "affirmative determinateness as the in-itself with which something . . . remains congruous in face of its entanglement with the other by which it might be determined, maintaining itself in its self-equality, and making its determination hold good in its being-for-other." (123) To translate, in Figure 3(a), Something was Something/Other. Only external reflection can tell whether it was Something or Other. Whatever external reflection chooses, that determination by external reflection is Something/Other's Being-for-other. Now external reflection chooses. With the accent on Being, Something is *determined* as Something. Determination, then, stands for dependence on external reflection. Something is Something (and not Other) because it is *determined* as such by an outside force. Yet it could not be so determined unless it were already "in itself" so determinable. An object needs outside force to be what it is. But the object is not *purely* a subjective product. Determination is a compromise between Being-in-itself and Being-for-other. Between the object and the determining subject is a "play of forces."[64]

Figure 3(c)
Determination of the In-itself

As an example of Determination, Hegel writes: "The *determination* of man is thinking reason." (123) Reason distinguishes man from brute. Yet bruteness exists within man as his Being-for-other. Brutality is to man what nature is to spirit. In Kantian moral theory, inclination is

---

[64] In the *Phenomenology*, knowledge of the object is shown to be a "play of forces" between the knowing subject and the object. PHENOMENOLOGY, *supra* note 48, ¶¶ 138-43.

natural, reason is spiritual. Morality consists of suspending nature so that reason can speak.[65] So when parents procreate, they produce a brute. Bruteness is what the baby is for the parents – not to mention the neighbors. The baby also has Being-in-itself. This is *reason*. The job of the parents is to bring forth the in-itself of the child. If they succeed, the child is "determined" to be a person. Determination is the product of an external reflection. The child cannot raise herself. But education works only because reason is the "in-itself" of the child. Thus, the determination of man is thinking reason.

Constitution. In Figure 3(c), the in-itself [4] of the determined Something [4, 5] is to be distinguished from what is only Being-for-other [4, 6]. [4] retains against [6] "the form of immediate, qualitative being." (123) Hegel assigns to [6] the name Constitution.

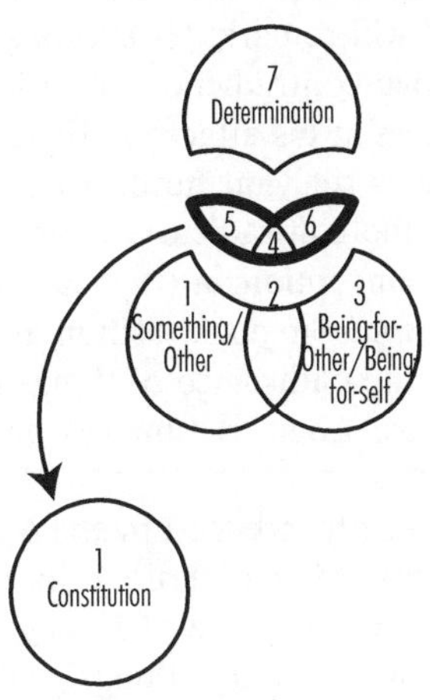

Figure 4(a)
Constitution

> That which something has *in it*, thus divides itself and is from this side [3] an external determinate being . . . , but does not belong to the something's in-itself [2]. The [implicit] determinateness is thus a *constitution* [*Beschaffenheit*].
>
> Constituted in this or that way, something is involved in external influences and relationships. This external connection on which the constitution depends, and the circumstances of being determined by an other, appears as something contingent. But it is the quality of something to be open to external influences and to have a *constitution*. (124)

Constitution, then, is alien imposition. It represents the tyranny of the Understanding – of external reflection.

In Figure 4(a), the Understanding proposes that the universe is *constituted* – mediated by an external reflection that works on immanent material. Structurally this move resembles what we saw in Figure 3(a). In it, the Understanding seizes upon [4, 5, 6], the mediated portion of the middle term. This will be the quintessential move of the Understanding across the three sections of Finitude. In effect, the Understanding focuses on the *negative* side of Determinate Being. Notice how this fits

---

65 *See* Jeanne L. Schroeder & David Gray Carlson, *Kenneth Starr: Diabolically Evil?*, 88 CAL. L. REV. 653 (2000).

perfectly with the *silent fourth*. Constitution is the confession that Being cannot constitute itself. It needs the silent fourth to complete it.

The negative part of Something is isolated in Figure 4(a), and so negativity has migrated from the right side of the diagram over to the left. These are the seeds and weak beginnings from which will sprout the self-destruction of the Doctrine of Being.

Taylor's Challenge. This transition is challenged by Charles Taylor, who insists that the brief mortality of things may cohere with our *experience* but is not *logically* required.[66] In effect, Taylor accuses Hegel of the inductive fallacy – drawing universals from experience. Any ground in experience defeats Hegel's claim that he has generated a *Logic*.

It is Taylor, however, not Hegel, who is guilty of appeal to experience. Taylor has experienced that *some* things (for the moment) endure. On this basis, he is unwilling to accept the premise that Being logically cannot sustain itself. Later, Hegel will remark: "It shows an excessive tenderness for the world to remove contradiction from it." (237) Taylor is guilty of just such a tenderness in his attack on Figure 4(a).[67] A remark from the end of the Logic is relevant here: "formal thinking makes identity its law, and allows the contradictory content before it to sink into the sphere of ordinary conception, into space and time, in which the contradictories are held *asunder* in juxtaposition and temporal succession." (835) In other words, the endurance of things is just a trick that time and space play on us. Logic is timeless and spaceless and quite immune from this trick.

Taylor's taste for subsistence will soon be amply indulged by the *SL*. Self-subsistence is the hallmark of True Infinity. The True Infinite *ceases to be* but *remains what it is.*. Later, in the Doctrine of Essence, enduring "things" will appear. At this stage of the Logic, "things" turn out to be contradictory, negative unities of multiple properties. The very negativity that Taylor opposes turns out to be the savior of "things." But self-subsistence is too advanced an idea for the evanescent Doctrine of Quality. It must await the arrival of essential Existence.

Nor is there anything wrong with Hegel's methodology in Figure 4(a). Hegel's technique is to focus the Understanding's vulture eye on the middle term. Even Taylor admits that [4, 5, 6] of Figure 3(c) – that

---

66 TAYLOR, *supra* note 13, at 236.

67 For a similar refusal to believe that contradictions are in things (rather than simply in our minds), see INWOOD, *supra* note 54, at 302-7.

which is negative, compared to [7] – is a constituent part of any Determination. Why can't the Understanding consider [4, 5, 6] as such? If it does, and if we develop the logic of the negativity within the Determination, then the Logic proceeds along its necessitated way. I see nothing illegitimate in Hegel's methodology here, nor should we concede that Hegel covertly relies on the experience of things not enduring. Rather, it is Taylor who insists that the Understanding must *not* make the move of Figure 4(a), lest it disturb his experience that some things persist.

Indeed, the very next move in Figure 4(b) makes Taylor's own point. Being does not go out of existence just because the negative camel nose of Constitution is in the tent of Being. Determinations *do* survive the isolation of negative activity. Rather, under the law of sublation, they are destroyed *and* preserved.

Taylor makes an additional criticism of Figure 4(a). Constitution – a positivization of [2, 3] in Figure 3(b) – has two senses. Constitution is (a) negation as contrastive frontier. It is also (b) negation as "interactive" influence or causal pressure (which might destroy Something). Of Figure 4(a), Taylor writes:

> This argument arouses our suspicion, and rightly so. For it trades on a number of confusions. First the two senses of negation, the contrastive and interactive are elided in the term frontier (*Grenze*). Something only has determinate being through its contrastive frontier with others. Its frontier is in this sense constitutive of it. "Something [*Etwas*] is only what it is in its frontier and through its frontier."[68]
>
> But this frontier is common with the other contrasted properties. It also defines and is constitutive of them. Hence in containing it each contains what negates it as well as what essentially constitutes it.
>
> If we now shift to the [interactive] sense of frontier . . . we can give this "negation" a concrete as well as just a contrastive logical sense, and it looks as though each entity essentially contains the seeds of its own destruction. But of course however much we may be tempted to speak of something containing its negation in the contrastive sense, when we move to the frontier at which things "negate" each other by interaction, it is just false to say that each contains its own negation. Quite the contrary, to the extent that they maintain themselves, they hold their "negations" off. If they fail to do so, of course, they go under, but they are not essentially determined to do so by the very way in which they are defined.[69]

In other words, things may change because of outside pressure, but they do not *necessarily* change because of internal pressure. Hegel is

---

[68] *EL* § 92 Addition.

[69] TAYLOR, *supra* note 13, at 236.

supposedly guilty of conflating these two senses of Limitation. Taylor implies that Hegel was wrong to locate Constitution at the heart of Determination. It should have been left on the outside. Taylor goes so far as to announce the *SL* is a failure, because of this very point.[70]

Taylor concludes his line of inquiry by judging that Hegel's doctrine of the immanent self-erasure of being is "not established by a strict proof."[71] Yet, in using Something/Other and Constitution to introduce negativity into the heart of being, Hegel proceeds logically in this sense: In Figure 2(a), the Understanding exhausted the possibilities of seizing upon the immediacy to be found in Figure 1(c). Now it pursues the study of mediation, which brings negativity into being. Negativity is now the "in-itself" of being, which, when it becomes "for itself," spells the end of Finite Being. To my eye, this is "a strict proof;" Taylor has not destroyed Hegel's enterprise.

Determination. Hegel claims that, if Something alters, the alteration occurs within its Constitution. Yet, in the face of alteration, Something preserves itself. Alteration is only a surface change in Something. Constitutional change does not run deep. "[S]omething in accordance with its determination, is indifferent to its constitution." (124) Here Hegel agrees with Kant that only the permanent is changed.[72] "This remaining-in-conformity-with expresses itself in the being of something . . . as the 'beginnings' of a power over and against becoming-other, and thus reveal [Constitution] to be powerlessness."[73] Constitution [1] represents only the *mediated* parts of Determination [4, 5, 6]; the immediate version of Determination [7] is immune to Constitution. It is Constitution's negation. Hence, Hegel opposes unconstituted Determination (in its negative version) [7] to Constitution.

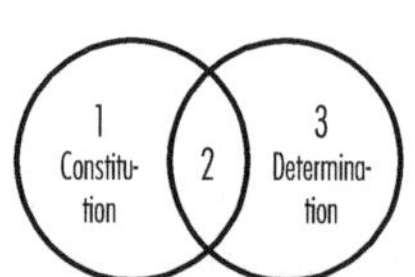

Figure 4(b)
Constitution v Determination

In Figure 4(b), the extremes of the syllogism act in their usual manner: "[D]etermination spontaneously passes over into constitution, and the latter into the former." (124) This is the chiasmic exchange of properties that we saw in Figure 1(c). Hegel describes this connection between Constitution and the negative version of Determination as

---

70 *Id.* at 348.

71 *Id.* at 239.

72 IMMANUEL KANT, CRITIQUE OF PURE REASON A182-9/B224-33 (Paul Guyer & Allen W. Wood trans., 1990).

73 MARCUSE, ONTOLOGY, *supra* note 21, at 52-3.

follows: "[I]n so far as that which something is *in itself* is also present *in it*, it is burdened with being-for-other." (124) This was already true in Figure 3(b), where [2] was the pair of Being-for-other and Being-in-itself. Being-for-other was therefore a constituent part of Determination, in its positive sense, as shown in Figure 3(c). "[H]ence the determination is, as such, open to relationship to other." (124)

This openness justifies the negative version of Determination as the right-leaning term in Figure 4(b). In this position, it is Being-for-other to Constitution. First, Determination in Figure 3(c) was "reduced to constitution" [1] (124) Second, Determination was "reduced" to [3] in Figure 4(b). "Conversely, being-for-other isolated as constitution [1] and posited by itself, is in its own self the same as the other [2] . . . in its own self." (124) Constitution is thus a "*self-related* determinate being" [1], but it also has Being-in-itself [2] "with a determinateness, and therefore a *determination*." (124) Constitution is taken immediately [1] but is also a determinateness [1, 2]. Figure 4(b) shows Constitution and Determination as mutually dependent. Constitution imposes Determination from the outside, but it is simultaneously on the inside. It has its effect only because it is the "in itself" of Determination [2]. Constitution – originally negative – is now on the side of *Being* in Figure 4(c). That which *alters* is now "*posited* in the something." (125)[74] With Constitution, "being-within-self includes the negation within it [2], by means of which alone it now has its affirma-tive determinate being." (125) This means that being-within-self has become "negation of its other," (125) and "the non-being of . . . otherness." (125) Here is a development that will culminate in the demise of the Finite. Positive Being is now a negative activity – "*the ceasing of an other in it*." (126) Coming-to-be is now Ceasing-to-be, which becomes the theme of Being's tongue.

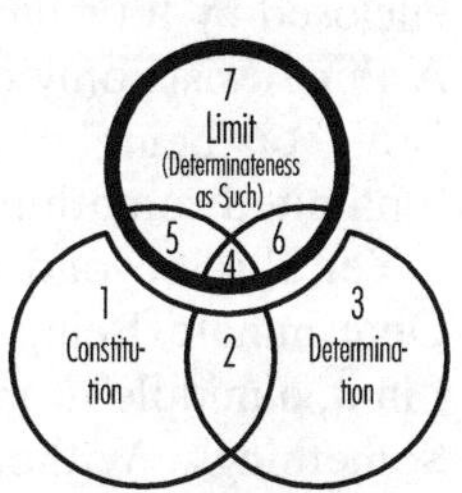

Figure 4(c)
Limit (Determinateness as Such)

Limit. In Figure 4(b), Constitution and Determination share a common element [2], which becomes Determinateness as Such [7] in Figure 4(c). This Hegel renames Limit (*Grenze*) – "where the thing stops, or . . . what the thing is not."[75] In Limit, "the

---

[74] Constitution stands for *change*, which becomes the inherent dynamic of the Something. The Something now changes itself. BURBIDGE, LOGIC, *supra* note 3, at 50.

[75] PHENOMENOLOGY, *supra* note 48, ¶ 3.

non-being-for-other becomes prominent." (126) The Other [4, 6] is kept apart from Something [4, 5]. "[I]n the limit, something limits its other." (126) But the Other [4, 6] is likewise a Something; it claims Limit as much as the affirmative Something does. Limit [4] is a little like the border between France and Germany. This border is a line, but does the line belong to Germany or to France? Since a line is not spatial, it is a non-entity, so far as spatial France and Germany are concerned. Limit is in fact the *negative unity* between the two Beings, as [4] in Figure 4(c) shows.[76]

Because Limit is the non-being of the other, Something "*is* through its limit. It is true that something, in limiting the other, is subjected to being limited itself; but at the same time its limit is, as the ceasing of the other in it, itself only the being of the something." (126) Limit is nothing else but a *beyond*. In Figure 4(c), this "beyond" is [7]. Thus, the Somethings [4, 5, 6] have their Determinate Being (in part) "*beyond* their limit." (127) Furthermore, Limit has *non-being* in the Somethings. The Somethings are therefore different from their Limit, an idea illustrated by some simple geometric terms: "the line appears as line only outside its limit, the point; the plane as plane outside the line; the solid as solid only outside its limiting surface." (127)

By way of example, take Line *AZ* (comprised of infinitely numerous points). *A* and *Z* are the limits of this line. The line only appears "outside" *A* and "outside" *Z*. So it is with the plane. Imagine a square, enclosed by four lines. This plane exists only "outside" the four lines. A thing exists only outside its limit, and this "outside" constitutes the "stuff" or "being" of Limit. Indeed, Hegel states that Limit implies an "unlimited something." (127).

Yet this beyond of the limit – the unlimited something – is a Determinate Being indistinguishable from its Other – [4, 5]=[4, 6]. Limit, a middle term, is both the *unity* and *distinguishedness* of the two Somethings. Without Limit, the two Somethings are the same;

---

[76] Limit is *internal* to Determinateness. EL § 92 ("We cannot . . . regard the limit as only external to being which is then and there. It rather goes through and through the whole of such existence.") Limit implies the negativity of Being – a negativity that underwrites the independence of the thing from outside oppression. But this can be turned around. Limit also prevents the thing from truly *being* what it is. Žižek exploits this aspect of Limit and uses it to explain the Lacanian idea of ex-timacy: Limit implies there is a nothingness in the soul of the subject which it can never overcome in order to be truly an object. This nothingness is the subject's "*internal* limit – that is, the bar which itself prevents the subject's full realization." SLAVOJ ŽIŽEK, THE FRAGILE ABSOLUTE – OR, WHY IS THE CHRISTIAN LEGACY WORTH FIGHTING FOR? 29 (2000).

Something owes its Determinate Being to Limit. Yet Limit and Determinate Being are each the negative of the other. This means that Something [4, 5] expels itself [4] from itself and banishes this material to Limit [7].

The idea of the universal Something expelling its being to a "beyond" is portentous for Hegel's entire theory. It signals the end of "reality" and the birth of "ideality." Ceasing-to-be is now the very heart of Hegel's entire system.

Contradiction. After introducing Limit, Hegel invokes the ominous concept of "Contradiction" – a term officially introduced only in the Doctrine of Essence. Limit is in a state of unrest – just as Becoming was. Unrest – Contradiction – is what impels Something to surpass its Limit. A geometric point – which is Limit to the line – goes outside itself and *becomes* the line – an unlimited progression of points. The Limit of the plane is the line – a plane is nothing but an unlimited array of lines. Hegel thus defines the line as "the *movement* of the point," and the plane is "the movement of the line." (128)

As Limit to the line, the point is the beginning of the line which spontaneously repels itself from itself to create the line. Yet, in spatial or linear terms, "*there is* no such thing as a point, line or plane" – taken as limit to line, plane, or solid. (129) As Limit, they exist *outside* the line or the plane or the solid. Limit is a Determinate Being but also a nothing. As such, it very much resembles Becoming, which starts from Nothing and "becomes" a Determinate Being.

But is it true that the point spontaneously produces the line? Why can't I ignore the line and hold the point fixed and isolated? The answer is that, *if* the point is Limit, it must limit *something* (just as, earlier, Other had to be Other to something). Something *must* be "beyond" Limit. The very idea of Limit compels a transcending. Hence, the geometric point, *when conceived as Limit*, necessarily produces the line *spontaneously*.

(c) Finitude

We are still not done with Finitude, the chapter's middle section. In Determinate Being – the first third of the chapter – we made a circle, but the work was all done to the left of the diagram. The initial move of the Understanding was [7] → [1]. In Finitude, the move has been [4, 5, 6] → [1], which isolates *mediation as such*. We have been occupied with the diagram's right side. We need two more mediated turns before moving on to Infinity.

Limit transcends itself necessarily. "Something with its immanent limit . . . through which it is directed and forced out of and beyond itself, is the *finite*." (129)

As Finite, Something has Being that is determined but limited. "[I]ts quality is its limit, and, burdened with this, it remains . . . an affirmative, stable being." (129)[77] But Limit, as negative to Something, must develop its negativity – a negativity that is now the being-within-self [4] of Something. This development is *ceasing-to-be* – the Something's Finitude:

> When we say of things that *they are finite*, we understand thereby that . . . finite things are not merely limited – as such they still have determinate being outside their limit – but that . . . non-being constitutes their . . . being. Finite things . . . send themselves away beyond themselves, beyond their being. They *are*, but the truth of this being is their *end*. The finite not only alters, like something in general, but *ceases to be*; and its ceasing to be is not merely a possibility . . . but the being as such of finite things is to have the germ of decease as their being-within-self: the hour of their birth is the hour of their death. (129)

The meaning of this famous passage[78] is this: We think of ourselves as finite beings. We know that we shall die. So death is already embedded within us. Death is our Being-in-itself. We only await our Being-in-itself to posit itself as actual. At that point life ends, and we shuffle off this mortal coil to encounter what dreams may come.[79]

For God, there is no time; birth is *simultaneously* death. God sees our lives as the constant modulation of Being into Nothing. To God,

---

[77] *See* BURBIDGE, LOGIC, *supra* note 3, at 51 (Limit "prevents the introduction of changes that would destroy its specific qualities and would make it into something else").

[78] MARCUSE, ONTOLOGY, *supra* note 21, at 55 ("for the first time the concept of finitude is removed from the theological tradition and placed on the ground of pure philosophical ontology . . . From this point on, Hegel opens the wholly new dimension of the universal *historicity* of beings and clears the way for understanding the essence of the *historical*"); MARCUSE, REASON, *supra* note 30, at 136 ("a preliminary enunciation of the decisive passages in which Marx later revolutionized Western thought").

[79] "We say, for instance, that man is mortal, and seem to think that the ground of his death is in external circumstances only; so that if this way of looking were correct, man would have two special properties, vitality and – also – mortality. But the true view of the matter is that life, as life, involves the germ of death, and that the finite, being radically self-contradictory, involves its own self-suppression." EL § 82 Addition. A false note is sounded by Nancy, who writes: "the negation of the given or of Being-in-itself, in other words, its entry into becoming, into manifestation and desires, goes toward nothing other than freedom . . . " NANCY, *supra* note 57, at 70. Being-in-itself *is* negation as such and *is* the fate of any given.

we are born and we die in the very same "hour." Like Shakespeare, Hegel too generously accords us an *hour* to strut and fret upon the stage. To God this hour is nothing at all.

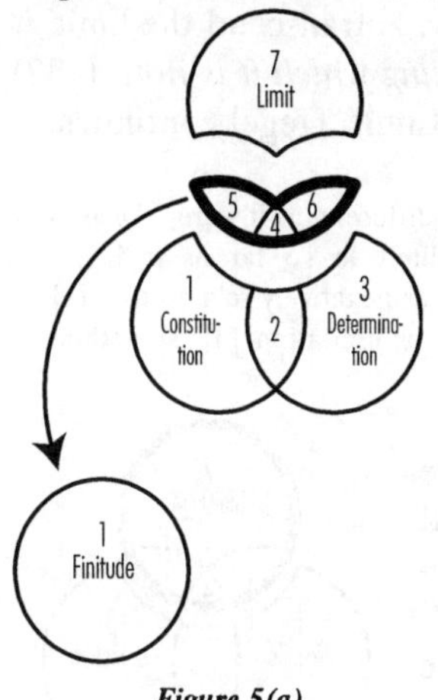

Figure 5(a)
Finitude

(α) The Immediacy of Finitude

The thought of Finitude brings sadness. "[T]here is no longer left to things an affirmative being *distinct* from their destiny to perish." (129) The other negatives – Negation, Constitution, Limit – reconcile themselves with their Other. But Finitude is negation *"fixed in itself*, and it therefore stands in abrupt contrast to its affirmative." (130) Yet Finitude is likewise an affirmative thing. "The understanding persists in this sadness of Finitude by making non-being the determination of things and at the same time making it *imperishable* and *absolute*." (130)

In Figure 5(a), [4, 5, 6] represents the "beyond" of Limit – its non-being. The Understanding makes this into [1]. Finitude, or death, is eternal and fixed. For this reason, Finitude is "the most stubborn category of the understanding." (129)

But Dialectical Reason comes to the rescue with an optimistic note: "[C]ertainly no philosophy or opinion, or understanding, will let itself be tied to the standpoint that the finite is absolute; the very opposite is expressly present in the assertion of the finite; the finite is limited, transitory." (130) So Finitude gets a taste of its own medicine. Under the laws of sublation, Finitude *itself* ceases to be.

(β) Limitation and the Ought

Figure 5(b)
Limitation

The Understanding suppresses the negative voice [2] of Finitude, which Dialectical Reason brings forth and calls Limitation (*Schranke*), the *beyond* of the Finite. If the Finite is limited, there must be a *beyond*.

Limitation, Hegel warns, must not be confused with the earlier stage of Limit (*Grenze*): "Something's own limit thus posited by it as a negative which is at the same time essential, is not merely limit as such, but *limitation*." (132) In short, Limitation is a negative version of Limit.

Hegel writes of Figure 5(b): "In order that the limit . . . should be a limitation, something must at the same time . . . transcend the limit, it must . . . *be related to the limit as to something which it is not*." (132) Limitation, then, is [3], the beyond of [1]'s Limit. Hegel continues:

> The determinate being of something [1] lies inertly indifferent, as it were, *alongside* its limit [2]. But something only transcends its limit in so far as it is the accomplished sublation of the limit, is the *in-itself* [2] as negatively related to it [1]. And since the limit [2] is in the [Finite] itself as a limitation [3], something transcends *its own self*. (132)[80]

Hegel immediately follows with the middle term – the Ought, Finitude's most advanced moment. It shows that the Finite is "something *which is not what it ought to be*." (248)[81] Finite things "do not possess the complete reality of their Notion within themselves, but require other things to complete it . . . That actual things are not congruous with the Idea is the side of their *finitude* and *untruth*, and in accordance with this side they are *objects*." (757)

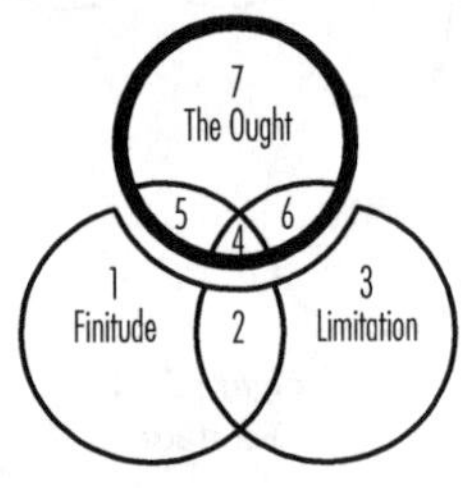

Figure 5(c)
The Ought

The Ought is "posited as the in-itself." (132) The *Ought* of the Finite is that it *ought* to cease to be. This is the "in itself" of Finite things. So long as they have not passed away, they are not what they should be.[82]

---

[80] In defending Hegel against charges of totalitarianism, William Maker emphasizes that Logic limits itself and posits its own beyond. WILLIAM MAKER, PHILOSOPHY WITHOUT FOUNDATIONS: RETHINKING HEGEL 139 (1994). Limitation proves "the necessity for thought of thinking something as having the character of not being determined by thought." *Id.* In Maker's view, the self-determinations of Logic leave nature intact and irreducible and also explain nature's necessity from within the perspective of Logic.

[81] Marcuse uses this remark to enlist Hegel for leftwing causes. MARCUSE, REASON, *supra* note 30, at 66 ("Hegel's dialectic is permeated with the profound conviction that all immediate forms of existence – in nature and history – are 'bad,' because they do not permit thing to be what they can be").

[82] *See* Thomas E. Wartenberg, *Hegel's Idealism: The Logic of Conceptuality*, in THE CAMBRIDGE COMPANION TO HEGEL 106 (Frederick C. Beiser ed. 1993) ("all finite beings are dependent beings and thus not fully real. But if finite beings are dependent, it follows that there must be some nonfinite being upon which they are dependent.").

The Ought

What is *commonly* meant by "ought"? Suppose I say: "You ought to take piano lessons." This observation states what *is* and what is *not*. Thus, I have really said: "You have the potential to be a better piano player. For this reason, lessons are advisable. Your potential *is*." Also, I have said: "Frankly, right now, you're not yet a good piano player. That's why lessons are in order. Your talent is merely potential and is not now actual. In terms of actuality, your talent is *not*." In both cases, something (potentiality) is present and something (actuality) is absent. These statements are full of Becoming. The potential should cease-to-be what it is and should become something else. Actuality should come-to-be and should cease being only potential.

Empiricism says that you cannot prove an *ought* from an *is*. It suppresses the in-itself and never advances beyond the Understanding. This is quite wrong-headed, says Hegel. Anything that ought to be "is." The Ought "is" in the present. If not, then it will never come-to-be. The proof of the Ought is precisely whether it *does* come-to-be. If it never does, it was never possible. In the eye of God, the Ought *always* comes-to-be and is indistinguishable from the "is." Probability theory agrees: given infinite time, what is possible *will* become actual.[83] Hegel's point is no different. The Ought becomes the "is" in the eye of God:[84] "What ought to be *is*, and at the same time *is not* . . . The ought has, therefore, essentially a limitation." (132-3) This Limitation is the *not* of the Ought. Its significance is that the Ought represents the positing of the unposited in-itself. Being-in-itself logically *must* become "for-itself." The potential *must* become the actual.

For the moment, the Ought is *not yet*: "[t]he being-in-itself of the something . . . reduces itself therefore to an *ought-to-be* through the fact that [its] in-itself is . . . a *non-being*. (133)[85] The non-being of the Ought is [4, 5, 6] of Figure 5(c). Yet the Ought *transcends* its non-

---

[83] Physicists call this the "ergodic hypothesis."

[84] This point of view does much to illuminate Kant's *Critique of Practical Reason*. There, Kant defends, *inter alia*, belief in the immortality of the soul, because only this makes possible the attainment of absolute moral perfection. CRITIQUE OF PRACTICAL REASON, *supra* note 60, at 148. This moral perfection is an Ought to mortals, but to God, moral perfection *is*.

[85] MARCUSE, ONTOLOGY, *supra* note 21, at 58 ("With this determination, Hegel removes the concept of the 'ought' from the ahistorical sphere of Kantian ethics of duty . . . and places it on the ground of concrete happening").

being – its Limitation – in [7]. [7] is the Being-in-itself of the Ought – a paradox, because [7] is an *immediacy*, and Being-in-itself is always a mediated determinateness. In effect, Being-in-itself is "posited" as *expressly* implicit.

"The ought has recently played a great part in philosophy," Hegel muses, "especially in connection with morality and also in metaphysics generally." (133) Here Hegel alludes to Kantian moral theory, which announces: "You can because you ought."[86] Hegel counters, "it is equally correct that: 'you cannot, just because you ought.'" (133) The Ought contains Limitation, and so long as the Ought is before us, actuality is *not*. "[I]n the world of actuality itself, Reason and Law are not in such a bad way that they only *ought* to be – it is only the abstraction of the in-itself that stops at this." (136) The Ought is only the "standpoint which clings to finitude and thus to contradiction." (136)

To the Kantains who maintain that Limitation cannot be transcended, Hegel retorts, "To make such an assertion is to be unaware that the very fact that something is determined as a limitation implies that the limitation is already transcended." (134) Limitation is the negative of the Finite. As such, the Finite is *already* "beyond" Limitation, even before Limitation comes to be. It is in the nature of reason to transcend the Limitation of the particular and manifest what is universal.

In light of the above, if Limitation is already overcome in them, why don't rocks rise up from the earth and become self-conscious beings? Here is a question very likely to bother the beginner. If Hegel really raises the object to subjectivity in the *SL*, why don't the rocks speak to us?

Hegel assures us, "Stone and metal do not transcend their limitation because this is not a limitation *for them*." (134)[87] Rocks have already been expelled from spirit when physical nature was shown to be self-alienated spirit. Being finite things, "[t]hey cannot develop their potentialities except by perishing."[88] Limitation is a feature of sentient

---

[86] SLAVOJ ŽIŽEK, THE SUBLIME OBJECT OF IDEOLOGY 81 (1991).

[87] With regard to Hegel's credentials in metallurgy, the original 1807 edition of the *Phenomenology* has a title page identifying Hegel as "Dr. and Professor of Philosophy at Jena, assessor in the Ducal Mineralogical Society and member of other learned societies." Donald Phillip Verene, *Hegel's Nature*, in HEGEL AND THE PHILOSOPHY OF NATURE, *supra* note 53, at 209.

[88] MARCUSE, REASON, *supra* note 30, at 137.

beings. Yet Hegel goes on to say that perhaps stones and metals *do* transcend their Limitation. They have Being-in-itself. They "ought" to become something different. If oxidizable, they *potentially* can be burned. In the eye of God, they *will* be burned; God's timeless nature dissolves all difference between potential and actual. "[O]nly by force" (134) can unoxidized metal be kept from its rusty fate.

So this raises again the possibility that rocks *will* speak to us.[89] They will surmount their objectivity and become "subject." And indeed they do. Rocks crumble and become soil. Soil yields plants. Humans eat the plants and participate in thought. Meanwhile, there must be rocks. Objectivity is a valid moment that must be exhibited.[90] If all objects must become subjects over time, this already will have occurred long ago. Instead, alas, some objects must be left behind so that nature can make itself useful to spirit. We lucky humans are granted the privilege of subjectivity, in which self-consciousness constitutes objects, though, as humans, we cannot quite shake off our Finitude, which remains a valid moment in us. When the germ of our decease blossoms forth, we become as silent as the rocks.

(γ) Transition of the Finite into the Infinite

In the transition to the Infinite, Hegel introduces no *new* terms, yet, in a short space, a new advance is described. What we get are enriched observations pertaining to Figure 5(c).[91] First, the Understanding isolates the mediated portions of the Ought [4, 5, 6]. Here the Ought

---

[89] *See* HEGEL'S PHILOSOPHY OF NATURE 206 (M.J. Petry trans., 1970) ("the stones cry out and lift themselves to spirit"). Of this passage Errol Harris remarks that it "may be only poetic enthusiasm, but is nevertheless a notion full of scientific premonition." ERROL E. HARRIS, THE SPIRIT OF HEGEL 116 (1993).

[90] "The essence of the inorganic thing is in fact a particular determination, which is why it becomes concept only in its connection to other things. But the thing does not preserve itself in that connection; it is only *for-some-other*; it does not reflect on itself in the process of relating to other things . . . These elements are particular determinations, and they lack reflection on themselves, that is, they present themselves as being for-others." HYPPOLITE, GENESIS, *supra* note 49, at 240-1.

[91] According to Andrew Haas, "Assuming that the *Logic* is then a machine functioning along [an] immediacy/negation/mediation blueprint, divided into "trinities," into three subsections each with the moments, is misleading. In fact, the tripartite structure is continually interrupted; for example, in "Quality," the section entitled "Transition" is a supplement (it is not a third and has no three)." ANDREW HAAS, HEGEL AND THE PROBLEM OF MULTIPLICITY 79 (2000). I obviously disagree and find triunity in this subsection of chapter 2.

"contains limitation, and limitation contains the ought. Their relation to each other is the finite itself which contains them both in its being-within-self." (136) The being-within-self of the Finite is [4]. In [4], the Finite contains both the Ought and Limitation. By virtue of these observations, the Finite of the transition is more powerful than the Finite of Figure 5(c), in which the Ought and Limitation were merely implicit.

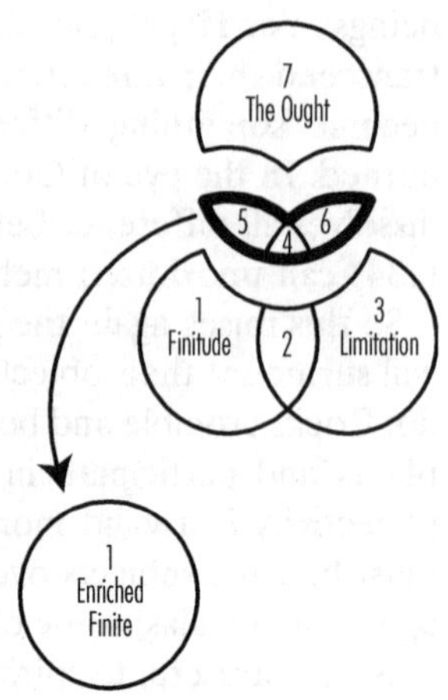

Figure 6(a)
Enriched Finite

Dialectical Reason emphasizes that what appears to be a self-identity [1] has a negative voice [2], which implies Another Finite [3]. As Finite, [1] *ceases-to-be* and the new Finite [3] *comes-to-be* as the first Finite's negative. The other Finite [3] likewise ceases to be and becomes the former Finite [1]. We have the ceaseless seething turmoil of [1] → [3] → [1].

Of this process of birth and death, Hegel says, "the finite in its ceasing-to-be . . . has attained its being-in-itself, is *united with itself*." (136) The in-itself has manifested itself in this ceaseless activity. The in-itself of the Finite is the act of dying. Here we have a harbinger preceding still the fates, and prologue to the omens coming on. Being is about to die.

Not only is the Finite *for itself* when it ceases to be, but it points to its other: "the ought transcends the limitation, that is, transcends itself; but beyond itself or its other, is only the limitation itself. The limitation, however, points directly beyond itself to its other, which is the ought." (136) So each extreme ceases to be and points to the other as what really *is*. Each extreme says, "I am not *it*." This is tantamount to saying, "My other is *it*." This negative "positing" is precisely the move of Reflection, much later in the Logic. It is presaged early in the Doctrine of Being as the posture of rightward leaning Finitude.

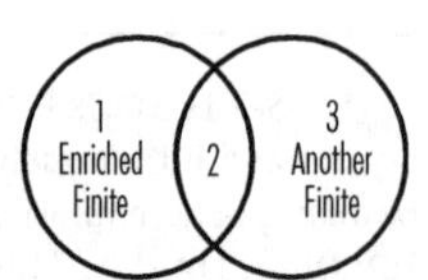

Figure 6(b)
Another Finite

In its activity, the Enriched Finite (which Hegel here calls the Ought) becomes what it is by ceasing to be and going beyond itself. "[I]n going beyond itself . . . it equally only unites with itself." (137) This going beyond while remaining united is Infinity, the middle term between the two Finites.

The Absolute. The Infinite is to be "regarded as a fresh definition of the absolute." (137) Here, for the first time Hegel associates the middle term with the "Absolute." As the Logic progresses the Absolute becomes increasingly richer, until it is Absolute Idea, which encompasses all mediations.

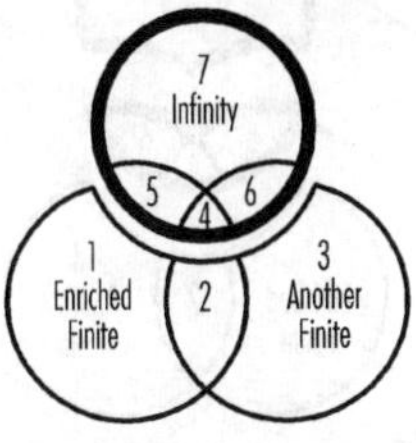

Figure 6(c)
Infinity

Of the Absolute, Hegel remarks, "The forms of *determinate being* find no place in the series of those determinations which can be regarded as definitions of the absolute, for the individual forms of that sphere are immediately posited only as determinatenesses, as finite in general." (137) The "forms of determinate being" are determinatenesses which Dialectical Reason describes in such dialectic forms as are shown in Figure 6(b). Only two circles are invoked here. The form of the Absolute is more advanced, as Figure 6(c) shows. It invokes all three circles.

In the *EL*, however, Hegel more broadly claims that every step of the way has been a proposed definition of the Absolute: "at least the first and third category in every triad may – the first, where the thought-form of the triad is formulated in its simplicity, and the third, being the return from differentiation to a simple self-reference."[92] The second step of Dialectical Reason, however, is merely a negative critique of the Understanding's proposition. On its own, it does not pretend to put forth a definition of the Absolute.

C. Infinity

Infinity is certainly the most overwritten, overlong section we have so far encountered in the *SL*. One gets the impression that Hegel received criticism for his view of the Infinite and responded with the weight of pure repetition in the hope of convincing his unnamed opponents.[93] In truth, by grace of what has preceded, the concept seems straightforward.

---

[92] *EL* § 85. Butler overlooks this passage when he announces, "Hegel is nowhere so indiscriminate as to say that qualitative being is a definition of the absolute." BUTLER, *supra* note 4, at 110.

[93] The 1831 version of the *SL* includes a much expanded section on Infinity. John W. Burbidge, *Hegel's Logic*, in HANDBOOK OF THE HISTORY OF LOGIC 165 (2004).

(a) The Infinite in General

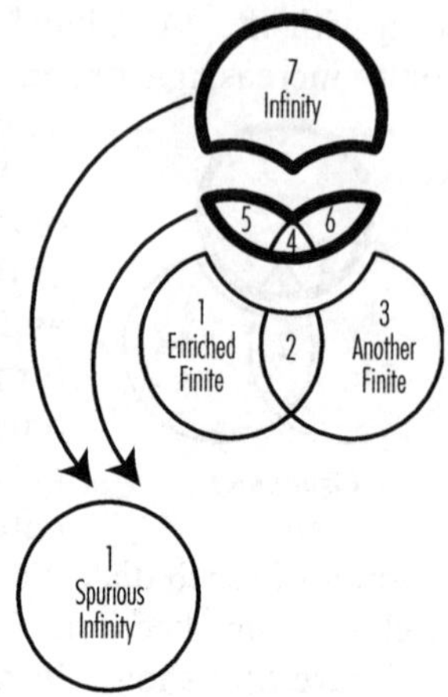

Figure 7(a)
Spurious Infinity

The Infinite of Figure 6(c) still suffers from Limitation and Finitude. So far it is "Spurious Infinity" (*Schlecht-Unendliche*). It is spurious because it names only the endless autistic alternation between being and non-being.[94] It is not to be confused with quantitative infinity, which will be a *true*, not a spurious, infinite.[95]

In Figure 7(a) the Understanding is in charge. It sees only Infinity's self-identity. It cannot see that, within Infinity, one finds Limitation.

(b) Alternating Determination of the Finite and the Infinite

Dialectical Reason intervenes to point out Spurious Infinity's history. The Infinite has negated the Finite. This means that the Infinite is a Determinate Being, with negation inside it. This internal negation is the Infinite's Limit [2]. In Figure 7(b), "the finite stands opposed to the infinite as a *real determinate being*; they stand thus in a qualitative relation, each *remaining* external to the other." (138)

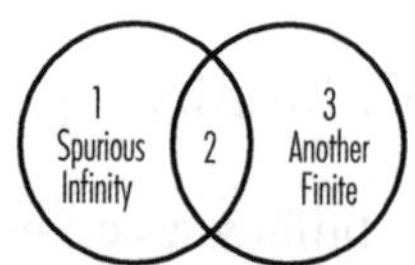

Figure 7(b)
Spurious Infinity and Its Other

Something is wrong with Spurious Infinity. It was supposedly Infinite – in the sense of having no borders. But [2, 3] is Limit to [1]. Figure 7(b) reveals the Spurious Infinite to be just as finite as the earlier Finites. It is "burdened with the opposition to the finite [2]." (139) It is only the "*finitized infinite*." (145) It has

---

[94] "[W]henever we find the spurious infinite that runs away into a progression, we are faced with a contradiction of *qualitative being* and an *impotent ought-to-be* that goes out and away beyond it; the progression itself is the repetition of the demand for unity in opposition to the qualitative, and the persistent relapse into the limitation which is inadequate to that demand." (673)

[95] *Infra* at 174. Though more advanced than the *qualitative* Spurious Infinite, Hegel is no admirer of this version of infinity either.

> only the first, immediate negation for its determinateness relatively to the finite. [E]ach is *assigned* a *distinct* place – the finite as determinate being here, on *this* side [3], and the infinite, although the *in-itself* of the finite [2], nevertheless as a beyond in the dim, inaccessible distance, *outside* of which the finite is and remains [3]. (140)[96]

Hegel compares Spurious Infinity to a line that continues indefinitely in both directions. Such Infinity is "only where the line – which is determinate being – is not." (149) The line well describes the defect of Spurious Infinity. The "Infinite" is portrayed as never present in the line. If we extend the line to reach Infinity, we only find that Infinity has relocated and is still a beyond. Travelers know Spurious Infinity in the form of the horizon. The traveler heads for it, but never reaches it. The horizon stubbornly relocates itself as we approach it.

Hegel warns that it is a mistake to view the Infinite [1] as the unconnected "beyond" of the Finite [3]. There *is* a connection:

> This negation [2] which connects them – the *somethings* reflected into themselves – is the limit of the one relatively to the other, and that, too, in such a manner that each of them does not have the limit *in it* merely relatively to the other, but the negation is their *being-in-itself*. (140)

Notice that the "somethings" – [1] and [3] – reflect themselves (or *collapse*) into [2], which stands for the *negation* of the Finite. Once again we see reflective shrinkage, a renunciation of inessential parts. [2] is Limit to [1] and [3], and [2] is Being-in-itself to both entities as well. [2] is where [1] and [3] withdraw. "[E]ach thus immediately repels the limit [2], as its non-being, from itself." (140) And just as [1] and [3] reflect themselves into [2], they likewise reflect themselves back into themselves – [2] into [1] or [3]. When this occurs, each extreme posits "*another being* outside it, the finite positing its non-being as this infinite and the infinite, similarly, the finite." (140) Once again, reflection shows itself to be negative but productive. When [1] withdraws into itself, it presupposes the existence of [2, 3].

This leads to the negation of the negation. The *unity* of the Spurious Infinities is that each goes beyond itself. *Ceasing to be* is the unity of the Finite and the finitized Infinite.[97] Spurious Infinity is [1] → [3] →

---

[96] *See* G.W.F. HEGEL, THE JENA SYSTEM, 1804-5: LOGIC AND METAPHYSICS 32 (John W. Burbidge & George di Giovanni trans. 1986) (the Spurious Infinite "can only express the striving to be itself; it cannot express itself in truth, for its essence is the absolute sublating of determinacy").

[97] Kosok, *supra* note 22, at 254 ("Unity is therefore the *transcendence* of that which

[1] in perpetual alternation. Hegel calls it the "external realization of the Notion. In this self-erasure is *posited* the content of the Notion, but it is posited as *external* as falling *asunder*." (143) Why "external"? If we contemplate [1] → [3] and [3] → [1], we have left out [2]. [2] has been "externalized" from the process. Yet [2] is also essential. Without [2], "neither is what it is." (144) Therefore, [1] and [3] are "external" to the essential content of the Notion [2], which is self-erasure.

In the infinite progression, [1] and [3] are isolated. But in truth, they are both determinatenesses. Both include [2] as a negative part of the whole. But [2] has different significance for [1] and [3]. To the Spurious Infinite [1], [2] is the connection to [3]. Even the Spurious Infinite purports to include the Finite.[98] To the Finite [3], [2] is Limit. It holds [3] apart from [1]. Yet, in spite of [2]'s dual function,

> both modes yield one and the same result: the infinite and the finite viewed as *connected* with each other – the connection being only external to them but also essential to them, without which neither is what it is – each contains its own other in its own determination, just as much as each . . . has its other present within it as its own moment. (144)

In other words, [1]'s view is that [2] connects it to [3]. [3] thinks [2] separates it from [1]. Yet, recalling that *nothing is, after all, something*, we can likewise say that *no relation is, after all, a relation*. Hence, both [1] and [3] agree that [2] is *a relation*.

The externalization of [2] "yields the decried unity of the finite and the infinite – the unity which is itself the infinite which embraces both itself and finitude – and is therefore the infinite in a different sense" (144) from the Spurious Infinite.[99] Taken alone, [2] posits [1] and [3]

---

is unified, and transcendence as a *movement* from an initial state (e) to its negation (-e) is a *unity* of both . . . ").

[98] The Finite cannot be excluded from even the *Spurious* Infinite. "In *saying* what the infinite is, namely the negation of the *finite*, the latter is itself included in what is *said*; it cannot be dispensed with for the definition or determination of the infinite. One only needs to *be aware of what one is saying* in order to find the determination of the finite in the infinite." (143)

[99] Why "decried" (*verrufene*)? This may refer to Jacobi's criticism of Hegel's derivation of the True Infinite. GIACOMO RINALDI, A HISTORY AND INTERPRETATION OF THE LOGIC OF HEGEL 106 (1992) Soon after the phrase quoted in the text, Hegel writes of rebutting "that idea of the unity which insists on holding fast to the infinite and finite in the quality they are supposed to have when taken in their separation from each other, a view which therefore sees in that unity *only* contradiction, but not also resolution of the contradiction through the negation of the qualitative determinateness of both."

as sublated. "[I]n their unity, therefore, they lose their qualitative nature." (144) Because the Finites terminate themselves and send their being into [2], the Finite "is exalted, and, so to say, infinitely exalted above its worth; the finite is posited as the *infinitized* finite." (145) "That in which the finite sublates itself [2] is the infinite as the negating of finitude; but finitude itself has long since been determined as only the *non-being* of determinate being. It is therefore only *negation* which *sublates* itself in the *negation*." (146) So the True Infinite is the negation of negation – something positive. It is what *endures*. Each Finite manifests its inherent non-being in [2], and this very activity is what the True Infinite is. "Thus, both finite and infinite are this *movement* in which each returns to itself through its negation; they *are* only as *mediation* within themselves." (147)

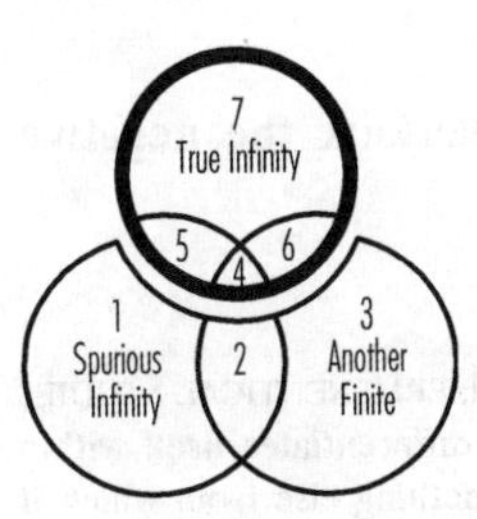

Figure 7(c)
True Infinity

(c) Affirmative Infinity

The Spurious Infinite and its finite beyond modulate back and forth. The name of the movement is the True Infinite. The process resembles Becoming, with which chapter 1 ended. Both chapters 1 and 2 culminate in modulation. Naturally, True Infinity is more advanced than Becoming. It is "now *further determined* in its moments." (148) Now, in True Infinity, the extremes themselves are in the process of Becoming. They are their own manifestation of their non-being – each independently from its own side.

The True Infinite is that which becomes something else while remaining what it is.[100] This proposition is absolutely vital for every succeeding step of the *SL* from now on. Indeed, Hegel calls the True Infinite the "fundamental concept of philosophy."[101] "The whole of the *Logic* [is] an extended proof that being is infinite . . . "[102] The contribution of

(144-5) Friedrich Jacobi (1743-1819) was the first president of the Academy of Sciences in Munich. In *EL* §§ 76-7, Hegel categorizes Jacobi as an intuitionist with great faith in "faith." In spite of these criticisms, Hegel and Jacobi were on friendly terms. KAUFMANN, *supra* note 23, at 175.

[100] *See* EL § 94 Remark (True Infinity "consists in being at home with itself in its other, or, if enunciated as a process, in coming to itself in its other"); PHENOMENOLOGY, *supra* note 48, ¶ 161 (infinity means "(a) that it is self-*identical*, but also . . . *different*; or it is the selfsame which repels itself from itself or sunders itself into two").

[101] EL § 95 Remark.

[102] QUENTIN LAUER, ESSAYS IN HEGELIAN DIALECTIC 142 (1977).

the True Infinite, this "eruption of the infinite in the finite as an *immediate transition* and vanishing of the latter in its beyond," (371-2) is that it encompasses both the Finite and its beyond. In True Infinity, Limit (between the Finites) and Limitation (the Other of the Spurious Infinite) are sublated.[103]

Hegel's critics, whom he generically names "the understanding," fail to follow along:[104]

> The reason why understanding is so antagonistic to the unity of the finite and infinite is simply that it presupposes the limitation and the finite, as well as the in-itself, as *perpetuated*; in doing so it *overlooks* the negation of both which is actually present in the infinite progress. (147)

It is ever the fault of the Understanding to overlook the negative process inherent in a concept.[105]

---

[103] HANS-GEORG GADAMER, HEGEL'S DIALECTIC: FIVE HERMENEUTICAL STUDIES 93 (Christopher Smith trans., 1976) ("insofar as that which differentiates itself within itself is not limited from the outside by the boundary of something else from which it differentiates itself, it is the infinite").

[104] In analyzing the True Infinite, Pinkard continues his error of holding that Determinate Being concerns the world of aggregated individual things. For Pinkard, the True Infinite is the "the underlying substrate that provides the background for the scattered plurality . . . " PINKARD, DIALECTIC, *supra* note 12, at 39. Pinkard portrays True Infinity as the common denominator of "things," but he does not portray it as an act of self-erasure, together with self-preservation. In fact, the True Infinite refers to the *one* universal thing which *ceases to be* but *remains what it is*. In the True Infinite, Being cancels itself and becomes its other – thought. All this is missing in Pinkard's account. Meanwhile, Inwood accuses Hegel of unconsciously slipping between seven different meanings to infinity. INWOOD, *supra* note 54, at 364-5. These are: (1) Because it is infinite, thinking is non-empirical. It does not depend on sensory data. (2) Infinite thought has no object; it is its own object. (3) Thought cannot assign final limits to itself. (4) Thoughts flow into one another. (5) Thought overreaches the other. (6) Thought is embedded in its other. (7) Thought releases itself into the empirical world without assistance. Yet the formula – the true infinite becomes something other while remaining what is – encompasses all of these supposedly different formulations.

[105] Inwood finds the reduction of the Infinite to mere finitude an

> apparently fallacious argument . . . of a type which occurs quite frequently in Hegel. We are told, for example, that if we form abstractly universal concepts, such as that of an animal, and distinguished [sic] them sharply from 'particular' concepts like that of a giraffe, then the universal will turn out to be just one particular alongside others. Such arguments involve a confusion of orders or levels. Universal, or generic, concepts may form a particular, or specific, type of concept co-ordinate with the particular type of particular concepts. But it does not follow from this that universal concepts are themselves merely particular concepts, that the concept of

The thing-in-itself. True Infinity, "the consummated return into self," (148) is "present before us. It is only the spurious infinite which is beyond." (149) This is another reproach to Kant, for whom the beyond was a thing-in-itself which we can never know: "to be thus unattainable," Hegel remarks, "is not its grandeur but its defect, which is at bottom the result of holding fast to the *finite* as such as a *merely affirmative being*. It is what is untrue that is unattainable." (149) In other words, Kant's doctrine of the thing-in-itself depends upon the self-identity of the phenomenal thing. Better to let the Finite do what it does best – cease-to-be. The very act of ceasing *is* True Infinity.

True Infinity, "contradiction as displayed in the sphere of being," (440) is a higher reality than Determinate Being. It has acquired a more concrete content and therefore better deserves the name "reality." *It is what endures*. The Finite is precisely what does *not* endure. It is *not real*.[106] Yet Hegel has second thoughts about invoking reality in connection with True Infinity. He invokes it, he says, because the term is familiar to "untrained thinking." (149) In truth, reality was opposed to a *first* negation in Figure 2(b). Now we have a negation of the

---

an animal, for example is co-ordinate with that of a giraffe . . . We would be making the same mistake, only in a more obvious way, if we were to infer from the fact that 'big' is a small word that big things are really only small.

INWOOD, *supra* note 54, at 162-3. Indeed, we *will* see that Hegel defines particularity as abstracted universality, and that genus *is* one of the species. *Infra* at 450. Inwood, however, does not attend to an obvious point: the infinite is that which has *no borders*. If the infinite is said to be at a different level from the finite, then a border separates it from the finite. The above remark reveals Inwood's inability to escape the dogma that concepts are self-identical.

With regard to universality, Hegel defines it as "absolutely fluid continuity." (639) If the universal is held absolutely different from the particular, as Inwood insists, the universal would not be fluid and not universal. Rather, it would be particular. Finally, the big-small distinction is inappropriate. Hegel is addressing the assumption that infinite-universal is *beyond* the finite-particular. Big-small operates at the phenomenal level and does not attend to the distinction between the phenomenal and the noumenal.

A great many of Inwood's criticisms are based on insisting that the Infinite is radically diverse from the Finite. In other words, Inwood attempts to rally common sense against Hegel's system. For those who, with Inwood, cannot see that the finite-excluding infinite is *itself* a mere finite, there is little hope of any speculative profit from the *SL*.

[106] KENNETH R. WESTPHAL, HEGEL'S EPISTEMOLOGICAL REALISM: A STUDY OF THE AIM AND METHOD OF HEGEL'S *Phenomenology of Spirit* 142 (1989) ("According to the sense of 'reality' Hegel adopts from the metaphysical tradition, something is 'real' only if it is self-sufficient, that is, ontologically independent. In contrast to this, Hegel holds that something is 'ideal' if (and only if) it is ontologically dependent on something else.").

negation, which is opposed to *both* reality and the first negation. A better word for True Infinity is *ideality*. Thus, "ideal being [*das Ideelle*] is the finite as it is in the true infinite" (149-50)[107] – a moment that is not self-subsistent.

Hegel is known as the ultimate idealist philosopher. Now we can grasp what that means. Not "reality" as the Understanding perceives it but a deeper, anti-empirical truth is at stake in Hegel's work.[108]

The Infinite Progress. Spurious Infinity is a contradiction, yet it is sometimes put forward as the final solution to metaphysics. Spurious Infinity is incomplete reflection. It has before it both alternating determinations of True Infinity, but it cannot bring them together in a unity. It only knows how to alternate them.

An example of Spurious Infinity is cause and effect. Every cause is an effect, and every effect a causes. We have a never-ending chain – a Spurious Infinity. (151) Indeed, we find that "cause and effect" is Kant's third antinomy,[109] which states that cause-and-effect is either a bad infinity that never gets resolved or a finite chain that is resolved by a first cause (which ends up being the Kantian autonomous subject).

Kant solves the antinomy by asserting that the two sides are both

---

[107] *See* JOHN W. BURBIDGE, REAL PROCESS: HOW LOGIC AND CHEMISTRY COMBINE IN HEGEL'S PHILOSOPHY OF NATURE 252 n.4 (1996) ("His spelling of this term (*Ideelle*) . . . showed that he was not referring to an ideal (*Ideale*) union of concept and object, but to something that is recognized and isolated only by thought").

[108] MARCUSE, ONTOLOGY, *supra* note 21, at 61 ("for Hegel idealism never means a simple epistemological principle but an ontological one"); MARCUSE, REASON, *supra* note 30, at 138 (idealism "consists of nothing else than the recognition that the finite has no veritable being. . . . For, philosophy starts when the truth of the given state of things is questioned and when it is recognized that that state has no final truth in itself"). Inwood asks, is there one or multiple infinite things? INWOOD, *supra* note 54, at 362. The answer is that there is one infinite thing *and* many infinite things. A sentence from the *Jena Logic* makes Hegel's position clear: "Quality, quantity, and quantum are quality or simple connection; each has as its essence the concept of this whole sphere, and, because this concept of the whole sphere has been cognized truly as infinity, each is itself infinite. But just for that reason this exposition of infinity is an impure one." JENA LOGIC, *supra* note 97, at 31-2. It is also possible to answer the claim of Kosok and Inwood that the *SL* is but one of numerically infinite logics that could have explicated, since each negation both returns to self and spins off other, completely diverse selves. INWOOD, *supra*, at 298-9; KOSOK, *supra* note 22; Michael Kosok, *The Dynamics of Hegelian Dialectics, and Non-Linearity in the Sciences*, in HEGEL IN THE SCIENCES 311, 321-2 (Robert S. Cohen & Marx W. Wartofsky 1984). This view represents a failure to attend to the logic of the True Infinite. There *is* no diversity outside the True Infinite and therefore no infinitely numerous logics. There is one whole, which the *SL* undertakes to explain.

[109] CRITIQUE OF PURE REASON, *supra* note 71, at A444-5/B472-5.

true but incommensurable. Autonomy is on the side of noumenon, cause-effect on the side of phenomena.[110] But for Hegel these antinomies "are only *moments*." (151) Present here are not moments but the *movement* between these alternating moments. In this movement "the finite is united only with itself; and the same is true of the infinite." (152) The negation of the negation by the True Infinite is thus the affirmation – the being – of *both* moments. This unity is the *ideality* of both moments – the resolution of the contradiction that Spurious Infinity is. We thus have before us Speculative Reason itself:

> In this detailed example, there is revealed the specific nature of speculative thought, which consists solely in grasping the opposed moments in their unity. Each moment actually shows that it contains its opposite within itself and that in this opposite it is united with itself; thus the affirmative truth is this immanently active unity, the taking together of both thoughts, their infinity – the relation to self which is not immediate but infinite. (152)[111]

Figure 7(c) is a perfect illustration of Speculative Reason. Each Finite had its Being-in-itself in its own erasure. This self-erasure was common to both of the extremes. It was their "active unity."

In his analysis of Essence, Hegel reveals something vital about the True Infinite. *It is external reflection itself*. "This external reflection in the sphere of being was the infinite; the finite ranked as the first, as the real; as the foundation, the abiding foundation, it forms the starting point and the infinite is the reflection-into-self over against it." (403)

The True Infinite *is* the silent fourth. What we have in Spurious Infinity is the inability of the realm of Being to sustain itself without the aid of subjectivity. The True Infinite *is* the subject, and the alternation of the Finites occurs only within it. For this reason, the True Infinite is the beginning of ideality and the end of reality.

Idealism

> The idealism of philosophy consists in nothing else than in recognizing that the

---

[110] Henry Allison shows how Kant's entire theory of practical reason stems from the appropriation of the "freedom" side of this Third Antinomy. HENRY E. ALLISON, KANT'S THEORY OF FREEDOM (1990).

[111] Kosok emphasizes that, once the moments of being and non-being have been idealized in thought, they can be thought together without contradiction. Kosok, *supra* note 22, at 239, 243-4. True Infinity is the point where co-existence becomes possible and self-identity can be sustained. MCCUMBER, *supra* note 54, at 43.

> finite has no veritable being. Every philosophy is essentially an idealism or at least has idealism for its principle, and the question then is only how far this principle is actually carried out . . . Consequently the opposition of idealistic and realistic philosophy has no significance. A philosophy which ascribed veritable, ultimate, absolute being to finite existence as such, would not deserve the name of philosophy. (154-5)

That this last assessment is true can be proved by the following test. Suppose a philosopher were to say, "Everything is finite and will come to an end. That is the absolute truth." By now, we have figured out how to respond: "But your own statement about finitude is put forth as infinite. Hence, not *everything* is finite, on your own logic." With this simple observation, we have defeated our *soi-disant* philosopher. Absolutizing the Finite is a sorry excuse for philosophy.

In common usage, the *ideal* means "what is simply *in* my conception" (155) – mere subjective fancy. Hegel certainly does not mean *this* when he invokes ideality. *His* ideal is *objective*. For the reduction of ideality to subjective fancy Hegel reserves the name *subjective idealism*. Subjective idealism (*i.e.*, Kantianism)[112] "concerns only the *form* of a conception according to which a content is mine; in the systematic idealism of subjectivity this form is declared to be the only true exclusive form in opposition to the form of objectivity or reality." (155-6) Subjective idealism keeps separate the thought of a thing (form) and the thing-in-itself (content).[113] Content is allowed to remain wholly within Finitude. Such philosophizing never gets beyond the Spurious Infinite.

---

[112] When Hegel speaks of subjective idealism, he is usually thinking of Kant and Fichte. THEODOR W. ADORNO, NEGATIVE DIALECTICS 39 (E.B. Ashton trans. 2000); *see* STANLEY ROSEN, G.W.F. HEGEL: AN INTRODUCTION TO THE SCIENCE OF WISDOM 48 (1974) ("the [subjective] Idealist fails to account for nature or *objectivity*, whereas the Realist cannot explain *subjectivity*. The problem, then is to overcome the separation between the subject and the object, without dissolving their intrinsic characteristics.").

[113] *See* W.H. Walsh, *Kant as Seen by Hegel*, in HEGEL'S CRITIQUE OF KANT 206, 210 (Stephen Priest ed., 1987) ("A true idealism must not stop half way but, as it were, go over into things").

3
Being-For-Self

The highest maturity, the highest stage, which anything can attain is that in which its downfall begins. (611)

Qualitative Being finds its consummation in Being-for-self. If chapter 1 generally stands for Being and chapter 2 for the negation of Being, chapter 3 constitutes a middle term between the two. It is the negation of the negation – "the primary definition of the Concept as such."[1]

Being-for-self is an ironic portion of the Logic. The chapter takes up with a positivization of the True Infinite, which is self-erasure as such. Being *ought* to erase itself. When it does, the in-itself is for-itself. Being is for-itself when it erases itself! As a result, Being-for-self is *form and no content*. Its content is entirely outside itself. Being has thus split in two. There is the empty oneness of Being, and there is its externalized content.

Although itself a "central" chapter, in terms of our convention in which the left side of our diagram is Being and the right side is Nothing, the chapter nevertheless contains a left, right and center bias. First, there is (A) Being-for-self, or the One. The One repulses itself from itself ([1] → [2]), yet stays within itself (in [1, 2]). It becomes (B) the One and the Many, and then (C) Repulsion and Attraction. These "collapse into equilibrium" (157) – that is, a middle term. Its name is Quantity – an entity with sparse Quality indeed. Quantity is Being with

1 ERROL E. HARRIS, AN INTERPRETATION OF THE LOGIC OF HEGEL 110 (1983).

all content outside of itself. It is a dialectic concept; Quantity is the negation of Quality.

A. Being-For-Self as Such

(a) Determinate Being and Being-For-Self

Something "is for itself in so far as it transcends otherness." (158) In Being-for-self, otherness is only a "moment" – historically significant, but now transcended. The Finite once *was*, but it has ceased to be; yet it is idealized, preserved in memory.

The Understanding grasps Being-for-self as "infinity which has collapsed into simple being." (158) In Figure 8(a), the Understanding sees the whole – the positive *and* the negative, the Finite *and* the True Infinite. The whole is a ceasing-to-be, now the very essence of being.

In Figure 8(a), we see a change in the Understanding's focus. Back in Figure 2(a), [7] → [1]. This pattern represented the Understanding's focus on the immediacy present in the middle term [7]. In Figure 3(a), [4, 5, 6] → [1], representing the Understanding's focus on the mediation within the middle term. Now, in Figure 8(a), the Understanding focuses on the *unity* of immediacy and mediation, [4-7] → [1]. The Understanding has grown wiser. It has progressed from the Understanding *as such* in Figure 2(a) to Dialectical Reason in Figure 3(a) and, now, to Speculative Reason in Figure 8(a). The Understanding now sees that the absolute is a True Infinity – a thing that stays what it is *and* becomes something else.

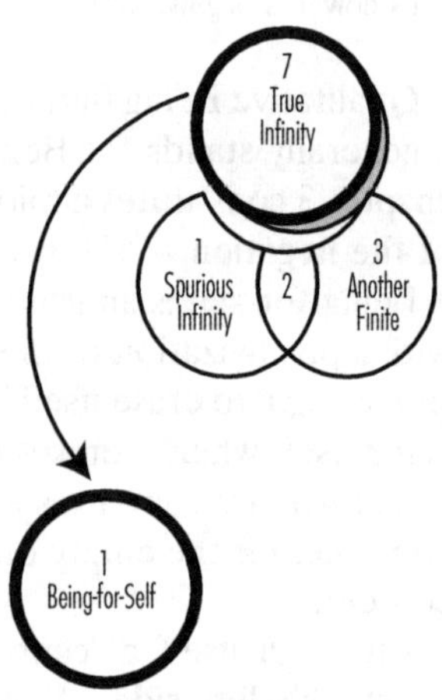

Figure 8(a)
Being-for-self

The True Infinite's double nature implies that Being-for-self is "the infinite *return* into itself." (158) How is this so? At the end of chapter 2, we saw that the True Infinite was comprised of two Finites – the Spurious Infinite and its other. The Being-in-itself of each was ceasing-to-be. The very act of ceasing-to-be was the unity of the two otherwise incommensurable entities. The two Finites blew themselves up. Self-erasing *movement* is the middle term; its name is True Infinity. True Infinity *is* itself and *returns* to itself when it becomes something other.

Furthermore, it is an "infinite" return in that this movement transcends Limitation. The return is infinite in the sense of having no borders – no Limitation.[2]

Being-for-self "is *determinate* being in so far as the negative nature of infinity . . . is from now on in the explicit form of the *immediacy* of being, as only negation in general, as simple qualitative determinateness." (158) This formulation is paradoxical. Surely the True Infinite is negative in nature. It was nothing but Finitude erasing itself from within. Yet this negative process is now presented in the form of an immediacy. This is what [1] in Figure 8(a) shows. But how can [1], an immediacy, be a negativity, which is a doubled figure? The answer is that this is so on the law of sublation. [1] is ever presented as a simple immediacy. This is the only way the Understanding can perceive things. Yet [1] has a history in determinateness and negation, of which the Understanding is now cognizant.

True Infinity represents the self-erasure of Finitude – transcendence above Limit. Limit, in turn, cleaves all determinatenesses in two. With Limit transcended, Determinateness erased is now present in immediate Being-for-self. The "negative nature of infinity" bears "in the explicit form of the *immediacy* of being, as only negation in general." (158)

Consciousness. Hegel compares Being-for-self with consciousness and self-consciousness. Mere consciousness *represents* to itself the object it senses. In other words, it renders the object ideal. "[I]n its entanglement with the negative of itself, with its other [*i.e.*, the idealized object], consciousness is still only in the presence of its own self." (158) That is, if consciousness is [1], the idealized object (*i.e.*, knowledge) is [2]. The "self" of consciousness is [1, 2]. Therefore, in knowledge of the object [2], [1] merely confronts its own self. In light of this structure, consciousness is "the dualism . . . of knowing [2] an alien object external to it [3], and . . . of being for its own self [1, 2], having the object ideally . . . present in it; of being [1] not only in the presence of the other [2, 3], but therein being in the presence of its own self [1, 2]." (158) In comparison, self-consciousness is "being-for-self as *consummated* and *posited*." (158) Self-consciousness contem-

---

[2] *See* HERBERT MARCUSE, HEGEL'S ONTOLOGY AND THE THEORY OF HISTORICITY 62 (Seyla Benhabib trans., 1987) ("Each being remains *for-itself* in this movement of becoming an other, in that it relates (*ver-hält*)") itself to others but remains self-same (*verhält*). It bends itself back in to itself out of the given multiplicity facing it, in such a way that it does not lose itself in this movement does not go beyond itself but remains precisely by itself.") (footnote omitted).

plates *only* itself. "[T]he side of connexion with an other, with an external object, is removed. Self-consciousness is thus the nearest example of the presence of infinity." (158)

Self-consciousness, however, is too advanced to introduce officially at this time. Being-for-self is still qualitative, but self-consciousness is not.[3] It is derived only at the end of the Doctrine of Essence. But consciousness is implicitly at stake in chapter 3 of the *Science of Logic* as the *silent fourth*, which, Hegel says, *is* the True Infinite in the realm of Being.

(b) Being-For-One

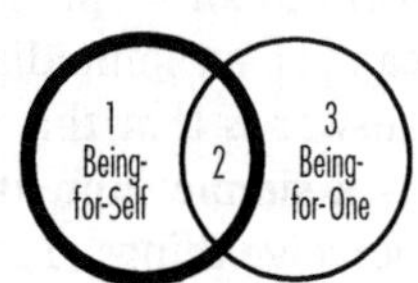

Figure 8(b)
Being-For-One

Dialectical Reason always brings forth the negative voice that the Understanding suppresses. It remembers that "determinate being is present in being-for-self." (159) Hegel names this negative recollection *Being-for-one*. "This moment expresses the manner in which the finite is present in its unity with the infinite." (159) The sublated Finite is now "an ideal being," (159) a moment that is not self-subsistent. By calling Being-for-one a moment, we can say that it *was* present, but isn't any longer. Caesar *was* in Gaul, but neither he nor Gaul is here now.[4] Only the memory is present – inside Being-for-self.

Figure 8(b) contains an insistence that [1, 2] is really *one*. Such an insistence implies that [3] is not even before us. Accordingly, I have

---

[3] CHARLES TAYLOR, HEGEL 245 (1975). Taylor, however, offers an unwarranted criticism of Hegel's transition from Being-for-self to Quantity. According to Taylor, when Being-for-self expels its content, Logic should regress to the beginning – Pure Being and hence Pure Nothing. Instead Hegel illegitimately presses on to Quantity. "In this of course," Taylor writes, "Hegel seems to be having his cake and eating it, retaining those prerogatives of the subject he needs for his argument while remaining in the sphere of Being; but let us waive this objection in order to follow his argument." *Id*. Taylor thus takes Being-for-self as a prerogative of the subject, out of place in the objective transition to Quantity. This is erroneous. Being-for-self is a necessary predicate of consciousness, not a prerogative that is derived *from* consciousness. The logic of Being-for-self is to expel all its content. In doing so, Being-for-self does not retrogress. It retains its Being and becomes Quantity. Here Taylor fails to comprehend the difference between Quantity and Pure Being. Pure Being stands over against nothing at all. Quantity stands over against all its content. Quantity is a determinate indeterminacy, more advanced than Pure Being.

[4] EL §193, at 257 ("Thus, to say, Caesar *was* in Gaul, only denies the immediacy of the event, but not his sojourn in Gaul altogether . . . ").

drawn [2] and [3] as faded presences, compared to the bolder assertion of Being-for-self's immediacy. Why won't Hegel admit that Being-for-one is a determinateness? The answer is that, in the left-leaning emphasis of "Being-for-self as Such," determinateness is sublated. We cannot refer to it without regressing. For this reason, "Being-for-one and being-for-self are, therefore, not genuinely opposed determinatenesses." (159)

Such a muted presence, however, seems inconsistent with the dialectic spirit, which *emphasizes* the history of the concept in mediatedness. Dialectical Reason accuses the Understanding of suppressing otherness. Now it seems to *conspire* with the Understanding to repress the other. This odd posture of Dialectical Reason can be explained as follows: Dialectical Reason recalls the history of the process, which the Understanding suppresses in the name of promoting immediacy. But the Finite is now *sublated*. So when Dialectical Reason emphasizes the history of Being-for-self, it can only assert a sublated negativity, which, properly speaking, is not equal in dignity to the affirmativity that the Understanding promotes.

Hegel provides another justification for Dialectical Reason's subdued nature. Being-for-self is *negativity* and, therefore, is precisely *not* a universal Something. "[H]ere there is not something," Hegel says. (159) Rather, Being-for-self is "not yet a one." (159) The One must await Figure 8(c). Rather, Being-for-self is mere indeterminate *being* for the One that is to come. It is the prehistoric, merely implicit One. Because it is pre-One, "what we have before us is still an undistinguishedness of the two sides." (159) For this reason, Being-for-one and Being-for-self are "not genuinely opposed determinatenesses." (159) Hegel denies that we can even acknowledge that Figure 8(b) is a determinateness: "there is only *one* being-for-other, and because there is only *one*, this too is only a Being-for-one; there is only the *one* ideality of that, for which or in which here is supposed to be a determination as moment." (159)

Ideal Being is subordinated in Being-for-one. Yet, by the law of sublation, we can equally affirm that Limit *is* present in Figure 8(b), because everything in chapters 1 and 2 is canceled *and* preserved. Hegel permits us hypothetically to assume a difference between Being-for-self and Being-for-one, as we are sorely tempted to do as we gaze upon the concreteness of Figure 8(b). In such a case, "we speak of *a* being-for-self." (159) That is, [1] exists separately from [3] and is "the sublatedness of otherness." (159) As such, it "relates itself [1] to itself [2] as the sublated other [3], and so is '*for one*.'" (159) It is *not* "for an other." Thus, we simply cannot admit that [2] is Being-for-other – *i.e.*,

[2, 3]. It is only Being-for-one, the in-itself [2] of Being-for-self.

Was für ein Ding?

Hegel has already expressed his delight with the speculative ambiguity of German.[5] In a Remark following Being-for-one, he lauds the German phrase, *was für ein Ding*, which means "What kind of a thing is that?" *Literally* translated, however, it means "What for a thing?" Hegel thinks that this phrase illustrates Being-for-one. The question does *not* ask, "What is *A* for *B*?", or "what is *A for me*?" It asks, "What is *A* for *A*?" In this question, Being-for-one returns to the thing: "that which is, and that *for which* it is, are one and the same." (160)

Ideal entities enjoy "infinite self-relation." (163) "Ego is for ego, both are the same, the ego is twice named, but so that each of the two is only a 'for-one,' [the ego] is ideal." (160) The infinite *Ding* referred to in *was für ein Ding*, whether it be ego or any other Infinite, is both an *identity* and an *ideality*. That is, [1, 2] in Figure 8(b) is to be taken as an immediacy. But any otherness is *ideal*. "Ideal," in general, designates "being" as it exists after it graduates from the college of True Infinity – "being" reduced to a mere moment or memory.[6] In True Infinity, reality erases itself and becomes the deeper negative substance that lies beneath.[7] "Ideality attaches . . . to the sublated determinations [or reality] as distinguished from that *in which* [*i.e.*, from which] they are sublated." (160) In other words, reality is in the logical past and is now only remembered by Dialectical Reason as a by-gone moment.

Of [1, 2] in Figure 8(b), Hegel states that the ideal is *one* moment; reality is another. Both moments "are equally only *for one* and count only for *one*." (160) The ideality is also one reality – a reality without

---

[5] *Supra* at 30.

[6] G.W.F. Hegel, Hegel's Philosophy of Mind § 381 Z (William Wallace & A.V. Miller trans., 1971) (ideality is "the reduction of the idea's otherness to a *moment*, the process of returning – and the accomplished return – into itself of the idea from its other").

[7] Ermanno Bencivenga, Hegel's Dialectical Logic 31 (2002) ("everything that was alleged to be real ('itself and not another thing') has been turned into an ideal moment (itself *and another* – indeed every other – thing")). The phrase "indeed every other" should have been deleted from this quote. Ideality is not metonymy – the notion that a thing is simply the empty space left by the context of all other "things." Ideality is rather the memory of what once was but is now *not*. What is "other" to a thing is its own self – not other things.

distinction (and for that very reason an ideality). That is, it is a reality on the laws of sublation (but not otherwise). Nevertheless, reality is a definite "moment" in the ideality. In slightly different words, we saw in chapter 2 that "reality" implied a linkage of being with nothing. Hence, a reality without distinction suggests that reality is sublated and hence is now only a memory – an ideality.

To return to the too-advanced example of consciousness, it encounters reality, but it idealizes what it encounters. It is therefore implicated in a difference between itself and other. This is equally true for self-consciousness, which has *itself* as object, against which it nevertheless stands as observer. Hegel suggests that observing consciousness produces conceptions, which are idealities taken as realities.

Nevertheless, Hegel warns against thinking of thought *only* as ideal being. This would presuppose "the standpoint from which finite being counts as the real, and the ideal being or being-for-other has only a one-sided meaning." (160) In other words, an empiricist, who counts only finite being as real, would view ideality as merely subjective. Hegel wants to say that the real requires the ideal, and what is ideal is part of the definition of objectivity itself. Indeed, recall that the *history* of the ideality is steeped in reality. Ideality has been produced in the course of analyzing *Being*. What we are saying about ideality is so far very much *in the object*. This is, after all, only chapter 3 of the *Objective* Logic. As of yet, subjectivity has not been derived (though, as the silent fourth, it is implicitly with us). Hence, there can be no question of isolating reality from ideality, or of identifying the ideal as subjective.

(c) The One

In Figure 8(b), Being-for-self refuses to acknowledge [3]. Even skeptical Dialectical Reason concedes that the relation between self and other is "ideal" – occurring totally on the "being" side of the ledger. This coheres with the basic "leftist" bias of which the first third of Hegel's "Quality" chapters is guilty. Thanks to this bias, "[t]here is before us only a single determination, the self-relation of the sublating." (163)

Hegel explains: "The *moments* of being-for-self have collapsed into the *undifferentiatedness* which is immediacy or being, but an *immediacy* based on the negating which is posited as its determination." (163) In other words, Speculative Reason interprets Being-for-self and Being-for-one as inherently negative. In this negativity, [3] was not acknowledged as present. *Refusing* to acknowledge the Other is now the middle term. Refusal to acknowledge is now posited as the One.

Some questions may arise as to why I have drawn the One in this fashion. Did we not just ignore [3] altogether? Why now do we say that Being-for-one is [3], when [3] has been abolished? For that matter, why did Figure 8(b) show [3] as Being-for-one, if the point was to abolish [3]?

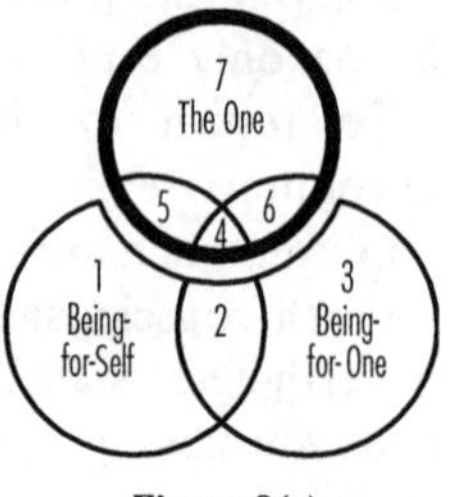

Figure 8(c)
The One

The answer: refusing to recognize something is the surest way of recognizing it; therefore [3] was never abolished. Throughout much of the last half-century, the United States refused to "recognize" Red China. Yet Red China was a peculiar obsession of Americans. They scarcely did anything else but focus on Red China during the time they were supposedly not recognizing it. Similarly, the One stands for the ongoing act of refusing to recognize otherness [3], and [3] is very much recognized. Hence, the One becomes the pure notion of refusal to recognize. Or, as Hegel puts it, the One is "an *immediacy* based on the negating which is posited as its determination." (163)

With regard to Figure 8(c), Hegel remarks:

> Attention may be drawn in advance to the difficulty involved in the following exposition of the *development* of the one and to [this difficulty's] cause. The *moments* which constitute the Notion of the one as a being-for-self fall *asunder* in the development. They are: (1) negation in general [3], (2) *two* negations [2, 3, 4, 6], [4-7], (3) two that are therefore the *same* [1] = [3], (4) sheer opposites [1], [3], (5) self-relation, identity as such [1, 2, 4, 5], [2, 3, 4, 6], [4-7] (6) relation which is *negative* and yet to *its own self* [7]. (163)

Hegel states that the reason for separating these moments is to draw attention to the fact that the One is not just Being-for-self as such but *a* Being-for-self that, in effect, recognizes other Beings-for-themselves by refusing to recognize them – a plurality that will be expressly recognized in the next section. Thus, "*each moment is posited* as a *distinct, affirmative determination*, and yet they are no less *inseparable*." (164) In other words, the pretense of the One is that it has *no relation* with the other Ones to which it is unconnected. Yet nothing is always something, and no relation is very much a *species* of relation. By not recognizing [3], the One recognizes [3], and so it becomes *a* One, rather than One as such. Because it is merely *a* One, there is perforce another One. Indeed, there are Many, as we are about to discover.[8]

B. The One and the Many

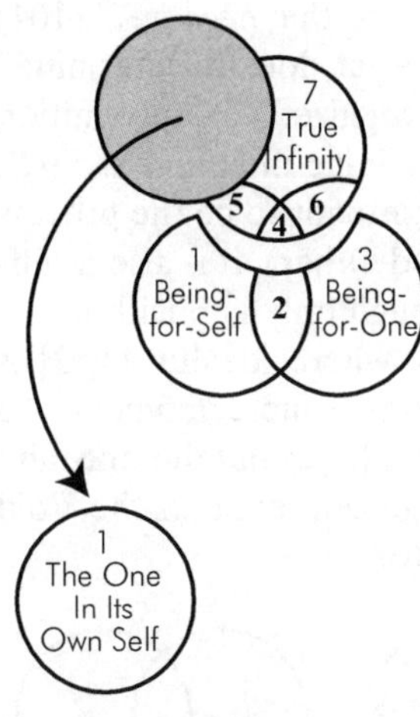

Figure 9(a)
The One in Its Own Self

In Figure 9(a), the Understanding moves the empty space of the middle term over to the left. Whereas, in Figure 8(a) we moved the middle term as such, now we move the place where the middle term ought to have been. Hegel describes that move as follows: "The one is the simple self-relation of being-for-self in which its moments have collapsed in themselves and in which, consequently, being-for-self has the form of *immediacy*, and its moments therefore now have a *determinate* being." (164) Figure 9(a), then, represents a seizure of the "collapsed moments" by the Understanding.[9] The end result is the immediacy that Hegel names the One in Its Own Self. It *does* have Determinate Being – but only as its

---

[8] In the above account, the One is the name given to the pure refusal of Being to recognize the other as its constituent part. Charles Taylor has a different interpretation, which he admits departs from Hegel's "fanciful" derivation of the One:

> [A] being of this kind can only be picked out, that is, distinguished from others, by some numeration-like procedure. In other words, we can only identify a particular being of this kind by attributing to it some number in a series, or some ordinal position. For all beings of this kind are identical in being without determinate quality, they can only be distinguished numerically.
>
> Of course, in this argument I am taking for granted that identifying "the one" is the same as distinguishing it from others, that a being of this kind is only conceivable as one among many. How else can a being without internal differentiation by identified, except in contrast with others?

TAYLOR, *supra* note 3, at 245. Taylor borrows thoughts about Number and Degree as he worries about identifying One from some other One. He entirely misses the upcoming derivation of the Many from the One, which is a necessary precondition to ordinal numbers. This derivation will depend on the One's status as a True Infinite.

[9] ANDREW HAAS, HEGEL AND THE PROBLEM OF MULTIPLICITY 105 (2000) ("Here the one is in its own self . . . abstractly posited as the being-in-itself . . . wherein all difference and multiplicity . . . have disappeared").

moment. We have only the recollection of that moment – not Determinate Being as such, which has been sublated.

The One of Figure 9(a) is "self-relation of the *negative*." (164) Furthermore it is a *process* of *determining*. What does it determine? The very Other [3] it has been refusing to recognize. Non-recognition is always a recognition. This process of determining the other is a *self*-determining. It is self-determining because it intends to be the process of recognizing *only* itself (and not the excluded Other). It is also a self-determination because its other *is* itself (though only implicitly).

One's duality is portrayed in Figure 9(b), where ideality [1, 2] is before us. Otherness [2] is within the One as a mere moment – a recollection of the past. Yet [1] also *determines* [2] as *not* the one, and hence [3] comes into existence. This "unrecognized" entity is the Void (*das Leere*). In the Void, sublated "reality" (or Limit) reasserts itself. Of this reappearance of reality at the expense of ideality, Hegel writes: "The *ideality* of being-for-self as a totality thus reverts . . . to *reality* and that too in its most fixed, abstract form, as the *one*." (164) The One stands over against the void but *is* the Void – just as much a One as the One was.

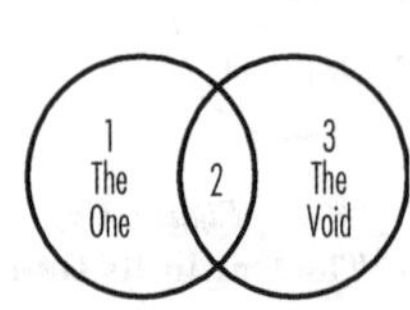

Figure 9(b)
The One and the Void

Hegel describes "The One and the Void" as the epitome of Dialectical Reason, which always brings forth [2] as the voice of [1]. [2] is the "in-itself" of the One:

> [W]hat the one [1, 2] is *in itself* [2] is now only *ideally present in it*, and the negative [2, 3] consequently is an other distinct from it [1]. What shows itself to be *present* as distinct from the one [3] is its [1] own self-determining. . . . [T]he unity of the one with itself [1, 2] as thus distinguished from itself [1] is reduced to a *relation* [2], and as a *negative* unity it [1] is a negation of its own self as *other* [2], exclusion of the one [2, 3] as other from itself [1]. (164)

In other words, Dialectical Reason focuses on [2], which implies [3]. But since [2] is the genuine voice of the One, the One itself has produced the Void.

(a) The One in Its Own Self

The One is unalterable. "In its own self the one simply *is*; this its being is neither a determinate being, nor a determinateness as a relation to an other, nor is it a constitution; what it is, in fact, is the accomplished negation of this circle of categories. Consequently, the one is not capable of becoming an other: it is *unalterable*." (164) The One is not Determinate Being, determinateness, or Constitution, as these have been reduced to idealities – mere moments. The One of Figure 9(a) is simply the bare refusal to recognize the Other – and nothing else. But why unalterable? This is key for what follows. The one is a True Infinite. It *stays what it is* (*i.e.*, is unalterable) while *becoming something else*. Unalterability will be important for generating the Many Ones.

The One is indeterminate – but it is not the same indeterminacy that Pure Being was. The One's indeterminateness is a *determinateness*, as Figure 9(b) shows. The One is related negatively to its self [2]; it is "a self-related negation." (165) That is, [1] is the negation of [2] yet [2] is [1]'s own voice. Difference is therefore in the One.

The One [1] negates itself [2]. It flees from its Other – [2], "but this movement is immediately turned back on itself, because it follows from this moment of self-determining that there is no other to which the one can go." (165) The premise of the One is that it absolutely refuses to recognize the Other. Hence, [1] flees [2], but it cannot, consistent with its principle, move to [3]. It must retreat back to [1] and be *unalterable*. In light of this retreat, "the mediation of determinate being and of ideality itself, and with it all difference and manifoldness, has vanished. There is *nothing* in it." (165)[10] In effect, the One has holed itself up in [1] and refuses even to recognize its own content – [2]. As [1], the One has distinguished itself from its own being-within-self [2]. The One is therefore contentless.

This state of being without content makes the One unalterable, because things alter only as a result of a dynamic that depends on Dialectical Reason recalling that [2] exists. But the One has now expelled [2], and, with it, any hope of alteration. This is what Hegel means when he says that the One is "indeterminate but not, however, like being; its indeterminateness is the determinateness which is a relation to its own self, an absolute determinateness – *posited* being-within-self." (164-5) Absolute determinateness connotes *relation as such*, separate and apart from the parts it relates. "Relation" isolated from its parts is an entity that is all form and no content.

---

[10] Harris suggests, "being-for-self is simply one – not one among many, but one differentiating itself into and as many internal moments . . . Being-for-self is a differentiated whole." HARRIS, *supra* note 1, at 115. It is rather more true that the One expels its many moments into the Void and remains an empty shell *without* internal moments. That, at least, is what Being-for-self is "for itself."

If the One as [1] is this absolute determinateness – a relation without parts – then why is it also posited being-within-self, which we have associated with [4] (part of [2] in Figure 9(b)? The answer is that being-within-self is the suppressed negative voice of the Understanding. Dialectical Reason, through recollection, brings [2] to the fore. Yet, what was [2]? It was always that which unified [1] and [3]. But if we now wish to consider [2] as a relation but without any reference to its parts, then [2] would be relation as such. But that is what we are saying [1] is. [1] = [2], and both are "posited" as being-within-self as such – relation without any content to unify.

The One [1] has isolated itself from its being-within-self [2]. The One, a nothing, is "the abstraction of self-relation" (165) – a relation isolated from its parts. Yet it is to be distinguished! The One posits itself as nothing, and therefore it also posits being-within-self as its absolute other. "[T]his being-within-self no longer has the simple character of something but, as a mediation, has a concrete determination." (165) That is, being-within-self is [2, 3] in Figure 9(b) – concrete and mediating.[11]

The One has expelled its own being-within-self, and this implies that its being is entirely outside of itself. But the expelled material [2, 3] is actually the One's own self. [2] continues to be the One, but, as expelled, and as mediation, it must latch onto [3], which is revealed to be just as much *in* [1] as *not* in [1]. In short, [1] = [3]. This is the very hallmark of the True Infinite, which becomes something else while remaining what it is.

Hegel has already named [3] as the Void. By virtue of the equality just expressed, the Void is "posited as *in the one* . . . The void is thus the *quality* of the *one* in its immediacy." (165)[12]

---

[11] One might say at this point that [2] – which implies [2, 3] – has Being-for-self. But if [2] is indifferent to [1], we come close to Errol Harris's remark: "This being for itself of its other [2], this *grasp of the relation between self and other*, as for one and for itself, is the essence of ideality." HARRIS, *supra* note 1, at 111. Harris is correct that [1]'s "other" is [2] and that [2] has Being-for-self. But, besides having Being-for-self, [2] is the essence of ideality because [2] stands for a recollected "moment" of [1, 2]'s history in reality. Hence, contrary to its Being-for-self, [2] has sublated Being-for-other. On the basis of this paradox, Harris's formulation can be affirmed.

[12] *See* SLAVOJ ŽIŽEK, FOR THEY KNOW NOT WHAT THEY DO: ENJOYMENT AS A POLITICAL FACTOR 52 (1991) ("the Void is not external to One, it dwells in its very heart – the One is itself is 'void': the Void is its only 'content'").

(b) The One and the Void

In this section Hegel explicitly discusses Figure 9(b), where the One confronts the Void. But in fact [1] = [3]. Hence, "[t]he One *is* the void as the abstract relation of the negation to itself." (165) In other words, the One and also the Void are relation as such, without reference to any parts. They are thoroughgoing negatives.

Even though [1] = [3], [1] and [3] are also different. The One has affirmative being. The Void does not. Their difference is "posited" by Dialectical Reason. What is the difference? Nothing more than this: "as distinct from the affirmative being of the one, the nothing as the void is *outside* it." (165) Thus, the One has content – it is simply *not the Void*. And, of course, the Void has content – it is *not the One*.

In light of this difference, Figure 9(b) is once again infected with Determinate Being. "The one [1] and the void [3] have negative relation to self [2] for their common, simple base. The moments of being-for-self emerge from this unity, become external to themselves." (165) Thus, taken by themselves, the One and the Void are isolated and have renounced their connection with being-within-self. Speculative Reason will see the truth. The renunciation is a fraud. The One (and the Void) are retrogressive Determinate Beings.[13]

Atomism

By now it should be apparent that Hegel opposed any philosophy that presupposes the self-identity of objects. For Hegel, at the deepest

---

[13] Harris confesses that he does not fathom the transition from the One to the Void. "But Hegel makes a very complex and obscure transition from the One to the Void, by drawing a distinction within the One between abstract self-relation as empty . . . and its concrete affirmative being." HARRIS, *supra* note 1, at 116. This would appear to be a misreading. The One [1] *expels* the Void [2, 3]. At least at the level of Figure 9(b), the distinction is not *within* the One. Nor is the affirmative being of [1] "concrete" following the expulsion of the Void. It is, ironically, the void that is concrete. Affirmative self-relation is empty, precisely the opposite of what Harris says.

Harris goes on to suggest that, according to Hegel, [1] "reverts" to determinateness. *Id*. More accurately, when [1] expels [3], [3] automatically implies [2, 3] – a determinateness. But [3] is likewise the One. As such, it expels [2] which automatically implies [1, 2]. Hence, [1] does, in a sense, *become* a determinateness – indirectly, because of [3]'s action, but it definitely does not *revert* to a determinateness. [1, 2] – the product of [3]'s act of repulsion – is in fact a *different* entity than the [1] that expelled [2] and created [2, 3]. The One is about to become the Many in the very next section. Our discussion there will make clear why "reversion" is inappropriately invoked.

core of the object is a modulating unity of being and nothing. It follows, then, that Hegel would not be enamored of "atomism." "Hegel's main criticism of [atomism] is that it permits of no inner of *self*-determination."[14] Hegel calls it an example of "figurate conception." (166)[15] "Picture thinking" is ever Hegel's *bête noir.*

Hegel states that the atomism of the ancient Greeks was the exaltation of the One and the Void. Admittedly, atomism was an advance over Parmenides's "being" or Heracleitus's "becoming." But, in the end

> it is equally easy for figurate conception to picture *here* atoms and *alongside* them the void. It is, therefore, no wonder that the atomistic principle has at all times been upheld; the equally trivial and external relation of *composition* which must be added to achieve a semblance of concreteness and variety is no less popular than the atoms themselves and the void. The one and the void is being-for-self, the highest qualitative being-within-self, sunk back into complete *externality*; the immediacy . . . of the one . . . is posited as being no longer . . . alterable; such therefore is its absolute, unyielding rigidity that all determination, variety, conjunction remains for it an utterly external relation. (166)

In other words, atomism asserts the utter indifference of one atom and another; it has no theory (other than subjective composition) to explain why atoms must be joined together.[16]

Atomic thinkers, Hegel continues, did not remain wedded to the brute externality of the One and the Void. The Void was recognized as the source of movement, which means that the One and the Void did not have a purely external relation. The One can move only into unoccupied space – not into space already occupied by a One. But this "not . . . trivial" (166) observation means only that the Void is the presupposition or condition of movement – not its explanation. Indeed, the very idea that atoms *move* is presupposed. Presupposition signifies that no *logical* connection between the One and the Void is yet recognized. The more profound view is "that the void constitutes the ground of movement . . . [I]n the negative as such there lies the ground of becoming, of the unrest of self-movement." (166) Notice, however, that Hegel shifts the ground of movement. Hegelian atoms do not

---

[14] Murray Greene, *Hegel and the Problems of Atomism*, 11 INT'L STUD. PHIL. 123, 125 (1979).

[15] "[V]orstellende Reflektieren." [I:156]

[16] John W. Burbidge, *Chemistry and Hegel's Logic*, in HEGEL AND NEWTONIANISM 609 (Michael John Petry ed., 1993).

move about the void; movement consists in dialectics of self-erasure.

Hegel concludes by complaining, "Physics with its molecules and particles suffers from the atom, this principle of extreme externality, which is thus utterly devoid of the Notion, just as much as does that theory of the State which starts from the particular will of individuals." (167)[17] Physics has wised up since 1815. Today, physicists cheerfully divide the indivisible atom into electrons, nucleons, quarks, etc. Liberal political philosophy, however, has never escaped its reliance on the self-identity of the free (*i.e.*, adult, white, male) individual, for whom the state is merely "useful." Any kind of utilitarian or contractarian philosophy is fundamentally atomistic in its outlook. Such philosophies do not get past the One and the Void.[18]

(c) Many Ones: Repulsion

"The one and the void constitute the first stage of the determinate being of being-for-self," Hegel writes. "Each of these moments has negation for its determination." (167) Indeed, the One and the Void are nothing *but* negation as such. But each stands over against the other: "the one is negation in the determination of being, and the void is negation in the determination of non-being." (167) This pure

---

[17] In the *EL*, Hegel complains that the atomists presume to think they are not being metaphysical:

> At present, students of nature who are anxious to avoid metaphysics turn a favourable ear to Atomism. But it is not possible to escape metaphysics and cease to trace nature back to terms of thought, by throwing ourselves into the arms of Atomism. The atom, in fact, is itself a thought; and hence the theory which holds matter to consist of atoms is a metaphysical theory. Newton gave physics an express warning to beware of metaphysics, it is true; but, to his honour be it said, he did not by any means obey his own warning. The only mere physicists are the animals: they alone do not think: while man is a thinking being and a born metaphysician.
>
> The real question is not whether we shall apply metaphysics, but whether our metaphysics are of the right kind: in other words, whether we are not, instead of the concrete logical Idea, adopting one-sided forms of thought, rigidly fixed by understanding, and making these the basis of our theoretical as well as our practical work. It is on this ground that one objects to the Atomic philosophy.

EL § 98 Remark.

[18] "In modern times the importance of the atomic theory is even more evident in political than in physical science. According to it, the will of individuals as such is the creative principle of the State: the attracting force is the special wants and inclinations of individuals; the Universal, or the State itself, is the external nexus of a compact." *Id.*

positionality vis-à-vis each other is their "thin" claim to "being."

Figure 9(b) has the now familiar attribute of motion, a motion that travels through [2]:

> The being-for-self of the one [1] is, however, essentially the ideality of determinate being [2] and of other [3]: it [1] relates itself not to an other [3] but only *to itself*. But since being-for-self is fixed as a one, as *affirmatively* for itself [1], as *immediately* present, its *negative* relation *to itself* [2] is at the same time a relation to an *affirmative* being [3]. (167)

In this difficult passage, Hegel emphasizes that [2] is [1]'s own voice. Yet [2] always implies [3]. Dialectical Reason brings [2] to the fore, but [2] is always yet another "being" – a [3]. Hence, [3] = [1], but also [1]'s relation to [3] is, at the same time, "a relation to an *affirmative* being" – *i.e.*, [3] is radically different from Being-for-self, which can be defined as [1, 2]. Thus, [3] is "a *determinate being* [2, 3] and an *other* [3]." It is also as much an affirmative Being-for-self as [1] was.

So [1] expels [2]. But [2] implies [3]. And [3] is just as much One as [1] is. "The one is consequently a *becoming of many ones*." (167) Is the conclusion justified? Have we not simply produce a *single* other One – to wit, [3]? In Figure 9(b), do we but witness [1] → [3] → [1] *ad infinitum*? If so, we have mere alternation, not infinite multiple production. Such an alternation is mere Spurious Infinity.

Such a move would be retrogressive. The Spurious Infinite is already sublated. Hence, [3] → [1] violates the Logic of [1] and constitutes an "external reflection" on *our* part. (168) We are tempted to say that [1] infinitely produces the same [3] and vice versa. But the standpoint of the One is absolute indifference to the other Ones. It is *we* who proclaim the many Ones as a single One. Logic does indeed produce *many* Ones, which imperialist thought insists on unifying.

Only external reflection denies the plurality of Ones. To prove this, Hegel compares Figure 9(b) to *Becoming* in Figure 2(b). In Figure 2(b), [1] → [3] constituted "Ceasing-to-be." That is, [1] went out of existence, but was soon re-established by [3] → [1]. What we had was primitive alternation. Figure 9(b), however, is not a simple Becoming. In Figure 9(b), when [1] → [3], [1] expelled its otherness *and continued to be*. It did not *just* "cease-to-be." [1] in Figure 9(b) is *unalterable*, whereas [1] in Becoming had no resilience whatever. What occurs in Figure 9(b), then, is that the One [1, 2] repels itself [2] *from itself*. Yet, in so doing, [1] *is*, and it remains what it *is*. [1] does not cease-to-be.[19]

---

[19] *See* Alan H.T. Paterson, *The Successor Function and Induction Principle in a*

When [3] likewise repels itself from itself, [3]'s product is *not* [1] *as such*. If it were, then, in [1] → [3], [1] must have ceased-to-be, such that [3] can create [1] anew. Rather, [3] becomes *yet some other [1]* – a [1*]. If *we* insist upon [3] → [1], we have reduced Hegel's Repulsion of the Ones into mere Ceasing-to-be.

Hegel calls [3] → [1*] "repulsion according to its Notion, repulsion *in itself*." (168)[20] He calls the *illegitimate* move of [3] → [1] the "second repulsion," which is "what is immediately suggested to external reflection: repulsion not as the *generation* of ones, but only as the mutual repelling of ones presupposed as already *present*." (168) In the false move, [3] presupposes that what it produces is [1], when it is not licensed to say *anything* about what its Other is – except that it is *not* [3].

Of what [3] produces, Hegel writes, "the products of the process are ones, and these are not for an other, but relate themselves infinitely to themselves. The one repels only *itself* from itself, therefore does not *become* but *already is*." (168) If we had said [3] reproduces the original [1], then we admit that [3] contains Being-for-other: "If plurality were a relation of the ones themselves to one another then they would limit one another and there would be affirmatively present in them a being-for-other." (168) This proposition cannot be true. [3] is the One and is strictly "for itself," just as [1] was. Thus, [3] cannot be said to reproduce [1]. Rather it produces some *other* One. And, for that matter, [1] reproduces "many" [3]'s. As both [1] and [3] are infinite processes, they instantaneously[21] fill the universe with Many Ones. "The plurality of

---

Hegelian Philosophy of Mathematics, 30 IDEALISTIC STUDIES 25, 41 (2002) ("the ones therefore *are* only insofar as they repel each other"). Why then did not this attribute of changing-while-remaining appear with Being-for-one? Being-for-one was the first dialectic step after the derivation of True Infinity. Being-for-one refused to recognize otherness at all. It was not until the One emerged over against the Void that the [1] acknowledged [3]. Only then did the extremes have the opportunity to show mutual resilience against its other.

[20] This account of the birth of multiplicity is absent from many analyses of Being-for-self. *E.g.*, HAAS, *supra* note 9, 104-9 (discussing "Becoming Many Ones"); TERRY PINKARD, HEGEL'S DIALECTIC 43 (1988). Pinkard reads Hegel as only establishing, from the notion of Being-for-self and the One, the *possibility* that many ones exist. But Hegel *does* show that distinct units are a direct consequence of True Infinity which stays what it is as it becomes something else. Taylor entirely misses the derivation of the Many from the One, and so it is not surprising that he names Repulsion as "another example of a detour [from] essential notions." TAYLOR, *supra* note 3, at 246. Taylor is stuck on what Hegel called the "second repulsion" of external reflection, which is not productive of the Many.

[21] *I.e.*, in no time at all. Since the Logic does not occur in time, the universe is

ones . . . unconstrainedly produces itself." (169) Of these mutually indifferent Ones, Hegel writes: "The void is their limit but a limit which is external to them, in which they are not to be *for one another*." (168) It should be apparent that Limit [2] is external to [1], which continues to "be" as pure negativity toward the other Ones.

This negative shedding of content is called, at this stage, Repulsion. Repulsion is the middle term between the One and the Void. It names the very movement by which [1] – and also [3] – shed [2], so that [1] and [3] can be truly One. Repulsion is "a simple relating of the one to the one, and no less also the absolute absence of relation in the one." (169) Repulsion is an active process (as all middle terms are). In Repulsion, the One sublates *all* its otherness. It becomes a purified being. But as such, *it has no content at all*! Whatever content the One has is somewhere outside it. This is what Hegel meant when he indicated that the One's Limit [2] was entirely external to the One.

C. Repulsion and Attraction

(a) Exclusion of the One

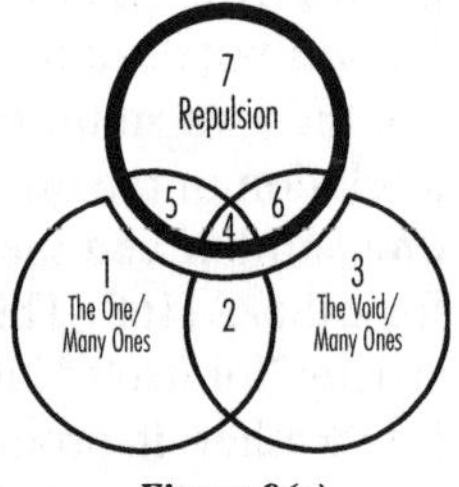

Figure 9(c)
Repulsion

We now face some heavy weather. Virtually every turn of phrase within every sentence shall require special attention. There is no other way to follow Hegel through the underbrush of this difficult subsection.[22] The basic trajectory to follow shows the One repulsing the Many. These, however, are fused back into One by an external reflection, which Hegel associates with Attraction. Attraction, however, cannot function without the Repulsion by the One of the Many. The equilibrium of Attraction and Repulsion yields Quantity – Being with its content outside itself (*i.e.,* in external reflection).

The One is a non-relation – a relation without parts, suggesting *absolute indifference* of the One toward any other One. The Ones are free-floating entities in the Void. Their Determinate Being is external

---

instantaneously full of Many Ones.

[22] John Burbidge's "fragmentary" comment on the Logic takes a vacation just before this spot. JOHN W. BURBIDGE, ON HEGEL'S LOGIC: FRAGMENTS OF A COMMENTARY (1981). Harris finds it "difficult to understand and interpret." HARRIS, *supra* note 1, at 116. Terry Pinkard calls this part of the Logic "boisterously obscure." Terry Pinkard, *Hegel's Philosophy of Mathematics*, 41 PHIL. & PHENOMENOGICAL RES. 453, 457 (1980-1). An excellent essay on the upcoming transitions, however, is Greene, *supra* note 14.

to them. The Ones are therefore "this negative relation to themselves as [well as] to *affirmatively present* others – the demonstrated contradiction, infinity posited in the immediacy of being." (170)

What does it mean for a One to be a "negative relation to itself"? Fundamentally, it is the posture of the entity that says, "I am not *that*," when it *is* that. "As self-relating in its determining, it is *itself* that which it posits as a negative." (558) Thus, the One says, "I am not the Void." In fact, the One is nothing *but* this announcement of what it is not. And what it is *not* is its very Being-in-itself [2], which it has repulsed.

This is ironic. The One, in its self-hatred, has expelled its own determinateness from itself and has propagated the many Ones. As relation without parts, One is no doubt an absurdity – Hegel's "demonstrated contradiction." It should also be clear why the One is an "infinity posited in the immediacy of being." The One is certainly *immediate*, and, in addition, the One is an Infinite. Recall that the True Infinite was a pure movement of the Finites exceeding their Limitations. This is what the One has accomplished. In effect, the One has gone beyond its Limitations and is nothing at all.

Repulsion now finds itself facing what it repelled – the Many Ones, which, though plural, are taken as a unified whole (even as each of the Ones is completely indifferent to each other One). In Figure 10(a), [4, 5, 6] represent the Many Ones, as produced in Figure 9(b). These are what Repulsion has excluded.

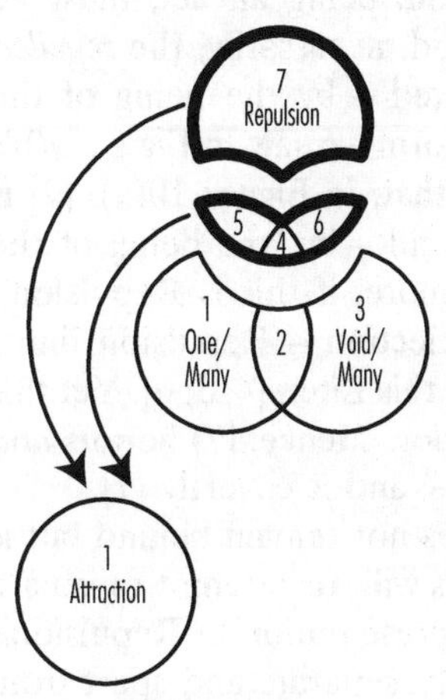

Figure 10(a)
Attraction

In Figure 8(a), the entire middle term was taken as an immediacy, and it became Being-for-self. In Figure 9(a), the mere negation of the middle term was taken – the ghostly *negative* version of [4, 5, 6]. It became the One. Now Figure 10(a) seemingly shows a retrogression – an expulsion of the mediated part of the middle term. This seizure of "mediation" by the Understanding was the characteristic move in chapter 2. Have we retrogressed?

We have not. In Figure 4(a) (Constitution), Hegel designated a role for an external reflection not itself logically derived. This was the silent fourth that makes the system progress. Determination by external reflection was what it meant for Being to be "constituted." Yet we progressed only because external reflection acted on the middle term's immanent materials. Now, in Figure 10(a), Repulsion does all the work of alienating the Many Ones. External reflection has been displaced by the operations of the One. In Figure 10(a), Repulsion itself generates the force needed to expel the Many Ones.

In Figure 10(a), the One, taken as [7], "repels from itself only the many ones which are neither generated nor posited by it." (170) Does this contradict what was said with regard to Figure 9(b), where the One generated (and posited) the Void? There we learned that the Void, in turn, was not only another One but was Many Ones. Hence the Void was posited. In Figure 10(a), however, that which Repulsion excretes was *not* posited. The contradiction is resolved because Repulsion is at a higher level than the positing activity of Figure 9(b). Repulsion is a *unity* between the many Ones – not the producer of the Ones. For this narrow purpose, Repulsion does not generate or "posit" the Many Ones. The Many ones were posited earlier, by the Ones themselves. Indeed, Repulsion *itself* was posited by the Many Ones. What Repulsion does in Figure 10(a) is to isolate the Ones, thereby *unifying* them. This grouping of all the diverse Ones is what Hegel will call Attraction.

Hegel next states: "This mutual or all-round repelling is relative, is limited by the being of the ones." (170) Why is Limit – a sublated term – invoked here? It denotes that Repulsion, being an act, must be correlative.[23] There is the repelling One and, necessarily, the *repelled* One. Being correlative, Repulsion is limited – by the being of the Ones. In other words, repelling takes the form we saw in Figure 9(b).

By invoking Limit here, Hegel explains that, in Figure 10(a), [7] is left behind. Thus, [7] is limited – left behind – by "the being of the ones;" the ones now become [1]. Furthermore, if this is Repulsion's own work – not the work of external reflection – Repulsion limits itself. [7] refuses to recognize itself beyond this Limit [4, 5, 6]. Yet this refusal to recognize is the perfect recognition. Hence, [7] honors *and exceeds* its Limit, like the good Infinity it is, and is covertly [1].

This means that, in Figure 10(a), [7] does not remain behind but is swept along with the Many Ones against its will. Its attempt to isolate itself fails. We can view this failure as a representation of Repulsion's inability to sustain itself as an isolated entity, separate and apart from Attraction. Its dependence on Attraction will soon be explicit.

---

[23] Limit, it will be recalled, was correlative. For this reason, the point (as limit to the line) spontaneously generated the line. *Supra* at 85-6.

Of [1], Hegel writes that "[t]he plurality is, in the first place, non-posited otherness." (170) That [4, 5, 6] are not posited we have already seen. Repulsion found the Many Ones *given* to it. Repulsion therefore proceeded to expel non-posited materials. [4, 5, 6] is Limit to [7]. And, in addition, we know by the law of sublation that the plurality is also the Void, as shown in Figure 9(b). This implies that [4, 5, 6] are the Many Ones, but also an immediacy – the Void. We thus have further justified the design in Figure 10(a), where the Many Ones became an immediacy, standing over against [7] – another immediacy.

The Many Ones "*are* . . . in the void." (170). Yet each One is in the process of "repulsing" the Void. Hence, Repulsion "is the posited *determinate being* of the many ones." (170) But it is not the Being-for-self of the Ones, "for according to this they would be differentiated as many only in a third." (170) What does this mean? Being-for-self refuses to recognize otherness. It cannot acknowledge a relation of One to the Void (and hence to another One). Relations, after all, *expressly* depend on otherness. If the Ones [4, 5, 6] had Being-for-self and *also* a relation to another One [7] (as Repulsion shows), then external reflection ("a third") would have to assert the relation. Repulsion's very task is to deny all relation. To hear Repulsion tell the tale, the relation would not be immanent to the Ones themselves. But Repulsion is a liar. Instead, their *own* differentiating preserves the Ones. (170) That is, the Ones are in the process of expelling the Void from themselves – in Figure 9(b). This process as such is the middle term in Figure 9(c). In this middle term, the Ones [4, 5, 6] are preserved – though now expelled in Figure 10(a). So the ones *are* in relation after all.

The Ones also "posit one another as being only *for one*." (170) Being-for-one, it will be recalled, was idealized Being-in-itself – mere memory of a determinateness, brought forth in Figure 8(b) by Dialectical Reason. Now, however, the One [1, 2] expels [2]; [2] becomes the Void and hence one of the Many Ones. In this expulsion, "the being-for-one as determined in exclusion is, consequently, a being-for-other." (170) This remark is best understood as referring to Figure 9(b) – not the current Figure 10(a). In Figure 9(b), Being-for-one [2] is expelled and hence is in effect Being-for-other. But if so, then [1] is "other" to Being-for-other. This allows Hegel to suggest that [2, 3] likewise expels [1]. [1] is now "not *for itself* but *for-one*, and that another one." (170) In other words, [1] is "for" [2, 3].

Also, if it is true that [2, 3] has now expelled [1] as its other, then, likewise, in Figure 10(a), the Many Ones [4, 5, 6] have expelled [7], which is the advanced version of the One. The Many Ones now take the initiative. They have said to [7]: "You can't fire us. We quit!"

This initiative is the "being-for-self of the many ones." (170) It is "their self-preservation," (170) which is achieved by the *mutual* repulsion of the One and the Many Ones. That is, [7] fires the Many Ones, and the Many Ones fire [7]. Not only does the union of the Many Ones repel [7], but within [4, 5, 6], the Many Ones repel each other. In other words, the Ones simultaneously preserve and negate themselves – the hallmark of True Infinity and of sublation itself.

The ones "maintain themselves by their reciprocal exclusion." (171) This is their Being-for-self, and it is shown by [1] in Figure 10(a). Being-for-self, then, is the *process* of repulsing Being-in-itself. Yet the expelled Being-in-itself [2] ended up being the One [2, 3] just as much as the expelling One [1, 2] was. All the Ones are [2]: "they are in their being-*in-itself* the *same*." (171) Furthermore, [1] negates its own Determinate Being [2, 3]. But, once again, all the ones do this! In this regard, they are all the same. "Consequently, as regards both their being and their positing, they are only *one* affirmative unity." (171) This again is seen as [1] in Figure 10(a). This "sameness" is the Attraction of the supposedly diverse Ones to each other.

The Ones are attracted to each other in Figure 10(a). But Hegel states that this dissolution of all difference in Figure 10(a) and the assertion of [1] as an immediacy is "a comparison made by us." (171) *External* force welds the Ones together. Earlier I suggested that Repulsion's expulsion of the Many Ones was *not* externally caused. Yet the dissolution of all difference in [1] *is* external. This appears at first to be contradictory, but the two statements indeed can be reconciled. External reflection no longer wrenches a piece from the middle term; the middle term expels those pieces on its own. But external force is still needed to weld the pieces together. They could still fly apart as in Figure 9(b). But such a move is retrogressive. Instead, *we* the audience decide to move on, which requires the formation of [1]. So external reflection works on unifying [1] but not on the expulsion of [4, 5, 6, 7].[24] Attraction presages the outside mathematician[25] who breaks up magnitude in general into sets of Units and unifies them again.

---

[24] This replicates Hegel's critique of Leibnizian monads. According to Hegel, monads ideate themselves, but their relation-to-other is externally supplied. (161) Leibnizian idealism "does not grasp [the ideating monad] as a *repulsion* of the monads." (169)

[25] *Infra* at 138.

The sameness of the Ones may be *our* act of comparison, but "we have also to see what is *posited* in them in their *inter-relatedness*." (171) This is the role of Dialectical Reason. Dialectical Reason discovers that the Ones of Attraction nevertheless maintain themselves as Ones by mutual Repulsion. In remaining aloof in this way, they negate their own negatedness – their own act of repulsing [2] from [1, 2]. But the Ones *are* in [1, 2] "only in so far as they negate." (171) By negating their negation, they negate their own being. Since negation is their mode of returning into themselves, the negation of their negation prohibits this return. Hence, the Ones repulse Repulsion – their own Being.

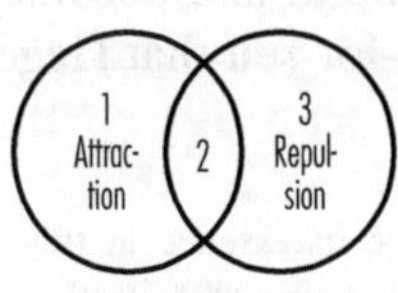

Figure 10(b)
Attraction and Repulsion

The Unity of the One and the Many

Hegel lays bare the great irony of what has happened:

> Self-subsistence pushed to the point of the one as a being-for-self is abstract, formal, and destroys itself. It is the supreme, most stubborn error, which takes itself for the highest truth, manifesting in more concrete forms as abstract freedom, pure ego and, further, as Evil. (172)

The One has expelled all being from itself. What was supposed to be perfectly self-subsistent and *liberated* from the other has surrendered *all* its being to the Other. This, Hegel says, is *egotism* and *evil*. In one of his late works,[26] Kant admitted that the famous categorical imperative – "Act so that the maxim of thy will can always at the same time hold good as a particular of universal legislation"[27] – was a mere procedure, which called for a person to suppress her pathology (*i.e.*, emotion, inclination, or being-for-other) so that only the voice of universal reason (being-for-self) could speak. The test of morality was independent of its content. This raised the question, what if the voice of reason spoke absolute evil for its own sake, not for the sake of inclination? Kant had to admit that the resulting evil could not be

[26] IMMANUEL KANT, RELIGION WITHIN THE BOUNDARIES OF MERE REASON (Allen Wood & George Di Giovanni trans., 1998).

[27] IMMANUEL KANT, CRITIQUE OF PRACTICAL REASON 46 (T.K. Abbott trans., 1996).

distinguished from morality. Kant called this possibility "diabolical evil."[28]

Kant confesses that the highest morality flips around and becomes the worst evil. This reversal *is* the dynamic of Being-for-self that Hegel has described. Of diabolical evil, Hegel writes:

> It is that freedom which so misapprehends itself as to place its essence in this abstraction [of Being-for-self], and flatters itself that in thus being with itself it possesses itself in its purity. More specifically, this self-subsistence is the error of regarding as negative that which is its own essence, and of adopting a negative attitude towards it. Thus it is the negative attitude towards itself which, in seeking to possess its own being destroys it, and this its act is only the manifestation of the futility of this act. (172)[29]

Hegel's advice to the egotistical self is to *let go* of Being-for-self and submit to the jurisdiction of the big Other – the symbolic realm of law and language. Thus, the final lesson that reason has to give (before ostensibly announcing itself as spirit) is that "law is law," and it just has to be accepted, because who are we, after all, to proclaim, through the law of the heart, that we are above the law? Similarly, in the *Philosophy of Right*, morality ends in the nightmare of Being-for-self.[30] What the free individual must do is to submit to *Sittlichkeit* (Ethical Life). There, traditions of the family, the market, and the state will anchor the individual to prevent Being-for-self from turning mad.

Returning to the theme of the One and the Many, Hegel ponders the "ancient proposition that the one is many and especially that the many are one." (172) The truth of this, Hegel claims, cannot be expressed in fixed propositions. Truth exists "as a becoming, a process, a repulsion and attraction – not as being." (172) We mortals know only the traces of this movement and try, by our Understanding, to fix the movement in "propositions."

---

[28] *See generally* Jeanne L. Schroeder & David Gray Carlson, *Kenneth Starr: Diabolically Evil?*, 88 CAL. L. REV. 653 (2000).

[29] Clark Butler quotes Hegel as saying, "evil is to be apprehended as the existence of contradiction." CLARK BUTLER, HEGEL'S LOGIC: BETWEEN DIALECTIC AND HISTORY 56 (1996), *quoting* G.W.F. Hegel, *Review of Göschel's* Aphorisms, 17 CLIO 387 (1988). According to Butler, "the fallen individual soul persistently acts on the contradictory belief that it exists like an atom whose existence or good is detached both from that of other individuals and from the community of individuals in which it has been reared." BUTLER, *supra*, at 56.

[30] G.W.F. HEGEL, ELEMENTS OF THE PHILOSOPHY OF RIGHT § 139 Addition (Allen W. Wood trans. 1993).

It is too easy, Hegel warns, to assume that there are "many" that are welded by the Understanding into the One (just as modern utilitarians assume that the "good" is an aggregate of human preferences). This given one is presented as a self-sufficient atom – a "*fact*, and all that has to be done is to grasp this simple fact." (173) Of course, Hegel strongly opposes any such atomistic dogmas.

(b) The One One of Attraction

At this point, the Many Ones have no relation *inter se* – a negative relation. This relation "is without effect because [the Ones] presuppose one another as affirmatively present." (173) When this relation is posited as Repulsion – in Figure 9(c) – the relation is "only the *ought-to-be* of ideality." (173) By this Hegel means that the relationship of Repulsion is not (but ought to be) self-subsistent. Repulsion's ideality is realized in Attraction. "Repulsion passes over into attraction, the many ones into *one* one." (173) That is, Repulsion [7] is present in Attraction [1], but only as a memory, not as an express immediacy. This is shown in Figure 10(a), where Repulsion sought to stay aloof but covertly traveled along and became part of [1]. Attraction now has a resilience that Repulsion lacks. The Many Ones are now One One.

But now repulsion and attraction must be considered in relation, as shown in Figure 10(b). Repulsion is said to be "the reality of the ones." (173) Attraction is "their posited ideality." (173) In Repulsion, the Ones are negatively related. Hence, the Ones demonstrate their Determinate Being – being in relation with nothing. In Attraction as such in Figure 10(a), this negative relation is sublated. It is only a memory. For the Ones, relation is a "posited ideality." Thus, Hegel can say:

> The relation of attraction to repulsion is such that [Attraction] has [Repulsion] for *presupposition*. Repulsion provides the material for attraction. If there were no ones there would be nothing to attract; the conception of a perpetual attraction, of an absorption of the ones, presupposes an equally perpetual production of them. (173)

Repulsion is therefore the truth of Attraction, as Dialectical Reason discovers in Figure 10(b). But for the constraint of repulsing force, Attraction long ago would have gathered all the ones into a single inert One. When this is hypothetically accomplished – when we achieve the "One One of Attraction" – Attraction abolishes itself and goes out of existence. Attraction therefore must have negativity within itself: "attraction is inseparable from repulsion." (173)

In Figure 10(a), Attraction was our license to say that the Many

Ones were *one*. In order to say this, we had to presuppose that the Many Ones were *diverse*. In short, Attraction is a force[31] – an activity. But it cannot be permitted to succeed. Otherwise, our license to unify abolishes itself. This important point is called the "play of forces" in the *Phenomenology*.[32] The idea of it is that force is never perceptible unless another force opposes it. Otherwise, the first force would have obliterated everything long ago. The same point can be made about society. If we view personality as a becoming – a force – it must have another force – another person – to oppose it. Otherwise it could not recognize itself. Human beings are forces that need other human beings to recognize them as such. Persons, in Hegelian psychology, are not self-sufficient but social for this very reason.

Hegel warns against an illegitimate view of Attraction. In Figure 10(a), Attraction is the name Hegel gives to the unity of all the Ones. The One One of Attraction is the result if Repulsion is not present in Attraction as a negative moment. Hence, Figure 10(a) could be taken as a diagram of this One One, whose impossibility is posited only in Figure 10(b). What Hegel warns against is to picture the One One as king of the Ones – a *primus inter pares* with "precedence" (173) over the peasant Ones. Such a picture is wrong for several reasons.[33] First, "attraction belongs equally to each of the many ones as *immediately* present." (173) Furthermore, the illegitimate picture grants self-identity to all the Ones, including the *primus inter pares*, which Hegel describes as "an equilibrium of attraction and repulsion." (173) Self-identity is always an error. The illegitimate picture also suggests "a specific difference" between the One One and the Many Ones, when Attraction is supposed to be "the positing of the immediately present undifferentiatedness of the ones." (174) Nevertheless, on the law of sublation, the Many Ones are idealized and are indeed within the One One. In Figure 10(b), the Many Ones are [2] in the unity of [1, 2]. In an earlier guise, they were [4, 5, 6] in Figure 9(c); for this reason, Hegel says of the Many Ones that "through their posited negation arises the one of attraction, which is consequently determined as mediated, the *one posited as one*." (174) In other words, [1] in Figure 10(a) depends on the suppression of what becomes [2] in Figure 10(b).

---

[31] Hegel later warns that the word "force" is not to be used in connection with Attraction, if force is taken to mean a self-subsisting, self-identical meaning. (178-80) I use the word "force" here, but not in the disapproved manner Hegel describes.

[32] G.W.F. HEGEL, PHENOMENOLOGY OF SPIRIT ¶ 138-43 (A.V. Miller trans. 1977).

[33] This picture turns out to be Intensive Magnitude in Figure 14(b).

Hegel has said that the One One of Figure 10(a) is "determined as mediated" and "*posited as one*." How can this One One be determined as mediated, when it is shown in Figure 10(a) as an *immediacy*? The answer is that Hegel refers to Repulsion's *act* of positing. In Figure 10(a), we saw Repulsion repelling itself from itself. This act is mediated – it implies the actor (Repulsion) and the excrement (the Many Ones). Of course, Repulsion itself *denies* that it is positing at all. Rather, it claims that it is merely refusing to recognize the Many Ones. But Repulsion has already been revealed to be a liar. "For us," we know that Repulsion has de-posited the Many Ones. The Understanding now intervenes. It peers into the toilet and interprets the excremental materials as the One One. In other words, the act of positing is mediated and concrete, but the *result* is an immediacy.

The Many Ones were sublated in Figure 10(a), but they return as [2] in Figure 10(b). Repulsion *is* the Many Ones. And the Many Ones are the negative internal voice of Attraction [1, 2] itself. Thus, Attraction "does not absorb the attracted ones into itself as into a centre." (174) Rather, Repulsion, from the inside of Attraction, "preserves the ones as many in it." (174)

(c) The Relation of Repulsion and Attraction

In chapter 3's final subsection, the difference between the One and the Many is a difference of their *relation* to one another. This relation is now cleft in twain – Repulsion and Attraction. In Figure 10(b), each is different yet essentially connected. Repulsion appeared first, initially as immediate [7] in Figure 9(c). Many Ones were repulsed and, in this action, de-posited as immediate – as the unitary Void, or as Attraction. Thus, the Many Ones became a relation – Attraction. The two immediates – Repulsion and Attraction – were, at that point, indifferent to each other. Attraction – the unity of the Many Ones – was "externally added to it as thus presupposed." (174)

We must pause to consider: what does it mean to say that Attraction was presupposed? Here Hegel echoes his comments on atomism, in an earlier Remark.[34] Atomists presuppose the Void in which the atoms move about. Hegel, however, dialectically established in Figure 9(b) that the Void *is* the Many Ones. The Many Ones, in Attraction, are made into the One One in Figure 10(a). So just as atomism

---

[34] *Supra* at 115-7.

presupposes the Void (Attraction), Repulsion also assumes the Void (Attraction) when it expels the Many Ones.

In Essence, the very act of positing is always coupled with presupposition. If an entity announces, "I am not that" (the act of positing), it *presupposes* a "that" from which it differentiates itself.[35] If it posits itself as *not* the Many Ones, Repulsion must presuppose that there *is* such a thing as the Many Ones. Repulsion is an *activity*. Activity requires an actor and a thing acted upon. So Repulsion is a slave to what it repulses. "[R]epulsion and flight is not a liberation from what is repelled and fled from. [T]he one as excluding still remains *related* to what it excludes." (175)[36]

This moment of relation is Attraction itself and thus implicitly is *inside* Repulsion. In Figure 9(c), Attraction can be viewed as [4, 5, 6]. In this capacity, Attraction negates "abstract repulsion" [7]. (175) If Attraction as internal to Repulsion, Hegel likewise emphasizes that Repulsion is internal to Attraction in Figure 10(b). There, Repulsion is [2]. But if Repulsion is Attraction's negative voice – the voice of Dialectical Reason – then Hegel likewise implies that, in Figure 10(c), Repulsion is just as much Attraction, and Attraction is just as much Repulsion. Instead of placing Attraction on the left, we could have placed it on the right, and *vice versa*.

The extremes, then, cannot distinguish themselves. It took outside determination to name them. We saw something similar to Figure 3(b), where the leftward extreme was Something/Other and the rightward extreme was Being-in-itself/Being-for-other. There also an outside force had to determine whether "being" was truly on the left or on the right. This helpless state of the extremes portends no self-subsistence.

This is the great irony of Being-for-self in general. It purports to expel otherness so that it can be "for itself." Yet, in the end, it has no idea what it is. Only an outsider can assign to Being-for-self a content. Hence, in the *Phenomenology*, Hegel refers to the unhappy

---

[35] *Infra* at 268-73. The point is vital for the commencement of the *Philosophy of Right*, *supra* note 30, Hegel's dialectic of liberal freedom. There, he starts with the most negative of negative freedom – the self freed of all inclination, desires, and even embodiment. The self is indeterminate. But, Hegel emphasizes, if such a self is indeterminate, there must be "determinacy." So the self announces, "I am not *that* – the determined." Determinacy is thus presupposed by the liberal subject. *Id.* § 34 Addition.

[36] This is a Lacanian truth – the repressed is a bloody instruction that always returns to haunt the inventor. What is foreclosed in the symbolic returns in the real. SLAVOJ ŽIŽEK, THE INDIVISIBLE REMAINDER: AN ESSAY ON SCHELLING AND RELATED MATTERS 191 (1996).

consciousness as having Being-for-self and not Being-in-itself. The unhappy consciousness perceives that he is nothing and God is everything.[37]

Repulsion and Attraction are inseparable. "[A]t the same time each is determined as an ought and a limitation relatively to the other." (175) As mere Oughts, they *ought* to exceed their Limitations.[38] The Ought of these opposing forces is "their abstract determinateness in the form of the *in-itself*" [2] (175) Taken abstractly, [2] – the very determinateness of both Attraction and Repulsion – is the in-itself to both forces. From [2] will spring the new middle term. For the moment, however, Hegel draws attention to the fact that, in [2], "each [i.e., Attraction or Repulsion] is simply directed away from itself and relates itself to the *other*. [E]ach *is* through the mediation of the *other* as *other*." (175) In other words, [1] repulses [2] – its very being. Hence, [1] *is* because its essence [2] is utterly other. The obverse is true of [3], which likewise repulses [2]. At this point, these forces are self-subsistent only in the sense that each is "posited for the other as a *different* determining." (175) But, simultaneous to "being for other" in [2], each is "for self" in [1] and [3] respectively. Thus, "in this interdependence the mediation of each through the other [2] is rather negated, each of these determinations being a self-mediation." (175)

In what sense a self-mediation? Of [1] and [3], Hegel writes that "each presupposes *itself*, is related only to itself in its presupposition." (176) This is fully implied in Figure 10(b), which emphasizes the relatedness of Attraction and Repulsion. Attraction (now revealed to be just as much Repulsion) expels [2] – its own self. It says, "I'm not [2]." In saying this, [1] presupposes there *is* such a thing as [2] to expel. And furthermore, [2] is just as much Attraction as [1] was. Attraction therefore presupposes itself *and* is related *only* to itself. The same could have been said about Repulsion (which is just as much Attraction as Repulsion).

In Figure 10(a), Repulsion repelled the Many Ones. Attraction became the Many Ones, unified by the force of external reflection. Now Hegel says that the Many Ones have not disappeared. They are Repulsion itself – taken as the negative of Attraction. Figure 10(b), then, could have been drawn as the opposition of the One and the

---

[37] PHENOMENOLOGY, *supra* note 32, ¶ 231 ("For the Unhappy Consciousness the in-itself is the beyond of itself").

[38] "[A]s the *ought*, something is *raised above its limitation*, but conversely, it is only as the *ought* that it has its *limitation*." (133)

Many. Thus, the Many Ones were presupposed by Repulsion in Figure 10(a), but now Repulsion *is its own presupposition*. This will become the archetypical move of Reflection in the Doctrine of Essence. Reflection typically expels itself from itself only to become precisely what it repelled. This has now happened to Repulsion. It expelled the Many Ones. Now it *is* the Many Ones – the opposite of the One One of Attraction and the very failure of Attraction to unite the Ones.

Both sides at this point are identical in their activity. Each side self-presupposes. It posits itself as the negative of itself. It sheds its Being-in-itself [2] and attributes it to the other. This shedding activity is Repulsion – a self-preservation. Within [1] or [3] it is a self-identity – Attraction. Each thus has both moments of Repulsion and Attraction – self-preservation and self-alienation. Each expels itself into the other. In this activity, each "is the transition of each out of itself into the other." (176) Each posits itself as its own other:

> The one as such, then, is a coming-out-of-itself, is only the positing of itself as its own other, as many; and the many, similarly, is only this, to collapse within itself and to posit itself as *its* other, as one, and in this very act to be related only to its own self, each continuing itself in its other. (176)

Being-for-self has now reached its conclusion in a middle term which names the activity of repelling all content: Quantity. Quantity is "[t]he one as *infinitely self*-related." (177) What does this mean? Recall that the Infinite is what goes beyond all Limitation. So, in Figure 10(c), Repulsion/Attraction has gone beyond its Limitation. It is "the mediation in which [the One] repels from itself its own self as its absolute (that is, abstract) *otherness*." (177) Quantity, then, becomes itself when it becomes other.

Figure 10(c)
Quantity

Quantity is the thinnest of entities. All its content is expelled; it is a mere ghost of Being. For Quantity, its expelled Quality is its very non-being. Yet Quantity was impoverished through its own initiative. It is, in Republican terms, the "undeserving poor." Quantity "is only self-relation," and a "*becoming* in which it is no longer determined as having a *beginning*." (177) Quantity has sublated immediacy itself.

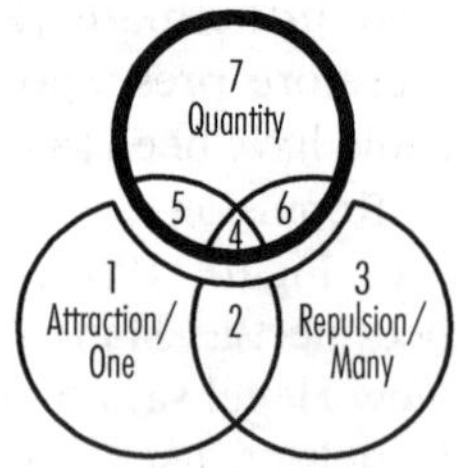

Among the things outside itself are the Many Ones. This is ironic. We are inclined to think of Quantity as *numbers*, but, so far, distinguishable integers are too advanced for us. We must think of

Quantity *as such,* with no Determinate Being of its own. Thus, Quantity is a sublating that is "at first determined as only a relative sublating of the *relation* to another determinately existent one." (177) This non-relation is even less than an "indifferent repulsion and attraction." (177) Repulsion and Attraction are, after all, posited as relations. Quantity has moved beyond relation (or so it thinks). But in its radically negative attitude toward its own being, Quantity

> equally displays itself as passing over into the infinite relation of mediation through negation of the external relations of the immediate, determinately existent ones, and as having for result that very process of becoming which . . . is the collapse . . . into simple immediacy. (177)

Thus, by negating immediacy, Quantity is – what else could it be? – nothing *but* mediation. Indeed, if you think of it in the more advanced notion of ordinary numbers, Quantity does nothing but relate various qualities. The number "three" can refer to three houses, three roses, three bears, etc. The number three is a great mediator of "things."

Quality is now Quantity, and Hegel reviews the moments of the transition. The fundamental determination of Quality – the first three chapters of the *Science of Logic* – was "being and immediacy." (178) In these chapters, "limit and determinateness are so identical with the being of something, that with its alteration the something itself vanishes." (178) Here, Hegel summarizes the trajectory of Something, which alters itself and becomes an Infinite Being. Infinite Being has now repelled from itself its own being, and hence it too has now vanished. This was foretold when the Something became the Finite. The very Ought of the Finite was that it must cease-to-be. In Quantity, its destiny is fulfilled.[39]

Quantity as an immediate unity, "in which the *difference* has vanished

---

[39] Failure to grasp that the Ought predicts the abolition of being leads Charles Taylor to announce that this transition from being-for-self to Quantity is "a little strained." TAYLOR, *supra* note 3, at 244. Of this transition, Taylor writes: "It offers another example of a twist we have often noticed in the Hegelian dialectic: where Hegel 'goes back' from the advanced point he has reached in order to take up and 'feed into' his dialectic some other important range of concepts or transitions." *Id*. Taylor takes the True Infinite to be both ceasing-to-be and coming-to-be, and he implies that Hegel privileges one over the other solely in order to produce Quantity – the realm in which the content of being is strictly beyond itself. Yet, if we concentrate on the feature of the Ought – that it names ceasing-to-be as the soul of the Finite – then the pursuit of ceasing-to-be at the expense of coming-to-be – is (like the quality of mercy) not strained.

but is *implicitly* present in the unity of *being* and *nothing*." (178) It is pure *relation without parts* – a contradiction. Yet, by virtue of being a relation without parts – an immediate unity – Quantity *implies* its parts. Hence, Quantity cannot remain an immediacy but must make express what it is: "This relation to other contradicts the immediacy in which qualitative determinateness [*i.e.*, Quantity] is self-relation." (178) In other words, having expelled its being, Quantity must now recapture it by bringing Quality back within itself.

Conclusion

> The most enduring result of Hegelian logic is that the individual is not flatly for himself. In himself, he is his otherness and linked with others.[40]

In its journey, Being started by placing an accent on its affirmative side. But this accent was no more than the announcement of what Being was not: Being is not nothing. The substance by which Being manifested itself was therefore beyond it. Being sustained itself only by refusing to recognize the other. It became nothing else *but* this refusal,[41] and hence it enslaved itself to its other. It became the very act of expelling its own content. As this expelling force, it is Quantity.

This expulsion of content from what "is" immediately is of the utmost spiritual significance. It is the heart of idealism, as opposed to materialism. Hegel's idealism "ascribes being to the infinite, the Spirit, God [and] denies that things and the finite world have true reality."[42] Thus, if Quality has chased its being elsewhere, it does so only to retrieve it at a deeper spiritual level.

Quality, then, does not lose all. It retains Being-for-self – empty though this is. This retained Being-for-self was responsible for the very idea of multiplicity. Because the True Infinite never entirely gave up its place, its expelled content, itself a Being-for-self that expels content, counted as a new One, which in turn produced another One, etc.

Later, in Quantity, being will discover that its other is really itself. Quantity continues to go outside itself but recognizes that its destination is still its own self.[43] This realization, culminating in

---

40 THEODOR W. ADORNO, NEGATIVE DIALECTICS 161 (E.B. Ashton trans. 2000).

41 "*Dasein* is a determinately qualitative finite being determined by what it excludes." HARRIS, *supra* note 1, at 136.

42 LUCIO COLLETTI, MARXISM AND HEGEL 7 (Lawrence Garner trans., 1973).

43 *Id.* at 137 ("Moreover, its other is not a qualitative other, but is an extension of

Measure, is the threshold to Essence, where return-to-self is named Reflection. Here, Being's vanishedness implies a deeper soul that has "staying power." The essential thing endures, but the thing that merely *is* is finite and therefore must become (and always already is) what *is not*. What is and is not serve as the stuff for Hegel to make paradoxes.

---

itself beyond its own limit, and is still indifferently the same all over again, the limit notwithstanding.").

PART II
QUANTITY

4
Pure Quantity

Upon reaching the realm of Quantity, a word of comfort is in order for readers suffering from "math anxiety." Such readers have nothing to fear from Hegel. With the exception of some notorious (and quite extraneous) remarks on calculus, nothing in his analysis extends beyond rudimentary algebra, knowledge of which I will *not* presuppose. Hegel was no great champion of mathematics – though his education in it was formidable.[1] In fact, he had contempt for its spiritual worth.[2] Nevertheless, Quantity enjoys an important role in the *SL*. In this fourth chapter,[3] Hegel equates Pure Quantity with time, space and the ego – deeply metaphysical ideas.

---

[1] For the educational details, see Michael John Petry, *The Significance of Kepler's Laws*, in HEGEL AND NEWTONIANISM 476-83 (Michael John Petry ed., 1993).

[2] Hegel calls mathematics a "subordinate science." (27) Its claim to necessity is inadequate, and its practitioners do nothing but ward off heterogeneity, an act itself tainted with heterogeneity. (40) In these remarks, and many others, Hegel anticipates Gödel's critique of mathematics as inherently incomplete. *See* Michael Kosok, *The Formalization of Hegel's Dialectical Logic: Its Formal Structure, Logical Interpretation and Intuitive Foundation*, in HEGEL: A COLLECTION OF CRITICAL ESSAYS 263 (Alasdair MacIntyre, ed., 1972) ("dialectic logic can be taken as a way of generalizing Goedel's theorem, and instead of regarding it merely as a *limitation* to the expression of consistent systems in ordinary logical structures, it now becomes the *starting point* for a dialectic logic, which regards these limitations as the essence of its structure").

[3] Hegel renumbers his chapters after every section, so there is no "chapter 4." I take the liberty of renumbering them. Hence, we are reading chapter 4 and will continue straight through to chapter 27.

For Hegel, Quality precedes Quantity, reversing Kant's preferred order.[4] "[H]itherto," Hegel observes, "the determination of *quantity* has been made to precede *quality* . . . for no given reason." (79)[5] Errol Harris, however, suggests why Kant led with Quantity:

> Kant gives quantity precedence over quality but that is because he maintains that the categories are applicable only to sensuously intuited experience the *a priori* forms of which are space and time. Space and time, therefore, take precedence over that which fills them, and space and time are quantitative schemata . . . [6]

For Kant, space and time are subjective. They are added to the object by consciousness.[7] For Hegel, space and time are Pure Quantity, derived from the concept of Quality: "the *externality of space and time* [exists] absolutely on its own account without the moment of subjectivity." (843) Space and time belong to the object itself. Indeed, space and time are the opening moves of the Philosophy of Nature; they stand for the logical Idea beginning to externalize itself.[8] For this reason, space and time are properly *beyond* the realm of Logic.

In chapter 3, Quality became Being-for-self – utterly indifferent to otherness and hence radically free. Being-for-self was Repulsion of its own content – a *relation* without *parts*. Yet "it cannot be conceived of as something which is entirely without relations . . . as was the more basic category of pure being."[9] Relation *requires* parts, so, ironically, Being-for-self found itself completely dependent on otherness to define itself. It became "absolutely identical with being-for-other." (185) Instead of being radically free, it was radically unfree.

Quantity is still a determinate being, but one devoid of all content. It is "indifferent to its affirmative determinateness." (372) It represents

---

4 IMMANUEL KANT, CRITIQUE OF PURE REASON A142-3/B182-3 (Paul Guyer & Allen W. Wood trans., 1990).

5 Fichte, however, preceded Hegel in privileging Quality over Quantity. H.S. Harris, *General Introduction*, in G.W.F. HEGEL, THE JENA SYSTEM, 1804-5: LOGIC AND METAPHYSICS xvii (John W. Burbidge & George di Giovanni trans. 1986).

6 ERROL E. HARRIS, AN INTERPRETATION OF THE LOGIC OF HEGEL 124 (1983).

7 Kantians have complained, however, that Kant nowhere demonstrates this. ROBERT PIPPIN, KANT'S THEORY OF FORM: AN ESSAY ON THE *CRITIQUE OF PURE REASON* 55 (1982).

8 HEGEL'S PHILOSOPHY OF NATURE § 259 (Michael John Petry trans., 1970) ("The *present, future, and past,* the dimensions of time, constitute the *becoming of externality as such* . . .").

9 Gerd Buchdahl, *Hegel on the Interaction Between Science and Philosophy*, in HEGEL AND NEWTONIANISM, *supra* note 1, at 67.

the idea of simply *not being Quality – i.e.*, not being independent from outside determination.[10] The job of Quantity over the next three chapters is to recapture its Quality. When it succeeds, it will resist (but be open to) outside determination and pass over to Measure.

By way of preview to the first chapter of Quantity (which is Chapter 4 of this book), we begin with Pure Quantity, which must be distinguished from its more complicated successor – Quantum. The challenge here is to remember that Quantum – *i.e.*, "Number" – is too advanced. We must first isolate the deeper substance of numbers.[11]

Pure Quantity "develops a determinateness" and becomes Quantum. (185) Quantum is "indifferent determinateness, that is, a self-transcending, self-negating determinateness." (185) It self-erases and lapses into a Spurious Infinity – the mathematical infinite of the never-ending number line.

Spurious Infinity amounted to the pure act of self-erasure. This act is what the finitized infinite did.[12] The unity between the Finite and the Spurious Infinite was precisely self-abnegating activity, whose name was True Infinity. Something similar happens to the mathematical infinite. The vanishing of integers will emerge as True Infinity, an indiscernible. Since Quality *is* resistance to outside determination, the emergence of the Infinitely Small (δx) or Large Quantum signifies that Quantity has taken back its Quality.

---

[10] Alan H.T. Paterson, *The Successor Function and Induction Principle in a Hegelian Philosophy of Mathematics*, 30 IDEALISTIC STUDIES 25, 41 (2002) ("quantity is *both* simple immediacy and infinite mediation)."

[11] A criticism is offered by Terry Pinkard, who writes that Hegel "followed the tradition of his time in his assumption that the elements and principles of mathematical thought were those related to quantity and number. [M]ore recent developments show that a whole set of mathematical ideas must be defined without reference to quantity . . . To make matters worse for Hegel, the traditional quantitative conception of measurement to which he appeals is not necessarily tied up with a conception of quality per se." TERRY PINKARD, HEGEL'S DIALECTIC 42 (1988). In fact, Hegel's *exact* point is that mathematics had insufficiently appreciated the role of quality in the constitution of quantity. Pinkard's remark about Measure could not be more wrong. *See* TOM ROCKMORE, HEGEL'S CIRCULAR EPISTEMOLOGY 9 (1986) ("it would be a mistake to argue that if [Hegel's view of mathematics] can be refuted, which cannot be shown, the position as a whole could be rejected. For whatever fate of the critique of mathematics, it is no more than an illustration of the more general point that a form of thought which is divorced from the movement of reality, and hence feeds only on itself, is necessarily one-sided and abstract, or linear.").

[12] See Figure 7(b).

A. Pure Quantity

In chapter 3, Quantity was "the repelling one." (187) Repulsion said: "I am not *that*." In so announcing, it confessed it *was that* after all: it "treats the other as identical with itself, and in doing so has lost its determination." (187) The excreta, however, were united in Attraction.[13] Attraction consisted of a unity imposed on the many ones by *external reflection*.[14] Repulsion was *indifferent* to this unity. External reflection made the One One out of the Many, but it equally could have made *two* ones or a million ones. Since external reflection is outside the logical sequence, Repulsion's principle is not offended. Repulsion was "indifferent to attraction which is externally added to it as thus presupposed." (174) What now can be revealed is that Attraction *is the will of the mathematician* who makes of magnitude[15] whatever she wants. Quantity is *open* to this force of Attraction and is indeed dependent on it. Yet the mathematician is not utterly free. Attraction "is at the same time determined by the immanent repulsion." (187) Quantity is the *unity* of Attraction and

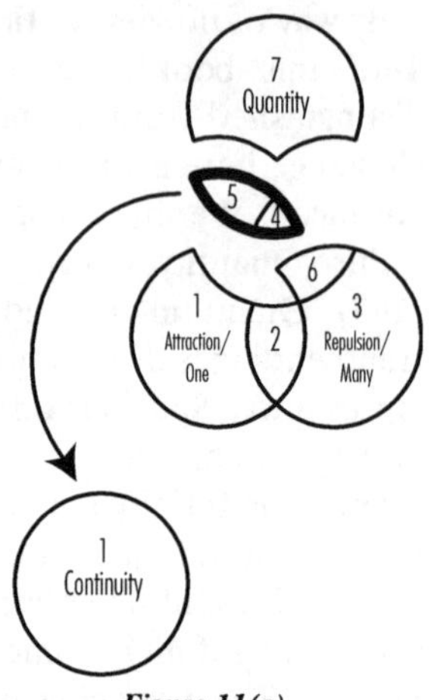

Figure 11(a)
Continuity

---

[13] In Figure 10(a), [7] posited the Void/Many Ones as not itself. Covertly, [7] – Repulsion as an immediacy – was swept along and was not left behind. Hence, [7] entered into Attraction as an immediacy, but Dialectical Reason retrieved it in Figure 10(b).

[14] *See supra* at 127-9.

[15] Magnitude (*Größe*) means Quantum – not Quantity. It is too advanced for the concept of Pure Quantity, because it implies a more developed determinateness. In common mathematical discourse, "[a] magnitude is usually defined as that which can be increased or diminished." (186) This, Hegel finds, is a poor definition. What does "increase" mean? It means "make the magnitude more." What does "diminish" mean? It means "make the magnitude less." Covertly, the word defined ("magnitude") appears in the definition. Nothing is learned from such a definition, except that magnitude is magnitude. It is nevertheless clear, in this definition, that "the *more* or *less* can be resolved into an affirmative addition" (186) – or subtraction – which is externally added or subtracted. "It is this *external* form both of reality and of negation which in general characterizes the nature of *alteration* in quantum." (186) In other words, Quantum cannot alter itself.

Repulsion. Reminiscing about this relationship, the Understanding announces that Attraction is the moment of Continuity in Quantity. In Figure 11(a), Quantity has expelled its content [4-7]. Therefore, the "content" of Figure 11(a) must be found amidst the expelled entities. Attraction [4, 5] is plucked from the exiles and made the Understanding's focus of attention. It becomes Continuity [1].[16] Continuity is

> simple, self-same self-relation, which is not interrupted by any limit of exclusion; it is not, however, an *immediate* unity, but a unity of ones which possess being-for-self. The *asunderness of the plurality* is still contained in this unity, but at the same time as not differentiating or *interrupting* it. (187)

The above passage shows a significant change of perspective. The first chapters of the *SL* were the realm of "being" – the realm of *immediacy*. There, [1] was always immediate. Now, beyond the realm of immediacy, [1] is simple and not interrupted, but *not simply immediate*. The Understanding continues to learn. It grasps [1] as a simple view of a complex *mediated* entity. Mediation now breathes and reigns in the extremes of Understanding and of Dialectical Reason. If immediacy exists within Continuity, it exists as a *moment* – a memory of its origin in reality. Indeed, Hegel will often use the word "immediate" in this and the following chapters. The Understanding knows, however, that immediacy is now an ideal moment. The Understanding has left the crude realm of reality and exists now in the realm of the ideal.[17]

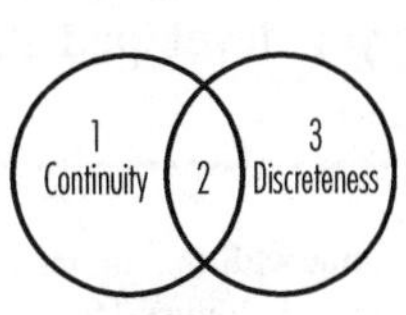

Figure 11(b)
Discreteness

Dialectical Reason is now rather less patronizing of the Understanding. Acknowledging that the Understanding sees that Continuity contains mediation within it – the distinction of Many Ones – Dialectical Reason proposes to shift attention to the moment of difference. Of Figure 11(b), Hegel writes: "In continuity, therefore, magnitude immediately possesses the moment of *discreteness* – repulsion has now a moment in quantity." (187) The word "immedi-

---

16 Continuity has the attributes of Attraction. That is, Continuity is a plurality held together by an external will. HARRIS, *supra* note 6, at 126.

17 *See* Paterson, *supra* note 10, at 43 ("The turbulent 'pulling in' and 'forcing away' of attraction and repulsion . . . have become quiescent in continuity and discreteness through the transgression of limit in quantity, each permeating the other conceptually").

ately" must be taken in its ideal sense, for the reason just stated.

We are beyond the realm of immediacy. "Hence, discreteness on its side, is a coalescent discreteness, where the ones are not connected by the void, by the negative, but by their own continuity and do not interrupt this self-sameness in the many." (187) In other words, [3] is not immediate, except in an ideal sense. The Many Ones are acknowledged in Discreteness; and they are acknowledged as connected by Continuity.

Enriched Quantity is the unity of Discreteness and Continuity. Hegel does not use this phrase. I have added this to distinguish Figure 11(c), which brings Continuity to the fore, from Figure 10(c).[18] Enriched Quantity will turn out to be the same thing as time, space, and the ego.[19]

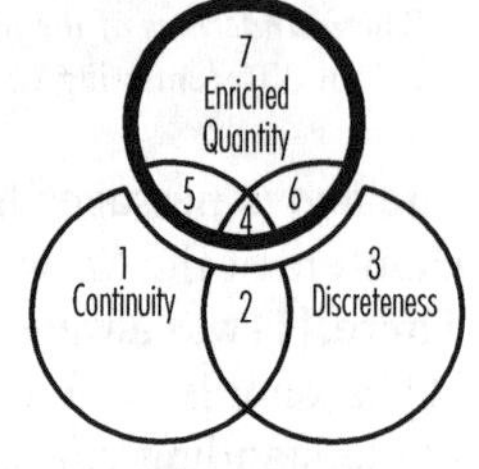

Figure 11(c)
Enriched Quantity

Enriched Quantity is "the unity of these moments of continuity and discreteness, but at first it is so in the *form* of one of them, *continuity*, as a result of the dialectic of being-for-self, which has collapsed into the form of self-identical immediacy." (187) Here we have reference to [1] in Figure 11(a) – Continuity as an *immediacy*. But this must be taken as ideal or "recollected" immediacy. Continuity is "this simple result in so far as being-for-self has not yet developed its

---

[18] Could Figure 11(c) be viewed as *the same* as Figure 10(c), but with the names of the extremes changed? I did something similar once before. In chapter 1, Figure 1(c) was Pure Being, Pure Nothing, and Becoming. Then the names changed, without an advance. Figure 1(c) became coming-to-be, ceasing-to-be, and Determinate Being. Nevertheless, an advance to Figure 11(c) is justified. In Figure 10(a), [1] was Attraction – precisely a stubborn unity that nevertheless covertly implies Repulsion. In Figure 11(c), Continuity shows no such stubbornness.

[19] Hegel gives this useful example of Continuity and Discreteness:

> It may be said, the space occupied by this room is a continuous magnitude, and the hundred men assembled in it form a discrete magnitude. And yet the space is continuous and discrete at the same time; hence we speak of points of space, or we divide space, a certain length, into so many feet . . . which can be done on the hypothesis that space is also potentially discrete. Similarly . . . the discrete magnitude, made up of a hundred men, is also continuous; and the circumstance on which this continuity depends is the common element, the species man, which pervades all the individuals and unites them with each other.

EL § 100 Remark.

moments and posited them within itself." (187) Quantity, taken as a mere immediacy, is retrogressive – a throwback to the last part of chapter 2. This immediacy, however, is precisely what Being-for-self expelled by the end of chapter 3. Quantity, as portrayed in Figure 11(a), *contains* the moments of Being-for-self "posited as it is in truth. The determination of being-for-self was to be a self-sublating relation-to-self; a perpetual coming-out-of-itself. But what is repelled is itself; repulsion is, therefore, the creative flowing away of itself." (188) This "creative" flowing of content out of Being-for-self is precisely what Continuity is. Thus, Being-for-self flows into all the other Ones: "On account of the self-sameness of what is repelled, this distinguishing or differentiation is an uninterrupted continuity." (188)

Thanks to Discreteness, Continuity – [4,5] in Figure 11(c) – "without being interrupted, is at the same time a plurality, which no less immediately remains in its self-identicalness." (188) Immediacy, then, is an *ideal* moment. The Understanding has a simple, yet mediated, view of Quantity as a substance that continues itself in all things.

Quantitative Limit

Pure Quantity does not yet have a Limit. On the contrary, Quantity "consists precisely in not being bounded by limit." (188) It is "limit which is just as much no limit." (185) Limit has been sublated, rendered ideal. By virtue of it, Quantity is distinguishable from Being. Being is no limit, and so Quantity suffuses or "continues" into the heart of external being with no opposition.

Limit *is* determinateness. But its significance differs for Quality and Quantity. When Quality exceeds its Limit, it changes radically. Limited Being is Finite. Its fate (*i.e.*, its Being-in-itself) is to erase itself and send its being *beyond* its Limit. Not so with quantitative limit:

> If, however, by limit we mean quantitative limit, then when, for example, a field alters its limit it still remains what it was before, a field. If on the other hand its qualitative limit is altered, then since this is the determinateness which makes it a field, it becomes a meadow, wood, and so on. (186)[20]

Hegel gives this example: "Red" is a quality of something – its color.

---

[20] *Cf.* CHARLES TAYLOR, HEGEL 247 (1975) ("It is thus a mark of the quantitative, says Hegel, that we are dealing with such indifferent limits, that the things can increase or decrease in extension without changing their nature").

Let's make the thing brighter or paler red. It remains red all the same. But let's paint the thing blue. The thing has now undergone a *qualitative* change, not a mere quantitative change.[21]

With regard to red that waxes and wanes, Hegel states that its degree is its magnitude. In magnitude, redness "has a permanent substratum of being *which is indifferent to its determinateness*." (186) In other words, red as such continues to be red even as the brightness or paleness (its determinateness) is manipulated by outside forces.

It requires an outside manipulator to make a thing *more* or *less* of what it is. Of "more or less," Hegel remarks: "In that imperfect expression . . . one cannot fail to recognize the main point involved, namely the indifference of the alteration, so that the alteration's own *more* and *less*, its indifference to itself, lies in its very Notion." (186) The essence of Quantum, then, is that it is indifferent to being changed by outside forces.

This last observation is significant. Common sense, fearful of affirming something absolutely, refers to its proposition as "more or less" true. What it aims for is a switch from brittle qualitative Limit to robust quantitative Limit. If the audience acquiesces to this transition, then the common sense proposition will be harder to refute. Of course, we should not fall for this trick. If common sense is making a qualitative point, then it is not entitled to the ease and comfort that quantitative Limit affords.

Alteration of Quantum, then, is accomplished only externally – hence inessentially. This is the penalty Being-for-self pays for driving out all content. Only strangers can tell the Quantum what it is – until chapter 6 reveals a moment of integrity within Quantum, from which will spring forth the slave-rebellion Hegel calls Measure.

In bad philosophy – "thinking that is not based on the Notion" (188) – Continuity quickly devolves into "mere *composition*, that is, an *external* relation of the ones to one another, in which the one is

---

[21] *See* HERBERT MARCUSE, HEGEL'S ONTOLOGY AND THE THEORY OF HISTORICITY 64 (Seyla Benhabib trans. 1987) ("A being which is immediately identical with its respective quality such as to remain the same throughout all its qualitative transformation is no longer qualitatively but quantitatively determined"); *see also* EL § 80 ("Quality is . . . the character identical with being: so identical that a thing ceases to be what it is, if it loses its quality. Quantity. . . is the character external to being, and does not affect the being at all. Thus *e.g.* a house remains what it is, whether it be greater or smaller; and red remains red, whether it be brighter or darker."). Hegel further remarks that "in quantity we have an alterable, which in spite of alterations still remains the same." *Id* § 106 Addition.

maintained in its absolute brittleness and exclusiveness." (188) For Hegel, "composition" is a derogatory term, suggesting that the unity is not immanent to the entities but is imposed upon them from the outside.[22] Compositional philosophy fails to see that the One "essentially and spontaneously . . . passes over into . . . ideality." (188) This spontaneous action was documented at the end of chapter 2 (when True Infinity appeared) and throughout chapter 3.

Atomism – much denounced in chapter 3 – holds that Continuity is external to the One, an idea that "ordinary thinking finds it difficult to forsake." (188) (Here, as we shall soon discover, Hegel is thinking about the concept of time and space.) Mathematics, however, rises above this naive view. It "rejects a metaphysics which would make time [or space] *consist* of points of time [or space]. It allows no validity to such discontinuous ones." (188) A plane may consist of the sum of infinitely many lines, but the Discreteness of the lines is only a moment. The sublation of this moment is implied by the infinite plurality of the lines.

Time, space, matter,[23] the ego – these are examples of Pure Quantity. They are "expansions, pluralities which are a coming-out-of-self, a flowing which, however, does not pass over into its opposite, into quality or the one." (189) Space is "absolute *self-externality* which equally is absolutely uninterrupted, a perpetual becoming-other which is self-identical." (189)[24] Time likewise is "an absolute coming-out-of-

---

[22] According to Hegel, composition is "the worst form in which anything can be considered . . . That the form of the untruest existence should be assigned, above all, to the ego, to the Notion, that is something we should not have expected and that can only be described as inept and barbarous." (615)

[23] In the *Philosophy of Nature*, Hegel identifies matter as the unity of Attraction and Repulsion, which is, of course, exactly what Quantity is. Host-Heino Von Borzeszkowski, *Hegel's Interpretation of Classical Mechanics*, in HEGEL AND NEWTONIANISM, *supra* note 1, at 79, *citing* PHILOSOPHY OF NATURE, *supra* note 8, § 262. Hegel also *distinguishes* Pure Quantity and matter. Quantity is a determination of pure thought. Matter is the same thing, but in outer existence.

[24] Space (Pure Quantity) is the starting point for the *Philosophy of Nature*, just as consciousness is the starting point for the *Phenomenology* and the autonomous individual is the starting point for the *Philosophy of Right*. *See* Lawrence S. Stepelevich, *Hegel's Conception of Space*, 1 NATURE AND SYSTEM 111 (1979). On the changes in the *Philosophy of Nature* between the first and second editions, where space goes from a mathematical to a mechanical idea, see Cinzia Ferrini, *Framing Hypotheses: Numbers in Nature and the Logic of Measure in the Development of Hegel's System*, in HEGEL AND THE PHILOSOPHY OF NATURE 283 (Stephen Houlgate ed., 1998).

In chapter 2, Hegel derived nature as other to Spirit. We now may add that nature so

itself." (189)[25] It generates the "now" – the present – but then immediately annihilates it. Time is the "continuous annihilation of this passing away" and the "spontaneous generating of non-being." (189) But time *itself* does not disappear. In its pure destructivity, self-devouring time is "a simple self-sameness and self-identity." (189)[26]

The ego is a Pure Quantity. It is "an absolute becoming-other, an infinite removal or all-round repulsion to the negative freedom of being-for-self." (190) The ego always says, "I am not *that*." No proposition ever captures all of the ego, which is nothing at all but Continuity over time – "utter simple continuity." (190) That the ego is Continuity (which *is* time itself) Hegel expresses this way: the ego is "the continuity of . . . being-with-self uninterrupted by the infinitely manifold limits, by the content of sensations, intuitions, and so forth." (190) The equation of the ego with being-with-self (*Bei-sichsein*, which I interpret to be the same as "being-within-self," or *Insichsein*) is significant. In chapter 2, we saw that being-within-self equates with [4] – the only numbered segment to appear in all three circles of the Borromean knot. It connoted immanence and hence freedom from outside compulsion. The birth of being-within-self in chapter 2 was therefore the seeds and weak beginnings of human self-consciousness – though that concept was too advanced for chapter 2 or even now.

The ego continues through its content – "sensations, intuitions, and so forth." None of these things, however, is adequate to the ego. The ego is always *beyond* these things and so never fully present to itself. But neither is the ego Pure Nothing. In fact, the ego is always suspended between its content and Pure Nothing. For this very reason, it is constantly restless.

Those familiar with Jacques Lacan's theory of the subject can glimpse

---

expelled by Spirit is Pure Quantity. G.R.G. MURE, THE PHILOSOPHY OF HEGEL 116 (1965). ("Quantity is conspicuous in Nature, since self-externality as opposed to the self-possession of spirit is the distinctive character of Nature"); PHILOSOPHY OF NATURE, *supra* note 8, § 257 Remark, at 231 ("*Only* that which is natural . . . is subject to time").

[25] *See* ANDREW HAAS, HEGEL AND THE PROBLEM OF MULTIPLICITY 252 (2000) ("the 'now' . . . exemplifying the immediacy of sense-certainty (that does not yet think 'time and space'), is not the now – for the now is no longer at precisely the moment when it is now; it is far more a not-now, a having-been: '*now*'; it has already ceased to be in being shown; the *now* that *is*, is another now than the one shown, and we see that the now is just this; already when it is, to be no more"), *quoting* G.W.F. HEGEL, PHENOMENOLOGY OF SPIRIT ¶ 106 (A.V. Miller trans. 1977).

[26] *See* RICHARD DIEN WINFIELD, AUTONOMY AND NORMATIVITY 59 (2001) (calling time "this self-devourer").

it prefigured in Hegel's theory of Pure Quantity. Lacan held that the subject was "split" between the realm of the Symbolic – the external realm of "being" – and the Real, the obliterative concept of Pure Nothing. The Lacanian subject constantly tries to fill in the gaps so that it can fully "be." This is precisely what "desire" is – the drive to be complete and whole. Yet desire must fail. For the subject to be whole would be for it to surrender its very essence – Continuity that stays forever free from the external realm of "being."[27]

Kant's Second Antinomy

In a Remark following Pure Quantity, Hegel makes his famous criticism that there are not merely four antinomies, as Kant alleged, but infinitely numerous antinomies; *every* concept is a union of opposites – as Becoming implies.[28]

In Kant's second antinomy, there is (1) a undividable simple, and (2) no simple; everything can be further subdivided.[29] Hegel states that Figure 11(c) gives rise to this antinomy, which "consists solely in the fact that discreteness must be asserted just as much as continuity. The one-sided assertion of discreteness gives . . . an indivisible, for principle; the one-sided assertion of continuity, on the other hand, gives infinite divisibility." (190) Discreteness (indivisibility) and Continuity (divisibility) are *both* necessary moments. Figure 11(c) diagrams the antinomy itself. Kant thought both sides of the antinomy to be false, because each can be disproved by *apagogic reasoning* – reason by process of elimination. The Kantian solution to the antinomies, Hegel says, was to make the contradiction subjective, where it remained unresolved.[30] The genuine solution, however, is to recognize that each side of an antinomy is one-sided and not valid on its own. "[O]n the contrary, they are true only as sublated." (192)

Before demolishing the antinomies, Hegel praises them as "the

---

[27] These thoughts summarize JEANNE LORRAINE SCHROEDER, THE VESTAL AND THE FASCES: HEGEL, LACAN, PROPERTY, AND THE FEMININE (1998). In her book, Schroeder draws rigorous parallels between Lacanian and Hegelian thought.

[28] *See* EL §48 ("Antinomies . . . appear in all objects of every kind, in all conceptions, notions and ideas").

[29] CRITIQUE OF PURE REASON, *supra* note 4, at A434-7/B462-5.

[30] Harris states that the understanding holds the two sides of the antinomy "incommunicado," and that the result is "logomachy" – a war on words. HARRIS, *supra* note 6, at 128.

downfall of previous metaphysics." (190) They helped to produce the conviction that finite things are null in content. Nevertheless, they are far from perfect. Hegel accuses Kant of choosing these antinomies (from the infinite set of them) to match his four categories of the understanding, earlier developed in the *Critique of Pure Reason*.[31] This was done, Hegel remarks, to provide a "show of completeness." (191)[32]

Hegel sets forth this memorable denunciation of Kant:

> The Kantian antinomies on closer inspection contain nothing more than the quite simple categorical assertion of *each* of the two opposed moments of a determination, each being taken on its own in isolation from the other. But at the same time this simple categorical, or strictly speaking assertoric statement is wrapped up in a false, twisted scaffolding of reasoning which is intended to produce a semblance of proof and to conceal and disguise the merely assertoric character of the statement. (192)

To make good on this criticism, Hegel paraphrases one side of Kant's second antinomy as follows: "Every composite substance in the world consists of simple parts, and nowhere does there exist anything but the simple or what is compounded from it." (192) The truth of the thesis is to be established by apagogic reasoning. Thus, if Kant can prove that infinite divisibility is impossible, he has proved that a "simple" exists.

---

[31] Here is how the categories of understanding match up with the antinomies:

Categories of the Understanding	Antinomies
Quantity	Beginning/No Beginning in Time
Quality	Infinite Divisibility/Simple
Relation	Freedom/Causation
Modality	Absolutely necessary God/No God

The categories are said to belong *a priori* to the understanding. CRITIQUE OF PURE REASON, *supra* note 4, at A79/B105. According to Kant, we cannot think any object except by means of the categories. We cannot cognize any thought except by means of intuitions corresponding to these conceptions. *Id.* at B165. They are the mere forms of thought for the construction of cognitions from intuitions. *Id.* at B288.

[32] HERBERT MARCUSE, REASON AND REVOLUTION 69 (1999) ("Hegel announced in his criticism of the Kantian philosophy that the task of logic was 'to develop' the categories and not merely 'to assemble' them"). Ironically, Hegel renders his theory of Judgment quadratic (not triadic) so that it conforms with Kant's Table of Logical Functions in Judgement. *Infra* at 461.

Hegel, however, claims that the demonstration is superfluous; Kant brings forth the very presuppositions he introduced into the model, so that nothing is achieved. Here is Hegel's appraisal of Kant's *real* argument for proving indivisible simplicity: (1) Assume there is such a thing as substance. (2) Now assume that composites do not have simple parts. (3) Now think away all composition. Nothing remains. (4) This contradicts the assumption that there is substance. (5) Ergo, there must be atoms. This, Hegel complains, does not move the argument. Kant could have begun this way: Composition is merely a contingent relation of the substance – a relation externally imposed on substance and not immanent to it. If composition is external, then substance is simple. In short, substance is a "thing-in-itself," which, in chapter 2, Hegel suggested, was a simplex.

Composition. Hegel likewise attacks the demonstration that everything is infinitely divisible, which he calls "a whole *nest* (to use an expression elsewhere employed by Kant) of faulty procedure." (195)[33] To disprove simplicity, Kant's apagogy argues: (1) Composites exist in space. (2) Space is infinitely divisible. (3) Since a simplex can occupy only one space at a time, it too must be equally divisible, to conform to the many spaces it occupies. (5) Ergo, simplicity does not exist.

Hegel complains that this argument assumes that whatever is substantial is spatial. It also assumes without proof that space is infinitely divisible. Indeed, space *is* Quantity, in Hegel's view. As such, it is Continuous *and* Discrete. Furthermore, the second move suggests that simplicity is *not* spatial. Simplicity, by definition, does not have complexity within it. Composition is outside it. If composition is outside the simple, so is space, and simplicity is not spatial. Only composition is. Yet, if simplicity is not spatial, Kant's demonstration falls apart.[34]

Hegel accuses Kant of *quaternio terminorum*: "There is also involved here a clash between the continuity of space and composition; the two are confused with each other. [Space is] substituted for [composition]

---

[33] Hegel refers here to Kant's critique of the cosmological proof of God, which Kant calls "a perfect nest of dialectical assumptions." CRITIQUE OF PURE REASON, *supra* note 4, at A609/B637.

[34] John Llewelyn complains that Hegel "misrepresents Kant's proof of the antithesis." John Llewelyn, *Kantian Antinomy and Hegelian Dialectic*, in HEGEL'S CRITIQUE OF KANT 90 (Stephen Priest ed., 1987). Spatiality, he says, *includes* compositeness but is not exhausted by it. This may be what Kant intended, but the indivisibility of the simple *proves* the simple is not spatial. If so, it is useless to apply the divisibility of space to disprove simplicity.

(which results in a *quaternio terminorum* in the conclusion)." (196) A *quaternio terminorum* is a syllogism with four terms instead of three. It has the following form:

A=B
C=D
A=D[35]

How is Kant guilty of *quaternio terminorum*? The criticism is that Kant changes the meaning of "space." Earlier in the *Critique of Pure Reason*, Kant said that space is sole and single. It does not have discrete parts.[36] It was properly equated with Continuity. But in the second antinomy, this point has been forgotten. Now space has infinite parts and is itself a composition of them. Hence, Kant's proposition is (A) all composites are in (B) space (conceived as continuous); (C) space (conceived as made up of parts) is (D) infinitely divisible. Therefore, (A) composites are (D) infinitely divisible.

Furthermore, Kant held that we know only phenomena – never the thing-in-itself. Space is a condition for the possibility of phenomena. Hence, if "substance" means sensuous material, we are discussing only phenomenal substance, not substance-in-itself. So the disproof of simplicity amounts to this: sensual experience shows us only what is composite. What is simple is not empirically discoverable.[37]

When Kant's argument is liberated from "all pointless redundancy and tortuousness," (197) the proof of the antithesis ("everything is divisible") assumes space is Continuity, because substance is placed in space. In the proof of the thesis, however, space is not continuous. Rather, "substances are *absolute ones*." (197) The thesis asserts Discreteness. The antithesis asserts Continuity. When substance, space, time, etc., are taken as discrete, their principle is the indivisible One. When they are taken as continuous, infinite division is possible.

Continuity contains the atom within it, however. If division is always a possibility, there must be some atom to divide. A discrete thing must

---

[35] For example, (A) all politicians are (B) managers; (C) all administrators are (D) sybarites; therefore all (A) politicians are (D) sybarites. IRVING M. COPI & CARL COHEN, INTRODUCTION TO LOGIC 206 (11th ed. 2002).

[36] CRITIQUE OF PURE REASON, *supra* note 4, at A22-3/B37-8.

[37] Thus, in the thesis, "the sensible (continuity and parts of space) is intellectualized (by composition and the concept of substance) and [in] the antithesis the intellectual is sensibilized." Llewelyn, *supra* note 34, at 90.

exist before divisibility, with its golden axe, cleaves it in twain. Likewise, Discreteness contains Continuity. In it, the ones are purely simple and hence identical to each other. The sameness of the ones is precisely Continuity. As Figure 11(b) shows, "each of the two opposed sides contains its other within itself and neither can be thought without the other." (197) Neither side, taken alone, has the truth. The truth lies only in their unity – which is shown in Figure 11(c).

In the end, Kant leaves the solution of the antinomy to one side. According to Hegel, each side of the antinomy should have nullified itself (as each is by now a True Infinite). In this activity, each side is "in its own self only the transition into its other, the unity of both being *quantity* in which they have their truth." (199)

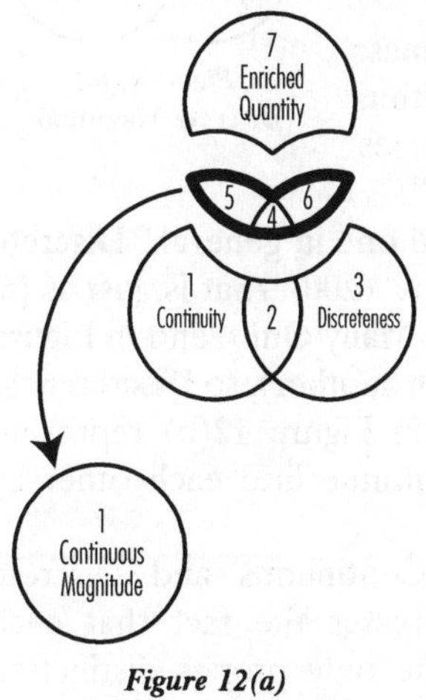

Figure 12(a)
Continuous Magnitude

B. Continuous and Discrete Magnitude

Continuity "requires the other moment, discreteness, to complete it." (199) Yet Continuity is not merely the *same as* but is *distinct from* Discreteness. Hence, we must extract *difference* from the middle term and consider it in isolated form. Of Figure 12(a), Hegel writes that Quantity is "a concrete unity only in so far as it is the unity of *distinct* moments. These are . . . not to be resolved again into attraction and repulsion, but are to be taken as . . . remaining in its unity with the other, that is, remaining in the *whole*. (199) Here Hegel emphasizes that Figure 12(a) is more advanced than Figure 10(b), which featured Attraction and Repulsion. Attraction and Repulsion exhibited Being-for-self. Each expelled its other so that each could be by itself. Now Continuous Magnitude is part of a community, even as it asserts its individuality within that community. As Continuous Magnitude, Continuity is "no longer only a moment but the whole of quantity." (199) The addition of the word "magnitude," then, signifies "determinateness in quantity." (201) Accordingly, Figure 12(a) shows an advance over Figure 11(a), where the positedness of the extremes was not yet manifest. This justifies the isolation of Figures 12(a) and (b) as separate official steps in the Logic.

Continuous Magnitude is *immediate* Quantity – taken as a whole. But immediacy is only a sublated, *ideal* immediacy: "immediacy is a determinateness the sublatedness of which is quantity itself." (200) When we place the emphasis on this recollected Determinateness, we obtain Discrete Magnitude. Like Continuous Magnitude, Discrete Magnitude is to be taken as a unified whole, with a double moment of Continuity and Discreteness within it:

> Quantity is in itself asunderness, and continuous magnitude is this asunderness continuing itself without negation as an internally self-same connectedness. But discrete magnitude is this asunderness as discontinuous, as interrupted. (200)

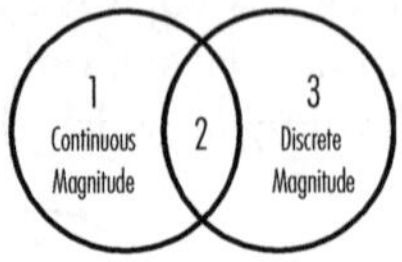

Figure 12(b)
Discrete Magnitude

Notice the new domesticity of the extremes. Each now admits to its subordinate role within a community, whereas, earlier, the extremes selfishly insisted on being "for themselves."

If Continuous Magnitude is "the manifold one in general," Discrete Magnitude is "posited as the *many of a unity*." (200) That is, just as [5, 6] in Figure 9(c) was both the Void and the Many Ones, and in Figure 10(c) [5, 6] was Repulsion (of each One from another), so Discreteness in Figure 11(b) and Discrete Magnitude in Figure 12(b) represent *many* discrete ones which nevertheless continue into each other by virtue of their complete sameness.

There is a "usual" interpretation of Continuous and Discrete Magnitude that Hegel disfavors. It suppresses the fact that each extreme contains its fellow inside it.[38] The only proper distinction between Continuous and Discrete Magnitude is that, in Continuous Magnitude, determinateness is merely implicit, while in Discrete Magnitude, determinateness is posited. "Space, time, matter, and so forth are continuous magnitudes in that they are repulsions from

[38] Terry Pinkard, who calls for a complete rewriting of Hegel's analysis of Quantity, is guilty of this fault. Pinkard denies that Hegel's Continuity is connected to the modern mathematical notion. PINKARD, *supra* note 11, at 44. This is precisely wrong. The continuity of a curve (which makes it differentiable) is exactly what is at stake here. Pinkard wants to recast Hegel in the language of Bertrand Russell's set theory: "Continuity would only be another way of talking of the one, and discreteness would only be another way of talking of the many." *Id.* at 44. This misses the main point. Continuity is the activity of a thing going outside of itself and into the other while remaining itself. This is the hallmark of True Infinity, which is missing from Pinkard's account.

themselves, a streaming forth out of themselves which at the same time is not their transition or relating of themselves to a qualitative other." (200) Each one of these possesses the *possibility* that, at any time, the One may be posited in them. Time's One would be *presence*. As a Continuous Magnitude, time holds open the possibility that it can be frozen. (Indeed, since time annuls all moments, there must be a moment before it to annul.) Discrete Magnitude, on the other hand, *expressly* posits presence as a necessary component of time.[39]

C. Limitation of Quantity

Discrete Magnitude is One. It is also a plurality of Ones that repel each other. But each of these Ones is quite the same as any other. Hence, the Ones "continue" from one into the other. When we focus on the oneness of Discrete Magnitude, we behold an "*excluding* one, a limit in the unity." (201) But Limit has long been sublated. Hence, Discrete Magnitude is "immediately not limited; but as distinguished from continuous magnitude, [1] is a determinate being [2, 3], a something, with the one [3] as its determinateness and also as its first negation and limit." (201) Not only is Discrete Magnitude plainly a determinateness, considered as [2, 3], but even in its isolated form [3] it is still a determinateness, because Discrete Magnitude fully remembers its ideal moment of being the Many Ones. Furthermore, even as [3] is posited as the Many Ones, still it is One and, as such, is Limit and first negation to its own being-in-itself [2].

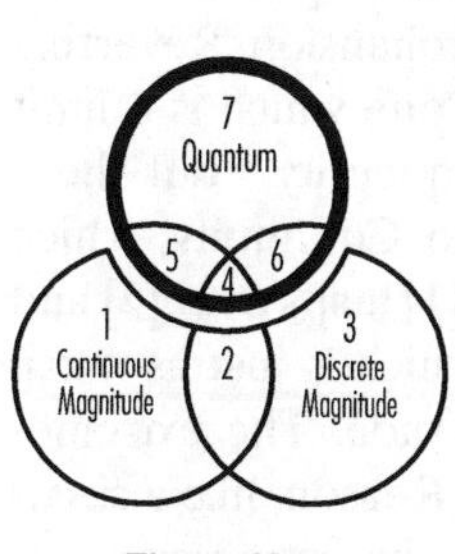

Figure 12(c)
Quantum

[39] Joining Walter Kaufman, who denies the triune structure of the Logic, Andrew Haas complains that "'Continuous and Discrete Magnitude' has only two moments and not three." HAAS, *supra* note 25, at 79; WALTER KAUFMANN, HEGEL: A REINTERPRETATION 33 n.97 (1978). This is technically accurate. The opening chapter on Quantity has three principal sections but only two revolutions. The truth of Continuous and Discrete Magnitude will be revealed in the last section of the chapter. The test, however, should not be whether each revolution is honored by a subhead, but whether the revolutions, wherever they occur, are driven by a rigorous sequence of the Understanding, Dialectical Reason, and Speculative Reason. We have already seen that Hegel does not always dedicate a subsection to a single revolution. Several subsections have already had multiple revolutions. Some – such as this one – have less than one full revolution.

If we take [3], in Figure 12(b), as "enclosing, encompassing limit," (201) it is self-related and is the negation in Discrete Magnitude [2, 3]. [3] is "the negative point itself." (201) But Discrete Magnitude is also Continuity, "by virtue of which it passes beyond the limit, beyond this one [3], to which it is indifferent." (201) This speculative moment leads to Figure 12(c), of which Hegel writes: "Real discrete quantity is thus *a* quantity, of quantum – quantity as a determinate being and a something." (201) Quantum is to Pure Quantity what Determinate Being was to Pure Being,[40] and chapter 5 is to Quantity what chapter 2 was to Quality – a display of Dialectical Reason. Quantum is, in effect, determinate Quantity.

Does Speculative Reason work in Figure 12(c) in the same way it did in the Quality chapters? Recall that, at first, the extremes modulated back and forth. Speculative Reason then named the movement and produced the middle term. Later, the extremes turned on themselves and self-erased (the Finites). Speculative Reason named this self-erasure as the True Infinite. Now it appears that Speculative Reason has operated on [2, 3] without considering the role of [1].

Hegel ends the chapter by correcting this misapprehension. Reverting back to [3] for a moment, Hegel holds that this "one which is a limit includes within itself the many ones of discrete quantity." But these Many Ones are sublated. [3] serves as a limit to Continuity, which Continuity leaps over with ease. Since Continuity [1] leaps over [2] and enters into [3], [3] likewise leaps back into [1], which is just as much Discrete Magnitude as it was Continuous Magnitude. The extremes equally leap out of themselves, and so Speculative Reason, like a circus ringmaster, still names the activity it witnesses in the extremes.

---

[40] As Hegel specifically emphasizes. EL § 101 Remark.

5
Quantum

We now commence what is, by far, the longest,[1] most maddening chapter in the *SL* – Quantum. At the end of chapter 4, Hegel derived Quantum. Quantum becomes Number – "quantity with a determinateness or limit in general." (202) Quantum/Number will melt, thaw, and resolve itself into a pair of terms unfamiliar to the modern ear – Extensive and Intensive Quantum, sometimes called Extensive and Intensive Magnitude. Intensive Quantum is also called Degree. Degree is indeed the ladder to all high design. Quantum's intensity will yield Quantitative Infinity and the infinitely small or large number, which can never be named. When we reach this unnameable thing, Quantum has recaptured its Quality. Quality *is* independence from outside determination. Whereas as the middle chapter of Quality saw Being chasing away its own content, the middle chapter of Quantity will do the opposite – it will recapture some measure of its content.

A. Number

Quantum has Limit, but only in *ideal form*: "The very nature of quantity as sublated being-for-self is *ipso facto* to be indifferent to its limit. But equally, too, quantity is not unaffected by the limit or by being quantum; for it contains within itself . . . the one, which . . . is its

---

[1] Henry Paolucci, *Hegel and the Celestial Mechanics of Newton and Einstein*, in HEGEL IN THE SCIENCES 55, 63 (Robert S. Cohen & Marx W. Wartofsky 1984) ("book-length").

limit." (202) So Quanta are Continuous and indifferent to Limit but they also have Discreteness. Ten is distinct from nine. But ten what? The number ten has no content *except that* it is not nine or eleven.

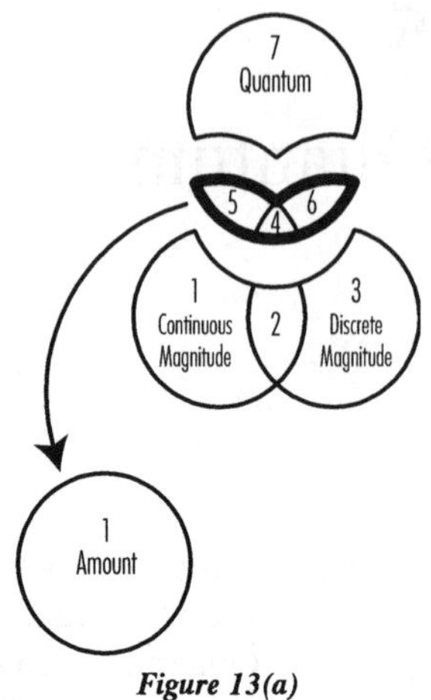

Figure 13(a)
Amount

Quantum, then, contains within itself the moment of the One.[2] "This one is thus the principle of quantum." (202) It is "(a) *self-relating*, (b) *enclosing* and (c) *other-excluding* limit." (202) When posited in all these three determinations, Quantum is Number.

The Understanding sees Quantum as *a continuous discrete magnitude* – "limit as a *plurality*." (203). It isolates this plurality as Amount. In Figure 13(a), Quantum contains the Many Ones. Across this plurality, Number is continuous. In Amount, Quantum determines itself as unique from other pluralities. "Ten" proudly boasts that it is uniquely "ten" and *not* some other number.

Amount is a plurality – of what? Units![3] Hence, "ten" is really ten units, or *10 = 10x1*. Hence, we immediately derive Figure 13(b). "*Amount* and *unit* constitute the *moments* of number." (203) This brings us to Number in Figure 13(c).

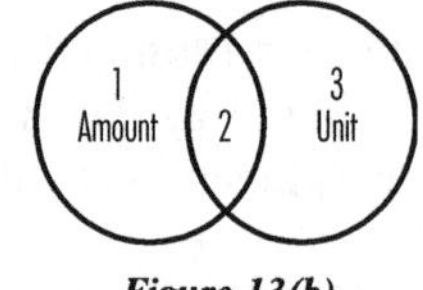

Figure 13(b)
Unit

Number, Hegel, says, is a "complete positedness." (203) Positedness represents a self-erasing True Infinite that presupposes there *is* an other that constitutes its content. Thus, ten is simply *not* nine or eleven; it *posits* its being in all the other numbers. The existence of these numbers is presupposed. It is also a "complete *determinateness*, for in it the limit is present as a specific *plurality* which has

---

[2] One commentator goes so far to suggest that the first three chapters of the *SL* are entirely dedicated to establishing this one proposition. Michael John Petry, *The Significance of Kepler's Laws*, in HEGEL AND NEWTONIANISM 485 (Michael John Petry ed., 1993).

[3] G.R.G. MURE, THE PHILOSOPHY OF HEGEL 119 (1965). ("Any whole number is the 'discerning' of a sum within a continuous multiplicity of self-equal units, within an endless flow in which the unit endlessly repeats itself").

for its principle the one, the absolutely determinate." (203) Determinateness represents a cruder stage – "being" which admits a unity with non-being but which refuses to self-erase: "In the sphere of determinate being, the relation of the limit to [Determinate Being] was primarily such that the determinate being persisted as the affirmative on this side of its limit, while the limit, the negation, was found outside of the border of the determinate being." (203) Putting these points together, Number is a True Infinite. It becomes something other (positing); its being is determined externally, by all the numbers it is not. Yet it also stays what it is (Determinate Being); for this very reason, ten does not change into nine or eleven.[4]

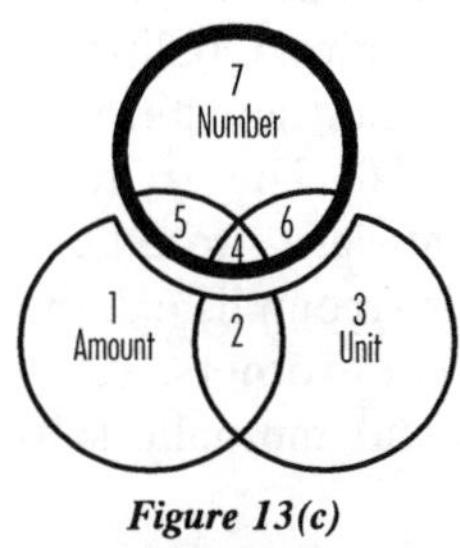

Figure 13(c)
Number

Hegel has said that Number is a "complete determinateness" because of continuity. How so? Because, just as Attraction fused the Many into One,[5] so Continuity fuses the plurality into One. Hence, Number [4-7] is made into One by Continuity. Yet this One refers both to itself and all the other Units within it. Equally, this One's being might be viewed as continuous plurality [4, 5, 6] or the negative unity [7] that holds it together. Either way, because it is complex, Number is a determinateness. Quantum is now beginning to recapture some of the content that Being-for-self shed from itself in Repulsion.

With regard to Amount, Hegel asks how the Many Ones (of which Amount consists) are present in Number. In effect, Amount assumes an external counter, who breaks off Amount for his own purposes and isolates it from the many other Amounts that could have been isolated.[6] For example, the counter, for reasons of his own, counts to 100. This amount is thus isolated from 99 or 101 by some external "counting" force. Of counting to 100, Hegel writes:

> In the quantitative sphere a number, say a hundred, is conceived in such a manner

---

[4] ANDREW HAAS, HEGEL AND THE PROBLEM OF MULTIPLICITY 117 (2000) ("The concept of quantum . . . is not merely quantitative. Indeed, if number can show itself as qualitative, then it is because every quantitative difference (numerical e-quality and inequality) is always also a qualitative difference").

[5] Figure 10(a).

[6] "[T]he breaking off [in the counting] of the many ones and the exclusion of other ones appears as a determination falling outside the enclosed ones." (203)

> that the hundredth one alone limits the many to make them a hundred . . . [But] none of the hundred ones has precedence over any other for they are only equal – each is equally the hundredth; thus [the units] all belong to the limit which makes the number a hundred and the number cannot dispense with any of them for its determinateness. (203-4)

Unit, then, is Limit to Amount. 100 is simultaneously *one* Unit, but it also implies 100 equal units contained therein, each one of which lays equal claim to being the 100th.[7]

Number has a limiting Unit – the 100th Unit. By this, 100 differs from 99 or 101. The distinction, however, is not qualitative. Qualitative distinctions are self-generated. Quantitative distinction is externally imposed. The units do not count *themselves* to 100. They require "comparing *external* reflection" (204) – a mathematician – to do the counting. 100 is thus externally derived. Once this is accomplished, the 100th one "remains returned into itself and indifferent to others." (204) All of the Units within the Amount are equal and mutually self-repelling.

Hegel emphasizes that Number is an "absolutely determinate" Unit, "which at the same time has the form of simple immediacy and for which, therefore, the relation to other is completely external." (204) In 5+7=12, nothing inherent in 5 demands that it be brought into relation with 7. Besides being this immediacy, Number is also a determinateness – a mediation. Its moments are Amount and Unit.

Geometry and Arithmetic

In a long Remark, Hegel distinguishes and relates geometry and arithmetic. Geometry, the science of spatial magnitude, has Continuous Magnitude as its subject matter. Arithmetic trafficks in Discrete Magnitude. Perhaps this can be seen in the Cartesian plane. On the Cartesian plane, $xy=100$ is a rectangle and so is continuous through its allotted space. The arithmetical 100 is, like valor, the better part of discreteness. It is simply neither 99, 101, nor any other Number.

Spatial geometry nevertheless implies and continues into arithmetic. Hegel returns to the "point" that from the geometric point springs the

---

[7] A related point was made by Hegel earlier with regard to Attraction. In chapter 3, Hegel stated that the Many Ones were fused into One by Attraction. We were not, however, to assume that, amidst the Many Ones, a single Caesar had risen to become the imperial One. Rather, each of the Many Ones had an equal claim to the laurel crown of One. *Supra* at 128. So it is with the Units in Number.

line of its own accord, when the point is *Limit* of the line. Limit is a correlative term; when point is designated as Limit, we must think of what point *limits* – the line.[8] Hegel thinks that this demonstration indicates that spatial magnitude – *i.e.*, geometry free and clear of Number – generates numerical magnitude. Spatial magnitude (the point, which is also a numerical *one*) immediately sublates itself and continues on to become the line of many Ones. Accordingly, geometry is never entirely isolated from arithmetic, just as Continuity is never entirely isolated from Discreteness.

Arithmetic trafficks in Number without contemplating what Number is. To arithmetic, Number is "the determinateness which is indifferent, inert; it must be actuated from without and so brought into a relation." (205) Arithmetic is the tool of an outside will. Numbers do not add themselves.

Arithmetic has various modes of relation – addition, multiplication, etc. Arithmetic not being a speculative enterprise, the transition from one of these modes to another is not made prominent. These modes can, however, all be derived from the very concept of Number: "Number has for its principle the one and is, therefore, simply an aggregate externally put together, a purely analytic figure devoid of any inner connectedness." (205) Thus, an external "counter" breaks off the counting at, say, 100, thereby isolating this Number from the infinite others the counter may have preferred. All calculation is essentially counting.[9]

Suppose we have two numbers chosen by the counter. Whatever relation these two numbers have must also be supplied by the counter. The counter must decide whether to subtract or divide these numbers. Number has qualitative difference within it – Unit and Amount. But the identity or difference between these Numbers is entirely external.

Numbers can be produced in two ways. We can count up the units and produce a number. Or we can subdivide from an aggregate already given. That is, given 100, we can negate 70 of the Units and isolate 30. In both cases, counting is implicated. One is positive counting. The other is negative counting.

In counting, the Amount of the Unit is set arbitrarily. We can count five single Units. Then we can decide to count some more – seven more units are added, or 7+5=12. In this expression, the relation of

---

8 *Supra* at 85-6.

9 Hegel calls mathematical operations as "telling a tale" about numbers. EL § 103.

7 and 5 is a complete contingency. These two Numbers are quite indifferent to each other. They were simply put together by the mathematician for her own private purposes – an arranged, not a romantic, marriage.[10]

We can also count six Units of two (multiplication). So multiplication also counting. What counts as a Unit (one, two, etc.) is externally decided by the mathematician. Counting, however, is tedious and so, to save time, we learn by rote what the products of two numbers are.

The sum 7+5=12 is chosen by Hegel because Kant used this very sum to demonstrate that arithmetic is a *synthetic* proposition.[11] Hegel, however, thinks it is analytic:

> The sum of 5 and 7 means the mechanical . . . conjunction of the two numbers, and the counting from seven onwards thus mechanically continued until the five units are exhausted can be called a putting together, a synthesis, just like counting from one onwards; but it is a synthesis wholly analytical in nature, for the connection is quite artificial, there is nothing in it or put into it which is not quite externally given. (207-8)

It is not clear to me why Hegel is so heated in denouncing Kant's arithmetic's synthetic nature. Was Kant not simply saying that 5 and 7 do not add themselves – that mathematical knowledge "is obtained not through definition but through intuition and construction"?[12] And is not Hegel in complete agreement that addition is a matter for the external counter? In short, "synthesis" to Kant is what "externality of content" is for Hegel.[13]

Hegel also objects to Kant's view that arithmetic is *a priori*, *i.e.*, not derived from experience.[14] If we synthesize *experience*, then knowledge

---

[10] In analyzing "analysis," Hegel will summarize this point by announcing that arithmetic is basically "one" – magnitude as such. If this "one" is rendered plural, or unified into a sum, this is done externally. "How *numbers* are further combined and separated depends solely on the positing activity of the cognizing subject." (790)

[11] IMMANUEL KANT, CRITIQUE OF PURE REASON A10/B14 (Paul Guyer & Allen W. Wood trans., 1990).

[12] Lewis White Beck, *Can Kant's Synthetic Judgments Be Made Analytic?*, in KANT: A COLLECTION OF CRITICAL ESSAYS 3, 21 (Robert Paul Wolff ed., 1967).

[13] Hegel thinks that 5+7 already contains the command to count 7 more beyond 5. The result contains nothing more than what was in 5+7 – the command to keep counting. So arithmetic is analytic only. *Infra* at 581-2. The difference between Kant and Hegel could be put this way. Kant focuses on the fact that a mathematical sentence must be constructed. Hegel focuses on what the sentence requires *after* it is constructed.

[14] CRITIQUE OF PURE REASON, *supra* note 11, at A76-7/B102.

is merely empirical, contingent, and *a posteriori*. Hegel attacks the very distinction of *a priori* and *a posteriori*: every sensation "has in it the *a priori* moment, just as much as space and time, in the shape of spatial and temporal existence, is determined *a posteriori*." (208) This plaint is related to Hegel's criticism of the unknowable thing-in-itself. For Hegel, our knowledge of objects is always a unity of our perception (*a posteriori*) and the authentic integrity of the object (*a priori*).[15]

Hegel praises, after a fashion, Kant's notion of the synthetic *a priori* judgment as belonging "to what is great and imperishable in his philosophy." (209)[16] But what he likes about it is the speculative content Kant never brought to light. In the synthetic *a priori* judgment, "something differentiated . . . equally is inseparable." (209) Identity is "in its own self an inseparable difference." (209) If arithmetic is *a priori* synthetic, then 7+5 can be kept apart and also *not* kept apart simultaneously. Difference and identity each have their moments in 7+5=12. But this identity of identity and difference[17] is no mere property of the *a priori* synthetic judgment. It is just as much present in intuition – *a posteriori* judgment. Hence, the compliment to Kant is, at best, ironically tendered.

In any case, Hegel attacks Kant's assertion that Euclidean geometry is synthetic. Kant conceded that some of its axioms[18] are analytic, but he held as synthetic the proposition that the shortest way between two points is a straight line.[19] In contrast, Hegel has held that, at least if

---

[15] These demonstrations are made in the early chapters of the *Phenomenology*. G.W.F. HEGEL, PHENOMENOLOGY OF SPIRIT (A.V. Miller trans. 1977).

[16] *See* RICHARD DIEN WINFIELD, AUTONOMY AND NORMATIVITY 43 (2001) ("As Kant recognized, philosophy could obtain new knowledge of what was necessarily and universally the case only insofar as concepts could be set in binding relation to what was not their immediate identity").

[17] The identity of identity and difference – a key Hegelian slogan – is expressly considered in the Doctrine of Reflection. *Infra* at 284-98.

[18] Euclid gave these four postulates upon which all geometry is based: (1) a straight line segment can be drawn joining any two points. (2) Any straight line segment can be extended indefinitely in a straight line. (3) Given any straight line segment, a circle can be drawn having the segment as radius and one end point as center. (4) All right angles are congruent. DOUGLAS R. HOFSTADTER, GÖDEL, ESCHER, BACH: AN ETERNAL GOLDEN BRAID 90 (1979). A fifth was added, but it turned out to be subjective, not objective: (5) If two lines are drawn which intersect a third in such a way that the sum of the inner angles on one side is less than two right angles, then the two lines inevitably must intersect each other on that side if extended far enough. *Id*. The suspension of the fifth postulate leads to non-Euclidean geometry.

[19] CRITIQUE OF PURE REASON, *supra* note 11, at A10/B14.

point is *Limit*, the line generates itself. This self-generated line is inherently simple. "[I]ts extension does not involve any alteration in its determination, or reference to another point or line outside itself." (208) Euclid was therefore right to list amongst his postulates the *analytical* proposition that the shortest way between two points is a straight line. Because this definition includes nothing heterogeneous to geometry, Euclid's proposition is analytic.[20]

Subtraction and Division. Subtraction and division are negative counting. In subtraction (*i.e.*, 12-5=7) the Numbers are indifferent or "generally unequal" to each other. That is, given a line segment of 12 units, we could have subdivided the line as 7 and 5, or 9 and 3, or 11 and 1, *etc*. The two Numbers into which a line of 12 units is subdivided bear no relation to each other. If we make the two Numbers (qualitatively) equal, then we have entered the province of division. Suppose we isolate a Unit – say, 6. The Number 12 now has a Unit of 6 and an Amount of two.

Division is different from multiplication, however. In multiplication, where 6·2=12, it was a matter of indifference whether 6 counted as Amount or Unit.[21] Division would seem to operate on another principle. 12/6 is not the same as 6/12. But, remembering that negative counting takes 12 as given, it is likewise immaterial whether the divisor (6) or quotient (2) is Unit or Amount. If we say 6 is Unit, we ask how often 6 is contained in 12. If we say that the quotient (2) is Unit, then "the problem is to divide a number [12] into a given amount of equal parts [here, 6] and to find the magnitude of such part." (210)

Exponents. In multiplication and division, the two Numbers are related to each other as Unit and Amount. Yet Unit and Amount are "still immediate with respect to each other and therefore simply *unequal*." (210) If we insist that Unit and Amount be equal, we will complete the determinations immanent within Number. This last mode of counting is the raising of Number to a power. Take 6^2=36. Here, "the several numbers to be added are the same." (210) Should not Hegel have said the *two* numbers (6 and 6) to be *multiplied* are the same? No. Hegel has said that multiplication is counting, like addition. Hence, we shall count six units. Each unit has six in it. In short, we count from 1 to 6. Next we count from 7 to 12, and so forth. Eventu-

---

[20] Antonio Moretto, *Hegel on Greek Mathematics and the Modern Calculus*, in HEGEL AND NEWTONIANISM, *supra* note 2, at 154.

[21] This is the "commutative" property of multiplication (*ab* = *ba*).

ally we reach 36. The point is that in squaring 6, Amount equals Unit.

The square is "in principle those determinations of amount and unit which, as the essential difference of the Notion, have to be equalized before number as a going-out-of-itself has completely returned into self. [T]he arithmetical square alone contains an immanent absolute determinedness." (211) Here we have a preview of what, in chapter 6, will be called the *Ratio of Powers*. The premise is that if we insist that Unit equals Amount, Number resists outside manipulation and thereby shows its *quality*. If $x^2=36$, then *x must* be {6, -6}. The Ratio of Powers is the last stage of Quantity. Here is where Quantum recaptures its integrity and wins independence from the counters who have tyrannized it prior to that point.[22]

Hegel concludes the Remark with this observation:

> It is an essential requirement when philosophizing about real objects to distinguish those spheres to which a specific form of the Notion belongs . . . [O]therwise the peculiar nature of a subject matter which is external and contingent will be distorted by Ideas, and similarly these Ideas will be distorted and made into something merely formal. (212)

This warning means that speculative philosophy and higher mathematics each has its sphere. Each should be wary of permitting the other to interfere unduly with its project.

Number is "the absolute determinateness of quantity, and its element is the difference which has become indifferent." (212) The indifference of Number implies that Number finds its content imposed upon it from the outside. Thus, arithmetic is an analytical science. It does not contain the Notion. Arithmetical combinations are not intrinsic to the concept of Number "but are effected on it in a wholly external manner." (212) It is therefore "no problem for speculative thought, but is the antithesis of the Notion." (213) When thought engages in arithmetic, it is involved in activity which is the "extreme externalization of itself, an activity in which it is forced to move in a realm of thoughtlessness and to combine elements which are incapable of any necessary relationships." (213)

Numbers are supposed to be educational, but Hegel thinks this is overrated. Occupation with numbers "is an unthinking, mechanical one.

---

[22] *See* G.W.F. HEGEL, THE JENA SYSTEM, 1804-5: LOGIC AND METAPHYSICS 122 (John W. Burbidge & George di Giovanni trans. 1986) ("However, a square is precisely not a quantum, not a part, not something externally limited").

The effort consists mainly in holding fast what is devoid of the Notion and in combining it purely mechanically." (216) Calculation dulls the mind and empties it of substance. It is so thoroughly debased, Hegel notes, "that it has been possible to construct machines which perform arithmetical operations with complete accuracy." (216)

B. Extensive and Intensive Quantum

(a) Their Difference

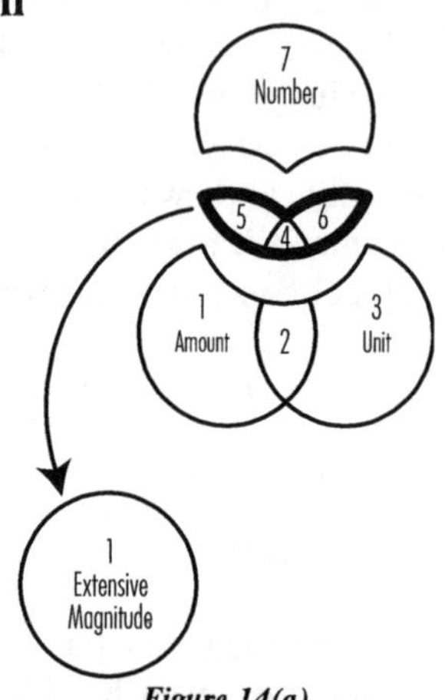

Figure 14(a)
Extensive Magnitude (Extensive Quantum)

In Figure 13(c), Number's determinateness is isolated in Amount [4, 5, 6].[23] [7] is Number's Unit, which can be taken as a plurality, since Amount continues right on through it. Number is nothing *but* Limit – five is nothing but *not* six or four. Accordingly, Quantum, "with its limit, which [Limit] is in its own self a plurality, is *extensive magnitude*." (217) If 100 represents a Unit (or set) of 100 Units, Extensive Magnitude represents the 100 individuals within the set. Extensive Magnitude is "an amount of one and the same *unit*." (217) Number, in contrast, was a *plurality* – not yet fused by the Understanding into Unit.

Dialectical Reason complains that Extensive Magnitude cannot alone account for the determinateness of Number: "the many as a plural asunderness or discreteness does not constitute the determinateness as such." (218) There is an "externality which constituted the ones as a plurality." (218) A *counter* has determined to stop counting at 100 Units. But there is inherently in Number a being-for-self that resists externality, which now "vanishes in the one as a relation of number to its own self." (218) Thus, 100 is *many* but it is also *one*. This "intensive" quality of Number is Intensive Magnitude or Degree.

Of Figure 14(b), Hegel writes, "the limit of quantum, which as extensive had its real determinateness in the self-external amount, passes over into *simple determinateness*." (218) Extensive Magnitude

---

[23] [6] is beyond Amount proper. But, since Unit is just as much Amount as Amount, [6] can be included as part of the determinateness which Hegel names as Amount.

says, "I am not a unity." Unity therefore flees the precinct of Extensive Magnitude and takes sanctuary in the temple of Intensive Magnitude.

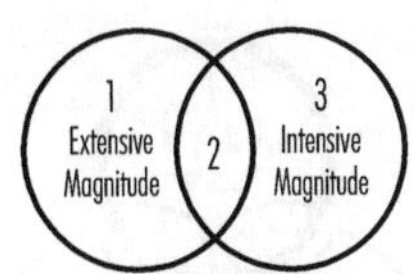

Figure 14(b)
Intensive Magnitude (Degree)

Earlier, Number was Amount – a plurality made into one. Within Amount, each of the Many Ones was equal to any other. None was *primus inter pares*. If Amount is 100, each One could claim to be the determining 100th. Amount did not exhibit determinateness as such (Limit), and so Amount collapsed into Unit.

Degree, in contrast, is a specific magnitude. It is the 100th One, selected by the counter as the determinant. As such, it "is not an aggregate or plural *within itself*." (218) Rather, it is a "plurality only in principle." (218) In Degree, "determinate being has returned into being-for-self." (218)

The determinateness of Degree must be expressed by a Number. It must be, for example, the 100th One. In this expression, 100 is not Amount. It is only unitary (or a Degree). Now, a single One emerges as *primus inter pares* over all the other Ones.

Upon what meat does this Degree feed that it hath grown so great? Degree has Being-for-self. It resists Continuity in a way that, in the earlier stages of Quantity, the Many Ones could not. But, at the same time, its content is external to itself. If it is the 100th, the "100" is outside of it. Hegel gives the example of a circle with 360 degrees. The determinateness of any one degree "derives essentially from the many parts outside it." (222) One degree of the circle depends on its relation with the others.[24]

Extensive Magnitude owns plurality – the externality of Degree.[25] Although this plurality is likewise One, Extensive Magnitude could not express this truth. It sheds unity to its outside (Degree), just as Degree sheds plurality to *its* outside. So Degree [3] and Extensive Magnitude [1] are doing the same thing – expelling their own content, which we

---

[24] Justus Hartnack writes "If we talk about . . . a room temperature of 20° C, then the degrees below 20° never formed an extensive magnitude that was absorbed in that degree of temperature . . . " JUSTUS HARTNACK, AN INTRODUCTION TO HEGEL'S LOGIC 32 (Lars Aagaard-Mogensen trans., 1998) The opposite is true. The Extensive Magnitude of 20° is *precisely* all the degrees that 20° excludes.

[25] HAAS, *supra* note 4, at 118 (multiplicity "is interior to extensive quantum . . . Here number reveals the quality of quantum: determinate *indifference* . . . to is own multiplicity (within or without)").

can now interpret as [2]. "Although extensive and intensive quanta are differentiated according to the ways in which they express the multiplicity that forms their other, they are identical insofar as they both are characterized by qualitative indifference".

The expulsion of [2] yields a middle term: "Number as a one . . . excludes from itself the indifference and externality of the amount [*i.e.*, the plurality] and is self-relation as *relation through itself to an externality*." (219) The self-erasure of Number is on display.

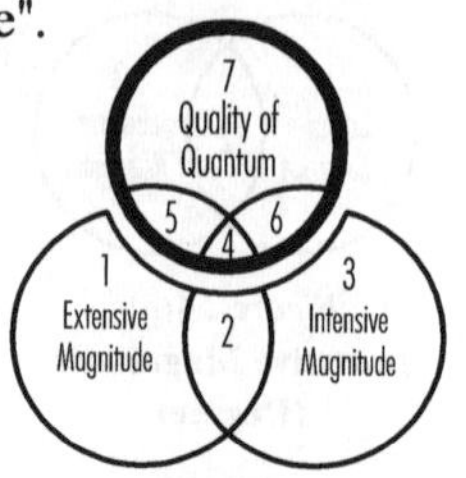

Figure 14(c)
The Quality of Quantum

In this middle term, "quantum has a reality conformable to its Notion." (219)[26] Speculative Reason shows that the soul of Quantum is that its content is imposed from the outside, even as it has a unitary nature that resists imposition.[27] And what is the nature of its resistance? Quantum cannot be made to surrender its absolute openness to outside determination. "[E]xternality itself is its specific 'quality,' its 'being-in-itself.' Its quality is thus the very negation of Quality's possibility . . . "[28]

Hegel also hints at a shift in the nature of Degree's content that should be made explicit. Extensive Magnitude referred to a set of individuals entirely within the set (but not the set itself).[29] In our earlier example, it referred to the 100 individuals corralled together. Degree, however, does not refer *just* to those 100 individuals. It refers to *all* the other degrees in the universe: "degree is a unitary quantitative determinateness *among* a plurality of such intensities which, though differing from each other, [are] essentially interrelated so that each has its determinateness in this continuity with the others." (219) A Degree's meaning, then, depends on the infinite set, not on any specific set designated by an outside will. Continuity between Degrees makes possible an "ascent and descent in the scale of degrees of a continuous progress, a flux, which is an uninterrupted, indivisible

---

[26] "Reality" must be taken loosely here, as it gave way to ideality in chapter 2.

[27] HAAS, *supra* note 4, at 123 ("the qualitative aspect of quantity means qualitative opposition, that is, having determinateness in another, by means of its non-being, having its being by virtue of its nothing . . . ").

[28] GIACOMO RINALDI, A HISTORY AND INTERPRETATION OF THE LOGIC OF HEGEL 166 (1992).

[29] This is what set theory calls a *fusion*, as opposed to a *collection*, which adds *entity*. MICHAEL POTTER, SET THEORY AND ITS PHILOSOPHY 20 (2004).

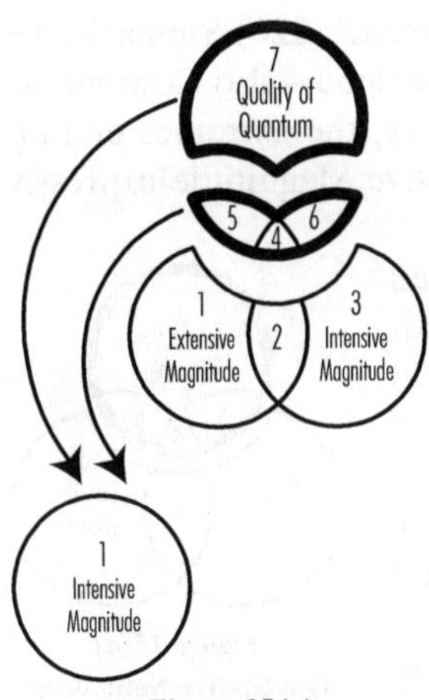

Figure 15(a)
Intensive Magnitude (Degree)

alteration; none of the various distinct degrees is separate from the others but each is determined only through them." (219) The Quality of the Quantum may in general stand for the dependence of Quantum on otherness for its determinateness, but it also puts on the table the infinite set of Quanta.

(b) Identity of Extensive and Intensive Magnitude

The last section addressed the *difference* between Extensive and Intensive Magnitude. Ironically, this difference was gathered together in a middle term: the very Quality of Quantum is indifference to Quality, to content. Now we explore this Quality-as-indifference and discover the self-identity lurking within Figure 14(c).

Our next move is the positive version of Intensive Magnitude, according to which "Degree is not external to itself within itself." (220) If Degree [1] sheds its content [2, 3], it equally retains what it sheds. Unlike Number, which has Amount in general, Degree has a *particular* amount.

Degree sheds all the other degrees, with which it is continuous. Thus, 20° sheds all the other degrees, even while it retains for itself the "20" – which uniquely distinguishes 20° from all others. These excluded degrees[30] can be called, collectively, Extensive Magnitude (or Extensive Quantum) – this time taken negatively.

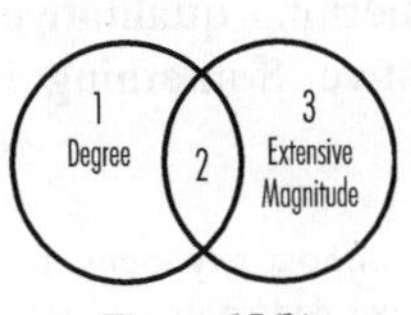

Figure 15(b)
Extensive Magnitude

Thanks to the analysis of the Quality of Quantum, we can see that "extensive and intensive magnitude are thus one and the same determinateness of quantum; they are only distinguished by the one having amount within

[30] HAAS, *supra* note 4, at 167 (Degree implies "a reference to a numerical series, to a quantitative manifold; but this latter is posited 'outside' its self-identity . . . whereas in the case of Number it was posited 'within' in").

itself and the other having amount outside itself." (220) Similarly, we previously saw that Unit and Amount were the same – also Continuous and Discrete Magnitude. Throughout Quantity, the extremes end up being each other – here Intensive and Extensive Magnitude expressly have swapped places.

The middle term of the obversely charged extremes is the Qualitative Something. This unity is "self-related through the *negation of its differences*." (221) This is the standard move of Speculative Reason, as developed in and after the True Infinite. It names the very act of the extremes in erasing themselves and stating what they are not.

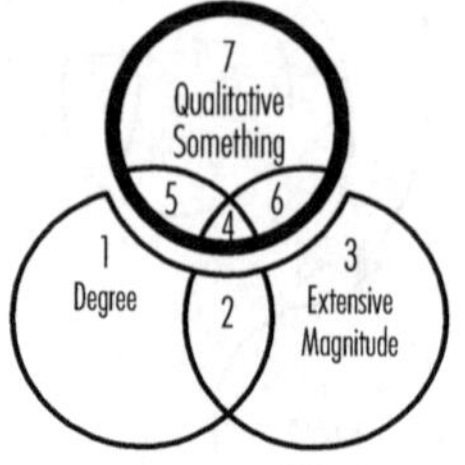

Figure 15(a)
Qualitative Something

Something appeared in Figure 2(c) – the unity between Quality and Negation. Furthermore, *Quality* has long been sublated. Why does Hegel use the phrase "*qualitative something*" (221)? Why not the *quantitative* something?

Quality was supposed to have stood for independence from otherness. Degree (in both its ummediated and mediated forms) still has its content outside itself. The Qualitative Something is precisely that content – but taken negatively as simply the opposite of Quantum. Degree depends on that Qualitative Something to define what it is.[31] The Qualitative Something should be taken as the infinite set of Numbers. Degree depends on negating some of these so that it can be some specific Amount. But whatever Amount Degree takes on, the Qualitative Something remains what it is. Such a Something is indifferent to its quantitative limit in Degree. Degree can be increased or decreased without affecting the Something (since the Something is the infinite set of Numbers). That makes the Something qualitative, even though made up of Quanta. The Qualitative Something is therefore substrate to the more primitive quanta.

> Quantum, number as such, and so forth could be spoken of without any mention of its having a something as substrate. But the something now confronts . . . its determinations, through the negation of which it is *mediated* with itself, as *existing*

---

[31] *See* ERROL E. HARRIS, AN INTERPRETATION OF THE LOGIC OF HEGEL 138 (1983) ("The contradiction of Quantum is that its internal determination rests in a limit which in its very nature posits an external other, on which the precise magnitude of the quantum is as much dependent as it is on what precedes the limit").

> *for itself* and, since it has a quantum, as something which has an extensive and an intensive quantum. (221)

As Quantum, the Qualitative Something is subsistent; the original Something of Figure 2(c) was not. Quantum is, after all, a True Infinite. *It stays what it is as it becomes something different.* In the Qualitative Something, we have a Something that positively resists the transgression of its Limit – which the original Something could not achieve.[32]

(c) Alteration of Quantum

Middle terms have proved to be names for *activities*. Accordingly, the Qualitative Something names the inability of Extensive and Intensive Magnitude to stand on their own. These self-erase and transfer their being to other Quanta – to the infinite set of Quanta on which Number's meaning is dependent.

The Qualitative Something is contradictory. It is posited as being "the simple, *self-related* determinateness which is the negation of itself, having its determinateness not within itself but in another quantum." (225) In other words, if the Qualitative Something is going to express itself, it *must* express itself in some Quantum. After all, it is the infinite set of Quanta. It has its entire determinateness outside of itself and in these Quanta.

If the Qualitative Something has its determinateness outside of itself, then it is "in absolute continuity with its externality, with its otherness." (225) From this perspective (while admitting that the Qualitative Something is immune from other quanta), the Qualitative Something can *both* "transcend every quantitative determinateness" (225) *and* be altered. In fact, Hegel says its external aspect *must* alter. More precisely, any Quantum that is proposed to be the "final" member of the infinite set can be displaced by a larger Quantum. The identity of this final member is therefore bound to alter.

In the Qualitative Something, Quantum reveals its "express character" (225) of impelling itself beyond itself into its external guise. That is, the Qualitative Something is quantitative determinateness. It consists in

---

[32] HAAS, *supra* note 4, at 119 ("quantum is infinite self-negation, production, creation, self-expulsion, a coming-out of itself as increase/decrease, that is, the moving, growing, living limit . . . that determines quantity insofar as it infinitely supersedes, determines and takes care of itself").

undergoing increase or decrease: "The quantitative determinateness continues itself into its otherness in such a manner that the determination has its being only in this continuity with an other; it is not a *simply affirmative* limit, but a limit which *becomes*." (225) When Quantum impels itself beyond itself, it becomes another Quantum. But this new Quantum is "a limit which does not stay." (225) The new Quantum becomes yet another Quantum, *"and so on to infinity."* (225)[33] With this we are ready to move onto Hegel's monumental treatment of Quantitative Infinity, an untravelled country from whose bourne few travelers return.

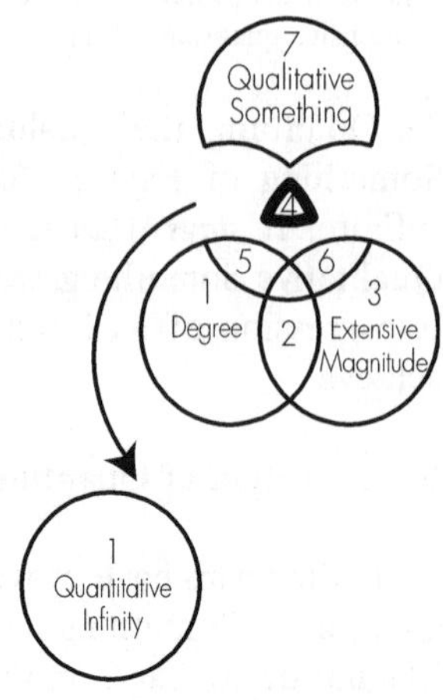

Figure 16(a)
Quantitative Infinity

C. Quantitative Infinity
(a) Its Notion

The Understanding sees the Qualitative Something as Quantitative Infinity, an *activity* wherein Quantum goes beyond itself and remains with itself. The beyond is a Quantum – the Infinitely Great or Infinitely Small Number, depending which way we are counting. This beyond "is

---

[33] Alan Paterson complains that the "successor function" and "induction principle" are not accounted for in Hegel's logic. Alan L.T. Paterson, *The Successor Function and Induction Principle in a Hegelian Philosophy of Mathematics*, 30 IDEALISTIC STUDIES 30 (2002). But are not these very ideas the stuff of the Qualitative Something? (The successor function is "the function that sends a natural number to its successor. The induction principle (roughly) says that we can assert a fact about *all* natural numbers if we know that it is true for the first one (0) and that its truth is preserved when we go from a number to its successor." *Id*. at 26).

Does Hegel have an account of ordinality in his theory of number? Paterson suggests the answer is no, and he may be right. Perhaps the concept of "more or less" is simply supplied by external reflection of the counter. *See* JENA LOGIC, *supra* note 22, at 23-4 ("And the rise and fall on the ladder of degree or of extensive magnitude is only to be regarded as an external indicator"). This is not to say that externally arranged numbers have no unique qualities. In the *Jena System*, Hegel gives as an example the fact that $8 = 2^3$ and $9 = 3^2$. By adding one, we travel from 2^3 to 3^2. But the addition of one to some number other than 8 reveals no such quality. *Id*. at 24.

not only the other of a particular quantum, but of quantum itself." (225) This remark, which looks forward to the Infinitely Great/Small Number two steps hence, raises a question. Given that Quantum inherently finds its being outside itself and given that this outside (the Qualitative Something) must be expressed as some Number, why does it follow that these numbers must get progressively larger or progressively smaller? Why can't, for instance, the Qualitative Something alternate from 10 to 11 back to 10 *ad infinitum*?

There are several answers to why an infinite process should be motivated toward a highest or smallest number. First, it is the nature of the Understanding to hazard a *complete* proposition of the absolute. In order to complete the infinite set of Quanta, it therefore becomes necessary to head for the Infinitely Great/Small Number that would (if it existed) complete the set. Second, Quantum goes outside itself, but the return trip is not to the original Number but to some *other* Number *ad infinitum*. This conclusion is compelled by the lesson learned in the One and the Many. There, the old One from which the new One springs does not go out of existence. Rather, the new One produces yet another One, creating infinitely Many Ones. Through the law of sublation, the same result must occur in Quantitative Infinity, though Hegel nowhere says so explicitly. Finally, there is our old friend the silent fourth, which is entitled to go forward or backward in the logical steps but elects to go forward in order to make the system unfold. For at least these reasons, Quantitative Infinity is *purposive* activity. It therefore *chooses* to aim for the goal of completion. Accordingly, Hegel says that Quantitative Infinity is "an ought-to-be; it is by implication determined as being for itself, and this being-determined-for-itself is rather the being-determined-in-an-other, and, conversely, it is the sublation of being-determined-in-an-other, is an *indifferent* subsisting for itself." (226) Completion, then, is the theme of Quantitative Infinity – one that is doomed to fail. Quantitative Infinity is the "impulse to go beyond itself to an other in which its [final] determination lies." (226)[34]

What is the difference between Qualitative and Quantitative Infinity? In Qualitative Infinity, [1] and [3] stood abstractly opposed to each other. Their unity was only "in-itself" – implicit. Quantitative Infinity,

---

[34] *See* HAAS, *supra* note 4, at 136 ("And as the continuity of quantum expresses itself equally in endless extensity and in endless diminution, the progression is interminable either way, though neither the infinitesimal nor the infinite is ever attainable").

in contrast, continues within itself even as it passes into its beyond. It is a True Infinite.[35]

(b) The Quantitative Infinite Progress

In Figure 16(b), Dialectical Reason denies that Quantitative Infinity is capable of completion. It points out that the complete expression of the infinite set of Quanta requires some Infinitely Great Quantum, but, as it is Quantum, this too must go out of itself. In this dialectical stage, the extremes fall into a Spurious Infinity – a senseless modulation toward a new Infinite Great/Small Quantum that is supposed to complete the set of Quanta. This time, the Spurious Infinite takes place within the context of a True Infinite: "in the sphere of quantity the limit [*i.e.*, Quantum] continues itself into its beyond and hence, conversely, the quantitative infinite too is posited as having quantum within it." (227) In other words, at the level of Quantity, the Infinite goes beyond itself *and* stays within itself as it travels into this beyond.

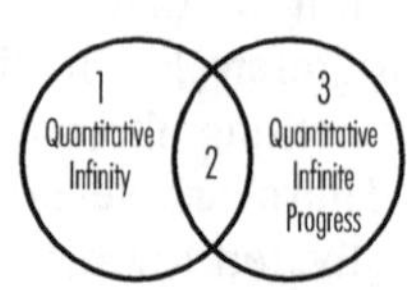

Figure 16(b)
Quantitative Infinite Progress

The Quantitative Infinite Progress intends but never reaches the Infinitely Greatest/Smallest Number. A *qualitative moment* prevents Quantitative Infinity from reaching completion. In fact, Hegel emphasizes, there can be no question of getting *nearer* to the goal of the Infinitely Great/Small, since it is by definition unreachable.[36] "No matter how much the quantum is increased, it shrinks to insignificance." (228) The Quantitative Infinite Progress is "not a real advance but a repetition of one and the same thing, a positing, a sublating, and then again a positing and again a sublating, an

---

[35] It is possible to quibble with Errol Harris's remark that, to resolve Quantum's contradiction, "the externality of the other must somehow be internalized to produce a true infinity." HARRIS, *supra* note 31, at 136. At this stage, the extremes each have long since been True Infinites. What Quantum must express is that it is as much its other as it is its own self. Hence, Harris is right that the external must be internalized, but the external must also *stay* external as it becomes internal. Furthermore, it is already a True Infinite and therefore need not, at this late stage, become one.

[36] Lacanians will recognize this qualitative moment as structurally similar to trauma – a stumbling block, or piece of the Real, which prevents the patient from completing his fantasy. BRUCE FINK, THE LACANIAN SUBJECT: BETWEEN LANGUAGE AND *JOUISSANCE* 26 (1995).

impotence of the negative, for what it sublates is continuous with it, and in the very act of being sublated returns to it." (228)

What is the bond between the two extremes of Figure 16(b)? Simply that each flees from the other, "and in fleeing from each other they cannot become separated but are joined together even in their flight from each other." (228) The alternating Quanta are in a *relationship* (*Verhältnis*).

The High Repute of the Progress to Infinity

No admirer of Quantitative Infinity, Hegel complains that "in philosophy it has been regarded as ultimate." (228) With Kant obviously in mind, Hegel remarks, "this *modern* sublimity does not magnify the *object* – rather does this take flight – but only the *subject* which assimilates such vast quantities." (229) In *The Critique of Judgment*, Kant defined sublimity as a subjective feeling that one could actually know the thing-in-itself (which is impossible).[37] Hence, the sublime exalts the subject (and not the object). What makes thought succumb to the shock and awe of the Quantitative Infinite Progress "is nothing else but the wearisome repetition which makes a limit vanish, reappear, and then vanish again . . . giving only the feeling of the *impotence* of this infinite or this ought-to-be, which *would* be master of the finite and *cannot*." (229)

Kant compares the sublime to the withdrawal of the individual into his ego, where absolute freedom opposes the terrors of tyranny and fate. At this moment, Hegel says, the individual knows himself to be equal to himself.[38] Of this ego's self-equality, Hegel agrees that it is "the reached beyond; it has *come to itself*, is *with* itself, here and now." (230) This negative thing – the ego – has "determinate reality . . . confronting it as a beyond." (231) In this withdrawal, "we are faced with that same contradiction which lies at the base of the infinite progress, namely a returnedness-into-self which is at the same time immediately an out-of-selfness, a relation to its other as to its non-being." (231) How is this so? Recall that Quantitative Infinity stayed within itself, but this "in-itself" had no content. All content was in the beyond. Simultaneous with its being-for-self, Quantitative Infinity was

---

[37] IMMANUEL KANT, CRITIQUE OF JUDGMENT 100-1 (J.H. Bernhard trans., 1951); *see also* IMMANUEL KANT, CRITIQUE OF PRACTICAL REASON 142 (T.K. Abbott trans., 1996).

[38] This is probably a reference to *Critique of Practical Reason*, *id.* at 191.

pure flight into the beyond and hence a constant modulation between the moment of flight and the moment of return. Ego, it turns out, is the same thing.

Here we have the Lacanian view of the subject as suspended between the realm of the Symbolic (*i.e.*, being) and the Real (*i.e.*, nothing).[39] The subject finds part of its selfhood in its beyond. The subject desires wholeness but cannot achieve it. This is what the Lacanians called symbolic castration.[40] Hegel saw this some 150 years before Lacan. For Hegel, the relation of the subject to its non-being (*i.e.*, the Symbolic realm) "remains a *longing*, because on the one side is the unsubstantial, untenable void of the ego fixed as such by the ego itself, and on the other, the fulness which though negated remains present, but is fixed by the ego as its beyond." (231)

Hegel especially complains that Kant equates morality with Quantitative Infinity. The antithesis just described – autonomy *v* heteronomy – is a *qualitative* opposition. Kant supposes that the subject, suspended between them, can get closer to moral autonomy but can never reach it:

> the power of the ego over the non-ego, over sense and outer nature, is consequently so conceived that morality can and ought continually to increase, and the power of sense continually to diminish. But the perfect adequacy of the will to the moral law is placed in the unending progress to infinity, that is, is represented as an *absolutely unattainable* beyond, and this unattainableness is supposed to be the true sheet-anchor and fitting consolation; for morality is supposed to be a struggle, but such it can be only if the will is inadequate to the moral law which thus becomes a sheer beyond for it. (231)

Here is a concise critique of Kant's doctrine of "radical evil." According to Kant, the ego is forever tainted with pathology. It can never finally purge itself of pathology but can only struggle for moral purity.[41] Kant even goes so far as to deduce the immortality of the soul from the very fact that all eternity is required for the soul to reach perfection.[42]

---

39 FINK, *supra* note 36, at 59 ("*The subject is nothing but this very split*"). Kant, in turn, describes the "I" – the *universal* aspect of personality, which Lacanians insist is *not* the subject. Mladen Dolar, *The Cogito as the Subject of the Unconscious*, in SIC 2: COGITO AND THE UNCONSCIOUS 12 (Slavoj Žižek ed., 1998).

40 SLAVOJ ŽIŽEK, THE INDIVISIBLE REMAINDER: AN ESSAY ON SCHELLING AND RELATED MATTERS 46-7 (1996).

41 *See* Jeanne L. Schroeder & David Gray Carlson, *Kenneth Starr: Diabolically Evil?*, 88 CAL. L. REV. 653 (2000).

42 CRITIQUE OF PRACTICAL REASON, *supra* note 37, at 148, 155.

Hence, Kant is guilty as charged. He has reduced morality to Quantitative Infinity.

With regard to Kant's opposition of morality and nature, Hegel complains that they are put forth as "self-subsistent and mutually indifferent." (231) "At the same time, however, both are moments of *one and the same being*, the ego." (232) Hence, the very constitution of the Kantian subject is the Lacanian split subject.[43] This contradiction is never resolved in the infinite progress. "[O]n the contrary, it is represented and affirmed as unresolved and unresolvable." (232) This Kantian standpoint is "powerless to overcome the qualitative opposition between the finite and infinite." (232) The subject counts it as nothing that it has supposedly progressed toward the unattainable perfection of pure morality.

Kant's Antinomy of the Limitation of Time and Space

We have seen that Hegel has small regard for Kant's four antinomies of reason. Now he repeats his conclusion that the antinomies are spurious qualitative infinities, each side of which is a one-sided view of the truth. The antinomy at hand is Kant's first – the world is (or is not) limited in time and space.[44] This antinomy is the one Kant associates with the category of quantity[45] (which is why Hegel discusses it here).

Hegel's first proposition about this antinomy is that the "world" could have been left out of the discussion. Kant could have addressed time as such and space as such.[46] Hegel also proposes that Kant could have restated his antinomy as follows: (1) there is a limit, and (2) limit must be transcended – two things Hegel says are true of Quantity generally.

The Thesis. In terms of *time*, Kant proves the thesis (the world has a beginning) by showing that the antithesis is impossible. If time has no beginning, then at any given point of time, an "eternity" – an infinite series of temporal measures – has lapsed. The lapse of an infinite

---

[43] Lacanians give Kant the greatest credit for this. Schroeder & Carlson, *supra* note 41, at 671-80.

[44] CRITIQUE OF PURE REASON, *supra* note 11, at A426-7/B454-5. Of this antinomy, Henry Allison remarks, "These are the most widely criticized of Kant's arguments . . . ." HENRY E. ALLISON, KANT'S TRANSCENDENTAL IDEALISM: AN INTERPRETATION AND DEFENSE 36 (1983).

[45] *Supra* at 150 n.31. Kant calls time and space "the two original *quanta* of all intuition." CRITIQUE OF PURE REASON, *supra* note 11, at A411/B438.

[46] Henry Allison disagrees and thinks that synthesis of a *world* out of infinite moments is central to Kant's argument. ALLISON, *supra* note 43, at 39.

series is impossible. Therefore, time must have a beginning.

Hegel proposes that Kant's proof of the thesis is only the direct assertion of what was to be proved. With regard to time (it has a beginning), the very assertion that time has *points* presupposes that time is already limited. One point in time is "now." It designates the end of the past and the beginning of the future. With regard to the past, "now" represents a qualitative limit. But why, Hegel implicitly asks, should "now" be a *qualitative* limit? Suppose we say that "now" is a *quantitative* limit. Time would then continue on from the past, over the "now," and into the future, because Quantitative Infinity always leaps o'er the vaunts and firstlings of any limit. Quantitative Infinity "not only must be transcended but *is* only as the transcending of itself." (235) If time is Quantitative Infinity, "then the infinite time series would not have *passed away* in it, but would continue to flow on." (235) A switch from qualitative to quantitative limit destroys Kant's argument.

But, Hegel continues, let us concede that *now* is a qualitative limit to the past. It would then also be the beginning of the future. But this is precisely the thesis to be proved – that time has a beginning. So what if this beginning was preceded by a deceased past? This does not affect the point. The past is conceived as radically separate from the future. Hence, the very introduction of "now" – a point in time – presupposes time's beginning.

The antithesis. Kant also proves also proves the antithesis by ruling out the opposite (apagogy). In terms of *time*, suppose the world has a beginning. Before the beginning, the world does not exist. An existing thing, however, cannot originate from nothing. Nothing comes from nothing. Kant's argument for the antithesis likewise merely asserts what must be proved, Hegel thinks. Kant's argument presupposes that, just because the world exists, it must have "an *antecedent condition* which is in time." (236) This is the very antithesis to be proved. Also, when Kant insists that nothing can come from nothing – when "the *condition* is sought in empty time" (236) – this means that the world is taken as temporal and hence limited. Something always precedes the "now" of the world. There is always a yesterday. All of this, Hegel charges, is presupposed. It is the antithesis itself.

Kant's demonstration of the antithesis in terms of space is likewise rejected. A limit in space implies there must be a "void space." We thus have a relation of the finite world to void space. But this is a relation of things to *no object*. A thing cannot have a relation to nothing – nothing is not a *thing*. Consequently the world is not limited in space.

Hegel finds again that Kant has merely restated the proposition – not proved it. Kant assumes that space is not an object, and that, in order to prevent the impossible relation of object to non-object, the object must continue itself as far as space does. This means that Kant thinks space must never be empty – the world must continue into it. Yet this is precisely the antithesis restated.

Hegel concludes this remark by criticizing Kant for "subjectivizing" contradiction. For Kant, the four antinomies do not occur in nature. Rather, they occur in consciousness. (Time and space, Kant says, are the very conditions of possibility for subjective intuitions).[47] Of this subjectivization of the first antinomy, Hegel writes:

> It shows an excessive tenderness for the world to remove contradiction from it and then to transfer the contradiction to spirit, to reason, where it is allowed to remain unresolved. In point of fact it is spirit which is so strong that it can endure contradiction, but it is spirit, too, that knows how to resolve it. (237-8)

The "so-called world" (238) *is* contradictory, Hegel insists. The world "is unable to endure it and is, therefore, subject to coming-to-be and ceasing-to-be." (238)

(c) The Infinity of Quantum

The middle term between Quantitative Infinity and its Infinite Progress is the Infinitely Great and/or Infinitely Small (*i.e.*, the differential δx in the derivative $\delta y/\delta x$) The Infinitely Great/Small is the destination that the Quantitative Infinity implies. It is a Quantum, but "at the same time it is the non-being of quantum. The infinitely great and infinitely small are therefore pictorial conceptions which, when looked at more closely, turn out to be nebulous shadowy nullities." (238) This should be clear even to non-speculative thinkers. In the Quantitative Infinite Progress, the counting mathematician aims to reach infinity. That infinity has "being" is thus presupposed by the counter who aims to reach this end. Yet this end will never be reached. It is a non-being. This contradiction – the non-being of infinity – is now

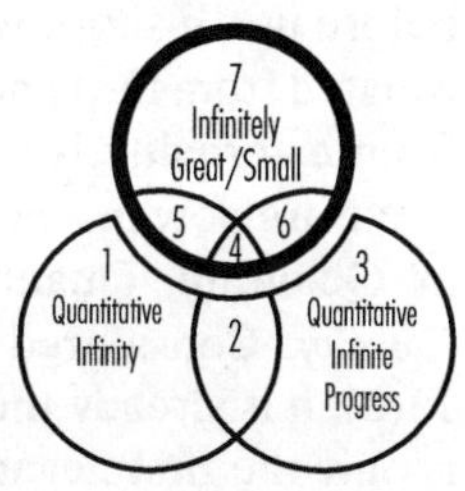

Figure 16(c)
Infinitely Great and Infinitely Small

---

[47] CRITIQUE OF PURE REASON, *supra* note 11, at A22-4/B37-9

explicitly present, and so is the very nature of Quantum.

When Quantum reached Intensive Magnitude (Degree), Quantum "attained its reality." (238) Degree is "unitary, self-related and determinate within itself." (238) As unitary, Degree sublated (*i.e.*, negated) its otherness and its determinateness. These were external to Degree. This self-externality was the "*abstract non-being* of quantum generally, the spurious infinity." (238) In other words, Degree yielded the Qualitative Something which in turn yielded Quantitative Infinity. If we now examine Figure 16(b), we witness each of the extremes erasing itself and establishing its non-being in the other, while expressly continuing itself in the other, so that each was a Quantum as well as not a Quantum. Hence, "this non-being of quantum, infinity, is thus limited, that is, this beyond is sublated, is itself determined as quantum which, therefore, in its negation is with itself." (238)

The in-itself of Quantum is therefore self-externality.[48] Externality determines what Quantum is. The Infinitely Great/Small thus illustrates the notion of Quantum. It is "not there" and yet treated as if it *is* there: "In the infinite progress as such, the only reflection usually made is that every quantum, however great or small, must be capable of vanishing, of being surpassed; but not that this self-sublating of quantum, the beyond, the spurious infinite itself also vanishes." (239)

How is this claim justified? Why has the Spurious Infinite vanished? Consider what the Infinitely Great/Small is: the end that the Quantitative Infinite Progress could never reach. If we have that end before us, then we do *not* have the Quantitative Infinite Progress before us. In short, we can take Figure 16(c) in terms of [7] – which is isolated from the vanished Quantitative Infinite Progress. This isolation from externality is a sign that *Quantity has recaptured its Quality*.

We are now in a position to summarize the progress across the realm of Quantum. Quantum (via Quantity) is the negation/sublation of Quality. Considered immediately, as in, say, Figure 11(a) or Figure 13(a), it is already the first negation – in *positivized form*. But Quantum is only the first negation *in principle*. It is posited as a "being," and "its negation is fixed as the infinite, as the beyond of quantum, which remains on this side as an *immediate*." (239) But it is the "beyond" that is *overtly* the first negation. In the Infinitely Great/Small, "quantum [is] determined in conformity with its Notion, which is different from

---

48 *Cf.* the Ought in Figure 5(c), where the in-itself of the Finite was that it must cease to be and become other.

quantum determined in its immediacy." (239) The Infinitely Great/Small is externality itself, brought inward as a moment of Quantity. For this reason, "externality is now the opposite of itself, posited as a moment of quantity itself – quantum is posited as having its determinateness in another quantum by means of its non-being, of infinity." (239) Because Quantum has brought its externality inward, "it is *qualitatively* [what] it is." (239)

Quantum "has reverted to *quality* [and] is from now on qualitatively determined." (239) Its quality (per Hegel, its "peculiarity") is that its determinateness (or content) is external. Quantum is "indifferent" to outside determination. But the outside is now in: "Quantum has infinity, self-determinedness, no longer outside it but within itself." (239)

In Figure 16(c), Quantum is "posited as repelled from itself, with the result that there are two quanta which, however, are sublated, are only as moments of *one unity*." (240) In chapter 6, Quantum will now appear as double – as Quantitative Ratio. This ratio is the relation between Quality (internality) and Quantity (externality). Quality forms a partnership with Quantity. The middle term between this partnership is Measure – the stuff of chapter 7.[49]

Calculus

At the end of chapter 5, Hegel inserts three long Remarks, the first

---

[49] Charles Taylor expresses his dissatisfaction with Hegel's entire discussion of Quantum, and we are now in a position to answer his queries. Taylor writes:

> But one might think that Hegel is a little cavalier in his transitions here. Granted that Quantity is the realm in which things are indifferent to their limit, how does that show that quanta must go beyond themselves, and change? (whatever that means). And even if they do so endlessly, even granted Hegel's dislike for the "bad" infinity of the endless progress, does this show a contradiction requiring resolution by a higher category?

CHARLES TAYLOR, HEGEL 248 (1975). The answer to the first question is, since quanta are True Infinites, their very function is to go beyond their limit (while staying what they are). This act is the Quality of the Quantum. But this does not necessarily mean that numbers change and that arithmetic is promiscuous and subjective. Quanta have limits within themselves. Three does not melt into two. If the limit external to a quantum is exceeded, it is exceeded spiritually, not empirically. The answer to the second question is that the bad infinity's modulation between quanta is itself the higher category. As always, Speculative Reason names the autistic modulation of Dialectical Reason and underwrites progress to a higher level.

two of which are by far the longest Remarks in the *SL*. They cover the subject of calculus, which endlessly fascinated Hegel, because the differential δx – the Infinitely Small – embodies his theory that Being is in the process of vanishing.[50] In the main, Hegel will criticize nineteenth century calculus for its lingering dependence on geometrical ideas, and for the quantification of δx, which Hegel views as an undefined *quality* (not a quantity). Future generations of mathematicians would tend to agree.[51]

The calculus remarks are usually dismissed as "digression, at best"[52] and a self-indulgence – not unfair observations.[53] I have found few references to Hegel's views on the calculus, which nevertheless seem prescient for his day. Because these commentaries digress from the logical progression, analysis of these challenging Remarks is omitted.[54]

---

[50] The differential δx stands for the change in the variable *x*. As such, it is undefinable, because it is supposed to be infinitely close to (but distinguishable from) zero. Yet δx given δy (or $\delta y/\delta x$) is fully determinate. This point is important in understanding why the Infinitely Great/Small is a ratio. δx has its being in δy, and *vice versa*. The two become visible only when brought into conjunction.

[51] In this regard, Hegel remarks that mathematical necessity is inadequate. Mathematics does nothing but ward off heterogeneous elements – an effort that is itself "tainted" with heterogeneity. (40) The heterogeneous element warded off by mathematicians is the qualitative nature of δx. One commentator views the point of the calculus discussion as follows: Calculus cannot "yield the mathematics of nature which Hegel was looking for. [S]uch a mathematics can only take over what is qualitative from experience, it cannot develop it out of itself." Host-Heino Von Borzeszkowski, *Hegel's Interpretation of Classical Mechanics*, in HEGEL AND NEWTONIANISM, *supra* note 2, at 76.

[52] MURE, PHILOSOPHY, *supra* note 3, at 118.

[53] *E.g.*, CLARK BUTLER, HEGEL'S LOGIC: BETWEEN DIALECTIC AND HISTORY 110-1 (1996) ("Suspecting Hegel of wishing in part to demonstrate his mastery of mathematics and science to contemporaries and colleagues . . . "). Those who prefer scorn to thought will find merit in Bertrand Russell's dismissal:

> Hegel (especially in his *Greater Logic*) made a quite different use of mathematics. [He] fastened upon the obscurities in the foundations of mathematics, turned them into dialectical contradictions, and resolved them by nonsensical syntheses. It is interesting that some of his worst absurdities in this field were repeated by Engels in the *Antidüring*, and that, in consequence, if you live in the Soviet Union and take account of what has been done on the principles of mathematics during the last one hundred years, you run a grave risk of being liquidated.

Bertrand Russell, *Logical Positivism*, in LOGIC AND KNOWLEDGE: ESSAYS 1902-1950 368-9 (Robert Charles Marsh ed., 1950).

[54] For a detailed analysis, see David Gray Carlson, *Hegel's Theory of Quantity*, 23 CARDOZO L. REV. 2027, 2093-148 (2002).

6
Quantitative Relation

Quantum is an infinite being. It changes *quantitatively* but it remains what it is *qualitatively*.[1] Ergo, "the infinity of quantum has been determined to the stage where it is the negative beyond of quantum, which beyond, however, is contained within the quantum itself. This beyond is the qualitative moment as such." (314) At this stage, Quantum is a *unity* of the qualitative and the quantitative.

Quantum in its advanced stage is *relation* (*Verhältnis*), which Hegel's translator calls *Ratio*. The relation or Ratio in question is Quality and Quantity. Ratio is "the contradiction of externality and self-relation, of the affirmative being of quanta and their negation." (315) Its distinct feature is that it is "qualitatively determined as simply related to its beyond." (314) Quantum is continuous with its beyond, and the beyond is another Quantum. The relation between Quanta, however, is no longer externally imposed. These related Quanta have recaptured an integrity that more primitive Quanta did not have.

And what is their integrity? Their integrity is that they have no integrity. In becoming other, these Quanta show their true selves: they are as much other as they are themselves.

---

1 HERBERT MARCUSE, HEGEL'S ONTOLOGY AND THE THEORY OF HISTORICITY 64 (Seyla Benhabib trans. 1987) ("A being which is immediately identical with its respective quality such as to remain the same throughout all its qualitative transformations, is no longer qualitatively but quantitatively determined").

> The flight of quantum away from and beyond itself has now therefore this meaning, that it changed not merely into an other, or into its abstract other, into its negative beyond, but that in this other it reached its determinateness, finding *itself* in its beyond, which is another quantum. (314)

Here Hegel implies that Quantum cannot distinguish itself without the aid of the Other. Therefore, the Other is as much the stuff of *self* as it is Other. Hence, in distinguishing the other, Quantum finds itself.[2] The quality of Quantum, then, is "its externality as such." (314)

At stake here is not just one Quantum and its beyond (another Quantum), but the *relation* between these two quanta. Quantum "is not only *in* a Ratio, but it is itself *posited as a ratio*." (314) Each extreme, then, has to be taken as a singularity and *also* as a mediation. The extremes have grown concrete.

Hegel trifurcates his Ratio chapter. First, we have Direct Ratio ($A/B=C$). Here the qualitative moment is not yet explicit. Rather, it shows the retrogressive mode of having its externality outside itself. Direct Ratio shows all the defects of the Understanding. Second is Indirect Ratio, or Inverse Ratio ($AB=C$). Here, where Dialectical Reason holds forth, modulation occurs between the quanta as they negate each other. Third is the Ratio of Powers ($A^2=C$). Here quantum (A) reproduces itself. When this middle term is posited as a simple determination, we have reached Measure – the unity of Quantity and Quality. At this moment, the rightward leaning chapters of Quantity give way to the centrist chapters of Measure.

The culmination of this chapter, then, is the Ratio of Powers – $A^2=C$. The middle term, however, is a definition of the absolute.[3]

---

[2] In this passage, Hegel echoes the most famous passage he ever wrote – the Lord-Bondsman dialectic in the *Phenomenology*. G.W.F. HEGEL, PHENOMENOLOGY OF SPIRIT (A.V. Miller trans. 1977). In this dialectic, two warriors try to subjugate each other. One succeeds and becomes the master, the other the slave. But the master discovers that the other is truly himself. The master is thus reduced to dependency. Likewise, in ratio, Quantum attempts to distinguish itself by expelling the Other, only to find that the Other is as much itself as itself is.

Errol Harris calls "The Quantitative Relation or Qualitative Ratio" a chapter that is "more technical than philosophical. ERROL E. HARRIS, AN INTERPRETATION OF THE LOGIC OF HEGEL 140 (1983). But perhaps he underestimates its importance. In any case, the Ratio of Powers, with which the chapter ends, is a very lucid and powerful demonstration of the qualitative moment in the heart of Quantity.

[3] Every proposition of the Understanding and Speculative Reason is a vision of the Absolute. Dialectical Reason, in contrast, is purely a critique of the Understanding's proposition. *Supra* at 92-3.

Shall we say, then, that the universe (*C*) is A^2? Yes, in a sense, if *A* stands for some "thing" (or Unit). This chapter – Quantitative Relation – in effect argues that all "things" define all other things, even while remaining a thing-in-itself. Hegel is therefore describing a universe of deeply contextual metonymic "things."[4]

A. The Direct Ratio

In Figure 17(a), Direct Ratio is immediate. An infinite being, it has qualitative being-for-self. To illustrate, take *2/7=C*. Hegel insists on calling *C* the exponent – a confusing choice of words. For mathematicians, *C* is a quotient. Where $A^3=C$, 3 is the exponent. What Hegel means by "exponent," however, is simply the relation between two quanta in a ratio.[5]

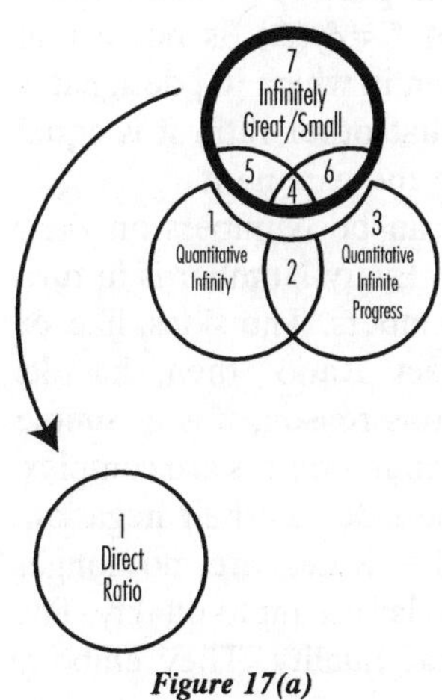

Figure 17(a)
Direct Ratio

In *2/7=C*, *C*'s value survives the increase of 2 and 7. For example, *4/14=C*. (For this reason, 2 and 7 have a *direct*, not an *inverse* relation.) This example shows that *C* has a "being" separate and independent from the sides of the ratio. Furthermore, 2 and 7 have nothing to do with each other. They were "combined" by the will of the mathematician. Given $C \neq 0$,[6] *any* pair of numbers could have been selected to represent *C*.

Yet Direct Ratio is also a relation of *quanta*. These quanta are *other*

---

[4] Terry Pinkard is scathing about the ratio of powers. He proclaims it "so idiosyncratic to Hegel's system that it offers little insight to anyone who has not accepted the entire Hegelian outlook – lock, stock and barrel. It is not one of the things that even Hegelians have seen fit to develop, and there is good reason for this lack of interest." TERRY PINKARD, HEGEL'S DIALECTIC 52 (1988) This criticism is out of order. If Hegel is developing a theory of metonymic meaning, this chapter – substrate to the concept of Measure – should not necessarily be expected to yield "useful" dividends to common sense. This "lemmatic" chapter does indeed further develop what Quality and even freedom are.

[5] Thus, "the exponent, simply as product, is *implicitly* the unity of unit and amount." (320-1)

[6] Zero, of course, is not a quantum but is the negation of quantum.

to the Direct Ratio, and so the determinateness of the ratio lies in an other. As a Quantum, *C*, in $C=A/B$, is the unity of Unit and Amount, per the law of sublation. Unit stands for Being-for-self; Amount stands for "the indifferent fluctuation of the determinateness, the external indifference of quantum." (315) Earlier, Amount and Unit were moments of Number. Hegel therefore refers to the sides of Direct Ratio as *less* than *C*, the exponent that determines their being. The integrity of the Direct Ratio therefore implies the servile dependence of the sides. Recall that Direct Ratio is the Understanding's interpretation of the Infinite Great/Small in Figure 16(a). The infinitely Small (δx) was unnameable. And when δy is part of a Direct Ratio ($C=\delta y/\delta x$), *C* is perfectly determinate. Yet $C=\delta y/\delta x$ "is not a real equation; it is rather an incomplete expression in which [*C*] designates only a ratio of which we do not yet know that other ratio it is equal to."[7] The sides of the ratio do not complete the exponent.

Yet the sides of the ratio, as in $2/7=C$, can be Numbers on their own. Hence, an infinite regress is before us. Every Number is in turn an Amount and Unit, which are in turn Numbers. The sides, like δx and δy, are never entirely present. Direct Ratio, then, has its qualitative and quantitative moments. For this reason, it is a "simple determinateness" (316) – a paradox, as determinatenesses are complex.

Hegel refers to this incompleteness of the sides as their negation. What this means is that the sides of the Ratio are no longer independent. Only the exponent of the Ratio lays claim to quality. The sides of the Ratio are the negative to that quality. They embody quantitative difference.

But, if the sides are incomplete, this does not mean that the *exponent*[8] is complete. *C* can be reduced to Unit or Amount which means that it too is incomplete. If $A/B=C$, then $A=BC$. *C* can take *A*'s place with ease. When it does, it becomes one of the sides – incomplete. *C*, therefore, is "not posited as what it ought to be. . . the ratio's qualitative unity." (317)

B. Inverse Ratio

If Figure 17(a) emphasizes Ratio's immediacy, Figure 17(b)

---

[7] Alain Lacroix, *The Mathematical Infinite in Hegel*, 31 PHIL. FORUM 298, 322 (2000).

[8] Here Hegel calls exponent "quotient." (317)

emphasizes its incompleteness, which Hegel names a sign of negativity. Direct Ratio's fault was its failure to be immediate and immune from outside manipulation. An external reflection had to determine whether *C* was exponent or one of the subordinate sides. Thus, in $C=A/B$, *C* is exponent. But it is Unit/Amount in $A=BC$.

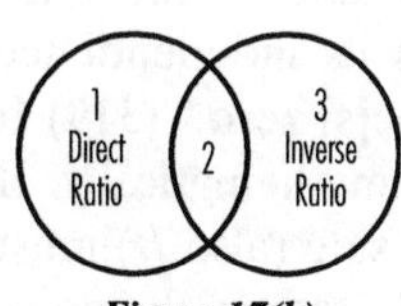

Figure 17(b)
Inverse Ratio

In the Inverse Ratio, the exponent is some *fixed* Quantum. The exponent does *not* migrate over to the other side of the equal sign. Apparently, we are not to multiply $A=BC$ by $1/C$, which would reveal the exponent to be no different from the Unit/Amount. Rather, we are to consider *A* as fixed.

Certainly it is odd that the fault of Direct Ratio – its openness to outside manipulation – becomes the virtue of Inverse Ratio, which depends on outside fixity to differentiate it from Direct Ratio. But recall that the Quality of the Quantum is precisely Quantum's openness to outside manipulation. In other words, the integrity of Quantum is its *lack* of integrity. That is what the fixity of the exponent represents.

When $C=A/B$, *A* and *B* had a *direct* relationship. If *C* stayed constant and *A* is increased, *B* also increased. Now, $A=BC$. If the exponent stays fixed, *B* and *C* are in an inverse relationship. If *B* increases, *C* falls in value. Indeed, *B* and *C* can fluctuate wildly. Fluctuation "is their distinctive character – in contrast to the qualitative moment as a *fixed* limit; they have the character of *variable* magnitudes, for which the said fixed limit is an infinite beyond." (320) But there is a limit to this inverse relationship. Whereas the mathematician can cause *B* to fall and *C* to rise, the mathematician cannot force *B* to zero. Otherwise, the exponent, which is supposed to be fixed, is destroyed.[9] This resistance of *B* (or *C*) to the mathematician's will is a sign that Inverse Ratio has recaptured its Quality.

Speculative Reason seizes upon this resistance of *B* and *C*. In this refusal of *B* and *C* to go to zero, they are *equal qualities* – immune from outside manipulation at least to this one small extent. Since $B=C$ as a qualitative matter, the in-itself of $A=BC$ is $A=BB$, or $A=B^2$ – the Ratio of Powers. Here the first *B* determines the value of the second *B*. The second reciprocally determines the value of the first. If $A=16$, the mathematician has no option but to admit that $B=\{4,-4\}$.

---

[9] Geometrically, *B* and *C* are in a hyperbolic relation. As one approaches zero, the other approaches an infinitely large number.

Each side of the Inverse Ratio, then, "limits the other and is simultaneously limited by it." (319) Yet once the side of the ratio achieves its in-itself – its potential – it establishes its independence from the other side. "[T]he *other* magnitude become[s] zero." (319) It vanishes. Obviously this last point cannot be taken mathematically. If one side (*B*) of the product (*BB*) is zero, the other side (also *B*) must likewise be zero, and B^2 is no longer equal to $A > 0$. Rather, the point is that the first *B* enjoys Being-for-self. It is indifferent to the second *B*, for whom it is a nothing – a void. But since $B=B$ qualitatively, *both* *B*'s are zero. They erase themselves and remove their being to a middle term.

Hegel summarizes the Inverse Ratio as follows: "the whole, as exponent, is the limit of the reciprocal limiting of both terms and is therefore posited as *negation of the negation*, hence as infinity, as an *affirmative* relation to itself." (320) Thus, the exponent is limit to the sides and the sides are likewise limit to the exponent. The negation of the negation is precisely the refusal of either side to disappear and become zero. A limit is now located in the sides of the ratio. These sides negate the superiority of the exponent. Previously incomplete, the sides now speak for themselves as to what they are (within the confines of the externally fixed exponent).[10]

Of the sides, Hegel makes two points: (α) Ratio has an "affirmative aspect," (321) – immunity or fixity in general. Yet, because each side of the ratio cannot be raised to equality with the exponent, each side is, in a sense, "fixed." This fixity – the refusal of *B* or *C* to equal *A*[11] – means that each side "is *implicitly* the whole of the exponent," (321)

---

[10] I disagree with Mure's analysis of Direct and Indirect Ratio, the sum total of which is as follows: "In Direct Ratio . . . the two quanta unified in the constant exponent increase or diminish together. In Indirect Ratio they vary inversely and so in closer relation." G.R.G. MURE, THE PHILOSOPHY OF HEGEL 120 (1965). The two sides of the Indirect Ratio are *not* in "closer relation;" the function of the Indirect Ratio is to emphasize the qualitative (not the quantitative) difference between either side and the exponent.

[11] Hegel writes that *B* and *C* "can increase and decrease relatively to each other; but they cannot become equal to the exponent . . . As thus the limit of their reciprocal limiting, the exponent is (α) their beyond, to which they *infinitely* approximate but which they cannot reach." (319-20) Rinaldi asks, if $A=16$ and $B=1$, does not $A=C$, contrary to what Hegel has said? GIACOMO RINALDI, A HISTORY AND INTERPRETATION OF THE LOGIC OF HEGEL 185 n.35 (1992). The answer is that *equality* cannot mean numerical equality. Rather, Hegel has in mind a qualitative inequality. *C* cannot fix itself, like *A* can. It can become infinitely large as *B* becomes infinitely small, but it can never be "for itself," like the exponent.

since the Inverse Ratio is all about fixity.[12] Yet (b) the same refusal is a negative moment. *B* and *C* are constituted by a Spurious Infinite, which frustrates the mathematician who strives to make them equal to the exponent. This resistance to manipulation is "the *negation* of the self-externality of the exponent." (321) This very resistance is the resultant middle term, which is "posited as preserving itself and uniting with itself in the negation of the indifferent existence of the quanta, thus being the determinant of its self-external otherness." (321)[13]

C. The Ratio of Powers

The Ratio of Powers ($B^2=16$, for example) is shown in Figure 17(c). It is a "quantum which, in its otherness, is identical with itself and which determines the beyond of itself." (321) That is, given the requirement of B^2 and the exponent of 16, the one *B* determines itself and its other. At this point, Quantum "has reached the stage of being-for-self." (321) Quantum is "posited as returned to itself." (322)

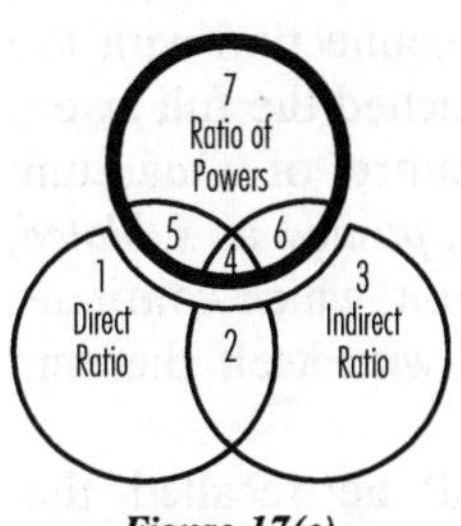

Figure 17(c)
Ratio of Powers

Earlier, we could never tell whether *B* or *C* was Unit or Amount. Now $B=B$, so that Unit *is* Amount. For this reason – and also because Unit stands for Quality – the Ratio of Powers is "posited as determined only by the unit." (321-2) The quantum (*B*) may undergo alteration, separate and apart from the Ratio of Powers, "but in so far as this alteration is a raising to a power, this its otherness is limited purely by itself." (322)

Hegel refers to the Ratio of Powers as qualitative yet external – an apparent contradiction. Where the exponent is fixed, the variable *B* is

---

[12] This "equality" of a given side of the ratio with the exponent justifies Mure's remark: "In Ratio of Powers, where one [*i.e.*, the exponent] is a higher power of the other [*i.e.*, a side of the ratio], they relate, if I follow Hegel, so closely that they are fully equivalent to the exponent, and the total expression is true infinity." MURE, PHILOSOPHY, *supra* note 10, at 120. A True Infinite becomes other and remains the same. Hence, the sides become the exponent, in the sense that each is *fixed*. Fixity stands for quality here.

[13] Andrew Haas points to Inverse Ratio as evidence that Hegel's Logic does not have a triune structure. He writes, "in the 'Inverse Ratio' . . . the second moment has only two sub-moments . . . ." ANDREW HAAS, HEGEL AND THE PROBLEM OF MULTIPLICITY 79 (2000). This is not a fair point. The *entire chapter* is triune. The three moments are Direct, Inverse and Power Ratios.

determined by the other *B*. Hence, its determinateness is external. But it is equally *internal*: "this externality is now posited in conformity with the Notion of quantum, as the latter's own self-determining, as its relation to its own self, as its *quality*." (323) "[I]n so far as the externality or indifference of its determining . . . counts," (323) the Ratio of Powers is still Quantum. At this moment it "is posited *simply* or *immediately*." (323) But also at this moment "it has become the other of itself, namely, quality." (323) In going outside itself, Quantum stays within itself, "so that *in this very externality quantum is self-related*" and hence "is *being* as quality." (323)

We have given $B^2=16$ as an example of the Ratio of Powers. In it, *B* limits itself and thus has recaptured its Quality. But is it not the case that outside forces can erase 16 and choose, say, 25 instead, thereby changing *B*? Of course, Hegel allows for this possibility, but nevertheless the Ratio of Powers "has a closer connection with the *Notion* of quantum." (322) In it, Quantum has reached the full extent of its Notion. It expresses the distinctive feature of Quantum: "Quantum is the *indifferent* determinateness, i.e., *posited* as *sublated*, determinateness as a limit which is equally no limit, which continues itself into its otherness and so remains identical with itself therein." (322)

Why is Quantum a determinateness? It will be recalled that Determinateness was another name for Limit.[14] It stands for a unity of being and nothing. So Quantum, as Number, is the unity of Amount (being) and Unit (nothing). Number – an early version of Quantum – was indifferent to its Quality. It depended on external reflection to determine which of its parts was Amount and which was Unit. But now that indifference is sublated. Number as the Ratio of Powers resists outside manipulation. Nevertheless, Amount and Unit are indistinguishable precisely because they are equal ($B=B$). Each side of the ratio stays what it is and yet it determines itself in its other. It both remains identical with itself and goes outside itself.[15]

---

[14] *Supra* at 83-4.

[15] Trying hard to tart up an otherwise dry chapter, Haas writes that the Power Relation is "a relation of *potencies* . . . The mathematician cannot help but speak (always) the words of the philosopher and the sexologist: the decent, respectable power ratio is (also) the indecent language of fornication, the multiple obscenities of the polygamist." HAAS, *supra* note 13, at 131. *Verhältnis* does have the alternative meaning of romantic affair. At least we can go along so far as to confirm that the Ratio of Powers is the inseparable unity of two quality-quantities.

Quantum is also said to be "the difference of itself from itself." (322) How is this so? If we contemplate, *BB=16*, clearly the first *B* is distinguishable from the second *B*. Nevertheless, *B*=*B*, and so, if the first *B* is different from the second *B*, it is different *from itself*. It is no self-identical entity, of which Hegel is so thoroughly critical.

To have a selfhood that is different from itself is what it means for Quantum to be a Ratio. At first, Direct Ratio showed itself in immediate form. There, "its self-relation which it has as exponent, in contrast to its differences, counts only as the fixity of an amount of the unit." (322) This means that, in Direct Ratio, where Unit is fixed, Amount is fixed. Yet the exponent itself was not qualitatively different from Unit or Amount. Direct Ratio was not what it ought to have been. In the Inverse Ratio, the exponent is only *in principle* the determinant of the sides of the ratio. In fact, *B* and *A* can fluctuate greatly, but they never quite become zero. For this reason the exponent is affirmative in that it has an independence from its sides. That is, the Quantum which is exponent relates itself to itself. In the Ratio of Powers, however, self-relation extends to the sides of the Ratio as well as the exponent.

A summary. Hegel now summarizes the Quantity's journey. Quantity was at first *opposed* to Quality. But Quantity was itself a Quality – "a purely self-related determinateness distinct from the determinateness of its other, from quality as such." (323) Ironically, Quantity learned to resist Quality, and in its resistance, it showed itself to be a Quality. By hating its other, it *became* its other. Quantity, therefore, is "in its truth the externality which is no longer indifferent but has returned into itself." (323)[16] But Quantity is not just a Quality. "[I]t is the truth of quality itself." (323) Without Quantity, there could be no Quality.

On the brink of Measure, Hegel notes that a double transition was necessary – a chiasmic exchange of properties.[17] Not only does one determinateness continue into the other but the other determinateness continues into the original one.[18] Thus, Quality is contained in Quantity, "but this is still a one-sided determinateness." (323) The

---

16 Mure remarks, "In Ratio the endless impotent self-externalizing of Quantity became a self-relation as near to true infinity as Quantity can rise to. It has developed an internal systematicness, which is only thinkable as qualitative." MURE, PHILOSOPHY, *supra* note 10, at 121. Mure errs in implying that Quantity is not itself always already a True Infinite.

17 *Supra* at 46-7.

18 That is, in $x^2=y$, x stays an x and determines the other side of the ratio as x.

converse is true as well – Quantity is contained in Quality. "This observation on the necessity of the *double* transition," Hegel remarks, "is of great importance throughout the whole compass of scientific method." (323) "It is clear that within this frame, whatever transition may happen, no dissolution or vanishing can any longer be expected; the terms remain permanently related."[19] The name of the partnership between Quality and Quantity is Measure.

Conclusion

"A main result of the science of logic is to repudiate quantitative definition of the absolute, and to retrieve qualitative definition."[20] Across the "quantity" chapters, we have seen how an exclusive quantitative perspective falls apart. At first, Being expelled otherness so that it could be all by itself – independent from the negative. But it discovered that, in this mode, Being expelled all its content and became Quantity. Quantity stands for the very act of expelling all content.

Quantity discovers, however, that it has an integrity that it cannot expel – a limit that preserves its content within itself. "This inability to reach its bourne Hegel describes as *eine Ohnmacht des Negativen* – a weakness of the negative – in that what it abolishes by its own cancelling immediately reasserts itself."[21]

This reappropriation of what is canceled is nevertheless reappropriation of an "other." Hence, in Quantitative Infinity, Quantum goes outside itself to a beyond. The infinitely big or small number can never be named. Yet, in going beyond its limit, Quantum discovers that its *own content* is beyond the limit. In this sense, Quantum returns to itself when it exports its content to the other. It shows what it is when it shows it is nothing. This return will later be called reflection-into-self

---

[19] Cinzia Ferrini, *Framing Hypotheses: Numbers in Nature and the Logic of Measure in the Development of Hegel's System*, in HEGEL AND THE PHILOSOPHY OF NATURE at 296 (Stephen Houlgate ed., 1998). The double transition of Measure, Ferrini, suggests was not present in the 1812 version of chapter 6, which suspended the reflective trope to the end of Measure. *Id*.

[20] CLARK BUTLER, HEGEL'S LOGIC: BETWEEN DIALECTIC AND HISTORY 143 (1996).

[21] HARRIS, *supra* note 2, at 136; *see* (228) ("impotence of the negative"). Adorno refuses to accept any weakness of the negative and so disagrees with Hegel's entire system. But this amounts to a dogmatic insistence on the self-identity and irreducibility of the negative, an irony of which he seems unaware. THEODOR W. ADORNO, NEGATIVE DIALECTICS 119 (E.B. Ashton trans. 2000).

– the hallmark of Essence. For now, it can be noted that the nature of Being has changed. Whereas in the first three chapters Being constituted expelling the negative, now Being constitutes expelling its own self and therefore, in this act of expulsion, accomplishing a return to itself. This return is still implicit and will remain so throughout Measure, the last portion of Being. The return becomes explicit in Hegel's theory of Reflection.

PART III
MEASURE

7
Measure and Specific Quantity

Measure is the last province in the kingdom of Being. After traversing it, we arrive at the gate of shadowy Essence – a negative, correlative underworld.

Hegel proclaims the development of Measure "extremely difficult," (331)[1] and commentators have concurred.[2] We can nevertheless des-

---

[1] This has been found "a particularly significant observation, since such modesty is not often encountered in his writings." Louis Fleischhacker, *Hegel on Mathematics and Experimental Science*, in HEGEL AND NEWTONIANISM 209, 211 (Michael John Petry ed., 1993). Cinzia Ferrini finds in this remark, added to the 1831 version of the *SL*, a complex story involving Hegel's renunciation of his notorious early dissertation, *De Orbitis Planetarum*, where he logically deduced the ratio of the distances between planets. Ferrini notes that Hegel simply renounced this conclusion in the 1817 "Heidelberg" Encyclopedia, but omitted the renunciation in the later Berlin editions. The Heidelberg version was based on a "single" transition from Quality to Quantity, and a "single" transition back. In this single transition, only vanishing was emphasized. Hence, Hegel could flatly renounce *De Orbitis*. But in the 1827 and 1830 Berlin editions of the *Encyclopedia*, Hegel realized that there was the "double" transition described at the end of chapter 6. In the double transition, each side of the syllogism vanishes *and* sustains itself. This leads Hegel to withdraw his renunciation of his earlier work, since empirical quanta are not *entirely* unrelated to Logic. Cinzia Ferrini, *Framing Hypotheses: Numbers in Nature and the Logic of Measure in the Development of Hegel's System*, in HEGEL AND THE PHILOSOPHY OF NATURE 283 (Stephen Houlgate ed., 1998). On Hegel's notorious dissertation, see Olivier Depré, *The Ontological Foundations of Hegel's Dissertation of 1801*, in *id.* at 257.

[2] Errol Harris judges Measure to be "extraordinarily difficult . . . so obscure as to

cribe the theme of Measure easily enough: *change*; more precisely, an exploration of the difference between qualitative and quantitative change.

Change has itself changed over our logical journey. At first, change was *transition*. Being became Nothing. Determinate Being became Negation. The Finite ceased to be. Starting with the True Infinite, however, change itself changed. The True Infinite did not cease to be. It stayed what it was even while it became something different. This was the beginning of *ideality*. In True Infinity, immediate Being ceased to be *and* preserved itself in an idealized form.

When Being ceased to be and survived as an ideal memory of immediacy, we entered the realm of Quantity – Being with all its content outside of itself. Quantity is determined by outside intellect. Quantitative change is change imposed from the outside. The very quality of Quantum was that it was open (and therefore indifferent) to change imposed upon it from the outside.

Qualitative change is self-imposed change from the inside. We will learn, however, that genuine qualitative change depends on quantitative change. Nature does make great leaps, but only after indifferently undergoing incremental quantitative change.[3] Liquid water, as it gets colder due to outside force, indifferently stays liquid, but, at 0° centigrade, liquid, radically and all at once, turns solid.

Measure emerged in the Ratio of Powers ($x^2 = y$), which showed itself to be "self-related externality." (327) In $x^2 = y$, the identity of the first (internal) x is determined by the second (external) x. The first x is in the thrall of externality. Nevertheless, $x = x$, and so it is self-related, not just externally determined. As self-related, the Ratio of Powers (which we now call Measure) is "a *sublated* externality." (327) Under the law of sublation, externality is canceled *and* preserved; Measure "has within itself the difference from itself." (327) Because this is so, Measure will sublate itself in favor of its measureless beyond.

When difference was simply external, we had before us quantitative difference. But now, having been captured by Measure, this difference is a qualitative moment. The quantitative report of a Measure is the

---

be, for the most part, hardly intelligible, and, while it contains some astonishingly prescient scientific comments, it also indulges in what, to us in the twentieth century, must appear ill-informed and perverse polemic against sound scientific insights." ERROL E. HARRIS, AN INTERPRETATION OF THE LOGIC OF HEGEL 143 (1983).

[3] For this reason, "a seemingly innocent change of quantity acts as a kind of snare, to catch hold of the quality . . . " EL § 108 Remark.

thing's own authentic report of itself. When the mode is external but essential, Measure is before us.[4] As John Burbidge remarks:

> *Measuring* . . . introduces an explicit act of relating. It brings together two realities, indifferent to each other. This conjunction is recognized as valid, however, only if each term allows for, and indeed encourages, the association. Since mutual reference is now an inherent characteristic of the concept, one passes beyond simple immediacy.[5]

Essence. Measures are brought together by an external measurer. Nevertheless, they are *ready* to be brought together. Measure therefore is "the *immanent* quantitative relationship of *two* qualities to each other." (340) Each Measure, however, imposes quantitative change on the other. Each Measure has a qualitative resilience against the change imposed upon it from the outside. If this resilience is isolated and considered on its own, we have the Measureless – or Essence. So Hegel provides his first definition of Essence – "to be self-identical in the immediacy of its determined being." (329) In the realm of Essence, things mediate themselves. They are not mediated by outside forces. The "Determinations of Reflection"[6] are destined to enjoy a self-subsistence and independence from the qualitative and the quantitative.

For the moment, Quality and Quantity are still with us, but in mediated form. Each of these extremes in the syllogism of Measure is equally the one and the other. This was not so before. In Quality, the Understanding grasped Being as an affirmative immediacy. In Quantity, the Understanding learned that the negative, quantitative moment of

---

[4] "In the Hegelian system, the quantities involved in measurement, which from an epistemological point of view are a means to cognition, are ontologized and treated as natural objects, that is to say as the objects of an overriding analytical cognition. What is more, the equalities in behaviour constituting the substance or content of the quantities measured are interpreted as being things. As a result, the natural world as determined by Hegel corresponds to the view of nature developed by *mechanicism*, the world-view of the mechanistically-minded popularizers of natural science." Renate Wahsner, *The Philosophical Background to Hegel's Criticism of Newton*, in HEGEL AND NEWTONIANISM, *supra* note 2, at 83. 1993.

[5] JOHN W. BURBIDGE, ON HEGEL'S LOGIC: FRAGMENTS OF A COMMENTARY 63 (1981). In his later book on chemistry, however, Burbidge less plausibly remarks: "Measuring uses a quantity to specify a quality. That definition sets the logical task." JOHN W. BURBIDGE, REAL PROCESS: HOW LOGIC AND CHEMISTRY COMBINE IN HEGEL'S PHILOSOPHY OF NATURE 53 (1996). This formulation threatens to obscure the fact that, for Hegel, a Measure's quality *is* its quantity – accurate reportage of what the thing is.

[6] *Infra* chapter 11.

Continuity was the truth of Being. Now the Understanding sees that the qualitative and the quantitative are two houses both alike in dignity. The difference between them is "indifferent and so is no difference." (330) The difference between Quality and Quantity has been sublated. In Ratio, Quantity showed itself to be a return-into-self, an indifference to mere quantitative change. This reflection-into-self *is* Quality. It is not mere Being-for-self (which self-destructed and became nothing). Rather, this form of Being – reflection-into-self – is "being-in-and-for-self" (330) – the attribute of Essence. Thus, Hegel introduces in Measure the portentous new brand of substance – being-in-and-for-self.

Being-in-and-for-self, however, is so far merely implicit. Measure is still "the *immediate* [*seiende*] unity of quality and quantity; its moments are determinately present as a quality, and quanta thereof." (330) Immediate Measure is a mediation of qualitative and quantitative moments. But soon Measure will turn out to be always a *ratio* of Measures. Within the ratio, each side will further reveal itself to be a "*ratio* of specific quanta having the form of self-subsistent measures," (330) yielding an infinite regression or "bad infinity." The sides of every ratio have mere quantitative difference from each other. This implies that each measure continues into the other and so beyond itself entirely. The name of this beyond is the Measureless.

The Measureless is Measure's negativity. The indifference of the Measureless to determinations of Measure is the final result of Real Measure.[7] Measure becomes an "*inverse ratio of measures*." (330) In this Ratio, which must remain largely mysterious until chapter 9, the Measureless is shown to be continuous with its Measures – quantitatively related but qualitatively distinct. Qualitative Measures are superfluous to the Measureless. They sublate themselves and yield their being to Essence, "which is their reflection-into-self." (331) At this point, externality sublates itself, and Being's journey draws to a close.

Measure and the social sciences. Because Measure entails external imposition upon a phenomenon that is partly free and immune from outside oppression, Hegel is able to set forth a hierarchy in the natural sciences in terms of conduciveness to Measure. "The complete, abstract

---

[7] "Real," for Hegel, tends to be a dialectical word, denoting a determinateness. *See* JOHN W. BURBIDGE, HEGEL ON LOGIC AND RELIGION: THE REASONABLENESS OF CHRISTIANITY 44 (1992); RICHARD DIEN WINFIELD, AUTONOMY AND NORMATIVITY 50 (2001) ("reality is the determinacy something in virtue of its contrast to something else"). Here, Real Measure is the second, "dialectical" chapter of Measure.

indifference of developed measure . . . can only be manifested in the sphere of *mechanics*" wherein matter is abstract. (331) In the inorganic and even more in the organic spheres, Measure is "subordinated to higher relationships." (332)[8] The free development of Measure according to logic is still less to be found in politics or constitutional law – "the realm of spirit." (332) It may be that the Athenian constitution is suited only to city-states, "but all this yields neither laws of measure nor characteristic forms of it." (332) In this sphere "there occur differences of *intensity* of character, *strength* of imagination, sensations, general ideas, and so on." (331) The "measure" of such phenomena never goes "beyond the indefiniteness of *strength* or *weakness*." (332) Ordinal, not cardinal, measures are the most political science can expect to achieve.

Hegel terminates his introduction to Measure with a blast against empirical psychology – of late passing under the name of behavioralism: "How insipid and completely empty the so-called laws turn out to be which have been laid down about the relation of strength and weakness of sensations, general ideas and so on, comes home to one on reading the psychologies which occupy themselves with such laws." (332)[9] Hegel, I think, objects to empirical psychology because it proposes to reduce human freedom to a set of inviolable laws.[10] Any such attempt to measure freedom is what Hegel attacks elsewhere as mere phrenology.[11]

Modality. Early in his treatment of Measure, Hegel addresses a topic seemingly unrelated to physical measurement – Kant's notion of modality. At the beginning of the *SL*, Hegel wrote: "Measure can also,

---

[8] Ferrini suggests that these observations were designed to answer Goethe, who questioned the propriety of measuring organic processes. She reads Hegel as *not* entirely rejecting measures of organic life, in the nature of Goethe, but conceding the limitations of doing so. Cinzia Ferrini, *On the Relation Between "Mode" and "Measure" in Hegel's* Science of Logic: *Some Introductory Remarks* 20 OWL OF MINERVA 20, 47-8 (1988).

[9] Kant agrees: "If we took principles from psychology, i.e. from observations about our understanding . . . this would therefore lead to the cognition of merely *contingent* laws. In logic, however, the question is not one of *contingent* but of *necessary laws*." IMMANUEL KANT, LOGIC 16 (Robert S. Hartman & Wolfgang Schwarz trans., 1974).

[10] STANLEY ROSEN, G.W.F. HEGEL: AN INTRODUCTION TO THE SCIENCE OF WISDOM 18 (1974) ("Modern science yields necessary or certain knowledge of the body, but if that knowledge is applied to the mind or soul, the result is a loss of freedom, and even further, of Syllogism of Necessity or subjectivity").

[11] G.W.F. HEGEL, PHENOMENOLOGY OF SPIRIT ¶309 (A.V. Miller trans. 1977). On social science's hatred of freedom, see Jeanne L. Schroeder, *The Stumbling Block: Freedom, Rationality and Legal Scholarship,* 44 WM. & MARY L. REV. 263 (2002).

if one wishes, be regarded as a modality; but since with Kant modality is supposed no longer to constitute a determination of the content, but to concern only the relation of the content to thought, to the element, it is a quite heterogeneous relation." (80) This passage in effect accuses Kant of believing that thought has no effect on the object measured.[12] Hegel now elaborates on this criticism.[13] Modality – where thought meets object – is the "sphere of coming-to-be and ceasing-to-be." (329) By this, Hegel means to comment on Kant's claim that the gap between subject and object is unbridgeable. Hence, subjectivity "ceases to be" in the thing-in-itself. And the thing-in-itself "ceases to be" in subjective experience. In Hegel's view, objects "come to be" in the measure of thought. Kantian modality is faulted for *not* being Measure to the extent thought leaves the object unaffected.[14]

For Kant, modality, fourth in his table of categories,[15] is the choice of possibility or impossibility, existence or non-existence, necessity or contingency. In his table, Kant leads with "quantity" and "quality" – a

---

[12] *See* IMMANUEL KANT, CRITIQUE OF PURE REASON A219/B267 (Paul Guyer & Allen W. Wood trans., 1990) ("The categories of modality . . . do not augment the concept to which they are ascribed in the least, but rather express only the relation to the faculty of cognition").

[13] Ferrini suggests that Hegel's identification of modality as a form of measure constitutes "the essence of Hegel's response to the challenge of the way in which transcendental idealism treated determinate being." Ferrini, *Mode*, *supra* note 8, at 40. According to Ferrini, most commentators wrongly view the discussion of modality to be a digression that has nothing to do with Measure.

[14] *Id.* at 43.

[15] Kant's categories are as follows:

(I) *Of Quantity*	(II) *Of Quality*
Unity	Reality
Plurality	Negation
Totality	Limitation

(III) *Of Relation*
Of Inherence and Subsistence (substantia et accidens)
Of Causality and Dependence (cause and effect)
Of Community (reciprocity between the agent and patient)

(IV) *Of Modality*
Possibility–Impossibility
Existence–Non-existence
Necessity–Contingence

CRITIQUE OF PURE REASON, *supra* note 12, at A80/B106.

priority Hegel reverses. For Kant, quantity comes first. Within quantity, "unity" stands over against "plurality." The unity of unity and plurality is "totality." Quality is second. Within Quality, Kant opposes reality to negation; their unity is limitation. The triplicity that Hegel so much favors is confined by Kant within a given category. No triplicity inheres between the concepts themselves. For this very reason, Hegel writes, Kant "was unable to hit on the third to quality and quantity." (327)

Hegel implies that "modality" was Kant's true third. If so, then we can see why Hegel equates modality with Measure. "Relation" – Kant's nominal third – is dismissed as an "insertion."[16] Kantian modality, Hegel says, is "the relation of the object to thought." (327)[17] Kant perceived thought as entirely external to the thing-in-itself. The first three categories belong to thought alone – though "to the *objective* element of it." (327) Modality involves the relation of thought to object. It contains the determination of reflection-into-self, meaning that, by encountering objects, modality renders the objects into thoughts and brings them under the jurisdiction of the mind. This signifies that the objectivity common to the other categories is lacking in modality. The modalities – possibility, existence and necessity – do not add to the determination of the object. They only express the relation of the object to the faculty of cognition. In short, for Kant, thought leaves the object unaffected.

For Spinoza, "mode" was third after substance and attribute. Mode was the affectations of substance: "that element which is in an other through which it is comprehended." (327) Accordingly, mode for Spinoza is "externality as such." (327) Because external, mode is untrue. It is "the non-substantial generally, which can only be grasped through an other." (328)[18] Modal being for Spinoza is precisely what does *not* endure. Yet when the modal *thought* of substance disappears (back into

---

[16] Gadamer suggests that Relation in Kant corresponds to Essence in Hegel's Logic. HANS-GEORG GADAMER, HEGEL'S DIALECTIC: FIVE HERMENEUTICAL STUDIES 81 (Christopher Smith trans., 1976).

[17] *See* Ferrini, *Mode*, *supra* note 8, at 36 ("for Kant, modality was concerned solely with the meaning of the verb "to be," as is used in order to indicate or establish a connection between an object and a proposition, and this use had to be based upon the faculty of cognition in that the modality is understood as *de re* and not *de dicto*.").

[18] *See* 1 HARRY AUSTRYN WOLFSON, THE PHILOSOPHY OF SPINOZA: UNFOLDING THE LATENT PROCESSES OF HIS REASONING 370-99 (1934). On Hegel's personal history with Spinozism, see Hans-Christian Lucas, *Spinoza, Hegel, Whitehead: Substance, Subject and Superject*, in HEGEL AND WHITEHEAD: CONTEMPORARY PERSPECTIVES ON SYSTEMATIC PHILOSOPHY 39 (George R. Lucas, Jr., ed. 1986).

substance), nothing of mode remains. Spinoza thus "failed to see that if every determination is a negation, that negation is genuinely expressed (for-itself and no longer only in-itself) only in the mode."[19]

The Hindus had a similar triune system, leading to comparisons with Christianity, but, Hegel insists, the comparison is misleading. In Hinduism, the unity of Brahma disperses but does not return. The supreme goal is "submergence in unconsciousness, unity with Brahma, annihilation." (329) In Christianity, "there is not only unity but union [*nicht nur Einheit, sondern Einigkeit*], the conclusion of the syllogism [which] is a unity possessing *content* and *actuality*, a unity which in its wholly concrete determination is spirit." (328) Like the Brahmans, Spinoza does not manage return-into-self. Mode is external and untrue. Truth lies only in substance. "But this is only to submerge all content in the void, in a merely formal unity lacking all content," Hegel says. (328)

In Spinozism, mode is abstract externality, "indifferent to qualitative and quantitative determinations." (329) These "unessential elements are not supposed to count," but, nevertheless, "everything depends on the kind and manner of the mode." (329) This dependence shows that the mode belongs to the essential nature of a thing – "a very indefinite connection but one which at least implies that this external element is not so abstractly an externality." (329)

A. The Specific Quantum

At the end of chapter 6, Quantity had recaptured its Quality – its immunity from outside manipulation. Measure is the *unity* of Quality and Quantity. Our first step, then, is Immediate Measure.

Immediate Measure is "an immediate quantum, hence just some specific quantum or other," but it is equally an immediate *quality*, "some specific quality or other." (333) It is therefore appropriate to represent *mediatedness within* Immediate Measure. The Understanding therefore presents Measure as a mediated immediacy [1, 2]. Immediate Measure is brittle. The slightest *quantitative* change yields qualitative change. In Measure, Quantum is no longer "a limit which is no limit; it is now the determination of the thing, which is destroyed if it is increased or diminished beyond this quantum." (333-4)

Quantitative change is externally imposed change. Yet Quality is

---

[19] JEAN HYPPOLITE, GENESIS AND STRUCTURE OF HEGEL'S *PHENOMENOLOGY OF SPIRIT* 106 (Samuel Cherniak & John Heckman trans., 1974).

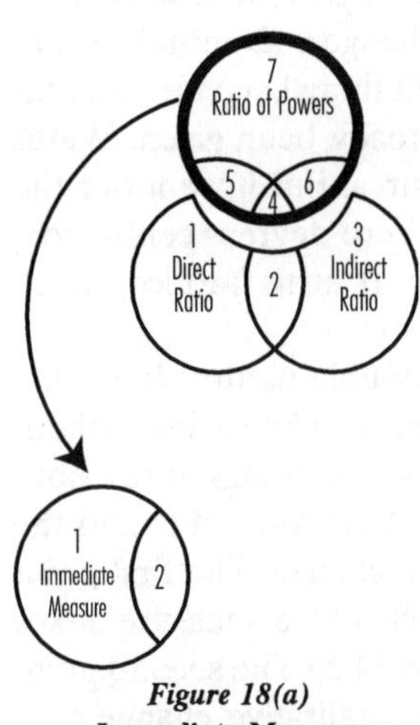

Figure 18(a)
Immediate Measure

supposed to be *immunity* from quantitative change. Dialectic Reason therefore brings forth the *qualitative* moment that Immediate Measure suppresses. The Quality of a measure *is* the extent it can withstand quantitative change without succumbing to qualitative change. Quantum, Hegel says, is a "a self-related externality [and] thus itself quality." (333)

Why Immediate Measure is a self-relation should by now be apparent. [2] represents the mediation between [1] and [3] and is the very being-within-self of the concept of Measure. But why is this self-relation an externality? The answer lies in the True Infinite nature of Measure. True Infinitude requires that [1] go out of itself and into [2], which, as always, instantly implies that [2] is an externality – represented by [3]. Hence, the externality of Immediate Measure is both inside and outside – [2] and [3]. Accordingly, Hegel says of the Quantum [1] that it is distinguished from Quality, but "does not transcend it, neither does the quality transcend the quantum. [Measure] is thus the determinateness which has returned into simple identity with itself." (333)

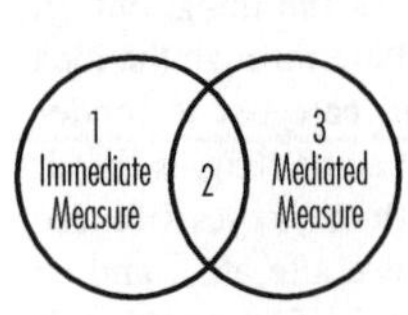

Figure 18(b)
Mediated Immediate Measure

These last two steps represent the claim that "all that exists has a measure" (333), the proposition of the Pythagoreans.[20] Quantum "belongs to the nature of the something itself." (333) It is inherent in Being – its being-within-self [2]. Accordingly, Being is not indifferent to its magnitude. If its magnitude is altered, the quality of the thing in question alters as well: "Quantum, as measure, has ceased to be a limit which is not limit; it is now the determination of the thing, which is destroyed if it is increased or diminished beyond this quantum." (333-4)

---

[20] CLARK BUTLER, HEGEL'S LOGIC: BETWEEN DIALECTIC AND HISTORY 111 (1996).

A measured thing is supposed to exhibit a degree of resilience. It remains what it is even though its quantum changes. Eventually there comes a dramatic moment when the measured thing becomes qualitatively different. The example of water has already been given. Water has a liquid quality over a range of temperatures. But if we lower the quantitative side of water's Measure to below zero degrees centigrade, water undergoes a sudden cataclysmic change. It turns into ice, which is qualitatively different from liquid water.

Quantitative determinateness, then, has a double nature. It is "that to which the quality is tied" and also "that which can be varied without affecting the quality." (334) Immediate Measure brings forth both moments – the idea that quantitative change destroys quality and the idea that quality *is* indifference to quantitative change. The first point states that "the destruction of anything which has a measure takes place through the alteration of its quantum." (334-5) The second point states that not every quantitative change is a qualitative change.

The idea of quantitative change resulting in qualitative change is captured by the common sense notion of gradualness. Suppose we lower the temperature of water with a view of destroying its quality as liquid (*i.e.*, we make some ice cubes).

> On the one hand this destruction appears as *unexpected*, in so far as the quantum can be changed without altering the measure and the quality of the thing; but on the other hand, it is made into something quite easy to understand through the idea of *gradualness*. The reason why such ready use is made of this category to render conceivable or to explain the disappearance of a quality or of something, is that it seems to make it possible almost to watch the disappearing with one's eyes, because quantum is posited as the external limit which is by its nature alterable, and so *alteration* of (quantum only) requires no explanation. But in fact nothing is explained thereby; the alteration is . . . essentially the transition of one quality into another, or the more abstract transition of an existence into a negation of the existence; this implies another determination than that of gradualness which is only a decrease or an increase and is a one-sided holding fast to quantity. (335)

In short, incremental change is simply easier to accept as a psychological matter, compared to radical qualitative change. Behind every incrementalist strategy, however, lies the radical program of obliterating what exists and installing something new. Hegel asks:

> [D]oes the pulling out of a single hair from the head . . . produce baldness, or does a heap cease to be a heap if a grain is removed? An answer in the negative can be given without hesitation since such a removal constitutes only a quantitative difference, a difference moreover which is itself quite insignificant; thus a hair, a grain, is removed and this is repeated, only one of them being removed each time

> in accordance with the answer given. At last the qualitative change is revealed; the head . . . is bald, the heap has disappeared. In giving the said answer, what was forgotten was not only the repetition, but the fact that the individually insignificant quantities (like the individually insignificant disbursements from a fortune) *add up* and the total constitutes the qualitative whole, so that finally this whole has vanished; the head is bald, the purse is empty. (335)

In the next chapter, Hegel suggests that the gradual, quantitative side of change is external to the thing:

> On the qualitative side . . . the gradual, merely quantitative progress . . . is absolutely interrupted; the new quality in its merely quantitative relationship is, relatively to the vanishing quality, an indifferent, indeterminate other, and the transition is therefore a *leap* . . . People fondly try to make an alteration *comprehensible* by means of the gradualness of the transition; but the truth is that gradualness is an alteration which is merely indifferent, the opposite of qualitative change. (368)

Hegel goes on to complain that gradualism quantifies and therefore externalizes qualitative change, thereby robbing it of its immanence. (370-1) Gradualness subjectifies what should be an objective process.[21]

Common sense errs, then, when it thinks that removal of a single hair does not produce baldness. The mistake is "assuming a quantity to be only an indifferent limit, i.e. of assuming that it is just a quantity in the specific sense of quantity." (336) Quantitative change is thought to have no bite. What common sense misses is that "quantity is a moment of measure and is connected with quality." (336) When Quantum is taken as an indifferent limit of a thing, it leaves the thing "open to unsuspected attack and destruction." (336) Gradual quantitative change *can* lead to a catastrophic *coupure*. Accordingly, Hegel writes, "It is the cunning of the Notion to seize on this aspect of a reality where its quality does not seem to come into play; and such is its cunning that the aggrandizement of a State or of a fortune, etc., which leads finally to disaster for the State or for the owner, even appears at first to be their good fortune." (336)

---

[21] For example, in an attempt to save the American legal system from the nihilism of Critical Legal Studies, Andrew Altman announces that we "more or less" live under a rule of law. I had occasion to suggest that the invocation "more or less" is designed to lend the American system some "give," so that counter-examples of lawlessness cannot blow apart the argument. David Gray Carlson, *Liberal Philosophy's Troubled Relation to the Rule of Law*, 43 U. TORONTO L. J. 257 (1993).

B. Specifying Measure

If Measure undergoes qualitative change at the alteration of magnitude, we are in the realm of Immediate Measure. But if we admit that *some* quantitative change can occur within a range without *any* qualitative change, then we are in the more advanced realm of Specifying Measure. Here Quality has some independence from Quantum.

As always, Speculative Reason names motion. Gazing back at Figure 18(b), it notices that Measure can undergo some limited amount of quantitative change without also undergoing qualitative change. How does Hegel derive the resilience of quality from quantitative change? Simply by pointing out that, at this point, resilience *is* quality:

> As a quantum it is an indifferent magnitude open to external determination and capable of increase and decrease. But as a measure it is also distinguished from itself as a quantum, as such an indifferent determination, and is a limitation of that indifferent fluctuation about a limit. (334)

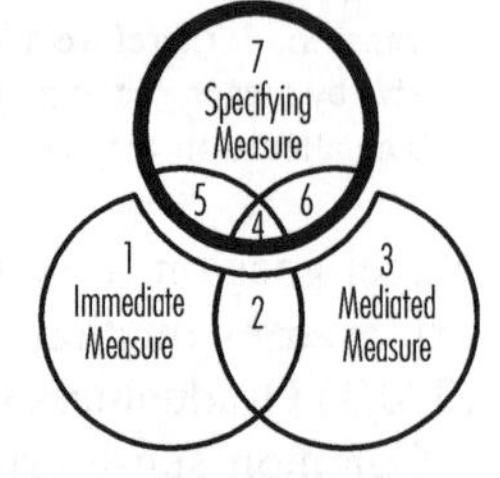

Figure 18(c)
Specifying Measure

But this does not mean that Quality is now independent of Quantity (the source of change). Under the law of sublation, Immediate Measure stood for susceptibility to change. Specifying Measure is therefore susceptibility to change *and* resilience. Accordingly, "the quantitative determinateness of anything is thus twofold – namely, it is that to which the quality is tied and also that which can be varied without affecting the quality." (334)

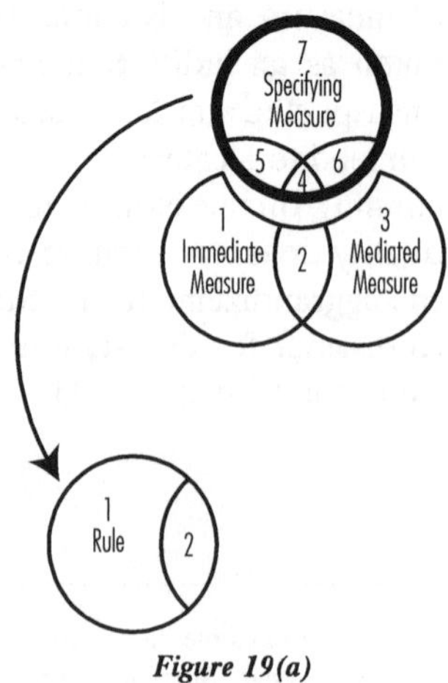

Figure 19(a)
Rule

(a) Rule

The Understanding names the range of quantitative change that Measure might undergo without suffering qualitative change. Rule is "measure which is external with reference to mere quantum." (336) Rule [1] is what's *specified* by a *Specifying Measure* that produces a report of itself.

Rule in Figure 19(b) is external to what it measures [2, 3]. We therefore have before us an act of comparison – an inferior brand of knowledge. Rule is "an arbitrary magnitude which in turn can equally be treated as an amount (the foot as an amount of inches)." (337)[22] Measure, however, is not merely external Rule. "[A]s a specifying measure [3] its nature is to be related in its own self [2] to an other which is a quantum [1]." (337)

Rule is an important concept for jurisprudence, with its emphasis on negative freedom and the rule of law. In the typical American vision, the human subject is a natural phenomenon, with preferences that are simply accepted as given. This natural subject is free to do what he will within the bounds of positive law, which are imposed on the subject externally. The function of the law is to protect the rights of the next fellow from the exuberance of the natural subject. In this vision, the negative freedom of the subject accorded by positive law is the range of quantitative change that a person can enjoy without qualitative change. But if a subject transgresses the rule of law, the subject undergoes qualitative change – from lawful to criminal.[23]

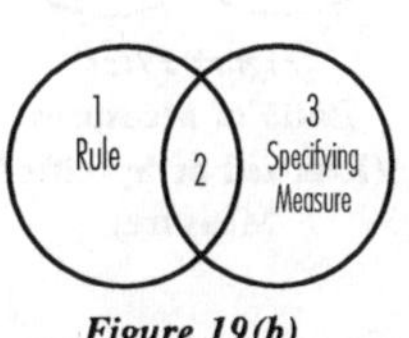

Figure 19(b)
Rule Measuring Its Other

Hegel endorses the proposition that God is the measure of all things. Presumably this means that God Rules. God as Measure "is an external kind and manner of determinateness, a more or less, but at the same time it is equally reflected into itself, a determinateness which is not indifferent and external but intrinsic; it is thus *the concrete truth of being*." (329) So God is not *just* external to things but is also implicit *in* things. This relates to Hegel's characterization of nature as the non-spiritual – a necessary *otherness* to God, which nevertheless implicitly is spiritual. The inherent spirit in nature is why it ultimately gives rise

---

[22] Hegel remarks that it is "foolish to speak of a *natural* standard of things." (334) Universal standards of measure serve only for external comparison. The adoption of a universal standard is merely conventional – "a matter of complete indifference." (334) A "foot" might be an internal measure – where a foot means literally the length of a human being's foot. But where that same foot is applied to some thing other than itself, it is only an external measure. On the conventionality of measurement, Harris protests that "today the physicist, following Eddington, will claim that there is indeed a natural standard of length, namely, the radius of curvature of space." HARRIS, *supra* note 2, at 146.

[23] *See* Carlson, *supra* note 21, at 268-73.

to man, reason and mind.

(b) Specifying Measure

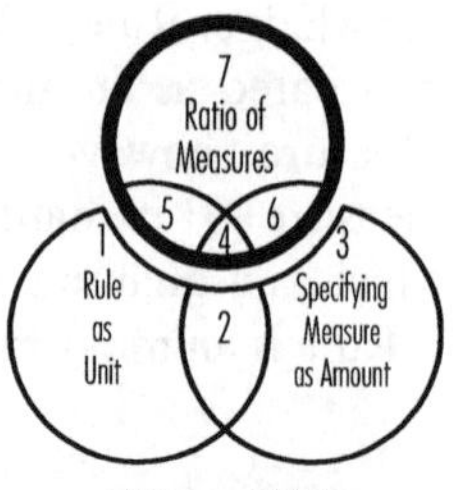

Figure 19(c)
Ratio of Measures
(Realized or Specified Measure)

Rule was external, indifferent magnitude "posited by some other existence in general in the measurable something." (337) It signifies the dependence of Measure [2, 3] on externality, a silent fourth who *measures*. Yet Specifying Measure, subject to external Rule, is likewise an internal *qualitative* Quantum, a "being-for-other to which the indifferent increasing and decreasing is proper." (337) This internal Quantum [2] is, to a degree, indifferent to Rule [1]. Accordingly, [2] can equally be taken as the *Quality* of [2, 3]. Likewise, since [2] is also Rule, Rule is in some sense the content of Specifying Measure. In effect, [2, 3] and [1, 2] are two Measures – two separate unities of Quality and Quantity – facing each other. *Measure has split itself in two.*

Why is Rule now a Measure? Because Measure involves physical intrusion. The Rule is itself a Quality with a Quantum. If one sticks a thermometer into water, the temperature of the water is not unaffected. Ruled matter [3] (*e.g.*, the water) reacts against externally imposed matter (the heat of the thermometer) and "behaves towards the amount [2] as an intensive quantum." (337) Why this reference to Intensive Quantum (Degree), negatively shown in Figure 14(b) and positively shown in Figure 15(a)? In Degree, Quantum recaptured its Being-for-self. It stood over against Extensive Magnitude. It represented the Unit that Extensive Magnitude was not. In Degree, "determinate being has returned into being-for-self." (218) Ruled matter (Specifying Measure as Amount) likewise has being-for-self [3] which resists externally imposed change. Of course, it is not *entirely* immune. The water heats up when the thermometer is put in, but it does so at its own pace. It does not assume the temperature of the thermometer, nor does the thermometer precisely assume the temperature of the water.

The resistance of ruled matter also explains Hegel's earlier remark that Measure, in its more developed form, is necessity, or fate. Nemesis attacks the presumptuous, who think themselves too great. By reducing the presumptuous to nothing, "mediocrity is restored." (329) Fate is Specifying Measure as Amount, which resists the subjective will of presumptuous rulers. Human society insists on its own rate of quantitative (and eventually qualitative) change. Those who insist on speeding up the rate of change are taught a hard lesson that the people has a *quality* of its own. Its quality is its own unique rate of change. Nevertheless, human institutions do change, and they require patient reformers to work hard in order to effectuate that change.[24]

Ratio of Measures. In Figure 19(b), two Measures face each other and form a unique Ratio of Measures which is an "exponent"[25] different from either Measure. (337) The Ratio of Measures, sometimes called Realized Measure or Specified Measure, is shown in Figure 19(c). Here, the two Measures, each having a Rule within which neither undergoes quantitative change, produce yet a third Rule which is different from the "incommensurable ratios" (138) that make it up. Alteration of the Measure, then,

> consists by itself in the addition of such a numerical one and then another and so on. If in this way the alteration of the external quantum is an arithmetical progression, the specifying reaction of the qualitative nature of measure produces another series which is related to the first, increases and decreases with it, but not in a ratio determined by a numerical exponent but in a number of incommensurable ratios, according to a determination of powers. (338)

This new, third range of values is the qualitative moment of the Ratio of Measure, "the qualitative moment itself which specifies the quantum as such." (338) So when a Measure is observed (or Specified), its reality is *validly* observed. Yet Measure in part escapes observation – the unmeasured thing [6] lies beyond the Ratio of Measures that is actually observed [4, 5]. To measure a thing is to change it.[26]

---

[24] The point about mediocrity may refer to the fall of Napoleon. In a private letter, Hegel commented on the event: "There is nothing more *tragic* . . . . The entire mass of mediocrity, with its irresistible leaden weight of gravity, presses on, without rest or reconciliation, until it has succeeded in bringing down what is high to the same level or even below." JACQUES D'HONDT, HEGEL IN HIS TIME: BERLIN, 1818-1831 30 (John Burbidge trans., 1988). A believer in historical greatness, Hegel lacked patience for those who sought to remove the halo from heroes by pointing out base motives for their great acts. "If heroes of history had been actuated by subjective and formal interests alone, they would never have accomplished what they have." EL § 140 Remark.

[25] Recall that Hegel uses the term "exponent" to describe what we might call a quotient. Thus, if A/B = C, Hegel calls C the exponent.

[26] Hegel compares Figure 19(c) to the progress concerning Intensive Quantum and Extensive Quantum. In Figure 14(a), Extensive Quantum was presented as representing Amount. Then a single Degree was brought to the fore as *primus inter pares* of all the

Hegel gives temperature as an example of the Ratio of Measures. In temperature, "two sides of external and specified quantum are distinguished." (338) The temperature of a body is registered in the external quantum of yet another body – mercury in a thermometer, for instance. Yet the body of a sick child and the thermometer differ in the rate at which they absorb temperature. The child's temperature affects the thermometer, but (it is forgotten) the thermometer affects the temperature of the child, "and the change of temperature in any one of them does not correspond in a direct ratio with that of the medium or of the other bodies among themselves." (338-9) Each body has a "specific heat."[27] Temperature is in fact a ratio that differs from the temperature of either side of the ratio of child and thermometer.

The Ratio of Measures must not be viewed as the relation of Quantity to Quality. Rather, two complete Measures face each other and produce yet another Measure which is a middle term – though mistakenly taken to be the truth of the Specifying Measure.

(c) Relation of the Two Sides as Qualities

In Figure 19(c), the qualitative side of the Ratio of Measures is intrinsic yet determinate (*i.e.*, constituted by Quantity). The quantitative side is external [5]. But this externality has become internal [4, 5]. The internal side, Hegel concludes, "has a quantum for its presupposition and its starting point." (339) In other words, Quality presupposes an externality, and, as we are still in the realm of Being, this externality is still taken as the starting point for determining what the thing is.

The external Quantity, however, has a Quality of its own and so is qualitatively distinguishable from its other. This very difference is their unity. This qualitative difference [4] is now sublated in the Ratio of

---

numbers – *i.e.,* the 100th degree. Dialectical Reason showed that Degree was dependent on plurality for its identity. The 100th degree was incoherent without a reference to 1st-99th degree, etc. Throughout this process, "the quantum lying at the base suffers no alteration, the difference being only an outer form." (338) Specifying Measure is different. Here, "the quantum is taken in the first instance in its immediate magnitude [1], but in the second instance it is taken through the exponent of the ratio [2] in another amount [3]." (338) The point is that each Measure alters the other (through quantitative change). Measure therefore has physical consequence, whereas the alteration between Extensive and Intensive Magnitude did not.

27 Specific heat is the ratio of (a) the quantity of heat required to raise the temperature of a body one degree to (b) the quantity of heat required to raise the temperature of an equal mass of water one degree.

Measures. It is "now to be posited in the *immediacy* of being as such, in which determination measure still is." (339) That is, externality is sublated, and Measure embraces immediacy.[28]

Each of the two sides is quantitatively related and yet each is itself a Determinate Being, both qualitative and quantitative. The unity of the two extremes (each a Measure) is likewise a Measure. "Measure is thus the *immanent* quantitative relationship of *two* qualities to each other." (340) In this guise of distinguishing itself – [1] or [3] – from itself [2], each Measure "now appears as a Determinate Being which is both one and the same (e.g. the constant temperature of the medium), and also quantitatively varied (in the different temperatures of the bodies present in the medium)." (340) Measure is both the Ratio of Measures and *not* the Ratio of Measures.[29]

In Realized Measure, one side of the ratio is Amount, "which increases and decreases in an external arithmetical progression." (341) This is the external Measure which is applied against the measured material. This is, for instance, the thermometer in the child. The other side is the measured material – Unit to the external Amount, or the child. But which side is which? Since the child affects the thermometer and the thermometer affects the child, only external reflection can discern the difference. For themselves, "it is immaterial which is regarded as increasing or decreasing merely externally in arithmetical progression, and which, on the other hand, [is] specifically determining the other quantum." (341) Nevertheless, both must be present. One side of the ratio must be "extensive," while the other is "intensive." Extensiveness stands for externality, Amount, power, and becoming-other. Intensiveness stands for Unit, being-within-self and immunity from, "negative relatively" (341) to, the other.

The Law of Motion. Hegel compares the Ratio of Measures to the

---

[28] In his account of Measure, John Burbidge tends to say things like "measurement is . . . nothing but a proportion between two numbers." BURBIDGE, REAL PROCESS, *supra* note 5, at 46. But it is very important to see the extremes as, not just numbers, but themselves independent Measures, the middle term of which is a metonymic "average" which we take to be the measure of a thing.

[29] For this reason, the Ratio of Measure, or Realized Measure, is like variable magnitudes in mathematics. (340-1) The variables $x^2=y$ can be anything the mathematician chooses to make them. Yet the relation of x and y restricts choice. The restriction is qualitative and the freedom is quantitative. As with variables, the Ratio of Measure provides the measurer some freedom; any two Measures can be brought together to produce the Ratio. But the Realized Measure also restricts the measurer's freedom; the Ratio has a quality of its own.

laws of motion. Particularly, he denies that time and space are properly two Measures which produce a third Realized Measure. In motion, space and time are inseparable from the Ratio. This is most easily seen in "free motion" (342) – the motion of planetary orbit. In free motion, the quantitative relationship of time and space is "the being-for-self of measure." (343) These cannot be rendered asunder; time and space bear the relation that $\delta y/\delta x$ bears in calculus.[30]

Historically, the determination of the laws of planetary orbit was based on unifying empirical data through general formulae. "It is a great service to ascertain the empirical numbers of nature, e.g. the distance of the planets from one another," (343) Hegel writes. It is "an infinitely greater" (343) service when empirical numbers disappear and universal natural laws are manifested.[31] "But yet a still higher *proof* is required for these laws." (343) The proper laws must be proven from the notions of time and space themselves. "Of this kind of proof there is still no trace in the said mathematical principles of natural philosophy." (343)[32]

Hegel refers to Gallileo's formula for falling bodies, "a conditionally free motion," (342) which moves according to $s = at^2$. This is a Ratio of Powers – a qualitative "natural" feature of all bodies that fall. As a mathematical expression, however, it is merely a Direct Ratio; space and time are indifferently brought together.

The velocity (s/t) of an accelerating body is an expression of space

---

[30] This point is Einsteinian. To quote Bertrand Russell: "The scientific merit of Einstein's theory lies in the explanation, by a uniform principle, of many facts which are unintelligible in the Newtonian system. The philosophical itself lies chiefly in the substitution of the single manifold, space-time, for the two manifolds, space and time." Bertrand Russell, *Introduction*, in A.V. VAILIEV, SPACE, TIME, AND MOTION xv-xvi (1924); *accord*, HARRIS, *supra* note 2, at 146 (proclaiming Hegel to be Einsteinian).

[31] This may be a reference to Hegel's early dissertation *De Orbitis Planetarum*. *Supra* at 197 n.1.

[32] For a description of Hegel's attempt to "notionalize" Galileo's law, see Stefan Bütner, *Hegel on Galilei's Law of Fall*, in HEGEL AND NEWTONIANISM, *supra* note 1, at 337-8. Hegel complains of Newton's attempt to deduce the physics of the natural world from calculus, a point Hegel covers in his calculus commentaries. "These proofs *presuppose* their theorems, those very laws, from experience; what they succeed in doing is to reduce them to abstract expressions and convenient formulae." (343) Hegel does, however, give Newton important credit: "Undoubtedly the time will come when, with a clearer understanding of what mathematics can accomplish and has accomplished, the entire, real merit of Newton as against Kepler . . . will clearly be seen to be restricted to the said transformation of Kepler's formula." (343-4) (footnote omitted)

traversed in the very first Unit of time.[33] That is, the accelerating body has an *average* velocity, which is never its true speed. In the statement of velocity (for example, 25 MPH) – space is Amount as "determined by the specifying measure." (345) That is, the falling object does not demand that it fall 25 miles. This criterion is imposed upon it. Yet, since the law of falling bodies is a Direct Ratio, space is just as much exponent as Amount or side of the Ratio. The velocity found by the measurer is "the merely formal velocity which is not specifically determined by the Notion." (345) The velocity at the first unit of time does not actually exist, nor does the velocity at the last unit of time. Velocity is merely an average parading as the true velocity at any given unit of time.[34] "[T]his so-called unit of time is itself only an assumed unit and has as such atomic point no real being." (345-6)[35]

The real Being-for-self in velocity is the constant *a*. "The same co-efficient *a* remains in all the following units of time," (345) Hegel notes. Here is what is really internal to velocity. Space and time are externally imposed. Yet *a* is Being-for-self "only in so far as this moment is *unexplicated* [*an sich*] and hence an immediacy." (346) In short, the Being-for-self of the Specified Measure is precisely *not* its empirical measure.

C. Being-for-Self in Measure

The Ratio of Measures has Being-for-self [4], which will constitute the very negation of its being, in analogy to chapter 3 of Quality. In Figure 19(c), the extremes had quantitative elements that were qualitatively distinguished. Each extreme in the Ratio of Measures was itself a Measure, as shown in Figure 19(c). These extremes have an

---

[33] Why is time Unit? According to one commentator, "the qualitative moment of time constitutes a being-for-self, time being negatively related to itself in a manner which is still entirely abstract. It is because of this that it qualifies as the relational unit and therefore as a denominator." Bütner, *supra* note 32, at 338.

[34] Fall is "a truly uniformly accelerated motion [only] if the radius of the Earth were infinite, or . . . if the height of the fall were zero. Paradoxically enough, only if the movement it involves were not a fall, would the law governing it be realized as a uniformly accelerated motion." *Id.* at 336 (footnote omitted),

[35] "This certainly indicates that he thought that the concrete sciences . . . are dealing only with a sort of outer appearance, that the inner reality of the measurements and calculations by means of which they make their subject matter intelligible has to be sought here in the *Logic*." Arnold Vincent Miller, *Defending Hegel's Philosophy of Nature*, in HEGEL AND NEWTONIANISM, *supra* note 1, at 112.

existence that exceeds Realized Measure – [5] and [6] in Figure 19(c). As such, these surpluses are "so far posited only as immediate, *merely different* qualities." (344)

If [5] and [6] are immediate Qualities, [4] must be the quantitative side of Measure. But [4] is just as immediate – qualitative – as [5] and [6] are. Simultaneously, [4] is also part of [4, 5] and [4, 6] respectively. Hence, the immediate Quality is just as much immediate Quantum.

The quantitative aspect of the Ratio of Measures is what can be altered externally. Consequently, the Ratio of Measures is in part beyond itself – subject to outside control. "[E]xternally given" (345) Quantum is part of the Ratio. This givenness by an external measurer (who replaces the external mathematician in the Quantity chapters) is "the negation of the qualitative determination of measure." (345)

This negation of the qualitative aspect is nevertheless *inside* the Ratio of Measures – on the law of sublation. Hence the Ratio's qualitative heart is its quantitative promiscuity via outside manipulation. The negativity at the heart of the Ratio of Measures is its Being-for-self. For this reason, "[t]he qualitative element thus masks itself, specifying not itself but the quantitative determinateness." (344) In short, the Ratio of Measures is telling us what it is *not*. It is *not* free from outside manipulation, and this susceptibility is precisely its Quality.[36]

Specifying Measure is still specified. It is the qualitative "unit appearing as empirical, in the quantitative side of measure." (345) But, even if its empirical Unit is given to it, its true Being-for-self is hidden. Its freedom from externality is not yet truly "for-itself." For now, it is still a Determinate Being – "the quotient or exponent of a direct ratio between the sides of the measure." (345)

Measure is now "a specified quantitative relation which, as qualitative, has in it the ordinary external quantum." (346) But Measure is not just this "fixed exponent." (346) Measure also has an integrity against the measurer. This qualitative aspect of the Measure belies the quantitative expression. For example, no quantum can ever state the true speed of the falling body at any given moment. Thus, Measure has two sides – each of which is a Measure. One side is "immediate and external, and the other immanently specified." (347)

---

[36] Writing of the passage just explicated, Cinzia Ferrini remarks, "It is clear that for Hegel the empirical numbers of nature are now '*an sich*' captured by the conceptual net . . . which reveals something basic to them: namely, the qualitative aspect." Ferrini, *Framing*, *supra* note 1, at 299.

The unity of these moments in Figure 19(c) "means that measure is now . . . *realised.*" (347) In this realization, however, the "self-determination of the relation is thus *negated.*" (347) Its explicit determinateness comes from its external other. Measure was supposed to be qualitative in its own self, "but possesses in truth such qualitative determinateness only in the other side of the relation." (347)

Measure is thus merely a negative unity – "a *real being-for-self*, the category of a *something* as a unity of qualities which are related as measures." (347) Although the Specified Measures are external and given, the Specifying Measure nevertheless is "a complete *self-subsistent* something." (347) Meanwhile, the two extremes constituting this ratio are each repulsed "into *distinct self-subsistent* somethings," (347) and hence are Measures (and Ratios of Measures) unto themselves. And each side of these internal ratios are themselves Measures and Ratio of Measures. A bad infinity of Measures is in the offing.

8
Real Measure

Measure is now "a correlation of measures." (348) Its dialectical fate now occupies our attention.[1]

In chapter 7, relations concerned "abstract qualities like space and time." (348) These were said to be inseparable. (342) Now concepts like specific gravity and chemical properties take the stage – "determinations characteristic of *material* existence." (348)[2] Because the Ratio of Measures is the puck over which two resilient Measures

---

[1] Harris and Mure proclaim this chapter to be incomprehensible and announce that they will analyze the simpler discussion of the *EL* only. ERROL E. HARRIS, AN INTERPRETATION OF THE LOGIC OF HEGEL 145 (1983); G.R.G. MURE, THE PHILOSOPHY OF HEGEL 121-2 (1965). John Burbidge provides a lengthy and sympathetic account of this chapter. He reports that the chapter was substantially revised in the 1831 edition of the *SL*, to account for new developments in chemistry since 1813. JOHN W. BURBIDGE, REAL PROCESS: HOW LOGIC AND CHEMISTRY COMBINE IN HEGEL'S PHILOSOPHY OF NATURE 56-8 (1996).

[2] Clark Butler suggests that chapter 7 concerned physics, while this chapter stands for chemistry: "The *Logic* distinguishes between ideal measurement by stipulated units of a universal physical variable (such as force) and real measurement by natural units of a particular element of compound (such as water or salt). Ideal measures are found in physics, real measures in chemistry. Chemistry distinguishes particular material compounds, while physics (mechanics) distinguishes universal properties of matter everywhere." CLARK BUTLER, HEGEL'S LOGIC: BETWEEN DIALECTIC AND HISTORY 112 (1996). It must be added, however, that "real measures" are also ideal. On the law of sublation, we have been in the realm of the ideal ever since True Infinity arrived upon the scene. As for "natural units" in chemistry, Butler has in mind atoms – a dangerous claim, since Hegel was vociferously anti-atomic, even in chemistry.

face off, the Measures can now be considered separable. Eventually, they will dissolve into the middle term.

Hegel begins by summarizing the crosses borne and perils to ensue. Real Measure is first "a self-subsistent measure of a material thing which is related to others." (348)[3] It specifies these others as well as being specified by them.[4] These Specified Measures are in turn specifying, and so an entire series of Measures is implied. "[S]pecific self-subsistence does not continue as a single direct relation but passes over into a specific determinateness which is a series of measures." (348)

The specified series are the "Elective Affinities" of Specifying Measure. When opposing Measures are each viewed as Elective Affinities, each Measure can sustain a certain amount of quantitative change without undergoing qualitative change. But eventually, qualitative change ensues. Hegel calls this face-off of quantitative properties, as qualitatively limited, the Nodal Line. The Nodal Line stands over against the Measureless. Together, the Nodal Line and the Measureless constitute "the *infinity* of measure. In this, the self-exclusive and self-subsistent measures are one with each other." (349) In Measure's Infinite-for-itself, the extremes of Measure sublate themselves, and their Being flees to the middle term, where "self-subsistent measure enters into a negative relation with itself." (349)

---

[3] Materiality is "qualitative nature and subsistence." (347) Ulrich Ruschig complains that Real Measure's materiality is simply assumed *sub silentio*, not derived from prior categories, such as Pure Being. Ulrich Ruschig, *Logic and Chemistry in Hegel's Philosophy*, 7 INT'L J. PHIL. CHEMISTRY 5, 7 (2001). But this overlooks the fact that Pure Being *is* material. ERROL E. HARRIS, THE SPIRIT OF HEGEL 119 (1993) ("Being is the actual existing world as well as a logical category"). This material is rendered ideal at the end of chapter 2. We now have merely the thought of materiality to which the thought of Measure is applied. Not merely assumed, materiality is the residue of Pure Being and hence is derived. To be sure, there is the "givenness" of the beginning of the Logic, which Hegel concedes and carefully discusses. *Supra* at 26-39. Ruschig means something different in his criticism, which cannot be judged as well taken.

[4] What makes the Measure "real"? Butler suggests that chemicals dictate their own proportions and therefore can be considered "natural units." BUTLER, *supra* note 2, at 113. In physics, which involves inseparable time and space, there are no natural units. "Since force and other physical variables vary continuously in quantity, there is no objective unit of force." *Id*. Butler implies here that time or space are infinitely divisible, so that the unit of time – hour or second – is conventionally chosen. Hegel does say in general that space "is an external, real whole as such – hence amount – whereas time, like volume, is the ideal, negative factor, the side of unity." (342) *Infra* at 222-3.

A. The Relation of Self-Subsistent Measures

The Measures have become self-subsistent. They can withstand, to some degree, the power of quantitative change. This is evidence that Quantity has recaptured its Quality. We are on the verge of checking out from the transient hotel of Being altogether, in order to take up a permanent self-subsistence in the realm of Essence, where "things" endure over time.

Measures are actually relations of Measures, which are themselves relations of Measures. In this first section of Real Measure, the relation undergoes three changes. (a) At first, the relation is immediate and separate from its extremes (the Specifying and Specified Measures). (b) These separate Measures, however, are also quantitative, which means they continue on into the relation which is their middle term. (c) The quantitative aspect of these Measures represents the range of quantitative change each Measure can undergo without suffering qualitative change. Each Measure is a series facing another series in a determinate way. Hegel calls this Elective Affinity. Here Measure's indifferent willingness to be externally applied to other Measures becomes exclusive to certain others and hence constitutes a qualitative Being-for-self.

(a) Combination of Two Measures

The ensuing section emphasizes the externality inherent in the idea of combination. A measurer combines substances, which, like school children at a cotillion, are indifferent to the choice of a partner. Each of the combined measures is self-subsistent. Each "exists apart in particular things and their *combination* is effected *externally*." (349) Hence, this section stands for the move of the Understanding (but within the context of a dialectical chapter), as Figure 20(a) shows. The lesson is that, at first, Measure is a compound of other Measures. Specifying Measure is thus alienated from what measures it.

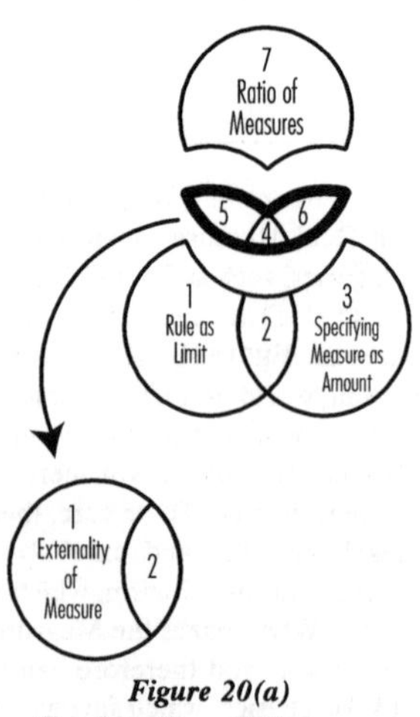

Figure 20(a)
Combination of Measures

Hegel begins by reminding us that a Measure is a relation of

Measures. As such, it is a unity between what is internal and what is external. Inwardness (or being-within-self) is exemplified by weight.

The internal, intensive side is joined to an external appearance – "the abstract, ideal element of space." (349) The external appearance is quantitatively determined (and space, it will be recalled, is Pure Quantity itself). The relation of these external qualities – their negative unity – "constitutes the qualitative nature of the material something." (349-50) In other words, a measurer, who joins the external qualities together in a quantitative way, puts them together in a Measure, but a unity transcending the Measure constitutes the true quality of the thing. Hegel aims here at the negative constitution of things that will be emphasized in the doctrine of Essence.[5]

Specific gravity – the ratio between weight and volume – is given as an example of Figure 20(a). Weight is portrayed as more authentic to the thing than volume. As proof, Hegel points out that, when two indifferent substances – say, gold and silver – are mixed together, the weight of the combination is the sum of the two weights. A pound of gold mixed with a pound of silver weighs two pounds.

Not so with volume. Volume is spatial – the ideal aspect of the thing. Why ideal? Recall that ideality stands for reduction to thought – the mere memory of a moment that has passed away through sublation. If we consider a physical object as constructed of molecules whizzing about but somehow held together by Attraction in a shape – this object is mostly space (or Repulsion) and very little "substance." The space infused between the molecules of a thing cannot be perceived. It is negative, and negative things are deduced, not perceived. Space is

---

5 Ruschig draws a different conclusion. He has Hegel claiming that specific weight (or density) is more "real" than the Ratio of Measures in Figure 19(c). "Yet it is doubtful if the transition to the "real" and allegedly more intrinsic measure can be regarded as a step in the logic of measuring without referring to a particular material. It is also doubtful if there is a merely logical reason that the direct ratio of mass and volume is the correct one for such a measuring." Ruschig, *supra* note 3, at 10. Ruschig suggests, to the contrary, that density fails to characterize the complete truth of a substance. "[C]haracterization by external comparison turns out to be superficial," he writes. *Id*. I think this is precisely Hegel's point. Hegel is not saying that density is *closer* to measuring the real thing than Rule was, which produced the Ratio of Measures in Figure 19(c). Rather, in density (for Hegel a mere *example* of Real Measure) an external force is necessary to accomplish the measuring, but there is some unique quantity in the measured material which is truly essential to it. The material is not *totally* open to outside manipulation. Hegel is working on bringing out the "measureless" essence of the thing. He is not trying to measure the measureless, as Ruschig implies.

simply a thought and hence ideal, not "real."

To prove that space is ideal, Hegel invokes again the admixture of two indifferent substances. A pound of gold and a pound of silver makes an alloy of two pounds. But if we add a *cup* of gold to a *cup* of silver, we get less than two cups. The joint volume of a compound may be less than the sum of the individual substances. This is true because the substance is a mixture of material and non-material – or empty and filled space. Hence, when liquid gold is added to liquid silver, some of the silver atoms slip into the space that pure gold would have preserved, so that the joint volume is less than the sum of the individual volumes.[6]

Not only is volume taken as ideal, it is also to be taken as Unit. Why? Recall that, in the early career of Quantity, the part of Number that was Amount and the part that was Unit were arbitrarily designated by the mathematician. Measurers have no such discretion accorded to them; space's unitary status reflects the negative constitution of things. It is the negative unity of qualities that is the qualitative nature of the thing. "Unit" stands for Discreteness, content, being, etc. All these concepts tend to the right of the diagram early in Quantity. Now the thing is conceived as Ratio – a negative unity of independent Measures. This negativity is to be equated with space – and with the ideality of things in general. Volume is therefore the "being" of the material thing. It is to be taken as leaning to the left of the diagram. "[I]t is space itself which constitutes the subsistence of matter in its external separated existence." (351)

If volume is Unit because it is spatial, extensive, external, and subjective, then weight (in specific gravity) is Amount. This is the intensive aspect, "which manifests [the thing] quantitatively." (350) For instance, a cubic inch of gold weighs 19.3 times as much as one cubic inch of water, when water is at its maximum density at 4° C, and when the densities of both gold and water are obtained by weighing the substances in air. Hence, we can say that for every unit (*i.e.*, cubic inch of water), gold of like unit manifests itself by the unique amount of 19.3. Quantity is therefore intrinsic to the physical object. Nevertheless, this Amount, although intrinsic, is negative, because negativity is the constitution of all things. Gold is *not* inherently 19.3, but is so only

---

6 Later, Hegel will criticize such naive descriptions as I have provided for assuming the existence of atoms without metaphysical proof. (360) I am undoubtedly guilty as charged. My point simply is that solid objects are made up mostly of empty space.

under very specified conditions to which gold itself is indifferent. Hence, Amount leans to the right of our diagram.

Here is no Ratio of Powers, however. Ratio of Powers stood for the relation that is immune from manipulation of the mathematician. So long as the exponent 16 stayed fixed in $x^2 = 16$, x determines itself as {4, -4}. This cannot be said of specific gravity. Nothing inherent in gold requires its comparison to a cubic inch of water at 4° C. Hegel says of Measures like specific gravity that "with the self-subsistence of the material thing immediacy has returned and in this the specific magnitude is an ordinary quantum whose relation to the other side is likewise determined as the ordinary exponent of a direct ratio." (350) 19.3 depends not only on the gold but on the water.

Why has immediacy returned? Because Measure is a negative unity of diverse Measures brought together externally to define the thing. Of course, the Specified Measures are diverse and subjectively chosen, but the fact that the unity of them *is* the thing suggests that the thing is immediate. If the Specified Measures are stripped away and the mediating unity alone is considered, it would be an immediacy. Yet Specifying Measure is at the mercy of the measurer. For that reason, we do not have the self-determining Ratio of Powers before us but highly manipulated quanta of the sort that we witnessed in Direct Ratio.

The intrinsic Quantum of gold, to continue with that example, is an "immediate quantum," (350) and it is specific to the thing. But it is likewise determined "only in the *comparison* with other exponents of such ratios." (350) Here Hegel emphasizes the conventionality of Measure. In chapter 7, Hegel remarked that it is "foolish to speak of a *natural* standard of things." (334) Universal standards of measure are merely conventional – "a matter of complete indifference." (334) Yet even if specific gravity is conventional, it likewise captures *the actual thing* which manifests itself quantitatively: "The exponent constitutes the specific intrinsic determinedness, the inner characteristic measure of something; but because this its measure rests on a quantum, it too is only an external, indifferent determinateness." (350) Gold's unique weight of 19.3 becomes something entirely different if comparison of gold is to another metal (*i.e.*, mercury) rather than water at 4° C. Accordingly, the intrinsic magnitude of the thing is *alterable*.

As the section heading indicates, specific gravity is "The Combination of Two Measures" (349) A cubic inch of water at 4° C (Unit) with the weight of 1 (Amount) is one Measure that faces off against gold, a second Measure, which has the same Unit (cubic inch) but a different

Amount (19.3). In this encounter, "each of the two measures, just because it is a measure, preserves itself in the alteration which it ought to suffer through the externality of the quantum." (350) Thus, self-preservation is "an alteration of the measure itself" and nevertheless "a reciprocal specification." (350) Yet "this self-preservation is itself a negative relation toward this quantum." (350) In other words, there is some quantitative aspect of gold which is *not* 19.3. Whatever this unnameable Quantity is, it is quite alienated from 19.3. Yet this Quantity likewise specifies 19.3, when gold and water are compared. Measure, then, is simultaneously a liar *and* a truth-teller about things.

Hegel has not finished with weight and volume (the two sides of specific gravity). Weight may be more authentic to a thing than volume. A pound of gold and a pound of silver weighs two pounds, but a cup of gold and a cup of silver do not make two cups. That weight is doubled is evidence that weight is "a real being-for-self" and "fixed determinate being" of the substance. (351) But even weight's exponent is subject to alteration, since the exponent expresses the qualitative aspect of the compound. Hegel has already said that the qualitative aspect of material things is the negative unity of their external parts. This implies that the substance can undergo quantitative change *without* undergoing qualitative change. The quality of a substance is its very indifference to outward quantitative measure. Accordingly, the exponents "are subject to alteration since they are the expression of the qualitative aspect of the compound." (351)[7]

Weight, then, does not, after all, represent the immanent determining of the quantitative element of the thing. Immanence is in fact on display with regard to volume, even though the volume of the compound is exempt from the rigor of addition. Its indifference to addition suggests that volume is not the real Being-for-self of substances. Nevertheless, as established in chapter 3, Being-for-self is precisely the *non-immanence* of a thing's content. Volume represents immanence because *space* "constitutes the subsistence of matter in its external separated existence." (351) In other words, what subsists in a Measure is its negativity to outward Measure – negative space.

Being negative, subsistence "lacks intrinsic being." (351) Evidence of this is that the quantitative volume of the compound is "subject to alteration." (351) The upshot of "this immanent determining of the

---

[7] Perhaps this likewise means that the *perceived* number of pounds or grams that a substance yields is external to the thing that is being weighed.

quantitative element" in volume is that "space is posited as what it truly is, an ideal being." (351) Space is not a *real* being but simply the thought of a past moment of the substance. That it is merely an absence is why addition does not apply.

The lesson from "The Combination of Two Measures" is that all things have a Measureless aspect that escapes merely external Measure. But Hegel does not wish to concede that there is an unknowable thing-in-itself in the Kantian manner. Measure says something true about the thing as well, thanks to the contribution of Dialectical Reason in the next section.

(b) Measure as a Series of Measure Relations

Metonymy is the theme of this new section's tongue. Metonymy is the inability to name the thing directly – only the context of the thing. In metonymy, if the entire context is described, the unnameable thing becomes a ghostly space the existence of which is simply inferred from context.

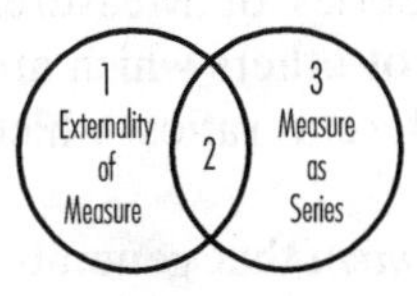

Figure 20(b)
Measure as a Series of Measure Relations

In the current section, Hegel suggests that a thing is ultimately the series of quanta produced when the thing is measured by all the other things that surround it. Specifying Measure is therefore a vacant place that is beyond direct, unmediated knowledge, but nevertheless indirectly knowable.

In praise of degree, Shakespeare's Ulysses says: "Take but degree away, untune that string, And, hark, what discord follows! each thing meets In mere oppugnancy." Hegel[8] agrees: "If two things forming a compound body owed their respective specific natures only to a simple qualitative determination, they would only destroy each other when combined." (351) The quantitative element is what permits a thing to survive combination. *Quantity* is the key to self-subsistence. Self-subsistence requires that the thing be combinable with another thing. That is, a Measure is affected quantitatively by another Measure and yet remains what it is qualitatively. Its quantitative manifestation *is* the quality of

---

[8] An ardent admirer of Shakespeare. WALTER KAUFMANN, HEGEL: A REINTERPRETATION 253 (1978); T.M. Knox, *The Puzzle of Hegel's Aesthetics*, in ART AND LOGIC IN HEGEL'S PHILOSOPHY 4 (Warren Steinkraus & Kenneth I. Schmitz eds., 1980).

the thing. Hence, a thing's quality is "masked in the quantitative element and is thus also indifferent towards the other measure, continuing itself in it and in the newly formed measure." (352) A thing, then, both contributes to and escapes detection of its Measure.

Measure functions because a measurer imposes a Specified Measure on a Specifying Measure. The result is a predictable Quantum that is nevertheless external to the "true" Measureless thing. Measure is not an arbitrary Quantum, as Figure 20(a) implied. Rather, it contributes to a unique middle term between two Measures which nevertheless fails to express the complete being of the Specified Measure.

It takes two sub-Measures to produce a third observable Measure. Only when a self-subsistent Measure is compared to some other Measure does its unique exponent make itself apparent. This exponent, however, is a "neutrality," not a direct expression of the *real* exponent. Neither sub-Measure is *entirely* reflected in the observable third Measure. Nevertheless, the observed Quantum in the Ratio of Measures is an accurate report of the Specifying Measure.[9] Furthermore, every Measure has a series of unique quanta that relates it to any given sub-Measure brought forth. A Series of Measures defines a thing: "This combination with a number of others which are likewise measures within themselves, yields different ratios which therefore have different exponents." (352)

The empty metonymic center or *quantitative exponent* that generates a series of neutral exponents is to be taken as Unit – the qualitative being of the thing. The external quantitative series – its relations with other Units – is Amount. Many Units face each other. Which is truly Unit and which Amount? Only the external measurer can determine this. As we are in a dialectic mode, undecidability reigns between the extremes and also *within* each of the extremes in Figure 20(b).

An infinite regress is present. A Unit is only fully known if brought into comparison with every other unit. In this infinite regress, Hegel

---

[9] Such truth, of course, is merely one-sided. Yet "being is a result of measurement; that is, 'to be' means 'to already have a measure' – for being is merely an abstraction from concrete measurement, or a reduction and fixing of immeasurable singularity." ANDREW HAAS, HEGEL AND THE PROBLEM OF MULTIPLICITY 139 (2000). In short, things *are* only to the extent they are measured by consciousness.

It does not follow, as Ruschig suggests, that "the quality of a substance can be characterized more precisely by comparing its initial density with the densities of its combinations with substances." Ruschig, *supra* note 3, at 11. Hegel is not aiming to define *precise measurement*. Rather, he is trying to show that, no matter how precise the measurement, a measureless aspect always escapes.

sees a return to Degree. The Specifying Measure and also the series it generates are "simple or unitary." (354) But, just as the 100th Degree was defined by the Extensive Magnitude outside it, so the Specifying Measure, as Unit, is defined by all the Measures outside such a Specifying Measure. The Unit is surrounded by "a circle of quanta," (354) and each quantum is itself surrounded by a circle of quanta. Specifying Measure is metonymic, unknowable directly, known only by what it is not. Within these wheels-within-wheels "the self-determinedness of measure lies." (354)[10]

Of metonym, Hegel writes, "Its self-relation is . . . an *immediate* relation and therefore its indifference to an other consists only in the quantum." (354) In other words, the quality of the thing is quantitative. Like a Quantity, its content is supplied by the circle of Measures that surrounds it. But Measure as Series is too advanced to be a Quantity indifferent to its own integrity: "this relation in which two specific measures specify themselves in a third something, the exponent, also implies that the one has not passed into the other; that therefore there is not only *one* negation, but that *both* are posited as negative in the relation." (354) The Specifying Measure, being a True Infinite, stays what it is even as it yields an appearance in a series.[11] In this guise, the Specifying Measure announces, "I am not any one of the quanta in the series." Yet the Specified Measure which generates the quantum

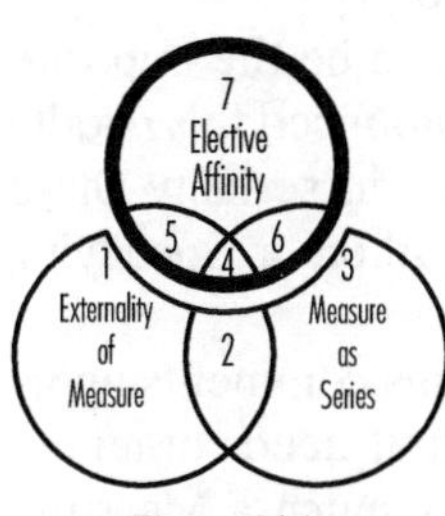

Figure 20(c)
Elective Affinity

[10] "Combination of Two Measures" stands for the indifference of Specifying to Specified Measure; "Measure as a Series of Measure Relations" represents the dependence of a thing on Measure in general. The middle term will stand for the unity of indifference and dependence of things to their Measure. In contrast, Ruschig thinks that "Combination of Two Measures" stands for density of unchanged substances, while "Measure as a Series" stands for neutralized (hence changed) substances. "Only if we refer to the chemical content, the logical transition is comprehensible as well as conclusive." Ruschig, *supra* note 3, at 7. Obviously, I disagree. Hegel is aiming for the metaphysics of Measure, for which density and stoichiometry are but examples. Hegel may shift from examples pertaining to density to examples pertaining to stoichiometry (the quantification of neutralizing relations), but this does not affect the integrity of his logic.

[11] Enduring externality is the feature that separates ordinary chemistry from the advanced category of Chemism at the end of the Logic. *See* John W. Burbidge, *Chemistry and Hegel's Logic*, in HEGEL AND NEWTONIANISM 609-11 (Michael John Petry ed., 1993).

in the Series is saying the same thing. It likewise says, "Neither am I the quantum in the Series that the Specifying Measure generated."

At this point, Speculative Reason observes that each Measure – [1] and [3] – claims not to be the Series [2]. Yet [2] is authentically each of the Measures. Hence, [1] and [3] have something in common. Hegel names this serial commonality Elective Affinity (*Wahlverwandtschaft*). Of Figure 20(c), Hegel writes: "This their qualitative unity [4] is thus a self-subsistent *exclusive* unit [7]." (354) This [7], which Hegel calls "the neutral relationship," (354) proves that the exponents in the Series have a qualitative nature, reflecting the truth of the thing. Obviously, [7] is a Measure; Measure is quantitative *and* qualitative, and so [7] reflects that the difference between [4] and [6] is quantitative. Of this quantitative basis, Hegel says that the self-subsistent Measure – [4] or [6] – is indifferent to [7]. This indifference is the very quantitative basis that permits [4] or [6] to go outside itself and into [7].

To summarize, then, [1, 2] and [2, 3] turned out to be the opposite of what they were supposed to be. The extremes renounced this middle term – seriality – and held themselves aloof. Yet in seriality these extremes have an *affinity*, because, without its other, a Specifying Measure could not manifest what it is.

Although Hegel is "chemical" in his discussion, his comments apply to love. A human being stands aloof from others but needs others to inform him what she is. Human personality is very much a Measure, which is why people alternate aloofness with affinity towards their Specified Measures.[12]

(c) Elective Affinity

Affinity and neutrality refer to chemical relationships. A chemical substance "has its specific determinateness essentially in its relation to its other and exists only as this difference from it." (355) Affinity is not

---

[12] The connection between Elective Affinity and love was not lost on the Greeks. "Empedocles was of the opinion that the particles of the four elements – earth water, air, and fire, passed to and from one another by means of love and hatred." Cees de Pater, *Newton and Eighteenth-Century Conceptions of Chemical Affinity*, in HEGEL AND NEWTONIANISM, *supra* note 11, at 619. Goethe, Hegel's patron, also had a popular novel in 1809 entitled *The Elective Affinities.See* JOHANN WOLFGANG VON GOETHE, ELECTIVE AFFINITIES (R.J. Hllingdale trans., 1971). For a review, see H.A.M. Snelders, *The Significance of Hegel's Treatment of Chemical Affinity*, in HEGEL AND NEWTONIANISM, *supra*, at 631.

just affinity to some other substance but to the series of *all* substances. The series is nothing but the quanta that the Specifying Measure holds in common with every other Measure. They identify "a self-subsistent measure [that] relates itself to self-subsistent measures of a different quality and to a series as such." (367) Specifying Measure is *indifferent* amongst the many Measures to which it is compared. Simultaneously, each member of the series is itself an *exclusive* Measure between the Specifying and any given Specified Measure.

Elective affinity, however, singles out these exclusive Measures and proclaims some "better" than (or at least qualitatively different from) some of the others. "In elective affinity as an exclusive, qualitative correlation [7]," Hegel writes, "the relationship is rid of [its] quantitative difference." (355) In this series of exclusive relations, numbers have lost their continuity with each other. These relations are therefore qualitative (yet not entirely qualitative).

How does Hegel derive this qualitative preference for one Measure over another? The derivation has to do with the *extensive magnitude* of the substances in the series of Measures that define the metonymic thing. Extensive Magnitude, it will be recalled, stood over against Degree. If Degree was the 100th, Extensive Magnitude was all the numbers implicitly excluded by the 100th degree and by which Degree is defined. But Extensive Magnitude and Degree ended up being the same thing. The 100th Degree had its Extensive Magnitude within it as well as without it.

Intensity suggests that the series of neutralizing Measures that define the Specifying Measure can be arranged by the intensity with which they "neutralize" the Specifying Measure. The Specified Measures therefore differ in the quantity needed to neutralize the Specifying Measure. This ends up being the Specifying Measure's very quality. Music is Hegel's example of this. The musical notes can be arranged into scales, and each note has an affinity with the other notes. Musical "compositions" are therefore Elective Affinities.

The relation of a Specifying and Specified Measure is unique and hence qualitative. Now the measured thing graduates to "the relationship . . . of *more* or *less*." (356) But there is still a sense in which the Specified Measure is indifferent as to whether it is neutralized by one rather than another Specifying Measure (even as the amount necessary to neutralize differs). The qualitative relation of

Elective Affinity is therefore still external and quantitative.[13]

B. Nodal Line of Measure-Relations

In Elective Affinity (or neutrality), the exclusive and hence qualitative nature of Specifying Measure's relation to Specified Measure was emphasized. Yet a Measure has a series of Affinities. These can be distinguished only quantitatively.[14] The amounts needed to neutralize a Specified Measure vary. Because it is quantitative, Affinity *is* continuity from one neutrality into another. To the extent we arrange the Affinities quantitatively, this is externally imposed on them. Neutrality is "*separable into the moments* which united to produce it." (366) Yet externality "in the form of a comparison" (366) is not their only moment. Affinity may be continuous, but "it is as self-subsistent somethings that these [two Measures] enter into relation indifferently with one or the other of the opposite series, although combining in different, specifically determined amounts." (366-7) Hence, says Dialectical Reason, not only is Affinity continuous, but it is "infected with its own indifference; it is in its own self something external and alterable in its relation to itself." (367) Beyond the external Affinity is "an affirmatively present [*seiende*], qualitative foundation – a permanent, material substrate which, as also the continuity of the measure *with itself* in its externality, must contain in its quality the principle of the specification of this externality." (367) We thus have a unity of Continuity *and*

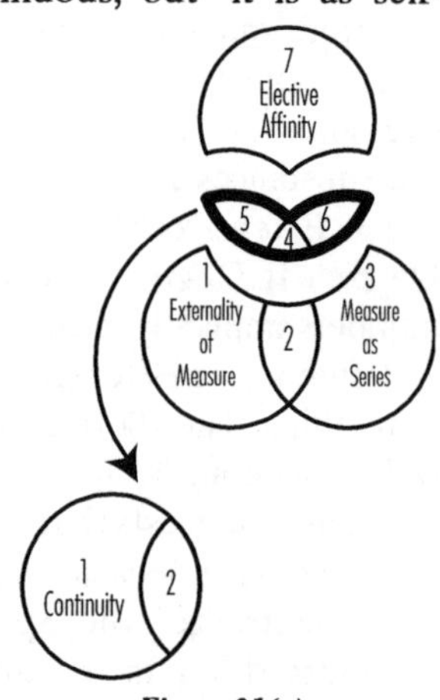

Figure 21(a)
Continuity of Affinity

[13] Following Elective Affinity, Hegel indulges in a long comment, added in the 1831 revision, on contemporary chemistry. BURBIDGE, REAL PROCESS, *supra* note 1, at 65. For Hegel, "elective affinity is the cause of the origin of chemical substances." Snelders, *supra* note 12, at 637. As with calculus, the fault is that chemistry inadequately distinguishes Quantity and Quality. For a detailed analysis, see David Gray Carlson, *Hegel's Theory of Measure*, 25 CARDOZO L. REV. 129, 174-7 (2003).

[14] Hence, eighteenth century chemistry made tables of Elective Affinities a major research project. Snelders, *supra* note 12, at 640.

Indifference, which Hegel names Substrate. The Indifference of Affinity implies the "relation *to itself* of the measure relation." (367) As such, it is qualitative.

Significantly, self-relation now appears at this stage on the right, *negative* side of the page – a sign that Essence is nigh. This was already the case in Measure as Series, which was likewise implicitly a metonym – an indifference to any given Measure but nevertheless the sum total of them all. Now we have a *posited*, "affirmatively present" (367) indifference to Measure. What is posited is what Being is *not*. This will be the quintessential character of Essence, which starts officially in chapter 10 but already shows itself here.

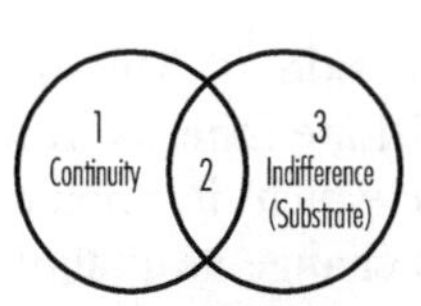

Figure 21(b)
Continuity and Indifference (Substrate)

The Substrate is a qualitative continuity. It remains the same, even as its outward appearance changes. To borrow Hegel's favorite example, water becomes ice if its quantitative temperature falls too low, steam if the temperature becomes too high. But, in all these different states, it remains H_2O. H_2O is Substrate to its liquid, solid or gaseous forms. Yet Substrate is continuous with its external Measure. It "must contain in its quality the principle of the specification of this externality." (367)

In a dialectical mode, the extremes – [1] and [3] – deny [2] and thereby confirm [2] as their true being: "The exclusive measure [1] is external to itself in its being-for-self [2] and hence repels itself from itself, positing itself both as another measure relation and also as another, merely quantitative, relation; it is determined as in itself [2] a specifying unity which produces measure relations within itself." (367)[15] The isolation of [2] as the essence of the extremes is the move of Speculative Reason.

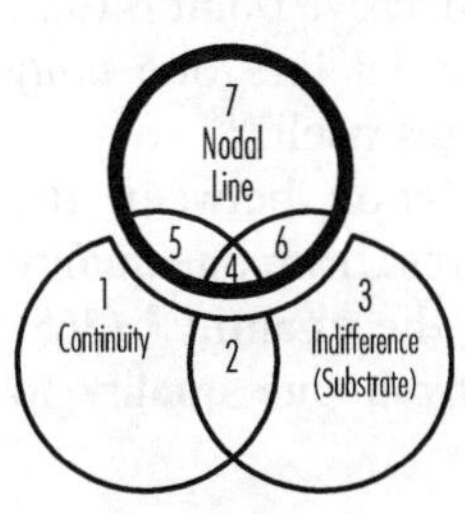

Figure 21(c)
Nodal Line

The Nodal Line (*Knotenlinie*) differs from Elective Affinity. In Affinity, "a self-subsistent measure relates itself to self-subsistent measures of a different quality and to a series of such." (367) At that point, the concept of Substrate had not yet been devel-

---

15 *See* HAAS, *supra* note 9, at 155 (Measure "shows itself as the between of that which it seeks to exclude").

oped. Now the series in Figure 21(c) is recognized as taking place "in *one and the same* substrate within the same moments of the neutrality." (367)[16] Measure has become self-repelling. It has exiled its Measures [4, 5, 6] to the extremes, from which it is quantitatively *and* qualitatively different [7]. The Substrate, then, organizes the series of Measures into "a nodal line of measures on a scale of more and less." (367)[17] Substrate is a being-for-self, which needs external quanta to express what it is. Because of this need, it is "open to externality and to quantitative alteration." (367)

Substrate constitutes one side. On the other side is Measure generally, organized in the Nodal Line. The Nodal Line inherits from Rule the character that "it has a range within which it remains indifferent to [quantitative] alteration and does not change its quality." (367) Because of this range of quantitative change that invokes no qualitative change, "there enters a point in this quantitative alteration at which the quality is changed and the quantum shows itself as specifying, so that the altered quantitative relation is converted into a measure, and thus into a new quality, a new something." (367) Quantitative change, then, leads to qualitative change. Nevertheless, underneath the qualitative change lies a Substrate indifferent to *both* quality and quantity. In qualitative change, two qualities have no connection. One is *not* the limit to the other. Each is completely external to the other. But a Substrate underlies all the changes. "The new something has therefore not emerged from or developed out of its predecessor but directly from itself." (367-8) The decisive point is that, "in this 'infinite progress' of a self-continuing nodal line one *unity* remains nonetheless, one 'self-sameness' constitutes itself."[18]

Meanwhile, on the side of Measure, the relation between the qualities is quantitative. This means that "the progress from one quality [to another] is in an uninterrupted continuity of the quantity." (368) Yet, at some dramatic moment, nature *leaps* from one quality to

---

16 Wolfgang Bonsiepen, *Newtonian Atomism and Eighteenth-Century Chemistry*, in HEGEL AND NEWTONIANISM, *supra* note 11, at 607 ("In his theory of elective affinity, [Hegel] seems to be operating without any presupposed substances. Since there is no chemical substratum, simply a variety of chemical reactions, the chemical elements are regarded as being completely determined by means of their mutual inter-relationships.").

17 HAAS, *supra* note 9, at 155 ("If 'exclusion' marks the elective affinities of self-sufficient measures, then 'inclusion' marks them when they take on the form of a knotted line").

18 HERBERT MARCUSE, HEGEL'S ONTOLOGY AND THE THEORY OF HISTORICITY 66 (Seyla Benhabib trans. 1987).

another, even if the quantitative change is reassuringly gradual. Gradualness, however, is the opposite of qualitative change. In gradualness, the quality of the thing is indifferent to the quantitative change.

The nodal line is like a knotted string. Between the knots is quantitative difference, to which quality is indifferent. Each knot represents a qualitative change. "The system of natural numbers already shows a nodal line of qualitative moments which emerge in a merely external succession," Hegel writes. (368) Each number in the line bears a quantitative relation to the one before or after it. But these numbers likewise have specific relations with specific numbers when the question is power or root. (This specific relation of a number and its, say, square root would be an Elective Affinity).

The musical scale is a nodal line. A note is indifferent to the one before or after it, but, in harmony, the notes have specific relations with other notes, analogous to the specific relations between roots and powers. As one plays notes, each successive one seems unrelated to the one before, when "there suddenly emerges a *return*, a surprising accord, of which no hint was given by the quality of what immediately preceded it." (369) The harmony constitutes "a sudden interruption of the succession of merely indifferent relations which do not alter the preceding specific reality. [A] specific relation breaks in *per saltum*." (369)[19]

Qualitative leaps occur in chemical combinations. Water, for example, instantly freezes when it reaches 0° C It "does not gradually harden as if thickened like porridge [*breiartig*], gradually solidifying until it reach the consistency of ice." (370)[20] "Every birth and death, far from being a progressive gradualness, is an interruption of it and is the leap from a quantitative to a qualitative alteration." (369-70)

Hegel ends his analysis of the Nodal Line of Measure with a blast at gradualness seemingly at odds with the early chapters on Being but, on further reflection, is not. It will be recalled that, in the Ought, Being ceases to be – a cessation which is the in-itself of Being; the Finite *ought* to cease to be. This led efficiently to the True Infinite, which ceases to be what it was and yet remains what it was.[21] Now Hegel

---

[19] This material on harmony was added in the 1831 edition of the *SL*. BURBIDGE, REAL PROCESS, *supra* note 1, at 57.

[20] The rendering of *breiartig* (pasty or viscous) into "like porridge" reveals the translator's poetic side.

[21] *Supra* at 97.

complains that gradualness is based on the assumption that what comes to be is already actually in existence, but not yet perceptible because of its smallness. Under the rule of gradualness, "coming-to-be and ceasing-to-be lose all meaning." (370) The complaint is that Being-in-itself is quantified in gradualist discourse, and quantification is, in Measure, the externalist position. Rather than denying the True Infinite here, Hegel is merely complaining that, in gradualism, the True Infinite undergoes change *externally*, not immanently.

Gradualness, Hegel says, threatens morality. Stealing starts off as wrong, but perhaps dodging bus fare is not a crime, and so on. "It is through a more and less that the measure of frivolity or thoughtlessness is exceeded and something quite different comes about, namely crime, and thus right becomes wrong and virtue vice." (371) Since gradualness represents the external position (not the immanent one), gradual change in morality subjectivizes the process. The reality of the situation – the radical change from the legal to the criminal – becomes obscured in quantitative measures.

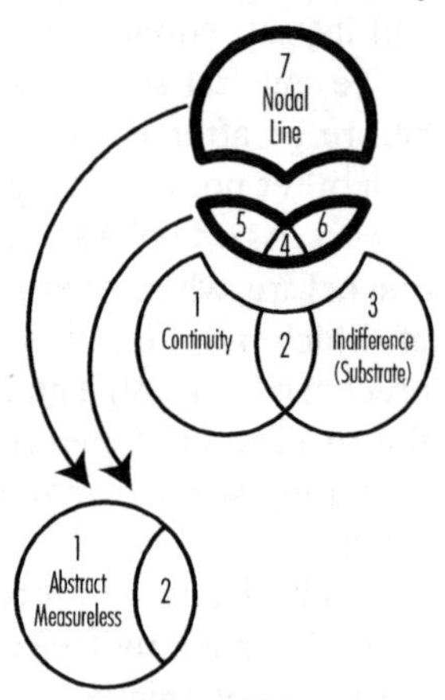

Figure 22(a)
Abstract Measureless

C. The Measureless

The Nodal Line is a sequence of Rules within which Quality is indifferent to quantitative change. Yet quantitative change is potentially lethal. "Magnitude is that side of determinate being through which it can be caught up in a seemingly harmless entanglement which can destroy it." (371) None of this concerns the Substrate, however. The Understanding therefore proposes that travel up and down the Nodal Line is a Spurious Infinity [4, 5, 6] to which the Substrate is indifferent: "Thus there is posited the alternation of specific existences with one another and of these equally with relations remaining merely quantitative – and so on *ad infinitum*." (371) This Spurious Infinity cannot teach us what the substrate [7] is. The Substrate is therefore Measureless.

Quality "is impelled beyond itself into the *measureless* and is destroyed by the mere alteration of its magnitude." (371) How does this follow? If we lower the temperature of liquid water from 1° to -1° C, the liquid quality is impelled beyond itself, but do we not end up with a *new* quality – solid ice? Yes; that represents the Spurious Infinity of the Nodal Line. But liquid quality is discontinuous with the solid quality. *Both* these qualities are, however, continuous with the Abstract Measureless Substrate. So when the liquid quality erases itself, its being is sent to the Substrate, not to the new, discontinuous solid quality. The Abstract Measureless therefore represents the Continuity between the Substrate and the Nodal Line. It is "the quantum as such which lacks an inner significance and is only an indifferent determinateness which does not alter the measure." (371) By this Hegel means that the Abstract Measureless Substrate cannot determine its own state on the Nodal Line. An external measurer is in charge of Quantum; for this reason the Abstract Measureless is *itself* a Quantum – open to outside determination and lacking "inner significance." It depends on the measurer for its appearance in the Nodal Line of Measures.

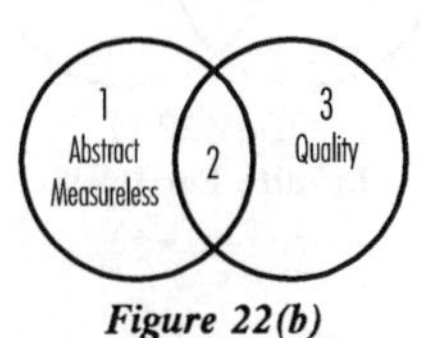

Figure 22(b)
Quality of the Abstract Measureless

The Measureless is quantitative.[22] Yet, Dialectical Reason counters, the Abstract Measureless "is equally a quality on its own account." (371) Its quality is that it has no quality, if quality is what changes via quantitative pressure. Hegel gives this new step no name other than the qualitative aspect of the Abstract Measureless.[23] Once again, Quality appears on the rightward side of the page – the side of nothingness.

In this alternation, [1] proclaims itself not qualitative. It sees the Substrate as immune from quantitative pressure. [3] proclaims itself not quantitative. Both of them export what they are not to [2]. Speculative

---

[22] Michael Baur sees the Measureless as an illusion: "But any Measurelessness merely provides the grounds for the generation of a new set of Measure-relations. This new set persists until its Quantities once again change beyond a certain point to produce yet another apparent Measurelessness. This process repeats itself indefinitely, and so Measure, too, has developed a bad infinite oscillation, only this time between Measure and the Measureless." Michael Baur, *Sublating Kant and the Old Metaphysics: A Reading of the Transition from Being to Essence in Hegel's* Logic, 29 OWL OF MINERVA 139, 145 (1998). This assumes that the Measureless is just another Measure in disguise, but I think the Measureless describes the essence of Substrate – that which underlies the Nodal Line. Accordingly, the Measureless is a *beyond*. The modulation in question is between syllogistic extremes which each deny the influence of quantitative change. It is this negation which places the Infinite for Itself beyond the realm of Measure proper.

[23] "Hegel is hard put to find names for his categories which will distinguish them satisfactorily." HARRIS, *supra* note 1, at 170.

Reason agrees that [2] is *neither* quality nor quantity. This concrete version of the Measureless is *beyond* Quality and Quantity. The name Hegel assigns to this speculative step is the Infinite For Itself.[24]

Hegel compares this new Infinite to earlier versions. Most primitive was the Qualitative (Spurious) Infinite. This was "the eruption of the infinite in the finite as an *immediate transition* and vanishing of the latter in its beyond." (371-2) What the Spurious Infinite lacked was continuity. In Figure 7(b), the Spurious Infinite went out of existence and became Another Finite. The True Infinite, in contrast, stayed what it was *and* became something different.

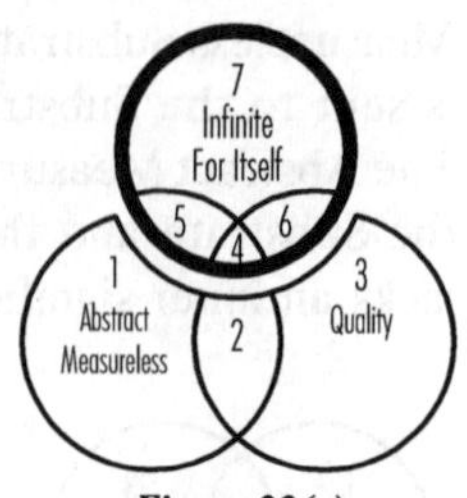

Figure 22(c)
Infinite For Itself

Quantitative Infinity was more advanced. It had continuity. It expelled itself from itself, as did the Spurious Infinite. But, as a True Infinite, the Quantitative Infinite also remained what it was. The Quantitative Infinite was already "in its own self its beyond and *points beyond itself*." (372) A True Infinite is both inside and outside of itself.

The Infinite For Itself, in contrast, "*posits* both the qualitative and quantitative as *sublating* themselves in each other." (372) In short, the Infinite For Itself represents Measure returned to itself, and, in this reflection-into-self, the Infinite For Itself shows itself to be *dehors* the realm of Being.

The Infinite For Itself is beyond the concept of qualitative change. So long as Measure is open to quantitative change, it is slave to something external – not yet free. Yet in the Abstract Measureless, externality sublated itself, converting itself into "that which is

---

[24] John Burbidge's account is different. He views the Nodal Line as giving rise to absolutely discontinuous qualities, conceived as distinct neutral compounds. BURBIDGE, REAL PROCESS, *supra* note 1, at 47. But this leaves out the whole notion of Substrate, which is the very point of the Nodal Line. Burbidge then writes: "Since there is no qualitative boundary the two [neutral compounds] share – at least to the extent that thought can anticipate it – they are simply external to each other. So we are far removed from even a minimal account that would enable us to understand the relation. From this perspective no explanation is possible. We cannot conceive what is involved; it is immeasurable." *Id.* (footnote omitted). Thus, for Burbidge, what is immeasurable is qualitative change. *Id.* at 48 ("The transformation of one quality into another is defined as immeasurable"). This seems off point. There is nothing inconceivable about the Measureless. It represents the substantial Substrate which is immune from qualitative change through quantitative manipulation. It does not represent a property of qualitative transformations.

determined in and for itself." (372)

Here we have for the first time the concept of "in and for self," the very essence of Essence. Being-in-itself is mere implicitness. Its job is to become for itself. Being-for-self expelled its content and became Quantity. Quantity had to recapture its Quality in order to subsist. But openness to qualitative change still portended an inability to subsist.[25] Only when Quality and Quantity are both sublated can a thing subsist. The state that is beyond quantitative and qualitative transition is being-in-and-for-self. "This unity which thus continues itself into itself in its alternating measures is the truly persisting self-subsistent material substance or thing." (372)

An important consideration must not be missed. Quality and Quantity have a beyond in a Measureless Infinite For Itself, but the Infinite For Itself *has no beyond*. It is a totality that "has an identity that is more than then the sum of its parts . . ."[26] A non-reflexive relation adheres between Measure and the Infinite For Itself. Measure has its beyond in the Infinite For Itself, but the latter has no beyond. It is a bit like this. When Determinate Being was negated, negation was Limitation to Determinate Being, but Negation was not ultimately Limitation to Determinate Being. Rather Negation was immanent within Determinate Being. At first, Negation – the product of Dialectical Reason – was reified and opposed abstractly to Determinate Being; Negation *was* a Determinate Being and accordingly had Limitation. But now the true nature of Negation has been revealed. It is Determinate Being's inner stuff. So the Infinite For Itself is no Determinate Being limited by Measure. Rather it is unlimited, Infinite and for-itself. *Measure* has a beyond, but the Infinite For Itself does not.

Hegel concludes with three propositions about the Infinite For Itself. The first is qualitative, the second quantitative, the third the beyond of these concepts. (α) There is now posited a "perennial substrate" (372) underlying all quantitative and qualitative change. This is a "severance

---

[25] *See* Cinzia Ferrini, *On the Relation Between "Mode" and "Measure" in Hegel's* Science of Logic: *Some Introductory Remarks* 20 OWL OF MINERVA 20, 33, 34 (1988) ("The precise nature of "measure" is shown to be that of superseded externality which constitutes totality in that it reinstates the sublated being-for-self. [M]easure has still to be regarded as an externality, a more or less, the determination of the concrete truth of finite being.").

[26] ROBERT M. WALLACE, HEGEL'S PHILOSOPHY OF REALITY, FREEDOM AND GOD 154 (2005).

of being from its determinateness." (372) The Measures which manifest the Substrate are "qualitative self-subsistent measures," (372) separate and apart from the Substrate. (ß) Nevertheless the difference between Substrate and Measure is *quantitative*. The Substrate is continuous with them. (γ) If qualitative change is merely quantitative (*i.e.*, has no bite), then quality itself is negated. And since quantity requires quality, quantity goes too. The Substrate negates both its qualitative and its quantitative moments. There is now a distinction between Measure and the Substrate that underwrites it. The meaning of the infinite progress up and down the Nodal Line is "only to *show* or to *posit* the *determinate being* " (373) of the Substrate. "Consequently, the measures and the self-subsistent things posited with them are reduced to *states*. The alteration is only change of a *state*, and the *subject* of the transition is posited as remaining the *same* in the process." (373)

To summarize our progress, first, in chapter 7 (Specific Quantity), the extremes were not self-sufficient Measures. Only the middle term was. In Ratio of Measures, the extremes became Measures in themselves. In Elective Affinity, Measure was revealed to be a series of Measures. The metonymic thing "shows itself to be an immanent specifying unity of a self-subsistent measure distinguished from its specifications." (373) But it is still a slave to externality.

> [I]t is not yet the free Notion which alone gives its differences an immanent determination: it is as yet only a substrate, a material, and for its differentiation into totalities, i.e., into difference embodying the nature of the unchanged substrate, it is dependent solely on the external, quantitative determination which shows itself at the same time as a difference of quality. (373-4)

What the Measureless must now do is escape this dependence on externality altogether.

9 The Becoming of Essence

Measure posits a substrate beyond itself, but we are not yet finished with the realm of Being. There remains the short third chapter of Measure[1] which previews the Doctrine of Essence. Real Measure ended with Measure external to the Substrate; the point now is to show that externality is equally internal.[2]

A. Absolute Indifference

The Understanding contemplates the Infinite For Itself in Figure 22(c) and proclaims its principle to be Absolute Indifference (*Indifferenz*).[3] Absolute Indifference is "the indifference which, *through the negation* of every determinateness of being, i.e., of quality, quantity, and . . . measure, is a process of *self-mediation* resulting in a simple unity." (375) It stands for the proposition that the Substrate and its Nodal Line are in perfect unity. By now the Substrate is posited as immune from externally imposed change. Its external manifestation is merely its *state* – "something qualitative and external which has the

---

[1] This chapter is omitted entirely from the *EL*.

[2] According to another summary of this chapter: "everything manifests itself externally, it being of its very essence to do so. Its indifference to this external self-manifestation is, therefore, only opposed in a relative manner to its identity with it. The distinction of quantity and quality constitutes a relative opposition which expresses an absolute identity." Louis Fleischhacker, *Hegel on Mathematics and Experimental Science*, in HEGEL AND NEWTONIANISM 209, 221 (Michael John Petry ed., 1993)

[3] Rinaldi claims this category is "nothing else than an analysis and critique – of unexcelled profundity, lucidity and rigor – of the ultimate foundations of Schellingian metaphysics . . . " GIACOMO RINALDI, A HISTORY AND INTERPRETATION OF THE LOGIC OF HEGEL 178 (1992).

indifference for a *substrate*." (375)

The *state* of the Substrate is qualitative, external, and "a vanishing determinateness." (375) Heretofore, Quality has been the integrity of the Specifying Measure against quantitative manipulation. But now Quality has been externalized. An externalized internality is a contradiction. "[Q]uality as thus external to being is the opposite of itself and as such is only the sublation of itself." (375) Outward determinateness (or *state*) is now posited as "an empty differentiation." (375) The *inner* life is the true thing. Nevertheless the inner is nothing without the outer. Therefore, "each of the two sides is posited as having to be itself *in principle* . . . this whole." (376)

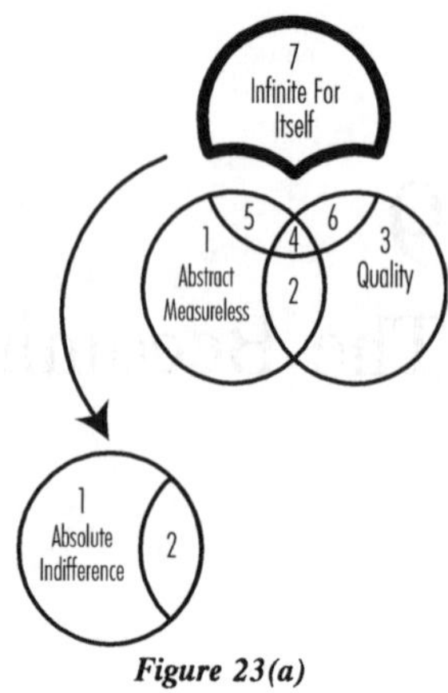

Figure 23(a)
Absolute Indifference

Absolute Indifference is "concrete, a mediation-with-self through the negation of every determination of being." (375) "Concrete," we know, implies a mediation between being and nothing. It is the opposite of "abstract," which implies no indwelling Spirit. Now, mediation between being and nothing (Quality and Quantity) is entirely within the selfhood of the Substrate. Externalities wreak no effect on the thing. The Substrate is beginning to taste freedom. "As this mediation [the Substrate] contains negation and relation, and what was called state is its immanent, self-related differentiation." (375) "Contains" here must be read in the double sense of having it within *and* preventing it from escaping. The external is not truly external but is the very manifestation of the Substrate. Because of this containment, the Substrate "ceases to be only a substrate and *in its own self* only abstract." (375)

B. Indifference as Inverse Ratio of Its Factors

Dialectical Reason reminds the Understanding of its history. The Understanding emphasized the immediate sameness between Substrate and Measure; Dialectical Reason emphasizes the difference of the two sides. It concedes the relation of Measure and Substrate [1, 2], but it asserts that Measure [3] is also different from Substrate. [3] is said to be "fixed measure." (376) It represents the *limit* to the Substrate. By this Hegel means that *all Measure relations* are now conceptually present to define the thing. Since it is *metonymic*, Substrate is finally manifested only when *every Measure relation is accountedfor*. Of course, this is empirically impossible, but this is just to say that empirical knowledge of things is always partial. If we are *really* to understand the Substrate, all its measures must be present and accounted for. And if all these Measures are present, the Substrate has gained an immunity from the will of the Measurer. Since the measurer has nothing to add, the role of external reflection is over. A "determination of indifference is posited within the indifference itself and . . . the latter is therewith posited as being for itself." (375) Hegel names the complete totality of Measures the Inverse Ratio of Its Factors (*umgekehrtes Verhältnis ihres Factoren*).

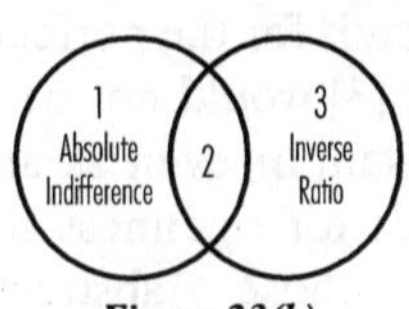

Figure 23(b)
Inverse Ratio of the Factors

Inverse Ratio is a term from chapter 6. In $xy = 16$, an increase in x led to a decrease in y. The variables x and y were open to external manipulation by the mathematician. But there was a limit to the mathematician's power over x and y; she couldn't make x or y equal to 16. This resistance helped reestablish Quality in Quantum.

In Inverse Ratio, the exponent 16 stayed fixed, through the will of the mathematician. Now, fixed measure [3] has become limit, which implies immunity from the will of a measurer. Hegel describes the difference between the primitive and more advanced Inverse Ratios as follows: "here the whole is a real substrate and each of the two sides is posited as having to be itself *in principle* [*an sich*] this whole." (376) The point is ultimately simple. Measure is fixed. The entire series of Measures "the indivisible self-subsistent measure which is *wholly* present." (376) Each side – Measure and Substrate – purports to be the *whole thing and its organizing other*. Recall that Quantity stands for openness to external determination. So if the Inverse Ratio of the Factors is the whole thing, a measurer can only add an extra measure by subtracting from the whole a comparable Quality and Quantity. This is why the Factors are in an Inverse relation. Something new is added only at the expense of something old. This implies that external determination has been canceled. According to Michael Baur:

> Thought finds itself condemned to a perennial and arbitrary interplay of qualitative and quantitative alterations which lack any stable substance or truth of their own. In order to overcome this bad infinite regress, one cannot appeal to yet another kind of external determination, for the mere appeal to another determination as such can only perpetuate the infinite regress. The problem can be overcome only when one succeeds in articulating a kind of relation which is not a relation to Other

> at all, but rather a kind of self-relation. That is, once the sphere of Being has shown itself in its nullity, one must enter a sphere where all transition is no transition at all.[4]

Hegel at first presents the Inverse Ratio of the Factors as a quantitative ratio, but we are not to think that the Substrate is therefore the *sum* of these quanta. Quantity here stands for the perfect continuity of [3] with [2], "in such a manner that it [3] would not be . . . a quantum or opposed in any way, either as a sum or even as an exponent, to other quanta." (376) Quantum stands for openness to externality of the Ratio of Measures [2], whose "abstract determinateness . . . falls into indifference." (376) We are beyond that now.

The sides of the Inverse Ratio of the Factors are quantitative and continuous, but they are still presented as different; each is a *Quality*. Suppose one side is put forth as a Quality. Hegel suggests that the other side must surrender its Quality and be merely quantitative. Two Qualities cannot meet each other as "mere oppugnancies," in Shakespearean terms. One must strike the other down. Thus, of the two Qualities, Hegel says that "one of [them] is sublated by the other." (376) But they are unified in a ratio nevertheless. And, Hegel further says, "neither is separable from the other." (376) So the assertion of one Quality at the expense of the other is a useless endeavor.

Externality by now is defeated, and everything is in everything else. "[T]herefore each side of the relation, too, contains both sides within itself and is distinguished from the other side only by a more of the one quality and a less of the other, and *vice versa*." (376) Yet, in spite of universal interpenetration, the two sides "are thus at the same time posited as self-subsistent relatively to each other." (377) This self-subsistence of the sides is a fault that cannot carry over into the Doctrine of Essence. So far the Substrate is not *expressly* the unity that holds together external appearances. The moments of the ratio "are not yet explicitly *self-determined*, i.e. are not yet determined as sublating themselves into a unity *within themselves* and *through one another*." (377) The indifference of the unity is also indifference to self. We must now also see posited an indifference toward indifference – a negation of the negation.

Of the pre-essence stages of Absolute Indifference and Inverse

---

[4] Michael Baur, *Sublating Kant and the Old Metaphysics: A Reading of the Transition from Being to Essence in Hegel's* Logic, 29 OWL OF MINERVA 139, 146 (1998).

Ratio, Hegel speaks of three deficiencies. First, the determinate being of the Substrate is "groundlessly emerging in it." (377); the Substrate still displays a moment of logical *unconnectedness* to its Nodal Line. No *self*-repulsion is on yet display. This is the *qualitative* fault.

Second, external reflection can assign to the Substrate the role of quality or quantity, in which case the other is quantity or quality respectively. Difference between the sides is imposed externally, whereas essence must be in *and for* itself. This is the *quantitative* fault; each side can be determined as quality or quantity.

Third, since the sides can be assigned a qualitative or quantitative role, the sides are *themselves* in an inverse relationship. One side is indifferently Quality or Quantity. This implies that each side is inherently already *both* Quality and Quantity. "Hence each side is in its own self the totality of the indifference." (378) Each side therefore contains an opposition. This is the speculative fault of the pre-essence stages.

Because each side is the totality, neither can go outside itself. To go into other is only to go into self. The pre-essence stages now pass beyond Quantity, which by definition always goes *beyond* itself. Going into the beyond (transition) has now gone into the beyond. Yet if there is no transition and hence no Quantity, there can be no Quality. Quality isolated is Pure Being. Pure Being is Pure Nothing, and so Quality too sublates itself.

In the penultimate paragraph of this section, Hegel tries for a very subtle point. The determinateness of the factors (in their zero-sum mode) requires a distinct difference between Quality and Quantity. The complete interpenetration suggests that the determinateness of the factors vanishes. This point presupposes his Remark on centripetal and centrifugal force. It is best to defer analysis pending Hegel's critique of these countervailing forces.

Hegel concludes by saying that the dialectic opposition in Figure 23(b) is "a contradiction in every respect." (379) Figure 23(b) "therefore has to be *posited* as sublating this its contradictory nature and acquiring the character of a self-determined, self-subsistent being which has for its result and truth not the unity which is merely indifferent, but that immanently negative and absolute unity which is called essence." (379)

Centripetal and Centrifugal Force. The last section described the "relationship of a whole which is supposed to have its determinateness in the quantitative difference of two factors determined qualitatively against each other." (379) This relation is exhibited by the movement of the planets. According to the pre-Newtonian theory, centripetal force draws the planets toward the center. Centrifugal force drives the planets away from the center. Their equilibrium is an elliptical orbit.

These forces, Hegel implies, are *not* an example of Inverse Ratio of the Factors. Such a ratio is constituted by Specified Measures which are complete unto themselves, indifferent to each other, yet diffused with Substrate. Instead, Hegel says, centripetal and centrifugal force are "only two qualities in inverse relation to each other." (379)

The inverse relation of centripetal and centrifugal force, Hegel claims, destroys the basic facts of astronomy. "[O]r," Hegel writes, "if, as is proper, the fact is retained it escapes notice that the theory proves to be meaningless in face of the fact." (379-80)

According to Kepler's second law, planets in elliptical orbit sweep equal areas with every increment of time.[5] Accordingly, "velocity is accelerated as [planets] approach perihelion and retarded as they approach aphelion." (380)[6] This fact, Hegel writes, "has been accurately ascertained by the untiring diligence of observation, and further, it has been reduced to its simple law and formula. Hence all that can properly be required of a theory has been accomplished." (380) But for Hegel this is insufficient. The theory assumes the forces are qualitatively opposed moments. Quantitatively, however, one increases and the other decreases, as the planets, in their evil mixture, pursue their orbits. At some point, the forces reverse in dominance, until the next tipping point is reached.

Separation of centripetal and centrifugal force is untenable, however. Each force only has meaning in relation to the other. Neither can exist on its own.[7] To say, then, that one of the forces preponderates is to say that the preponderant force is out of relation with its fellow to the extent of the surplus. But this is to say that the surplus does not exist:

> It requires but little consideration to see that if, for example, as is alleged, the body's centripetal force increases as it approaches perihelion, while the centrifugal force is supposed to decrease proportionately, the [centrifugal force] *would no longer be able* to tear the body away from the former and to set it again at a distance from its central body; on the contrary, for once the former has gained the preponderance, the other is overpowered and the body is carried towards its central body with accelerated velocity. (380-1)

---

[5] James W. Garrison, *Metaphysics and Scientific Proof: Newton and Hegel*, in HEGEL AND NEWTONIANISM, *supra* note 1, at 8.

[6] Perihelion is the closest distance from the sun. Aphelion is the farthest.

[7] This recalls Hegel's critique of calculus, where δy or δx were qualitative and meaningless outside the ratio $\delta y/\delta x$. *Supra* at 181-2.

Only an alien force could save centrifugal force from being overwhelmed. And this is tantamount to saying that the force that guides the planets *sans check* cannot be explained.

The alternation of the forces implies that "each side of the inverse relation is in its own self the whole inverse relation." (381) The predominant force implies its opposite, servient force. The servient force never vanishes. "All that recurs then on either side is the defect characteristic of this inverse relation." (381) Either each force is wrongly attributed a self-identical existence free and clear of the other, "the pair being merely *externally* associated in a motion (as in the parallelogram of forces)." (381)[8] Or neither side can achieve "an indifferent, independent subsistence in the face of the other, a subsistence supposedly imparted to it by a *more*." (382)

Vanishing. Prior to his remarks on centripetal and centrifugal force, Hegel makes a point that can now be more conveniently apprehended. Hegel has said that, if centripetal force were really predominant, it would sublate centrifugal force once and for all, causing the planet to fly mothlike into the sun. Hegel indicates in the prior section that, in Measure generally, this sublation must logically occur. The Inverse Ratio of Factors is immune from outside manipulation because it represents the entire world of outward appearance – all the Measures there are. Yet there are two sides – Substrate and the Measures by which Substrate manifests itself. Any attempt of external reflection to intervene in order to call one side or the other qualitative is like the astronomer who intervenes to break down orbit into constituent parts. The Inverse Ratio of Factors, like the orbit, is now immune from outside intervention. "Each of these hypothetical factors vanishes, whether it is supposed to be *beyond* or *equal* to the other." (379) The mere isolation of these, in the face of a perfect equilibrium, implies their sublation in general. This self-abolition of Quality and Quantity "constitutes itself [as] the sole self-subsistent quality." (379) This argument, if valid, establishes [2, 3] in Figure 23(b) as an "inherent incompatibility with itself, a repelling of itself from itself." (384) This self-repulsion is the step that Speculative Reason identifies.

Is the argument valid? My conclusion is yes. At the point where the argument is hazarded, the Substrate was metonymic. It was a negative

---

[8] The parallelogram of forces describes the phenomenon that if two forces exist as vectors, their average vector forms a parallelogram with the original vectors, provided one of the original vectors is multiplied by the imaginary number, -√1.

unity of *all* the Measure relations with all other Substrates in the world. Measure, being fixed, does not permit quantitative disequilibrium. The very attempt of any such surplus to manifest itself is self-destructive. Any such manifestation puts the surplus – a qualitative proposition – in a lethal isolation from the thing. This self-identity is thus radically incommensurate with any other thing, including itself. Such an entity destroys itself by its very logic.

C. Transition into Essence

"Absolute Indifference," Hegel says, "is the final determination of *being* before it becomes essence." (382) This must be read in a technical sense. The Understanding makes affirmative propositions. Absolute Indifference is the final attempt by the Understanding to state what *is*. In our conventional mode of depicting the official moves in the *SL*, the Understanding shifted the middle term over to the left side of the diagram. This is the last such move. In the Doctrine of Essence the Understanding shifts the middle term over to the right, to explain what is *not*. In effect, the Understanding *becomes* Dialectical Reason. Later, it will *become* Speculative Reason (in the Subjective Logic).

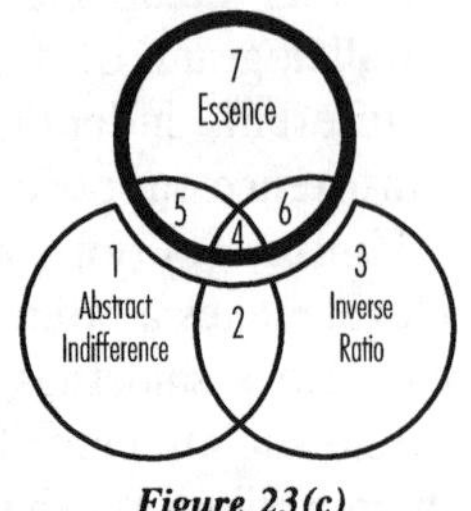

Figure 23(c)
Essence

Absolute Indifference is not yet Essence. An external reflection still distinguishes a Substrate from the complete set of Measures called the Inverse Ratio of Its Factors; "it still contains difference as an *external*, quantitative determination; this is its *determinate being*." (383) Absolute Indifference is "only *implicitly* the absolute, not the absolute grasped as *actuality*." (383) Actuality, Hegel says, requires that the differences be posited as indifferent. The further step that is needed "is to grasp that the reflection of the differences into their unity is not merely the product of the *external* reflection of the subjective thinker, but that it is the very nature of the differences of this unity to sublate themselves." (384)

Speculative Reason always names the activity that unifies the sides. This unity is that the sides sublate themselves. Hegel therefore identifies the unity of the existential differences as "absolute negativity." (384) This negativity (Essence) is a truly radical indifference. It is an indifference to Being, which is therefore an indifference to itself, and even an indifference "to its own indifference." (384)

Essence is the repulsion of itself from itself. It is an active principle, in the nature of Pure Quantity. Indeed, at the beginning of Essence, Hegel confirms: "In the *whole* of logic, Essence occupies the same place as quantity does in the sphere of being; absolute indifference to limit." (391) Essence is therefore a return to quantity, but in an enriched form – a form which never leaves itself as it repels itself from itself. Quantity, in contrast, had a definite *beyond* into which it continued. Quantity was in effect the announcement, "I am whatever my radical Other says I am." Essence is the opposite. It announces, "I am *not* my external being, my appearance."

Essence is therefore a negative version of Quantity. It names the act of expelling its own Being. What is the fate of expelled Being? These *dejecta* "do not emerge as self-subsistent or external determinations." (384)[9] They are borne by and retained as ideal moments of the essential thing. Things "*are* only through their repulsion [of their Measures] from themselves." (384) Appearances are *authentic* to the Essence of the thing. But they are not what they are affirmatively. This is the now superseded error of the Understanding. Rather, these beings are "sheer *positedness*." (384)[10] A positedness, in Essence, is what determinateness was in the realm of Being. It is a relation between the affirmative and the negative, with the understanding that the affirmatives are really negations of negations.

Being has now abolished itself. It has, to paraphrase Romeo, cut off its own head with a golden axe and exiled itself to a negative beyond. And in this self-banishment, the presupposition with which the entire Logic began has sublated itself. Being turns out to be "only a moment of [Essence's] repelling." (385) The self-identity for which Being strived so assiduously "*is* only as the *resulting coming together with itself*." (385) Being is now Essence, "a simple *being-with-self*." (385)

---

[9] "In the sphere of Essence one category does not pass into another, but refers to another merely. In Being, the form of reference is purely due to our reflection on what takes place: but it is the special and proper characteristic of Essence. In the sphere of Being, when some[thing] becomes another, the some[thing] has vanished. Not so in Essence: here there is no real other, but only diversity, reference of the one to *its* other. The transition of Essence is therefore at the same time no transition: for in the passage of different into different, the different does not vanish: the different terms remain in their relation." EL § 111 Remark.

[10] ROBERT M. WALLACE, HEGEL'S PHILOSOPHY OF REALITY, FREEDOM, AND GOD 155 (2005) ("The great divide between the sphere of being, which we have now left behind, and the sphere of essence, is that in the latter, things are determinate only insofar as they are 'posited,' and thus only *in relation* to . . . essence").

Conclusion

Hegel's theory of measure differs starkly from that which emanates from analytic philosophy, in that Hegel identifies Quality as a constituent part of Measure. According to one example: "Most scientific theories – if one is willing to translate predicates into characteristic functions [*i.e.*, universal truths] one could say *all* scientific theories – express relations among quantities. To test a theory or to apply it therefore requires measurement."[11] In this account, there is no definitional work on what quantity is, let alone quality.[12] It concerns itself with a theory of error in order to describe the gap between observation and axiomatic truth. But to put the problem in this way is to reinscribe the dogma of axiomatic truth as the ultimate criterion after all. There can be no gap if there is no truth.

For Hegel, the gap between measure and background truth is constitutional. In the background is the very gap that analytic philosophy would subjectivize by attributing it to the observer. For Hegel, measurement cannot *possibly* be accurate, because any "thing" is, at its core, *Measureless*. There can be no question of correcting, once and for all, the errors of measurement.

---

[11] HENRY E. KYBURG, THEORY AND MEASUREMENT 9 (1984).

[12] Kyburg seems to equate "quantity" with Hegelian Measure. Thus there are "kinds of quantities." *Id.* at 19. In general, the concept of "quantity" is treated as self-evident. Quantity at times seems to be nothing other than language stripped of its connotative penumbra. *Id.* at 20 ("*if* it *were* the case that we could speak without a background fund of information and convention concerning the application of language, then it *would* be possible for us to develop notions of quantity analogous to those with which we actually operate").

PART IV
REFLECTION

10
Illusory Being

What is the *essence* of a thing? To common sense, essence means some *affirmative quality* to be distinguished from equally affirmative *inessential* qualities.

This view is completely rejected by Hegel, for whom essence was no affirmative, discoverable quality of a thing. For Hegel, essence is simply *not appearance – not the thing's immediate Being*. It has no more content than that.

From Hegel's definition, it is evident that when Essence manifests what it *is*, it shows that it is *not*. *Essence erases itself*. Oddly, when Essence erases itself, it *actualizes* and *preserves* itself and becomes what it ought to be.[1] This comprises the *entirety* of Hegel's theory of Essence. The hardest part of Essence is to see how very simple it is. This is why, in Hegel's opinion, Essence is "the most difficult branch of Logic."[2]

Essence stands at the empty center of the *SL*. In the first third, immediate being revealed itself to be semblance – *not* the truth. On its own logic, Being imploded upon itself. It showed itself to be *finite*. Essence is the residue left over after being erases itself. Now it is time

[1] For this reason, Marcuse calls the process "intro-reflection. HERBERT MARCUSE, REASON AND REVOLUTION 133 (1999). That is, what is reflected out is also reflected within.

[2] EL § 114. "[A]nd his treatment of it in the Greater Logic certainly makes it so." ERROL E. HARRIS, AN INTERPRETATION OF THE LOGIC OF HEGEL 157 (1983).

to look beyond what merely *is* to see what deeper truth lurks behind.

And what is the deep truth behind the world that merely *appears* to be present? The big secret is – there's nothing behind the veil at all! With Hegel, it is *appearances all the way down.*[3] "The only secret . . . is that there is no secret."[4]

Knowledge of Essence is knowledge of *what is not*. Yet *what is not* cannot be directly perceived. Knowledge of what is not can only be gained by watching what *is* disappear. Yet not everything *has* disappeared. Knowledge of Essence therefore cannot be induced but must be inferred by reflection on the nature of things. Knowledge of the negative is purchased at the expense of immediate intuition – the hallmark of the world of Being. From now on, "knowledge is a mediated knowing." (389)

> Since knowing has for its goal knowledge of the true . . . it does not stop at the immediate and its determinations, but penetrates it on the supposition that at the back of this being there is something else, something other than being itself, that this background constitutes the truth of being. (389)

But what is this "something else"? Simply that Being must erase itself and become Essence. For this reason, Hegel describes Essence as "absolute *being-in-itself*" (390).[5] "Being-in-itself" means implicitness. Regarding finite entities, what is implicit is that they should cease to be. The *disappearance* of finitude is the only true, actual thing.[6] A finite

---

[3] ERMANNO BENCIVENGA, HEGEL'S DIALECTICAL LOGIC 41 (2002) ("Reality is structure (form) all the way down").

[4] JEAN HYPPOLITE, LOGIC AND EXISTENCE 90 (Leonard Lawlor & Amit Sen trans., 1997); *see also* 1 JEAN HYPPOLITE, FIGURES DE LA PENSÉE PHILOSOPHIQUE 159 (1971) ("Hegelian philosophy rejects all transcendence. It is the attempt at a rigorous philosophy that could claim to remain within the immanent, and not to leave it. There is no other world, no thing in itself, no transcendence, and yet finite human thought is not condemned to remain a prisoner of its finitude. It surmounts itself, and what it reveals or manifests is being itself."); ROBERT B. PIPPIN, HEGEL'S IDEALISM: THE SATISFACTIONS OF SELF-CONSCIOUSNESS 211 (1989) ("there are no 'essences' beyond or behind the appearances, at least none that can do any cognitive work. There are just the appearances . . . ").

[5] CLARK BUTLER, HEGEL'S LOGIC: BETWEEN DIALECTIC AND HISTORY 125 (1996) (identifying being-in-itself as "a code term for 'essence'").

[6] For this reason, Marcuse recruits Hegel for leftwing causes. *See* MARCUSE, REASON, *supra* note 1, at 27 ("the given facts that appear to common sense as the positive index of truth are in reality the negation of truth, so that truth can only be established by their destruction . . . To Hegel, the facts possess no authority.") Yet, with equal justice, it could be said that a philosophy in which "all that exists dissolves into

thing is not what it ought to be (*i.e.*, dead) so long as it stubbornly lives on.

The in-itself, however, must become *for*-itself. But since what is implicit in Being is ceasing-to-be, then Being is "for itself" when it is no more. It no longer has *any* affirmative content. In Being-for-self, all content is forfeit and expelled to the outside. At this point, Being-for-self is Quantity – Being without any content of its own.

When "for itself," Essence will express what it is *in* itself – self-erasure. When Essence cancels itself, it is *actual*. When Essence is actual, Being – which has canceled itself – is finally recaptured. Essence is accordingly "the completed return of being into itself." (390) Upon completing this return Essence passes into the realm of universality and self-presence – the realm of Notion.[7]

Because Essence identifies what it is by announcing what it is *not*, I introduce here a change in the explanatory protocol. In the realm of Being, the Understanding constantly pulled the middle term over to the left side of the diagram – the side of being. Now the Understanding pulls the middle term to the right side – the side of negation. Whereas the Understanding earlier tried to discover the nature of its affirmative being, it now investigates what it *was* but now *is not*.

Negation always implies correlation – the negation *and* the thing negated. Accordingly, essentialisms "are always mere pairs of correlatives . . . "[8] With essence, "negation is built into the concept itself."[9] "[I]n Essence there is an inherent contradiction, a diremption

---

spirit . . . such a philosophy will apologetically take the side of what exists . . . ." THEODOR W. ADORNO, HEGEL: THREE STUDIES 85 (1999).

[7] *See* Richard Dien Winfield, *From Concept to Judgement: Rethinking Hegel's Overcoming of Formal Logic*, 50 DIALOGUE 53, 59 (2001) ("whereas the universal enjoys its characteristic unity as a one over many, bridging any gulf between itself and the particulars in which it communes with itself, essence maintains its defining primacy over its appearance not by relating a plurality of appearances to one another, but by preceding them all as their positor").

[8] EL §112; *see* Stephen Houlgate, *Why Hegel's Concept is not the Essence of Things*, in HEGEL'S THEORY OF THE SUBJECT 21 (David Gray Carlson ed., 2005) ("Essence is the relation of two terms, each of which is *not* the other, but each of which is a constitutive moment of the other . . . Here categories come in pairs, such that one is explicitly *included* in the other as *excluded* from it. The one does not just pass over into the other, but each is present *in* the other as *not* actually present in or part of it.").

[9] JUSTUS HARTNACK, AN INTRODUCTION TO HEGEL'S LOGIC 86 (Lars Aagaard-Mogensen trans., 1998); *see* HYPPOLITE, LOGIC, *supra* note 4, at 61 ("Hegel's originality is to put reflection into the Absolute, and, consequently, to surmount dualism without suppressing it").

into two mutually opposed and even repugnant abstractions, which are nevertheless mutually dependent . . . "[10] The Understanding now resembles Dialectical Reason. It always sees a doubleness. The Inessential is paired with the Essential. The Grounded is paired with Ground, and so forth.

Recollecting Essence's history in sublated Being, Dialectical Reason opposes the Understanding's negativity with a recollection of what *was*. In effect, Dialectical Reason says, "You say you are *not*. But you suppress the fact that *once you were*." From now on, Dialectical Reason appears on the left side of the diagram – on the side of being. In short, the convention is the opposite of what it has been heretofore. The Understanding proposes what is not, and Dialectical Reason recollects *what is*. Speculative Reason continues to reconcile the two views in a new synthesis.

This review of Hegel's methodology underscores the importance of memory.[11] If Essence is simply *not Being*, and if Being has imploded itself in the earlier stages of the Logic, then Essence (*Wesen*) can only be found through the process of recollection (*Erinnerung*) of what *was* but now is *not*. *Erinnerung* can also be translated as *inwardization*. Hegel remarks: "Not until knowing *inwardizes, recollects* [*erinnert*] itself out of immediate being, does it through this mediation find essence." (389) Recollection, inwardization, and memory tie directly into the concept of *ideality*. What is ideality? It is nothing but recollection of Being that is already past.[12] Ideality, first established with True Infinity, stood for Being that has abolished itself, thereby reducing itself to thought. In this vein, Hegel can exploit something true in German but not English. The word for essence in German is *Wesen*. This is related to *gewesen*, or "was," the past participle of "to be."[13] For Hegel, "essence

---

[10] HARRIS, LOGIC, *supra* note 2, at 157.

[11] *See* BENCIVENGA, *supra* note 3, at 56 ("Hegel's logic is one of recollection, of memory, its necessity is the internal consistency of what is remembered . . . ") (footnote omitted).

[12] Recollection "has nothing to do with the psychic phenomenon which we today mean with this term. It is a universal, *ontological* category." HERBERT MARCUSE, HEGEL'S ONTOLOGY AND THE THEORY OF HISTORICITY 68 (Seyla Benhabib trans. 1987).

[13] EL §112 Remark. Andrew Haas gets it wrong, I think, when he comments, "When it appears in the text [of the *SL*], essence has already been; it is past." ANDREW HAAS, HEGEL AND THE PROBLEM OF MULTIPLICITY 252 (2000). In fact, essence is *present* because *being* is past. *See* MARCUSE, ONTOLOGY, *supra* note 13, at 73 (essence is "an always present having-been").

is past – but timelessly past – being." (390)[14] Hegel's philosophy is all about retrospectivity, which is why he famously announces: "When philosophy paints its grey in grey, a shape of life has grown old, and it cannot be rejuvenated, but only recognized, by the grey in grey of philosophy; the owl of Minerva begins its flight only with the onset of dusk."[15]

Essence, Hegel says, is to the entire Logic what Quantity was to the realm of Being – the negative residue left from the self-destruction of the affirmative moment. Essence is thus "the *first negation of being*." (391) And so was Quantity. Nevertheless there is a key difference. Quantity was indifferent to determination by the Understanding. Any limit to be found within Quantity was imposed on it from the outside – i.e., "*affirmatively present* in it." (391) In contrast, Essence determines itself. Quantitative Determinateness "is not free." (391) Now, Determinateness is "*posited* by essence itself." (391)[16] Essence "is what it is through a negativity, which is not alien to it but is its very own, the infinite movement of being." (390) It is self-identity following negation[17] – the very hallmark of True Infinity.

Essence has much work to do before it is truly "for itself." At first, Essence is indeterminate – analogous to (but more advanced than) Pure Being. The determinateness of Essence is present "*in principle* . . . but [is] not *posited in it*." (390) Essence will determine itself, but in a different way, compared to self-determination in the sphere of Being. In the sphere of Being, the Finite "ceased to be." It became something radically "other" than what it was – *transition*.[18] But "transition" is not proper to the realm of Essence,[19] which does not permit its content to

---

[14] *See* EL § 112 ("Essence we may certainly regard as past Being, remembering however meanwhile that the past is not utterly denied, but only laid aside and thus at the same time preserved").

[15] G.W.F. HEGEL, ELEMENTS OF THE PHILOSOPHY OF RIGHT 22 (Wood trans. 1993).

[16] *See* ROBERT M. WALLACE, HEGEL'S PHILOSOPHY OF REALITY, FREEDOM AND GOD 155 (2005) ("The great divide between the sphere of being . . . and the sphere of essence is that, in the latter, things are determinate only insofar as they are 'posited.'").

[17] JOHN W. BURBIDGE, ON HEGEL'S LOGIC: FRAGMENTS OF A COMMENTARY 249 n.6 (1981)

[18] *See id.* at 63 ("In the logic of *being*, thinking simply passed from one concept or category over to another"). There is an aspect of this last quote with which I disagree. Hegel is not claiming that, *in our thought*, being passes from one category to another. He is claiming that *being itself* is in the process of this transition. In sublating itself, being *continues directly into our thought*.

[19] Hegel nevertheless uses the term in his Essence chapters. For example, he says that the movement of Essence "is the *transition* from being into the Notion." (391)

go forth into something else.[20] Essence retains its "content" (which content is nothing else but the act of self-erasure).[21] It develops its content within a totality.[22] "[I]ts determining remains within this unity and is neither a becoming nor a transition." (390) Its determinations are not "other" but overtly its own.[23]

In lieu of transition (or ceasing-to-be), the movement proper to Essence is Reflection.[24] Hegelian Reflection is not user-friendly, so it might go easier if we start with Locke, according to whom the two sources of ideas are *sensation* and *reflection*. Sensation entails data received from outside the mind – what we see, hear, and feel. Reflection is "that notice which the mind takes of its own operations . . ."[25] When reflective thought senses an object, it realizes that its own self (thought) is precisely *not* the object sensed. The object given by sensation is, in effect, negated by thought when thought realizes that it is "not the object." Reflection is therefore thought's highly negative statement, "I am not *that*."[26] Reflection – the negation of what *is*, essence "estranged from its immediacy" (399) – is the name of the process by which thought's immediate Being erases itself. Essence "does nothing but signify the process by which the concept of *being* cancels

---

[20] Rodolphe Gasché refers to Hegelian Reflection as "(1) the dissolving force of understanding, (2) the totalizing power of the speculative process, and (3) one moment within that process." RODOLPHE GASCHÉ, THE TAIN OF THE MIRROR: DERRIDA AND THE PHILOSOPHY OF REFLECTION 35 (1986).

[21] *See* William Maker, *Hegel's Logic of Freedom*, in HEGEL'S THEORY OF THE SUBJECT, *supra* note 8, at 10 ("In the logic of essence being no longer *dis*appears in its others, but *appears* in and through it, and is determined in virtue of the self-contrasting, as a result").

[22] *See* EL § 115 ("The Essence lights up *in itself* [and] is only self-relation, not as immediate but as reflected. And that reflexive relation is *self-Identity*"). In Reflection, "the negative is thus confined within an enclosed sphere in which, what the one is *not*, is something *determinate*." (639)

[23] MARCUSE, ONTOLOGY, *supra* note 13, at 421 (essentiality "must therefore be understood as a process of letting-spring-forth . . . of the manifold").

[24] It is sometimes asserted that Hegel regretted his analysis of Reflection and so omitted it from the *EL*. BURBIDGE, LOGIC, *supra* note 17, at 105; GIACOMO RINALDI, A HISTORY AND INTERPRETATION OF THE LOGIC OF HEGEL 194 (1992). But I agree with Pippin, who sees the *EL* as "a textbook summary." PIPPIN, *supra* note 4, at 213. According to Errol Harris, the *EL* "is [not] really a divergence from that of the Greater Logic, because there Contradiction is immediately resolved as Ground." HARRIS, LOGIC, *supra* note 2, at 159 (footnote omitted).

[25] 1 J. LOCKE, AN ESSAY CONCERNING HUMAN UNDERSTANDING 124 (1959).

[26] BUTLER, LOGIC, *supra* note 5, at 204 (essence "explicitly refers to its necessary correlate as contradictorily being unnecessary to it").

its own immediacy in thought. It is the negative movement of dissolution".[27] Reflection is therefore not an *artefact* but a process[28] – a *disappearance*.

These remarks should clarify why Reflection is "the negativity of essence." (391) The trick in Hegel's Reflection is that the object ("*that*") which Reflection negates ("I am not *that*") is *Reflection's own selfhood*. Reflection's attribute is that it is *not its own self*. It is *self-negating, self-erasing*, a statement of what *was* (recollection) together with what *is not* (the thought of what *was*).[29] A reflective concept is one that is self-repelling ("I am not *that*"). In this capacity of making express what it is *not*, Essence shows what it is: "at one with itself in this its own difference from itself." (390) Reflection is a movement that "consists in positing within itself the negation [of itself] thereby giving itself *determinate being*." (391) When Essence has given itself Determinate Being (the "*that*"), it is truly *for itself*. It is *Actual*. Ironically, its Actuality *is* its self-erasure. It really *is* – *not that*!

Essence's selfhood – its Determinate Being – is merely *posited*. If Essence is *not that*, then there must be a *that* against which Essence can stand. Essence's determinations are "*given* by essence to itself . . . and consequently still distinct from the Determinate Being of the Notion." (391) Essence is "a still imperfect combination of immediacy and mediation."[30] It sees itself as a unity of (a) itself and (b) a presupposed other.[31] Together, this unity is a *positedness*. Ultimately, Essence's successor, the Notion, overcomes mere positedness. It will see itself as a unity of (a) itself, (b) its other, and (c) the unity of itself and other.[32] When Notion arrives, Reflection and positedness will be

---

[27] BURBIDGE, LOGIC, *supra* note 17, at 63 (1981). Butler puts it this way: Being was an act. Act proves potency. Essence is the recollection of the act and the identification of potency. "[B]eing which is actually for itself proves its potentiality to be for itself: it is in itself actually for itself." BUTLER, LOGIC, *supra* note 5, at 127.

[28] WALLACE, *supra* note 16, at 177 ("As such a self-supersession, essence is very much a *process* rather than an immediately given identity").

[29] *See* HYPPOLITE, LOGIC, *supra* note 4, at 173 ("The distinction between the essential and the inessential is, at the level of essence, only a reminiscence of immediacy . . . ").

[30] EL §114.

[31] *See* Houlgate, *supra* note 8, at 22 ("Each determination is different from and opposed to the other. Yet each is also (as Derrida might put it) 'haunted' by the other within itself.").

[32] Hyppolite calls this triad "the rational minimum." HYPPOLITE, LOGIC, *supra* note 4, at 61. To reach it, Hegel "makes logic go through a torsion in order to make it capable of expressing this duality in unity and this unity in duality." *Id*.

passé.[33] They will give way to *development*.[34] If (1) transition is proper to Being, and if (2) positedness is proper to Essence, (3) development is proper to Notion (or subjectivity).

Essence starts with Reflection, where "essence *shines* or *shows within itself*." (391) Appearance and Actuality (manifestation of what *is*) follow. At the macro-conceptual level, Reflection is the position of comparative immediacy – the position of the Understanding. Appearance is dialectic; Essence stands over against Appearance. Actuality is speculative – the unity of Reflection and Appearance.

Reflection itself is subdivided. First is Illusory Being (*Schein*), sometimes translated as semblance or "seeming." Second are the Determinations of Reflection, covering the important concepts of Identity, Difference and Contradiction. The final part considers Ground and its relation to what is Grounded. From Ground emerges the Thing and *advanced being* – what Hegel calls Existence.

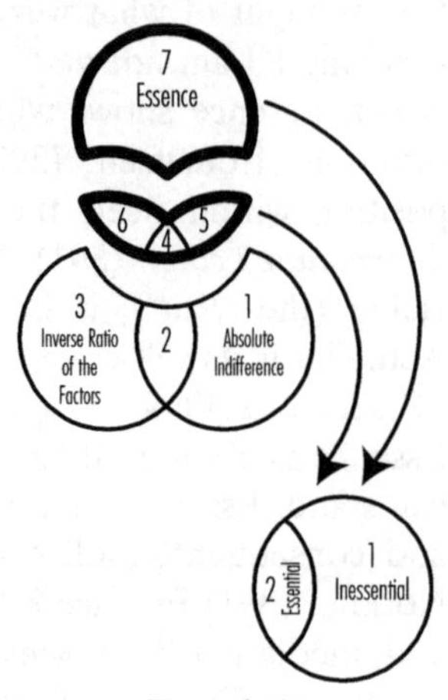

Figure 24(a)
The Essential and Unessential

A. The Essential and the Unessential

Essence is the recollection and negation of what was – Being. Essence is *not* Being and has no further content than that. This is not what common sense thinks. For common sense, Essence is "the *indeterminate*, simple unity from which what is determinate has been eliminated in an *external manner*." (389) According to this false procedure, Essence is found by subjectively wishing away appearances in an exercise of abstraction.[35] The leftovers are affirmative essence. In this process, appearance is simply located in one place and Essence in another; Essence is just as much an immediate being (and hence an

---

[33] Houlgate, *Concept*, *supra* note 8, at 24.

[34] EL § 161. More precisely, positedness will be *contained* within Notion. Hegel does not hesitate to use the word, however, throughout the Subjective Logic.

[35] The target here is *abstract* essence, not essence as such. BUTLER, LOGIC, *supra* note 5, at 126. This is a point Adorno manages to miss. THEODOR W. ADORNO, NEGATIVE DIALECTICS 169 (E.B. Ashton trans. 2000).

appearance) as appearance was. Subjective abstraction leaves "the determinatenesses of being" with "the affirmative character they had before." (390) So considered, Essence is "only a product, an artefact." (390) It is "neither *in itself* nor *for itself* . . . . Its character . . . is to lack all determinate character, to be inherently lifeless and empty." (390)[36]

This false view informs the Understanding's first proposition about Essence: the Essential *v* the Unessential. "In this determination, essence itself is *simply affirmative* . . . immediate essence, and being is only a negative *in relation to* essence, not in and for itself." (394) That is to say, Essence here is identified *contingently*. The Essential is what the Unessential is not.

The Understanding misidentifies Essence as yet another affirmative Being, which is precisely *not* Essence.[37] Therefore, the Unessential is both (1) the Essential's external appearance, which has by now abolished itself and is only remembered, and (2) the Understanding itself. Both of these are the same thing. Recall that Being is the realm of immediacy and hence of the Understanding. In Figure 2(a), Being's own voice asserted its immediacy and its freedom from otherness. In effect, the Understanding *is* Determinate Being. Thus, when Being finally repealed itself at the end of Measure, the Understanding likewise repealed itself (and preserved itself). Now it returns as an abolished, humbled entity, which asserts its own inessentiality, compared to the Essential.[38]

---

[36] "[I]f essence is defined as the *sum total of all realities*, then . . . this sum total reduces to empty oneness." (389-90) Here Hegel perhaps refers to his argument that the Kantian thing-in-itself is unitary. Stripped of all appearance, it is impossible to distinguish between multiple things-in-themselves. *See supra* at 75.

[37] Elsewhere, Hegel memorably denounces the "common sense" position: "These empty abstractions of . . . an "essence" that is linked with something unessential [are] often called "sound common sense." This "sound common sense" . . . is always at its poorest where it fancies itself to be the richest. Bandied about by these vacuous "essences," thrown into the arms first of one and then of the other, and striving by its sophistry to hold fast and affirm alternately first one of the "essences" and then the directly opposite one, it sets itself against the truth and holds the opinion that philosophy is concerned with mental entities. As a matter of fact, philosophy does have to do with them too . . . but in doing so, recognizes them *in their specific determinateness* as well, and is therefore master over them, whereas perceptual understanding . . . takes them for the truth and is led on by them from one error to another." G.W.F. HEGEL, PHENOMENOLOGY OF SPIRIT ¶ 131 (Arnold V. Miller trans. 1977).

[38] Charles Taylor concurs that Essence makes implicit reference to a subject of knowledge, which becomes express in the Subjective Logic, many chapters hence. CHARLES TAYLOR, HEGEL 297 (1975).

To put this in other terms, the Inessential is the position of the person who *sees* the essence of a thing and assumes it is really out there. Such a person takes her own thought to be *inessential* to the existence of the Essential.[39] Because the Unessential is simply *not* the Essential, the Unessential is drawn on the right side of Figure 24(a) – the side of nothingness. From its perspective, the Understanding beholds the Essential, which is comparatively on the left – the side of Being. We have before us *essentialism*, which takes what is subjective to be objective.

Retrogression. In Figure 24(a), the immediacy of the Inessential, on the right, and of the Essential, on the left, "has caused essence to relapse into the sphere of *determinate being*." (394) Essence is merely assigned the attribute of being-in-and-for-self as "a further determination external to determinate being itself." (394-5) "Such a division does not settle what is essential and what is unessential. It originates in some external standpoint." (395) The Essential exhibits only being-for-other, not being-in-and-for-self.

The Understanding has slipped from Essence back to the sublated realm of Being. We have seen like slippage before. In the beginning, the Understanding retrogressed in its interpretation of Absolute Knowledge. Absolute Knowledge was the unity of immediacy and all mediations. The Understanding dismantled this unity and one-sidedly interpreted Absolute Knowledge as Pure Being. This was how the *SL* got started – by the Understanding's retrogressive move. In truth, *every* move of the Understanding has been a retrogressive step backwards. The Understanding always fails to see speculatively, compared to the step that preceded it. Yet this retrogression is absolutely necessary if Dialectical Reason is to perform its function of opposing the history of the process against the Understanding's misinterpretation, and if Speculative Reason is to deliver a higher speculative truth that combines the Understanding's proposition with the dialectical recollections.

Insofar as the Understanding is concerned, immediate Being (which *is* the Understanding) has abolished itself, but it has preserved itself as well, under the law of sublation. It is therefore present as an absence.[40] It in effect says, "I am *not*. The Essential *is*." The

---

[39] This is the position of *analysis* (as opposed to synthesis) – two positions considered in chapter 26.

[40] STANLEY ROSEN, G.W.F. HEGEL: AN INTRODUCTION TO THE SCIENCE OF WISDOM 108 (1974).

Understanding does nothing other than to assert its own immediacy and that of the Essential. This move is retrogressive, but there is no other choice. The Understanding must reduce Essence to its own level.

In Figure 24(a), Essence is supposed to be *for itself*. But, according to the Understanding, "essence is only the *first* negation." (395) Negation, however, violates the premise that Essence is being-in-and-for-self. Negation implies something to negate – the Inessential. Hence, the Essential has no genuine independence from otherness. It is the opposite of what it is supposed to be. The Essential is therefore "*in and for itself* a nullity; it is only a *non-essence, illusory* being." (395)

B. Illusory Being

The section entitled *Der Schein* (Illusory Being or "seeming")[41] is not Hegel's most lucid moment. Adorno, for instance, calls it one of the "cryptic chapters." [42] The basic idea of it is familiar enough, though. Dialectical Reason takes the Understanding's proposition about the Essential and shows the opposite to be true. The Essential is actually Unessential. But if there is an Unessential, there must be an Essential. Neither the Understanding nor Dialectical Reason can fix its location, however. At one moment it is here. At another moment it is there.

The issue in Figure 24(b) is the status of the middle term [2]. The Understanding thinks [2] is Essential. Dialectical Reason thinks [2] is an immediate being and Unessential. So where is the Essential? Neither the Understanding and Dialectical Reason are about to confess that *it* is the Essential. From the perspective of being-in-and-for-self, each is external and distinctly not essential to Essence. Hence, two nothings have between them a third nothing. Illusory Being "is the negative posited as negative." (395)

There can be an *Essential* only if there is also an *Unessential*. If Dialectical Reason recharacterizes the Essential, calling it Illusory

---

[41] John Burbidge disfavors the term Illusory Being and substitutes "seeming." His reason: Illusory Being turns out to be Essence after all and hence not merely illusory. BURBIDGE, LOGIC, *supra* note 17, at 248 n.4.

[42] ADORNO, *supra* note 3, at 95. Rinaldi suggests that Hegel dropped it from the *EL* because it was unconvincing. RINALDI, *supra* note 24, at 194. Pippin everywhere shows his frustration with Hegel's style, but justly remarks of Illusory Being that Hegel "is trying to say everything at once (again), and so describes its [Illusory Being's] insufficiency in ways that cannot possibly be clear on this point and will require much explanation later." PIPPIN, *supra* note 4, at 204.

Being and putting it forth as *nothing*, then, from the perspective of being-in-and-for-self, it must also be saying that the *Understanding* was Essential. The Essential *must* stand over against Illusory Being [2]. It must therefore be located in [1] or [3]. In short, Illusory Being reveals what it is (Unessential) by announcing what it is not.

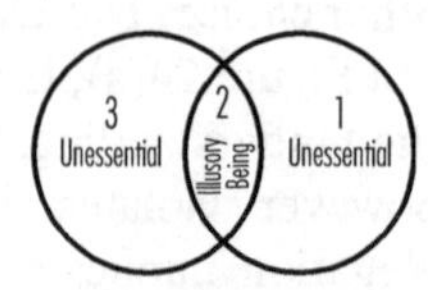

Figure 24(b)
Illusory Being

Figure 24(b) portrays the familiar modulation between the extremes. Each is *not* the Essential; each asserts the *other* is really the Essential one. The farced title of Essence is tossed like a hot potato by the extremes across the middle term.

Speculative Reason names this movement Reflection. It knows that, although Illusory Being has an "immediate side that is independent of essence and . . . simply an other of essence," it is equally mediated. Immediacy is the hallmark of Being (now sublated). Illusory Being, "is all that still remains from the sphere of being." (395) Immediacy, then, is an *ideal* moment – a recollection of what once was but now is *not*. Illusory Being is therefore a "*reflected* immediacy" (396) – a *mediated* immediacy. "Reflected" means that it is an product of some "other" announcing what this other is *not*.[43] The Unessential, in effect, says, "I am not Essential." To Dialectical Reason, Illusory Being *seems* immediate, but Speculative Reason knows that such an appearance is one-sided. Illusory Being is mediated *and* unmediated.

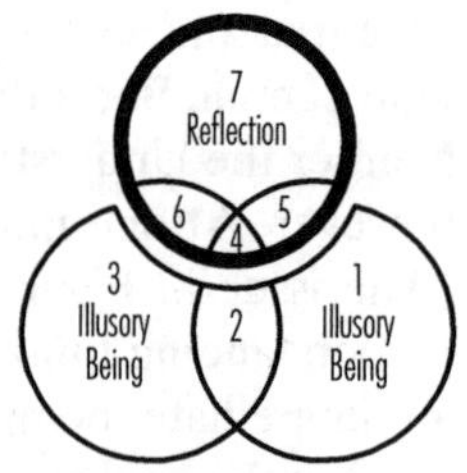

Figure 24(c)
Reflection

Burden of proof. Illusory Being [2] has a moment of independence from Essence ([1] or [3]), which Hegel calls "an immediate presupposition." (397) What is the significance of this claim? That Illusory Being [2] is "immediate" is merely to say that it is *different* from the Unessential (now co-rival to the honor of Essentiality). That

---

[43] Deborah Chaffin, *The Logic of Contingency*, in HEGEL RECONSIDERED: BEYOND METAPHYSICS AND THE AUTHORITARIAN STATE 146 (H. Tristram Engelhardt, Jr., & Terry Pinkard eds., 1994) (reflection "is the mediating other of immediate being . . . "); *see also* JOHN F. HOFFMEYER, THE ADVENT OF FREEDOM: THE PRESENCE OF THE FUTURE IN HEGEL'S LOGIC 11 (1994) ("Hegel developed the identity of determinacy and negation to show that determinacy is relation to other. Reflection is the other of presupposed immediacy").

Illusory Being is a presupposition follows because the Essential and Unessential exist correlatively: if the Unessential [1] announces what it is *not*, it necessarily presupposes the *existence* of the other thing [2] from which it distinguishes itself. As we discover in Positing Reflection,[44] presupposition of otherness is a major analytic technique in the analysis of Essence. Yet presupposition is the enemy of philosophy. *It must be overcome*;[45] indeed, Hegel says "the sublating of its presupposition is essence itself." (402) How might this be accomplished?

Hegel acquits himself of the task of showing that Illusory Being sublates itself and withdraws into Essence. This task has already been performed in the previous nine chapters: "[B]eing in its totality has [already] withdrawn into essence." (397) All Hegel has to show is that (1) Being's distinction from Essence is the "determination of essence itself," (397) and that (2) "this *determinateness of essence* which illusory being is, is sublated in essence itself." (397) If Essence gives rise to Illusory Being and then sublates it, then Essence has being-in-and-for-self and is not merely finite Being, dependent on otherness.

The second burden is met simply by showing that a new middle term arises from Figure 24(b). Sublation is what Speculative Reason always does to Dialectical Reason's discovery. As to the first challenge, how can Hegel show that Illusory Being's difference from Essence is Essence's own determination?

The mode of answering will resemble the proposition that, if it walks like a duck, sounds like a duck, and looks like a duck, it *is* a duck. Similarly, if Hegel shows that Illusory Being has all the properties of being-in-and-for-self, then (contrary to what has been alleged) Hegel has proved that Illusory Being is Essence.[46] The trialogue will go like this:

The Understanding: To find the Essential, peel away all the Unessentials. *Dialectical Reason*: You will never find the Essential by peeling away all the Unessentials. *Speculative Reason*: That *is* the essence of the matter – that you will never find the essence of the matter. Essence erases itself.

The argument proceeds as follows: First, Illusory Being was supposed

---

[44] *Infra* at 268-73.

[45] PIPPIN, *supra* note 4, at 213-4.

[46] BURBIDGE, LOGIC, *supra* note 17, at 65 ("Supposed to be other than *essence*, *seeming* [Illusory Being] has the same defining characteristics").

to be Essential, but only because it was assigned this role by external Understanding. The Understanding announced, "I am Unessential; the other is the Essential." Dialectical Reason then pointed out that the so-called Essential had no being-in-and-for-self and was therefore Illusory Being – a nothing. In this dialectical observation, Illusory Being is counted as an immediacy and, further, an immediacy that is *not*. But this is precisely what Essence is – *not being*. Hence, Illusory Being, which announces "I am not Being," reveals itself to be Essence after all. Illusory Being announces what it is not, and *this* is the hallmark of Essence. In Illusory Being, "the negativity of essence [is] present." (397) From this it follows that the disputed immediacy of Illusory Being is "essence's own absolute being-in-itself." (397)[47] In effect, [2] shows itself to be Reflection [7].

Immediacy – a moment of Illusory Being – is (by definition) equality with self. "[I]t is through this that essence itself is being." (397) In other words, the being of Essence is precisely its independence (immediacy) from being. Essence is nothing but the statement, "I am not Being." Non-being is therefore Essence's mode of being. But this immediacy is "not simply affirmative." (397) Affirmativity is retrogressive at this stage. Instead, immediacy is "purely mediated or reflected immediacy." (397) The immediate "being" of Illusory Being is merely a *moment*. Its *other* moment is mediation.

There are in fact two moments in Illusory Being. There is (i) "the nothingness which yet is" (mediation), and (ii) "the being which is only a moment" (397) (immediacy). Reflection, then, has the structure of Becoming – a unity of nothing and being. This structure means that Reflection is on the move; it is "the movement of becoming." (399)

Immediacy (*i.e.*, difference from Essence) is a moment of Illusory Being, which is now equally a moment of Essence. This immediacy, Hegel says, "is essence's own absolute being-in-itself." (397) What does this imply? Being-in-itself is mere implicitness. Hegel is thus saying that immediacy is not yet posited by Essence but must eventually be posited if Essence is to be *for-itself*. Essence must *recapture* its lost immediacy. Paradoxically, immediacy is Essence's legacy from Being, under the law of sublation, but so far, the sublated immediacy is merely "in-itself." Thus, Hegel says, "Being has preserved itself in essence in so far as

---

[47] As Burbidge puts it, Essence is "that which seems to be a seeming." BURBIDGE, LOGIC, *supra* note 17, at 66. Since "seeming" is not being, seeming to be a seeming is a reestablished kind of negative being.

[Essence] in its infinite negativity has this equality with itself; it is through this that essence itself is being." (397) In short, immediacy is recollected from the logical history of Essence, but is not present *now*.

Immediacy, then, is Essence's own immediacy, and, when Dialectical Reason distinguishes Illusory Being as an immediate nothingness, it "recollects" the history of Illusory Being as sublated immediacy.[48] But as merely an *ideal* (*i.e.*, recollected) moment, "the immediacy is not simply affirmative" but is "purely mediated or reflected." (397)

The import of this exercise is that Illusory Being and Essence enjoy a unity. This implies that Essence is "determinate within itself." (398) Determinateness signifies a duality. The determinateness of Essence is also "distinguished from its absolute unity." (398) In short, we can *know* Essence (determinateness) through, *and* distinguish Essence (as immediacy) from, its appearances (though not in an immediate way).

Because Illusory Being is self-related *and* other-related, it is "the negative that has a being, but in an *other*, in its negation." (398) Illusory Being is a True Infinite that sends its being elsewhere *and* retains its being. But Hegel adds a twist. Illusory Being's being is negative, and its "other" is likewise a negative – as [1] or [3] (as compared to [2]) in Figure 24(b) suggest. This habit of sending its anti-being elsewhere means that Illusory Being is "a non-self subsistent being" (which, as a True Infinite, nevertheless subsists), "self-sublated," and "null." (398) As such, Illusory Being is "the negative returned into itself." (398) Or, since [1] or [3] is just as much a participant in Illusory Being, the send-off of Being from [2] is only a return to [1] or [3]. And because the relation to other is self-relation, we can confirm that Illusory Being is an immediacy – "the purely *self*-coincident negative." (398) Its self-subsistent indeterminateness means that Illusory Being "is essence itself." (398) [2] thereby becomes [7] in Figure 24(c). Essence is accordingly the "negativity that is identical with immediacy and immediacy that is identical with negativity." (398)

Notice the contradiction in this last definition of Essence. Negativity has always been correlated to the thing negated.[49] It is always a

---

[48] *See* MARCUSE, ONTOLOGY, *supra* note 12, at 71 ("Vis-à-vis [immediate being], essence always has been; at the same time it is always present in being. Concretely this means that being-there is at one and the same time a presupposition . . . and a consequence of essence."). What is presupposed in essence is that being *was*.

[49] Negation "in its truth is a *relation* or *relationship*; for it is the negative, *but the negative of the positive*, and includes the positive within itself. It is therefore the other, but not the other of something to which it is indifferent – in that case it would not be

mediation. But now Essence is both negative-mediated *and* immediate. This coheres with the claim that Essence is to the whole of Logic what Quantity was to Being.[50] As such, Essence is negative to *and* correlated with Being. But Essence *is*, and as such it must be an immediacy. Both immediacy and mediation are valid moments of Essence.

Hegel concludes his description of Illusory Being by comparing the dynamic of Essence to that of Being. Pure Being was an immediacy. It turned into Pure Nothing, likewise an immediacy. Their truth was Becoming. In Essence, the Essential first opposed the Unessential. Two immediacies faced each other. Accordingly, the Essential revealed itself to be Unessential (*i.e.*, Illusory Being). Illusory Being [2] drove from itself its negative being – [1] or [3]. This self-repulsion *is* the essence of Essence. And the name of this self-repulsion is Reflection.

Illusory Being is therefore a *movement* that determines its own immediacy as negativity and its negativity as immediacy. This, Hegel says, is "the reflection of itself within itself." (399) Reflection is the self-movement of Essence. If Essence is taken as the entirety of Figure 24(c), then reflective movement contains itself within itself. Later, Hegel will summarize the above by saying: "Essence at first reflects an *illusory being* within itself, within its simple identity; as such it is abstract reflection, the pure movement from nothing through nothing back to itself." (499) Reflection, in short, is a negation of a negation.[51]

C. Reflection

Essence is non-being and nothing more. What a thing is *not* constitutes it more profoundly than what it is. Reflection is the name of the negating act by which Essence shows what it is *not*: "For illusory being that has withdrawn into itself and so is estranged from its immediacy, we have the foreign word *reflection*." (399)

Reflection sends its affirmative being outside itself. But, per the rules

---

an other, nor a . . . relationship – rather it is the *other in its own self*, the *other of an other*; it includes *its* own other within it and is consequently a contradiction." (834-5)

[50] *Supra* at 255.

[51] HARRIS, LOGIC, *supra* note 2, at 159 ("The 'two nothings' are the abstract aspects distinguished by reflection, each of which by itself is the negation of immediate being, and as such is a mere shadow. Yet each is correlative to (and 'shows' in) the other, and each reflecting into each to reveal an inner essence issuing in outer disclosure or self-expression.").

of True Infinity, the expelled material is just as much retained as expelled. Reflection therefore names not only the act of withdrawal of Being *from* itself and but also the withdrawal of being *into* itself. But where is Reflection located? In common parlance, if *I* reflect about a thing, *I* turn it over in my mind and discover a deeper essence that may contradict the immediate appearance of the thing. Does Reflection therefore exist in my mind, or does it exist in the thing? Contrary to Kant,[52] Hegel locates Reflection in the thing.[53] Hegel would rewrite "I reflect on a thing" to read: "The thing reflects its deeper truth in my mind."[54] Earlier the Understanding viewed the Essential as an immediate Being. Unable to sustain itself, this immediate Being showed itself to be merely the *appearance* of Essence. The fate of appearance is to disappear; the dissolution of the Essential was therefore no subjective exercise, but something that logically happens to an immediate Being posited as beyond thought.

Reflection is *movement*, and so Hegel compares it to Becoming: "At the base of becoming, there lies the determinateness of being, and this is relation to *other*. The movement of reflection, on the other hand, is the other as the *negation in itself*, which has a being only as self-related negation." (399) This last statement must be read with care. The *movement* is *other*. To what? Other to what it negates – static Illusory Being. In Figure 24(c), we can view [7] as the negating movement: Reflection's "immediacy is only this movement itself." (399) Movement [7] negates [4, 5, 6], all of which are inessential Illusory Being. Furthermore, [7] is the "negating of the negation." (399) [4, 5, 6] can

---

[52] IMMANUEL KANT, CRITIQUE OF PURE REASON A260/B316 (Paul Guyer & Allen W. Wood trans., 1990).

[53] *See* MARCUSE, REASON, *supra* note 1, at 143. ("for Hegel reflection . . . denotes an objective as well as subjective movement. Reflection is not primarily the process of thinking but the process of being itself.").

[54] *See* HYPPOLITE, LOGIC, *supra* note 4, at 88 (speculative logic "is the reflection of the determinations in the medium of the universal and not the subjective reflection of consciousness as such"). Michael Kosok defines Reflection as "a generating process in which an initially unformed element *becomes* formed, making the reference to the element impossible without reference to the act of reflection. The activity of reflection becomes an integral aspect of the element reflected and a process of continual reflection amounts to *self*-reflection – the initial element embodying reflection as its form." Michael Kosok, *The Formalization of Hegel's Dialectical Logic: Its Formal Structure, Logical Interpretation and Intuitive Foundation*, in HEGEL: A COLLECTION OF CRITICAL ESSAYS 237, 239 (Alasdair MacIntyre, ed., 1972) In other words, Reflection transforms Being, but operates from *within* Being. From the perspective of the thing, Reflection is always reflection of self.

be viewed as modulating negative activity, each segment announcing that it is not its other, Essence. Reflection negates them all. In Figure 24(c), all portions of the diagram are negative. [7] is therefore negation of the negation "in such wise that it has its being in its negatedness, as illusory being." (399) It *is* by virtue of its negating [4, 5, 6], yet [4, 5, 6] is preserved as the veritable determinateness of [7]. In this manner Hegel emphasizes the moment of immediacy and self-relation in Essence as "the *movement of nothing to nothing, and so back to itself.* [T]he *other* that . . . comes to be, is not the non-being of a being," as in earlier stages, "but the nothingness of a nothing." (400)

The immediacy of Essence is the *movement* of Reflection [7]. Hence, immediacy has become a middle term. In the Doctrine of Being, immediacy was "a *first* from which the beginning was made and which passed over into its negation." (399) Now immediacy is the *result.* Accordingly, this derived immediacy is not to be viewed as "an affirmatively present substrate." (399)[55] The new immediacy is strictly a negative concept – a negation of the negation.

(a) Positing Reflection

Reflection determines itself into (a) Positing (or Absolute), (b) External, and (c) Determining. Positing Reflection emphasizes the *negative immediacy* of Reflection – a paradox, since negativity is always correlative. In Positing Reflection, Hegel develops the notions of positing (*setzen*), presupposing (*vorrausetzen*), and return-into-self.

Reflection announces what it is *not*. This negative enunciation is what Hegel calls *positing*.[56] Positing requires "otherness" to function. When Illusory Being said, "I am not Essence," it *presupposed* there *is* such a thing as Essence. Positing Reflection must have within it an other – a "that" if the statement "I am not *that*" is to make sense. Positing therefore *presupposes*.[57] *What* Positing Reflection presupposes, however, is precisely the opposite of what the Inessential presupposes.

---

[55] Affirmitivity should be taken as dogmatic, not immanently derived.

[56] "Speculative contradiction is the contradiction of the Absolute itself that negates itself by positing itself; but this meaning of negation, which is not only subjective but also inherent to being, is the decisive point of the Hegelian dialectic . . . " HYPPOLITE, LOGIC, *supra* note 4, at 92.

[57] In Determinate Being, Hegel argued that, if a point is *limit*, then the line arises spontaneously, since limit is a correlative term. *Supra* at 85-6. Similarly, positing requires a "posited," because it is inherently correlative.

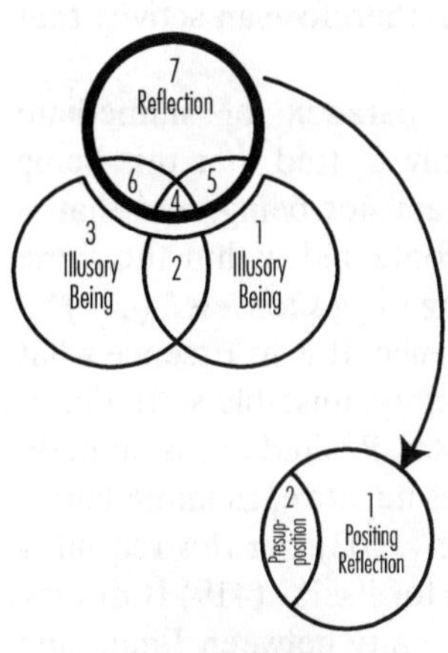

Figure 25(a)
Positing (Absolute) Reflection

The Inessential presupposed Essence. But now Essence has been derived. It is Reflection. So Positing Reflection *is* Essence. It presupposes its own Determinate Being.[58]

What Positing Reflection presupposes is itself *already derived*. Its other is *sublated* being – its own atemporal past. Accordingly, Positing Reflection represents "a relation of what is prior and what is posterior."[59] We already know, on the law of sublation, that this sublated other *was*. Accordingly, Hegel states, "*Determinate being is merely posited being or positedness*; this is the proposition of essence about determinate being." (406)

Positing Reflection is an immediacy encompassing correlativity. The presupposed other is *internal* to Essence. The Essence of Positing Reflection is "its own equality with itself." (400) Self-equality implies that Positing Reflection *forgets* its own mediated structure, even as it *finds* its other before it. Because Positing Reflection is an immediacy, negativity has disappeared, for the moment. This leaves Positing Reflection in a state of contradiction. "[I]t is itself both the negative, and simple equality with itself or immediacy. It consists, therefore, in *being itself* and *not itself* and that, too, in a single unity." (400) Essence is now to be conceived as return-to-self *and* as self-negation. As such, it is a self-contained totality, with no outside. If anything is negated, it is Essence's own negations *within* the totality.

Presupposing is how Positing Reflection "relates itself to itself, but to itself as negative of itself." (401) In this sense, Positing Reflection resembles the Cartesian *cogito ergo sum*. The active "I think" distingui-

---

[58] Stephen Houlgate, *Hegel's Critique of Foundationalism in the "Doctrine of Essence"*, GERMAN PHILOSOPHY SINCE KANT 27 (Anthony O'Hear ed. 1999) ("It is here at the end of the section on 'seeming' . . . that the profound reversal in our conception of the essence of things occurs; for it is here that we first see the essence play a positive – indeed, generative – role, rather than a purely negative one. Here in other words, we first see negativity negate itself into positivity.").

[59] HOFFMEYER, *supra* note 43, at 11.

shes itself from its thoughts. Yet its thoughts are proof that it *is*. Hence, a passive "I am" is posited. Thinking is therefore an activity that presupposes a static end to its activity.

Positedness. Positing Reflection is the paradox of immediate mediation. It sends its being from itself only to find that this being returns. Positing Reflection announces, "I am not being, *and* that is what I am." Negativity *and* positivity are contained within the same concept. Hegel calls this mode "*posited being* or *positedness*." (401)[60]

Positedness is key in Hegel's theory of Essence. It is to Essence what determinateness is to Being. It is a contradictory, unstable state that is nonetheless necessary if essence is to be known. Positedness is immediate but mediated because it is "determined as negative, as immediately *opposed* to something, therefore to an other." (402) For this reason, a positedness is "an identity that is not in and for itself." (419) It differs, however, from determinateness, which is a unity between Being and Nothing. In a positedness, a negative faces a negative other. The two negatives differ yet constitute an immediate unity.

Return-into-self. Connected to positedness is the equally important notion of return-into-self (*Rückkehr in sich*), reflection-into-self (*Reflexion-in-sich*), or reflectedness-into-self (*Reflectiert-sein in sich*), as Hegel indifferently calls it. Reflection sends its being from itself by announcing what it is not. But the otherness to which its being is sent is identical and internal to the address from which being is shipped. If there is a sending, it is strictly inter-office mail. By traveling to the other, being merely delivers itself to itself. Reflective movement is thus "an *absolute recoil* upon itself." (402) Every sending is a return. Yet, if so, the starting point is itself a presupposition. Positing Reflection presupposes itself as well as its other. This is precisely what Positing Reflection forgets. For this reason, Reflection "is the movement that starts or returns only in so far as the negative has already returned into itself." (401)

Positing is "immediacy as a returning movement." (401) What does immediacy imply? In this moment, Positing Reflection sublates the

---

[60] *Id.* at 44 ("Positing reflection remains indeterminate because it swallows up immediacy in the movement of reflection. The determinate relation of priority and posteriority established in the act of presupposing turns out to be illusory, since that which is presupposed disappears in the reflection that posits it."). Perhaps Positing Reflection's indeterminacy sounds the wrong note, since it is supposed to be a correlation of what is and is not. But the swallowing of the presupposition is exactly right. Positing Reflection privileges positivity over negativity.

negative and therefore its other. Yet its other *is* immediacy – *i.e.*, Being. If Positing Reflection sends forth its Being to an other, this other insists upon *its* moment of immediacy – an honor once accorded in the realm of Being. But because Positing Reflection is itself immediate, the immediacy of the other cannot subsist. Immediacy cancels immediacy.

This leaves Positing Reflection as a movement – a cancellation of otherness ("I am not *that*!"). Positing Reflection is therefore active. This constitutes an advance for the Understanding. At first, the Understanding saw passive stasis or *Being*. But slowly it grew inured to the fact that what it perceives is *active*. The Understanding is beginning to resemble Dialectical Reason, which is capable of seeing a contradiction between passivity and activity.[61]

Lacanian implications. What follows is a most difficult passage: "It is only when essence has sublated its equality-with-self that it is equality-with-self. It presupposes itself and the sublating of its presupposition is essence itself." (402) What can this mean? Recall that Being strove to be self-equal (*i.e.*, free). But self-equality destroyed itself and became Essence. Ironically, in its failure, Being actually achieves its goal of self-equality in Positing Reflection. This is the moment that Positing Reflection expresses.

The point here is Lacanian. In Lacanian theory, we succeed by failing. The Lacanian subject feels alienated from his being. Out there is some missing thing (the phallus) that would make the subject feel whole. What is missing is strictly "sublime" – a negative. Through sublimation, this negative becomes associated with some positive thing, such as unrequited love or winning an election. These are the sublime objects of our desire. In pursuing them, we pursue self-equality. If we can just get a date or win an election, we think that we can recapture our missing being. But the endeavor must logically fail. Constitutionally, we are not self-identical (as Hegel everywhere emphasizes in the *SL*). Rather, we *are*, as Kant puts it, a "faculty of desire."[62] We are not what we desire, and that is what we are. Achievement of our desire

---

[61] Later, the Understanding will begin to resemble Speculative Reason. It will propose that the Notion is itself (immediacy), its other (dialectic), and the unity between itself and other. See chapter 19. *See also* G.W.F. HEGEL, THE DIFFERENCE BETWEEN FICHTE'S AND SCHELLING'S SYSTEM OF PHILOSOPHY 95 (H.S. Harris & Walter Cerf trans., 1977) (reason seduces the Understanding "into producing an objective totality.").

[62] IMMANUEL KANT, CRITIQUE OF PRACTICAL REASON 32 (T.K. Abbott trans., 1996).

would be catastrophic. We succeed by failing.

The thing we desire is not really the point. It masks over a negative thing that is beyond us *and* constitutive of us and hence in us.[63] Psychoanalysis teaches us to surrender or sublate the aspiration to self-equality. When we do, we paradoxically achieve self-equality. Desire is best fulfilled when it is renounced – when the subject says to desire, "I am not *that*!"

Hegel continues: "Reflection *finds before it* an immediate which it transcends and from which it is the return." (402) The verb "to find" is important. Reflection does not say, "I am just making this all up. There is no 'other' out there." Rather, Positing Reflection discovers what really *is* (or *was*). But by insisting upon its moment of immediacy, Positing Reflection equally transcends its discovery and reappropriates the very being it had sent forth, since presupposition is also a return.

In short, return and presupposition mutually constitute each other. One cannot exist without the other. Accordingly, Hegel remarks, "But this return is only the presupposing of what reflection finds before it. What is thus found only *comes to be* through being *left behind*; its immediacy is sublated immediacy." (402) What this passage means is that *presence* (Positing Reflection) is constituted by an *absence* (Being that is both found and left behind). Again, the point has significance for psychoanalysis. Human subjects who feel empty and alienated have *found* that they have *lost* their grace (*i.e.*, original sin). Once they had it but now they don't. The loss comes to be only when the subject feels that a missing piece has been left behind. This feeling of loss is what Lacanians call "castration." But this is "false autobiography."[64] We never had what we lost. Loss is presupposed.[65]

---

[63] This negative non-thing is Lacan's *objet petit a*. The *a* stands for *autre*, or *other*. "Object *a* can be understood here as the *remainder* produced when that hypothetical unity [of the self] breaks down, as a last trace of that unity, a last *remainder* thereof. By cleaving to that rem(a)inder, the split subject, though expulsed from the Other, can sustain the illusion of wholeness; by clinging to object *a*, the subject is able to ignore his or her division." BRUCE FINK, THE LACANIAN SUBJECT: BETWEEN LANGUAGE AND *JOUISSANCE* 59 (1995).

[64] Jeanne L. Schroeder, *Pandora's Amphora: The Ambiguity of Gift*, 46 UCLA L. REV. 815, 899-903 (1999).

[65] Psychoanalysis therefore tries to achieve a "loss of a loss" – a realization that what is lacking in ourselves is simply presupposed. SLAVOJ ŽIŽEK, FOR THEY KNOW NOT WHAT THEY DO: ENJOYMENT AS A POLITICAL FACTOR 168 (1991). Stephen Houlgate, however, interprets this passage differently. He views it as marking the point at which Essence stops being the *product* of Being and becomes the *producer* of Being. "Positing

(b) External Reflection

External Reflection, the quintessence of Dialectical Reason, emphasizes difference at the expense of identity.[66] It accuses Positing Reflection of having found in the stones the very sermons it placed there. It says, "You claim you *are* by virtue of your return from sublating Being. That's just a presupposition. You've just imagined it all. You have found nothing objective."

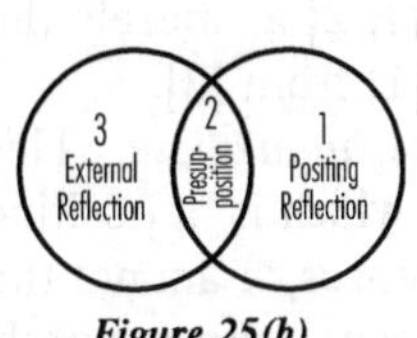

Figure 25(b)
External Reflection

External Reflection makes "what is prior independent of what is posterior."[67] It is "subsequent and synthetic" and "necessarily external to the relations it considers."[68] It arises because Positing Reflection "*has* a presupposition and starts from the immediate as its other." (402)[69] The "other" to Positing Reflection is its own immediate Being, which Positing Reflection itself presupposes. Dialectically, we can now see that Positing Reflection "reflects its illusory being within itself and presupposes for itself only an illusory being, only positedness." (402-3)

External Reflection [3] views presupposition [2] as "the negative of reflection [1], but so that this negative *as* negative is sublated." (403) That is to say, External Reflection accepts [2] as sublated Being, as derived in earlier chapters. What it denies is the *return* and hence the being of Reflection. Accordingly, External Reflection

> is the syllogism in which are the two extremes, the immediate and return-into-self; the middle term of the syllogism [2] is the connection of the two, the determinate immediate, so that one part of the middle term, immediacy, belongs only to one of

---

is thus a deeply paradoxical movement: for it *is not* simply prior to positedness, but only *comes to be* prior to positedness in and through the activity of producing that positedness. It does not simply come first, but, as it were, *ends up* preceding what it posits . . . This reflects the paradox at the heart of essence itself: for essence is that which is primary and prior to being, but that which only turns out *at the end* to have come first. It is that to which posited being can only ever *point back*." Houlgate, *Concept*, *supra* note 8, at 21.

[66] HOFFMEYER, *supra* note 43, at 15 ("All the second members of triads . . . should bear a basic similarity to external reflection").

[67] *Id*. at 12.

[68] JOHN W. BURBIDGE, HEGEL ON LOGIC AND RELIGION: THE REASONABLENESS OF CHRISTIANITY 25 (1992).

[69] BUTLER, LOGIC, *supra* note 5, at 135 (External Reflection should be called "presuppositional reflection," because it is reflection aware of its own act).

the extremes, the other, determinateness or negation, belongs only to the other extreme. (403)

This passage describes Figure 25(b). Positing Reflection [1, 2] is Reflection's immediate moment. External Reflection [3] – a return-into-self – is on the left side of the syllogism – the side which *is* (as opposed to the side which is not). It stands against Positing Reflection [1] and immediacy [2]. It sees the immediacy of [1, 2] as merely the product of Positing Reflection and so decouples [1] from [2].

Hegel calls the middle term the *determinate immediate*. This immediacy is presupposed by External Reflection, which is "a positing of the immediate." (403) External Reflection announces, "I am not the immediate. Rather, [2] is immediate." The immediate "consequently becomes the negative or the determinate."(403)

But External Reflection is likewise "immediately also the sublating of . . . its positing." (403) This sublating was also a feature of Positing Reflection. According to this activity, Positing Reflection forgot its own positing activity. Now External Reflection does the same. External Reflection "*pre*supposes the immediate; in negating, it is the negating of . . . its negating." (403)[70]

External Reflection is *both* what Positing Reflection was (on the law of sublation) – that is to say, not a positing – *and* a consciousness of positing activity.[71] We have a version of Dialectical Reason's standard flaw. It denounces the position of the Understanding but replicates it.

As conscious of the other's immediacy, External Reflection is not truly external. It is a genuine unity with its negative. This union, like all unions, implies a moment of genuine immediacy. The realization that External Reflection is "not external but is . . . the immanent reflection of immediacy itself" (403) is the contribution of Speculative Reason. "Reflection is thus *determining reflection*." (404)

(c) Determining Reflection

Determining Reflection is the unity of Positing and External

---

[70] *See* HYPPOLITE, LOGIC, *supra* note 4, at 86 ("Because external reflection starts from immediate content, it does not see that it presupposes itself, and that the content reflects itself into what grounds it"), 117 ("external reflection does not reflect on itself; it is beyond the compared things, it is subjective").

[71] "In this way, the immediate is not only *in itself* – that means, for us, or in external reflection – *identical* with reflection, but this identicalness is *posited*." (404)

Reflection. From Illusory Being Dialectical Reason had elicited the confession that it was not Essential; it did not have being-in-and-for-self. Speculative Reason responded, "But that is what Essence is. It is the act of stating what it is *not*." With that observation, Illusory Being was born again as Reflection. Infuriated in defeat, Dialectical Reason accuses Positing Reflection of presupposing itself. Speculative Reason once again says, "But that is all there is. Essence presupposes what it *is*. The job of Essence is to be. And it *is* by announcing what it is *not*."[72] What is added is *consciousness* of positing activity.[73] For Speculative Reason, self-presupposition is no embarrassment. Rather, it is the birth of *freedom*. *Creatio ex nihilo* is Determining Reflection's theme.[74]

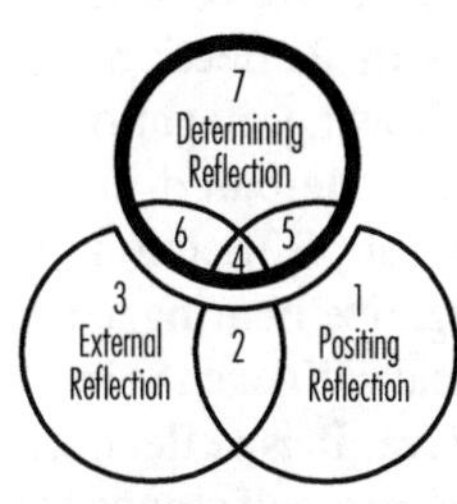

Figure 25(c)
Determining Reflection

Determining Reflection accepts the fact that reflective activity is always positing a presupposition. For this reason, Hegel says that positedness is a middle term mediating between Essence and Determinate Being. External Reflection announces that the determination of Positing Reflection is "*only* a positedness." (406) This can have two meanings. Either it is (1) a positedness opposed to a real, substantial Determinate Being, or it is (2) a positedness *of Essence*. With regard to (1), External Reflection takes Determinate Being to be superior to positedness; positedness is a dream ascribed to "the subjective side." (406) But Determining Reflection knows that *there is no Determinate Being beyond the positing of it*.

Positing "is now in unity with external reflection." (406) Whereas External Reflection would not permit a return to self, Determining Reflection permits the return to occur. This means that "the boundary between 'positing' and 'external' reflection falls, not between

---

[72] HOFFMEYER, *supra* note 43, at 11 ("Determining reflection articulates that which positing reflection makes so clear, but which external reflection covers over; namely, the presupposition is reflection's own positing. On the other hand, determining reflection articulates that which external reflection brings to bear, but which is absent from positing reflection.").

[73] For this reason, Hyppolite writes, "Speculative thought is dogmatic like naive thought and critical like transcendental thought." HYPPOLITE, LOGIC, *supra* note 4, at 87.

[74] For the view that Positing, External and Determining Reflection represent Greek religion, Judaism and Christianity respectively, see SLAVOJ ŽIŽEK, THE METASTASES OF ENJOYMENT: SIX ESSAYS ON WOMAN AND CAUSALITY 38-43 (1993).

appearance and essence, but within essence itself."[75] Hence, Determining Reflection is "the positing of the determinateness *as determinateness of itself*." (406) Primitive determinateness is immediate relation to other. Determinate Being is simply affirmative negation. Being undergoes *transition* into Nothing; it cannot sustain itself and is not equal to its negation; Quality is not equal to itself. Positedness too is a relation to other, but *that* other is now internal to the concept – *relatively* other, not *radically* other. Determinations of Reflection are free from transition.[76] They are self-identity following negation.[77] This enables the negative to persist. Transitoriness is defeated.

Like all "essential" tropes, a Determination of Reflection is correlative; there are two sides – "a positive and negative bearing, each being posited as exclusive, and only *implicitly* identical with each other." (638) First, a Determination of Reflection is *positive*. It is reflection-into-self and, as such, equality with itself. Reflection-into-self stands for subsistence – the accomplished sublation of positedness. This side is *not* reflected into its other – its non-being. "*By virtue of this reflection-into-self* the determinations of reflection appear as free essentialities floating in the void without attracting or repelling one another." (407)[78]

Second, the determination "is positedness, negation as such." (407) The *negative* side acknowledges otherness. As a positedness, a Determination of Reflection is "a non-being over against an other, namely, *over against* absolute return-into-self, or over against essence." (408) Positedness stands for sublatability and instability; it is "an immediacy that is *in itself* sublated, that is not distinct from the return-into-self and is itself only this movement of return." (402) But, because it is only sublated *in itself*, it is not yet *expressly* sublated. Hence, we have before us the correlation of positedness and sublation of positedness.

Hegel had earlier pointed out that Essence is to the whole of Logic

---

[75] SARAH KAY, ŽIŽEK: A CRITICAL INTRODUCTION 37 (2003).

[76] Kant disagreed. He "went so far as to call the determinations of reflection 'amphibolic' and he excluded them from his table of categories because they have an equivocal function in the determination of objects." GADAMER, *supra* note 56, at 81. An "amphiboly" is the confusion of noumenon and phenomenon. CRITIQUE OF PURE REASON, *supra* note 53, at A270/B326.

[77] BURBIDGE, LOGIC, *supra* note 17, at 249 n.6.

[78] The freedom of "free essentialities" will turn out to be a one-sided freedom, "characterized by subjugation and domination." HOFFMEYER, *supra* note 43, at 13. Freedom will be vastly enriched in future developments.

what Quantity was to the doctrine of Being.[79] How did Quantity get its start? By presupposing an other to which its expelled content was assigned. Into this other Quantity continuously flowed. Now Reflection does something similar. It presupposes a return from an other which, in its now more advanced state, is internal to the concept – not external, as Quantity's other was. The other to Reflection (purely the *act* of announcing what it is *not*) is Illusory Being. Essence is discovering that its very existence is correlative.[80] It needs *appearance* in order to show what it is – the act of announcing that it is *not*.

---

[79] *Supra* at 255.

[80] BURBIDGE, LOGIC, *supra* note 17, at 65 ("*essence* is not a simple concept that can be isolated in the way [Determinate Being] can be isolated. *Essence* signifies a much more complex process of thought: in . . . negating what is immediate given, it remains identical with itself.") (footnote omitted).

11
Determinations of Reflection

A Determination of Reflection (*Reflexionbestimmung*) has a dual structure. It is a positedness, which implies a relation with otherness. It is also an immediacy, which perseveres in impious stubbornness even after it negates its other and hence itself. Because of this double structure, a Determination of Reflection is "infinite return-into-self" and "negative simplicity." (409) By now Hegel's meaning should be clear. The True Infinite sends its being elsewhere while remaining what it is. Determinations of Reflection behave in just this way. Being is sent off when Essence announces, "I am not *that*," but the bad penny of Being infinitely returns. Essence is mediated yet paradoxically simple – a negative *non-simple* simplicity. Accordingly, a Determination of Reflection "has a positive and negative bearing, each being posited as exclusive, and only *implicitly* identical with the other." (638)

Hegel previews the fate of the *Reflexionbestimmungen*. First, immediacy is taken up – the concept of Identity. Identity already contains Difference. Second, mediatedness is considered – Difference as such. Difference has two natures – Diversity (*i.e.*, complete and utter difference) and Opposition (dependent or mediated difference). The middle term between Identity and Difference is Contradiction – the Ground of all things.

Identity is the province of the Understanding. Dialectical Reason champions Difference. Speculative Reason sees the identity of Identity and Difference, or Ground. Meanwhile, all Determinations of Reflection have a double structure (including the Understanding's account of

Identity). The double structure fits in with the fact that we have before us the second, dialectical chapter of Reflection. Whereas chapter 10 stood for immediacy, this chapter stands for mediation. The next chapter – Ground – stands for reconciliation.[1]

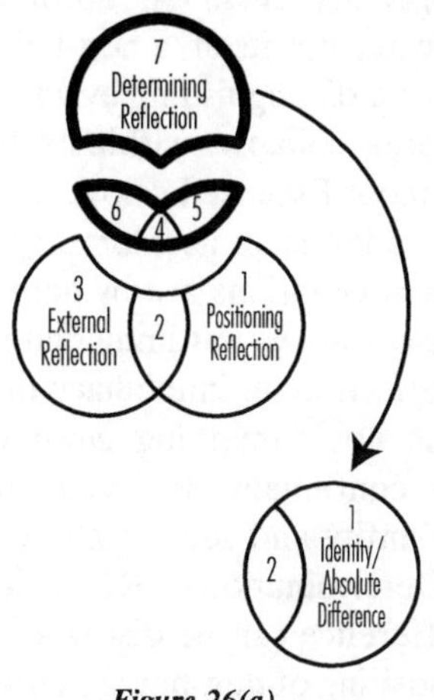

Figure 26(a)
Identity
(Absolute Difference)

A. Identity

According to the Understanding, Identity – one of the moments in a Determination of Reflection – already has Difference within it. In this guise it is Absolute Difference. Though negative, Absolute Difference is Essence's moment of "simple immediacy." (411) As we are well past the doctrine of Being, immediacy is now mediated. Identity is therefore "self-equal in its absolute negativity." (411) Negativity, as always, implies mediatedness. Hence this Identity is the self-identity of a True Infinite.[2] A True Infinite is that which *endures* while *becoming something different*. Accordingly, Identity is itself *and* its other, but with the accent on endurance. We do not have an abstract Identity but an Identity "that has brought itself to unity, not a restoration of itself from an other, but this pure origination from and within itself." (411)

"Thinking that keeps to external reflection" (412) (*i.e.*, common sense) never gets past abstract identity. "In its opinion, reason is nothing more

---

[1] According to Stanley Rosen, Identity stands for the "in itself" – the merely implicit. Being strives for Identity, but fails. Identity remains merely an ought-to-be. Difference is "for itself." Reflection is the statement, "I am not *that*." It is the pose of negative Difference. Essence is identity after self-differentiation. It is in-and-for-self when it is the unity of Identity and Difference. "In order to bring together the in-itself and the for-itself, we require a reconciliation of identity and difference within the ground . . . When this is achieved, being may be said to have recollected itself, or accomplished its truth. This accomplishment may also be described as the reconciliation of essence with its appearances . . ." STANLEY ROSEN, G.W.F. HEGEL: AN INTRODUCTION TO THE SCIENCE OF WISDOM 107 (1974).

[2] *See* JOHN W. BURBIDGE, ON HEGEL'S LOGIC: FRAGMENTS OF A COMMENTARY 73 (1981) (Identity "is an equivalence to itself that is maintained through a process of change").

than a loom on which it externally combines and interweaves the warp, of say, identity, and then the woof of difference." (412) If it proceeds analytically, it isolates identity here and difference there, failing to see that Identity and Difference are interdependent.[3]

Of Identity in its speculative form, Hegel observes: "As absolute negation it is the negation that immediately negates itself, a non-being and difference that vanishes in its arising, or a distinguishing by which nothing is distinguished, but which immediately collapses within itself." (412) These should be familiar sentiments about Essence by now. In its moment of unity, a Determination of Reflection is an absolute negation – a negation rendered immediate (when negations are by nature correlative). Its other moment – positedness – arises but immediately collapses, leaving the Determination of Reflection an immediacy that contains difference within it. "Identity is not something *given* or derived: it is something that has to be continually achieved and reaffirmed, involving the anxiety of non-identity and self-negation."[4]

With regard to the other moment of the Determination of Reflection – the moment of positedness, in which difference can be discerned – Hegel remarks: "The distinguishing is the positing of non-being as non-being of the other. But the non-being of the other is sublation of the other and therewith of the distinguishing itself." (412)[5] In other words, Reflection is the statement, "I am not *that*." It is always a reference to an other. This other is, by now, a negative non-being. But, in its announcement, Essence erases or sublates the other and returns to itself. Meanwhile, the other *is* the self of Essence. Essence distinguishes itself

---

[3] Taylor can be criticized for limiting this truth: "Hence the identity of a thing with itself – so long as we are not talking about an entity which is defined in terms of a single property, but rather about something which can bear many properties – properly understood bears on the underlying substrate which not only can undergo change, but is the necessary source of change itself. This identity thus has difference as an essential moment . . . " CHARLES TAYLOR, HEGEL 261 (1975). For Taylor, some things *are* self-identical – things with only one property. But even here the thing with one property has *more* than one property. There is (1) the thing and (2) the one property of the thing, from which the thing is distinguished. Even uniproprietal things are not self-identical.

[4] Michael Kosok, *The Formalization of Hegel's Dialectical Logic: Its Formal Structure, Logical Interpretation and Intuitive Foundation*, in HEGEL: A COLLECTION OF CRITICAL ESSAYS 237, 269 (Alasdair MacIntyre, ed., 1972).

[5] These last quotes are from a mysterious paragraph 2. There is no paragraph 1 in this Remark. This problem stems from the German original. BURBIDGE, LOGIC, *supra* note 2, at 250 n.1. Possibly this paragraph was not intended to be part of the Remark but was the second paragraph to the general section on Identity. Miller illegitimately assigns a numeral "2" to the paragraph just above the Remark.

from itself. Identity, then, is reflection-into-self and internal repulsion. It is "difference that is identical with itself. But difference is only identical with itself in so far as it is not identity but absolute non-identity." (412) In short, we have a version of Hegel's key slogan – the identity of identity and difference, "the bond that holds together opposites in the very activity of opposing them or holding them apart".[6]

The First Original Law of Thought

> Few topics have occasioned more irritated criticism of Hegel than his views on the Laws of Thought in formal logic, not least what he says about the Law of Identity.[7]

Audaciously, Hegel attacks the very notion of $A = A$ – the presupposition of self-identity. Self-identity is taken as one of the universal laws of thought "that lie at the base of all thinking, that are absolute in themselves and incapable of proof." (409)

Hegel sees no reason why thinking should begin with *A* is *A*. Why not begin with the proposition "*A is*"? We would then begin, as Hegel had done, with "all the determinatenesses of the sphere of being." (409) Being is the universal predicate. Of course, Being turns into its opposite, implying that negative Being is just as necessary as affirmative Being. If $A = A$, it is likewise true that $A \neq A$. Neither Identity nor Difference, then, can assert a privilege over the other.

Determinations of Reflection have two moments: Identity and Difference. As relational and therefore determinate, they contain the propositional form (*i.e.*, $A = A$). A proposition expresses a relation. But the other moment of the *Reflexionbestimmungen* is self-identity, to which the propositional form is superfluous. Even within their proper domains, propositional forms are retrogressive. They simply privilege affirmative Quality at the expense of Negation. Judgment, in contrast, "transfers the content to the predicate as a universal determinateness

---

[6] ROSEN, *supra* note 1, at 24 (footnote omitted). The identity of identity and difference is a Schellingian slogan, but, for Schelling, the Absolute, which mediates between identity and difference, is a complete indifference, which leads Hegel to characterize the Schellingian absolute as "a night in which all cows are black." *Id.* at 59; *see* G.W.F. HEGEL, PHENOMENOLOGY OF SPIRIT ¶ 16 (A.V. Miller trans. 1977) ("To pit this single insight, that in the Absolute everything is the same, against the full body of articulated cognition, which at least seeks and demands such fulfillment, to palm off its Absolute as the night in which, as the saying goes, all cows are black – this cognition is reduced to vacuity").

[7] ERROL E. HARRIS, THE SPIRIT OF HEGEL 82 (1993).

which is for itself and is distinct from its relation, the simple copula." (410) This presages Hegel's analysis in the subjective Logic.[8]

In any case, the so-called laws of thought – everything is the same, everything is different – contradict each other. If everything is identical, then nothing is different, and nothing has any ground.[9] Or, if no two things are the same, everything is different from everything else. Then $A \neq A$, but A is not opposed to A either. That is to say, if A is completely diverse from A, they are not opposed but are self-identical (and hence not different from each other).[10] Either one of these laws rules out the other. They can only be enumerated one after the other.

$A = A$ is supposed to be an empty tautology. "It has therefore been rightly remarked that this law of thought has *no content* and leads no further." (413) It is the favorite slogan of those who think identity and difference are different (and not the same). "They do not see that in this very assertion they are themselves stating that *identity is different*; for they are saying that *identity is different* from difference." (413) That is to say, it is in the nature of identity to be different.[11]

Many will say of $A = A$ that it is merely a formal truth, "which is *abstract, incomplete*." (414) But such an assertion implies that *complete* truth requires the unity of Identity and Difference. In other words, if $A = A$ is only formal, then truth must have a form like $A = B$. This is obviously the assertion that A is different from B – they have different names, shapes, positions on the page, etc. Yet the equal sign signifies that these different symbols are nevertheless the same.

In effect, what people mean by "identity" is absolute separation. Identity is "*nothing for itself* but is a moment of *separation*." (414) In other words, identity cannot even be expressed except in terms of difference.

---

[8] See chapter 20. Hegel suggests that judgment transforms verbs into participles. (410) For instance, "she sleeps" becomes "she is sleeping." But Determinations of Reflection are propositions, not judgments. In them, "the propositional form itself lies immediately at hand." (410) In propositions, the subject and the predicate are "diverse," but in judgment they are not.

[9] "The result is a universe of nonarticulated monads, each indistinguishable from the others. Hence each collapses into the others, and the result is . . . the Parmidean One . . . " ROSEN, *supra* note 1, at 116.

[10] This was the lesson of Being-for-self at the end of chapter 3. Also, I am borrowing from Hegel's critique of Diversity and Opposition, *infra* at 285-98.

[11] *See* G.W.F. HEGEL, THE JENA SYSTEM, 1804-5: LOGIC AND METAPHYSICS 182 (John W. Burbidge & George di Giovanni trans. 1986) ("The self-equivalent is something other").

$A = A$ is taken as self-evident, and its truth is established by an appeal to universal experience. But this appeal

> is a mere manner of speaking. For it is not pretended that the experiment with the abstract proposition $A=A$ has been made on every consciousness. The appeal, then, to actually carried-out experiment is not to be taken seriously; it is only the *assurance* that if the experiment were made, the proposition would be universally admitted. (414)

In fact, what people experience, Hegel says, is $A = B$, and from this the proposition $A = A$ is abstracted. But this abstraction does not leave experience as it is, but rather alters it. The experience of $A = B$, Hegel says, "is the *immediate refutation* of the assertion that abstract identity as such is something true, for the exact opposite, namely, identity only in union with difference, occurs in every experience." (415)

The abstraction of $A = A$ as a universal rule of thought is disappointing.

> If anyone opens his mouth and promises to state what God is, namely God is – God, expectation is cheated, for what was expected was a *different determination*; and if this statement is absolute truth, such absolute verbiage is very lightly esteemed; nothing will be held to be more boring and tedious than conversation which merely reiterates the same thing. (415)

When someone says, "A plant is – ", the listener expects some real information. The expectation is that the plant as such will disappear and some essential predicate will take its place. "The propositional form can be regarded as the hidden necessity of adding to abstract identity." (416) Hence, if instead of "plant" we substitute "identity," identity will disappear and become something different.

How legitimate is this line of argument? Hegel is referring to the attempt to ground $A = A$ in experience. Since his unnamed opponents rely on experience, Hegel feels equally licensed to examine what experience requires – that identity requires difference. Of course, Hegel in general thinks experience to be a poor source for truth.

Identity, Hegel says, is the pure movement of Reflection. It identifies what it *is* by announcing what it is *not*. A is enunciated: it is not "not A" – a negation of the negation. "Not A" appears only to vanish immediately. A and "not A" are thus distinguished. "Distinguishedness" is the identity that A and "not A" share. In short, Identity in its speculative sense already contains difference within it – as Figure 26(a) shows. A is as much "not A" as it is A.

The law of identity, then, does not express a law of thought. The opposite is true. $A = A$ violates the way thought really functions. "[T]hese laws contain *more* than is *meant* by them, to wit, this opposite, absolute difference itself." (416)[12]

B. Difference

Even the Understanding saw that simple Identity is really a complex identity of Identity and Difference. The *difference* (*Unterschied*) between Identity and Difference is now the two hour traffic of our stage. The discussion is divided into three parts. The point of the three sections is to show that Difference is properly located first in [1] – in its Identity with Identity. This is absolute difference. So far, this is a continuation of Understanding's account of Identity. Next, Difference is *diverse* from Identity. This dialectical moment locates Difference in [3], where it is radically other to Identity. Hegel calls this moment "Diversity" (*Verschiedenheit*). Finally, Speculative Reason relocates Difference in the middle term [2], where it is called Opposition.

(a) Absolute Difference

In Figure 26(a), the Understanding saw that Reflection has two moments – the moment of positedness (which implies Difference) and the moment of immediacy (which implies Identity). If Reflection has said, "I am not Difference," the Understanding emphasizes that it *is* Difference by virtue of this very enunciation. "Difference is the negativity which reflection has within it." (417) When Identity speaks (*i.e.*, announces what it is *not*), Difference is the language spoken. Difference is internal to Identity and is to be located in [1], along with Identity. It is "not difference resulting from anything external," and for this very reason is "difference in and for itself." (417)

Absolute Difference endures. Unlike the otherness of Determinate Being, which was *inherently* internal, otherness is now *overtly* internal. In the realm of Being, Absolute Difference "revealed itself only as the *transition* of one determinateness into the other." (417) Now Reflection

---

[12] The point is precisely the *opposite* of what Justus Hartnack attributes to Hegel: "Nevertheless, Hegel's point is clear enough . . . 'A = A' is a tautology, and from a tautology nothing but tautologies follow." JUSTUS HARTNACK, AN INTRODUCTION TO HEGEL'S LOGIC 45 (Lars Aagaard-Mogensen trans., 1998) In fact, tautologies have "surplus" content yielding speculative progress. Tautology wins a special place in the logical progress in chapter 12.

moves *within* a totality. Difference may be different, but it is just as much Identity and holds itself together as such. "It is not transition into an other, not relation to an other outside it: it has its other, identity, within itself." (418) Difference is not different from an other, but is different *from itself*. And that which is different from Difference is Identity. Identity is as much Difference as it is Identity, and *vice versa*. Each is a genuine moment of the other.

Absolute Difference is the Understanding's moment, but dialectical dynamism exists in the two moments of Identity and Difference. The Understanding cannot distinguish between them; all things are the same *and* different. This dialectical modulation "is to be considered as the essential nature of reflection and as the *specific, original ground of all activity and self-movement*." (417) It signifies that the Understanding is beginning to merge with Dialectical Reason.

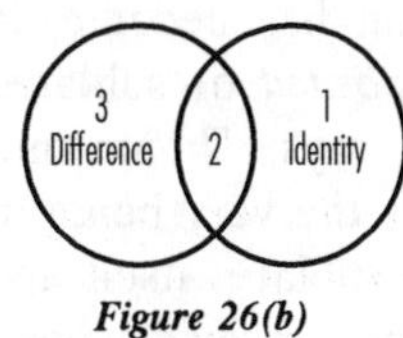

Figure 26(b)
Diversity

(b) Diversity

Because Absolute Difference is a positedness, it a "*determinate* difference." (418) This leads to Diversity, a key moment for the *SL*. In Diversity, "close relative of . . . atomism,"[13] Difference is *isolated* from Identity. When Difference is absolutely isolated and held to have no relation to its other, it is a finite Being. Finite Beings erase themselves. Difference needs otherness to endure;[14] it needs to be part of an Opposition. When a moment is merely Diverse, it has already vanished.[15]

---

[13] ROBERT M. WALLACE, HEGEL'S PHILOSOPHY OF REALITY, FREEDOM AND GOD 179 (2005).

[14] HARRIS, SPIRIT, *supra* note 7, at 253 ("Each partial and provisional element, therefore, fails to maintain itself in isolation, because its true and only nature is as a moment in the whole, so that it demands and goes over into its other to unite with it and to constitute a more complete and adequate exemplification of the ultimate universal principle of wholeness").

[15] Michael Inwood proclaims the rule of diversity invalid, because there *is* such a thing as immediate awareness or unmediated knowledge: "Any thing has a definite nature of which one might be aware without being aware of the processes and interactions responsible for it. We can, for example, easily know that Hegel is in Berlin without knowing how he got there . . . . [O]ne can be aware of the determinate character of a thing while ignoring the physical and/or logical relationships which underlie it." M.J. INWOOD, HEGEL 451 (1983) This objection constitutes a faith in the self-identity of objects and in the possibility of unmediated knowledge of them, which separates Inwood from Hegel, Kant and the entire speculative tradition.

Diversity is a dialectical moment. Whereas the Understanding proposes the *identity* of Identity and Difference, Dialectical Reason asserts their *difference*. "Identity *falls apart* within itself into diversity." (418) Difference is to be isolated in [3] of Figure 26(b), where, for just a moment, it stands over against Identity in [1].

In Diversity, there is no relation-to-other, only self-identity. Identity and Difference "are not different in themselves." (418) The irony is that "*difference* is *external* to them." (418) Accordingly, Difference is merely *imputed* to them by a third – an intelligence that takes concepts to be self-identities but nevertheless proclaims them alike or not alike. "There is no inner standard or *principle* that could apply to them, simply because *diversity* is the difference without unity in which the universality, which in its own self is absolute unity, is a merely external reflection." (606)

Since [3] or [1] is as much Difference as Identity, and since these self-identities are (by heritage) Reflections, "reflection has become, in general, *external* to itself; difference is merely a *posited* or sublated being." (419) "Posited" means that Difference says, "I am not Difference. I am a self-identity." Yet Difference is the very being of this self-identity. Hence, Difference – [1] or [3] – sublates itself and deposits its own being in a third [2]. Diversity, then, is just a pose. "When considered more closely, both identity and difference . . . are reflections, each of which is unity of itself and its other; each is the whole." (419)

Diversity's two moments. Determinations of Reflection are dualities – the union of positedness (otherness) and equality-with-self (immediacy). Diversity reflects this duality. Diversity is (1) reflection-in-itself (419); and (2) External Reflection. Reflection-in-itself [1, 2] stands for Identity; it is "determined as being indifferent to difference [3], not as simply not possessing difference." (419) It is Diversity proper. Yet immediacy in the absence of otherness self-erases; [1] and [3] represent the same reflective movement of self-erasure.

The second moment of Diversity – External Reflection – stands for the "*determinate* difference" between Identity and Difference. (419) According to External Reflection, [3] and [1] are different. The first moment (implicit Reflection), however, is indifferent to External Reflection's opinion. For this reason, the posture of Diversity is that Identity and Difference are "externally posited determinations, not determinations in and for themselves." (419)

Likeness and unlikeness is Hegel's term for external Identity and Difference. These are positednesses which lack being-in-and-for-self.

In this moment, the identities are indifferent to whether they are deemed like or unlike some other identity:

> Whether or not something is like something else does not concern either the one or the other; each of them is only self-referred, is in and for itself what it is; identity or non-identity, as likeness or unlikeness, is the verdict of a third party distinct from the two things. (419-20)

A thing's indifference to what *I* think it is like is the prejudice of skepticism. Likeness and unlikeness are but the mediocre tools of subjective comparison (*Vergleichung*). In comparison, the diverse thing "passes to and fro between likeness and unlikeness. But this relating to likeness and unlikeness . . . is external to these determinations themselves." (420) This modulation between [1] and [3] portends Dialectical Reason. We can think of this alternation occurring within [2], which participates in both [1] and [3] even as it is external to them.[16]

In their alternation, each extreme "stands forth immediately on its own." (420) The alternation that occurs is external to the extremes. We can view the alternation occurring in [2], taken as external to [1] or [3]. But [2] in truth is just as much *internal* to [1, 2] or [2, 3]. For this reason, when [2] is posited as external to [3] or to [1], Reflection is external to itself. In effect, [2] is a Diversity, just as [1] and [3] are, and so it must self-erase. Because they stand apart from the process of reflection-into-self, the moments of Identity and Difference "fall asunder and are related also as mutually external to the reflection-into-self confronting them." (420) *Three* Diversities now face each other.

Reflection has now alienated itself from itself. "The very thing that was supposed to hold off contradiction and dissolution from them, namely, that something is *like* something else *in one respect, but is unlike it in another* – this holding apart of likeness and unlikeness is their destruction." (420) Identity [1] has no meaning separate and apart from Difference [3]. Nor do "like" and "unlike" have meaning apart from each other either. "Like" is simply "not unlike" and no more than that. Yet, according to External Reflection, "likeness is only self-referred, and unlikeness similarly self-referred and a reflective determination on its own; each, therefore, is like itself; the Difference

[16] Robert Wallace finds an optimistic note in comparison, wherein objects are indifferent to what external reflection thinks. If things are indifferent to being like other things, they are at least *open* to comparison, and they imply, in general, *consciousness* capable of comparison. WALLACE, *supra* note 13, at 182-3.

has vanished . . . [E]ach therefore is only likeness." (420) The claim of like-unlike simply blows up – as skeptical External Reflection knows. Any external difference discerned "is the negativity that belongs to the comparer in the act of comparing." (421) The comparer *herself* is "*the negative unity*" (421) of both likeness and unlikeness. The comparer "lies beyond the compared and also beyond the moments of the comparison." (421) Comparison is "a subjective act falling outside them." (421)

But, Hegel suggests, the very fact that likeness and unlikeness do not function *is* their negative unity. Like and unlike, held apart by *and* from External Reflection, are mere finite beings that cease to be. If likeness ceases to be, then "likeness is not like itself." (421) Unlikeness, which also ceases to be, is therefore, in its finitude, just like likeness.

In this process, Diversity [3] expels and so unifies its positedness [1, 2]. This is the same as saying that External Reflection unifies likeness and unlikeness. "Likeness and unlikeness," Hegel asserts, "formed the side of *positedness* [1, 2] as against the compared or the diverse [3]," (421) and the compared/diverse [3] is implicitly the very Reflection that likeness and unlikeness posited as external to themselves. But, given the exercise of showing that likeness is unlikeness and vice versa, "this positedness . . . has equally lost its determinateness." (421) That is, [1] and [3] are precisely alike and cannot be distinguished. They are invisible.

Meanwhile, [1, 2], though expelled, is still a genuine moment of Diversity [3] – the implicit Reflection. Now that [1, 2] is identified with an indeterminate "like-unlike," Hegel can say that like-unlike is the genuine moment of Diversity after all.[17] Skepticism is defeated. "The merely diverse, therefore, passes over through positedness into negative reflection." (421)

Speculative Reason observes that Diversity defeats itself and embraces what (supposedly) External Reflection says of it:

> The diverse is the merely posited difference, therefore the difference that is no difference, and . . . the negation of itself. Thus likeness and unlikeness themselves, that is, positedness, returns through indifference or the implicit reflection back into the negative unity with itself . . . Diversity, whose *indifferent* sides are just as much simply and solely *moments* of one negative unity, is *opposition*. (421)

---

[17] "But likeness and unlikeness, the determinations of external reflection, are just this merely implicit reflection which the diverse as such is supposed to be, the merely indeterminate difference of the diverse." (421)

So Diversity abolishes itself because of its indeterminacy. It transports its being into the positedness it thought to exclude. It needed that otherness to be determinate.[18] This leads us to Opposition.

The Law of Diversity

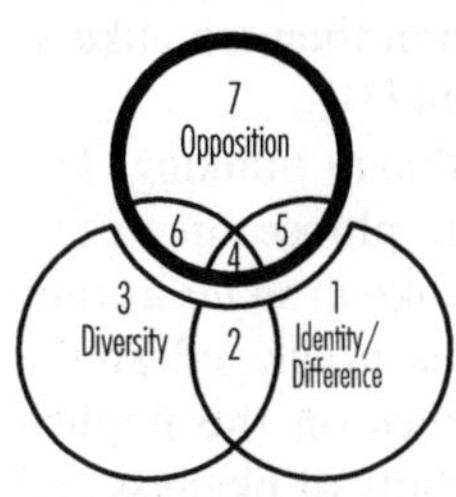

Figure 26(c)
Opposition

Identity expressed itself in the law of $A = A$. Diversity too has its law: "All things are different." (422) Hegel proposes that the law of diversity is opposed to the law of identity. If A is distinctive, it is so on its own principle. That means A has Difference within itself: "A is distinctive, therefore A is also not A." (422) The law of diversity, however, does not go so far as to say that A is different from itself. A is supposed to be different from some *other* and so is still self-identical. But Hegel has shown that self-identical (diverse) things are indeterminate. If A *is* determinate, then A must have negation inside it – "a difference of itself from itself." (422)

"Ordinary thinking," Hegel suggests, "is struck by the proposition that no two things are like each other." (422) Hegel invokes an anecdote which he tells in a slightly more charming way in the *EL*:

> The story is told that when Leibniz propounded the maxim of Variety, the cavaliers and ladies of the court, as they walked round the garden, made efforts to discover two leaves indistinguishable from each other, in order to confute the law stated by the philosopher. Their device was unquestionably a convenient method of dealing with metaphysics – one which has not ceased to be fashionable. All the same, as regards the principle of Leibniz, difference must be understood to mean not an external and indifferent diversity merely, but difference essential. Hence the very nature of things implies that they must be different.[19]

---

[18] "External reflection must see its contradiction in the content itself. It does this by considering the transition from diversity to opposition, no longer subjectively but objectively. Subjectively, the reflection of similarity in dissimilarity, and, reciprocally, the reflection of dissimilarity in similarity, is the opposition of the self to the self, but this opposition is also immediately the opposition in the thing; the [thing] is similar in its dissimilarity, dissimilar in its similarity. The things reflect one another, and this reflection is opposition." JEAN HYPPOLITE, LOGIC AND EXISTENCE 118 (Leonard Lawlor and Amit Sen trans., 1997).

[19] EL §117. This anecdote can be traced to *Fourth Letter from Leibniz to Clark*, in OPERA PHILOSOPHICA 755 (1959).

Yet, to the extent ordinary thinking believes in self-identity, it is committed to the proposition that all things are the same, since self-identical things cannot be distinguished.

If the law of diversity is to hold, then diversity must pass from likeness into unlikeness. "This involves the dissolution and nullity of the *law of diversity*." (423) If no two things are alike, then they are alike at least in this: "they are at once alike and unlike." (423)

Likeness and unlikeness are held asunder by ordinary thinking. The device that holds them asunder, Hegel says, is the phrase "in so far" (*das Insofern*). Thus "it is said that two things are alike *in so far* as they are not unlike." (423) One side of the relation is privileged at the expense of the other. Ordinary thinking thus relies on the implicit Reflection – [1, 2] in Figure 26(b) – to which the unity of likeness and unlikeness is removed from the thing, leaving the thing [3] a self-identity. In [1, 2], likeness and unlikeness turn into each other. Nevertheless, ordinary thinking is happy to have exported contradiction from the thing to the subjectivity of thinking:

> But the usual tenderness for things, whose only care is that they do not contradict themselves, forgets here as elsewhere that in this way contradiction is not resolved but merely shifted elsewhere, into subjective or external reflection generally, and this reflection in fact contains in one unity as sublated and mutually referred, the two moments which are enunciated by this removal and displacement as a mere *positedness*. (423-4)[20]

(c) Opposition

Difference was at first absolute and indistinguishable from Identity. Then it was diverse and, ironically, equally indeterminate. Once again, Dialectical Reason thought to improve upon the Understanding but only succeeded in repeating its mistakes. In Opposition (*Gegensatz*), "the *determinate reflection*, difference, finds its completion." (424)

Opposition is "the unity of identity and difference; its moments are different in one identity and thus are *opposites*." (424) In Opposition, "the moments of difference [are] held within." (424) Its moments – Identity and Difference – are said to be "*reflected* moments." (424) That is to say, each moment states what it is *not* – Identity is not identical, Difference is indifferent. By confessing what it is not, each moment

---

[20] This tenderness toward things and fear of contradiction echoes remarks quoted *supra* at 179.

establishes what it is.[21]

These moments in Diversity were mere immediacies *not* reflected into themselves; rather, they were indifferent "towards being-in-and-for-self as such." (424) The External Reflection that stood against them was a positedness – a unity of likeness and unlikeness. This positedness has Being, Hegel says. "[T]heir non-positedness is a *non-being*." (424) That is to say, the diverse moments posit their other – External Reflection (which is on the side of Being). The Diverse moment itself is a non-positedness which is *not*.

Self-identical moments, then, sublate themselves and pass over into External Reflection – and vice versa: [5] → [4, 6] and [6] → [4, 5]. Each Diverse moment was therefore, in the end, a "positedness reflected into itself or determination in general." (424) In plainer language, Essence requires external reflection for its determinacy. Things do not determine themselves. Essence is "where determinacy is determined by a determiner that it thereby reflects."[22] In chapter 1, I presented a schematic drawing of thought. In terms of Reflection, we can now see that the diverse object [3] sublates itself and transports itself into thought [2]. Likewise, the subject [1] sublates itself and transports itself to thought. In short, the subject is indeterminate *unless* it is thought. But once it is in thought, it is no longer subject as such. This vindicates the Lacanian criticism of the Cartesian *cogito ergo sum*. Properly, Descartes should have said, "I think, and I am not," or, alternatively, "I do not think, therefore I am."[23]

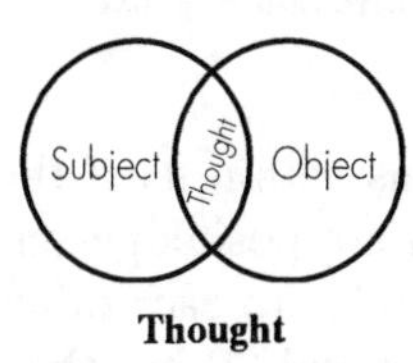

Thought

If Diversity posits an external reflection – an "implicit reflection" (419) – and if implicit Reflection is [4, 6] or [4, 5], then [4, 5, 6] can be analyzed as the unity of like-unlike, each of which turns into its opposite. These moments of [4, 6] or [4, 5] Hegel calls "the determinations

---

[21] JOHN W. BURBIDGE, REAL PROCESS: HOW LOGIC AND CHEMISTRY COMBINE IN HEGEL'S PHILOSOPHY OF NATURE 119 (1996) ("In an opposition . . . two things are explicitly antithetical to each other within a single framework . . . There difference is subordinate to, and governed by, their identity; it explicitly breaks up the general picture into incompatible particulars. So whatever opposes one body to another assumes some basic identity that they share.").

[22] Richard Dien Winfield, *The System of Syllogism*, in HEGEL'S THEORY OF THE SUBJECT 133 (David Gray Carlson ed., 2005).

[23] Jeanne L. Schroeder, *Three's a Crowd: A Feminist Critique of Calabresi & Melamud's* One View of the Cathedral, 84 CORNELL L. REV. 394, 396 (1999).

of opposition." (424) Each moment is as much *like* as *unlike*. Each requires the other for its coherence. "Therefore, each of these moments is, in its determinateness, the whole . . . [E]ach contains reference to its non-being, and is only reflection-into-self or the whole, as essentially connected with its non-being." (424) In terms of Figure 26(c), the whole is [4], and it is located fully within [4, 5] and [4, 6].[24]

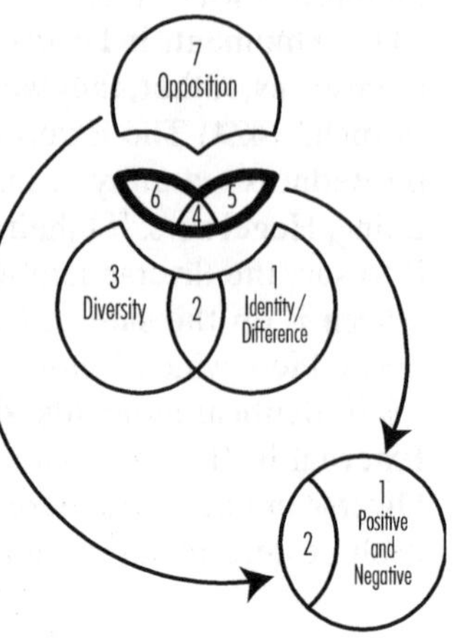

Figure 27(a)
Positive and Negative

Positive and Negative. The Understanding proposes that Opposition is Positive and Negative.[25] The Positive is "self-*likeness* reflected into itself that contains within itself the reference to unlikeness." (424) If it is self-identical, it is so "*through* excluding the negative."[26] The Negative is the obverse – "unlikeness that contains within itself the reference to its non-being, to likeness." (424) Both are positednesses. In Figure 27(a), Positive [4, 5] and Negative [5, 6] refer to each other even as they refer to themselves. So each is (1) itself and (2) its other. Furthermore, (3) "[e]ach is the whole." (425)

We have before us a portentous moment – *the beginning of the notional form*. Notion is the unity of (1) itself, (2) its other, and (3) the unity of itself and other.[27] Positive and Negative are now posited as

---

[24] TAYLOR, *supra* note 3, at 261 ("in polar opposition, each term is such that its interaction with another opposed entity is constitutive of its own reality").

[25] Wallace sounds the wrong note in suggesting that Essence and "its determinateness" (*i.e.*, appearance) stand to each other in the same relation as positive stands to negative . . . " WALLACE, *supra* note 13, at 184. In my view, Essence [2] stands over against Positive and Negative [1]. Essence is neither Positive nor Negative but that which sustains this Opposition.

[26] Wendell Kisner, Erinnerung, Retrait, *Absolute Reflection: Hegel and Derrida*, 26 OWL OF MINERVA 171, 174 (1995).

[27] Marcuse describes these three moments as the "unity as the remaining and persisting self, unity as the process of unifying, and the united manifold." HERBERT MARCUSE, HEGEL'S ONTOLOGY AND THE THEORY OF HISTORICITY 34 (Seyla Benhabib trans., 1987); *see also id.* at 205 (notional form is subject and predicate and "it is this *'relation' between subject and predicate* and this *conceptualization* . . . of itself as the unity of subject and predicate").

the unity of (1) themselves and (2) their other. Positive and Negative start to develop (3) – later to be identified as Individuality.

Dialectical Reason remembers that Positive and Negative are Diverse – not just unified Opposites. As Diverse, they are indifferent to whether they are designated as Positive or Negative. "Therefore, although one of the determinatenesses of positive and negative belongs to each side, they can be changed around, and each side is of such a kind that it can be taken equally well as positive as negative." (426) In other words, Dialectical Reason points out that Self-Subsistence is beyond the precincts of the Positive or Negative.

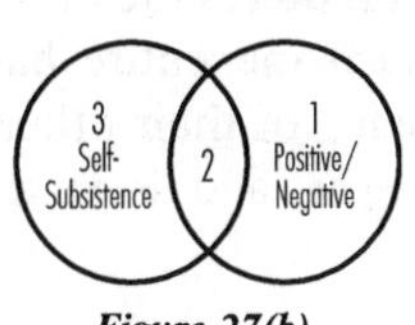

Figure 27(b)
Self-Subsistence

According to Dialectical Reason, each is the whole and each is as much the other as it is itself. So each is as much a *sublated* positedness as it is a positedness. As [1, 2], the Positive is a positedness – a reference-to-other. Taken as [1], it is a Diversity and not a positedness.

Positive and Negative, however, are not merely the like and unlike, which yielded their being to External Reflection. Even within the context of Figure 27(b), Positive and Negative [1, 2] each have self-subsistence [2] – reflection-into-self. They both have it [2] and *don't* have it [1].

But the Positive has this second moment – it negates the Negative. "[T]hus the negating reflection of the positive is immanently determined as *excluding* from itself this its *non-being*." (426) The third moment of Positive and Negative is that each is the unity of itself and other. Without this knowledge, "not a single step can really be taken in philosophy." (438) The point here is that the Positive (and hence the Negative) are in and for self. They are *not* merely diverse. Yet they are nothing in isolation from their other. This implies that the in-itself of Positive or Negative is *relation*. When taken in this way, Positive and Negative are in and for themselves.[28]

[28] Hegel says that, isolated, the Positive is an implicit Contradiction – a "positedness that is not a relation to an other" (432), a sublated positedness. As a sublated positedness, it is a relation without parts – an impossibility. It therefore *cannot be*, and is nothing. And, being negative, it refers to its other – to that which it negates. "It is thus the contradiction that, in positing identity with itself by *excluding* the negative, it makes itself into the *negative* of what it excludes from itself, that is, makes itself into its opposite." (432)

If the Positive is implicitly Contradiction, "the negative is the contradiction *posited*."

Nothing illustrates this point better than a bar magnet, one side of which is positive and the other negative.[29] Can the positive or negative side be isolated? If one snips the end of off a bar magnet in an effort to isolate the positive or negative, one replicates a new bar magnet. The small piece now has its positive and negative extremes. These moments of the bar magnet cannot be isolated. Each requires the other for its existence. Positive and Negative are as much the entire bar magnet as they are themselves or the mere non-being of their other. "Each therefore *is*, only in so far as its *non-being is*, and is in an identical relationship with it." (425)[30]

Opposite Magnitudes in Arithmetic and Ethics

Hegel's general critique of mathematics is that it doesn't sufficiently grasp the speculative content of its subject matter. As was the case throughout the interminable calculus commentaries of chapter 5, mathematics does not discern in the Positive and Negative the *qualitative* nature of its *quantitative* concepts.

Hegel states that there are "two *real* determinations of the positive and negative." (427) (1) Positive and Negative are pure opposition. Opposition is found in the notion that negative cancels positive, and vice versa. Thus, $+y-y=0$. "An hour's journey to the east and the same distance travelled back to the west, cancels the first journey." (428) A

---

(432) The Negative is a reflection-into-self and therefore in and for itself. It is a Negative with self-subsistence. It is therefore "determined as a non-identical, as excluding identity." (433) It excludes itself from itself while remaining identical to itself.

[29] *See* EL §119 Remark.

[30] Hegel compares the Negative to the early idea of Negation. *Supra* at 58. The Negative is correlated with the Positive – part of a pair. Like the Positive, it is a positedness; it states what it is not – the Positive. But its being *is* in the Positive. Hence, the Negative is unlike itself. It transfers its quality to the other and hence to itself. "[T]herefore its reflection into its unlikeness is rather its relation to itself." (432) Each extreme "is the same as its opposite." (432) Primitive Negation, in contrast, is "*immediate* determinateness." (432) It is not *related* to an other and not, strictly speaking, an opposite. But have we not been emphasizing that negation is *always* a correlate – a negation of *something*? How can this be reconciled with Hegel's claim that primitive Negation is an immediacy? The answer is that negation is correlative *for us* at the level of Figure 2(b). For *itself*, Negation stood for Dialectical Reason's positivization of what the Understanding left out in proposing that the absolute is Determinate Being. As such, Negation is considered *different* from Determinate Being. The conclusion that it is *also the same as* Determinate Being only comes later. This is Speculative Reason's conclusion in Figure 2(c).

debtor's negative liabilities cancels out her positive assets.

(2) Each sends its being into a third. In Figure 27(b), this third is [2]. Each is an immediate reflection-into-self, standing over against a positedness. Hegel calls [2] the *base*. With regard to $+a$ and $-a$, between these two opposites is a common base which is indifferent to the signs (+, -). That base is a (taken as neither positive nor negative), "which is indifferent to the opposition itself and serves here . . . as a dead base." (428) This base in effect announces that it is *not* opposition. From this perspective, the base is indifferent which of its extremes is deemed negative and which positive. "[E]ach side exists indifferently on its own." (428)[31]

The dead base is present in the travel example. Travelling east is not inherently positive. Nor is westerly travel inherently negative. East and west are indifferent to positivity or negativity. If I walk one mile east and then one mile west, I have walked two miles, *not* zero miles. "[I]t is a third point of view outside them that makes one positive and the other negative." (428)

In debtor-creditor terms, liabilities – negatives for a debtor – are not inherently so. To a creditor, the debtor's liability is an asset. In economics, the money supply is largely defined by countervailing bank credits. But this does not mean the money supply is always zero. The liabilities of one bank are counted as the positive wealth of another bank. In calculating the money supply, $+a-a=a$. (429)[32]

This second moment of non-opposition is a qualitative moment. To illustrate, Hegel points out that "an ordinate y is the same on which ever side of the axis it is taken; so far $+y-y=y$; it is only the one ordinate and it has only one determination and law." (429) In other words, $-y$ is "positively" on the y ordinate. As such, it is qualitative. So it is correct, in a sense, to write $+y-y=y$. In -8+3, eleven units (not five) are implicated.

---

[31] That $+a$ and $-a$ are different from a has been said to capture the entirety of Speculative Reason. Kosok, *supra* note 4, at 242 ("Reflection, in attempting to determine or assert [a], produces a self-negation of [a], involving a coupling of contraries: the *original* pre-formal *non*-positive and *non*-negative [a] becomes transformed into a formed self-relation . . . as a whole is written [+-a], i.e. something which is *neither* +[a] *nor* -[a] . . . "). Michael Wolff claims that Hegel's remarks led directly to the invention of $|a|$ by Hermann Graßmann, a student of the *SL*. *Id.* at 15. Michael Wolff, *On Hegel's Doctrine of Contradiction*, 31 OWL OF MINERVA 1, 15 (1999).

[32] Should Hegel should have written $+a-a=2a$? If a is defined as the infinite set of cardinal numbers, Hegel's formulation is perfectly correct. MICHAEL POTTER, SET THEORY AND ITS PHILOSOPHY 170-2 (2004) (describing transfinite arithmetic).

Arithmetic thinks opposite magnitudes are merely opposite and sees the net result as zero. But the intrinsically positive or negative are *qualitative* moments. When *a* bears no sign, it is meant to be taken as $+a$. "[T]he positive sign is given to it immediately, because the positive on its own has the peculiar meaning of the immediate, as self-identical, in contrast to opposition." (429)

When positive and negative magnitudes are added/subtracted, they are counted as positive and negative in their own right "and not as becoming positive or negative in an external manner through the relation of addition and subtraction." (429) That is, the signs (+, -) signal an arithmetic operation, but they also have a separate meaning in relation to their "dead base." "In 8-(-3) the first minus means opposite to 8, but the second minus (-3), counts as opposite *in itself*, apart from this relation." (430) In other words, the first minus is relational. It indicates that 8 is to be reduced by the integer that follows the minus sign. The second minus is not this pure opposition. Yet the function of the second minus sign is still partly oppositional. It works in reversing the prior minus sign, so that 8 enjoys an increase to 11 instead of a reduction to 5.

The qualitative nature of plus and minus becomes more apparent in multiplication and division. "Here the positive must essentially be taken as the *not-opposite*, and the negative, on the other hand, as the opposite." (430) They are *not* to be taken as merely the opposite of each other. Rather, each has a qualitative integrity against the other. In multiplication, the relation of the factors "is not a mere relation of increasing and decreasing as in the case of addition and subtraction." (430) That is, in addition +8-3 implies that +8 is to be decreased in magnitude to 5. In multiplication, the minus sign in +8(-3) indicates that the product has the quality of being opposite to +24. If plus and minus were to be taken as mere opposites of each other, with no qualitative integrity, "the false conclusion can easily be drawn that if $-a$ times $+ a = -a^2$, conversely $+a$ times $- a = +a^2$." (430) This would violate the commutative nature of multiplication.

Why does the minus tyrannize the plus in multiplication? Because the plus is "qualitatively determined against the *minus*." (430) The plus has a *non-oppositional quality*. The negative is also qualitative – it is "the intrinsically opposite as such." (431) It is in the very nature of the negative to *reverse*. The positive is something different – "an indeterminate, indifferent sign in general." (431) It has no power to reverse anything. Only the negative has power. When $-a$ times $-a$ produces $+a^2$, each minus sign orders us to take the other minus negatively. Here the mathematicians at last agree with Hegelian speculative philosophy – the negation of the negation is something positive.

Hegel gives some examples of the qualitative nature of Positive and Negative in ethical thought. These examples show that even "superficial thinking" (436) recognizes *both* the qualitative and oppositional nature of Positive and Negative. Virtue is taken as qualitative. It is *not* merely the lack of vice. But virtue is also negative – it has already negated vice. Vice is not merely the lack of virtue. Vice is *positively evil*. (437) Innocence is a qualitative concept, but it is related to its opposite as well. "[E]very nature emerging from its innocency, from its indifferent self-identity, spontaneously relates itself to its other and thereby falls to the ground or, in the positive sense, withdraws into its ground." (437)[33]

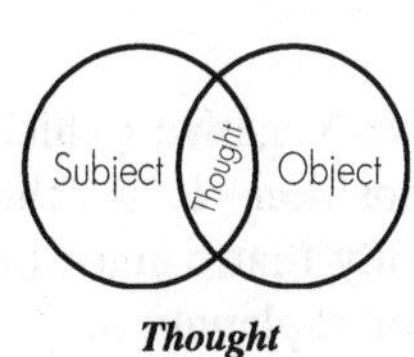

Thought

Truth is also qualitative. In the accompanying diagram, truth is knowing [2] that agrees with the object [3]. [2] becomes perfectly coincident with [3], thereby sublating the negative subject [1]. This operation Hegel would view as impossible. It is nevertheless the view of truth that ordinary thinking has. In fact, the subject [1] survives this operation as "not the object." Hence truth is qualitative but also refers to negative relation.

Like truth, error is qualitative. It is "opinion asserting what is not in and for itself." (437) Ignorance is viewed as standing over against either truth or error and is indifferent to it. Or, it is objective – an "impulse that is directed against itself, a negative that contains a positive direction within it." (438) Perhaps this means that ignorance must strive to preserve itself. Otherwise, it cannot help but turn into its opposite.

C. Contradiction

In common parlance, contradiction cannot *be*. It is impossible that *A*

---

[33] This last remark about innocence perhaps refers to Kantian radical evil, or, in Christian terms, original sin. Per Kant, pure morality and pure (diabolical) evil are impossible. Instead, because we cannot discern our own motives, we are constantly in doubt as to whether our acts were moral or motivated by inclination. *See generally* Jeanne L. Schroeder & David Gray Carlson, *Kenneth Starr: Diabolically Evil?*, 88 CAL. L. REV. 653 (2000). Here, Hegel refers to the soul emerging from innocence and falling to the ground. Since ground is the unity of opposites, the innocent person falls into a state of radical evil. PHENOMENOLOGY, *supra* note 6, ¶ 658 (analyzing the "beautiful soul").

should "be" *and* "not be." For Hegel, *A* is *and* is not. So Hegel has a rather different view of contradiction. It is precisely what endures – not an impossibility that passes away.[34] It is the "self-subsistent determination of Reflection that contains the opposite determination, and is self-subsistent in virtue of this inclusion." (431)

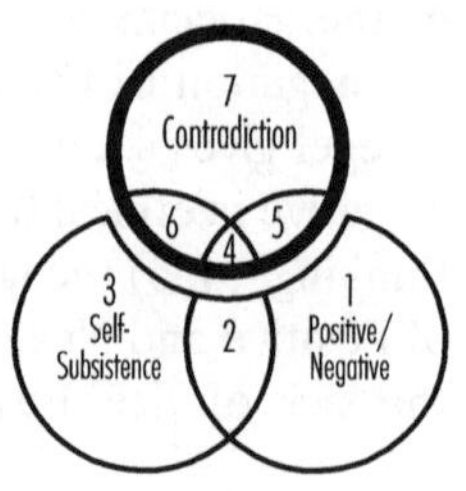

Figure 27(c)
Contradiction

Contradiction is the "relation between one of two opposed determinations [*i.e.*, positive or negative] and the substrate of logical reflection with regard to which the determinations are mutually opposed."[35] It is the unity between Positive/Negative (which cannot endure) *and* the self-subsistence of opposition. It is "the application of opposite categories to the same reality that cannot be maintained and requires the search for a ground or explanation."[36]

To review, in Diversity, Difference fell "*indifferently* apart." (431) *Opposition* united the two sides. There, each side opposes and so determines the other – though each side was equally "mutually indifferent." (431). On the law of sublation, the sides are diverse. They are the "*self-subsistent determinations of reflection*." (431) They are not *merely* opposition. But each was also the whole – a "self-contained opposition." (431) These attributes add up to Contradiction.

Contradiction endures because Self-Subsistence [6] is a Diversity that is *not* self-subsistent. It endures only when it joins with the non-self-subsistent Opposites. But while Opposition is included in Contradiction, it is also excluded, since Reflection always announces what it is *not*. Its negative being is sent forth *and* retained – the hallmark of True Infinity. A middle term, Contradiction is the name of an *act*.

"*Contradiction resolves itself*," Hegel promises (433). Positive and Negative self-erase. Each is the "self-transposition of itself into its opposite." (433) Hegel names this "ceaseless vanishing of the opposites into themselves" – this "*first unity* resulting from the contradiction" (433) – the Null (*die Null*).

---

[34] HARTNACK, *supra* note 12, at 48 (Contradiction is "not a defect associated with certain statements; on the contrary, it is an unavoidable . . . feature without which we would be left with the barren and sterile abstract identity"); ROSEN, *supra* note 1, at 233 ("The function of contradiction is not to cancel but to demonstrate the impossibility of coherent partiality or *apartness*").

[35] Wolff, *supra* note 31, at 18.

[36] BURBIDGE, REAL PROCESS, *supra* note 21, at 118.

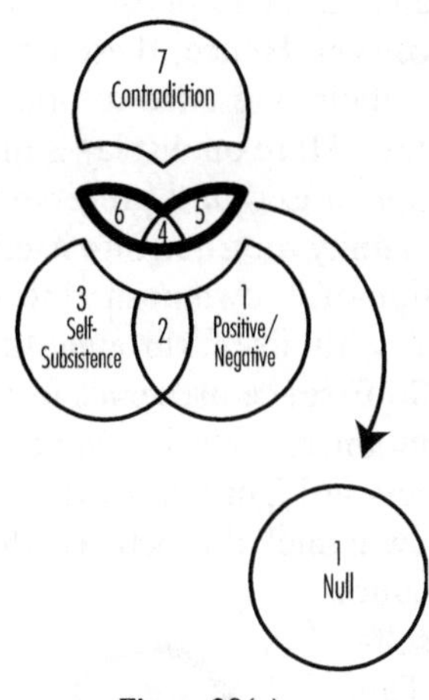

Figure 28(a)
Null

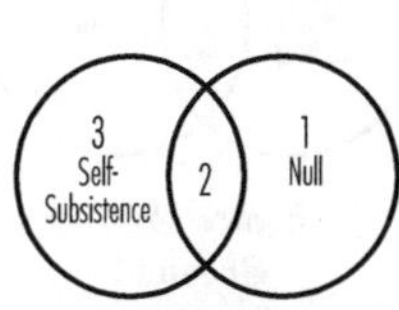

Figure 28(b)
The Positive Moment of Contradiction

Contradiction is not *merely* Null. Dialectical Reason intervenes to remind the Understanding that the Null is also positive; "the self-excluding reflection is at the same time *positing* reflection." (433) Positing Reflection was Reflection's *immediate* moment. It announced what it was *not*, and this affirmatively proved what it was. Contradiction, then, is Null but also something positive.[37]

Hegel describes this positive self-subsistent moment as follows. Positive and Negative "constitute the *positedness* of self-subsistence." (433) This can be seen in Figure 27(b), where Self-Subsistence stood over against Positive and Negative. There, Self-Subsistence said, "I am not *that*," and so Positive/Negative was its presupposition. As presupposed they were posited by Self-Subsistence and hence were *its* positedness. Positive and Negative, however, erase themselves. They are Null. When they exhibit their Nullity, they leave Self-Subsistence [2] standing alone. This activity of the Null in which Positive and Negative engage is the Positive Moment of Contradiction. In other words, what self-subsists is self-erasure – the very selfhood of essence. "Through this demise a genuine, non-exclusive self-subsistence is attained."[38] The subsistence of self-erasure is Ground *tout court*.

What is the difference between Figures 27(b) and 28(b)? In Figure 27(b), the sides were still opposites; they were only *implicitly* self-subsistent, still positednesses. Each side referred to its other. In Figure 28(b), the sides have explicitly excluded themselves from themselves in an act Hegel calls "excluding reflection." (433) At this point the sides

---

[37] ANDREW HAAS, HEGEL AND THE PROBLEM OF MULTIPLICITY 265 (2000) ("the null is only one side of the concept of contradiction wherein positive and negative are superseded . . . "); Kisner, *supra* note 26, at 174 ("To stop at the null would be to hold on to exclusion rather than releasing it into its self-demise").

[38] *Id.* at 176.

have a "negative relation" – that is, *no* relation – to their opposite. Self-subsistence is nevertheless posited by Opposition. Hence, these non-positednesses are positednesses by virtue of their reference to other. They are both self-identical *and* related to other. Here on display is the ordinary workings of sublation. Positedness is erased *and* preserved. Self-subsistence is "through *its own* negation a unity returned into itself, since it returns into itself through the negation of *its* own positedness. It is the unity of essence, being identical with itself through the negation, not of an other, but itself." (434) So Essence preserves itself and returns to itself by negating itself. It announces what it is *not* and thereby announces what it is. What we witness in Figure 28(b) is self-erasure of the sides. Speculative Reason now names this activity: the contradictory sides withdraw into their Ground.

Contradiction is "self-liquifaction."[39] It self-erases and sends its being elsewhere. The "place" to which its being is sent is *Ground*. As Hegel says later, "the significance of . . . every becoming is that it is the reflection of the transient into its *ground* and that the . . . *other* into which [the transient] has passed constitutes its *truth*." (577)

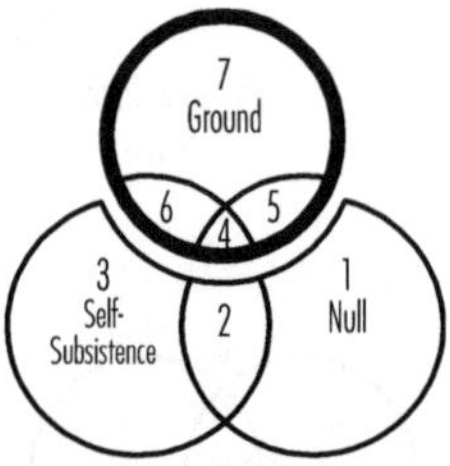

Figure 28(c)
Ground

Ground is negative. It is simply *not* the sides it opposes. It is "essence . . . *determined as undetermined*." (447)[40] It was *posited* by excluding reflection and is now the truer being of the self-erasing sides. Compared to Ground, the opposite sides – Positive and Negative – are reduced "to the status of *mere* determinations." (434) Each of these positednesses "has simply returned into its unity with itself." (434) Ground is thus "*simple essence*." (434) In fact, since essence is properly self-erasure, it is "posited as essence for the first time" in Ground.[41]

Ground, Hegel says, is "the excluding unity of reflection – a simple unity that determines itself as a negative, but in this positedness is immediately like itself and united with itself." (434) It should be clear by now what this means. In Figure 28(c) the extremes excluded themselves from themselves. Self-exclusion *was* their unity. This unity

---

[39] RODOLPHE GASCHÉ, THE TAIN OF THE MIRROR: DERRIDA AND THE PHILOSOPHY OF REFLECTION 140 (1986).

[40] For this reason, Contradiction is "*the structure of the absence of essence*." ROSEN, *supra* note 1, at 121.

[41] Kisner, *supra* note 26, at 176.

is negative to the extremes: [7] is a "beyond," from the perspective of [4, 5, 6]. In its negativity, [7] is nevertheless a self-identity. Yet, as negative, it is supposed to have an other. It is therefore in a state of contradiction – an immediate entity that implies relation-to-other. It is Essence determined as undetermined.

In chapter 2, we had such a contradiction – Limit. When "point" was taken as Limit to "line," the line sprang forth automatically.[42] In other words, Limit is a *relation*, so if a point is Limit, *there must be a line*; otherwise there is no Limit. Limit was therefore implicitly Ground. Ground's function is to bring forth the Grounded, as we shall see in the next chapter. Because of this function, Hegel calls ground "the *prius*, the immediate, that forms the starting point." (434) Obviously, it is not *the* starting point that Pure Being was. Rather, Ground is "*a positedness*, something that has become." (434)

Ground is "completed self-subsistence." (435) What endures is self-erasure. We now have the durability of things that Charles Taylor found wanting in Hegel's analysis of Being.[43] Taylor was too impatient in demanding that it be produced in the super-simple realm of Being. Ironically, what subsists is non-subsistence.

What makes Ground self-subsistent is that it is self-identical and hence positive as well as negative. In Ground, Opposition and Contradiction are "as much abolished as preserved." (435) These earlier unities were only implicitly Ground.

> [A]ll that was added to [Ground] was the determination of unity-with-self, which results from the fact that each of the self-subsistent opposites sublates itself and makes itself into its opposite, thus falling to the ground . . . ; but in this process [the opposite] only unites with itself; therefore, it is only in falling to the ground . . . that is, in its positedness or negation, that the opposite is really the essence that is reflected into and identical with itself. (435)

Essence is now the act of self-erasure and "falling to the ground" (*zugrunde geht*).[44]

---

[42] *Supra* at 85-6.

[43] *Supra* at 79-82.

[44] Rodolphe Gasché thinks the lesson of contradiction is that the

> Romantic dissolution of contradiction [was] within the realm of truth. [W]hat the Romantics aimed at was not so nihilistic after all. [T]he romantic idea of the medium of reflexivity, as well as that of the text as a medium of neutralization and annulment of concepts and strata, fails to achieve what it seeks: a unitary ground or essence in

The Law of the Excluded Middle

The law of the excluded middle (*Satze des ausgeschlossenen Dritten*) says, "*something is either A or not A; there is no third.*" (438) One need only look at *any* of the propositions of Dialectical Reason to see that Hegel disagrees with the validity of such a law. The "excluded middle" is [2]. If [2] is excluded, we would be left with the "diverse" entities *A* and *not-A*. These, Hegel says, cannot even be thought – they are mere Beings-for-self.[45]

The law of the excluded middle should be understood as follows: everything is an opposite. Everything should be determined as a positive or negative. This proposition is proven by the fact that "identity passes over into difference, and this into opposition." (438) Unreflective thinking does not understand the law in this sense. The law "usually means nothing more than that, of all predicates, either this particular predicate or its non-being belongs to a thing." (438) Things are either sweet or not sweet, green or not green.[46]

Hegel compares the law of the excluded middle to the law of contradiction, which states that *A* cannot be +*A* and -*A* at the same time. The law of contradiction implies the law of the excluded middle. Both claim that there is no third that is neither +*A* nor -*A* (even

---

which all self-subsistent opposites dissolve in order to ground themselves. Were they to achieve this goal, Romantic self-reflection and deconstructive criticism would represent a fulfillment of the telos of metaphysics. But Hegel's speculative critique of the movement of contradiction . . . shows that this movement produces only the simple or abstract idea of such a ground. As Hegel shows, such a unity cannot be achieved in a logically satisfactory manner within a logic of essence or reflection but only in the logic of the Concept or Notion, since only here can the determination of interdetermination by self-determination be completed.

GASCHÉ, *supra* note 39, at 141.

[45] HAAS, *supra* note 37, at 266 ("The logic of the excluded middle . . . insofar as it thinks only two ways of being/not-being or having/not-having, makes all things into dead things").

[46] The Law of the Excluded Middle stands for completeness, whereas the Law of Contradiction stands for consistency: "the notion of consistency demands that an elements and its negation cannot *both* be present, while the notion of completeness demands that an element and its negation cannot *both* be absent. Kosok, *supra* note 4, at 243. According to Kosok, Reflection represents the non-presence of two opposites, which is not inconsistent. Thus "not *A*" and "not not *A*" are equally "not present," which is not contradictory. However, the Law of the Excluded Middle is offended, because *either* A or *not* A *must* be present, which is not the case in Hegel's Reflection. *Id.*

though these laws overtly refer to *A* with no plus or minus sign in it). This third becomes the excluded middle for purposes of the law now under consideration. This third, "when taken more profoundly, is the unity of reflection into which the opposition withdraws as into ground." (438)

The Law of Contradiction

After criticizing the laws of identity, difference and opposition, Hegel proposes a *real* law to which he can subscribe his name. The true law of contradiction is "*everything is inherently contradictory*." (438) Here is a law that "in contrast to the others expresses rather the truth and the essential nature of things." (438)

Ordinary thinking "abhors contradiction, as nature abhors a vacuum," (442) It privileges Identity over Contradiction. This very preference distinguishes ordinary from speculative thinking. Speculative thinking is precisely thinking that "holds fast contradiction, and in it, its own self." (440) Ordinary thinking, in contrast, resolves contradiction into other non-contradictory determinations or into nothing.

"[I]n fact," Hegel remarks, "if it were a question of grading the two determinations and they had to be kept separate, then contradiction would have to be taken as the profounder determination and more characteristic of essence." (439) Identity is "merely the determination of the simple immediate, of dead being." (439) But Contradiction, Hegel says, is "the root of all movement and vitality; it is only in so far as something has a contradiction within it that it moves, has an urge and activity." (439) For this reason, contradiction "is not, so to speak, a blemish, an imperfection or a defect in something if a contradiction can be pointed out in it. On the contrary, every determination, every concrete thing, every Notion, is essentially a unity of distinguished and distinguishable moments." (442)

Hegel has already emphasized how unreflective thinkers like to keep Contradiction "aloof from things, from the sphere of being and of truth generally." (439)[47] Contradiction is removed from the objective world and made a subjective fault. "But even in this reflection, it does not really exist, for it is said that the *contradictory* cannot be *imagined* or

[47] Michael Inwood wreaks revenge on behalf of unreflective thinking. INWOOD, *supra* note 15, at 463 (claiming that Hegel "lacked the formal training to handle [contradiction] effectively"). For a rigorous counterdemonstration, see Wolff, *supra* note 31.

thought." (439-40) Contradiction "ranks in general as a contingency, a kind of abnormality and a passing paroxysm of sickness." (440)

All this is wrong, Hegel thinks. Contradiction is "the negative as determined in the sphere of essence, the principle of all self-movement." (440) External movement of a thing is "contradiction's immediate existence. Something moves, not because at one moment it is here and another there, but because in this 'here', it at once is and is not." (440)[48] Self-movement is "nothing else but the fact that something is . . . *self-contained and* deficient, *the negative of itself* . . . Something is therefore alive only in so far as it contains contradiction within it, and moreover is this power to hold and endure the contradiction within it." (440) On the other hand, if the thing is insufficiently strong to contain Contradiction, it falls to the Ground and ceases to be.

In Opposition, even ordinary thinking must acknowledge the self-subsistence of Contradiction. The relationship between left and right, for example, contains both right and not-right, left and not-left. but even here, ordinary thinking suppresses the speculative content of Opposition. It looks at "left" and "right" and "forgets their negative unity and so retains them merely as 'differents' in general. (441) Yet it cannot be denied that "left" and "right" are incapable of being isolated. The very notion of left refers to right and vice versa.

Ordinary thinking "everywhere has contradiction for its content," but "it does not become aware of it." (441) It "remains an external reflection which passes from likeness to unlikeness." (441) Or it focuses at one moment on the self-identity of opposites and then forgets in order to focus on the negative relation between the two terms. It refuses to think both moments at once.

Ordinary thought supposes that contradictions must dissolve into nothing. It "fails to recognize the positive side of contradiction where it becomes *absolute activity* and absolute ground." (442) Hegel, in contrast, has isolated this positive moment in Figure 28(b), where it stands against the Null – the one-sided view of ordinary thinkers.

The Null is nevertheless a genuine moment. Contradictory things erase themselves and withdraw into a negative Ground. This negative

---

[48] Recall that, in Hegel's Logic, there is no time. Everything unfolds instantaneously. If this is true, then movement is indeed problematic. The thing that moves *is* in two (or more) places at once. Contradiction solves the problem, because things are always present and absent simultaneously. In fact, historicization can be viewed as mankind's effort to remove contradiction from the world and make sense of it.

unity is precisely what a "thing" is. "[I]t is the *ground* that contains and supports [the] determinations" of the thing. (442) The thing is nothing but "resolved contradiction," but any such resolution is merely finite and therefore itself contradictory. "Finite things . . . are simply this, to be contradictory and *disrupted within themselves and to return into their ground*." (443)

Hegel's eventual goal is to derive the Absolute from the finite realm of Being. The truth is that absolute necessity arises from the very collapse of the finite thing. "[T]he true inference consists in showing that contingent being in its own self withdraws into its ground." (443) Hegel puts this point in different words: "the absolute is, because the finite . . . is *not*. [T]he non-being of the finite is the being of the absolute." (443)[49]

When the contradictory thing collapses, it returns to the Ground. "[B]y this withdrawal it posits the ground only in such a manner that it rather makes itself into a positedness." (443) That is to say, Ground is not the Absolute. Being a positedness, it refers to *something else* and for this very reason is not the last destination of the *SL*.

---

[49] Lenin apparently misinterpreted this passage from the *SL*. "It is a fact that Lenin, as well as Engels, sees in this page of the *Logic* the 'kernel' worth saving from Hegel's philosophy, the breaking through of a genuine realism in contradiction to the system's 'shell' and to the 'mystique of the Idea.' [¶] The 'reading' given by Lenin of these pages rests . . . on a basic misinterpretation. He tried to read Hegel 'materialistically' precisely at the place where the latter was negating matter." LUCIO COLLETTI, MARXISM AND HEGEL 24-5 (Lawrence Garner trans., 1973). Colletti sees this "dialectic of matter" as religious in character – not the anti-spiritual materialism of the Marxists. Yet, as chapter 12 will show, Colletti supports the interpretation that matter transports itself into form, so that there *is* a materialist aspect to Hegel's thought, contrary to what Marx thought.

12
Ground

Readers of Hegel have exceptional trouble with Ground,[1] so let me say off the top what it is. Ground is *self-erasure*, pure and simple. It is the result of Contradiction, which "falls to the ground." But self-erasure is what Essence turns out to be. On this basis, Ground is "essence put explicitly as a totality."[2]

Ground, the "most characteristic shape of essence,"[3] is prelude to Appearance and the realm of ordinary Things. Here, essence "excludes its own immediacy as that which it grounds."[4] It puts this immediacy out into the world of appearance and erases itself. According to naive metaphysics and common sense, things are *self-evident*. They just *are*. They are Groundless. But this illusion, Hegel will argue, comes about because the Ground of Things has self-erased. In truth, all Things are grounded in self-erasure. They are finite and must cease to be. Ground is therefore the *vanishing mediator* of Things. Because Ground self-erases – is self-erasure! – Things *seem to exist*.

Ground is where Contradiction withdraws after self-erasure. "The

---

[1] GIACOMO RINALDI, A HISTORY AND INTERPRETATION OF THE LOGIC OF HEGEL 200 (1992) ("the category of Ground . . . is likely to constitute the most conspicuous example of the shortcomings for which Hegel's critics are used to blaming his thought, excessive abstruseness, complicated artfulness . . . obscurity, etc. It can therefore come as no surprise that in the *Encyclopedia Logic* he himself decided to suppress it *in toto*.").

[2] EL § 121.

[3] Wendell Kisner, Erinnerung, Retrait, *Absolute Reflection: Hegel and Derrida*, 26 OWL OF MINERVA 171, 174 (1995).

[4] *Id.*

ground of a thing for Hegel is nothing other than the totality of its essence."[5] So, in retrospect, Reflection was Ground to Illusory Being, Essence Ground to Measure, and Quantity Ground to Being-for-self. Each of these concepts was a True Infinite. Each exhibited an expulsion of self from self and delivery of self to its Ground. Ground "*proceeds from* them *as* that which *precedes* them."[6]

Ground is the province of Speculative Reason.[7] Illusory Being represented an immediate-but-correlative chapter of the Understanding – correlative because Essence is the negative and hence dialectic stage of the entire Logic. In the negative-immediate stage, the Understanding saw itself immediately as Inessential (standing over against the Essential). The Essential revealed itself to be Illusory Being, which erased itself. But that is what Essence *is* – the erasure of what *seems* to be – the movement known as Reflection. In the second chapter of Essence, Determination of Reflection had the dual structure of Dialectical Reason: it was (1) an immediate and (2) a positedness – a Contradiction which has now fallen to the Ground. Ground, then, is the unity of Illusory Being (immediacy) and the Determinations of Reflection (positedness).[8] This dual structure means that Ground still has the dual structure of a Determination of Reflection.[9] But, Hegel says, "it is the last of them." (444)

Ground is the name of the act of self-erasure. As such it is "pure reflection . . . , the return of being into itself." (444) But this is so only "for us" (444) – not for itself. All Reflection does is to tell us what it is *not*, and *we* infer from that what it is. It is time, however, for Essence to posit itself in an affirmative manner. So far, "essence is lost in its negation." (444) *All* we have is self-erasure.

In Ground, the Determination of Reflection finds its true meaning, "namely, to be within itself the absolute recoil upon itself." (444)

---

5 HERBERT MARCUSE, REASON AND REVOLUTION 149 (1999).

6 Kisner, *supra* note 4, at 176.

7 *Cf.* CHARLES TAYLOR, HEGEL 262 (1975) (In Ground, "[w]e have in a sense only now come to the dialectic of Essence, after a lengthy introduction").

8 EL ¶ 121 ("the unity of identity and difference, the truth of what difference and identity have turned out to be – the reflection-into-self, which is equally a reflection-into-an-other").

9 According to Marcuse. "*while* it steps out of essence into 'existence,' it does not cease to have within itself the two dimensions of essence and immediate existence. The peculiar atemporality of the process unfolding in the *Logic* is based on this fact." HERBERT MARCUSE, HEGEL'S ONTOLOGY AND THE THEORY OF HISTORICITY 68 (Seyla Benhabib trans. 1987).

Essence, as ground, "is determined as the non-determined." (444) As such, Ground is "the restored, purified or manifested identity of essence." (444) All of these remarks are ways of saying that Ground is self-erasure pure and simple. *Self-erasure* is the ground of all finite things.

Ground is "*real mediation*" (445) of Essence with itself. "Real" is a reference to Self-subsistence, achieved in Figure 27(b). Thus, Ground is real mediation "because it contains reflection as sublated reflection." (445) Paradoxically, if the extremes of the Ground relation erase themselves, they erase their own erasure (because they *are* only the act of self-erasure). What results is the "*affirmative being*" (445) (*seiendes*)[10] of Ground. Accordingly, Ground is "essence that, through its non-being, *returns into* and *posits itself*." (445)

Yet Ground *mediates* – it requires a *Grounded*. Its reality portends a reference to other. Simultaneously, it is an immediacy. In other words, it is still a Determining Reflection.

This might be the place to object to the practice of deconstruction. According to Rodolphe Gasché, deconstruction "is distinguished from the speculative mode of resolving contradictions insofar as it maintains contradiction and resists its sublation into a higher unity."[11] By what authority may deconstruction resist the law of sublation? In privileging contradiction from sublation, does not deconstruction practice precisely the philosophy of presence that it opposes? In any case, Hegel does not *abolish* Contradiction through sublation. On the contrary, Contradiction is preserved, just as deconstruction would wish. Contradiction implies the self-erasure of structures, which is precisely what will occur throughout the balance of the Logic, until the final step of Absolute Knowledge. Deconstruction wishes the negative to stay negative.[12] But this transforms the negative into a transcendent thing-

---

[10] Here "affirmative" obviously does not mean imposed by External Reflection but rather immanently derived.

[11] RODOLPHE GASCHÉ, THE TAIN OF THE MIRROR: DERRIDA AND THE PHILOSOPHY OF REFLECTION 151 (1986); *see also* JACQUES DERRIDA, POSITIONS 40 (Alan Bass trans. 1971) ("If there were a definition of *différance* [*i.e.*, that which is never present and always deferred], it would be precisely the limit, the interruption, the destruction of the Hegelian *relève wherever* it operates") (footnote omitted).

[12] John Llewelyn, *A Point of Almost Absolute Proximity to Hegel*, in DECONSTRUCTION AND PHILOSOPHY: THE TEXTS OF JACQUES DERRIDA 87, 89 (John Sallis ed. 1987) ("Différance is an absolute exterior that no longer permits itself to be internalized") (citation omitted). This is also Adorno's position. THEODOR W. ADORNO, NEGATIVE DIALECTICS 119 (E.B. Ashton trans. 2000).

in-itself, with all the problems that noumena involve.[13]

Hegel's analysis of Ground proceeds on the following plan. The Understanding proposes that Ground is Absolute. Dialectical Reason sees Ground as Determinate. Speculative Reason sees that Ground presupposes Condition and Condition presupposes Ground. Their unity is the Unconditioned – the *Fact in itself*, or the "heart of the matter" (*Sache*). At this point Ground steps nimbly into Existence. In general, Hegel compares Ground – the unity of Positive and Negative – to Becoming. And since Becoming must become *something*, so Ground becomes what it ought to be – Appearance.[14]

A. Absolute Ground

(a) Form and Essence

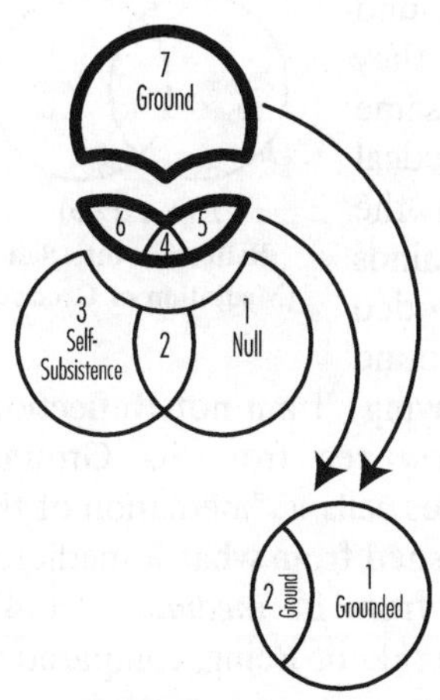

Figure 29(a)
Ground and Grounded

Since Essence is correlative, the Understanding sees things in pairs and so has picked up this attribute of Dialectical Reason. Accordingly, the Understanding correlates Ground with the Grounded.

This initial move of the Understanding is naive and crude, resembling the Understanding's opening move in Essence, where it perceived the Essential as an externality and reserved for itself the role of the Inessential. This was the naive "analytical" view that Essence can be known directly and that the Understanding has no constitutive role to play in the perception; hence it was Inessential. Dialectical Reason responded that the so-called Essential was a mere semblance of Essence – an Illusory Being.

Now something similar happens. The Understanding comprehends Ground as that which posits the Grounded but which is itself not posited in return. Thus, when the Understanding first contemplates Ground, it initially sees "an immediate determinate being in general,

---

[13] *See* Kisner, *supra* note 4, at 178 ("Now if we return to Derrida, it is quite striking to see him take over essentially . . . Kantian assumptions").

[14] *See* TAYLOR, *supra* note 7, at 263 ("we now see everything as emanating from its ground").

which forms the starting point." (447)[15] The Grounded is thoroughly Unessential.[16] It is viewed as a dead thing that does not participate in the constitution of Ground. That the Understanding at first perceives a *Determinate Being* counts as a defect. Determinate Being has already withdrawn into its Ground. It is already Grounded.

Meanwhile, the Grounded is posited by Ground but does not posit Ground in return.[17] As an unreflective immediacy, it is sublated in advance. In effect, the Grounded says, "I am not Ground," but it omits "and that is what I am." For us, *we* know that "presupposing is positing that recoils on that which posits." (447) For itself, however, there is no recoil.

Dialectical Reason takes over. Both Ground and Grounded are alike in one respect: they both sublate themselves. Both are the same thing – *not* Reflection-into-self. Dialectical Reason opposes Reflection-into-self to the immediacy of Ground/ Grounded.[18] It reminds the Understanding that the Grounded nevertheless has Reflection, just as Ground does. It takes Ground/Grounded to be saying, "I am not Reflection-into-self." Reflection-into-self thereby escapes from its Ground. Reflection-into-self, or, as Hegel sometimes calls it, "mediation of the ground" (448), is therefore to be distinguished from what it mediates. "[I]t is *essence as such* as distinguished from its *mediation*." (447) Significantly, Reflection-into-self is on the side of Being, compared to Ground/Grounded, which is a nullity.

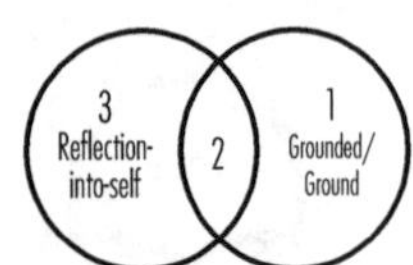

Figure 29(b)
Reflection-into-Self (Mediation of Ground)

[15] *See* ROBERT M. WALLACE, HEGEL'S PHILOSOPHY OF REALITY, FREEDOM AND GOD 310 (2005) ("since each Hegelian category mirrors within itself the totality of the Universe, and the most abstract and immediate thought-determinations *necessarily precede* the most concrete and comprehensive ones, the transition from a categorial totality into its dialectical opposite cannot but take the shape of an 'abrupt', seemingly 'irrational' overturning of the most concrete *Denkbestimmung* of the former into the most abstract (immediate) one of the latter").

[16] By way of example, one might say that the 14th amendment to the United States Constitution is Grounded in Article V of the Constitution, which permits amendments to be added. The obverse relation, however, does not pertain. There is a Constitution even in the absence of the 14th amendment.

[17] For this reason, "it is in the very nature of a ground to be in excess of what it accounts for . . . " GASCHÉ, *supra* note 11, at 155.

[18] JOHN W. BURBIDGE, ON HEGEL'S LOGIC: FRAGMENTS OF A COMMENTARY 86 (1981) ("for the formal relation between a *ground* and a *grounded* comes forward only after reflection dissolves its own activity").

Reflection-into-self is now in the embarrassing position of standing over against Reflection itself. That is to say, Dialectical Reason puts forth Reflection-into-self as an immediacy which is *not* reflective. Once again, Dialectical Reason exhibits the very fault it thinks it is criticizing – it isolates and renders immediate that which is really mediated. Because of its immediacy, Reflection-into-self is the opposite of what it should be. It has no Self-Subsistence.

This loss of Self-Subsistence is true of both extremes. Ground and Grounded have said, "We are not Reflection-into-self." Yet Reflection-into-self *is* Self-Subsistence *tout court*. Now Reflection-into-self, portraying itself as an indeterminate immediacy, likewise sublates itself. Both the extremes represent a *beyond* to Essence. Speculative Reason now names this "beyond" to be Form.

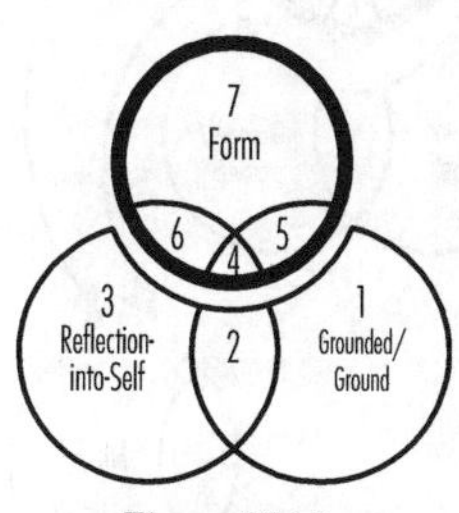

Figure 29(c)
Form (Ground Relation)

Form (sometimes called Ground Relation) is not the same as the earlier versions of Reflection. These were self-subsistent. Now Ground/Grounded has proven it has no Self-Subsistence[19] – *and this is its very Self-Subsistence*. The enduring thing about Form is that it does not endure. As Hegel puts it: "The determinations of reflection ought to have their subsistence within themselves and be self-subsistent; but their self-subsistence is their dissolution; they have it in an other; but this dissolution is itself this self-identity or the ground of their subsistence that they give to themselves." (448) Hence, Form recaptures (and *is*) the Self-Subsistence that the extremes renounced. Form is posited by its self-erasing extremes. Yet Form is not to be distinguished from the extremes (as Reflection-into-self was, in Figure 29(b)). Rather, Form *is* the extremes [4, 5, 6] as well as being distinguished from the Extremes [7]. That disappearing Form endures is important evidence that, with Hegel, it's appearances all the way down.

Nevertheless, the Understanding, gazing back at Figure 29(c), proposes that the extremes "constitute the *form as against essence*." (448) That is, the extremes have said, "We have no Self-Subsistence." This is the very confession of Form. Yet it is also true that Form [4, 6] has posited its Self-Subsistence – its Essence – as [7]. The

[19] *Id*. at 87 ("We have lost any distinct sense of *ground*").

Understanding therefore proposes that Form and Essence must always appear together as correlation.

"Essence *has* a form," Hegel says (448), meaning that Essence never exists on its own *without* Form. Therefore, the pair of Form and Essence always appears together – in a Ground Relation.[20] As portrayed in Figure 28(c), Essence as Ground had a fixed immediacy, but it was Essence "*determined* as *undetermined*." (447) Essence as Ground was a "*substrate*" (448) – "substrate" connoting an abstract, inactive beyond.[21] Simultaneously, Essence as Ground was pure movement – the movement of self-erasure. In Hegel's view, Essence is "inseparable from the movement of reflection itself." (448) One cannot say that this movement runs *through* Essence, nor can one say that Essence is the starting point of the movement. Essence "is not *before* or *in* its movement." (448) Rather, Essence *is the movement itself*, and the place to which it removes its self – its Being – is *Form*. Ironically, Form is an advanced version of Ground. Most philosophers would have thought the opposite to be true – that Form is grounded in Essence.

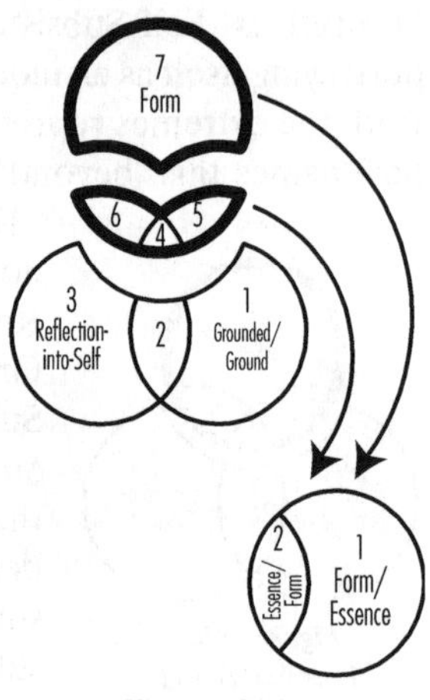

Figure 30(a)
Form and Essence

Essence announces it is *not* Essence, and this announcement is Form itself.[22] This allows Hegel to conclude: "A related determination only makes its appearance in ground conformably to the moment of sublated

---

[20] External reflection, Hegel complains, "usually does not go beyond this distinction of essence and form." (449) The Diversity attributed to Form and Essence itself implies a unity – the very distinction of one against the other. This unity is itself *not* coincident with Form or Essence. It is rather the Essence of Form and Essence (from the view of external reflection). Even for external reflection, Essence – this unity – expels itself from Form and Essence "and makes itself into a positedness." (449)

[21] Substrate is "the being that would be the inert support of . . . representations. JEAN HYPPOLITE, LOGIC AND EXISTENCE 139 (Leonard Lawlor and Amit Sen trans., 1997). Substrate is developed in Figure 21(b).

[22] *See* Deborah Chaffin, *The Logic of Contingency*, in HEGEL RECONSIDERED: BEYOND METAPHYSICS AND THE AUTHORITARIAN STATE (H. Tristram Engelhardt, Jr., & Terry Pinkard eds., 143, 147 (1994) ("form is self-relating negativity, and hence negates itself in its other").

reflection." (448) That is, only when Reflection erases itself does Essence appear in the guise of Form. When Essence is "related substrate" (as opposed to an isolated substrate), it is determinate; "by virtue of this positedness it contains form." (448) Or to say the same thing in different words, if we have before us the *form* of a thing, then, by definition, Essence *has already erased itself* in favor of form.

Yet, Hegel cautions, Essence – [2] in Figure 30(a) – still has a moment of indifference toward its own form determinations: "It is a form determination in so far as it is something posited and consequently distinct from *that of which* it is the form." (448) As form determinations have renounced Reflection-into-self, Essence – in its indifferent moment – is where Reflection-into-self has removed itself. Essence, then, continues to possess a self-identity that is not possessed by Form. It is "the *simple substrate* which is the *subsisting* of form" (449) (since Form by definition is not self-subsistent). Form posits subsistence to be in Essence. In Form, Essence is "made into something posited." (449) In Figure 30(a), "essence is essentially determinate and is thus once again the moment of ground-relation and form." (449)

Form and Essence are correlatives in Figure 30(a), but each is equally the whole that includes the other – as we saw in Hegel's analysis of opposites. Thus, Form is "the completed whole of reflection." (449) Still, it is "a sublated determination." (449) Sublation implies relation to an other that is *not* Form. In its moment of relation, Form [1] posits Essence [2], while Essence, as Ground, "is the indeterminate and *inactive* substrate in which the form-determinations subsist." (449) Yet, even while Essence excludes form, it likewise includes it. "Consequently, form has . . . essence, just as essence has in its negative nature absolute form. The question cannot therefore be asked, *how form is added to essence*, for it is only the reflection of essence into essence itself . . . essence's own immanent reflection." (449-50)

Form is not self-subsistent. It posits its Self-Subsistence to be in Essence. Yet Form is included in (and excluded from) Essence. In spite of its protest, Form is Essence after all. It "is in its own self equally the reflection that returns into itself, or identical [with] essence." (450) For this reason, it is incorrect to think that Form merely presupposes Essence, "as if separate from it." (450) This would be "the unessential determination of reflection that hastens without pause to destruction." (450) Form *is* Essence *and* is opposed to Essence – "it is itself the ground of its sublating or the identical connexion of its determinations." (450) In distinguishing itself from Essence, Form "sublates this very distinguishing and is the self-identity which essence is." (450) In short, Form is "the contradiction of being sublated in its positedness and of persisting in this sublatedness." (450) Form is as much Essence as it is Form. With Hegel, it is appearances all the way down.

(b) Form and Matter

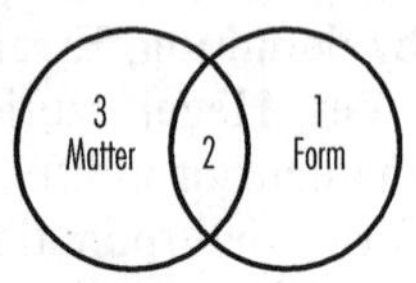

Figure 30(b)
Form and Matter

Dialectical Reason analyzes Essence as it stands over against Form (even while being Form itself). "[A]ccording to this moment, essence is the indeterminate for which form is an other. As such, it is not essence which is in its own self absolute reflection." (450) That is, at this moment Essence does not have being-in-and-for-self. Rather, it has being-for-other. It "is *determined* [by Form] as formless identity; it is *matter*." (450) In this dialectical moment, Matter (*die Materie*) is radically other to, or "diverse" from, Form. It is the "formless indeterminate." (450)[23] Nevertheless, because Form has expelled its Reflection-into-self, it must follow that Matter "constitutes the reflection-into-self of the form-determinations." (450) Matter is "the self-subsistent element to which [form-determinations] are related." (450)

In this guise, Matter is "determined as a *groundless* subsistence" (451) – seemingly separate from Form. "Form and matter alike are accordingly determined as being not posited by one another, as not being the ground of one another." (451) Matter in Figure 30(b) therefore resembles Reflection-into-self in Figure 29(b). In both these moments, self-subsistence is divorced from merely formal appearance. Furthermore, both Reflection-into-self and Matter are on the side of being (the lefthand side of the diagram); that which posits them is on the side of nothing. Thus, Matter "is not simple essence, which is immediately itself absolute reflection, but it is essence determined as the positive, that is, essence that only is as sublated negation." (451) The sublatedness of negation refers to the isolated immediacy of [3] in Figure 30(b), on the side of Being.

But this is just a pose, as Speculative Reason knows. Form (being negative) presupposes Matter as its indifferent other, but the two are not "externally and contingently opposite to one another." (451) Nor

[23] *See* BURBIDGE, LOGIC, *supra* note 18, at 87 (Matter "can be thought only by abstracting from *form* – all form").

are Form and Matter self-subsistent. "[N]either matter nor form is self-originated, or, in another terminology, *eternal*." (451)[24] Rather, they are mutually dependent. Their relation is "reciprocal presupposition." (452) Thus, Form withdraws into Matter. Matter is "real *basis* or substrate" to Form. (450) Matter is what is left after every form determination is abstracted from a thing. The nature of Form is to sublate itself, and so Form spontaneously reduces itself to Matter.

According to Hegel, Matter is passive and Form is active. Form dissolves itself as the non-self-subsistent, and withdraws into Matter. Form is thus "the self-related negative" – and "internal contradiction: it is self-resolving, self-repelling and self-determining." (451) Matter, in contrast is indifferent and passive. From the perspective of its moment, Matter is only "*implicitly* related to form." (451) That is, Matter does not posit Form. Rather, "Matter contains form locked up within it and is absolute susceptibility to form only because it has form absolutely within itself . . . *Matter must therefore be formed*." (451-2)

Form and Matter are different, but each is entirely the whole that includes the other. Matter is "the identity of ground and grounded, as a basis which stands over against [Form]." (451) Form is likewise ground and grounded – "the relation of the two as distinct sides." (451) Because Form "contains matter within it," Form's action on matter – the formation of matter – is "only *the removal of the illusion* of their *indifference*." (452)

If Form erases itself and transports itself to its other, and if Form also contains Matter, then Matter too is a self-erasure that sends its non-being into Form. Here is the usual see-saw between the extremes that typifies Dialectical Reason. Hegel names these self-erasures – this "mediation of each with itself through its own non-being" – (452) as inwardization of outwardness. What is outward inwardizes itself. Form is outward, and by self-erasing it moves inward. Deeper and deeper withdrawal and higher and higher intensity is the *whole point* of Logic. "Each new stage of *forthgoing*, that is, of *further determination*, is a withdrawal inwards, and the greater *extension* is equally a *higher intensity*." (840-1)

---

[24] An eternal thing cannot have been originated by another. Otherwise, there would have been a time when the eternal thing did not exist. But does it follow that therefore the eternal thing originated itself? Could it not be said that the eternal thing simply has no origin? I think what Hegel means here is that the eternal thing is grounded on nothing else but itself. Since ground is origin, the eternal thing is self-originating in this sense.

Each side of the syllogism, then, is Form transporting itself to its other. This, Hegel says, is "the *absolute* ground that *determines* itself." (452) Since Matter transports itself into Form (and vice versa), Matter makes itself into something determinate. The "*activity of form*" is therefore "no less a *movement belonging to matter itself*." (453) This moment supersedes the earlier point that Matter is passive. Speculative Reason sees that Dialectical Reason is again the pot that calls the kettle black. It accuses Form of self-erasure, but Matter is just as much self-erasure.

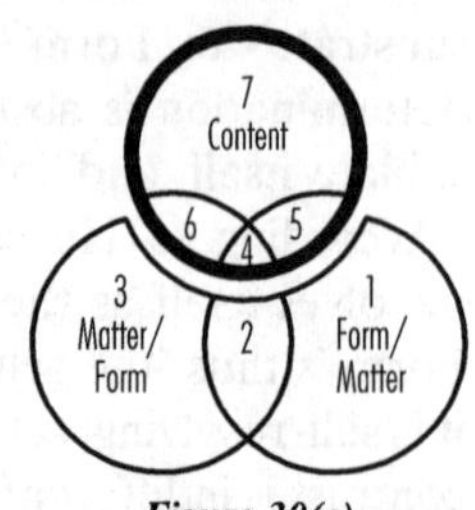

Figure 30(c)
Content (Inwardization of Outward Form)

Self-erasure is the unity – the *Content* – of Form and Matter. Matter was determined by Form, but Matter *is* Form. So Matter determines itself. Form is "simply material, subsistent form." (454) Thus the insight of Lucio Colletti is correct – that Hegel's idealism is not the anti-materialism the Marxists thought.[25]

Hegel reviews the journey traversed across Absolute Ground. First, Form was Ground Relation – the unity between itself and its Self-Subsistence (*i.e.*, Reflection-into-self). Then, dialectically, Form stood against Matter. Finally, Form was formed matter, or Content. Stated otherwise, in the development of Ground/Grounded, the Grounded (primitive Form) posited Ground. When Form stood against Matter, Form (Grounded) presupposed Matter. Now Form and Matter have been revealed to be the same: each posits Content, taken as self-erasure. Form has revealed itself as powerful.[26] "What was previously the self-identical – at first ground, then simple subsistence, and finally matter – comes under the dominance of form and is once more one of its determinations." (455)

---

[25] LUCIO COLLETTI, MARXISM AND HEGEL 52-67 (Lawrence Garner trans., 1973); *see also* ERROL E. HARRIS, AN INTERPRETATION OF THE LOGIC OF HEGEL 218 (1983) ("Hegel is as much a realist as, and effectively more so than, any other philosopher"); ERROL E. HARRIS, THE SPIRIT OF HEGEL 53 (1993) ("no dialectic can be materialistic, if that means, as is usually intended, that all forms of reality are reducible to finite, immobile, and dead matter. But if it means no more (nor less) than that matter is pregnant with life and mind, it must be the Hegelian and not the Marxian dialectic that operates in it . . . "); SARAH KAY, SLAVOJ ŽIŽEK: A CRITICAL INTRODUCTION 32 (2003) (idealism carried to the extremes "converts into dialectical materialism").

[26] SLAVOJ ŽIŽEK, TARRYING WITH THE NEGATIVE: KANT, HEGEL, AND THE CRITIQUE OF IDEOLOGY 134-5 (1993).

(c) Form and Content

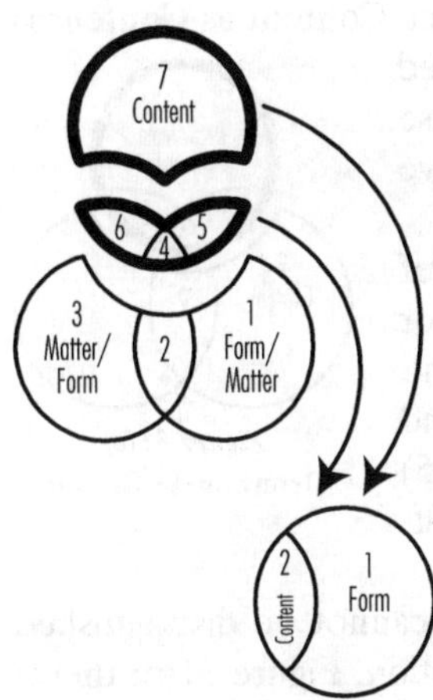

Figure 31(a)
Form and Content

Ground has now become "[f]ormed matter, or the form that has a subsistence." (454) On the one hand, it is "the absolute unity of the ground with itself." (454) This could be seen as [7] in Figure 30(c). On the other hand, it is *posited*, which refers to its otherness. Thus, [4, 5, 6] posit their Ground in [7] by self-sublating. In this explicit double guise, it is *Content*. The Content of Form is the inwardization of the outward. And what is Content? Nothing but self-erasure. As Hegel will say later, "form [*i.e.*, self-erasure] is the soul of all objectivity and all otherwise determined content has its truth in the form alone." (825)

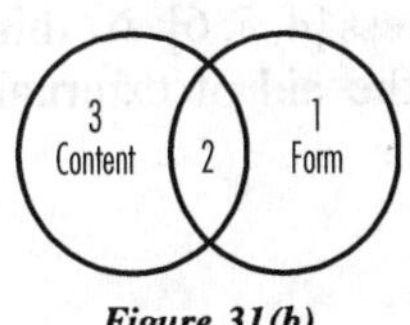

Figure 31(b)
Form v Content

The Understanding proposes that, given Form, there must be self-erasure, or Content. If the Understanding emphasizes the unity between Form and Content, Dialectical Reason reminds us of the difference. "There is thus a doubling of form. At one time it is reflected into itself; and then is identical with the content. At another time it is not reflected into itself, and then is the external existence, which does not at all affect the content."[27]

---

[27] EL § 133. Problematically, the above passage locates Form and Content in the realm of Appearance – two chapters hence. The significance of this relocation will be discussed in chapter 14. According to Errol Harris, "Hitherto essence has been expressed as the showing of an essential being in an external display or reflection. In matter and form, matter was the subsistent element and form its outward, contingent, inessential, showing forth." HARRIS, LOGIC, *supra* note 26, at 181. In fact, Essence has *never* overtly shown itself. Rather, the *inessential* constantly reveals what it is *not*. Self-erasure turns out to be how Essence appears. In these moments, Essence is presupposed. In any case, Harris is right to state that "essence is now embodied in material form." *Id*. But this does not mean that content is some positive thing coincident with form. *Id*. at 183 (suggesting that the content of falling bodies is the form of accelerating at 16 feet per second). Content is not something affirmative, like the law of falling bodies, but simply the act of form's self-erasure. In fact, the law of falling bodies will later be cited as *inessential* material. *Infra* at 366-7.

Speculative Reason sees that Form is as much Content as Content is Form. Any distinction between them is imposed externally. Form and Content therefore erase themselves and withdraw into their speculative result – Determinate Ground.

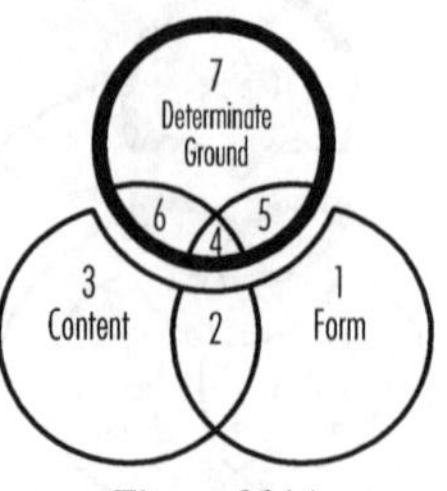

Figure 31(c)
Determinate Ground

Determinate Ground stands for the inability of Essence to manifest whether it is Form or Content. Nevertheless, Ground has a Content. "The content of the ground is . . . the ground that has returned into its unity with itself." (455) In other words, Determinate Ground is self-erasure itself. Its content *is* its form.

Determinate Ground has a content which cannot be distinguished from Form without the aid of external reflection. Figure 31(c) therefore has a double structure. First, it is immediate [7]. As such it is Form, standing indifferently over against Content. "[I]ts determinateness of being [is] external to the content." (456) At this moment, if Form goes together with Content, it is because an external reflection says so. Second, Determinate Ground is a positedness [4, 5, 6]. At this moment, Form is connected to Content *without* the aid of external reflection.

B. Determinate Ground

(a) Formal Ground

Formal Ground is the realm of tautological explanation, where Molière's physicians explain the *virtus dormitiva* of opium. In this relation of opium to dormitive force, opium is Grounded (or Form). Dormitive force is Ground (or Substrate). At this stage, ground is "negatively self-related identity, which thereby makes itself into a positedness." (456) How is this so? Negative self-relation is, by now, a familiar contradiction. Negation implies a doubleness at odds with immediacy. The self-relation is negative because it was produced when the extremes – Form and Content in Figure 31(b) – negated themselves. This immediacy, in Figure 32(a), has now made itself into a positedness. The Substrate presupposes that it has Form, even within the immediacy of [1, 2].

The Understanding sees that the job of Form is to self-erase and

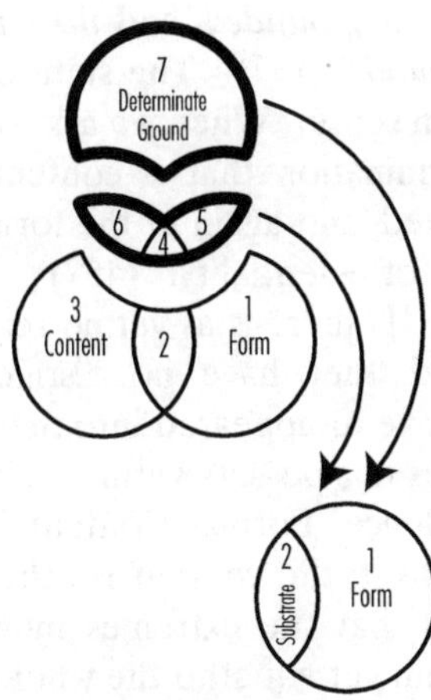

Figure 32(a)
Formal Ground

withdraw into Ground.[28] But Dialectical Reason sees that *both* sides are Form, "because each passes over into the other, mutually posit themselves as sublated in *one identity*; in doing so they . . . *presuppose* this identity." (456-7)[29] This identity Hegel names Formal Content, or Sufficient Ground.

Since the Formal Content of Form and Ground is that they erase themselves, the Self-Subsistence of Form or Ground is to be found in its other. Both sides, then, are simultaneously Ground and Grounded. "It does not matter which of the two determinations is made the first, whether the transition is made from the posited to the other as ground, or from the one as ground to the other as the posited." (457)

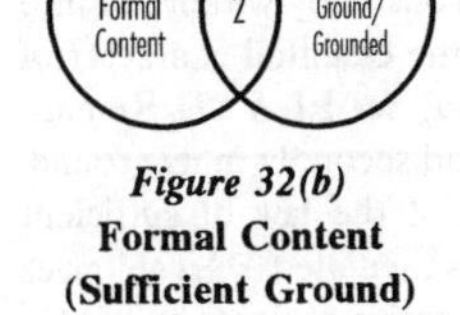

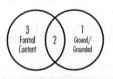

Figure 32(b)
Formal Content
(Sufficient Ground)

Meanwhile, Formal Content enjoys an immediacy [3] vis-à-vis the active extremes. In this immediate moment, it is "indifferent to this form; in both it is simply one determination only." (457) Once again, Self-Subsistence is held apart from Ground/Grounded. Ground and Grounded turn into each other. Neither can distinguish the other from itself. Formal Content stands to one side and laughs at the impotence of Ground and Grounded.[30]

Hegel also calls the Formal Content "sufficient ground" (457) – a Leibnizian phrase. In Figure 32(b), the parts are each other, the parts are themselves, the parts are the whole, and the whole is the parts:

---

[28] JOHN W. BURBIDGE, REAL PROCESS: HOW LOGIC AND CHEMISTRY COMBINE IN HEGEL'S PHILOSOPHY OF NATURE 117 (1996) ("in a formal ground, there is no difference in content between the ground and what is grounded by it. Any distinction is simply formal, a matter of superficial structure.").

[29] One consequence of this insight is that, if form mediates content, then "a merely formal theory of knowledge, such as epistemology sets forth, negates itself; it is not possible." THEODOR W. ADORNO, HEGEL: THREE STUDIES 66 (1999).

[30] In Žižek's view, this self-subsistence that comes into view here is the "exception" which will develop into subjectivity itself. SLAVOJ ŽIŽEK, FOR THEY KNOW NOT WHAT THEY DO: ENJOYMENT AS A POLITICAL FACTOR 48 (1991).

"*there is nothing in the ground that is not in the grounded*, and *there is nothing in the grounded that is not in the ground*." (457)[31] The state of sufficient ground is underwritten by common sense: "When we ask for a ground, we want to see the *same* determination that is content, double, once in the form of something posited, and again in the form of a determinate being reflected into itself, of essentiality." (457)[32]

Yet Sufficient Ground is pitifully deficient. "[T]here is as yet no real determination of the sides of the ground, they have no distinct content." (458) Figure 32(b), the extremes have disappeared into their unity [2]. This whole is too simple. "[I]t does not possess within itself the form of the ground-relation." (458) Hence, Formal Content is "indifferent to the form, which is external to it; the content is other than the form." (458) What must occur is that the extremes must *expressly* show themselves to be different from yet equal to the whole.

Pitiful Formal Ground may be, but it should not be missed that Formal Ground reveals the notional form. Notion is the unity of (1)

---

[31] In a short Remark, Hegel comments on Leibniz's concept of sufficient ground. The word "sufficient" (*zureichender*), Hegel suggests, is superfluous. *Insufficiency* means that it is not Ground at all. Leibniz insists that *everything* has a Ground. According to this concept, everything that *is* is posited by something else. "Being" is seen as a bad infinity, in which immediate appearance dissolves itself, and the thing constantly withdraws into its deeper, essential ground. "In the law of ground, therefore, the essential character of reflection-into-self in contrast to mere being is expressed." (446) *See* EL § 121 Remark ("we wish . . . to see the matter double, first in its immediacy, and secondly in its ground, where it is no longer immediate. This is the plain meaning of the law of sufficient ground, as it is called; it asserts that things should be viewed as mediated"). Hegel gives credit to Leibniz, who made sufficient ground "the basis of his entire philosophy." (446) At least this law expresses the idea that immediate being is not the truth of the thing. For Leibniz, *Ground* was assigned the honor of being "the true immediate." (446)

Leibniz distinguished the law of sufficient ground from causality. Causality is an external relation between cause and effect, not an immanent one. Sufficiency of ground had to do with immanent unity – final cause. In a paper dated 1697, Leibniz wrote: "In eternal things, even though there be no cause, there must be a reason, which, for permanent things, is necessity itself, or essence; but for the series of changing things, if it be supposed that they succeed one another from all eternity, this reason is . . . the prevailing of inclinations, which consist not in necessitating reasons . . . but inclining reasons." BERTRAND RUSSELL, THE PHILOSOPHY OF LEIBNIZ 32 (1997) An inclining reason is "the perception of the good, either by the substance itself, if it be free, or by God, if the substance be not free." *Id*. "But this," Hegel warns, "is not yet the proper place for this determination of ground." (446-7) Teleology is reserved a spot very late in the *SL*.

[32] In the *Phenomenology*, Hegel spends much time on tautology. But Hyppolite defends the expenditure of resources. The very structure of any explanation is that "it goes *from the same to the same*." JEAN HYPPOLITE, GENESIS AND STRUCTURE OF HEGEL'S *PHENOMENOLOGY OF SPIRIT* 133 (Samuel Cherniak & John Heckman trans., 1974).

itself (Universality), (2) its other (Particularity), and (3) the unity of itself and other (Individuality). Notion (or subjectivity) is indeed tautological or, to use the grander term, *free*.[33]

Tautology. At the stage of Formal Ground, "the assignment of a ground remains a mere formalism and empty tautology which expresses in the form of . . . essentiality the same content that is already present in the form of an immediate being." (458) This immediate being is taken as posited, and for that very reason we inquire into its ground. At this level, any talk of ground is empty. The sciences "are full of tautologies of this kind which constitute as it were a prerogative of science." (458) Why do the planets revolve around the sun? Science answers that the planets and the sun attract each other. "As regards content, this expresses nothing other than what is contained in the phenomenon, namely the relation of these bodies to one another, only in the form of . . . force." (458) What kind of force? "[T]he answer is that it is the force that makes the earth move round the sun; that is, it has precisely the same content as the phenomenon of which it is supposed to be ground." (458) Outside the sciences, such responses count as absurd: "To answer the question, why is this person going to town, with the reason, the ground, that is because there is an attractive force in the town which urges him in that direction, is to give the kind of reply that is sanctioned in the sciences but outside them is counted as absurd." (458-9)

Leibniz complained that Newton's gravity was an "occult quality," (459) but the opposite is true. Gravity "is a too familiar quality; for it has no other content than the phenomenon itself. What commends this mode of explanation is precisely its great clarity and intelligibility; for there is nothing clearer or more intelligible than that, for example, a plant has its ground in a vegetative, that is, plant-producing force." (459) But nothing is really explained by the invocation of such forces.[34]

---

[33] Ground is an activity – the act of self-erasure. Therefore, Clark Butler is correct in referring to Sufficient Ground as "the self-determination of an event which can be partially described but never sufficiently 'explained.'" CLARK BUTLER, HEGEL'S LOGIC: BETWEEN DIALECTIC AND HISTORY 169 (1996). If it could be explained, it would be determined by other causes and would not be *self*-determined.

[34] Hegel shows here his hostility to Newton, for whom he had "no very high opinion of Newton's ability to deal with thoughts." Renate Wahsner, *The Philosophical Background to Hegel's Criticism of Newton*, in HEGEL AND NEWTONIANISM 81 (Michael John Petry ed., 1993).

In this mode of explanation, "two opposite directions of the ground relation are present" (459) without being generally noticed. The ground is taken as reflection-into-self – "the content of the phenomenon which it grounds." (459) As a reflection-into-self, it is an immediacy. But it is likewise posited by the phenomenon. "It is that from which the phenomenon is to be understood." (459) Yet we know of the ground only because we inferred it from the phenomenon. This business of "converting the immediate phenomenon into the form of reflected being" (459) contributes nothing to knowledge. Any such movement "is confined within a difference of form which this same procedure inverts and sublates." (459) Explanation at this level, Hegel says, "is a distasteful business." (460) "The exposition begins with grounds that are placed in mid-air as principles and primary concepts; they are simple determinations devoid of any necessity in and for themselves." (460) Reason "is asked to treat what is groundless as a valid foundation. Success comes most easily when, without much reflection, the principles are simply accepted as *given* and one then proceeds to use them as fundamental rules of one's understanding." (460) When caught in this mode of explanation, "one finds oneself in a kind of witches' circle in which determinations of real being and determinations of reflection, ground and grounded, phenomena and phantoms, run riot in indiscriminate company and enjoy equal rank with one another." (461) Scientists have notoriously confessed that they do not understand the inner nature of forces like gravity. "This amounts," Hegel says, "only to a confession that this assigning of grounds is itself completely inadequate; that something quite different from such grounds is required." (461)

(b) Real Ground

Formal Ground was determinate, which means that it was double. It was part Substrate and part Form (or Ground Relation). But which was Ground and which Grounded? This could only be determined externally and arbitrarily, as Figure 32(b) showed. There, Ground/Grounded was quite external to Content. Yet Dialectical Reason can be made to confess that Content is essentially connected to Ground/Grounded. We are not ready to present the move of Speculative Reason, but perhaps Hegel borrows some lessons of Speculative Reason to point out that Figure 32(b) can be already viewed as Real Ground. In Figure 32(b), "the two are not external to one another." (461) The true content of both sides is that Ground and Grounded are truly in unity. Ground is Grounded (*i.e.*, is posited); Grounded is

Ground. "[E]ach is in itself this identity of the whole." (461)

Speculative Reason watches the Grounded withdraw into Ground and the Ground withdraw into Grounded (proving it was Grounded after all). In naming this activity Real (or "realized") Ground, Speculative Reason shows that Ground is no longer a stupid tautology. Earlier, tautology did not escape the confines of immediacy. Now, by definition, immediacy is transcended. Ground must be mediated. At this stage, "when we ask for a ground, we really demand that the content of the ground be a different determination from that of the phenomenon whose ground we are seeking." (462) Real Ground therefore implies a synthesis of new material not present in the Grounded.[35] In other words, Formal Content, standing over against what it grounds, represents the proposition that, in the search for Ground, something real and substantial takes place. Tautology is productive after all.

Underlying this last remark and, indeed, the whole idea of Real Ground, is that Form has many Essences. One of them is the true Ground. But which?

Real Ground is a disappointment. In effect, Real Ground knows there *is* a ground. It is the theater of sophistry – "argumentation from grounds." (466)[36] But it also knows that every Form implies a different ground. Which are the essential and which are the inessential grounds? Real Ground cannot tell, except that everything must have its ground.

Nevertheless, Real Ground plays a vital role in the progression of the Logic. Here, Ground is recognized as reflected into (and is the same as) Grounded. Grounded has its Self-Subsistence only in an other – in the Ground. But "grounded now has its own distinctive content." (462) This Content is the unity of Ground and Grounded. The Grounded thus displays the notional form – it is (1) itself, (2) its other, and (3) the unity of itself and other.

The trouble is that the Grounded thing is a unity of attributes that is separate and apart from the authentic Ground Relation; the unity of

---

[35] BURBIDGE, REAL PROCESS, *supra* note 28, at 117 ("in a real ground the process of grounding introduces a real change or transformation in the content. The result is not simply the sum of its constituents, but something qualitatively different. So the shift is not reversible.").

[36] *See* EL § 121 Remark ("To get no further than mere grounds, especially on questions of law and morality, is the position and principle of the Sophists . . . Sophistry lies in the formal circumstance of teaching it by grounds which are as available for attack as for defense. In a time so rich in reflection and so devoted to *raisonnement* as our own, he must be a poor creature who cannot advance a good ground for everything, even for what is worst and most depraved.").

Ground and Grounded is "empty, intrinsically contentless relation." (462) A thing is "an external combination" (462) of Ground/Grounded.

Two ideas are present in Real Ground. First, Ground is continuous with Grounded. Second, the Grounded has – and Ground does not have – "an unessential form, external determinations of the content which, as such, are free from the ground." (462) This is why we can never be sure empirically that the correct ground has been located. Ground dwells within the Grounded, "but does not posit itself therein in any difference of form." (462) It is an indifferent substrate, which means that, among the many attributes a thing has, the true Ground does not distinguish itself from the false grounds. "Ground, in determining itself as real, consequently breaks up, on account of the diversity of content which constitutes its reality, into external determinations." (463)

Explanations From Ground. Formal Ground is tautology. Real Ground is not. It plucks the one real Ground from the nettle of competing grounds. This means that Real Ground "brings with it the contingency and externality of the ground relation." (463) Real Ground knows that there *is* a Ground – but which Ground is the authentic one? The choice among Grounds seems to be free. The assigning of Real Ground is therefore just as much a formalism as Formal Ground.[37]

Sophistry is now before us:

> What Socrates and Plato call *sophistry* is nothing else but argumentation from grounds . . . [O]ne is as valid as another; because it does not embrace the whole extent of the subject matter, each is a one-sided ground. . . . [N]one of them exhausts the subject matter . . . . [N]one is a *sufficient* ground . . . [T]he door is wide open to innumerable *aspects* . . . lying *outside* the thing itself, on account of the contingency of their mode of connexion . . . The search for and assignment of grounds, in which argumentation mainly consists, is accordingly an endless pursuit which does not reach a final determination; for any and every thing one or more good grounds can be given, and also for its opposite; and a host of grounds can exist without anything following from them. (466)

Hegel gives some examples. The ground of a house is its foundation. Gravity is what unites house and foundation. But where does the distinction between house and foundation come from? It is externally imposed. The distinction is "a matter of complete indifference to the heavy matter itself." (464) Matter is not the ground of the distinction

[37] Formal Ground (tautology) is thus *sufficient* ground; Real Ground is *insufficient* ground. TAYLOR, *supra* note 7, at 264.

between foundation and house. Gravity is really in the foundation and in the house. But that one is house and the other foundation – this is not within the matter itself.

The concept of punishment has multiple grounds – deterrence, retribution, rehabilitation. These grounds are distinguishable from punishment. "[T]his concrete also contains those others which, whilst associated with the ground in punishment, do not have their ground in [punishment]." (465) In other words, punishment is overdetermined; it has *many* grounds.

Why does an official hold office? He has talent, charisma, the right friends. Each can be the ground of holding office. The leftovers are merely "posited" – attributed externally. The various grounds "are a diverse content which is joined together in a third." (465) That is, a thinking subject unifies the attributes of the official into a coherent thing. But among the attributes is a real Ground Relation – the true Form. The nature of a given attribute – whether it is essential or merely posited – is externally decided. Each of the attributes is essential in a sense, because they help make the officer an individual different from all other individuals. But the attribute that explains why the officer holds office is likewise external.

An action has many grounds. Actions may be motivated by morality or inclination. Among the many things that determine the action is the Real Ground of it. This is an important point for lawyers. Anglo-American jurisprudence has witnessed a war between legal realism and legal positivism. Legal realists suspect that, when a judge gives the law as her reason of decision, she is in effect choosing from one of many grounds. Hegel, however, gives some comfort, though perhaps it will seem cold porridge to those who suffer from "anxiety" – fear that the symbolic order will fly apart. The point is that, of all the many grounds a judge may have, one of them *is* the law. Therefore, the rule of law is not only a possible but a necessary Ground for judicial decision.[38]

(c) The Complete Ground

Complete Ground is Speculative Reason's reinterpretation of Real

---

[38] The true law is found when the judge suppresses her heteronomy and becomes the autonomous Kantian self through whom reason speaks. Unfortunately, no one's motives are completely transparent to one's own self, so we never quite know whether the judge has been autonomous or heteronomous. I develop these points in David Gray Carlson, *The Traumatic Dimension in Law*, 24 CARDOZO L. REV. 2287 (2003).

Ground, where Content (Ground in general) was only substrate – alienated from the Grounded. Ground as Content was posited as essential, but only by some external sophist intellect. Real Ground was therefore the theater of skepticism and even cynicism. In Real Ground, Content is merely posited by the reliance on external attribution. But Content *is* self-erasure. The sophist is defeated in advance.

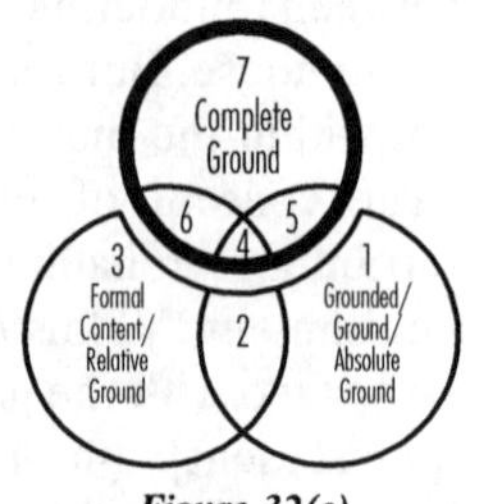

Figure 32(c)
Complete Ground

Since skepticism must be *self*-skeptical (if it is to be true to its principle), Real Ground can't be sure that [1] or [3] is the Real Ground. Speculative Reason now summarizes the situation. Each side is unified by its self-erasing activity. The true content of the extremes, then, is negative. Complete Ground is nothing but the inability of Ground to identify itself as Ground. Complete Ground simply says, "I'm not sure I'm Ground."[39]

Hegel summarizes the progress across Ground as follows. First, a thing has a Ground. It also has "a *second* determination, one which is *posited* by the Ground." (467) That is, it contains its other inside itself, but it is also determined by that other. Dialectical Reason notices that the thing now has two contents. Twoness requires a moment of indifference. At this moment, Ground is "not in its own self ground." (467) Ground is supposed to be a correlate, yet if it is immediate, its status as Ground is sublated. Nor, for the same reason, can we say that the other content is the Grounded. In its immediacy, each moment shows that it has its Ground in its other.

So Ground and Grounded have two relations. (1) They are *not* related (remembering that no relation is, after all, a kind of relation). The moments "are supported by a something which constitutes their merely immediate, not reflected, relation." (467-8) In other words, Ground requires an outside will to accomplish its relation to

[39] "Complete Ground" is sometimes interpreted as signifying the proposition that, unless *all* the grounds are present, then the thing is not really explained. TAYLOR, *supra* note 7, at 265. While not inconsistent with Hegel's ultimate view, I think this fails to capture the exact function of Complete Ground. According to this function, Complete Ground stands for the proposition that there *are* grounds, but, from the many contingencies which surround a thing, we are not sure which are mere contingencies and which are grounds. *See* BUTLER, *supra* note 33, at 168 ("Self-determination must be understood as a creative process, not as a Stoic acceptance of past necessity. This is the interpretation substantiated by Hegel's texts on the philosophy of ground").

Grounded. This dependence on outside will Hegel calls relative Ground.[40] In the skeptical moment of Real Ground, a thing is "only a relative ground in relation to the 'togetherness' in the other something." (468) Yet (2) the very idea of Relative Ground implies the necessity of an Absolute Ground. This leads to the other relation between Ground and Grounded. Since Ground is correlated with Grounded, they are *immediately* related.

The point is that there are two contents at stake – the skeptical and the "true" points of view inherent in Real Ground. One relation needs outside will to hold it together. The other is indifferent to this outside will, because it can hold *itself* together. The two things are separate, but they are simultaneously the *same* thing. Both things "stand in the identical ground-relation of form." (468) They are the one and the same whole content. They are distinguished only in this way. One relation is immediate. The other relation is posited – *i.e.*, made up.

But which relation predominates? Speculative Reason admits that it cannot tell. Undecidability *is* the shared content of the two things. Hegel states that the relationships – skeptical and apodeictic[41] – are distinguished "only *in respect of form*." (468) This can be taken in a double way. The difference between skeptic and apodeictic theories of Ground is formal only – not essential. And second, since the very job of Form is to erase itself in favor of Essence, the two somethings likewise erase themselves and withdraw into the Complete Ground.

Hegel further suggests that the two somethings can fairly be characterized as Ground and Grounded in and of themselves. Of course, Speculative Reason cannot tell which is which, but Hegel suggests that the *real* (apodeictic) thing is Ground. "One of the two determinations of the two somethings is therefore determined as being, not merely common to them as in an external comparison, but as being their identical substrate and the foundation of their relation." (468) This is the *essential* determination.

An essential relation inherently refers to a non-essential relation. The essential relation is therefore Ground, and the unessential relation is Grounded. The essential and inessential relations are therefore essentially related to each other. Inessentiality is thus mediated by essentiality. Hegel puts it this way:

---

[40] BURBIDGE, REAL PROCESS, *supra* note 28, at 177 (Real Ground "requires a middle term [*i.e.*, external will] to introduce what is novel").

[41] *I.e.*, certain and true.

> [I]n one something, the determination *B* is implicitly connected with determination *A*; therefore, in the second something to which only the one determination *A* immediately belongs, *B* is also linked with *A*. In the second something, not only is this second determination [*B-A*] a mediated one, but the fact that its immediate determination is ground is also mediated, namely, by the original connexion with *B* in this first something. This connexion is thus the ground of ground *A*, and the *whole* ground-relation is, in the second something, a posited or grounded. (468-9)

In the above syllogism, the first something contains *B* – the apodeictic relation of Ground and Grounded. The second something contains *A*, the skeptical relation. If *B* (Essence) exists, then *A* (the inessential) exists (because essence is always other to not-essence). *B* and *A* are therefore linked in the second, skeptical thing. *A* asserts that only external will connects the two somethings – external will thought to be the Ground of things. But *connection* with *A* is the true Ground. External will is therefore merely the Grounded. The second something is posited and therefore sublated by the first something. Real Ground, "the *self-external reflection* of ground," (469) is defeated, and, in Complete Ground, self-identity is restored.

On the law of sublation, this self-identity includes externality or Real Ground. Hence, Complete Ground is both self-sublating as well as self-positing. "[T]he ground relation mediates itself with itself *through its negation*." (469) Complete Ground is the very act of repelling self from self and so is in fact mediated by its other which is also itself. This next stage Hegel calls "conditioning mediation." (469)

C. Condition

(a) The Relatively Unconditioned

Complete Ground contained both the true and the externally imposed relationship. Hence, Complete Ground was the unity of the essential and the inessential. It leads directly to Hegel's theory of the Thing. A Thing, for Hegel, is a negative unity that really *is*, through the concatenation of all its appearances – here called Conditions.[42] The

---

[42] This Thing is "the thing before the development of the properties and features that, so to speak, define the thing in question or that constitute its essence. It is the state where these properties and features exist potentially but not yet actually. It is the internal structure that grounds the properties and features of the particular thing." JUSTUS HARTNACK, AN INTRODUCTION TO HEGEL'S LOGIC 58 (Lars Aagaard-Mogensen trans., 1998). Hegel would not, however, say that the properties of a thing constitute its essence. Rather, essence is simply not the being – not the properties – of the thing.

German verb "to condition" (*bedingen*) is portentous: it means to "be-thingify." And that is precisely what happens at this stage of the Logic: Conditions bring forth the Thing. Yet the Thing equally brings forth its Conditions. The thing is a *chiasmic exchange of properties* between internal Thing and external Conditions.[43]

John Burbidge describes succinctly the transition from Complete Ground to Condition:

> Earlier we drew a distinction between a formal ground, with the same content in both ground and grounded, and a real ground, with a difference in content. The latter requires a middle term to introduce what is novel. When the logic explores this relationship in detail, the middle term becomes as much a ground of what ultimately emerges as the original real ground. On their own, neither of them can ground; only in combination do they do so. Then, they are no longer *grounds*, but *conditions*.[44]

What Burbidge implies is that the middle term of Complete Ground is the sophistic external reflection that can ground a Form of a thing in its Essence. External reflection is where the outward Forms reside. External reflection *is* the Conditions that make up the thing. Yet external reflection cannot ground the thing alone, It requires an outside thing just as much as the thing requires the external reflection in which the Conditions are reflected.

The Conditions constitute and therefore are distinguishable from the thing. But, paradoxically, *they are themselves equally things*. Because this is so a bad infinity arises. With each Condition, "a fresh condition is asked for, and thus the usual *infinite progress* from condition to condition is introduced." (474) Why, Hegel asks, does a condition prompt us to ask for a fresh condition? "Because it is some finite determinate being or other." (474) That is to say, it cannot succeed as a complete determining; there must be some other Condition that makes it determinate.

The Thing is no-Thing without its outward Conditions. Yet the Thing is resilient. The Thing remains a Thing even if it loses one or more of its indifferent Conditions.[45] (Or if it loses too many of its conditions, it undergoes "qualitative change," and becomes a different thing from what it was.)[46]

---

[43] On chiasmic exchange, see *supra* at 46-7.

[44] BURBIDGE, REAL PROCESS, *supra* note 28, at 177.

[45] TAYLOR, *supra* note 7, at 269-70.

[46] Quantitative and qualitative change are the theme of Hegel's theory of Measure. *Supra* at 198.

Complete Ground was the statement, "I'm not sure I'm Ground." This modest act of self-sublation had a double content. It was either Relative or Absolute Ground. But Relative Ground posited Absolute Ground by its nature. In Figure 32(b), Relative Ground [3] withdrew into (and therefore posited and presupposed) Absolute Ground [1]. [3] was the moment of immediacy and relativity, and [1, 2] is what it is related to. Ground therefore "relates itself [3] to itself [1, 2] as to a sublated moment, to an immediate by which it is itself mediated." (470) This mediation is no external reflection. It is "the native act of the ground itself." (470) The ground-relation (by which Hegel means the "pre-Thing") is therefore "*self-external reflection*." (469)

In Figure 32(c), the relation between Relative [4, 6] and Absolute Ground [4, 5] contains a moment of immediacy [7] separate and apart from what it mediates – [4, 5, 6]. The Understanding sees this and names it Condition, which stands over against Ground. Conditions, on the one hand, posit that they are *not* the thing; the *other* (Ground) is the thing.[47] Conditions are therefore distinguishable *from* the thing. Hegel calls this the Relatively Unconditioned.

Condition, Hegel says, is "an immediate manifold something." (470) To the extent it is immediate, it is without a Ground. This immediacy is contradictory. It "ought to be, as condition, not for itself, but for something else." (470) But this other is not Ground to the Condition alone but is Ground "in some other respect." (470) By this last turn of phrase, Hegel hints that a thing – as negative unity of its conditions – is not Ground to *one* Condition but to many. The many conditions are the "other respect" to which Hegel refers.

Though immediate, Condition [1] nevertheless presupposes and posits Ground. When Condition is for other, it is for itself, since the very job of Condition is to be *for* the Ground. In other words, Condition is by its nature *for other*, but if we isolate it, Condition is *not* for other. Its propensity to sublate itself is itself sublated, when Condition is isolated as an immediacy. "[A] *something is indifferent to its being a condition*," Hegel writes. (470)[48]

---

[47] This accords with Burbidge's suggestion that the Conditions are external reflection itself. *Supra* at 329.

[48] *See* BURBIDGE, REAL PROCESS, *supra* note 28, at 178 ("condition on its own is not a condition at all, but only one existing among many. There is nothing inherent that points to any particular combination of conditions within a grounding relation. The synthesis that transforms it from a being to a condition has to be introduced from the outside.").

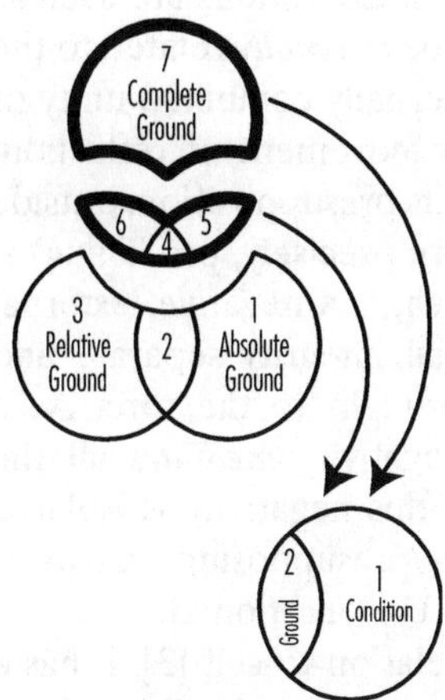

Figure 33(a)
The Relatively Unconditioned

Condition, then, has withdrawn into identity with itself and is consequently the Content of the Ground. We know this because Content *is* the withdrawal of Form to a place outside it-self. So Condition is not the mere "indifferent unity" (470) that Matter was in Figure 31(b). Rather, it inherently refers to its Ground (*i.e.*, to the Thing). By now Condition is more advanced than Form. Unlike Form, Condition has a self-subsistence. The externality introduced in Real and Complete Ground implies that Condition (*i.e.*, appearance of the Thing) has self-identity and independence from the essential thing. In short, Condition is *itself* a thing – *i.e.*, Ground. As such, Condition is only *implicitly* the content of the thing. Condition "constitutes *material* for the ground." (470)

(b) The Absolutely Unconditioned

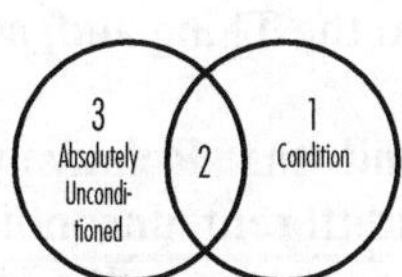

Figure 33(b)
The Absolutely Unconditioned

Condition ought to be for another. That is what Condition *is* in and for itself. But Condition, like a bad soldier, is in part indifferent to this relation. As such, it is the Absolutely Unconditioned.[49]

Dialectical Reason sees that a thing is not what it is because of its Conditions. Condition is not the Ground of a Thing. "Condition is the moment of unconditioned immediacy for the ground." (471) As [3], Condition is diverse from the Thing – the Relatively Unconditioned [*unbedingt*]. Notice that Condition, as Absolutely Unconditioned, is now the Form that endures – *on the side of Being*.

Remembering that Conditions are themselves *Things*, there is now an independence of the Thing from its conditions: "Something has, apart

[49] In the *Phenomenology*, "*unconditioned absolute universality*" is the moment at which mere perception gives way to the Understanding, which sees past the appearance of objects and into the laws by which the objects function. G.W.F. HEGEL, PHENOMENOLOGY OF SPIRIT ¶ 129 (A.V. Miller trans. 1977).

from its condition, also a ground." (471) When Conditions are seen as separate from the Thing, the Thing can only be *externally* related to the Conditions. The Thing is accordingly an externally combined unity of Conditions. The Thing displays "the empty movement of reflection, because reflection has the immediacy that is its presupposition, outside it." (471) In other words, the Thing (or, more precisely, pre-Thing) is a combination of its Conditions, and, as such, is a negative, external combination. Yet the Thing has an essential integrity separate and apart from its Conditions, which is now brought to the fore. As a negative unity, it is self-subsistent. This negativity *mediates* all the Conditions that make up the Thing. When this negativity is isolated from the Conditions, and when its positing/presupposing activity is suppressed or sublated, it is the Absolutely Unconditioned.

To the extent a Thing is a self-subsistent relation-to-self [3], it has a content peculiar to itself, compared to the content of its Conditions. The Thing announced, "I am not the Conditions. Rather, I am essentially formed." The Conditions are only the immediate material of the Thing. The relation of the material [1] is supposedly external to Ground/Absolutely Unconditioned [3]. Yet, in spite of this conceit, the Conditions are really the in-itself [2] of Ground. A Condition is a mixture of self-subsistent content with no relation to the Thing and, as its material, is meant to become a moment of it.

The two sides of the whole are Condition and the Relatively Unconditioned. At one moment the two sides are indifferent, unconditioned, and externally conjoined. But the two sides are also mediated. Condition [2] is the in-itself of Relatively Unconditioned [3]. But, for now, this is sublated. This in-itself is only a positedness – inessential to the moment portrayed in [3] of Figure 33(b). The "immediate determinate being [3] is indifferent to the fact that it is Condition" [2]. (471)

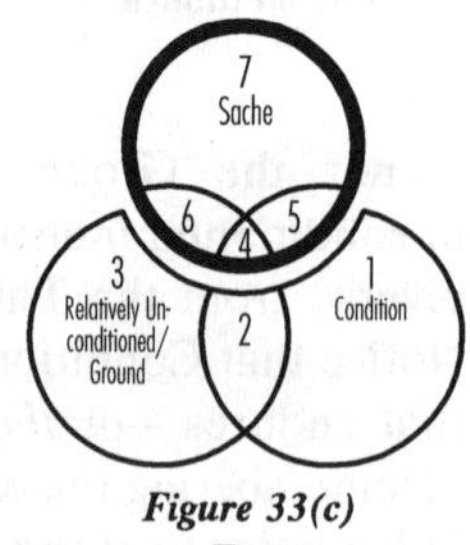

Figure 33(c)
Fact

In Figure 33(b), each of the two sides was Absolutely Unconditioned. That is, each side announced that it is not Condition. Though denying it, each side reflected itself into the other. There are now two Things before us. There is the Thing that is the negative unity of all its Conditions [3]. This is now unconditioned and immediate. In contrast, there are the Conditions of the Thing, each one of which is a *Thing* that is immediate and distinguishable from the Thing itself. These moments of immediacy and independence are what Hegel calls "the *truly unconditioned, the fact in its own self*" (474) Fact (*Sache*) is sometimes translated as the "Heart of the Matter"[50] – the true Thing.

Fact has two moments: (a) positedness and (b) the in-itself. According to its posited side, Fact is material, a "moment of the ground." (472) The posited side represents Condition [4, 5, 6]. The in-itself [7] represents Ground, "its simple reflection into itself." (472) In the Absolutely Unconditioned [7], the extremes of Figure 33(c) are external. Ground-relation is therefore sublated; the Thing exists as an immediacy [7].

From the perspective of [7], Fact has seemingly adopted the primitive position of Being, and so Hegel drops back to compare Determinate Being to Fact. The function of Determinate Being was only this: to sublate itself in its immediacy and fall to the ground. In making itself negative and hence correlative, Being became a positedness – "an identity which, through negation of itself, is the immediate." (472) The forms of positedness and self-identity, which Essence has borne all along, were therefore implicit in Determinate Being. Indeed, this structure of "othering" ("I am not *that*") and simultaneous self-identity is Reflection itself. Hence, Hegel concludes, Being is what it is through negation of itself. It only *is* – it only fulfills its destiny – through Ground. And Ground has shown itself to be self-erasure *tout court*.

Because of this history, one can't say that Condition is *just* mutual indifference and external combination into the Thing. These features of Determinate Being have been sublated. Condition is therefore "posited as that which it essentially is, namely, as moment, hence as moment of another." (472)[51] Condition is the whole form of the Thing. Without Condition, the Thing is no-Thing. Outward Condition is the presupposed in-itself of the Thing. Yet Condition is by definition *not the Thing*. Condition must therefore "repel itself from itself, in such a manner that it both falls to the ground and is ground." (473)[52] The Ground of the Thing makes itself into a positedness and is also a Grounded – all at the same time. What is present is the "*one* whole of

---

[50] BURBIDGE, LOGIC, *supra* note 18, at 100, 252 n.7.

[51] Heretofore Hegel has not emphasized that momentness is always correlative. It should be apparent, however, that, if we say any given stage of the Logic is a moment, then we are obviously implying that there are *other* moments as well.

[52] In this pun, according to Charles Taylor, "Hegel refers both to the demise of all finite things, and their necessary reference to an underlying ground, a necessity which deploys them." TAYLOR, *supra* note 7, at 262.

form, but equally only *one* whole of content." (473)

The Things that a Thing posits are its Conditions, which Hegel calls the "immediate determinate being" (473) of the Thing. Yet Condition is obviously not mere Determinate Being. It is "only condition through the presupposing reflection of the ground." (473) Yet the Thing is equally indifferent to Condition, which signals that the Thing has Self-Subsistence, even if it were to lose a few of its posited Conditions.

To summarize, Fact has two sides – Condition and Ground. The two sides erase themselves and transport themselves into their other. Thus, the Conditions of a Thing are themselves Things. As such, they are reflections; they (1) posit themselves as sublated, (2) relate themselves to what they negate, and (3) reciprocally presuppose one another. Reflection is the common content of both Condition and Ground; in this movement they are united.

Each side of the Fact – Condition and Ground – is "*the fact in its own self*." (474) Yet these two sides *presuppose* the totality of the Absolutely Unconditioned. Fact – the Thing, as negative unity of all Conditions – seems to arise from its Condition and from its Ground. These two sides have shown that they share an identity. When this identity is brought to the fore, the *relation* of Condition and Ground has vanished. These are reduced to an Illusory Being. The Fact, in its movement of positing and presupposing, is the movement in which this Illusory Being sublates itself. It is the Fact's own act to condition itself – and to put forth a material existence [4, 5, 6] – and, simultaneously, to oppose itself [7] to its Conditions.

(c) Emergence of the Fact [Sache] into Existence

In this final section of Reflection, Hegel introduces his concept of Existence. Existence is the state of a Thing over time. "*When all the conditions of a fact are present*, it enters into Existence." (477)

Fact is Ground that is identical with (yet different from) its Condition. As Ground, the Fact "relates itself negatively to itself, makes itself into a positedness." (475) That is, Ground announces that it is *not* Condition, thereby proving that it *is* Condition. Hence, Ground is a positedness, made up of Ground and Condition.

Each side of the positedness – Condition and Ground – is a complete, immediate identity. In this immediacy, Ground sublates itself. This is the side of the Conditions, which are "the *totality* of the determinations of the fact – the fact itself, but cast out into the externality of being." (475) In the Conditions, the sphere of Being is restored. The Thing comes into Existence. To the essential Thing [7], Condition [4, 5, 6] is "the *sphere of being itself.*" (475) "[T]he truth of determinate being is to be condition; its immediacy *is*, solely through the reflection of the ground-relation [7] which posits itself as sublated" (476) – into [4, 5, 6].

It would be a mistake, however, to view Condition as passive material spun off by the Thing itself, in order that the Thing (or, as Hegel now calls it, ground-relation) may exist. Condition makes *itself* a moment of the other through its own act. Its being-for-other is its being-for-self. The Conditions, then, are "the whole content of the fact, because they [4, 5, 6] are the unconditioned [7] in the form of formless being." (475) Yet Conditions have another shape. They appear "as a multiplicity without unity, mixed with non-essentials." (475) Thus, the Thing is *many* Conditions, some of which are unessential. Conditions are manifold: "the form, as a determinateness of being, goes on to multiply itself and thus appears as a manifold content distinct from and indifferent to the determination of reflection." (475)

The side of Ground other than the Conditions is the "ground-relation as such" – the Thing as negative unity of all the Conditions [7]. This is "determined as form over against the immediacy of the conditions and the content." (476) How is it that the Thing is Form, when the appearance of the Thing is in its Conditions? Because Form is *appearance* and Conditions are the *real* content of the Thing. This remark vindicates the view that, with Hegel, it is appearances all the way down. [7] *must* appear in the guise of [4, 5, 6].

This Form of the Thing "possesses within itself the unity of its form with itself, or its *content.*" (476) That is, the Form of the Thing has the constitution of Reflection. It is what it is by its own act (of self-sublation). And this is its Content – to assign its content to the Conditions. In this assignation, the Form of the Thing "reduces [the Conditions] to be a moment, just as, conversely, as essenceless form it gives itself the immediacy of a subsistence in this self-identity." (476) In this act, the Conditions – immediate in themselves – are *related* to the Thing and actually become what Conditions are supposed to be: conditioned.

In announcing that content is in the Conditions, the Form of the Thing is *itself* "the unconditioned fact." (476) Two things follow from this moment of mediated immediacy. First, the immediate Form sublates its own positing (since positing implies otherness). This is "the *vanishing of the illusion of mediation.*" (476) Second, positing is sublated and yet successful. The Form of the Thing *becomes* its content – the Conditions. Of this becoming, Hegel writes: "The process by which the fact is posited is accordingly an emergence, the simple entry of the fact *into Existence*, the pure movement of the fact to itself." (476-7)

Hegel now defines what he means by Existence – a state far in advance of primitive Being: "*When all the conditions of a fact are present*, it enters into Existence." (477) Existence, then, is about *presence*, or about immediacy. In Existence, the immediate Being of the Thing is restored in more adequate Form.

Hegel emphasizes: "The fact *is, before it exists*." (477)[53] It should be clear what this means. *Fact* (*Sache*, "the heart of the matter," or the thing) is the negative unity of all the Conditions. It posits the Conditions and therefore precedes them. Yet *until* it posits its Conditions, it does not *exist*.

In its Conditions, the Thing "has given itself the form of external groundless being because it is, as absolute reflection, negative self-relation." (477) At this moment, it "makes itself into its own presupposition." (477) For a moment, the Thing seems to be groundless and self-identical. It just *is*. (And, at this moment, we have the unreflective metaphysics by which most people live their lives.) At this moment, "this scattered multiplicity [*i.e.*, the multitude of diverse Conditions] *inwardizes* . . . itself in its own self." (477) That is to say, the Thing *really is* all its Conditions. The Form of the Thing erases itself. "The whole fact [is] present in its conditions . . . for *all* of them constitute the reflection." (477) When the Conditions inwardize, they *fall to the ground*. The Conditions, then, posit the Ground, just as much as the Ground (*i.e.*, the Form of the Thing) posits the Conditions. As a group, the Conditions sublate themselves and announce that the Being is in a single, negative unity. Ground likewise sublates itself and announces there is nothing *but* the Conditions. "[A]ccordingly, this emergence is the tautological movement of the fact to itself, and its mediation by conditions and ground is the vanishing of both. The emergence into Existence is therefore immediate in such a manner that

---

[53] Marcuse calls this "Hegel's famous proposition." MARCUSE, REASON, *supra* note 5, at 151. He interprets "the fact *is, before it exists*" in aid of his leftwing politics. All facts are conditions "Within the constellation of existing data. The existing state of affairs is a mere condition for another constellation of facts, which bring to fruition the inherent potentialities of the given." *Id.* at 151-2. While it is generally true that Hegel emphasizes the finitude of all states of affairs, it is not clear that Marcuse is correct in attributing this meaning to Hegel's "famous" proposition that a fact *is* before it exists. Rather, the point is better interpreted as a restatement of Hegel's basic theme that there is no inaccessible thing-in-itself. There are only phenomena all the way down.

it is mediated only by the vanishing of mediation." (477) Fact has now emerged from the Ground. But Ground does not remain behind as a mere substrate. It comes along into Existence (and hence vanishes as such). Ground is sublated – erased *and* preserved. "Through its *union* with the conditions, ground receives an external immediacy and the moment of being." (477) But this union is not externally imposed on it. The union is immanently produced.

To be sure, externality of late has played a major role in the Thing. But Speculative Reason has turned the tables on the external element present in the Absolutely Unconditioned. In the Absolutely Unconditioned, Condition and Ground could not tell which was which. Seemingly, it needed an outside determination to settle the matter. Now Speculative Reason says, "That's exactly the point. There *is* no meaningful distinction between Conditions and Ground. They are the same *Thing*." As Hegel summarizes the matter, the Thing (or *Fact*) "is not only the *unconditioned* but also the *groundless*, and it emerges from ground only in so far as ground has *fallen to the ground* and ceased to be ground: it emerges from the groundless, that is, from its own essential negativity, or pure form." (478) The self-identical Thing now *exists*.

Conclusion

In the three chapters on Reflection, we travelled from the simple idea of the Measureless to the realm of the Thing – Existence. The theme at every step along the way has been self-erasure. The very self-subsistence of Essence has been the inability to self-subsist.

Ground is Reflection sublated. Reflection may have sublated itself in the end, but the result is not nothing. If it were, knowledge of Essence would be separate from the result. The emerging Thing would not be a spontaneous emergence, an act starting only from itself. Instead, it would be an essentialist Thing that merely appears. That is to say, there would be a thing-in-itself beyond appearance, and also the appearance. Hegel's Copernican turn, however, is to redefine Ground as the act of self-erasure. The Thing-in-itself (Ground) erases itself. Only by erasing themselves do Things-in-themselves come into existence.

We have arrived at the world of discrete Things, but as the next Part shows, self-erasure is still the theme. "Things" are finite. They must pass away. When they do, we will have reached the realm of Actuality and self-consciousness.

PART V
APPEARANCE

13
Existence

Does God exist? Usually this question means to ask whether God exists as an immediate being beyond thought. For Kant the question was undecidable. For the empiricists, the matter is unprovable.

Hegel, "the Christian philosopher par excellence,"[1] rescues the inquiry by shifting the attention from the subject "God" to the predicate "existence." The problem in the question is not on the side of *God*. It is entirely in the concept of *Existence* – a state quite inadequate to God.

Existence is Hegel's word for advanced Being – "the immediacy of being to which essence has restored itself again." (499)[2] Existence, the realm of *Things*, is still a deficient realm. Things are finite. On their own logic, they are doomed to pass away. For this very reason, God is no mere *Thing*:

> It is the *definition of finite things* that in them the Notion is different from being, that Notion and reality, soul and body, are separable and hence that they are perishable and mortal . . . . The genuine criticism of . . . reason is just this: to make intellect aware of this difference [between Notion and Existence] and to prevent it from applying to God the determinations and relationships of the finite." (90)

Existence, in Hegel's system, arises autochthonously from Ground.

---

[1] ERROL E. HARRIS, THE SPIRIT OF HEGEL 223 (1993).

[2] "For being which is the outcome of *mediation* we shall reserve the term: *Existence*." (93)

Ground is strikingly analyzed by Hegel. It represents the idea that Form disappears. This active (f)act is the very *content* of Form. Ground represents this "deeper" content. It is the nature of Ground to erase itself. It is the "proto-thing" – a *vanishing mediator* of Things. When Ground self-erases, the Thing *just is*. It appears to be unproblematic and *self-identical* – an illusion that is necessary *and* inadequate to the nature of Things.

Although a vanishing mediator, Ground equally stands for the proposition that a Thing is both dependent on yet distinguishable from its external Conditions. Hegel calls this contradictory state *der Sache* – the heart of the matter of Things. *Der Sache* is "the immediacy which has proceeded from ground, but form is not as yet posited in it." (529) Having as yet no form, it remains for the Thing to *appear*.[3] When it does, it will be both independent from, yet dependent on, context. *Conditions* determine a Thing. Yet each Condition is likewise a "Thing," so that any one Thing is really a network of Things – a metonym.[4]

Existence comprises the first step in Hegel's overall theory of Appearance. In Existence, a thing has "an element of self-subsistence." (479)[5] The Thing at first is taken as self-grounded. But the immediate Thing "sublates itself and the Thing makes itself into positedness." (479) By "positedness," Hegel means that the Thing is presupposed by something else – by the network of Things, by the world of Appearance, which stands over against the "world that is reflected into itself, the *world of essence*." (479-80) "What appears . . . points to something *that* appears."[6] The worlds of Essence and Appearance stand in an Essential Relation. Still an imperfect union, this relation will piece out its imperfections and become *Actuality*.

We start, then, with the existent Thing, wherein all its Conditions are united with the Ground in an immediacy. The proposition of Ground has previously been: "whatever *is* has a ground." (481) That is to say,

---

3 Existence, as Clark Butler points out, is therefore "phenomenalistic." CLARK BUTLER, HEGEL'S LOGIC: BETWEEN DIALECTIC AND HISTORY 175 (1996).

4 *See* EL § 124 ("The existent therefore includes relativity and has . . . its multiple interconnections with other existents: it is reflected on itself as its ground. The existent is, when so described, a *Thing*").

5 In medieval usage, existence stood for duration over time and an objectivity outside of our minds to the thing. 1 HARRY AUSTRYN WOLFSON, THE PHILOSOPHY OF SPINOZA: UNFOLDING THE LATENT PROCESSES OF HIS REASONING 349, 354 (1934).

6 HERBERT MARCUSE, HEGEL'S ONTOLOGY AND THE THEORY OF HISTORICITY 104 (Seyla Benhabib trans. 1987).

everything is mediated. The proposition of Existence is twofold: whatever exists has (1) a ground and is conditioned, and equally has (2) no ground and is unconditioned. Ground is therefore a vanishing mediator that has sublated itself when the Thing emerges into Existence. The Thing seems to exist on its own – without a Ground. But this moment of self-evidence is just that – a moment. On its own Logic, the Thing must dissolve.

Returning to Anselm's question, "Does God exist?", for those wedded to the logic of self-identical Thinghood, the answer to this question can only be "problematic." In Kantian terms, God's existence is only a "permitted conclusion."[7] Kant famously divides the universe into phenomena and noumena. Knowledge is limited to matters empirical – to phenomenal Things. Concepts like God, free will, and things-in-themselves are noumenal. Of these we can know nothing. We can only *believe* in them. Yet belief is *not knowledge*. Indeed Kant was proud to have destroyed true knowledge in order to make room for faith.[8]

Kant's victory was Pyrrhic, confessing and even making a virtue of the ignorance of God. As Hegel puts it, "Knowing is supposed to have reached this conclusion, that it knows *nothing*." (482) Yet, given that Kant's allegiance to the dogma of ungrounded self-identity of the thing-in-itself – the thing *not* dependent on context – there was no other choice for him but to renounce knowledge. If noumenal "things" cannot be known, then the only possible result is atheism or dogmatism – each equally blind and each covertly the same. Each can be asserted only at the level of *belief*.

The *SL* is Hegel's ontological proof of God. By no means can this be accomplished at the level of Existence. Existence is the realm of finite Things, and God is no mere Thing. The proof of God belongs to the later stage of notional Objectivity. There a *necessary Being* invests itself in its predicate, so that there is a unity of Notion and Existence. This *mediation* of Notion and Existence is the proof of God. God can be known only through this (f)act. For this reason, "man was early instructed to recognize God in his *works*." (706) In Hegel's view, "conceptual activity (*der Begreifen*) is the most authentic being."[9]

---

7 IMMANUEL KANT, CRITIQUE OF PRACTICAL REASON 148 (T.K. Abbott trans., 1996).

8 IMMANUEL KANT CRITIQUE OF PURE REASON Bxxx (Paul Guyer & Allen W. Wood trans., 1990) ("I had therefore to remove *knowledge*, in order to make room for *belief*").

9 MARCUSE, ONTOLOGY, *supra* note 6, at 111.

Existence – the realm of finite *Things* – is (for Hegel *and* Kant) a *subjective* realm. For Kant, existence is entry of a self-identical thing "into the context of the totality of experience, that is, into the determination of an *otherness* and into relation to an *other*." (481) Something, as existent, is mediated by an other, and existence in general is on the side of its mediation. In different terms, a thing exists when it is *thought* about. Yet the thing that enters into existence is taken as self-related, with no mediation. Opposition is left out of the Kantian thing and invested into the subjectivity of the thinker.

On this definition, it is automatically apparent why the question, "Does God exist?", is unsatisfactory. On Hegel's definition, "Does God exist?" is the equivalent of asking "Is God a *thought*?". The very *posing* of this question shows that God *is* a thought. The question "Does God exist?" therefore answers itself in the very posing of it. Yet it is a mediocre question. Unicorns exist, on this definition. *Everything* exists, if we only think of it.[10] What we want to know, however, is the materiality of God – the place of God that is beyond mere finite, subjective thought.

Yet Existence plays an important *indirect* role in Hegel's notional proof. The question "Does God exist?" bids us to identify the *ground* of God – proof of its existence. The very question *limits* God to the status of a *grounded* – a *caused* thing that is not self-determined. Hegel's brilliant tactic is to show that *any adduced ground of God* is itself a finite Thing which must waft away. Once God's *ground* has wafted away, only God (yet to be proven) remains standing. Hegel's theory of Existence therefore clears the way for the notional proof of God later in the *SL*.

---

[10] The ability to think things into being is what Kant called an "intellectual intuition." Intellectual intuitions are an attribute to God. According to Charles Taylor:

> Hegel reproaches Kant for not having cleaved to the notion of an intellectual intuition, which he himself invented. This would be an understanding, which unlike ours did not have to depend on external reception, on being affected from outside, for its contents, but created them with its thought. This archetypical intellect Kant attributed to God; it was quite beyond us. But God's intellect is ultimately revealed to us for Hegel, it only lives in our thought. Hence we can participate in an intellectual intuition. God's thought is ours.

CHARLES TAYLOR, HEGEL 301 (1975). An intellectual intuition amounts to "the direct apprehension of things as they are . . . " STANLEY ROSEN, G.W.F. HEGEL: AN INTRODUCTION TO THE SCIENCE OF WISDOM 267 (1974).

Anselm's ontological proof adduces a ground for God's existence. But this does not purport to be an *objective* ground (for then God would be grounded and less than God.) The adduced ground "is merely a *ground for cognition*." (482) Such a *ground* is a finite thing and must vanish. But vanishing *is* God; when adduced grounds vanish, they become *indistinguishable from God*. Self-erasure, Hegel thinks, is a true mediation and hence a true proof that a thing exists. Proof for Hegel is nothing but "*mediated cognition*." (481)

This mediation, Hegel says, is unknown to the ratiocinative (*beweisende*) reflection that asserts the validity of Anselm's proof. By deeming the derived ground of God to be subjective only – a ground of cognition – the ontological proof "removes its mediation from God himself." (482) Anselm failed to see that Ground erases itself and becomes one with the Objective thing it posits.

The ontological proof should have posited the "true relationship" between God and subjective ground. God is *both* itself[11] *and* the subjective ground. The subjective ground is the result of God's self-externalization. God is a true infinite that becomes other (subjective ground) and stays what it is. *This* is what it takes to prove that God exists.

Perhaps thinking of Kant's fourth antinomy,[12] Hegel remarks: "the essence of God, it is said, is the *abyss* [*Abgrund*] for finite reason." (483) Hegel agrees with this, in so far as reason "surrenders its finitude . . . but this abyss, the negative ground, is the *positive* ground of the emergence of simply affirmative being – of essence which is in its own self immediate." (483) The self-erasure of God is therefore the *essential movement*[13] that brings God into Existence. In Existence, God-as-abyss is not left behind; the Ground is in *immediate union* with the existent thing. In this immediacy, mediation has vanished. Relevant

---

[11] GIACOMO RINALDI, A HISTORY AND INTERPRETATION OF THE LOGIC OF HEGEL 247 (1992) ("The *metaphysical* concept of 'God' . . . is devoid, in its Hegelian interpretation, of any . . . 'anthropomorphic' feature whatsoever, and rather coincides with . . . the *omnitudo realitatum*.")

[12] According to this antinomy, "To the world there belongs an absolutely necessary being," and "[t]here is no absolutely necessary being existing anywhere either in the world or outside the world as its cause." IMMANUEL KANT, CRITIQUE OF PURE REASON, *supra* note 8, at A452-3/B480-1.

[13] Essentiality should be understood as the propensity of a thought to erase itself. Essentiality signifies that a concept is only an appearance – "only a posited being, not a being in and for itself. This constitutes its essentiality, to have within itself the negativity of reflection, the nature of essence." (499)

here is Hegel's all-important earlier remark: "What is thus found only *comes to be* through being *left behind*." (402)

Here we have a preview of the Absolute Idea at the very end of the *SL*. Absolute Idea constitutes the final erasure of mediation and the institution of a thing – the one and only thing – that really, truly, and purely *is*. The key to the *SL* is that only self-erasure *exists*. Therefore, the self-erasure or self-sacrifice of God is proof that God exists.

Hegel retreats from Golgotha to observe, against Kant, that Existence is not the mere predicate or determination of Essence. In such a case, Essence itself would not "exist." Essence *actually* exists. "Existence is essence's absolute emptying of itself or self-alienation." (483) Essence has not remained behind. It *is* Existence and is not distinct from it. A True Infinite, "Essence has *passed over* into Existence in so far as essence as ground no longer distinguishes itself from itself as the grounded." (483)

Existence, then, "is essentially mediation-with-self." (483) The determinations of the mediation are present in it, "but in such a manner that they are also reflected into themselves and their subsistence is essential and immediate." (483) Existence "is a negative unity and a being-within-self." (484) We have arrived at the *Thing*, "a web of contradictions."[14]

A. The Thing and Its Properties

(a) The Thing-in-Itself and Existence

The previous chapter culminated in the Absolutely Unconditioned [*unbedingt*], "the something that has simply affirmative being." (484) It was "essentially that immediacy which has arisen through the reflection of mediation into itself." (484) The Absolutely Unconditioned was the last stop in Ground, and Ground stands for self-erasure. When the Ground of Things disappears, the result is the self-identical immediate Thing – the favorite of common sense.

The Understanding proposes that the Absolutely Unconditioned is a correlation between the Thing and its Properties. The Thing is essential and negative, leaning to the right side of the diagram. The

---

[14] JEAN HYPPOLITE, GENESIS AND STRUCTURE OF HEGEL'S *PHENOMENOLOGY OF SPIRIT* 102 (Samuel Cherniak & John Heckman trans., 1974). Existence – the realm of the Thing – corresponds with Hegel's discussion of perception in the *Phenomenology*. *See* G.W.F. HEGEL, PHENOMENOLOGY OF SPIRIT ¶ 111-31 (A.V. Miller trans. 1977).

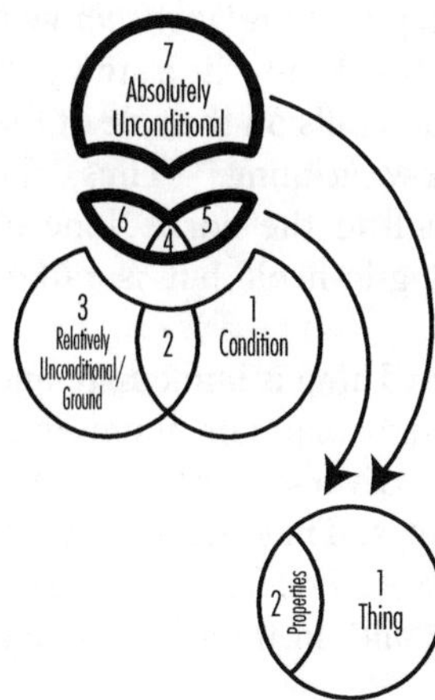

Figure 34(a)
The Thing

Properties are on the left side of "being." The Properties of a Thing represent a Thing's being-for-other.

Hegel associates Properties with a Thing's outward Existence – contrary to Kant, who defeated Anselm by asserting that existence is not an independent predicate of an object.[15] The difference between Existence and the Thing is that Existence "has within itself the moment of mediation." (484) So Existence [3] is where the thinker has the thought of the Thing. The Thing [1] is immediate. As immediate, it is the Thing-in-itself, "nothing else but the empty abstraction from all determinateness." (489)

Dialectical Reason holds that the difference between the Thing and its Existence "falls apart into *indifferent determinations*." (484) On the one side is the Thing-in-itself [1] as *"non-reflected immediacy."* (484) Contrary to Kant, who would say that the Thing-in-itself *causes* phenomena,[16] Hegel suggests that the matter is quite the other way around. The Thing-in-itself is the "simple reflectedness"(485) of Existence, which is to say that Existence *posits the Thing-in-itself*. The Thing-in-itself is not Ground to Existence, as Kant would have it. The opposite is true. Existence is Ground to the Thing-in-itself. Ground erases itself, so the Thing-in-itself (supposedly the Ground of phenomena) is "sublated mediation and therefore only the *substrate* of the determinate being." (485)

3
Existence
2
1
Thing
-in- Itself

Figure 34(b)
The Thing and Its Existence

Substrate stands for indifference; it stands in contrast to Ground, which is *related* to the Grounded. If the Thing-in-itself is substrate, Reflection – which stands for enduring notionality and "being-in-and-for-self – necessarily "falls *outside* the *thing-in-itself*." (485) The Thing-in-itself "is not supposed to contain within it any specific manifoldness;

---

[15] *Supra* at 39-40.

[16] As to the notion that the thing-in-itself causes sensations, Hegel points out that this implies sensation is beyond reason, and the thing-in-itself is an "extraneous impulse." PHENOMENOLOGY, *supra* note 14, ¶ 238.

and it therefore only obtains this when *brought into relationship with external reflection*." (485) That is to say, for Kant, if a thing is distinguished from another thing, the distinction falls on the side of the subject. Of the thing-in-itself, we can know nothing.[17] Thus, the Thing-in-itself has color only to the eye, smell to the nose. None of these properties is determined by the Thing-in-itself but is rather determined by an other.

Reflection is now external to the Thing. The Thing is immediate and aloof, and so is Existence. The two sides cannot maintain themselves as separate – this was the lesson of Diversity. Diverse things are "self-identical" – radically unrelated to other things. They are *immediate beings*. Immediate beings are wont to fade away. The Thing and Existence being diverse, they sublate themselves, and, in their immediacy, both sides are one and the same Diversity.

There is now a *plurality* of self-erasing Things-in-themselves. Two such things constitute the "extremes of a syllogism whose middle term constitutes their external Existence." (486) Because the Things-in-themselves sublate themselves, they send their being elsewhere – into a middle term toward which they are indifferent. In their indifference, the two Things-in-themselves collapse into one. "[T]here is only *one* thing-in-itself, which in external reflection is related to itself." (487)[18] Hegel calls this unitary Thing-in-itself the Totality of Existence. This collapse of the Things-in-themselves is the very determinateness of the Thing.[19] In other words, because the Thing-in-itself collapses

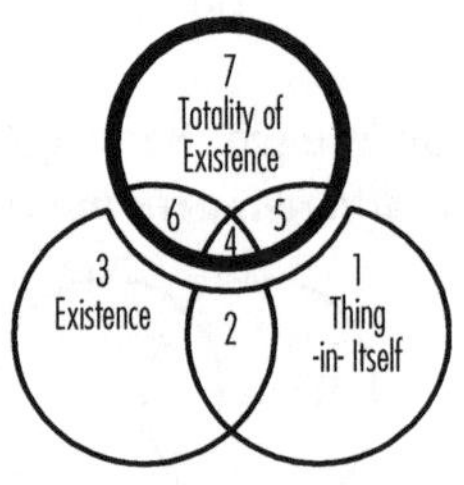

Figure 34(c)
The Totality of Existence

[17] The thing divorced from its existence is the Possible. (484) *See* chapter 16.

[18] In Hegel's penultimate chapter, the True becomes an logical official step. What is True is that Kant's notion of a transcendent thing-in-itself falls apart. *Infra* at 583.

[19] In the *EL*. Hegel complains that a thing "in itself" must become for itself, yet in Kant's usage, the thing-in-itself is inert. EL § 124 Remark. Here we see Hegel's Thing-in-itself does indeed become something by collapsing in on itself. Charles Taylor disagrees that the Thing-in-itself collapses. He holds that "things" might be the "peaceful coexistence of different properties in the thing." TAYLOR, *supra* note 10, 270 (1975); *see also id*. at 271 ("Hegel's claim that there is an unavoidable contradiction in the notion of the thing with properties is no stronger than his thesis that finite things in general are contradictory"). In his remarks, Taylor has not adhered to Hegel's analysis of Diverse things, nor has he escaped the fundamental prejudice that, in spite of everything, things *are* self-identical.

of its own accord, it enters into Existence and is, indeed, nothing *but* Existence. Hegel calls the Thing's determinateness "the *property of the thing*." (487) Though the point is still implicit, there is only *one* real Property of a Thing – self-erasure of its noumenal self and entry into the consciousness of the thinker (*i.e.*, Existence).

(b) Property

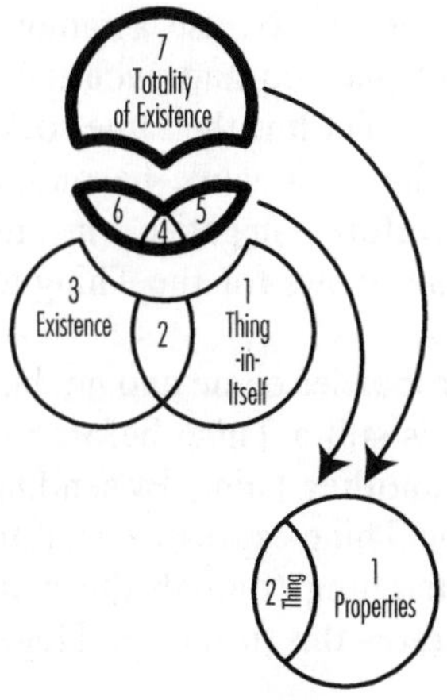

From Figure 34(c), the Understanding has gleaned that the Properties of a Thing are the Totality of its Existence. Property therefore succeeds to the position of negative essentiality. Property is now the "negativity of reflection through which Existence in general is an existent." (487) That is, the Properties announce, "We are *not* the Kantian thing-in-itself," thereby proving that they *are* the Thing-in-itself *tout court*. In other words, Properties are Things.

Figure 35(a)
The Thing and Its Properties

Between Figure 34(a) and Figure 35(a), Properties and Things have switched places. The Understanding is growing wiser. In Figure 34(a) it saw the Thing as a negative unity of positive Properties. Now it thinks there is no-Thing *apart* from its properties. The Thing is on the side of Being by grace of Properties which nevertheless are distinguishable from and therefore are *not* the Thing.

Figure 35(a) is a move of the Understanding, in the distinctive mode of Essence. Accordingly, Figure 35(a) is an immediacy that is both a "sublated mediation" and an "*identity-with-self*." (487) The Thing, as portrayed in the Totality of its Existence, is determinate, yet, in its relation to the other, it does not pass over into otherness; it is therefore free from alteration.

We now know, on the logic of Reflection, that the Properties are as much Thing-in-itself as the Thing-in-itself was. In Figure 35(a), the Properties (each one being a Thing) presuppose the Thing, and by the Properties the Thing appears. The Properties are therefore the determinate relation of one *Thing* to another *Thing*. Property is a mode of relationship. It is "the external reflection and the side of the thing's positedness." (487) That the Properties are implicated in a positedness is clear on the face of Figure 35(a). The externality of the relation signals that the Thing can now be perceived by outside consciousnesses. In short, the Thing now at hand is a sophisticated version of the self-identical thing. Common sense holds that Things project their Properties outward. Properties are reliable indicia of what a Thing is.[20]

Hegel says of this sophisticated self-identical Thing that it is "only a surface with which Existence is exposed to the becoming and alteration of being." (488) In short, the Properties of the thing come and go; they are mere Beings. But the Thing stays what it is.[21] To use a famous philosophical example, a sock is darned and patched and eventually contains no thread of its original manufacture. Yet it is the same sock. Such a sock is a True Infinite – it stays what it is while becoming something different. Thinghood is therefore negative in its constitution,[22] and this very negativity is what allows for the Thing to survive quantitative change in its Properties.

Yet Property is not lost in this. Specific Properties come and go, but Property as such remains, so long as there is still a Thing before us. Property is the power of the Thing to affect another Thing. By sending forth its Properties to the external world, the Thing expresses itself to another Thing – by implication a *conscious* Thing (though the conscious thing is not yet derived). "It demonstrates this property," Hegel

---

[20] Legal scholars have emphasized the relationality of the legal concept of property. Some have taken property's relationality to the extreme of saying that there are no "things" at all but *only* relations between persons. This justifies the conclusion that there is no separate legal doctrine of property, but rather only pure law that mediates between persons. Hegelian legal scholars, however, insist on the vital role of "things" separate and apart from persons as to which persons can have property relations. *See* JEANNE LORRAINE SCHROEDER, THE VESTAL AND THE FASCES: HEGEL, LACAN, PROPERTY, AND THE FEMININE 115-228 (1998).

[21] Hegel notes that the Thing passes from *being* to *having*: "As a term of relation, 'to have' takes the place of 'to be'. True, some[thing] has qualities on its part too: but this transference of 'having' into the sphere of Being is inexact . . . the character as quality is directly one with the some[thing], and the some[thing] ceases to be when it loses its quality. But the thing is reflection-into-self: for it is an identity which is also distinct from the difference, i.e. from its attributes. In many languages 'have' is employed to denote past time. And with reason: for the past is absorbed or suspended being, and the mind is its reflection-into-self; in the mind only it continues to subsist – the mind . . . distinguishing from itself this being in it which has been absorbed or suspended. EL § 125.

[22] The negativity of Constitution was memorialized in Figure 4(a). Constitution appeared on the left side of the page – the side of Being. But it represented the Understanding's proposal about the true nature of the universe – that it is composed by external reflection.

writes, "only under the condition that the other thing has a correspon-ding constitution." (488) In other words, the Thing is an immediate Thing-in-itself and so is the (conscious) Thing it affects. It therefore follows that the affected Thing – the conscious subject – likewise leaves the affecting thing not unaffected. Perception is a compromise between True Infinite Things. "[A]t the same time," Hegel emphasizes, "the property is *peculiar* to the first thing and is [the first thing's] self-identical substrate . . . [I]t is for this reason that this reflected quality is called *property*." (488)

In Property the Thing passes over into externality. Through its Properties the Thing eventually becomes Cause. Cause preserves itself in Effect. For the moment, however, "the thing is so far only the quiescent thing of many properties . . . [I]t is so far only the implicit reflection of its determinations, not yet itself the reflection which posits them." (488) In other words, the Thing is *passive* and its effect upon consciousness is implicit. But soon the Thing will be *active*. Eventually it will become self-consciousness itself. When that occurs, the Thing does indeed assert itself forcefully in the world.

But we run before our horse to market. For now, the Thing-in-itself is no longer merely the positedness of an external reflection. Kant's Thing was "substrate devoid of determinations and lying beyond of its external Existence." (488) Rather, the Thing's Properties are "its own determinations through which the thing enters into relationships in a determinate manner." (488) The thing is *present* (in the Derridean sense) in its Properties.[23] It is "identity-with-self in its positedness," (488) a positedness that is "a self-external reflection." (488) It is reflected out of itself by its Properties but is also reflected into itself and "is in itself only in so far as it is external." (488) At this stage "the whole is ground that in its repelling and determining, in its external immediacy, is self-related ground." (489)

(c) The Reciprocal Action of Things

The Thing-in-itself *exists*. After Figure 34(b), there are a plurality of Things, "distinguished from one another . . . through themselves." (490) Here at last we have the universe as aggregate of discrete Things – a

[23] Jacques Derrida is famous for his critique of "philosophy of presence" – that is, of the assumption of self-identity that excludes negativity (or *différance*, as Derrida calls it). For a description, see David Gray Carlson, *On the Margins of Microeconomics*, in DECONSTRUCTION AND THE POSSIBILITY OF JUSTICE 265 (D. Cornell et al eds. 1992).

state that Charles Taylor and others wrongly assumed to be at issue in chapter 2. Only here in chapter 13 do Things have staying power, through their *negative* (not affirmative) being.

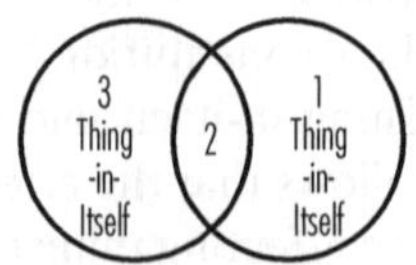

Figure 35(b)
Properties as Reciprocal Action

At this stage, Dialectical Reason asserts that, if a Thing has Properties, each Property is as much a Thing as the Thing was. Accordingly, a Property can only be known by *its* Properties, thereby launching a bad infinity in which every Thing has its Being beyond itself. In effect, the Thing-in-itself is back. Property does not correlate with its Ground in the Thing, as it is supposed to. Rather, two Things-in-themselves[24] face each other in Reciprocal Action through their Properties. Things are what they are because of the Properties, but Properties are also other *things*. Property now stands for the reciprocal relation between things. Reciprocal determination is therefore the middle term of the duelling Things-in-themselves.

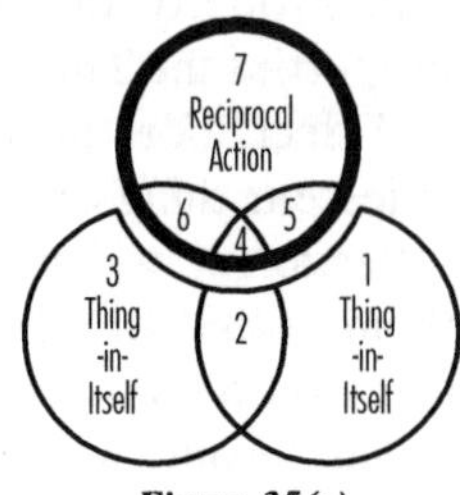

Figure 35(c)
Reciprocal Action of Things

The Things-in-themselves are supposed to remain indifferent to all relation – they are self-identical. Yet Things are entirely determined by their Properties. Apart from Property (now conceived as Reciprocal

[24] Kant thought that all determination fell outside of the thing-in-itself and instead was located in consciousness. To the thing-in-itself Kant opposed reflection. This claim, Hegel suggests, "is directly contradicted by the consciousness of freedom, according to which I know myself rather as the universal and undetermined, and separate off from myself those manifold and necessary determinations, recognizing them as something external for me and belonging only to things." (489) The ego conscious of its freedom represents the "true identity reflected into itself, which the thing-in-itself was supposed to be." (489) *Cf.* SLAVOJ ŽIŽEK, TARRYING WITH THE NEGATIVE: KANT, HEGEL, AND THE CRITIQUE OF IDEOLOGY 14-5 (1993) (protesting that the ego is even *less* than the thing-in-itself, because the thing-in-itself has a positive content, even though we can't perceive it). At this point of the Logic, however, the Thing-in-itself is not yet determined as consciousness or ego. Nevertheless, Hegel says that External Reflection is the thing-in-itself because it is presupposed as existing by the Kantian thing-in-itself. The Thing-in-itself is *not* opposed to, but *is* Reflection, "and determines itself to be a thing with its *own* determinations, a thing endowed with properties." (490) In other words, the Kantian thing-in-itself says, "I am not External Reflection," thereby proving it *is* External Reflection. In this way the *true* thing-in-itself demonstrates the falseness of the *abstract* thing-in-itself.

Action), the Thing is nothing. "Thinghood [*Dingheit*] is thus reduced to the form of indeterminate identity-with-self which has its essentiality only in its property." (490)[25] The Thing isolated from its Properties is merely quantitative – its being is entirely external to it. "There thus results a 'totality' of existing things, among which, each individual is a 'nullity.'"[26] The point, then, is that there *is* no essence beyond the appearance of the Thing. It is Appearance all the way down. Kant's metaphysical Thing-in-itself is a nullity. To the extent we think of it, it is just another phenomenon among phenomena. "[B]ehind the so-called curtain which is supposed to conceal the inner world, there is nothing to be seen unless *we* go behind it ourselves, as much in order that we may see, as that there may be something behind there which can be seen . . ."[27]

In Reciprocal Action, Things have a unity in the concept of Property, by which they are distinguished and related. Property is the *continuity* of one Thing into another. Yet every Property is itself a Thing. Without the Things called Properties, a Thing vanishes. Thinghood is therefore metonymic, as we first learned in Measure.[28] Any Thing is simply the empty space unifying other Things (its Properties). And yet these Properties are the forceful appearance of the Thing in the World.

As the unity of vanishing Things, Property itself is self-subsistent, and so Things have their self-subsistence in the concept of Property. The Thing is "in truth, only that unessential compass which, though a negative unity, is only like the one of something, namely an *immediate* one." (491) Previously, the Kantian Thing-in-itself was *made* into an unessential compass by an External Reflection, as seen in Figure 34(b). Even then, External Reflection supposed that the Thing-in-itself was "vaguely conceived as the essential," (491) that is, somehow not divorced from phenomenon. Now the Thing-in-itself makes *itself* unessential. It sublates itself and enters into its phenomenal Properties. "Hence property is now freed from the indeterminate and impotent

---

25 Thinghood is a phrase borrowed from Spinoza. HYPPOLITE, GENESIS, *supra* note 14, at 105.

26 MARCUSE, *supra* note 6, at 84.

27 PHENOMENOLOGY, *supra* note 14, ¶ 165. *See* TAYLOR, *supra* note 10, at 273-4; *see also* KENNETH R. WESTPHAL, HEGEL'S EPISTEMOLOGICAL REALISM: A STUDY OF THE AIM AND METHOD OF HEGEL'S *Phenomenology of Spirit* 165 (1989) ("If Hegel's arguments in the consciousness section [of the *Phenomenology*] are successful, then the world has been found to be cognitively accessible; there isn't anything more to the world than what it manifests").

28 *Supra* at 225.

connexion which is the one of the thing: it is that which constitutes the thing's *subsistence, a self-subsistent matter*." (491) Now, if there is to be a Thing, it is a Thing *constructed* out of *diverse* Properties. There are only "*various* self-subsistent matters of this kind and *the thing consists of them*." (492)

B. The Constitution of the Thing Out of Matters

In the Reciprocal Action of Things, Thinghood negated itself and became an unessential moment. Properties did the same (since they are Things). Properties in Figure 35(a) are the very means by which all things are different, yet, in Reciprocal Action of Things, shown in Figure 35(c), all difference between Things is entirely erased. If Difference exists, it is supplied externally, not by the Thing.

In the current section, Property, which distinguishes Things, is really the enduring mode by which Things are *continuous* with other Things. A Thing has its Properties, but it is *not* the only Thing with those Properties. Every Property is a *universal*. In its universal guise, particularizing Property is renamed Matters.

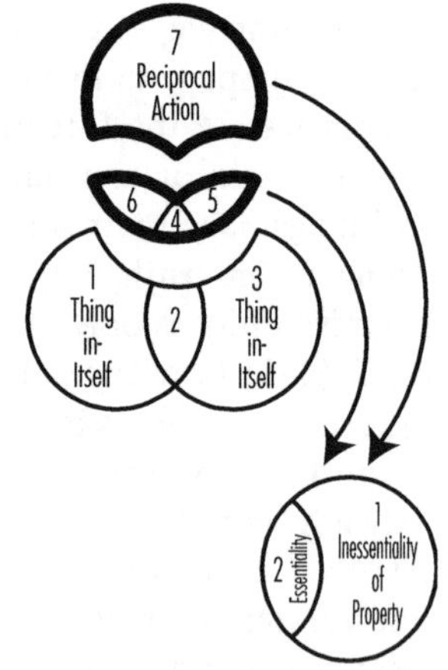

Figure 36(a)
Inessentiality of Property

At first, the Understanding, gazing back at Figure 35(c), proposes that Properties fail to distinguish one Thing from another. Property is therefore "in the element of unessentiality." (493) Property is not what distinguishes Things. External reflection does. What is essential in Things is this external reflection.

Dialectical Reason intervenes to point out that Property was previously shown to be a "unity of externality and essentiality, because it contains reflection-into-self and reflection-into-an-other." (493) This pairing of reflection-into-self and reflection-into-an-other is given the name This Thing and Matters, with reflection-into-self on the negative side of internal essence and reflection-into-other on the side of external Existence.

In Figure 36(a), Properties are reduced to moments. "[T]hat is, they are reflected into their negative unity as into a substrate distinct from them, namely *thinghood.*" (496) Properties defer to the Thing and were no-Thing on its own. Matters, in contrast, are more advanced. They are "self-subsistent *stuff*." (492) A Matter is "reflected into its own unity-with-self." (496) "This Thing" is now liberated from its Matters.

> Property was that by which things were supposed to be distinguished; but now that [Matter] has freed itself from this its negative side [1], of inhering in an other, the thing [1], too, has been freed from its being determined by other things and has returned into itself from the relation to other. (493)

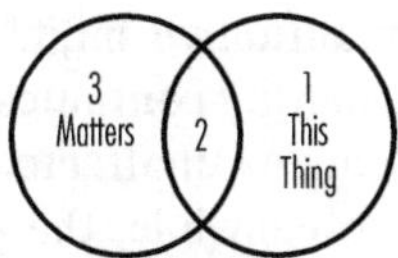

Figure 36(b)
This Thing and Its Matters

Matter is self-subsistent only when the Thing – the owner of the Property – is suppressed. If Matter is before us, the Thing is not. The Thing is "*abstract* identity, the *simply negative* Existence, or Existence *determined* as the *indeterminate*." (493) Matter negates This Thing and "therefore contains the moment of the negative, and its self-subsistence is, as this *negative unity*, the restored *something* of thinghood." (492)

On the law of sublation, Thinghood is negated by *and* preserved in the Matters. So the Matters are as much Thing as no-Thing. As a Thing, it cannot endure. Now that This Thing has once more been separated from its Matters, it is merely the Thing-in-itself again. It has "*become an other to itself*." (493) This Thing "is a self-identical negation only *as against* the positive continuity of the matter." (493)

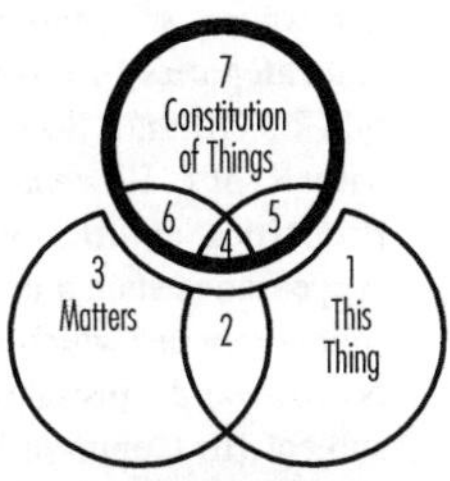

Figure 36(c)
Constitution of the Thing Out of Its Matters

Speculative Reason summarizes Things by saying that they exist only by a kind of differentiation of This Thing and its Matters. "The thing consists of self-subsistent matters which are indifferent to their relation in the thing." (493-4) The relation is seen as "only an unessential combination of them and the difference of one thing from another thing depends on whether and in what amount a number of the particular matters are present in it." (494) Matters now "pass *out of and beyond this* thing, continue themselves into other things, and the fact that they belong to this thing is not a limitation for them." (494) In short, a "Matter" is never unique to a Thing. If This Thing tastes bitter, bitterness *in general* is the property of many other Things as well. Property/Matter, supposed to signal the particularity of the Thing, is itself universal. Particularity, then, depends upon universality[29] (an idea Hegel emphasizes much further on).[30]

The Thing is therefore no limitation for Matters. And, since each Property/Matter is itself a Thing, they do not limit each other. For this reason, a Thing has many Properties. Nevertheless, every Property is a Thing-in-itself. "Therefore in their combination in [the Thing] they are impenetrable for one another, relate themselves in their determinateness only to themselves, and are a mutually indifferent manifoldness of subsistence." (494) Properties "are capable of only a quantitative limit." (494) Such a limit, it will be recalled, is *no* limit; Quantity continues itself into its beyond, while the Quality of the thing remains unaffected.

Meanwhile, the Constitution of the Thing is a "merely quantitative relation" (494) between the Properties. The Thing is cobbled together

---

[29] In the *EL*, the Matters coalesce into one Matter, which stand over against Form. There, Form takes the place of the Constitution of Things. EL § 128. In the *SL*, however, this pairing is placed earlier – in Ground. *See* chapter 12. According to Rinaldi:

> the superior speculative consistency of the deduction carried out . . . in the *Encyclopedia Logic* is undeniable. First, it does seem rather arbitrary and artful to consider (relatively) complex and *ontologically* "concrete" thought-determinations like those of Matter, Form, Content, Condition and the Unconditional as "subcategories of a (relatively) empty and abstract *logical-formal* principle such as that of Ground. Second, Hegel's concept of Appearance is substantially identical with Kant's. Its *content* coincides with the indefinite multiplicity of Things-and-Properties, and thus with Existence itself. Yet it differs from [Existence] in that in Appearance such a content is posited not as *positively* existent, but only as a simple "phenomenon" which is "in itself" merely *negative*, and can *appear* to be something positive and epistemologically valuable only to the consciousness of the "finite" subject (to Common Sense). Finally, Hegel's general conception of the categories of Essence as "determinations of reflections" . . . is that they constitute rather "couples" of (opposite) concepts than isolated thought-determinations. Now, Existence is unquestionably the "natural" immanent opposite of Essence, and therefore it seems quite appropriate to consider the two *Denkbestimmungen* as "moments" of a unique logical totality.

RINALDI, *supra* note 11, at 109-10. These points can be disputed. First, Content *is* the habit of form erasing itself; this is abstract and consistent with the Ground of Things (self-erasure). Second, Existence trafficks in multiple things, but Content is unitary – Form's self-erasure, appropriately treated in Ground. Finally, Existence may be the opposite of Essence, but Ground is correlative and so Form-Content is appropriately treated there. In addition, Form and Content ended up as the same thing, consistent with the speculative nature of Ground.

[30] *Infra* at 451-6.

by outside force and has no integrity of its own. The Thing "*consists* of some quantum or other of a matter, *also* of a quantum of another, and again of others; this connexion of having no connexion alone constitutes the thing." (494)

The Thing is about to dissolve. Externality of the Thing's constitution and its dissolution is the very "truth of what we call things." (39)

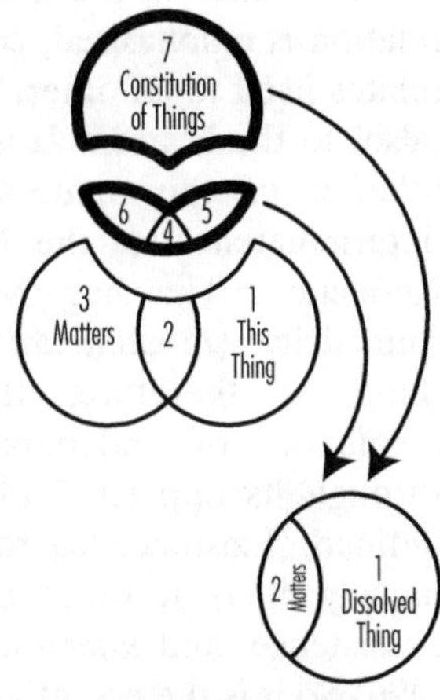

Figure 37(a)
Dissolution of the Thing

C. Dissolution of the Thing

So far, the Thing is "the merely quantitative connexion of free matters." (494) It is purely negative and has its being outside itself. This Thing is whatever external reflection makes of it. It is the mere afterthought or "also" of the Properties.[31] As such it is alterable. If too many of its qualities are taken away, or if too many properties are added, the Thing alters and becomes a different Thing than it was. Such a dissolution is also externally imposed. Meanwhile, "Matters circulate freely out of or into 'this' thing; the thing itself is absolute porosity without measure or form of its own." (494)

The Understanding now proposes that the Thing is unstable and alterable. On this view, the Matters are only self-related. They are unrelated to a Thing because the Thing is Dissolved.

---

[31] The thing as "also" recalls similar remarks in chapter 3 of the *Phenomenology*, where the Thing is both an Also and a One. PHENOMENOLOGY, *supra* note 14, ¶ 114 ("the differentiation of the properties . . . each property negating the others, thus falls outside of this simple medium; and the medium, therefore, is not merely an Also, an indifferent unity, but a *One* as well, a unity which *excludes* an other"); *see* Michael Baur, *Hegel and the Overcoming of the Understanding*, 22 OWL OF MINERVA 141, 142 (1991) ("it is the very nature of perceptual consciousness to be unable to reconcile the exclusive unity of the Thing with the presence in it of several distinct, sensible properties which can inhere in other Things as well. If perceptual consciousness attends to the distinctness of the properties in the Thing, then the Thing's unity itself becomes problematic, sinking into a mere 'Also.' If perceptual consciousness attends to the exclusive unity of the Thing, then such unity apparently excludes also the distinct properties which are supposed to inhere in the Thing.").

Dialectical Reason intervenes to assert that Matters partake of reflection-into-self. They *require* the Thing. Accordingly, the Matters are correlative to the Thing and connected to it after all. When this relation is emphasized, content as such is not reflected into itself. It relates itself to an other. The Thing is no mere "also" to the Matters. It is equally the negative relation of the matters. Because they are determinatenesses, the Matters are negative Reflection. The negative Reflection is the "puncticity" (*Punktualität*)[32] of the thing. "The thing is, therefore, the self-contradictory mediation of independent self-subsistence through its opposite." (495) In the Thing so defined, "Existence has reached its completion, namely it is intrinsic being or *independent* subsistence, and *unessential* Existence *in one*." (496) So it is the essential nature of things that they require outside help to be *things*. An outside will must gather up the Matters and unite them into thinghood; "the truth of Existence is to have its being-in-self in unessentiality." (496) Existence is merely Appearance.[33] Its ground or substrate is "its *own nullity*." (496)

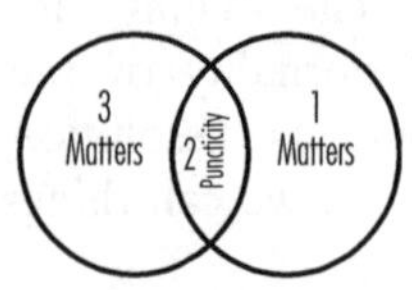

Figure 37(b)
Puncticity

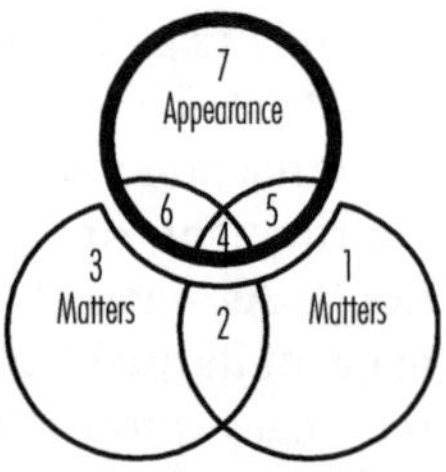

Figure 37(c)
Appearance

In the Dissolution of the Thing and its passage into Appearance, each Matter belonging to the thing had self-subsistence. Yet each Matter interpenetrated the Thing *and each other*, so that the self-subsistence of one Matter is the self-subsistence of *all* the Matters. This was the puncticity (negative unity) of the thing, in which every Matter, as well as the Thing itself, interpenetrates one another.

"[P]ictorial thinking" (497) wants to hold on to perception and have before it self-identical things. But Matter should not be conceived as

---

[32] Puncticity appears in no English dictionary. Presumably the translator thought that "punctuality" would mislead English readers.

[33] In the *Phenomenology*, puncticity or porosity of the Matters yields Force. PHENOMENOLOGY, *supra* note 14, ¶ 136. When the Force of the Thing vanishes into the Force of the Understanding, the Understanding arrives at the idea of a beyond, or Appearance. *Id.* ¶ 143. In the *SL*, however, Force is reserved for Essential Relation, two chapters hence – well after Appearance has made its appearance.

a self-identicality alongside its negation. Rather, in one and the same point lie self-subsistent Matter *and* its negation or porosity.[34]

Hegel brings home the point to the spiritual sphere. The soul is said to have forces or faculties. They interpenetrate the soul.

> Just as man in general is made to consist of soul and body, each of which has an independent being of its own, so too the soul is made to consist of so-called *soul forces* each of which has a self-subsistence of its own, or is an immediate, separate activity with its own peculiar nature. It is imagined that the intellect acts separately in one place and the imagination by itself in another, that intellect, memory, and so on, are each cultivated separately, and for the time being the other forces are left inactive on one side until perhaps, or perhaps not, their turn comes. (498)

Of course, modern science does not hesitate to locate some of these forces in precise segments of the brain. Yet metaphysically, such powers interpenetrate the entire being of a person and serve to identify the person as unique.

---

[34] Hegel thinks that the physical laws which state that gases expand to fill the volume in which it is contained are one-sided views. "They show . . . that for example a certain volume takes up the same amount of steam whether it is empty of atmospheric air or filled with it." (498) If two gases are in the volume, they interpenetrate. What is neglected is this: "in this thing one matter is present where the other matter is, and the matter that penetrates is also penetrated in the same point." (498) Is Hegel trying to deny atomism? For instance, does he argue that there is no oxygen and nitrogen but only "atmosphere"? This is not the point, I think. Rather, there might be Matters – oxygen and nitrogen – but the atmosphere is nevertheless a Thing pervaded with Matters. At no point is there *only* oxygen and no nitrogen. These matters pervade each other. Nothing – not even the atmosphere – is truly self-identical.

14
Appearance

At the end of chapter 13, autochthonous Existence emerged from Ground but then dissolved itself. At the end of its journey from ashes to dust, Existence posited itself as absolute negativity – a reflected immediacy. As such, it was Appearance – an "*essential* Existence." (499) The function of unstable Appearance is to *dis*appear. Appearance does not have being-in-and-for-self; it *must* self-erase. It is "the reality that does not correspond to the Notion." (756) Even in ordinary parlance, when we say that *X appears* to be the case, we are saying that *X may* be true, but *X* must erase itself in favor of a deeper truth.[1] If *X* turns out to be true, then it was no mere appearance. Nevertheless, this verdict can only be reached *after X*'s appearance sublates itself. Hence, *X* is appearance *only* when it self-erases.[2]

Yet disappearance implies a removal to *some place*. Appearance is therefore "equally immediately a sheer *positedness* which has a *ground* and an *other* for its subsistence." (500) Sublation has always meant

---

[1] EL § 131 Remark ("Still, to say that anything is *only* an appearance suggests a real flaw, which consists in this, that Appearance is still divided against itself and without intrinsic stability") . Hegel suggests "we have all reason to rejoice that the things which environ us are appearances and not steadfast and independent existences; since in that case we should soon perish of hunger, both bodily and mental." *Id*.

[2] Hegel should not be read to suggest that certain appearances are true and certain appearances are false. JUSTUS HARTNACK, AN INTRODUCTION TO HEGEL'S LOGIC 44 (Lars Aagaard-Mogensen trans., 1998) ("One difference between Plato's view and Hegel's is this: According to Plato, 'show' as it was conceived in the cave is necessarily false, whereas 'show' according to Hegel may or may not be false; whether it is, is a contingent matter"). Rather, the truth of appearance is in its disappearance. Truth is not correspondence with some thought or appearance to the "real" object. Rather, it is a *process*, and so is Appearance.

preservation as well as cancellation. Accordingly, Appearance's very essence is *dis*appearance in favor of some apparently deeper reality: "This constitutes its essentiality, to have within itself the negativity of reflection, the nature of essence." (499) We have before us a dialectic moment. "Appearance is accordingly the unity of illusory being [which erases itself] and Existence [which endures]." (500)

Appearance undergoes the usual three stages. First, the Understanding distinguishes Appearance from what endures. "[T]hese two sides enter into relation with each other." (500) The relation is put forth as "simple self-identity which also contains various content determinations." (500) In the flux of Appearance, this relation stays constant as the Law of Appearance, or so the Understanding asserts.

Dialectical Reason reinterprets the proposition of the Understanding: there must be two worlds opposing each other – the World of Appearance and the world of Existence. Each of these worlds will be a self-subsistent totality. Finally, Speculative Reason establishes that the two worlds collide. Essence is in Appearance, and vice versa. At this point "Appearance becomes *correlation* or *essential relation*." (500) In Essential Relation, Appearance establishes its being-in-and-for-self.

A. The Law of Appearance

In this section, Appearance is defined as that which withdraws into Law, with which it enjoys a unity. Hegel has scientific laws in mind, but what he has to say likewise applies to jurisprudence.

As indicated, the subsistence of Appearance lies in its non-subsistence: "Appearance is the existent mediated by its *negation*." (500) Disappearance is, paradoxically, the one permanent thing about Appearance.[3] This alone is the "law of the Medes and Persians, which altereth not."[4] In effect, sublation has been sublated. "The existent," Hegel says, "is accordingly the *return* of itself into itself through its negation and through the negation of this its negation." (500) In other words, by negating itself, Appearance shows what it is – a negation of negation. This subsistence of self-erasure shows that Appearance is *essential* (self-sublation being the very essence of Essence). Accordingly, "Appearance is Existence along with its essentiality." (500-1)

---

[3] HANS-GEORG GADAMER, HEGEL'S DIALECTIC: FIVE HERMENEUTICAL STUDIES 40 (Christopher Smith trans., 1976) ("Constancy . . . . is the truth of disappearance").

[4] Daniel 6:8.

If Appearance erases itself, there must be a place to which it removes – the deeper essence which merely "appears." This deeper essence is the Law of Appearance.[5] Yet this "other" is likewise a subsisting negative – a positedness. "In other words, the existent is, as an Appearance, reflected into an other which it has for its ground, which other is itself only this, to be reflected into an other." (501) Repeating a phrase introduced in chapter 10,[6] Hegel characterizes Appearance as "a return-into-self [as] the return of the nothing through nothing back to itself on account of the negativity of the moments." (501) Nothing is here *except* the negative. Appearance is therefore "*essential illusory show*." (501)

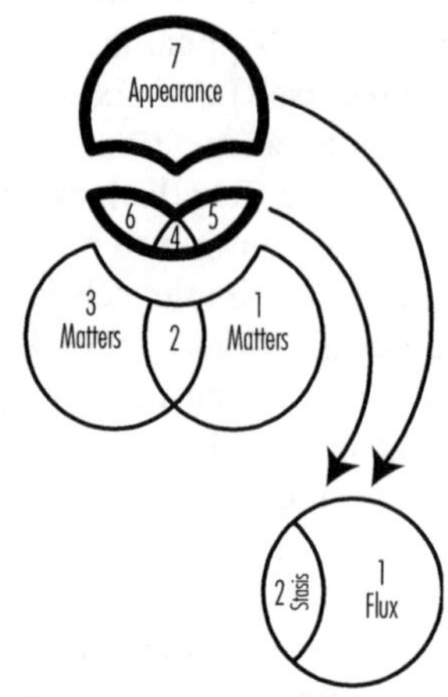

Figure 38(a)
The Law of Appearance

Yet Appearance is a *connection* of "reciprocally grounding existents." (501)[7] Each side of the relation appears only as it erases its other: "the subsistence of the one is not the subsistence of the other." (501) Since each side finds itself erased when the other side is emphasized, the true subsistence of the sides is in their *relationship* to each other.

Appearance is therefore a self-identity with two sides. First, it is in the form of "*positedness* or external immediacy." (501) On this side, Appearance is "a determinate being, but one which is contingent, unessential and, in keeping with its immediacy, subject to transition." (501) Second, Appearance is self-identical. This side is "exempt from

---

[5] The Law of Appearance corresponds to the first supersensual world of the *Phenomenology*. GADAMER, *supra* note 3, at 47; *see* G.W.F. HEGEL, PHENOMENOLOGY OF SPIRIT ¶ 157 (A.V. Miller trans. 1977). The later Law of Law and Appearance will conform to the second supersensuous world – the "inverted world" – of the *Phenomenology*. Meanwhile, Law does not, in the Logic, amount to a "world." GADAMER, *supra*, at 47. Worldhood must await its moment.

[6] There, Hegel described Reflection as "the *movement of nothing to nothing, and so back to itself*." (400)

[7] *See* PETER SIMPSON, HEGEL'S TRANSCENDENTAL INDUCTION, 128 n.9 (1998) ("It is important to see that appearance doesn't name simply the field of determinate things but the relation between that field and its unity. It is the difference between these moments that is appearance.").

flux, the *enduring* element" (501) of the Thing that appears.[8]

Figure 38(a) emphasizes the *unity* between flux and stasis of a Thing. Thus, the Thing is "the *one* and its *other*." (502) In this formulation, the other [1] is Appearance and the one [2] is the beyond of fluxional Appearance – a beyond that cannot exist on its own *without* appearing as the one. The beyond is therefore just as much present as absent. The Law of Appearance is that the Matters of the Thing "constitute *one* subsistence, but at the same time as a *diverse*, mutually indifferent content." (502) "The thing is a unity and at the same time a multiplicity."[9] Each side subsists in its other, as a unity. The Law [2] is the *positive* side of what appears. It remains when Appearance disappears.

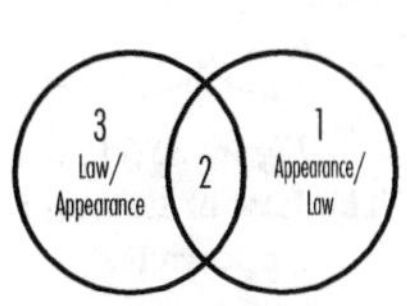

Figure 38(b)
Exclusivity of Law and Appearance

Dialectical Reason intervenes to emphasize that, in Janus-faced Appearance, the *presence* of the one side depends upon the *absence* of the other. Dialectical Reason says, "You say law is stable and Appearance is flux. But in truth, Law is just an appearance and therefore a flux." The unity is a failure. The Law is that each of the two sides exists in the sublating of the other. "[T]heir positedness as their negativity is the *identical, positive* positedness of both." (502)

Speculative Reason suggests that the content common to Appearance and Law is the Law itself. Another way of putting this is that, from the fluxional World of Appearance, the Understanding posits a stable realm of many laws. "But what the concept of law has not yet done is to account for what kinds of appearances or laws there are."[10] The

---

8 It has bothered some that Form and Content, the culmination of Absolute Ground in the *SL* (see chapter 12), is placed in the *EL* with the "Law of the Phenomenon (or Law of Appearance)." To be sure, the Content of Form is that Form self-erases. That is also the Law of Appearance. The two are obviously connected. It is sometimes overlooked, however, that in the *EL*, Hegel states that Form and Content, "in its mature phase is the *Law of the Phenomenon*." EL § 133. This suggests that, even in the *EL*, Hegel viewed Form and Content as more primitive than the Law of Appearance. In any case, as Mure remarks, "In the greatly simplified version of the [*EL*] not only does the articulation of the movement seem sometimes different, but often where it is clearly the same as in [the *SL*] the titles of the categories are nevertheless altered. Nowhere so much as in the Logic of Essence has the reader need to remember that these titles, however, indispensable for exposition, are mere 'compilations of external reflection.'" G.R.G. MURE, A STUDY OF HEGEL'S LOGIC 90 (1950); *but see id*. at 95 (changes in the *EL* intended as an improvement of *SL*).

9 HERBERT MARCUSE, REASON AND REVOLUTION 107 (1999)

10 SIMPSON, *supra* note 7, at 37.

many Laws *themselves* are unruly and unstable, and so the logic of the Understanding requires there to be a stable law of the many fluxional laws. So Speculative Reason reduces Law to Appearance and therefore subject to a meta-law.

Notice that the universal that unites the two sides is itself one of the sides. This stuttering trope has been seen before, in Hegel's difference and/or identity of Identity and Difference. There, the unity was also one of the sides. The trope tends to fit with the idea of no beyond – of a thoroughgoing presence, in which *genus* is present precisely as an absence.[11] This is the very nature of Notion, which is the unity of itself, its other, and the unity of itself and other.

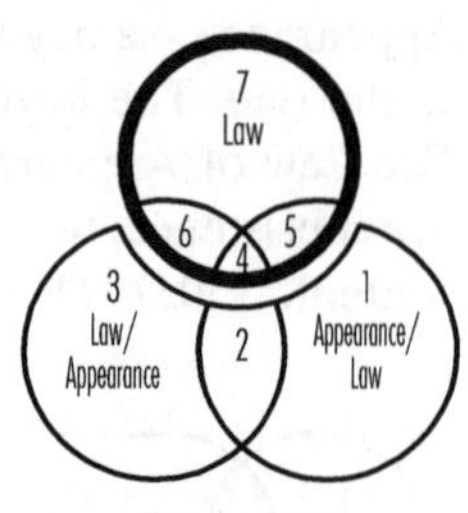

Figure 38(c)
The Law of Law and Appearance

The Subsistence of Appearance. In dissolving, the Thing has become an opposition, and Appearance is this very opposition. Yet both sides of the opposition are equally self-erasing Appearance. This is the proposition of Figure 38(c), where Speculative Reason suggests that Appearance is "conformable to its determination" (502) – *i.e.*, determined to be a relation between flux and stasis. This is so in three different ways, which correspond to Figures 38(a), (b), and (c).

(1) Subsistence [7] is opposed to the fluxionable immediacy of existence [4, 5, 6]. That is, immediacies are diversities which self-erase. But the Law of Law and Appearance [7] does not self-erase. On the positive side, the Law of Law and Appearance is identity-with-self [7]. But there is also a negative side [4, 5, 6] which announces it is *not* identity-with-self. Rather, it is a positedness.

(2) The Law of Law and Appearance [7] is just as much [4, 5, 6] – a positedness. At this point, Hegel exploits the etymological connection between Law (*Gesetz*) and positedness (*Gesetzsein*). "In this positedness lies the essential *relation* of the two sides of the difference which law contains." (502) In Figure 38(c), [7] represents the vanishing of the

---

[11] That "genus" is the absent member in the set of species is a Žižekian theme. SLAVOJ ŽIŽEK, THE METASTASES OF ENJOYMENT: SIX ESSAYS ON WOMAN AND CAUSALITY 97, 158 (1993) (attributing to Hegel the view that every genus has two species: itself and its species). He calls this the "paradox of *pas-tout*." SLAVOJ ŽIŽEK, FOR THEY KNOW NOT WHAT THEY DO: ENJOYMENT AS A POLITICAL FACTOR 44 (1991). Hegel will suggest that genus and species are the only two species in chapter 19.

sides. This vanishing is the unity between Appearance and the Law of Appearance.

(3) The Law of Law and Appearance is the unity of Law and Appearance in that both sides of the syllogism self-erase. Figure 38(c) stands for the proposition that "appearance and law have one and the same content." (503) Initially, this did not appear to be the case. Law was supposed to be the withdrawal from flux into deeper stasis. Appearance was supposed to be "the null *immediate*" (503) which opposes reflection-into-self. In truth, both sides self-erase; one is no more or no less Appearance than the other side. The "beyond" of Appearance is therefore a myth, a dogma.

The Understanding now interprets Figure 38(c). If Law is the unity of itself and Appearance, Appearance contains more than Law, namely, the unessential content of its immediate being.[12] The function of unessential content is to erase itself. Yet *Law* erases itself. So Law must be just as unessential as Appearance. The Law is that Law is only an Appearance. This is the Law that endures. "Accordingly, law is not beyond Appearance but is immediately *present* in it; the realm of laws is the *stable* image of the world of Existence or Appearance." (503) Before us is a single totality – the World of Appearance.

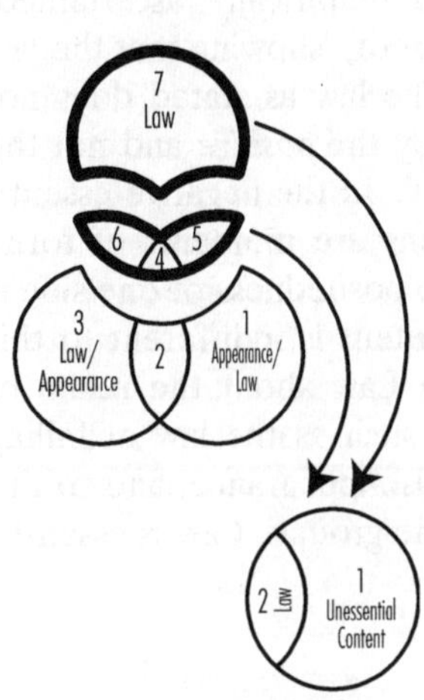

Figure 39(a)
The World of Appearance

The World of Appearance includes Law and lawlessness. Paradoxically, since Law is self-dissolution, lawlessness is what endures. Lawlessness constitutes the external connection of Appearance with a positive law. So the World of Appearance is full of multiple laws, none of which is adequate to its subject matter. Proper Law is self-erasure. Improper law is what science or

---

[12] This, according to Nancy, is where freedom proves to be "the law or the necessity that posits the self outside of itself. It is thus the law of what posits itself without law, whose law lies, precisely, in that positing. But this law . . . cannot be represented as a law, for a (physical or moral) law is always 'the stable image * * * unaware of the restlessness of negativity.'" JEAN-LUC NANCY, HEGEL: THE RESTLESSNESS OF THE NEGATIVE 68 (Jason Smith & Steven Miller eds. 1997), *citing SL* at 503-4.

jurisprudence puts forth as separate and apart from immanent logic.[13]

As an example of lawlessness, Hegel considers Galileo's law of the falling body: $s = at^2$, where s is space, t is time, and a is the acceleration effect of gravity. In this expression, spatial and temporal magnitudes are *brought* together empirically. Notionally, the unity of the two sides "would be their negativity." (504) The one would contain its other within itself. But this essential unity has not yet emerged in Galileo's law. The relation of time and space is merely *posited*. The Notion of space traversed by a falling body does not imply that time corresponds to it as a square. The determination of time – as it is "commonly imagined" (505) – does not imply a relation to space. Commonly, it is said that time "can quite well be imagined without space and space without time." (505) So conceived, the two are only externally related to each other. The magnitude by which time and space is related (a, in $s = at^2$) is also empirically ascertained. Philosophy, however, demands a notional proof, "showing that the law not only *occurs* but is *necessary*." (505)[14] The law as stated does not rest on its necessity. "Law is, therefore, only the *positive* and not the negative, essentiality of Appearance." (505)[15] In the negative essentiality of Appearance, content determinations are moments of form. They pass over into their other. In Law, the positedness of one side is the positedness of the other. Yet their content is indifferent to this relation. That is, when we assert the true Law about the realm of Appearances, we state some positive law, such as the law of falling bodies. The *real* law, however, is that Law is Appearance, and so this so-called Law of falling must itself fall to the ground. Law is essential

---

[13] This is Hegel's ultimate judgment of positive law. In the *Philosophy of Right*, "wrong" is defined as the positivization of right. Jeanne L. Schroeder & David Gray Carlson, *The Appearance of Right and the Essence of Wrong: Metaphor and Metonymy in Law*, 24 CARDOZO L. REV. 2481 (2003).

[14] For a description of Hegel's notional derivation of the law of the fall – undertaken in the *Philosophy of Nature* – see Stefan Büttner, *Hegel on Galilei's Law of Fall*, in HEGEL AND NEWTONIANISM 331 (Michael John Petry ed., 1993). In this proof, time is unit and internal space is amount and external. The fact that time is in a ratio of power and in velocity's denominator (s/t^2) shows that the Notion of falling bodies manifests itself externally in the space it covers. For other remarks by Hegel on Galileo, see chapter 7.

[15] If scientific explanation does not contain necessity, then it "is no really *explanation* at all, but merely *re-description* of the phenomena as they happen to appear to Consciousness, i.e., logically indifferent to one another." Michael Baur, *Hegel and the Overcoming of the Understanding*, 22 OWL OF MINERVA 141, 148 (1991).

in form – it self-erases. But, as expressed in $s = at^2$, it is not yet real Form which is reflected into its sides as content. Its self-erasure is merely implicit.[16]

Although Hegel is usually viewed as an opponent of English common law, his discussion of the Law of Appearance actually describes its basis perfectly.[17] In the common law tradition, the judge states the law, based upon his reading of the cases. But this statement is merely the appearance of law. Subsequent generations of judges must find their *own* law. If the original case is upheld, the original statement may *appear* to endure, but in fact it is the *new* statement, not the old one, which is the law. The original statement fades away into memory as wise saws and modern instances displace it. No one can ever state what the common law *is*, except in the sense of Hegel's Law of Appearance. The *true* common law, then, is that no statement of the law can endure.

In Galileo's case, every new empirical measurement of bodies in fall is the law – not Galileo's original publication of it. That is to say, empirical observation is king; should empirical observation depart from $s = at^2$, Galileo's law would be dead.[18]

---

[16] "Newton, for example, presents phenomena as diverse as the free fall of a body on earth and the general planetary movement around the sun . . . as universal gravitation. But ever since his Jena dissertation on planetary movement, Hegel had tried to show the error of such a reduction; it can only reach an abstract formula which, though it has, no doubt, the merit of setting forth lawfulness as lawfulness, completely obscures the qualitative diversity of the content." JEAN HYPPOLITE, GENESIS AND STRUCTURE OF HEGEL'S *PHENOMENOLOGY OF SPIRIT* 128 (Samuel Cherniak & John Heckman trans., 1974). According to Gadamer, the significance of Galileo's law is that, because of friction, the law (as it exists in the World of Appearance) is never pure but is always compromised or perverted. Galileo's law must therefore always be corrected by yet more law, in a bad infinity. GADAMER, *supra* note 3, at 43. But this does not mean Hegel discounts Galileo's contribution. Hegel praises the "immortal service" (343) which Galileo performed with his empirical discovery.

[17] On Hegel's covert sympathy for the common law process, see Arthur J. Jacobson, *Hegel's Legal Plenum*, in HEGEL AND LEGAL THEORY 97 (Drucilla Cornell et al. eds., 1991).

[18] Baur argues that Galileo's law has a static, nonrational, lawless moment in it: the amount of the fall is trivial compared to the earth's diameter. In effect, for Galileo's law the earth's diameter is infinitely wide. Only then can his law hold for all objects. For Newton, gravitational attraction works even if the "falling" object is significant compared to the earth's diameter, but space and time are immutably fixed. But this is because the things we observe moving do not approach the speed of light. For Einstein, space and time are mutable, but the speed of light is fixed. In the above examples, law cannot escape the irrational, unnecessary moment of fixity. "If that which must be assumed by the Understanding is truly non-reducible to the other relations specified within the law,

Hegel, then, turns the tables on H.L.A. Hart, who argued that the meta-law was the rule of recognition.[19] In effect, these rules tell the judge how to tell the difference between law and non-law. Of course, Hart is only able to give *examples* of such rules – such as, when the two houses of Congress enact a bill by the requisite majorities and the president signs it, the result is a law. He does not define the *entire* process of legal recognition, except to assure us that law *is* recognized, and that judges occasionally formulate the rule they supposedly followed in this act of recognition.

Hegel says something entirely different. He implies a rule of *non*-recognition. Whatever a rule of recognition empirically causes to be recognized, that appearance is precisely what law is *not*. The only real law is that empirical law – an Appearance – must disappear.

B. The World of Appearance and the World-in-Itself

"The existent world tranquilly raises itself to a realm of laws." (505) In Law, the World of Appearance has subsistence. And the Law is simply this: that Appearances must disappear; "its subsistence is therefore its dissolution." (505) When Appearance erases itself, Appearance shows what it is. When this occurs, "Law is this simple identity of Appearance with itself." (505)

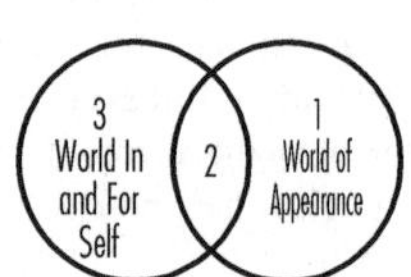

Figure 39(b)
World of Appearance; World In and For Self

But, Hegel says, Law is substrate, not Ground.[20] If Law is Ground, then Appearance is Grounded. Appearance would then withdraw into Ground when it disappears, and Law would enjoy a deeper meaning than mere appearance. Because Law is nothing *but* the activity of Appearance, there *is* no deeper realm of Law. Law and Appearance exist at the same level. Phenomenal things therefore have their grounds and conditions in other phenomenal things.

Nevertheless, Law has a different content from that of Appearance. Law reflects itself into Appearance, whereas Appearance reflects itself

---

yet nevertheless relevant to the truth of the law itself, then necessarily it must find its way back into the law." Baur, *supra* note 16, at 150.

[19] H.L.A. HART, THE CONCEPT OF LAW 94-5 (1961).

[20] "Substrate" implies diversity and denial of relation, whereas Ground is inherently a relation with Grounded. *Supra* at 301.

into Law. Because each self-erases, each is an "existent, which has its negativity for its ground." (505-6)

This very act of self-sublation is what Appearance and Law share. This act was the Law of Law and Appearance. We have ordinary Law (self-sublation of Appearance) *and* a meta-law (which requires that Law *and* Appearance self-sublate). Law is the "negative unity" (506) between itself and Appearance.

Each side is the unity of itself *and* the other.[21] This feature of containing itself, the other, *and* the unity of self and other, Hegel says, "is at first only their *inner* unity which stands in need of *proof* and *mediation*." (506) This merely implicit (or "negative") feature is now made express (or posited). Law and Appearance are different, even while each *is* the other. In spite of their identity, each is self-subsistent against the other. "[T]he identity of law is therefore now also a *posited* and *real* identity." (506) "Posited" and "reality" are dialectical words. Dialectical Reason therefore proposes that two worlds – Appearance and Law – are each diverse totalities unto themselves.[22]

About these two worlds, Hegel remarks:

> Existence has thus completely withdrawn into itself and has reflected itself into its absolute otherness in and for itself. That which was previously law is accordingly no longer only one side of the whole whose other side was Appearance as such, but is itself the whole. (506)

Because each side contains the other and is the whole unto itself, Law "now also contains the moment of unessentiality which still belonged to Appearance, but as reflected implicit unessentiality." (506) In other words, Appearance had formerly self-erased and announced itself inessential; this was the very essence of Appearance. Now Law, as a totality unto itself, is likewise inessential. But this unessentiality is its "essential negativity." (506-7)

Hegel next refers to the phenomenal appearance of a body of law: "As an immediate content, law is *determinate* in general, distinguished from other laws, and of these there is an indeterminate number." (507) In other words, when *immediately* perceived, specific laws can be

---

21 "This positedness of one in the other is their negative unity and each is *not only the positedness of itself but also of the other*, or, each is itself this negative unity." (506)

22 "However, what he means is, not that there are two distinct worlds, but that there are two laws applying to one and the same world. The second law states that the selfsame repels itself from itself and is not selfsame but posits itself as selfsame, whereas the first law states that the selfsame remains selfsame." HARTNACK, *supra* note 2, at 64.

discerned.[23] But law *as such* stands on a different ground. The Law of such contingent laws "now has within it essential negativity," and it "no longer contains such a merely indifferent, contingent content determination." (507) Rather, the content of the meta-Law is "all determinateness whatsoever, in an essential relation developing itself into totality." (507) In this passage, "essential relation" [2] must be understood as self-erasure. In self-erasing, the contingent laws show themselves to be mere appearance. But "Appearance which is reflected into itself is now a *world*, which *reveals* itself as a *world in and for itself* above the World *of Appearance*." (507)

All the contingent variations of self-erasing Appearance are now "the simple, changeless but varied content of the existent world." (507) Such a world contains the moment of "essenceless manifoldness." (507) Yet the world itself is self-subsistent. The self-subsistent world, beyond the contingencies of immediate perception, is the "*supersensuous world*, in so far as the existent world is characterized as *sensuous*, namely, as determined for intuition." (507) In the supersensuous World-in-and-for-itself, "*Essence* has as yet no determinate being; but it *is*, and in a profounder sense than being." (507)

This is a good point to introduce everyone's favorite quote from all of Hegel's works:

> The True is thus the Baccanalian revel in which no member is not drunk; yet because each member collapses as soon as he drops out, the revel is just as much transparent and simple repose. Judged in the court of this movement, the single shapes of Spirit do not persist any more than determinate thoughts do, but they are as much positive and necessary moments, as they are negative and evanescent.[24]

The point is that, as Appearance disappears, a stable world is created which does *not* disappear.[25] According to Gadamer, Hegel

> hits upon a brilliant formulation: the beyond, he says, is the appearance *as* appearance. That is, it is appearance which is not the appearance of something else, and which is no longer to be differentiated from something lying beyond it . . . On the contrary, it is nothing but appearance, and thus it is not appearance as opposed to reality, but rather appearance as the real itself.[26]

---

[23] In Hartian terms, rules are "recognized." HART, *supra* note 19.

[24] PHENOMENOLOGY, *supra* note 5, ¶ 47.

[25] *See* JEAN HYPPOLITE, LOGIC AND EXISTENCE 136 (Leonard Lawlor and Amit Sen trans., 1997) ("What we call substance, absolute truth, is undoubtedly translucent and simple rest as well as bacchanalian revel").

[26] GADAMER, *supra* note 3, at 41.

So far as Hegel is concerned, it is appearances all the way down.

Essential relation. Hegel concludes with the concept of the Essential Relation between the two worlds. Existence, it will be recalled, started with the *Thing*, "an immediacy that is not yet *posited* as essential or reflected." (507) But the Thing was also "not a *simply affirmative* . . . immediate. It is only as things of another, supersensuous world that things are posited . . . as veritable Existences." (507) In Things it is acknowledged that there is a being distinct from immediate being. Sensuous representation ascribes Existence only to the immediate being of feeling and intuition, but this is overcome in the deeper account of the Thing. Even sensuous representation has an unconscious sense that Things are not as they appear, but it is still not ready to acknowledge that "such determinations are not sensuous or simply affirmative immediacies, but reflected Existences." (507)

The World In and For Self is a totality; nothing is outside of it. "But since it is in its own self absolute negativity or form, its reflection-into-self is a *negative relation* to itself." (508) The World In and For Self shows what it is by expelling what it is not. This world "contains opposition and repels itself within itself into the essential world and into the world of otherness or the World of Appearance." (508)

Although a totality, the World In and For Self is also only *one side* of a totality. It is the self-subsistent world against the World of Appearance. This supersensuous world is the determinate ground of the World of Appearance. Two worlds coincide – the World of Appearance and the World In and For Itself. One is essential, one is inessential. But which is which? Outside forces must determine this. Because this is so "the *ground relation* has . . . been restored." (508) Ground Relation (or Form), it will be recalled, had no self-subsistence. But now we have before us the ground relation of *Appearance*. This is more than the relation of diversities. It is total relation – the relation of both worlds within the one world. Consequently, "each of the two sides of law is, in the negative unity, *in its own self its other* content." (508) The other is not an indeterminate other in general. It is *its* other. It too contains the content determination of the first. The two sides are opposed, yet each side contains the other.[27] Hence, we have "the *essential relation of opposition*." (509)

---

[27] "To grasp this world is to invert it into a "Beyond" (*Jenseits*); the effort to dwell in or explain the Beyond leads immediately to its inversion into this world." STANLEY ROSEN, G.W.F. HEGEL: AN INTRODUCTION TO THE SCIENCE OF WISDOM 147 (1974).

The ground relation of Appearance is "the opposition which, in its contradiction, has fallen to the ground." (509) Existence is, of course, the ground of Appearance. But in Figure 39(c), Existence has united with itself. It is the ground relation of opposed determinations, each of which is at the same time sublated ground. Existence has become the Appearance of Appearance, or the Appearance that does not disappear.[28]

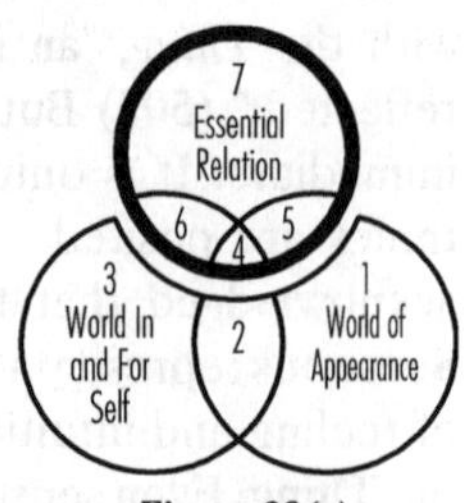

Figure 39(c)
Essential Relation

The Essential Relation between the two worlds is one of *inversion*. One of these worlds is Appearance. The other is transcendent. But which is which? This is undetermined. Nevertheless, Essential Relation is not to be taken as a mere opposition. The relation of the worlds is an opposition *and* an identity.

C. Dissolution of Appearance

The World In and For Self is a unity between the World of Appearance and the World-in-itself. But at the same time the World In and For Self is merely a side of its own self.

> The two worlds are therefore in such a relationship that what is positive in the world of Appearance is negative in the world in and for self. What is negative in the world of Appearance is the positive in the world in and for self. The north pole of one world is the south pole of the other. What is evil in the world of Appearance is *in and for itself* good. (509)

This is the topsy-turvy world.[29]

---

[28] *See* PHENOMENOLOGY, *supra* note 5, ¶ 47 ("Appearance is the arising and passing away that does not itself arise and pass away, but is in itself and constitutes the actuality and the movement of the life of truth").

[29] A decade before the *SL*, Hegel would identify the "inverted" world with the world of philosophy. G.W.F. Hegel, *On the Nature of Philosophical Criticism in General and Its Relation to the Present Condition of Philosophy in Particular*, quoted in WALTER KAUFMAN, HEGEL: A REINTERPRETATION 56 (1978). "In order to become aware of its task, philosophy must first have experienced the dissolution of the intelligible world. In contrast to the 'upright' world, the world of philosophy is an 'upside down' (*verkehrte*) world; in contrast to total appeasement, it is one of total restlessness." HERBERT MARCUSE, HEGEL'S ONTOLOGY AND THE THEORY OF HISTORICITY 12 (Seyla Benhabib trans. 1987).

With regard to Hegel's discovery of an inverted world, where the north pole is the south pole, Gadamer remarks, "Hegel is a Schwabian and startling people is his passion, just as it is the passion of all Schwabians."[30] But ultimately Gadamer proclaims the polar illustration or the good-evil point unhelpful. These are mere oppositions, not inverted worlds.[31] What inversion implies is that the world contains *both* law and the inversion of law. The topsy-turvy world is the world of satire, where opposites stand in for what should be, showing that things are not what they seem. Law is a possibility, but its inverse is also present in the world. As Hegel writes in the *Phenomenology*, "what is despised in the former [world] is honoured, and what in the former is honoured, meets with contempt" in the inverted world.[32] What is noble is smeared with what is ignoble. The evil is *also* the good because the world is both the World of Appearance and the World In and For Itself. The two worlds are not opposed but each is actually the other world in addition to being itself.[33]

In the opposition of the worlds, their difference has vanished. Each world is unable to sustain itself without the other world. Hence, the World of Appearance is determined as Reflection into otherness. The World In and For Self is likewise reflected into *its* other. This is the enduring fact of both worlds, and to this extent the worlds are "exempt from otherness and change." (510) Each world becomes "essenceless content, self-opposed and self-inverting." (510)

Each world is Ground to the other. The World of Appearance withdraws into the World In and For Self as to its Ground. But the Ground self-erases. The World In and For Self withdraws back into Appearance which is equally Ground. The two worlds engage in the

---

30 GADAMER, *supra* note 3, at 37.

31 *Id.* at 48.

32 PHENOMENOLOGY, *supra* note 5, ¶ 158.

33 That appearance does not always comply with law is why genera have species. Genera refer to species and species refer to individuals. But genera do not contain the principle of difference between the species. The world simply does not conform to the law. Inversion stands for the proposition that change, caprice and evolution are the law. GADAMER, *supra* note 3, at 45.

Ultimately, in the *Phenomenology*, the inverted world is what consciousness finds when it peers into the supposedly unknowable beyond. It finds a supersensible world that is no different from the World of Appearance. Such a world is self-moving. In short the beyond of consciousness *is* consciousness, and so the inverted world stands for the transition to self-consciousness. GADAMER, *supra*, at 52-3.

modulation that typifies the dialectic relation.

Yet each side is as much a totality as it is a mere side. A totality repels itself from itself and reveals itself to be two totalities – reflected and immediate. The self-subsistence of each is "now so posited that each is only as essential relation to the other and has its self-subsistence *in this unity of both*." (510)

In the Law of Appearance, two *contents* were related to one another – that of Appearance and that of Law. At the level of Figure 37(b), the identity of the two sides was only an inner identity, Hegel says. These two sides do not yet have the relation within themselves. This relation *is* the content of each world, and this content is so far only implicitly determined. In Figure 39(c), however, the content of each world is determinately present in the center. Now the sides must expressly capture this idea within themselves.

"'World' expresses in general formless totality of manifoldness." (511) The diverse worlds, however, have fallen to their ground – Essential Relation. "There have arisen two totalities of the content in the world of Appearance." (511) Each one is only a self-erasing Form. The essential relation is the consummation of their unity of form.

15
Essential Relation

The truth of Appearance is its Essential Relation with a supersensible world. The self-subsistent truth is that neither world can endure on its own without the other.[1] Furthermore, Logic cannot determine *which* world is Appearance and which world is "in and for self." The predominance of one over the other is a "*simply affirmative* . . . immediacy." (512) Any such predominance is simply assigned by external reflection. Yet, since the Essential Relation represents worldly self-erasure, and since reflection *is* self-erasure, the relation is "a self-identical reflection." (512)

The Essential Relation is not yet the true third to Reflection and Existence. This will be Actuality, which arises at the end of this chapter. Nevertheless, the Essential Relation already represents a union of Reflection and Existence – erasure and endurance. Both of these "have withdrawn from their indifference into their essential unity, so that they have this alone for their subsistence." (512) What Actuality will require is the unfolding of the middle term within the extremes of the syllogism.

For now the sides of the relation coincide with the totality of the

---

1 *See* KENNETH R. WESTPHAL, HEGEL'S EPISTEMOLOGICAL REALISM: A STUDY OF THE AIM AND METHOD OF HEGEL'S *Phenomenology of Spirit* 145 (1989) ("if [Hegel's] holism is correct, if things are what they are only through their contrast with and causal relations to other things, then there can be no epistemologically opaque metaphysical distinction between appearance and reality").

relation itself. Each side is at once itself, the other, and the whole. This feature has been present in the extremes since the Positive and Negative in chapter 10, but these mere "opposites" were impoverished, compared to the World of Appearance and the World In and For Self in Figure 39(c). In Positive and Negative, the sides had "no other determination but this their negative unity." (512) The sides of Essential Relation, in contrast, are entire worlds, each the inversion of the other. As "the unity of itself and its other, therefore a whole," each of the worlds is "self-subsistent Existence." (512)

Because of the inversion, however, each side of the Essential Relation is "disrupted within itself." (512) The worlds erased themselves in chapter 14 and sent their being into the Essential Relation. Consequently, each world has its self-subsistence falling outside of itself and in the relation. To this extent these worlds are not yet Actual. When the *relation* erases itself, we have achieved Actuality.

In this chapter, the Understanding proclaims the Essential Relation to be the Relation of Whole and Parts. This Hegel identifies as a relation between reflected and immediate self-subsistence. Each side in the relation conditions and presupposes the other. The Relation of Whole and Parts has this fault: neither side is "posited as moment of the other . . . ; their identity is not their negative unity." (513)

When this fault is addressed – when one side is moment and also ground of the other – then we have before us the Relation of Force and Its Expression. Yet such a relation will suffer from inequality. When that inequality is overcome, we have the Relation of Inner and Outer, the threshold of Actuality.

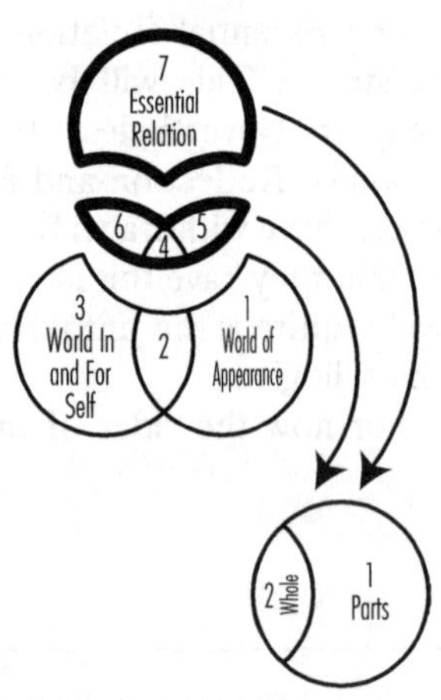

Figure 40(a)
Relation of Whole and Parts

A. Relation of Whole and Parts

The Essential Relation is simultaneously immediate and reflected. Being a relation, it is a *thing* separate from its parts. As such, it is the whole. But any relation depends on and hence posits its parts. Hence, the Essential Relation "is as much this identity with its opposite as it is its own self-subsistence." (513-4)

At first, the Understanding perceives

the immediacy of the *unity* of Whole and Parts. The unity [1, 2] is such that the Whole immediately posits the Parts, and vice versa. Hegel associates the Whole with the World In and For Self from Figure 39(b). The World of Appearance is associated with the Parts.

Earlier, Positive and Negative were said to have no self-subsistence on their own. But, by now, the sides of the relation are self-subsistent, "but in such a manner that each has the other reflected in it and at the same time only is as this identity of both." (514) Whole and Parts are simultaneously self-subsistent and *not* self-subsistent. Indeed, Hegel sounded this theme way back in chapter 1, where he announced that one cannot think the Whole and the Parts at the same time. One can think them in sequence only (105). This is the same as saying that each side of the unity subsists and does not subsist. The unity between them is simultaneously immanent *and* externally imposed. This is so on the law of sublation. In Figure 39(c), Essential Relation was the unity between immanence and external reflection.

Dialectical Reason seizes upon the negative unity inherent in the Relation of Whole and Parts. When the negative unity is emphasized, Whole and Parts are seen as diverse. From this perspective, the Whole is mere substrate – not Ground to the Parts.[2] Also from this perspective, the Whole is merely reflected self-subsistence – merely a moment, or a positedness.

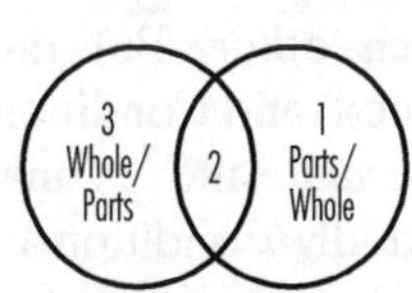

Figure 40(b)
Negative Unity of Whole and Parts

In the dialectic moment, "the whole is the reflected unity which has an independent subsistence of its own." (514) But its subsistence is equally repelled from it. The Whole is a *merely* negative unity of the Parts. The Whole is alienated from itself. It subsists only in the other. "*The whole accordingly consists of parts*." (514) It is not anything without them. What holds the whole together is External Reflection.

Like the Whole, the Parts exist on their own account. At one

---

[2] Michael Inwood finds Hegel wrong on this score and points out that refrigerators can be dismantled and reassembled, in which case they are Wholes once again. M.J. INWOOD, HEGEL 440-1 (1983) ("Hegel's categories seem insufficiently refined to handle such cases as this"). But Hegel's point is that Whole and Parts are not immune from outside determination and therefore do not suffice as a definition of the absolute. Hegel could respond to Inwood by pointing out that the disassembled refrigerator does not reassemble itself. It requires otherness and is therefore no totality.

moment, the relation of Parts to Whole is only an external moment, to which the Parts are indifferent. Yet "they have this whole as their moment within themselves . . . for without a whole there are not parts." (515) Dialectical Reason, then, proves that, if the relation contains the self-subsistence of the sides, it also contains their sublatedness.[3]

Speculative Reason intervenes to describe the unity between the position of the Understanding and that of Dialectical Reason. The truth is that the Essential Relation is *both* self-subsistent *and* diverse (*i.e.*, not self-subsistent). The relation is therefore conditioned – each cannot do without the other. As always, Diversity is untenable. The Parts "collapse within themselves." (515) Their Existence (apart from the Whole) is "reflectionless being." (515) The Parts have self-subsistence only in the Whole. The Whole is self-subsistent without the Parts. But the opposite is just as true. The Parts *are* subsistent without the Whole, and the Whole has its self-subsistence *in* the Parts.

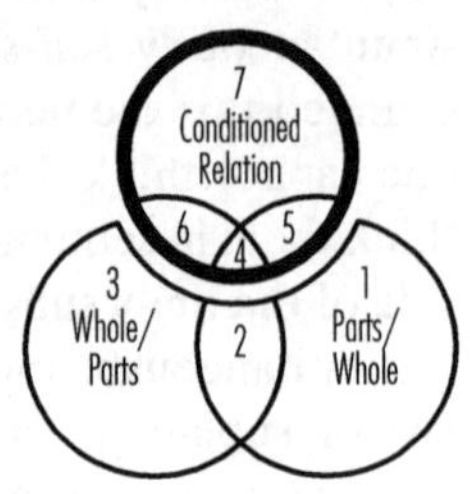

Figure 40(c)
Conditioned Relation

The Whole and Parts therefore condition each other. But the relation is higher than that of Ground (*i.e.*, conditioned) and Condition in Figure 33(a). There, Condition was "only the *immediate* and . . . only *implicitly* presupposed." (515) The Whole is admittedly Condition to the Parts, but it contains more. "[I]t, too, only is in so far as it has the parts for presupposition." (515) Thus, the *dependence* of Condition on the conditioned was merely implicit. Now it is "*realized*, that is, it is *posited* that condition is the essential self-subsistence of the conditioned in such a manner that it is *presupposed* by the latter." (515) Both sides of the relation are posited as conditioning each other. Each is an immediate self-subsistence within itself. But its self-subsistence is equally mediated or posited by the other.

Each side of the relation therefore has its self-subsistence in the other – as well as its own self-subsistence. What is present is only a single identity in which both sides are mere moments (and *more* than mere moments; each side is also self-subsistent and indifferent).

When unity is before us, "*the whole is equal to the parts and the parts*

---

[3] Errol Harris calls this dialectic relation of Whole and Parts "a mechanical correlation – the whole is the mere togetherness of the parts, yet if and so far as it is divided it ceased to be a whole; and if the parts are amalgamated they cease to be parts." ERROL E. HARRIS, AN INTERPRETATION OF THE LOGIC OF HEGEL 185 (1983).

to the whole. There is nothing in the whole which is not in the parts," and vice versa. (515) The relation has "an inseparable identity and one self-subsistence only." (516) The two infuse each other and cannot be considered apart. Nonetheless, the two sides are distinguishable.

Whole as Sum of Parts. According to common sense, the Whole is equal to the sum of the Parts. What is Hegel's position on this ancient nugget of wisdom? Naturally, he thinks common sense is confused: "although the whole is equal to the parts it is not equal *to them* as parts." (516) The Whole is a reflected unity – the Parts announce that they are *not* the Whole. The Whole is therefore a surplus that exceeds the Parts – as shown by [7] in Figure 40(c). Properly analyzed, "the equality of the whole and the Parts expresses only the tautology that *the whole as whole* is equal not to the parts but to *the whole*." (516) That is to say, since it is wedded to the error of self-equality (or internal differentiation, as Hegel calls it), common sense should see that the Whole is *not* equal to the Parts but is *different* from them. Yet, given self-equality, the Whole and Parts fall indifferently apart. Held apart, they necessarily destroy themselves.

Nevertheless, self-subsistence *is* present in Whole and Parts, just as common sense insists, but only as a moment. Reflection into other and hence into self is their other moment. Indeed, the truth of the relation is in mediation – not in self-sufficient immediacy. In the Conditioned Relation "both reflected and simply affirmative . . . immediacy are sublated. The relation is the contradiction which withdraws into its ground, into the unity which, as returning, is reflected unity." (517)

Whole and Parts have withdrawn into a simple immediacy [7], but within the immediacy is a negative relation, mediated through its other [4, 5, 6]. This immediacy [7] is equally posited by [4, 5, 6]. When we focus on the positedness, immediacy vanishes. Simple immediacy *is* only as sublated. Likewise, when we focus on the immediacy, positedness vanishes. Yet each moment is essentially related to the other.[4]

Infinite Divisibility. Hegel returns to the subject of Kant's second

---

[4] Inwood complains, "The concept of a whole containing parts is not very obviously applied by Hegel either to itself or to its immediate predecessor, appearance . . . [I]t is hard to find any regular, systematic relationship between the object-thoughts and the meta-thoughts." INWOOD, *supra* note 3, at 291. The idea of a concept applying itself to itself, however, belongs to Actuality – too advanced for Essential Relation. But it should be easy to see that the Relation of Whole and Parts *is* related to Appearance, which culminated in the insight that Existence and Appearance are in an Essential Relation. Existence is the Whole and Appearance is the Parts.

antinomy, which states, alternatively, that (1) everything is divisible, and (2) there are indivisible atoms.[5] Hegel's critique was that this antinomy represented Discreteness and Continuity. Discreteness presupposes the atom. Continuity insists upon divisibility. The antinomy thus consisted of taking a one-sided, isolated view of these contradictory concepts.[6] Hegel now suggests that Continuity and Discreteness were implicitly Whole and Parts. Continuity implies the *whole* of the number line. Discreteness is the Parts into which the number line is divided.

Accordingly, Kant's second antinomy can be reinterpreted as being an attempt to isolate a whole (a divisible thing) and Parts (indivisible things). "[T]he one moment in freeing itself from the other immediate introduces the other." (517)

Kant's simplex, however, cannot be a Whole, because then it would have Parts and would not be simple. Furthermore, as a simple, it excludes any relation with the Whole. Hence, the indivisible atom is not even a "part." We have before us a "part" only if we also have before us a "whole." These terms are strictly correlative. If, however, the simplex is not a part, it must be a Whole. Yet, if a Whole, it must have parts and not be a simplex – "*so on to infinity*." (518) This is a qualitative "spurious" infinity, as shown in Figure 7(b). Such infinities are the dismal reward for those who insist on self-equality of concepts.

The true meaning of Kant's antinomy is this:

> because the whole is not the self-subsistent, therefore the part is self-subsistent; but because the part is self-subsistent only *without the whole*, it is self-subsistent *not* as part, but rather *as whole*. The infinitude of the progress which arises is the inability to bring together the two thoughts which the mediation contains, namely, that each of the two determinations through its self-subsistence and separation from the other passes over into non-self-subsistence and into the other. (518)

In other words, "[a]ny effort to consider one moment in abstraction is defeated by the re-emergence in it of the other moment."[7] The Essential Relation is an advanced version of Spurious Infinity.[8]

---

5 IMMANUEL KANT, CRITIQUE OF PURE REASON A434-7/B462-5 (Paul Guyer & Allen W. Wood trans., 1990).

6 *Supra* at 149-50.

7 G.R.G. MURE, A STUDY OF HEGEL'S LOGIC 122 (1950).

8 CHARLES TAYLOR, HEGEL 277 (1975) ("the contradictions . . . that we see by looking at part and whole show that it is in movement, that it is constantly going over from unity to multiplicity and back again"). Michael Rosen faults Hegel for insufficiently dealing with the antinomies. MICHAEL ROSEN, HEGEL'S DIALECTIC AND ITS CRITICISM

B. Relation of Force and Its Expression

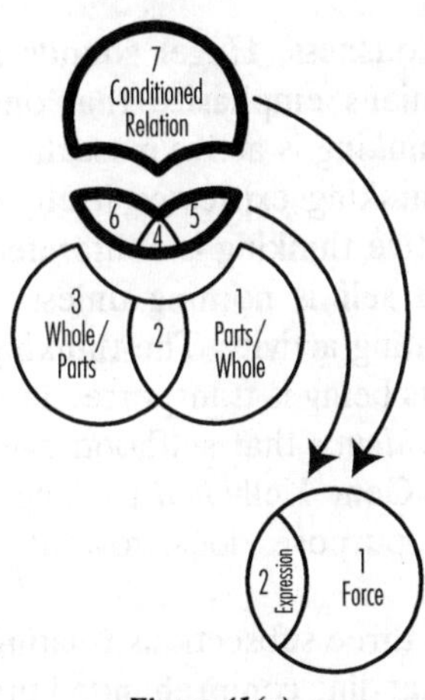

Figure 41(a)
The Relation of Force and Its Expression

The Understanding looks at Figure 40(c) and concedes that we no longer have before us a stable Relation of Whole and Parts. Even to refer to one side is to introduce the other side and so obliterate the first side. "This category, like every category of Essence . . . has itself the form of antithesis, of coupled opposition, and not of the whole triad."[9] This inability to express oneself without self-obliteration is the Relation of Force and Its Expression.[10] "In contradistinction to the thing, which has no link to its many properties, force makes sense only insofar as it manifests itself and poses what is inside itself outside itself."[11] Force "loses the determinateness given to

---

34 (1982). Since only immanent critique has bite, Hegel should have accepted Kant's standpoint as to the following: (a) Empirically, a thing either has or has not a property – the law of the excluded middle. (b) With regard to *cosmical* properties, a thing *can* have *and* not have a cosmic property. (c) There is a fixed border between empirical and cosmic properties. Cosmical conceptions for Kant were ideas that relate phenomena to the "absolute totality" – the stuff of the four antinomies. CRITIQUE OF PURE REASON, *supra* note 6, at A407/B434. By now it should be apparent that Hegel has dealt at length with the antinomies, and the entire *SL* is aimed at *denying* the law of the excluded middle for any entity – whether cosmic or empirical.

[9] MURE, LOGIC, *supra* note 8, at 122.

[10] Inwood suggests that Force and its Expression arbitrarily succeeds Whole and Parts. INWOOD, *supra* note 3, at 293. This is part of Inwood's general claim that Hegel's Logic is no logic but a string of thoughts connected contingently by Hegel's own external reflection. In fact, it is possible to comprehend the transition. Whole and Parts started out as a relation with self-subsistent sides. Speculative Reason, however, concluded that the relation is both self-subsistent *and* self-erasing. In proposing Force and its Expression, the Understanding surmises that it is impossible for one or the other side to be expressed without erasing the other side. If Whole and Parts stood for a complacent relation, Force and its Expression stands for the dialectical impossibility of it.

[11] JEAN HYPPOLITE, GENESIS AND STRUCTURE OF HEGEL'S *PHENOMENOLOGY OF SPIRIT* 120 (Samuel Cherniak & John Heckman trans., 1974); *see also* WESTPHAL, *supra* note 1, at 148 ("the gist of his view is that forces are exhausted by their manifestations").

it, for it passes over – or rather has already passed over – to the other."[12] This always-past nature of Force echoes Pure Being in chapter 1, which "does not pass over but has passed over – into *nothing*." (82-3)

On the verge of introducing self-consciousness, Hegel sounds a Lacanian theme *avant la lettre*. The Lacanians emphasize that one cannot think and "be" at the same time. Thinking is active/masculine. Being is passive/feminine.[13] The minute thinking expresses itself, it passes over into being. At that moment, active thinking is obliterated in favor of passive being. Yet the unified self is nothing unless it expresses itself. Thinking, therefore, is negating activity. The thinking thing erases its being as it expresses itself. Its being is transported into expression. Expression of self is *the only evidence* that selfhood ever existed. For this reason, writers *must* write. Gene Kelly *had* to dance. Yet Force "proceeds blindly, and not as purpose does, toward a rational end."[14]

This theme is implicated in the following three subsections relating Force and its Expression. When the Understanding comprehended the Relation of Whole and Parts, the whole was "a dead, mechanical aggregate." (518) The unity of Whole and Parts was an external relation. The new Relation of Force and Its Expression, however, "is the higher return-into-self" in which "the relation of the self-subsistent otherness ceases to be external." (518)

In Figure 41(a), immediate and reflected self-subsistence are sublated. In Figure 40(a), they were separate and independent. Now we have pure self-erasure. Force (*i.e.*, thinking)[15] erases itself instantly and passes over to Expression. The Expression *is* "only as borne and posited by force." (519) Each side of the relation is "not only a becoming and vanishing, but is a negative relation-to-self." (519) We have before us a vigorous True Infinite that becomes other and stays what it is. But now we are to view Force, "an internal excitation of

---

12 G.W.F. HEGEL, PHENOMENOLOGY OF SPIRIT ¶ 84 (A.V. Miller trans. 1977).

13 On the gender of thinking and being, see JEANNE LORRAINE SCHROEDER, THE TRIUMPH OF VENUS: THE EROTICS OF THE MARKET 259-61 (2004).

14 TAYLOR, *supra* note 9, at 277. For this reason, Hegel warns against the proposition that God is a Force. EL § 136 Remark.

15 Force is not to be taken as physical force in the Newtonian sense. "Force concretizes the 'potency' of being over and against being-there . . . and realizes the self-externalizing, self-manifesting motility in the dimension of existing beings which have emerged from essence." HERBERT MARCUSE, HEGEL'S ONTOLOGY AND THE THEORY OF HISTORICITY 92 (Seyla Benhabib trans. 1987).

formal moments,"[16] as more negative than ever. Now Force is *solicited* by its other, and its other is where Force begins.

(a) The Conditionedness of Force

Force has a complex nature. It is immediate, related to another (*i.e.*, attributed to some thing), and the negative unity of its own immediacy and its other. This accords with the notion that each side of the syllogism is by now itself, its other and the Whole of the unity between itself and other. "Each of those three movements is a way of relating to otherness, of mediating internal and external."[17]

Hegel considers Force in its immediacy. For common sense addicted to self-identity, Force is something merely attributed to a thing. Force and thing must therefore be distinguished. In Figure 41(b), Force is a reflected unity. It belongs to the Thing. But Force is not a form of the Thing, to which the Thing must attend. The thing is quite indifferent to Force. It contains no ground for having a Force. Force is external to the Thing according to common sense, which is shown in the question: How does a thing come to have force?

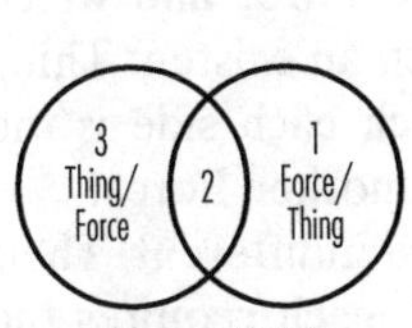

Figure 41(b)
The Conditionedness of Force

Although the Thing is supposed to be indifferent to the Force that is externally supplied to it, Hegel nevertheless says that Force is "a *quiescent determinateness of the thing*." (519) That is to say, Force does not express *itself* but speaks through the Thing.[18] Just as the Thing was once said to be made up of diverse Matters,[19] so Force is (by common sense) "designated as matter, and instead of magnetic, electrical, and other forces, magnetic, electrical, and other matters are assumed." (519)

But Force is an existent, which means that it has an affirmative

---

[16] STANLEY ROSEN, G.W.F. HEGEL: AN INTRODUCTION TO THE SCIENCE OF WISDOM 43 (1974).

[17] JOHN F. HOFFMEYER, THE ADVENT OF FREEDOM: THE PRESENCE OF THE FUTURE IN HEGEL'S LOGIC 26 (1994).

[18] Renewing the Lacanian theme, the subject is said to be the "thing that thinks." SLAVOJ ŽIŽEK, TARRYING WITH THE NEGATIVE: KANT, HEGEL, AND THE CRITIQUE OF IDEOLOGY 61 (1993).

[19] *Supra* at 354-7.

presence – an appearance. As an existent, it has both an affirmative immediacy and a reflected immediacy. And from this perspective, Force has being-in-and-for-self. The Thing in which Force is supposed to reside no longer has any meaning. Force is therefore not merely a "matter" to the Thing. The Thing has melded with its Matters and passed over to Appearance.[20] Force has more "staying power" than the Matters of a Thing.

In considering the dialectical moment of Conditionedness of Force, we have, on the one hand, the Thing indifferent to Force. We have, on the other hand, Force – equally a Thing – which is externally applied to the *passive* Thing. We cannot think of Force and the forced Thing simultaneously. One of these concepts self-erases when the other is asserted. Force is supposed to be active, but when the Thing is front and center, Force has erased itself and is passive. Once again, Dialectical Reason cannot tell which side is active Force and which side is passive Thing. Force is therefore just as much an existent Thing as the presupposed Thing was, "a relation in which each side is the same as the other." (520)[21] A Force always faces another Force.

At first the Forces are simply different and hence indifferent. Their unity is only inner. But each Force is conditioned; each requires the other to be what it is. Force is at first an act of presupposition, "a merely negatively *self*-relating act; this other force still lies *beyond* its *positing* activity." (521) Force, in this position, is merely diverse. As such, it erases itself and gives way to the unity between the two sides – a shared self-erasing activity.

(b) The Solicitation of Force

Force posits, and so is conditioned by, another Force.[22] It posits *and* is posited by another. As mere reciprocal presupposition, Force, if taken as an immediacy, erases itself. It cannot sustain itself without the aid of the other Force. Each Force shares this self-erasure as its truth.

---

[20] *Supra* at 358.

[21] HANS-GEORG GADAMER, HEGEL'S DIALECTIC: FIVE HERMENEUTICAL STUDIES 38 (Christopher Smith trans., 1976) ("eliciting and being elicited are the same process").

[22] This is at the very center of Hegel's theory of recognition, especially as formulated in the opening chapter of the *Philosophy of Right*. GEORG W.F. HEGEL, ELEMENTS OF THE PHILOSOPHY OF RIGHT § 34 Addition (Allen W. Wood trans. 1993); *see generally* David Gray Carlson, *How to Do Things With Hegel*, 78 TEX. L. REV. 1377 (2000).

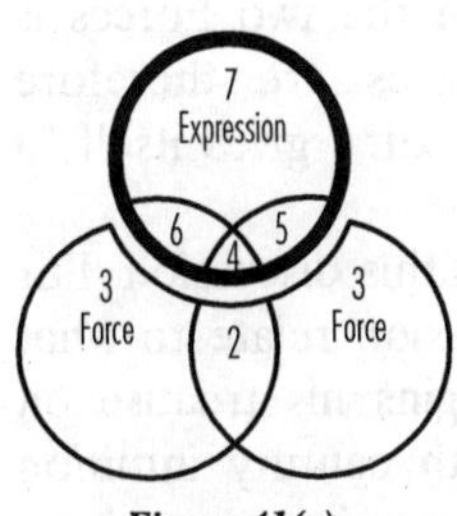

Figure 41(c)
Self-Externalization of Force (Expression)

When Force sublates itself, its being withdraws into [7], which, by this late stage, is as much inside itself [4, 5, 6] as outside itself. The truth of any Force is its self-externalization. But since diverse Force erases itself, and since Force is externality itself, externality is sublated when Force is sublated. The externality present in Force is "*its own presupposing activity*." (521)

Force [4, 5, 6] self-erases and withdraws into [7]. This means that externality as such is self-sublated. The outside is now *in*. Force-externality itself – says, "I am not the Thing," thereby proving it *is* the Thing. In this activity, Force/ externality expels itself from itself and is therefore "that which *in itself is null*." (521)

Impulse and Expression. Hegel says that, when a Force conditions its other, the other experiences it as impulse. In the face of impulse, the thing (which is also conditioned Force) pretends to be passive. By way of a psychological example, a person sometimes says, "The devil made me do it." The devil (impulse) absorbs the blame for the act of the subject. But impulse actually belongs to the supposedly passive Force. The passive Force is actually *active* Force. As active, the impulsive Force actually *solicits* the devil.[23] But this is not to say there is no devil. It is only to say that the devil solicits the subject's act if the subject is *open* to it, consistent with the comic book assumption that a hypnotist can never induce an act from the hypnotized subject unless he is open to it.

Under impulse, Force repels itself from itself. It projects the impulse "out there." The devil is made real, but the devil is the soliciting Force's own self. This other Force is thus the *Expression* of soliciting Force. When Force expresses itself, it makes itself external. And in making itself external, it *negates* externality. So, whether we start from supposedly passive Force or its impulse, the same unity in Expression results.

Expression has several sides to it. In expressing itself, Force at first sublates itself. But in reality, Force is two Forces – one soliciting, the other solicited. Which one is it really? It is impossible to say. Only an

---

[23] This is "weakness," one of the three Kantian evils (along with wickedness and impurity.) Each consists of the subject fooling herself about her true motives. Jeanne L. Schroeder & David Gray Carlson, *Kenneth Starr: Diabolically Evil?*, 88 CAL. L. REV. 653 (2000).

outside external reflection can tell. The truth of the two Forces is therefore their unity in Expression. The Forces are therefore "essentially mediated." (522) Expression is how Force gives itself "a determinate being-for-other." (523)

Many psychological implications are present in this discussion. For instance, the comments on Force and its Expression relate to what Charles Taylor calls "expressivism."[24] Taylor begins his treatise on Hegel with a description of an early nineteenth century intuition doubting that a self-identical personality precedes its expressions. Rather, it was intuited that a person is nothing *until* she expresses herself. We don't know what we think until we hear ourselves speaking about our thoughts. Expression is therefore a surprise to the speaker, who discovers what she thinks only as she begins to express herself. Everyone has had the sensation that, as one speaks, one changes her mind and is indeed transformed by the very act of speaking.

The themes sounded here also relate to the Lacanian concept of agency. A person acts. The act is Expression. The actor does not exist apart from the act. The very personhood of the actor is obliterated in the act. The actor cannot *do* and *be* at the same time. The *reasons* a person acts are only discovered epiphenominally, and they constitute a self-serving narrative that ascribes to the actor a pre-existing rationality that accounts for the act. In truth, our own motivations are opaque to us. We really don't know why we do the things we do. This inability to understand our own acts is precisely what makes us spontaneous and free (i.e., not "caused").[25]

(c) The Infinity of Force

In a short section, Hegel makes some final observations about Figure 41(c), which asserts that the truth of Force is in its Expression.

Force is finite when conceived in its moment of immediacy, Hegel says. From this perspective, its presupposing (external impulse) and its self-relation are distinct. Force is both passive and active. When passive, the other Force (impulse) is in charge. When active, the other Force is passive.

The two Forces, however, are one. This active unity is Expression

---

[24] TAYLOR, *supra* note 9, at 13-5 & n.1.

[25] *See* David Gray Carlson, *The Traumatic Dimension in Law*, 24 CARDOZO L. REV. 2287 (2003).

itself. In Expression, externality is sublated. There is no longer any distinction between the inner and outer truth of the Force. "Therefore what Force in truth expresses is that its relation to other is relation to itself, that its passivity consists in its very activity." (523) The impulse by which it is solicited into activity is its own soliciting. "In other words, what force expresses is this, that its *externality is identical* with its *inwardness*." (523)

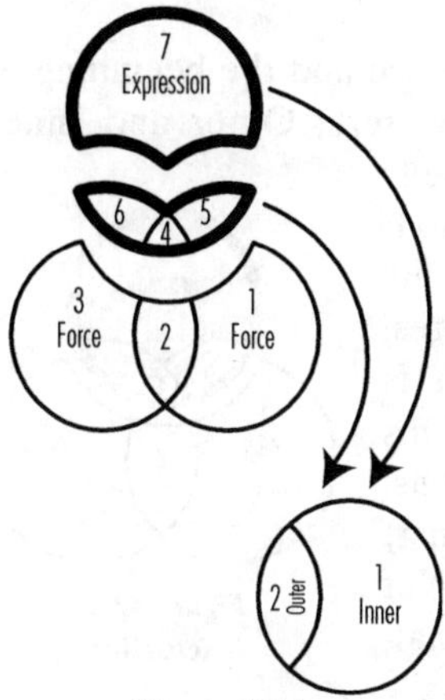

Figure 42(a)
Outer and Inner

C. The Relation of Outer and Inner

According to the Understanding, "Force in its expression . . . the determining which presupposes and the determining which returns into itself are one and the same." (525) That is, the Understanding interprets Expression of Force as an immediate unity of Outer and Inner. In this unity, Outer and Inner each have a self-subsistence. This is what differentiates Figure 42(a) from Figures 40(a) and 41(a). In Figure 40(a), Whole and Parts represented a complacent relation with self-subsistent sides. In Figure 41(a), the relation of Force and its Expression was a turbulent either/or. Now there is a self-subsistent unity between Outer and Inner. In short, we have moved from an immediate proposition through a dialectical proposition to a notional proposition.

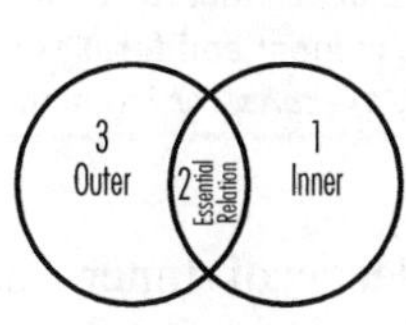

Figure 42(b)
Self-Subsistence of Outer and Inner

But, says Dialectical Reason, Outer and Inner equally "stand in essential relation." (524) When the negative unity between Outer and Inner is emphasized, neither the Outer and the Inner can self-subsist on its own. The self-subsistence of each is in the Essential Relation. Compared to this unity, Outer and Inner stand aside and are diverse from their own being. Self-subsistence is their indifferent substrate. Any distinction between Outer and Inner is therefore empty and transparent. Being diverse (compared to self-subsistence), Outer and Inner sublate themselves and remove their being to this unity only – a unity in Expression, which, at this point, we may officially call the Actual.

We have now reached the end of Appearance and the beginning of the last third of the Doctrine of Essence. Here, Outer and Inner cannot endure independently. Their self-subsistence is outside themselves in a relation. Yet the relation cannot endure without its constituent Parts. Neither extreme endures. Each side exists only in a totality which is Actual. Before us is one single *actual fact*. This fact is distinct from its form determinations. Form (which is in the business of self-erasing) is shed by and hence is external to the fact. Yet the fact is itself already established as externality itself. This means that external form is really *internal* to the fact – "an inner that is distinct from its externality." (524) In the Actual fact, Outer and Inner "are present as an interpenetrating identity, as a substrate pregnant with content (*inhaltsvolle*)." (524)

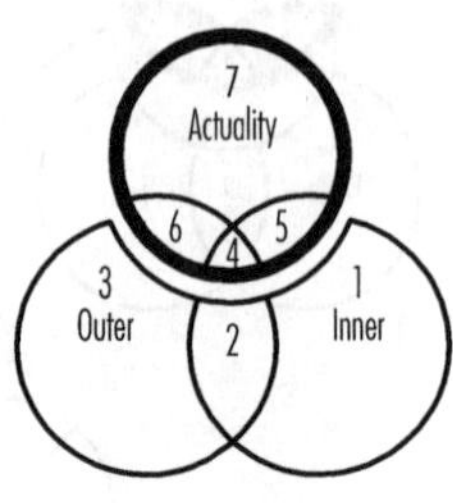

Figure 42(c)
Actuality

> What something is, therefore, it is wholly in its externality; its externality is its totality and equally is its unity reflected into itself. Its Appearance is not only reflection-into-an-other but reflection-into-self, and its externality is, therefore, the expression or utterance . . . of what it is in itself; and since its content and form are thus utterly identical, it is, in and for itself, nothing but this, *to express or manifest itself*. (528)

Essence, then, is *nothing but expression*. The dialectic of Inner and Outer "effectively puts an end to the duality posed in terms of elements and their link, for now the elements only exist as expression of the linkage."[26] Here Hegel finally ties together themes that have hovered about the discussion from the beginning. For Hegel, there is no mysterious beyond. Everything is appearance. The job of Essence is *precisely* to appear – which it has now done. Essence (Reflection) is in total unity with Appearance, and the result is that Essence is *actualized*. What was in itself has become for-itself. Essence *is* nothing but this drive to express itself in the outer world.

Inner and Outer, Hegel emphasizes, were *implicitly* actual. If Inner

---

26 TAYLOR, *supra* note 9, at 278.

and Outer were form-determinations,[27] they were equally *more* than mere form. Each was already the other. As Form, each erased itself and revealed itself to be itself, its other, and the unity of itself and other. What we get at the level of Outer and Inner is "not the real totality of the whole, but the totality or the fact itself only in the *determinateness* of form." (525) When Essence is said to be merely inner, a defect is implied. Non-defective Essence must have a perfect unity with the Outer. Each must immediately be its opposite *and* each must expressly be the unity between the two. Taken at their own level, Outer and Inner still lack "this identical substrate that contains them both." (526) "[T]his negative unity which links them together is the simple point devoid of any content." (526)

Actuality, in contrast, constitutes the totality of the fact. When actualized:

> each of the differences of form, the inner and outer, is posited within itself as the totality of itself and its other; the inner, as simple identity reflected into itself, is the immediate and accordingly is as much being and externality as essence; and the outer, as manifold, determinate being is only an outer, that is, is posited as unessential and as withdrawn into its ground, hence as an inner. This transition of each into the other is their immediate identity as substrate; but it is also their mediated identity; for it is precisely through its other that each is what it is in itself, the totality of the relation. (528)

Outer and Inner are not quite the Notion. "It is very important to notice that the unmediated *identity of form* is posited here without the movement of the fact itself, a movement pregnant with content." (526) Inner becomes Outer, but "there is also lacking that substrate which above was called the *fact*." (526) The thing is itself, its other, but not yet the express unity of itself and other. Or, as Marcuse put it:

> There remains something that is not absorbed into and fully displayed by immediate existence, something that is merely inward, despite the fact that or precisely because of the fact that it is one that exteriorizes itself. So long as something is still exteriorized, there remains something else which *has* not yet exteriorized itself and which is only at the interior. And so long as something is merely at the interior, actual being has not been attained.[28]

Notice that the Actual fact is *movement*. "The movement of essence

---

[27] Hegel comments that the Inner is the consummation of Essence "with respect to form." (525)

[28] MARCUSE, *supra* note 15, at 91.

is in general the becoming of the Notion," Hegel writes. (526) In Actuality, the extremes of the syllogism turn into each other instantaneously. Hegel compares this movement to the movement between Pure Being and Pure Nothing in chapter 1. There, Pure Being could not be kept apart from Pure Nothing. Here, something similar exists.

To be sure, in the beginning, Being "has not yet opposed and developed its moments." Even in Reflection it had "not yet *externalized* . . . and brought forth itself out of inwardness by its activity. It is therefore only an inner as *determinateness* against the outer, and only the outer as *determinateness* against the inner." (526) In short, Essence was merely in-itself but not for-itself. That the in-itself must become for-itself "makes itself apparent in all natural, scientific and spiritual development generally and it is essential to recognize that because something is at first only *inner* or also in its *Notion*, the first stage is for that very reason only its immediate, passive existence." (526) Science, Hegel implies, *is* rendering express and outward what is merely inward. Truth exists when Outer and Inner coincide.

So long as Essence remains inward, a thing seems like an aggregate of arbitrarily combined features with no inner unity. Hegel gives public instruction as an example of a jumble with no apparent inner unity.[29] Equally, if Essence is inward, a thing "is something *passive*, a *prey to otherness*." (527) The seed of a plant or a child is inwardly a plant or a man, but these may never grow into what they ought to become. For Hegel, there is no truck with what *might have been*. Logic is timeless and therefore what ought to be *will* be actual. And what is ultimately actual is that all "Things" must fade away.

---

[29] Hegel was the director of a public *gymnasium* (or high school) at the time he wrote these words. TERRY PINKARD, HEGEL: A BIOGRAPHY 342 (2000)

PART VI
ACTUALITY

16
The Absolute

What is rational is actual; and what is actual is rational.[1]

When Hegel published this notorious line in the *Philosophy of Right*, readers suspected him of Prussian apologism.[2] Was he saying that nothing could surpass the actual political state in whose employ Hegel was? Readers of the *SL* knew different. This was only Hegel's way of saying there is no unreachable, transcendental beyond.[3] Essence must appear. What is "in itself" (implicit) must become "for itself" (express). "When being posits its entire inwardness [*i.e.*, essence] outside itself, it becomes actual."[4]

Actuality is the state in which the in-itself of Essence finally becomes for itself. The Actuality chapters constitute the "speculative" truth of Essence. Reflection – "formless essence" (529) – was Essence's immediate moment. Appearance was dialectic. Actuality is the unity

---

[1] G.W.F. HEGEL, ELEMENTS OF THE PHILOSOPHY OF RIGHT 20 Addition (Allen W. Wood trans. 1993).

[2] *See* TERRY PINKARD, HEGEL: A BIOGRAPHY 342 (2000) (describing the contemporary reaction to the *Philosophy of Right*).

[3] CHARLES TAYLOR, HEGEL 279 (1975) ("It is external reality which is fully expression of the essence, and external reality which has nothing hidden behind it, because it is full manifestation of what is essential"); ROBERT M. WALLACE, HEGEL'S PHILOSOPHY OF REALITY, FREEDOM AND GOD 197 (2005) ("it is clear that Hegel [does] not interpret actuality as mere factual existence").

[4] HERBERT MARCUSE, HEGEL'S ONTOLOGY AND THE THEORY OF HISTORICITY 92 (Seyla Benhabib trans. 1987).

between Reflection and Appearance. Reflection and Appearance are Actual when they self-erase.[5]

Appearance ended with the unity of Inner and Outer in which "the content of both is only one *identical substrate* and equally only *one identity of form*." (529) This unity is the Absolute as such. Here, in the second shortest chapter of the *SL*,[6] "form has sublated itself and made itself into the *empty or outer difference* of an outer and inner." (529) This version of the Absolute, however, is "antithetical to difference."[7] So far, Reflection is external to the Absolute. It "merely contemplates rather than is the absolute's own movement." (529) Reflection must discover that it *is* "essentially this movement." (529) Only then will the Absolute be strong enough to encompass difference.

A. The Exposition of the Absolute

The Objective Logic soon yields the Subjective Logic. Accordingly, the next three chapters make psychoanalytic points. It is my thesis that the Exposition of the Absolute corresponds with what Hegel describes as madness in the third part of the Encyclopedia.[8] If the Absolute is taken as the subject, then the subject now begins to emerge from nature by madly obliterating it. Having done so, it is prepared to reconstruct a new world out of symbolic or conceptual materials. These symbolic materials are the determinations that subjectivity makes of its own self. But these determinations are never entirely adequate to the subject. The subject is therefore very much a Hegelian "thing" – a unity

---

[5] *See* Michael Kosok, *The Formalization of Hegel's Dialectical Logic: Its Formal Structure, Logical Interpretation and Intuitive Foundation*, in HEGEL: A COLLECTION OF CRITICAL ESSAYS 237, 239 (Alasdair MacIntyre ed., 1972) ("Reflection is thus a shift from a pre-formal to a post-formal situation, wherein a well-formed universe appears as an intermediate stage").

[6] The chapter on Chemism is shorter. There is no chapter in the *EL* corresponding to the Absolute. Marcuse thinks this shows that the *SL* is the superior, more complete exposition of Hegel's philosophy. The *EL* is only an outline, and "in this context the presence of a chapter on the absolute would only be confusing and unintelligible." MARCUSE, *supra* note 4, at 90. In Marcuse's opinion, chapter 16 stands for "[t]he comprehensive determination of the motility of actuality . . . " *Id*. at 104. "Motility" is the capacity for movement.

[7] JOHN F. HOFFMEYER, THE ADVENT OF FREEDOM: THE PRESENCE OF THE FUTURE IN HEGEL'S LOGIC 16 (1994).

[8] HEGEL'S PHILOSOPHY OF MIND § 408 (William Wallace, A.V. Miller trans. 1971). It is arresting that, for Hegel, human subjectivity is *born in madness*. *See generally* DANIEL BERTHOLD-BOND, HEGEL'S THEORY OF MADNESS (1995).

of diverse properties which the subject must shed if it is to manifest its truth.

From Actuality emerges the entire Subjective Logic,[9] which replays the Objective Logic and rebuilds a reality in which the subject can recognize itself. "There is no transition from 'actuality' to a more actual structure," Marcuse writes.[10] "There is no going beyond the absolute, only an 'exposition' of it, 'exhibiting what it is.'"[11] From now on the theme is development and exposition, not transition into otherness or the positing of an other.

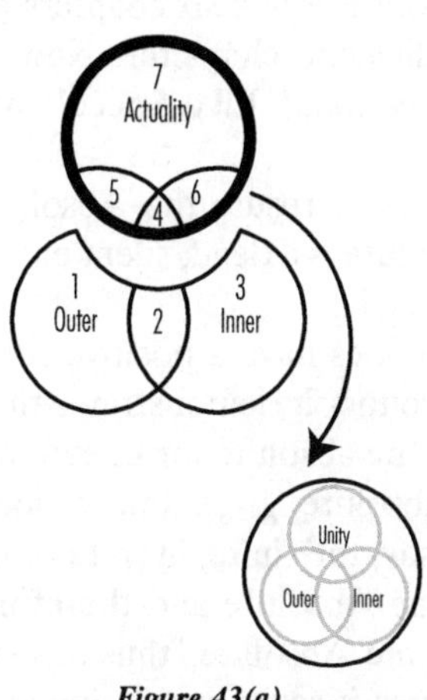

Figure 43(a)
Exposition of the Absolute

The Absolute is the perfect unity between Inner and Outer. The Understanding proposes that everything has dissolved itself into the Absolute. Neither Essence, Existence, nor Reflection can be distinguished any longer. "Accordingly, the process of *determining what the Absolute is* has a negative outcome." (530) The Absolute is merely "the negation of all predicates and [is] the void." (530) This is not to say that external reflection cannot discern an essence here or a deceptive appearance there. But it can, with equal ease, demonstrate the finitude and relativity of such determinations. What external reflection cannot do is "to raise either the [predicates] or the negations to a genuine unity." (530) The Absolute must *itself* display this unity.

The message of the Exposition of the Absolute is that the Absolute is *both* the extremes of the syllogism (inner and outer) *and* the middle term – all in one. Therefore, it is necessary to amend our expositional convention to reflect this fact. In Figure 43(a), the Understanding now sees "the *absolute form* . . . each of whose moments is within itself the *totality* and hence, as indifference to the form, is the complete *content* of the whole." (531) "Absolute form" is comprised of three overlapping

---

9 "Hegel's doctrine of the objectivity of essence postulates that Being is the mind that has not yet come to itself." THEODOR W. ADORNO, NEGATIVE DIALECTICS 168 (E.B. Ashton trans. 2000).

10 MARCUSE, ONTOLOGY, *supra* note 4, at 89.

11 *Id*. at 90.

circles. Nevertheless, the Understanding, as always, makes of the concrete relationship a single identity.[12]

The Understanding, at first simple and unschooled, has grown smarter. In the Doctrine of Being, it saw immediate identities. By Measure, it had learned to see double. Understanding at that point morphed into Dialectical Reason. Throughout the first six chapters of Essence, the Understanding sustained a dialectic character. Now it manifests further progress. It has become *notional*. Like Speculative Reason, it sees everything in threes.

In the Absolute, all distinction vanishes. As a result, the Absolute cannot determine or express itself. The Absolute is a dead, silent entity – "the *negative exposition* of the absolute." (531)

A failure, the Exposition of the Absolute does have a positive side: "for in so far as in it the finite falls to the ground, it demonstrates that [the finite's] nature is to be connected with the absolute, or to contain the absolute within itself." (532) The Absolute gives the various determinations their *subsistence*. That is to say, the finite, in spite of its propensity to erase itself, withdraws into the Absolute and therefore participates in eternity. The Exposition of the Absolute "thus arrests the finite before it vanishes and contemplates it as an expression and image of the absolute." (532)

But, Hegel warns, this positive side is "only an illusory activity." (532) It is *for us*. For itself, the Exposition of the Absolute is a failure. "Any further determinations that may occur [are] a nullity that the exposition picks up *from outside* and from which it gains a *beginning* for its activity." (532) For this reason, the Exposition of the Absolute "*begins from itself* and *arrives at itself*." (532) It does not account for its own Movement of Reflection, which Dialectic Reason sees as standing over against it.[13] Exposition of the Absolute is merely the negative of reflection and "something imperfect." (533) Yet the Absolute has swallowed all and therefore contains difference.

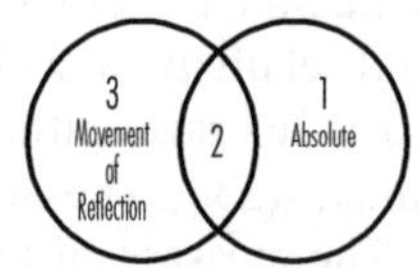

Figure 43(b)
Movement of Reflection

[12] We return to Absolute Form in chapter 27, when "content" has been abolished.

[13] *Cf.* Deborah Chaffin, *The Logic of Contingency*, in HEGEL RECONSIDERED: BEYOND METAPHYSICS AND THE AUTHORITARIAN STATE (H. Tristram Engelhardt, Jr., & Terry Pinkard eds., 154 (1994) ("Therefore, as self-related, the attribute is the determinate absolute. Yet the attribute is *also* reflection external to the absolute, since it is only by virtue of this characteristic that it is the determinateness of the absolute.").

Difference is movement. Difference must appear. Dialectical Reason suggests that, if the Understanding insists on the unity of the Absolute, it thereby excludes the Movement of Reflection.

The Movement of Reflection is self-erasure. In Figure 43(a), the Absolute accepted difference, but also destroyed it. Because difference was destroyed, Movement was banished and became "the beyond of the [sublated] manifold differences . . . , a beyond which *lies at the back of the absolute*." (531) This beyond proves that the Exposition of the Absolute is "only *arrived* at." (533) It is "only the *absolute of an external reflection*. It is therefore not the absolute absolute but the absolute in a determinateness." (533)

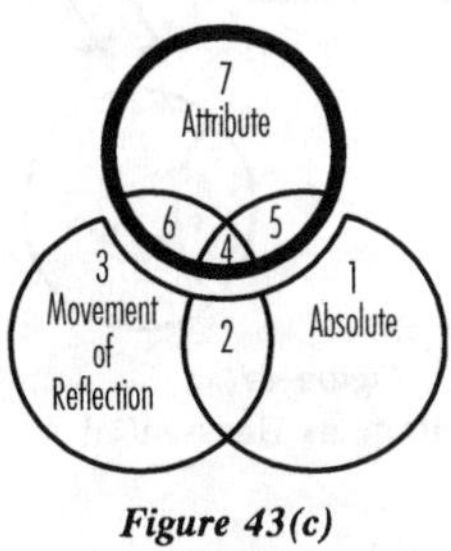

Figure 43(c)
Attribute

Speculative Reason points out that external reflection is not *merely* the beyond of the Absolute. It is also *in* the Absolute. This double status of the Movement of Reflection and Absolute Hegel names Attribute. Attribute stands for the dependence of the Exposition of the Absolute on external reflection. "In the attribute the absolute shows only in one of its moments, a moment *presupposed* and picked up by *external reflection*." (554)

B. The Absolute Attribute

The "absolute absolute" is not yet before us and does not arrive until the last chapter. Attribute is merely the *relative* Absolute – the Absolute in a form determination. In psychoanalytic terms, the Attribute is the investiture of the subject in the external world. Subjective Attribute is how a subject produces the means by which it might recognize itself as a subject (and, in a world of many subjects, be recognized by other subjects).

The Attribute is no mere product of Reflection. To leave the matter here would be to admit that Reflection is permanently external to Attribute. Inner and Outer are, by now, in unity. Reflection has already been shown to be equally *internal* to Attribute. Furthermore, the Attribute is the *whole content* of the Absolute. There is no "inner" any longer. Attribute is "the absolute as in simple *identity* with itself." (534)

Hegel compares the Attribute favorably to the World of Appearance and the World In and For Self of Figure 39(b). Each of these sides was itself, its other, and the whole of the relation. Nevertheless, each contained a moment of opposition. Each World insisted on its immediacy against the other. In the Exposition of the Absolute, however, immediacy is reduced to illusory being. That is to say, immediacy is an ideality or mere memory of a history long sublated. The "*true and sole subsistence*" is now the totality. (533-4)

Yet, since it is the determination of the Absolute, Attribute is "posited as *unessential* subsistence." (534) The Understanding now theorizes that the Absolute is the unity of all these sublations. Because Attribute is unessential, the Absolute can have multiple Attributes. Every one of them, however, is posited as sublated.

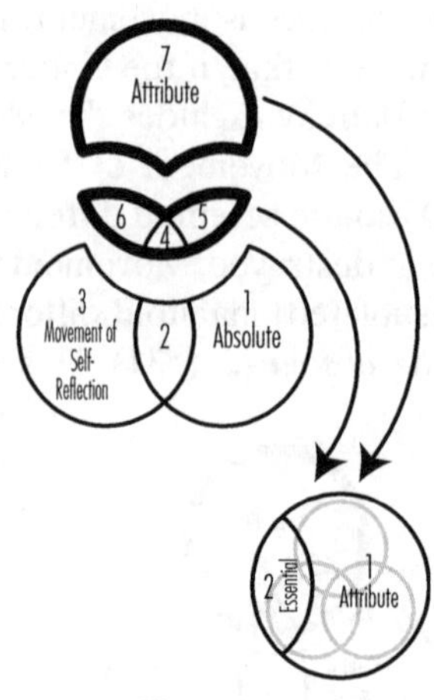

Figure 44(a)
Attribute as Unessential

Dialectical Reason points out that, in Figure 44(a), Attribute is held separate from the act of producing it.

> [S]ince it is as *inner* form that reflection determines the absolute into attribute, this determining is something still distinct from the externality; the inner determination does not penetrate the absolute; its utterance or expression is, as something merely posited, to vanish in the absolute. (534)

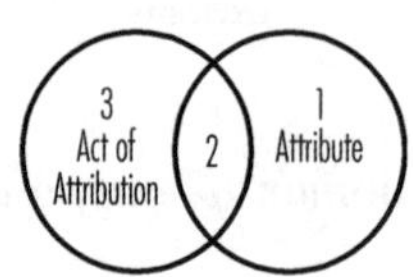

Figure 44(b)
Act of Attribution

The Attribute is now merely the "way and manner" (534) of the Absolute. The Absolute is *alienated* from its inessential ways and manners.

C. The Mode of the Absolute

In Figure 44(a), Attribute was "the absolute as in simple *identity* with itself." (534) But this implied that Attribute was *negation*, as seen in Figure 44(b). The side designated as [1, 2] is comprised of the two sides *and* the middle term that connects them. The side designated as [3], however, is "the reflection which is *external* to the absolute." (535) Yet [3] is just as much *in* [1, 2] as *out* of it. Therefore, to the extent that [3] is taken as external, the Absolute is *self*-external – "the loss of itself in the mutability and contingency of being, the accomplished transition of itself into opposites *without the return into itself*; the multiplicity of form and content determinations lacking the character of totality." (535)

In effect, the Absolute is recognized by an external reflection which is nevertheless as much a part *of* the Absolute as it is apart *from* the Absolute. The unity of the Attribute and the alienated Act of Attribution is what Hegel calls Mode. Mode represents the Absolute externalized. But it is not to be taken merely as the loss of totality. Mode is externality *posited* as externality. The Attributes recognized in the Mode constitute the authentic "way and manner" of the Absolute.

Speculative Reason always names a movement. So Mode is "reflective movement . . . posited as reflective movement." (535) In Mode, the Exposition of the Absolute has "completely run through all its moments." (535) At first an immediacy, then an opposition, it is now a unity of opposition and immediacy. Only this self-moving unity achieves "absolute identity." (535) Active Mode is not dealing with something external. Its products (Attributes) are Illusory Beings from which the "selfdissolving" Absolute (535) returns to itself. In its triplicity, Mode is the "first truly absolute identity" (541) and an "essenceless determination." (541) In Mode, the distinction between Essence and Appearance has been defeated. "The mode is therefore the externality of the absolute, but equally only as the reflection of the absolute into itself." (541)

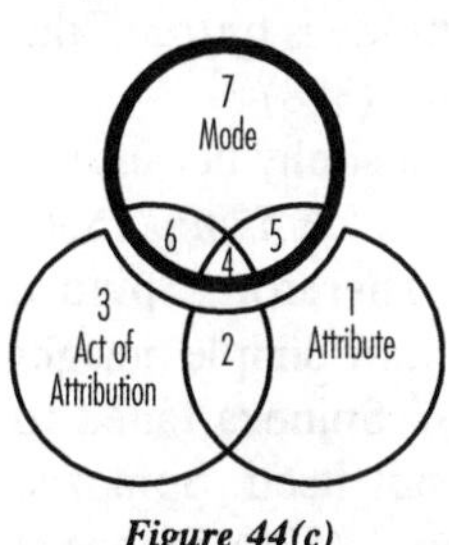

Figure 44(c)
Mode

What Hegel calls "expounding reflection" (535) is the *Spinozist* view of the Absolute. Expounding reflection begins from its own determinations which are taken as something external. These it merely *finds*. It then dissolves these "back into an indifferent identity." (535) Such an expounding reflection *terminates* its determinations but does not begin them.

The true Absolute contains within itself the determinateness from which the seemingly external determinations begin. Mode has not yet achieved this originary status. The determinateness of the Exposition of the Absolute belonged to the Movement of Reflection, as seen in Figure 43(b). Through this alone the Absolute is determined as having a form. It is not merely equal to itself. It *posits* itself as equal to itself.

The Mode is the Absolute's own reflective movement – a determining. But it does not make itself an other; it only makes itself what it already is. Externality is a *transparent* externality which is a self-manifestation. This outwardness is equally inwardness. It is a positing that is also absolute *being*.

So what truth does the Absolute manifest? Simply that the distinction between form and content is dissolved. The "content of the absolute is just this, *to manifest itself*." (536) The absolute *is* only as manifestation of itself for itself. "As such it is *actuality*." (536)[14] In Actuality the in-itself becomes for-itself.

Spinoza. Exposition of the Absolute stands for Spinozist substance. In chapter 7, Hegel criticized Spinoza's distinction between substance and attribute. The mediating "third" to these two oppositions was "mode" (*i.e.*, intellect). Mode for Spinoza was "externality as such," (327) the same as Hegelian Measure. As external, mode is untrue; "the rigid nature of substance lacks the return into self." (328)

Hegel now says that "Spinozism is a defective philosophy because in it reflection and its manifold determining is an *external thinking*." (536) Spinozist substance is *one*. It lacks determinateness. Therefore, Spinoza held that *determinateness is negation*; "this true and simple insight establishes the absolute unity of substance." (536)[15] Spinoza failed to see that the absolute negates not just its other but itself. Spinozist substance "*does not itself contain the absolute form*." (536) Spinozist substance may be the perfect unity of thought and extension (*i.e.*, being). But it contains thought "only in its *unity* with extension." (537) Thought does not separate itself from being but is treated as already separated. Thought is not reflective *activity*; it fails to return to itself.

Two consequences follow from this failure. First, "substance lacks the principle of *personality* – a defect which has been the main cause of hostility to Spinoza's system." (537) Personality is "the practical, objective Notion determined in and for itself which, as person, is impenetrable atomic subjectivity – but which . . . in its other has *its own* objectivity for its object." (824) Proper substance (Hegel's Absolute Idea) goes out of itself *and* returns to itself. Its other is itself. Absolute Idea therefore contains *all* determinations within itself. This feature of self-negation and return (personality) is missing in Spinozist thought.[16]

---

[14] Marcuse says that this passage "reinterprets the essential Aristotelian definition of Being as *energeia*, as well as defining the character of the movement of actual being." MARCUSE, ONTOLOGY, *supra* note 4, at 91. Hegel expressly invokes Aristotle's *energeia* in *EL* § 142 Remark.

[15] *See* Letter 50, in 2 CHIEF WORKS OF SPINOZA 370 (R.H.M. Elwes ed. 1955).

[16] This "is the principal difference between Hegel and Spinoza. For Spinoza, being is ultimately substance that is immanent in but also logically *prior* to its modes: it is the immanent *cause* of its modes. For Hegel, by contrast, being is ultimately concept that is wholly identical with its unfolding differences. Those differences belong to and constitute the concept itself. The concept is thus not their logically prior "ground" or "cause": it *is* simply the process of differentiating itself into those differences." Stephen Houlgate, *Why*

Spinoza's notions of substance, "profound and correct as they are, are [mere] *definitions*, which are *immediately* assumed at the outset of the science." (537) The absolute cannot be a *first*. It must be the *result*.[17]

On refutation of philosophical error. Later in the *SL*, Hegel, recalling the above criticism of Spinoza, reminds his readers that, though partly false, Spinozism is also partly true. "[O]ne must get rid of the erroneous idea of regarding the system as out and out *false*, as if the *true* system by contrast were only *opposed* to the false." (580) Spinozist substance is a genuine moment, "but *it is not the highest standpoint*." (580) The *true* system cannot merely oppose Spinozism, "for if this were so, the system, as this opposite, would itself be one-sided. On the contrary, the true system as the higher, must contain the subordinate system within itself." (580)

If a philosophy is to be defeated, "it must not proceed from assumptions lying outside the system in question and inconsistent with it." (580) A besieged philosophy "need only refuse to recognize those assumptions." (580-1) Rather, refutation must seize upon an assumption that the philosophy clearly honors, push it to the extreme, and show its destructive implications for the system. "The genuine refutation must penetrate the opponent's stronghold and meet him on his own ground; no advantage is gained by attacking him somewhere else and defeating him where he is not." (581)

The true system must preserve and honor vanquished philosophies as genuine moments in the system. The only way of refuting Spinozism is to honor it by "recognizing its standpoint as essential and necessary and then going on to raise that standpoint to the higher one through its own immanent dialectic." (581)

Spinozist substance (Hegel's Exposition of the Absolute) will yield the Notion. This result is "the sole and genuine refutation of Spinozism." (581)

Hegel's Concept is not the Essence of Things, in HEGEL'S THEORY OF THE SUBJECT 24 (David Gray Carlson ed., 2005); *see also id*. at 27 (Hegelian thought is "Spinozan metaphysics, freed from the dominance of essence").

[17] Stanley Rosen characterizes Hegel's critique of Spinoza as follows: "The finite is not reflected into substance because there is no interiority into which it could be received. Consequently, there is no 'third dimension' or Spirit within which substance and its attributes can be unified." STANLEY ROSEN, G.W.F. HEGEL: AN INTRODUCTION TO THE SCIENCE OF WISDOM 55 (1974). I disagree. Hegel thinks there *is* an inner to Spinozist substance; the problem is that it *stays* inner. Furthermore, spirit is not a third to substance and attribute. Spirit *is* substance, which will develop itself out of its subjective interior throughout the last third of the *SL*.

17
Actuality

Actuality is absolute form, with "no content save that of being self-manifestation." (541) "The utterance of the actual is the actual itself."[1] And what Actuality utters is *its own self-erasure*.[2]

Actuality posits the unity of itself, its other, and the unity of self and other.[3] Accordingly, the Actual "is not drawn into the sphere of *alteration* by its externality, nor is it the *reflecting* of itself in *an other*." (542) Yet Actuality has its moments, each "a further step in the logical breakdown between the internal and the external."[4] First, it is an immediacy with no essence – no reflection-into-self. The Actual thing just *is*. When immediacy is emphasized, Reflection is banished from Actuality. Hegel interprets banished reflection-into-self as Possibility (*Möglichkeit*). At this point, Essence is "capable of being actualized [and] is more precisely thought of as the possibility of the actual."[5]

In Possibility, the Actual becomes other, but, since it is expressly the

---

1 EL § 142.

2 *See* JOHN F. HOFFMEYER, THE ADVENT OF FREEDOM: THE PRESENCE OF THE FUTURE IN HEGEL'S LOGIC 55 (1994) ("Hegel does not understand manifestation as the 'expression' of something behind it or prior to it").

3 Hoffmeyer emphasizes that the structure of this chapter precisely embodies this slogan. *Id*. at 16. Actuality is "both the totality of the section and a moment within the section." *Id*. at 18. *See also* RICHARD DIEN WINFIELD, AUTONOMY AND NORMATIVITY 46 (2001) ("determinacy, determined determinacy and self-determined determinacy").

4 HOFFMEYER, *supra* note 2, at 17.

5 JOHN W. BURBIDGE, HEGEL ON LOGIC AND RELIGION: THE REASONABLENESS OF CHRISTIANITY 40 (1992).

unity of itself, its other and the unity of these two, Actuality only becomes itself when it becomes Possible.

The extremes will show that they cannot sustain themselves without the other. They are therefore imply a third term – Necessity.

The moments of Actuality must undergo the usual development of immediacy, duality and unity. The first of these is formal. The second is "real." The third is absolute.

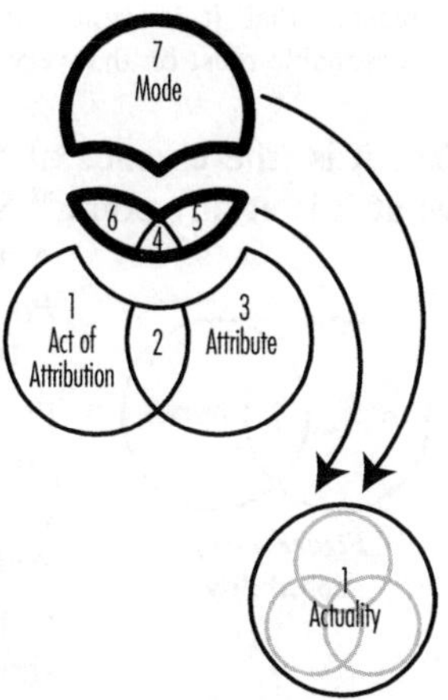

Figure 45(a)
Formal Actuality

A. Contingency

Formal Actuality is immediate and unreflected. It simply *is* – a phenomenon that "cuts itself off from the process that has led up to it . . . For this reason it appears as something that has no ground. Like anything that de facto *is*, it parades itself as self-sufficient. It has its own presence to guarantee for its possibility."[6]

Hegel denounces this "common sense" version of Actuality in the *EL*:

> Actuality and thought . . .are often absurdly opposed. How commonly we hear people saying that, though no objection can be urged against the truth and correctness of a certain thought, there is nothing of the kind to be seen in actuality . . . People who use such language only prove that they have not properly apprehended the nature either of thought or of actuality. Thought, in such a case is . . . the synonym for a subjective conception . . . just as actuality . . . is made synonymous with external and sensible existence. This is all very well in common life, where great laxity is allowed in the categories and the names given to them; and it may happen that, e.g., the plan . . . of taxation, is good and advisable in the abstract, but that nothing of the sort is found in so-called actuality . . . But when the abstract understanding gets hold of these categories and exaggerates the distinction they imply into a hard and fast line of contrast, when it tells us that in this actual world we must knock ideas out of our heads, it is necessary energetically to protest against these doctrines, alike in the name of science and of sound reason. For . . . Ideas are not confined to our heads merely, nor is the Idea . . .so feeble as to leave the question of its actualization . . . dependent on our will. The Idea is rather . . . active as well as actual . . . [A]ctuality is not so bad [as] muddle-brained would-be

---

6 George di Giovanni, *The Category of Contingency in the Hegelian Logic*, in SELECTED ESSAYS ON G.W.F. HEGEL 47 (Lawrence Stepelevich ed., 1993).

> reformers imagine. So far is actuality, as distinguished from mere appearance, and primarily presenting a unity of inward and outward, from being in contrariety with reason, that it is rather thoroughly reasonable, and everything which is not reasonable must on that very ground cease to be held actual.[7]

Yet it is "the essence of the actual to be always *more* and *other* than what it is at any point."[8] So Dialectical Reason proposes that Formal Actuality is *less* than the totality; it points to the *Possibility* of totality.

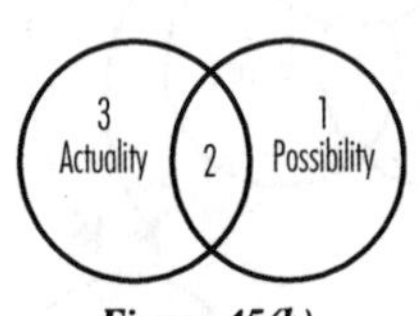

Figure 45(b)
Possibility

Possibility is here revealed to be the in-itself [2] of Formal Actuality.[9] "*What is actual is possible*," Hegel observes (542). Actuality proves Possibility. In Figure 45(b), Possibility and Actuality are in a relation. Before, they were in unity. Formal Actuality signals the realization that the Possible can only be derived retroactively from Actuality.[10] Possibilities never actualized are empty talk. Hegel memorably denounces foolish possibilities in the *EL*:

> [A]ny content, however absurd and nonsensical, can be viewed as possible. It is possible that the moon might fall upon the earth tonight; for the moon is a body separate from the earth – and may as well fall down upon it as a stone thrown into the air does. It is possible that the Sultan may become Pope; for, being a man, he may be converted to the Christian faith, may become a Catholic priest, and so on. In language like this about possibilities, it is chiefly the law of the sufficient ground or reason which is manipulated in the style already explained. Everything, it is said, is possible, for which you can state some ground. The less education a man has, or, in other words, the less he knows of the specific connections of the objects to which he directs his observations, the greater is his tendency to launch out into all sorts of empty possibilities . . .[11]

Possibility isolated from Actuality is empty. It is "*posited* as negative." (543) As negative, Possibility has two moments. First, it is a positive concept unto itself. As the in-itself of Actuality it is [2], but [2] always implies the immediacy of [3]. As [3], Formal Possibility is "the relation-

---

[7] EL § 142 Remark.

[8] HERBERT MARCUSE, HEGEL'S ONTOLOGY AND THE THEORY OF HISTORICITY 96 (Seyla Benhabib trans. 1987).

[9] *See* HOFFMEYER, *supra* note 2, at 68 ("Far from being made subordinate to actuality, possibility is actuality's essence").

[10] JEANNE L. SCHROEDER, THE VESTAL AND THE FASCES: HEGEL, LACAN, PROPERTY, AND THE FEMININE 31-2 (1998).

[11] EL § 143 Remark.

less, indeterminate receptacle for everything whatever. In the sense of this formal possibility *everything is possible that is not self-contradictory*; hence the realm of possibility is a boundless multiplicity." (543)[12] Possibility isolated from Actuality is *Diverse*. Diverse things negate themselves and pass into opposition. In isolation, Possibility is contradictory and turns into its opposite. "Possibility is therefore in its own self contradiction, or it is *impossibility*." (544)[13]

Possibility implies its own lack. It points to an other – Actuality – needed to complete itself. Possibility is ostensibly merely a moment in a totality. It is merely "the *ought-to-be* of the totality of form." (543) In effect Possibility confesses that its content might be *impossible*. It is possible that the Chicago Cubs might win the pennant. This implies it is equally possible they might not. Possibility *relates* these two otherwise indifferent remarks. Possibility is therefore the unity of the possible and the impossible. It is a contradiction and hence an *im*possibility.

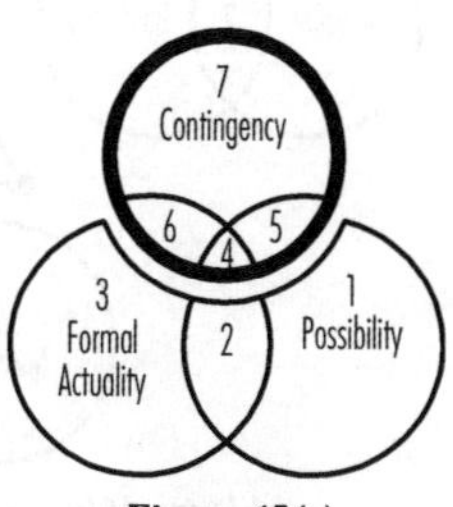

Figure 45(c)
Contingency

A contradiction, Possibility sublates itself. It announces, "I am not Actuality." But by this very act of self-effacement, Possibility *actualizes* itself. For Speculative Reason, Possibility is an Actuality and vice versa.[14] Taken as immediate, Actuality also implies that it is not Actual, only Possible. Speculative Reason names this self-renouncing activity to be Contingency.

"The contingent is an actual that at the same time is determined as merely possible, whose other or opposite equally is." (545) Accordingly,

---

[12] The definition of possibility as the non-contradictory is Aristotle's. G.R.G. MURE, A STUDY OF HEGEL'S LOGIC 134 (1950). Mure claims that the last part of the Actuality chapters "closely follows Aristotle's analysis in terms of potential and actual, contingent and necessary." *Id.* at 149.

[13] Michael Inwood overlooks this passage when he writes, "If the contradictory is not impossible, then what is? Hegel provides no satisfactory answer to this question." M.J. INWOOD, HEGEL 449 (1983) (footnote omitted).

[14] Stephen Houlgate writes, "Hegel thus agrees with the tradition that necessity lies in the foreclosing of possibility; but the twist he adds to this is that necessity lies in the foreclosing of the possibility that possibility itself might *not* be something actual." Stephen Houlgate, *Necessity and Contingency in Hegel's* Science of Logic, 27 OWL OF MINERVA 37, 42 (1995). In fact, the foreclosure (or actualization) of Possibility is more directly Contingency in Figure 45(c), which the Understanding, in Figure 46(a), will rename Necessity.

Contingency has two sides. First, it is immediate (Formal Actuality [7]). As such, it has no ground. It simply *is*. It is "only Existence." (545) Second, Contingency is a positedness [4, 5, 6]. As such it is grounded. So the Contingent is simultaneously grounded and ungrounded.[15] Causes may conspire to bring the Contingent into existence (in which case it is grounded). Or perhaps no cause precedes the Contingent; it may never be actualized. If not it is ungrounded.

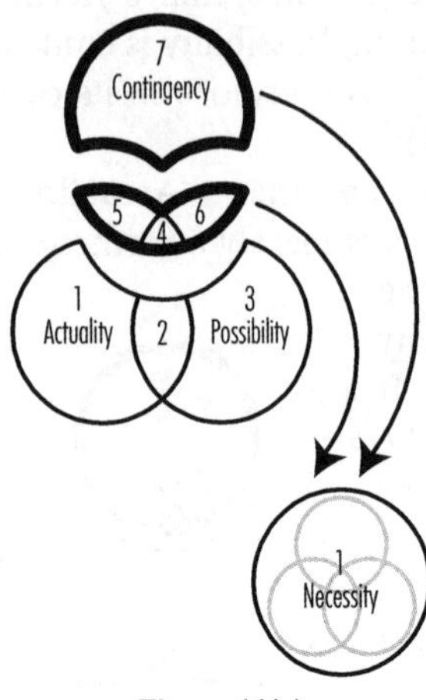

Figure 46(a)
Formal Necessity

Contingency is the name of the movement of Actuality into Possibility and back – "the *posited* unmediated *conversion* of inner and outer, or of reflectedness-into-self and being." (545)[16] Since Contingency is this movement, it cannot properly articulate *unity*.[17] By now, however, each extreme is itself, its other, and the unity between these extremes. Accordingly, Actuality and Possibility are Contingent as well as immediate. Each is nothing but the act of manifesting itself. So the Understanding proposes that Contingency is Necessity: "*Contingency is the matrix out of which necessity arises.*"[18]

Figure 46(a) is a reproach to those who see Hegel as a philosophical totalitarian. Contingency is *part of the totality*.[19] It is what's Necessary.

---

15 HOFFMEYER, *supra* note 2, at 23, 70.

16 Reflectedness-into-self refers to the act of Possibility renouncing its Actuality and Actuality renouncing its Possibility. By so renouncing, each brings Actuality into unmediated Being.

17 *Id.* at 41.

18 Di Giovanni, *supra* note 6, at 48.

19 EMIL L. FACKENHEIM, THE RELIGIOUS DIMENSION IN HEGEL'S THOUGHT 19 (1967); di Giovanni, *supra* note 6, at 43 ("Hegel is so far from denying the reality of contingency as actually to be the only speculative philosopher in history to attempt a demonstration of its inevitability") (footnote omitted); MARCUSE, ONTOLOGY, *supra* note 8, at 97 ("Necessity therefore is at bottom contingency!"). For this reason, Burbidge suggests that Hegel's philosophy is always retrospective; it cannot predict the contingencies of nature and history. BURBIDGE, RELIGION, *supra* note 5, at 69 ("Unreflective existence is thus not alien to thought, but a moment in its own process. For this reason, Hegel argues that contingency is necessary").

It is built in the system. Our future is *not* in the stars but in ourselves to rough-hew as we will. It is *necessary* that we be free, *i.e.*, contingent.

Necessity stands for the proposition that what *is* ain't necessarily so. Perhaps things are what they are through happenstance, or perhaps they *are* necessarily so. What is necessary is that things be subject to this very ambiguity.[20]

Here is what I think Hegel's point is *not*. A familiar nursery rhyme traces the loss of a kingdom to the loss of a nail. From history's perspective, the kingdom's loss required the loss of the nail, which, at the time, was a highly contingent matter. Everyone's actual state is brought about by a series of improbable circumstances. But this is not what Hegel means. Rather, he means that the determination of a finite thing (today's lost kingdom) is itself a contingency. Maybe it *is* lost, maybe it will come roaring back, like the Borbons in Spain. "[W]hat simply is, is not itself the necessary." (546)[21]

B. Real Actuality, Possibility, and Necessity[22]

In Figure 46(a), Necessity's moments were formal; Actuality and Possibility constantly turned into one another. Formal Necessity was "indifferent to its differences." (546) It confirmed that things are contingent, but it could not say whether a thing is possible or actual. It merely named the flux of formal moments, unable to distinguish between them. As flux, Formal Necessity did not have the form of self-subsistence.

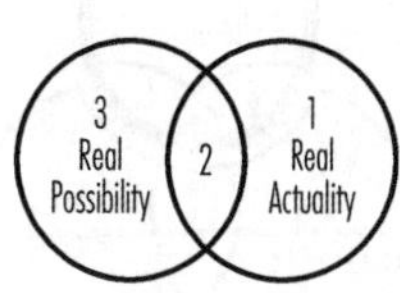

Figure 46(b)
Real Possibility

Dialectical Reason remembers that Necessity

[20] Burbidge thinks that there are three "necessities" for Hegel. This is the first. JOHN W. BURBIDGE, ON HEGEL'S LOGIC: FRAGMENTS OF A COMMENTARY 195 (1981) ("This sense of an immediate necessity is implicit in any appeal to self-evidence"). The second Necessity is that produced by a complete set of all Conditions – Real Necessity (Figure 46(c)). The third, most adequate Necessity is what exists when its contrary is self-contradictory. "Such a self-referential, negative determination specifies inherent (rather than external) conditions sufficient to rule out its own falsity." *Id.* at 196.

[21] This is lost on Michael Inwood, who thinks that necessity and contingency are mutually exclusive categories. Inwood reads Hegel as trying to *compartmentalize* contingency, so that *mostly* there is necessity. INWOOD, *supra* note 13, at 356-61.

[22] Hyppolite calls this section "perhaps the most illuminating of all the dialectics of essence." JEAN HYPPOLITE, LOGIC AND EXISTENCE 174 (Leonard Lawlor & Amit Sen trans., 1997).

is one with Possibility. Formal Necessity is now renamed Real Actuality and is paired with Real Possibility. "Real" for Hegel connotes mediation and determinability.[23] In Real Possibility, Necessity is negated Possibility and Possibility is negated Necessity. No term makes sense without its other.

According to Dialectical Reason, if Formal Necessity is isolated as [1], its content [2] is likewise isolated, on the side of Being. [2] is therefore Possibility. In conjunction with [1], [2] stands for the diverse determinations of the Actual thing "and is a *manifold* content in general." (546) Real Actuality [1, 2] is therefore "the thing of many properties, the existent world." (546) This notion ties into Hegel's view, presented in chapter 1, that knowledge is a collaboration between the subject and the object. Each of these is a force contributing to the middle term of knowledge. Thus, Real Actuality is the *forceful* object. "What is actual *can* act; something manifests its actuality through what . . . it produces." (546)

Real Actuality is more advanced than Existence as proto-thing. Actuality preserves itself in the manifold (whereas the "thing" of Existence dissolves).[24] Actual externality is authentic. "Its relationship to another something is the manifestation *of itself*." (546) No mere appearance, it is "exempted from transition."[25] Meanwhile, Possibility is the in-itself [2] of Real Actuality.[26] This in-itself, Hegel says, is "*pregnant with content*." (547) "Pregnant with content" (*inhaltsvolle*) is Hegelese for unity of Outer and Inner. Therefore, Real Possibility is an immediacy, but it also suffuses through Real Actuality.

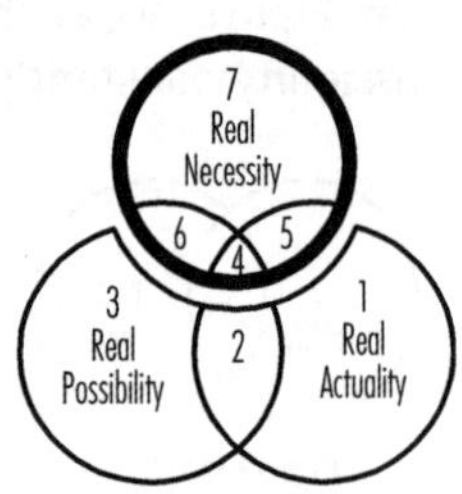

Figure 46(c)
Real Necessity
(Totality of Conditions)

When so taken, Real Possibility constitutes the *Totality of Conditions*. "When all the conditions of something are

---

[23] BURBIDGE, RELIGION, *supra* note 5, at 44. In chapter 1, "reality" was Quality paired with Negation. Real Measure in chapter 8 signalled Measure specifying the *specified*. Real Ground stood for the realization that Ground and Grounded define each other.

[24] *Supra* at 357-9.

[25] EL § 142.

[26] *See* HERBERT MARCUSE, REASON AND REVOLUTION 150 (1999) ("Possible is only that which can be derived from the very content of the real").

completely present, it enters into actuality." (548)[27] One Actual thing implies an entire world of actual determinate things, and every thing is *necessarily* what it is. It is now "impossible to distinguish possibility and actuality."[28] "Real possibility no longer has over against it *such an other*, for it is real in so far as it is itself also actuality." (548-9)

Real Possibility's duality is now sublated. In this negation of Real Actuality and Possibility, identity-with-self is achieved. "[I]n its sublating it is thus within itself the recoil of this sublating, it is *real necessity*." (549) Yet Real Necessity is still merely relative – not free. Real Actuality as such cannot exist on its own. It depends on all the circumstances implied by Real Possibility. Real Actuality is still merely possible, as is Real Possibility. Real Necessity, the unity between the two, is likewise only possible – "the totality which is *still external to itself*." (549) It has not yet broken free of otherness. In *form* it is Necessary, but "as regards content it is limited" (550) – hence Contingent.

If only Contingent, because it depends on its own force *and* the presence of all the circumstances in which its force must be expressed, how is it a Necessity at all? The answer is that Real Necessity is not a *thing*. It is an *event* – the name of the self-erasing move of Real Actuality and Real Possibility. It is necessary that these diversities manifest their inability to sustain the thing on their own.[29] Yet in this self-erasure, "*presupposing* and the *self-returning movement* are still separate." (550)[30] Because of this separateness, Hegel says that "necessity has not yet *spontaneously determined itself into contingency*." (550) So far, Contingency is merely Possible. It must become Actual.

---

27 This is Hegel's second Necessity, according to Burbidge. BURBIDGE, LOGIC, *supra* note 20, at 195-6.

28 BURBIDGE, RELIGION, *supra* note 5, at 46.

29 Marcuse cites this moment as proof of Hegel's leftwing political agenda: "The circumstances that exist in the old form are thus conceived not as true and independent in themselves, but as mere conditions for another state of affairs that implies the negation of the former . . . The concept of real possibility thus develops its criticism of the positivist position out of the nature of facts themselves. Facts are facts only if related to that which is not yet fact and yet manifests itself in the given facts as a real possibility." MARCUSE, REASON, *supra* note 28, at 152. Though Marcuse refers to Real Possibility, his point goes to Real Necessity.

30 "[D]ieses Voraussetzen und die in sich zurückkehrende Bewegung ist noch getrennt." [II:179] Miller's translation corrects Hegel's grammar here. Of the original, John Hoffmeyer remarks, "Hegel's use of the singular verb "is" anticipates the unity that will emerge from this externality." HOFFMEYER, *supra* note 2, at 41.

Real Necessity therefore exhibits externality.[31] "Whatever it is, it could have been otherwise."[32] Externality stands for form, and, to the extent it stands over against externality, Real Necessity has a content that is indifferent to its form. The Real Necessity of a thing is therefore some inner integrity, but the thing might have unessential forms that external reflection might perceive. "The really necessary is therefore any limited actuality which, on account of this limitation, is also only a *contingent* in some other respect." (550)

C. Absolute Necessity

The Understanding sees Real Necessity as a unity between the Actual thing and its entire context – "the unity of necessity and contingency." (550) This immediate unity is Absolute Actuality or Absolute Necessity. Figure 47(a) is Absolute because its being-in-itself is Necessity. It is "actuality which can no longer be otherwise," (550) "absolute self-mediation." (555) Nevertheless, as the unity of itself and Possibility, Absolute Actuality is "only an *empty* determination, or, it is *contingency*." (551) It is "a unity that does not do justice to the difference of actuality and possibility . . . ."[33] In its immediate form, it is "a *mere possibility*, something which can equally be *otherwise*." (551) Whatever it is, it has the capacity to be determined *absolutely* as either an Actual or as a mere Possible. These Hegel refers to as "free, inherently necessary actualities." (553) They may be compared to the Understanding's interpretation of Something. In Figure 3(a), it took Something to be *either* Something or Other. Now

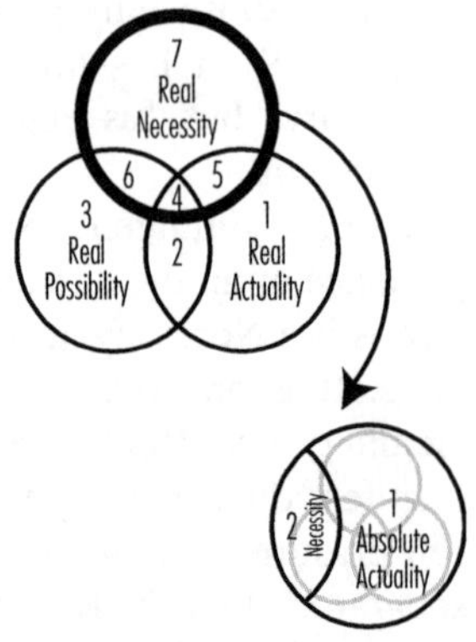

Figure 47(a)
Absolute Actuality
(Absolute Necessity)

[31] Hoffmeyer calls attention to the parallel between Real Necessity (or, in its guise as Figure 47(a), Absolute Necessity) and Determining Reflection in Figure 25(c). Determining Reflection stood for the acknowledgement that presupposition is all that there is. Likewise, Real Necessity stands for the absolute inability of anything to ground itself. HOFFMEYER, *supra* note 2, at 47.

[32] BURBIDGE, RELIGION, *supra* note 5, at 47.

[33] HOFFMEYER, *supra* note 2, at 40.

the Understanding takes Actuality to be the *unity* of either/or – the very capacity to be actualized (or not).[34]

Absolute Actuality is an advance over Real Necessity, where Contingency was merely implicit.[35] Contingency for Real Necessity was "the sublatedness of actuality in possibility" and vice versa. (551)[36] Now Contingency comes to be.[37] Actuality, as Real Necessity, was an *act* of self-erasure. Seeing this, the Understanding names self-erasure Absolute Actuality, which, ironically, underwrites the Contingency of things. What is Absolutely Actual, then, is Contingency.[38]

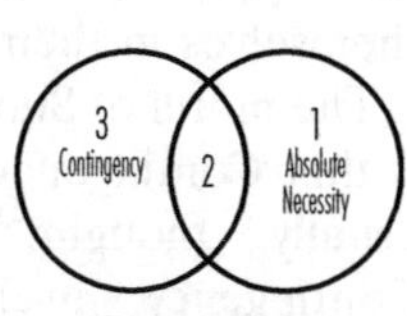

Figure 47(b)
Free Actualities

At this point, the "distinction of *content* and form itself has . . . vanished." (551) Form "has penetrated all its differences and made itself transparent." (551)[39] But Dialectical Reason points out that the Absolutely Necessary is *two* things – Actuality and Possibility, each identical to the other. From this perspective, Absolute Necessity is blind – "something merely *inner*." (581) It cannot tell what it is. Its essence is "*light-shy*, because there is in these Actualities no *reflective movement*, no reflex, because they are grounded purely in themselves alone." (553) But whichever it is – Actual or Possible – it is *necessarily* so.[40]

---

[34] *Id.*, *citing SL* at 551 ("It is indifferently the one or the other. Since it is both, that indifference is 'indifference over against itself.'").

[35] Nevertheless, the freedom of these actualities is a one-sided freedom that Hegel will soon criticize. HOFFMEYER, *supra* note 2, at 47.

[36] John Hoffmeyer finds significance in Hegel's use of a dative case. Actuality is sublated "in" Possibility, not "into." This signals that Actuality stays what it is even as it is "in" (not "moves into") Possibility. *Id.* at 42. The subtle grammar is a sign of Actuality's True Infinity.

[37] BURBIDGE, RELIGION, *supra* note 5, at 49 ("This new content of thought [Contingency] is what is actual period").

[38] For a different (and erroneous) interpretation, see GIACOMO RINALDI, A HISTORY AND INTERPRETATION OF THE LOGIC OF HEGEL 216 (1992) (interpreting Absolute Necessity as the complete negation of Contingency).

[39] Hoffmeyer warns, "Hegel does not mean by transparency that we see through the illusory surface of things to the reality behind them. The surface of things *is* their depth, and their depth is their surface." HOFFMEYER, *supra* note 2, at 46.

[40] *See* BURBIDGE, RELIGION, *supra* note 5, at 49 ("The distinction between possible and actual is reintroduced, not as a relation of contradictory opposites where both cannot be present at the same time, but as a relation of subcontraries whose meanings are distinct and opposite yet explicitly related within a larger universe of discourse").

Speculative Reason intervenes to observe that a Free Actuality is a diversity – an "absolute negativity." (553) It self-erases. Accordingly, Necessity "sacrifices movement to fixity," which yields "illusory notions of freedom."[41] "[T]he absolutes perish," Hegel says, and then "their *essence* will break forth in them and reveal what *it* is and what *they* are." (553) What we have is "the *freedom* of their reflectionless . . . immediacy." (553)[42] The Actualities (or beings) are identical with themselves in their negation. Hegel calls this unity Substance.

The moral of Substance – "[t]he *blind* transition of necessity" – (553) is that Contingency is not beyond reason, as is usually thought.[43] Absolute Necessity is Contingency itself.[44] It is rational that irrationality should exist.[45] "[F]or Hegel there are many things in the world that are not explicable by philosophy because, from the perspective of absolute reason, they are ultimately contingent and without ground."[46] Therefore, philosophy is condemned to "the endless process of overcoming the contingency that reasserts itself at the end of any process of explanation."[47] Every necessity is a contingency.

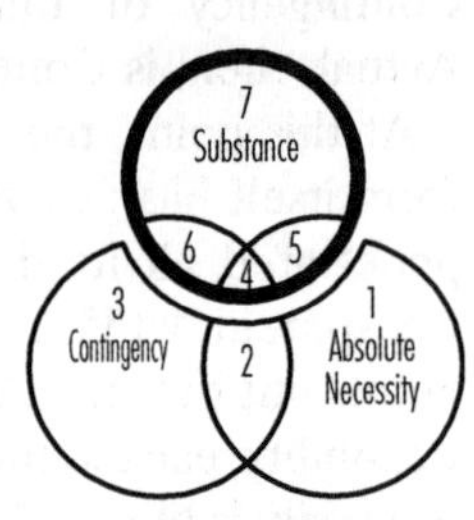

Figure 47(c)
Substance

Substance is still flawed. It stands for manifestation – for self-erasure of a finite entity. It can only articulate the relation between the free actualities and itself "by presupposing something external."[48] Substance

---

[41] HOFFMEYER, *supra* note 2, at 53.

[42] This is the third Necessity of Hegel. BURBIDGE, LOGIC, *supra* note 20, at 196.

[43] Di Giovanni, *supra* note 6, at 42.

[44] *See* Houlgate, *supra* note 14, at 48 (Absolute Necessity's lesson "is that the being and ceasing to be of finite, contingent things is absolutely *necessary* . . ."). Houlgate goes on to point out that "if being is only thought of as the realm of what is *necessary*, then . . . there is nothing that history can be *except* 'the slaughter-bench on which the happiness of peoples, the wisdom of states and the virtue of Individuals have been sacrificed." *Id.*, *citing* G.W.F. HEGEL, THE PHILOSOPHY OF HISTORY 21 (J. Sibree trans. 1991). Freedom, however, transcends necessity and is the very goal of history.

[45] *Id.* at 52; *see also* BURBIDGE, LOGIC, *supra* note 20, at 215 ("true knowledge can and must comprehend its contrary – excessive stupidity . . . ").

[46] Houlgate, *supra* note 14, at 42.

[47] Di Giovanni, *supra* note 6, at 53; *see also* MAURICE MERLEAU-PONTY, SENSE AND NON-SENSE 63 (Hubert L. Dreyfus & Patricia Allen Dreyfus trans., 1964) (Hegel "started the attempt to explore the irrational and to integrate it in an expanded reason which remains the task of our century").

[48] HOFFMEYER, *supra* note 2, at 50

still remains dependent on externality and hence is Contingent. "The movement beyond substantial otherness can only be a movement beyond necessity. For Hegel, to move beyond necessity is to move to freedom."[49]

John Hoffmeyer suggests that Substance – the result of the chapter – is "not deterministic for two reasons. First, the content of the determination is contingency. Second, the determination is not a process of unfolding from some prior given. The absence of any such given is what distinguishes freedom from necessity."[50] In fact, Substance is determined *and* not determined. It still depends on externality – the totality of conditions it faces. Substance will graduate into the Subject *not entirely free* but *not entirely determined*. The matter will leave off ambiguously. For this very reason, Actuality is not the end of the Logic.

[49] *Id*. at 51.

[50] *Id*. at 71 (footnotes omitted).

18
The Absolute Relation

Classically, Substance is "a subject of predication or bearer of attributes that cannot itself be borne by anything else. [It is] an enduring substratum of change."[1] For Hegel Substance is the subsistence of semblance,[2] "the final unity of essence and being." (555) Substance implies Appearance all the way down. There is no mysterious "beyond" that grounds Appearance. Appearance grounds itself. Appearance manifested – or Actuality – is finally in and for itself. Substance does nothing but manifest itself and it does this by erasing itself.[3]

The Understanding sees Substance as Absolute Relation – a unity in which all the moments of Substance appear together.[4] Here, as before,

---

[1] HENRY E. ALLISON, KANT'S TRANSCENDENTAL IDEALISM: AN INTERPRETATION AND DEFENSE 214 (1983).

[2] In his translation, Arnold Miller translates *Schein* as "illusory being" instead of semblance, for which he is sometimes criticized. JOHN W. BURBIDGE, ON HEGEL'S LOGIC: FRAGMENTS OF A COMMENTARY 248 n.4 (1981) (suggesting "seeming"). While Miller's translation is better at the beginning of Essence (because Illusory Being erases itself), by now Burbidge's choice is superior. There is nothing "illusory" about Substance, which is the appearance or semblance of Essence itself.

[3] Hegel compares Substance to light: "Just as the *light* of nature is neither *something* nor a *thing*, but its being is only its showing or shining . . . , so manifestation is self-identical actuality." (554)

[4] In the *Jena Logic*, Hegel identifies this unified account of Substance as the *soul*. G.W.F. HEGEL, THE JENA SYSTEM, 1804-5: LOGIC AND METAPHYSICS 147 (John W. Burbidge & George di Giovanni trans. 1986) ("As this negative *one* that excludes itself

the Understanding sees *all* the moments of the Notion. Absolute Relation is itself, its other and the unity of the two. Triunity is present in each extreme as well as in the unity of the extremes.

Even while it adheres to the notional form, Absolute Relation must undergo the usual moments of development – the immediate moment, the dialectical "real" moment, and the unity of these two. Absolute Relation in its immediacy is the relation of Substance and Accident. Here, the "absolute illusory being" (554) immediately vanishes within itself. Dialectical Reason contrasts Absolute Relation's being-for-self with its otherness. At this point, the Absolute Relation is *real*. This is the relation of Cause and Effect. This relation devolves into a Spurious Infinity, wherein it is impossible to say which extreme is Cause and which is Effect. Speculative Reason sees the two extremes in a relation of Reciprocity. At this point, "the indiscernability of determiner and determined factor transforms their relation into one of *self-*determination."[5] "[T]his *posited unity* of itself in its *determinations* which are *posited* as *themselves the whole* . . . is then *the Notion*." (555) When the Notion is derived, active substance "*acts*, that is, it now *posits*, whereas previously it only *presupposed*." (578) Reciprocity is the final stop in the Objective Logic.[6]

A. The Relation of Substantiality

At first, Absolute Relation is "not *being* as such, but *being because* it is, being as absolute self-mediation." (555) This is the Cartesian moment of self-certainty. There is nothing behind Substance. It is because it is. It subsists in and for itself, and of this it is certain.

But, just as Necessity reveals itself to be Contingency, so Substance reveals itself to be Accident. "[T]he accident *manifests* the *wealth* of substance as well as its *power*." (627-8) Indeed, Substance is *nothing* but

---

and in this exclusion is self-equivalent, the soul is substance . . . ").

[5] RICHARD DIEN WINFIELD, AUTONOMY AND NORMATIVITY 46 (2001).

[6] This chapter can be viewed as covering the Kantian analogies of experience. CHARLES TAYLOR, HEGEL 286 (1975). These are permanence (Hegel's Substance), succession (Causality), and co-existence (Reciprocity). IMMANUEL KANT, CRITIQUE OF PURE REASON A176/B218 (Paul Guyer & Allen W. Wood trans., 1990). Michael Inwood questions whether Causality is the opposite of Substance. M.J. INWOOD, HEGEL 296 (1983) ("Only rarely does the second term of a triad seem to be the opposite of the first. In what sense, for example, is causality the opposite of substantiality or quantity that of quality?"). Taylor's point provides the answer. Succession implies the sublation of permanence. A thing immortal has no successor.

manifestation. It must appear, and what it manifests is Contingent, Accidental. Substance is "*reflective movement*." (555) After it produces Accident,[7] Substance is still with itself and so is "only the *positedness* that is identical with itself." (555) Tying this to the Cartesian point, Accidents are the uncontrolled blind thoughts that belong to but are separate from the ego. Yet, Hegel makes clear, non-conscious things have Substance, too. This is the being-for-self of a perceived thing, which logically must reveal itself in its Accidents. We are not yet at the realm of conscious, rational thought, even though our current theme is applicable to the unconscious life of the mind.

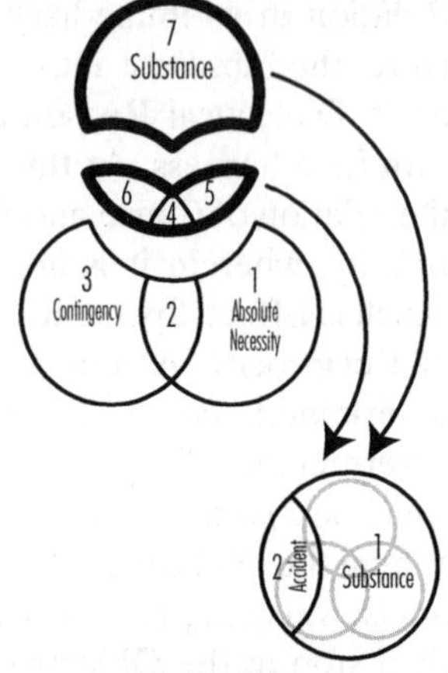

Figure 48(a)
Absolute Relation (Unity of Substance and Accident)

Because Substance is simple self-manifestation, Accident endures, even as individual Accidents vanish. Substance is a Becoming – a unity that names a ceaseless activity. In this movement (which Hegel calls *actuosity)*,[8] the one moment shows itself in the other moment. Accident is Absolute Relation and vice versa. In Cartesian terms, our thoughts are the proof of our Actuality.[9]

---

[7] *See* HERBERT MARCUSE, HEGEL'S ONTOLOGY AND THE THEORY OF HISTORICITY 99 (Seyla Benhabib trans. 1987) ("we can never comprehend substance except through the totality of its accidents").

[8] "[A] Spinozistic term that Hegel appropriates." George di Giovanni, *The Anti-Spinozism of Hegel: The Transition to Subjective Logic and the End of Classical Metaphysics*, in HEGEL'S THEORY OF THE SUBJECT 36 (David Gray Carlson ed., 2005).

[9] *See* Iain Macdonald, *The Concept and Its Double: Power and Powerlessness in Hegel's Subjective Logic*, in *id*. at 76. Justus Hartnack writes, "Hegel's substance neither is nor could be a cause . . . A concept cannot meaningfully count as a cause." JUSTUS HARTNACK, AN INTRODUCTION TO HEGEL'S LOGIC 80-1 (Lars Aagaard-Mogensen trans., 1998). In so asserting, Hartnack assumes a mechanistic notion of cause, wherein billiard balls, but not thoughts, can necessitate a new reality. In fact, Substance is nothing but self-manifestation, and therefore it is the spontaneous *causer* of Accidents. Nevertheless, Hartnack correctly emphasizes that Substance is *nothing* without Accidents, so that Accidents are in some sense the cause of Substance – the two are in reciprocal relation. But this is to jump ahead to Hegel's analysis of Cause and Effect. For the moment Accidents are *dead* things which Substance blindly *causes*. Substance is the *ground* of Accidents, but the reciprocal relation is not yet posited.

In Absolute Relation, Substance and Accident exhibit the unity of Being and Essence. Being was unsustainable immediacy. It erased itself in favor of Essence. Essence was the pure reflective movement of denying its own Being. By denying itself, Essence came to be. Like Being, Essence constantly passes away, but its Being must go somewhere on the law of sublation. The result is Substance – revealed to be nothing but its own manifestation *in* Accident.

Figure 48(b)
Substance v Accident

Accordingly, Substance has two aspects. First, it is "the *simple identity of being*." (556) Figure 48(a) shows the self-identity that ordinary Cartesian thinking takes consciousness to be. Dialectical Reason, however, insists that Substance and Accident are different. Substance itself must contain this second principle of difference.

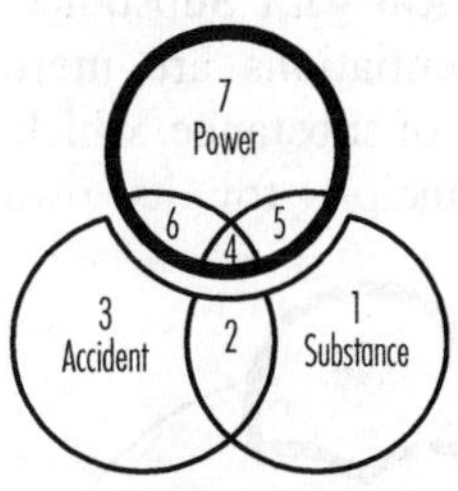

Figure 48(c)
Power (Substantiality)

Speculative Reason in turn sees that, when it comes to Substance and Accident, all we have before us is *movement* – the sheer Power (*Macht*) of Substance. Substance may differ from Accident, but speculatively it is also the same. It is nothing *but* Accident. We therefore have movement from Accident to Accident.

Substance is nothing but the necessity of self-manifestation. It "has *necessity* for its specific mode of relationship." (577-8) What is manifested is a great string of Accidents. But Accidents cease to be. Every ceasing to be is a withdrawal of being to *somewhere*, and this "somewhere" is *enduring* Substance. Accident, Hegel says, withdraws to itself – into its Possibility. But this in turn withdraws from itself to itself as Accident. The production of Accident is *creative* power.[10] The withdrawal from this product is *destructive* power. Yet they are the same Power: "the creation is destructive and the destruction is creative." (556) Meanwhile, Accidents are "things" on their own. Once created, they are indifferent to one another. To the extent they *do* exercise power over an other, it is really the power of Substance at work.

---

[10] Cf. 1 HARRY AUSTRYN WOLFSON, THE PHILOSOPHY OF SPINOZA: UNFOLDING THE LATENT PROCESSES OF HIS REASONING 421-2 (1934) ("Power . . . means to Spinoza the ability to exist and the ability to bring things into existence").

In Figure 48(b), no real difference is yet present between Substance and Accident. Substance is not yet posited according to its Notion. When Dialectical Reason distinguishes Substance in itself as opposed to Substance as totality of Accidents, Substance as Power is indirectly revealed. Power, a middle term, is the positive persistence of the Accidents in their negativity. The extremes have no subsistence on their own, except to the extent they are held together by the Power of Substance.

Substantiality is another name for Power – the movement between Accident and Accident. Substantiality is the Absolute Relation as immediately vanishing. Substantiality relates itself to itself, but not as a negative. It is the immediate unity of power with itself. Substantiality is "in the *form* only of its *identity*, not of its *negative essence*." (557) Only the negative vanishes. The moment of identity does not.

Meanwhile, Being (Accidentality) is Substance through the Power that puts it forth. But it is not posited as identical with Substance. "Substance is not subject so long as its differentiations are mere accidents, contents adding nothing to the identity of substance, which, for its part, can provide no determinate principle for its own modifications."[11] The Power relation is only the "inner of the Accidents;" (557) these exist only *in the Substance*. The speculative meaning of Substantiality is this – Substance manifests itself as formal Power. The differences are not substantial.

Substantiality is the *cause* of the Accidents, which are both substantial and *not* substantial. The relation of substantiality therefore passes over into the relation of causality.

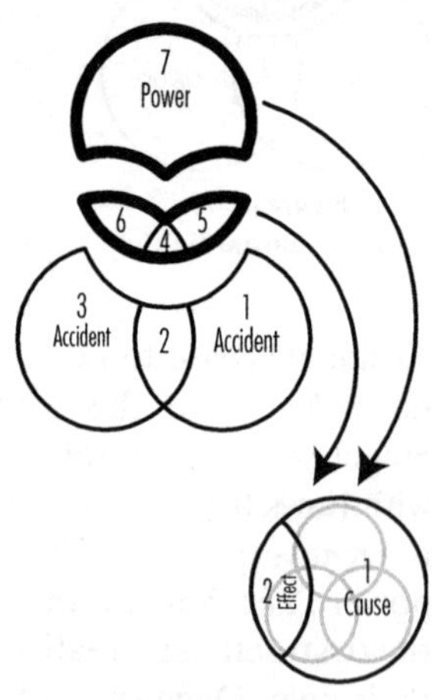

Figure 49(a)
Formal Causality

B. The Relation of Causality

Substance is intransitive Power – power over itself only. Nevertheless it posits determinations about itself and distingui-

---

[11] Richard Dien Winfield, *From Concept to Judgement: Rethinking Hegel's Overcoming of Formal Logic*, 50 DIALOGUE 53, 57 (2001).

shes itself from them, just as the thinker distinguishes herself from her thoughts. Thinking, then, is the negative of thought. Thoughts are just Accidents, and the thinker feels alienated from them. But, in announcing, "I'm not what I thought," the thinker shows what she *is* – thought.

In this reflective move ("I think, therefore I both am and am not"), Substantiality is on both sides of the equation. Accident separated from Substantiality is Effect. Substantiality united with Accident is Cause. Together, the Understanding proposes that Substantiality is Cause and Effect[12] – a sustaining *power* to cause that is also invested in Effect.[13]

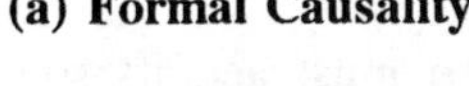

(a) Formal Causality

At first Cause is primary. It puts forth Effects, which are "sublated substantiality." (558) Effect is "only something *posited*." (558) Yet Cause without Effect is nothing. Each requires the other: "the two are *one* actuosity." (558)

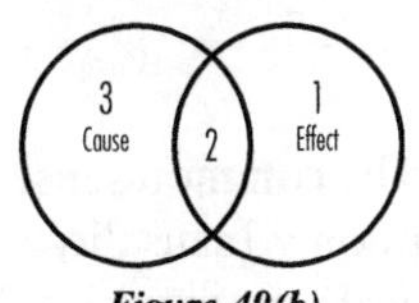

Figure 49(b)
Cause and Effect

Cause is more advanced than what produces Accidents. Accidents instantly vanish. But Effects endure so that Cause can endure. Effect is indeed the whole of Cause (and vice versa). In psychological terms, the thinker is now proud of her clever thoughts and does not feel alienated from them.

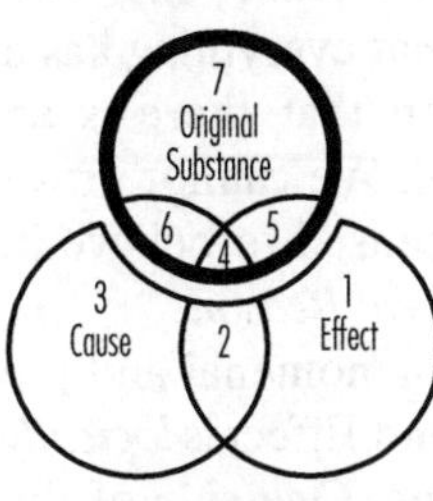

Figure 49(c)
Original Substance

Dialectical Reason observes that Cause and Effect are supposed to differ from each other. These in turn are opposed to the speculative moment; "substance as the non-posited original." (559) Hegel describes Figure 49(c) in these terms: "Because substance as absolute power is the return into itself, yet this return is itself a *determining*, it is no longer merely the *in-itself* of its accident but is also *posited* as this in-itself." (559) In other words, Cause and Effect more clearly announce their self-caused destruction than did Accident. And destruction *is* Substance: "It is therefore as cause that substance first

---

12 *See* EL § 153 Remark.

13 Taylor complains, "it is not clear how Hegel thinks he has done it" – *i.e.*, why Substance endures because of Causality. TAYLOR, *supra* note 6, at 289. To my mind, the transition is clear. Substance is the name for self-manifestation in external Accidents. This Power is what endures. Its name is Causality.

has actuality." (559)

Before us is Humean causal skepticism. In psychological terms, the thinker [7] is the Cause of Cause and Effect. Cause cannot cause itself. Nor is Effect its own Cause. All we have is the movement between Cause and Effect, a Spurious Infinity.[14] There, Hegel analyzed Kant's third antinomy, which states alternately that (1) everything has a cause, and (2) there is an uncaused (free) thing. Hegel's earlier point was that, since Kant is wed to self-identity, each antinomial side is finite. All one can do is alternate between two finites. This alternation is now precisely shown in [4, 5, 6] of Figure 49(c). This alternation is the Cause of Cause and Effect.

Substance is Cause, and, by definition, Cause must act; its sole function is to manifest Effects. Cause is therefore just as much Effect as Cause.

(b) The Determinate Relation of Causality

This section considers Cause and Effect as viewed by common sense. Its purpose, I think,[15] is to "solve" Kant's third antinomy (causality v. freedom). Unlike Kant's first two "mathematical" antinomies,[16] wherein opposites cannot both be true, the third and the fourth[17] "dynamic" antinomies are not contradictions, because the two propositions exist on different levels. The notion that everything has a cause exists at the phenomenal level. The notion that there is an uncaused (free) being exists at the noumenal level. We cannot prove the transcendental level to be true, but we are licensed to believe it. This license allows for the entire *Critique of Practical Reason*.[18]

Hegel rejects incommensurability between the phenomenal and the noumenal. Rather, the Spurious Infinity of Cause and Effect is *logically connected* to the notion of the free, uncaused thing. One side of the

---

[14] A point already made in chapter 2. *Supra* at 100-1.

[15] Citing Hegel's analysis of causality, Adorno remarks, "In the realm of great philosophy Hegel is no doubt the only one with whom at times one literally does not know and cannot conclusively determine what is being talked about, and with whom there is no guarantee that such a judgment is even possible." THEODOR W. ADORNO, HEGEL: THREE STUDIES 89 (1999).

[16] These are: the world has (or has no) beginning in time and space, and things are (or are not) infinitely divisible.

[17] There is or is not a necessary being (God).

[18] The "practical" is that which rests on the concept of freedom. CRITIQUE OF PURE REASON, *supra* note 6, at A315-6/B371.

antinomy implies the other.

In Figure 49(a), Cause and Effect were the same thing – an immediacy. In Figure 49(b), they were diverse. They fell apart and were extinguished. If they are *dis*tinguished, they are distinguished only externally. Cause and Effect in this state are "indifferent to the relation of cause and effect." (560) Figure 49(c) represents the self-erasure of Cause and Effect; these could not sustain themselves without the aid of an outside power. Formal Causality therefore lost its power. Causality is, ironically, contingent on a Humean third for subsistence. Contingency is the relation of Causality in its *"reality* and *finitiude*." (560)

Formally, Causality is "the infinite relation of absolute power whose content is pure manifestation." (560)[19] It is in the *business* of producing Effect and therefore *is* Effect as much as it is Cause. But *finite* Causality, as it *really* is, has a merely given content "and exhausts itself in an external difference," (560) even though its true content is to be identical with Effect.

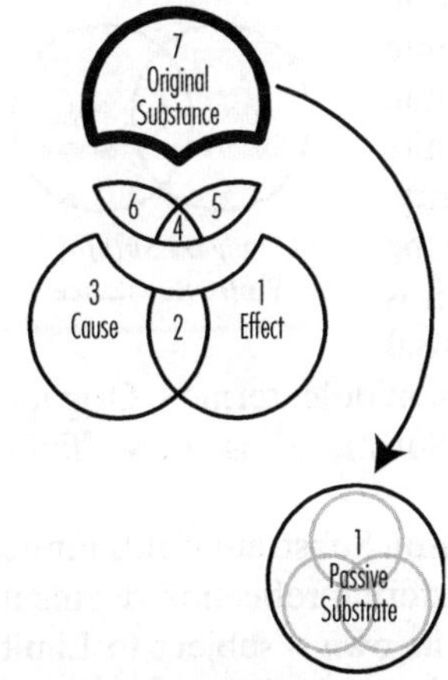

Causality in its real mode is merely "an *analytic* proposition." (560) In judgments of causation,

> [i]t is the *same fact* which presents itself once as cause and again as effect, there as something subsisting on its own account [Cause] and here as positedness or determination in an other [Effect]. Since these determinations of form are an *external* reflection, it is, *in point of fact*, the tautological consideration of a *subjective* understanding to determine a phenomenon as effect and from this to ascend to its cause in order to comprehend and explain it; it is merely a repetition of one and the same content; there is nothing else in the cause but what is in the effect. (560)

Figure 50(a)
Substance as Substrate

Thus, rain is the cause of wetness, pigment the cause of color. These tautologies show that the distinction between Cause and Effect is externally imposed. Cause and Effect cannot sustain themselves as distinct. The form of Causality (necessity)

---

[19] In an infinite relation, an entity becomes something else while remaining what it is. Thus, Cause becomes Effect while remaining Cause.

is distinct from the content of it (contingency).

Everything is indifferent to its determination as Cause or Effect, and from this is deduced the idea of Original Substance – the free, uncaused thing. This advanced Substance causes itself. Every "thing" has it; everything is at bottom free. This is true not just of conscious things, but of all things.

Yet, even if Cause and Effect are subjective, the form, taken on its own, has a content. The *formal* content of Cause and Effect is the dialectical point that Cause and Effect are different – precisely the opposite of their true content (according to which they cannot be distinguished without self-destruction). This content nevertheless implies that Cause and Effect are related. Their implicit identity is an immediacy – a Substrate. Because of this substrate, a thing is *open* to being made a Cause or Effect, even if indifferent to this relationship.[20] For example, water can be either rain (Cause) or wetness (Effect).

Dialectical Reason asserts that, since Causality causes nothing, it depends upon Substance. Causality is therefore Finite Substance, determined by an external reflection. Substance, it will be recalled, was the unity between Absolute Necessity and Contingency. So it is *necessary* that empirical Causality be contingent upon force of will. On its own, it is a Spurious Infinity. The Cause of causal determination, therefore, is Figure 49(c)'s middle term – Original Substance. This middle term, at first Substrate, is now "*finite* substance." (563)

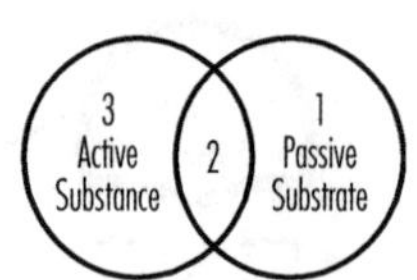

Figure 50(b)
Finite Substance

Finite entities erase themselves. So the reason Substrate yields Finite Substance is that it is indifferent whether external reflection deems it Cause or Effect. Substrate is what it is on its own – subject to Limit and therefore Finite. It causes its *own* demise, regardless of external reflection. *That* is why Substrate is Finite Substance, a "negative relation to *self*." (563)

Original Substance in Figure 49(c) was the Cause of the Causality. But it denied its originative role. It purported to *find* Causality in

20 Hegel usually employs the term "substrate" when he wishes to communicate an unsatisfactory relationship between some unknowable beyond and phenomenal appearance. See Figure 21(b).

nature. In short, it announces, "I am not Causality," thereby proving it *is* Causality. It is therefore a positedness – dependent on another – "because it is determined as an *immediately* actual." (563) Accordingly, the relationship banishes reflectiveness to its other. *Every* determination, Hegel insists, participates in this denial of its own Causality. It exports Causality to the Substrate of Figure 50(a). But the Substrate too denies its own Causality. It announces, "I am not Cause," thereby proving it *is* the Finite Substance of Figure 50(b).

The only thing that subsists in Substrate and Finite Substance is denial of Causal power:

> *[C]ausality* is external to [Finite Substance]; and therefore causality itself constitutes its *positedness*. Now since it is causal substance, its causality consists in relating itself negatively to itself . . . The action of this substance therefore begins from an externality, liberates itself from this external determination; and its return into itself is the preservation of its immediate existence and the sublating of its posited external, hence of its causality as such. (563)

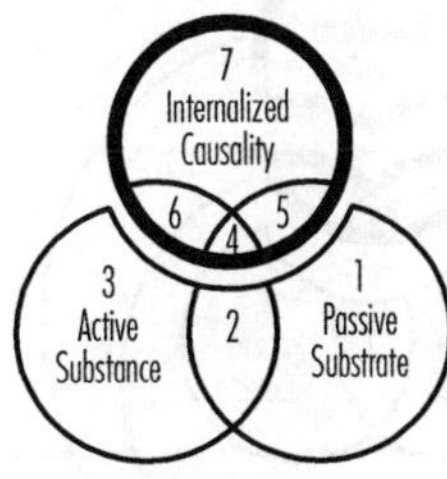

Figure 50(c)
Internalized Causality

To translate, Formal Cause and Effect announce that they are neither Cause or Effect. The *true* causality is external to them. This denial proves that the implicit Finite Substance is powerful. It *is* Causality. What it causes is self-erasure, or negative relation-to-self – "the innermost source of all activity, of all animate and spiritual self-movement, the dialectical soul that everything true possesses and through which alone it is true." (835) Therefore, what seemed external (Causality) is now internal. What Causality causes is its own demise. Figure 50(c) stands for the proposition that things cause their own sublation. Causality devolves to self-Causality.

Infinite regress. One side of Kant's third antinomy asserts the familiar regress in which every Cause is an Effect produced by yet another Cause. This regress comes about, Hegel says, because Causality is external to itself. In Figure 49(b), Cause announced that it was *not* Cause, and so it banished its Being to [2, 3]. [2, 3] was Cause, not [1]. Yet [2, 3] was supposed to be Effect. In fact, [2, 3] is *both* Effect and Cause. Being Cause, taken as [3], it must have its being elsewhere – in some other Effect [1, 2]. And so the Spurious Infinity begins. (565) What endures in Spurious Infinity is the ceasing-to-be of the Finite. Here Cause constantly ceases to be of its own accord. Hence, the true self of Cause is [2] and ultimately [7], which causes its own self – the infinite regress.

Effect likewise produces an infinite regress. It points to Cause as Cause. Being impotent, it "arrives at a substrate which is substance, an originally self-related subsistence." (565) So there are now two effects which mustn't be confounded. The first is the externally discovered effect. The second is the implicit effect of the self-causing Substance, a product of reflection-into-self. Only the first gives rise to a Spurious Infinity.

The outcome is that Cause is not merely extinguished in Effect. In being extinguished, it resurrects itself. There is no external transition here.[21] The becoming-other of Original Substance is its own positing. The unity of *empirical* Cause and Effect was only Substrate, posited over against the active Causality. Now there is Internalized Causality.

(c) Action and Reaction

The Understanding proposes that Substance has two natures – passive and active. Passive Substance (Substrate) is for another, not for itself. It is indifferent if some outside will designates it Cause or Effect. For this reason, passive Substance is "confronted by the power of accidentality as itself *substantial activity*." (566)

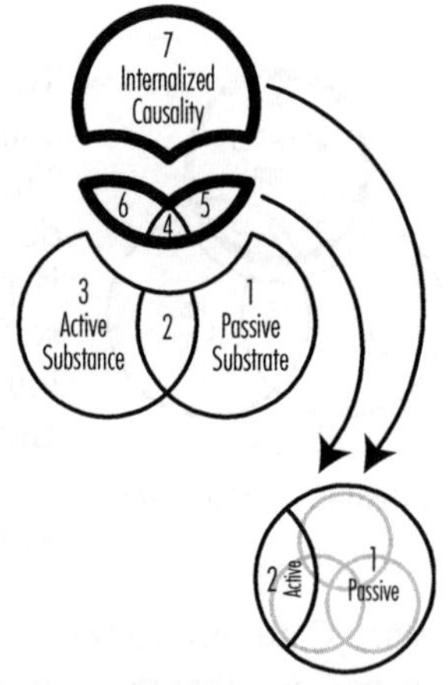

Figure 51(a)
Active and Passive Substance

Active Substance stands over against Passive Substance. Active Substance is Cause that has restored itself through the negation of itself. It is a reflected being – a *positing* activity, originative of causal relations. It "acts on itself as on an *other*, on the *passive substance*." (567) This act, Hegel says, is double. First, it sublates the other and returns to itself; it announces, "I am not passive." But its activity reveals a dependence

[21] There is, however, *transition*, in that Cause vanishes in Effect and vice versa. Later, Hegel will say that such concepts as force, cause and substance have actuality only in their effects; accordingly, "their activity is transition, against which they do not maintain themselves in freedom." (741) In Teleology, End does not vanish. It *develops* its other. See chapter 24.

on otherness. Its being is therefore in passivity.

Hegel equates the interaction of Active and Passive Substance with violence. When Active Substance announces that it is not passive, it sublates "the self-subsistence of the passive substance." (567) This "first sublating of it also appears in relation to the substance in such a manner that only *some determinations* in it are sublated and the identity of the passive substance with the active substance in the effect takes place externally in it." (567) To translate, Active Substance announces that it is not Passive Substance and thereby sublates it. This sublation requires that the passive other be determined. But, of the many determinations of Active Substance, only some are sublated. Active Substance says, "I am not *that* passive thing." In so saying, many passive things are unsublated, for the time being. For us, however, we know that Active Substance *is* Passive Substance, and negation of Passive Substance is self-negation. There is an identity of Passive and Active Substance, but this is only an external reflection at this point.

The sublation of Passive Substance is violence itself. "Violence is the *manifestation of power*, or power as *external*." (567) As an act of power, violence is visited "*only on an other presupposed by itself*." (567) Violence is the *proof* of Active Substance. Passive Substance proves itself passive by submitting to violence. "Therefore not only is it possible to do violence to that which suffers it, but also violence *must* be done to it." (567)

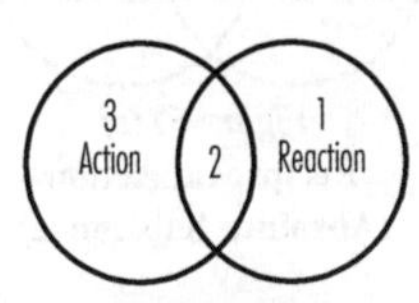

Figure 51(b)
Action and Reaction
(Conditioned Causality)

"Passive substance therefore only receives its due through the action on it of another power." (568) But this violence has its positive side. In it, Passive Substance loses its immediacy. It becomes a positedness, in which it shares an identity with Active Substance. This identity proves that violence is always self-violence. The externality of this violent power is an illusion. This is passivity's scant revenge.

When Active Substance shows its identity with its other, Passive Substance is "converted into cause." (568)[22] This conversion Hegel calls Reaction. There are two outcomes from the promotion of Passive Substance into Reaction. First, Passive Substance

---

[22] *See* Stephen Houlgate, *Why Hegel's Concept is not the Essence of Things*, in THEORY OF THE SUBJECT, *supra* note 8, at 34 ("This is the decisive move that takes us forward to the concept: for it introduces the strict *identity* of the positing and posited moments").

was supposed to be an immediacy, but it is now revealed to be a positedness. Cause always acts on an *other*, and this other is covertly in charge of the operation. Immediate passivity is now the real Cause.

The second outcome stems from the fact that the passive other on which reaction works is itself active. The active therefore becomes the passive. We have the typical dilemma of Dialectical Reason. Neither of the extremes can identify what they are on their own. "Since the two [extremes], then, are both passive and active, any distinction between them has already been sublated." (569)

Compare this with Cause/Effect in Figure 49(b). There, Effect turned into Cause of some new Effect. "But it did not react *against that cause*, but posited its effect again in *another* substance, giving rise to the progress to the infinity of effects." (569) In Action and Reaction (or Conditioned Causality), "the cause is *self-related* in the effect." (569) Active Substance more clearly works on its own self and "is thereby just as much a *becoming* as a positing and *sublating of the other*." (569) When Active Substance causes something, it "receives its effect back into itself as reaction, thus reappears as cause." (569) Instead of generating the infinite regress, action is "*bent round* and becomes an action that returns into itself, an infinite *reciprocal action*." (569)[23]

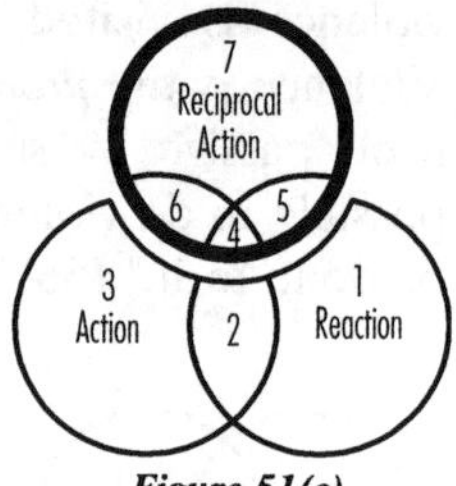

Figure 51(c)
Reciprocal Action
(Absolute Substance)

C. Reciprocity

Well, I'd like to know where you got the Notion.[24]

In finite Cause and Effect, two Substances were actively related to each other, but they were indifferent to the external attribution of Cause and Effect. The relation was merely mechanical. "*Mechanism* consists in this *externality* of causality." (569) In Reciprocity, mechanism

---

[23] It is unclear whether Charles Taylor sees the point that Cause acts only upon itself and is therefore also Effect – a Reciprocal Action. He thinks Hegel "throws in interaction" in order to give the appearance that chapter 18 coheres with Kant's analogies of experience. TAYLOR, *supra* note 6, at 288. In fact, Reciprocity is exactly the right note for Hegel to sound. Taylor also has Hegel confessing "interaction" "to be a rather inexact term . . . " *Id.*, citing EL § 156 Addition. But Hegel does no such thing. He simply announces that Reciprocal Action is not a satisfactory stopping place for the Logic – not that Reciprocity is "thrown in."

[24] The Hughes Corporation, *Rock the Boat* (1974).

is sublated. Reciprocity represents "the *vanishing* of that original *persistence* of the *immediate* substantiality" of [1] and [3]. (569) It stands for originativeness and self-mediation.

Reciprocal Action still distinguishes within itself two extremes, which are themselves free, and it distinguishes itself as the middle term distinct from the two sides.[25] The identity of being and appearance is still a merely "*inner* necessity." (571) This inner necessity must be made express.

The Understanding takes Reciprocity to denote passivity and aggressivity externally conjoined as the In-itself of Substance. This conjunction of the two Substances is merely the passivity of Substance showing through. Already passivity has proved to be the result of Substance's own activity. Passivity is the negation of Cause by Cause itself, which converts itself into passive Effect. Dialectical Reason therefore points out that the extremes are active, not passive. "[I]t is no longer *substrates* but substances that stand in relation to each other." (569-70) Hegel calls this the "being-for-self" of Substance. (578)

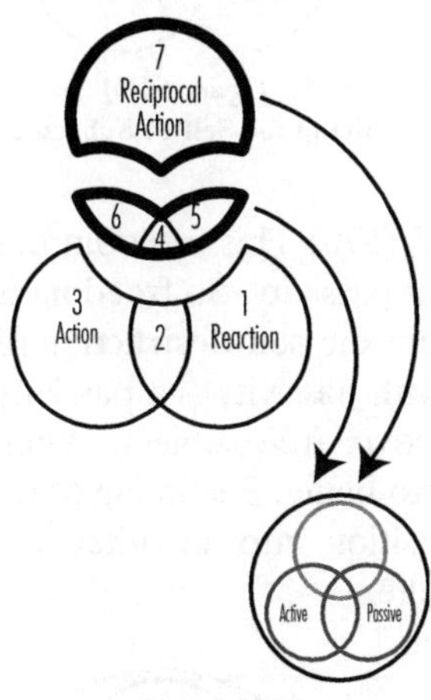

Figure 52(a)
In-Itself of Substance

The active movement in Figure 52(b) sublates the "still remaining *presupposed immediacy*" of the extremes. (570) Active Substance is now Cause; "it *acts*, that is, it now *posits*, whereas previously it only *presupposed*." (578)[26] But, precisely because the extremes move, they

[25] Michael Inwood describes the fault of Reciprocal Action in the following analogy: "The items . . . are conceived of as each having a nature which is independent of its relationship to the other. The nature of each item explains why it responds in the way that it does to the successive states of the other item. Each of two boxers, for example, makes movements – evasive, defensive, offensive and retaliatory – which are in part caused by the movements of the other. But equally each of the boxers is an entity with certain characteristics independent of his interaction with the other, characteristics which in part explain his responses to the other's movements. The course of the boxing-match is not therefore fully explained in terms of reciprocity." INWOOD, *supra* note 6, at 339-40.

[26] *See* EMIL L. FACKENHEIM, THE RELIGIOUS DIMENSION IN HEGEL'S THOUGHT 103 (1967) (Hegel's substance is "not a Substance which *is* independently of what it *does*").

are still *conditioned* by "the passivity of *being acted upon*." (570) Since this passivity is Cause's own being, Cause itself is passive. Cause acts upon itself and is therefore both conditioned and conditioning.

In acting on itself, active Cause aggressively asserts, "I am not passive." It therefore negates itself as passive and simultaneously converts itself into passive Effect. Cause *has* an Effect but also *is* the Effect. When this is realized, Causality has "returned to *its absolute Notion*" and "has attained to the *Notion* itself." (570)

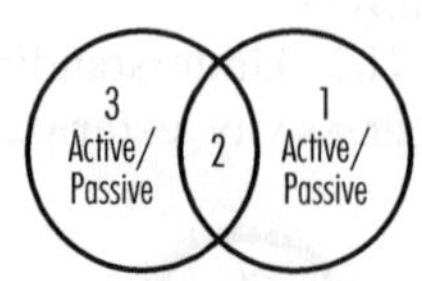

Figure 52(b)
Being-for-Self of Substance

The Notion (*der Begriff*) – often translated as Concept – is in the business of acting on itself and causing the manifestation of its own inner self. In its act of self-causation, where Cause produces Effect and Effect produces Cause, "necessity is raised to *freedom*." (570) This freedom has arisen from its self-negation – the negation of passivity. So freedom is properly active and positive, but it arises from the self-destruction of negative freedom, which can be identified with passivity – a passivity that is productive and originative of the active, free subject. When passivity passes away, true freedom comes into being. Becoming other is now revealed to be an illusion: "the transition into an other is a reflection into itself; the *negation*, which is the ground of cause, is its *positive union* with itself." (570)

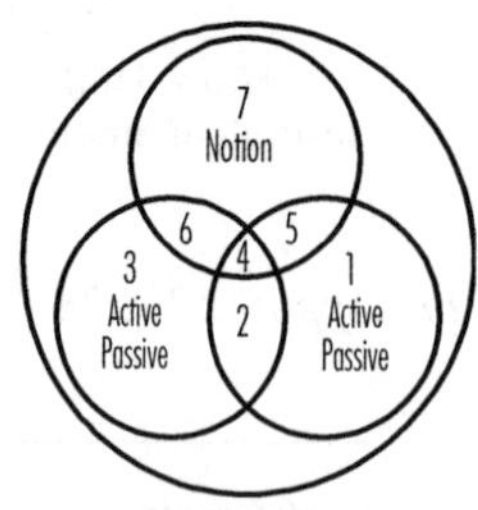

Figure 52(c)
The Notion

In Notion, "necessity and causality have vanished." (570) These contained both immediate identity and absolute substantiality of the sides. Now the substantiality of the sides is lost. The Notion "is the unity of the *two substances* standing in that relation; but in this unity they are now free, for they no longer possess their identity as something blind, that is to say, as something merely *inner*." (581) The extremes unified in the Notion are now "moments of reflection, whereby each is no less immediately united with its other or its positedness and each contains its positedness *within itself*, and consequently in its other is posited as simply and solely identical with itself." (581-2)

A truer necessity has unveiled itself. This version of necessity does not become freedom by *vanishing*. It becomes freedom because its inner identity is *manifested*. Manifestation is the identical movement of the different sides within themselves. Each of the sides moves in the same manifesting way. As Hegel puts it in the *EL*:

> For thinking means that, in the other, one meets with one's self. It means a liberation, which is not the flight of abstraction, but consists in that which is actual having itself not as something else, but as its own being and creation, in the other actuality with which it is bound up by the force of necessity. As existing in an individual form, this liberation is called I: as developed to its totality, it is free Spirit; as feeling, it is Love, and as enjoyment, it is Blessedness.[27]

If Necessity (*i.e.*, manifestation of the inner self) becomes freedom, so does Contingency, "for the sides of necessity, which have the shape of independent, free actualities not reflecting themselves in one another, are now *posited as an identity*." (571) These totalities are identical – they "are posited as only one and the same reflection." (571) So if Contingency stands for the indifference of the extremes to one another, this very indifference to otherness is what freedom is, and the manifestation of this freedom is precisely what the Notion is. It is *necessary* that the subject is a contingency. For Hegel, then, "freedom is the truth of necessity." (580)[28]

The Universal, Individual and Particular. Hegel concludes Essence by naming Reciprocal Action as Absolute Substance – one totality that is nevertheless distinguishable into the Universal, Individual and Particular. In this trinity – "the necessary categorial resources for determining self-determination"[29] – Absolute Substance "distinguishes itself from itself." (571) But it no longer *repels* itself from itself, nor

---

[27] EL § 159.

[28] Charles Taylor all but proclaims this transition to Notion a failure: "[W]e seem to have once more a case where Hegel is sure of an ascending transition because he is already sure of it; where he gives us what are only hints and traces of the higher reality which the lower is meant to be an emanation from, and takes these for a proof. The necessity to move to interaction or to the systemic perspective, can indeed be seen as a trace of the Concept; but it does not establish it. This conviction reposes rather elsewhere. The transition from interaction to causation out of totality is already there and is grounded on the whole earlier argument of the *Logic*, on the very conception of Essence as totality whose parts follow one on another of necessity." TAYLOR, *supra* note 6, at 294. In fact, as Notion is that which manifests itself, the transition is pristine. Cause sublates itself, thereby showing that it acts only upon itself, never upon another thing. Nor does Hegel move from totality to interaction to causation. Rather, the move is precisely the opposite. Cause shows itself to be reciprocal interaction between self and other, which is the totality known as Notion.

[29] WINFIELD, *supra* note 5, at 47.

does it "fall asunder into indifferent, self-external substances." (571)[30] Rather, it differentiates itself within a totality – not into alien parts.

The Universal is "negativity in general." (603) In its more developed form as the "I", the Universal stands for the abstraction of self-consciousness from all context. But, in negating all relations, it contains all relations – all positedness – even while it is self-identical.

The Individual is the negation of the negative Universal – "the negation or determinateness which is self-related." (582) It is pure abstraction reified into a thing, which is likewise the whole. The Individual is "*absolutely determined*, opposing itself to all that is other and excluding it." (583)

Universal and Individual are the same totality. The union of Universal and Individual, Hegel says, is Particularity. "These three totalities are, therefore, one and the same reflection." (571)[31] Each of the totalities devolves into the other two, but the difference between them, though real, is nevertheless "a *perfectly transparent difference*." (571) The three totalities before us are a single identity, a "determinate simplicity" and a "simple determinateness." (571) "This is the *Notion*," Hegel writes, "the realm of *subjectivity* or of *freedom*." (571) The Objective Logic has drawn to a close.[32]

---

[30] JOHN F. HOFFMEYER, THE ADVENT OF FREEDOM: THE PRESENCE OF THE FUTURE IN HEGEL'S LOGIC 11 (1994) ("The language of freedom does what the language of necessity can not do. It adequately articulates identity as movement and movement as identity.").

[31] Here Hegel names them out of order, compared to their development in chapter 19, where the sequence is Universal, Particular and Individual. But since each part reflects itself, its other, and the unity of self and other, this misordering presumably may be excused.

[32] "One is therefore tempted to conclude hastily that Hegel's thought is a 'panlogicism,' or the system of an inhuman mechanics of the absolute. But this is to forget that necessity must itself have a necessity, a sufficient reason: which, since its beginnings, is what philosophy has signified with *logos*. And this necessity of necessity is freedom." JEAN-LUC NANCY, HEGEL: THE RESTLESSNESS OF THE NEGATIVE 67 (Jason Smith & Steven Miller eds. 1997). Positive freedom is one of Hegel's great contributions to political theory. In the *EL*, he comments: "[W]hat a mistake it is to regard freedom and necessity as mutually exclusive. Necessity indeed, *qua* necessity, is far from being freedom: yet freedom presupposes necessity, and contains it as an unsubstantial element in itself. A good man is aware that the tenor of his conduct is essentially obligatory and necessary. But this consciousness is so far from making any abatement from his freedom, that without it real and reasonable freedom could not be distinguished from arbitrary choice – a freedom which has no reality and is merely potential. A criminal, when punished, may look upon his punishment as a restriction of his freedom. Really the punishment is not foreign constraint to which he is subjected, but the manifestation of

Conclusion

Across Essence, the whole "is presented over and over again as two correlated aspects reflected into each other."[33] Throughout these pairings, the Being in the extremes of our syllogism moved more and more clearly toward the center. Increasingly, the center displaced the extremes, even as the center revealed itself to be entirely dependent on the extremes. This movement can be viewed as the final obliteration of nature in favor of subjectivity. "The collapse of the distinction between determiner and determined has led to the threshold of self-determination where what determines and what is determined are indistinguishable." [34]

We now move on to the Subjective Logic. There Notion must reestablish reality, now obliterated. The Subjective Logic replays the entire Objective Logic, as subjectivity (or Notion) makes all the stages of being its own.

---

his own act: and if he recognizes this, he comports himself as a free man. In short, man is most independent when he knows himself to be determined by the absolute idea throughout." EL § 158 Addition. In other words, the truly free man is one with the law. The criminal who robs is the slave of impulse. The truer self of the criminal demands his own punishment as the reinstitution of the law that his crime has erased. *See* G.W.F. HEGEL, ELEMENTS OF THE PHILOSOPHY OF RIGHT § 100 Addition (Allen W. Wood trans. 1993) ("In so far as the punishment which this entails is seen as embodying *the criminal's own right*, the criminal is *honoured* as a rational being").

[33] ERROL E. HARRIS, AN INTERPRETATION OF THE LOGIC OF HEGEL 207 (1983).

[34] Winfield, *Concept*, *supra* note 11, at 63.

PART VII
SUBJECTIVITY

19
The Notion

> True thoughts and scientific insight are only to be won through the labour of the Notion. Only the Notion can produce the universality of knowledge which is neither common vagueness nor the inadequacy of ordinary common sense, but a fully developed, perfected cognition.[1]

The final nine chapters of the *SL* – the Subjective Logic – are the *result* – the grand middle term – of the first two-thirds. Quality was affirmative. Essence was the first negation. Notion is the second negation and a return-into-self from Essence.

Hegel's Notion should be very familiar indeed.[2] It is *subjectivity*. "The Notion, when it has developed into a *concrete existence* that is itself free, is none other than the *I* or pure self-consciousness." (583) Of course, the subject is not just the empirical ego, "but a mode of existence, to wit, that of a self-developing unity in an antagonistic process."[3]

From the foregoing, it is easy to piece together what the subject is for Hegel. First, it is the *erasure* of the natural world beyond thought.

---

[1] G.W.F. HEGEL, PHENOMENOLOGY OF SPIRIT ¶ 70 (A.V. Miller trans. 1977).

[2] Hegel proclaimed Essence "the most difficult branch of Logic." EL § 114. Therefore, the Subjective Logic must be less so. "Once the logic of being and essence is understood, the logic of the self-concept simply harvests the fruit of the most nearly true logical definition of the absolute." CLARK BUTLER, HEGEL'S LOGIC: BETWEEN DIALECTIC AND HISTORY 204 (1996).

[3] HERBERT MARCUSE, REASON AND REVOLUTION 8 (1999).

Second, it is the erasure of this erasure.[4] The subject therefore *is*. "Everything that exists is 'real' only in so far as it operates as a 'self' through all the contradictory relations that constitute its existence."[5] Accordingly, subject or Notion is "*being* once more, but being that has been restored as the infinite mediation and negativity of being within itself." (596)[6]

Whatever Notion is, it is the *outcome* of a self-repulsion that is "*unconditioned* and *original*." (601) "Becoming" was at first *transition* into other. Later, Reflection *posited* its other; it announced it was *not* Being; Being existed only in so far as Reflection implied its existence. Now Notion has posited *itself* into Being. Being "has restored itself as a being that is *not posited*, that is *original*." (601) Henceforth, "[t]he onward movement of the notion is no longer either a transition into, or a reflection on something else [*i.e.*, positing], but *Development*."[7] Development implies that "[i]n every transition the Notion maintains itself." (748)[8] Hegel, however, is not always scrupulous in his terminology. Thus, Idea becomes nature, Hegel will say. "But this determination [is not] a *transition*, as when . . . the subjective Notion in its totality *becomes* objectivity, and the *subjective end becomes life*." (843) Properly speaking, subjectivity-to-objectivity and teleology-to-life are developments, because the subject preserves itself in its predicate.

---

4 According to Marcuse, these are the two elements of free will. *Id*. at 186.

5 *Id*. at 8.

6 Haas wishes that Hegel had rearranged the Logic, so that Notion precedes Essence. ANDREW HAAS, HEGEL AND THE PROBLEM OF MULTIPLICITY 251 (2000). Such a move would violate the structure just described. It would mean that subjectivity is not derived but simply asserted as that which dissolves Being and discovers essences. Rinaldi errs in suggesting that Notion "*presupposes* the whole development of Being and of Essence as its *necessary* condition." GIACOMO RINALDI, A HISTORY AND INTERPRETATION OF THE LOGIC OF HEGEL 225-6 (1992). Notion is *not conditioned at all* but is *free*. What Rinaldi should have said is that the concepts of being and essence imply the Notion, as they cannot sustain themselves without it.

7 EL § 161; *see also id*. at § 161 Addition (notional movement is "to be looked upon merely as play").

8 ERROL E. HARRIS, AN INTERPRETATION OF THE LOGIC OF HEGEL 210 (1983) ("Transitions and reflection were premonitions, but not yet transparent exemplifications of development, and only now, from the viewpoint of the Concept, can they be seen as forms or phases of the same process"); MICHAEL ROSEN, HEGEL'S DIALECTIC AND ITS CRITICISM 88 (1982) ("It is natural to conceive of development as a making explicit of something that is implicit, and to think of this as something that is 'prefigured' or pre-existing in a 'logical space'").

Notion's task. Notion has subjugated Being and Essence.[9] It has swallowed reality whole. For this reason, "pure Notion is richer and higher than that metaphysical void of the *sum total of all reality*." (707) But Notion is not the end of the Logic; it is only the beginning of the *Subjective* Logic. Notion "must rise to the *Idea* which alone is the unity of the Notion and reality." (587) In order to accomplish this task, Notion's job is to build up the vanished reality from its own resources.[10] The Notion is incomplete precisely *because* there is no reality before it. In must be "poised to give itself determinacy, not by standing in contrast to some other, nor by shining forth in some subsidiary appearance, but by being identical with the difference it posits in virtue of being what it is."[11] Indeed, one could say with Slavoj Žižek that "there is Reality because and insofar as the Notion is inconsistent, doesn't coincide with itself."[12] Accordingly, "this Third Book of the Logic is devoted [to] the exposition of how the Notion builds up in and from itself the reality that has vanished in it." (591)

---

[9] Hegel equates this proposition with the proposition that Notion has subjugated psychological starting points (feeling and intuition). These are the starting points that Kant presupposes. They are psychological in the sense that feeling and intuition are precursors to consciousness, and are so treated in the *Phenomenology*. HARRIS, *supra* note 8, at 221. Notion, then, has subjugated phenomenology (sense certainty and perception). In connection with this, Hegel attacks the idea that *origin* is truth. "[I]n the order of nature, intuition or being are undoubtedly first, or are the condition for the Notion, but they are not on that account the absolutely unconditioned." (588) Their reality is sublated. Locating truth in origin may be a valid *historical* principle, which relies on narration. "But philosophy is not meant to be a narration of happenings." (588)

[10] *See* William Maker, *Hegel's Logic of Freedom*, HEGEL'S LOGIC OF THE SUBJECT 3-4 (David Gray Carlson ed., 2005) (free subjectivity involves "the absolutization of the subject, where the absolute subject produces objective reality from out of itself, and knows and is at one with itself therein"). *See Phenomenology, supra* note 1, ¶ 233 ("But self-consciousness is all reality, not merely *for itself* but also *in itself*, only through *becoming* this reality, or rather through *demonstrating* itself to be such").

[11] Richard Dien Winfield, *From Concept to Judgement: Rethinking Hegel's Overcoming of Formal Logic*, 50 DIALOGUE 53, 55-6 (2001). As Marcuse puts it, "There is no transition from 'actuality' to a more actual structure: the Subjective Logic means first, a 'repetition' of the exposition of 'actuality' in light of the *proper meaning* of actual being, and second, the exposition of that form of being which corresponds to this meaning of actuality. The subjective Logic is thoroughly concerned with the meaning of 'actuality.'" HERBERT MARCUSE, HEGEL'S ONTOLOGY AND THE THEORY OF HISTORICITY 89 (Seyla Benhabib trans. 1987); *see also id*. at 116 ("The entire third book of the *Logic* is devoted to showing how the concept 'forms' reality 'in and out of itself'").

[12] SLAVOJ ŽIŽEK, THE PUPPET AND THE DWARF: THE PERVERSE CORE OF CHRISTIANITY 66 (2003).

"Thought has reached the point where it explicitly thinks itself."[13] But the reality to follow "does not fall back again onto a ready-made reality confronting it." (591) Notion does not "take refuge in something which has shown itself to be the unessential element of Appearance because, having looked around for something better, it has failed to find it." (591-2) Rather, reality becomes *Notion's own reality*. "[F]rom now on, every category is self-referential."[14] For this very reason, "conceptual activity (*der Begreifen*) is the most authentic being . . . ."[15] This process of thinking its own self into existence is what Hegel calls "the proximate *realization* of the Notion." (623)[16]

It is now convenient to position Hegel in terms of a common philosophical dichotomy on the matter of truth. It is often suggested that one has either a "correspondence" or a "coherence" theory of truth.[17] Hegel is trying for both. Once Notion has raised itself to Idea, it *is* the truth in the "coherence" sense, since it is derived. But Notion has made its own reality, and therefore its truth is a correspondence theory as well. Thus, Hegel says that Logic is "*on its own account truth*, since [its] content is adequate to its form, or the reality to its Notion." (593) As Marcuse puts it: "we can readily see why logic and metaphysics are one in the Hegelian system. The *Logic*, it has often been said, presupposes an identity of thought and existence. The

---

[13] JOHN W. BURBIDGE, ON HEGEL'S LOGIC: FRAGMENTS OF A COMMENTARY 111 (1981).

[14] HARRIS, *supra* note 8, at 220.

[15] MARCUSE, ONTOLOGY, *supra* note 11, at 111.

[16] Taylor's formulation is questionable on this account: "Thus the subjective concept, by referring to particulars which are not produced out of it, essentially refers us to the judgement. A concept can have no use except in the making of a judgement. This is the short way to this conclusion which dispenses with the whole argument of this section, except of course that this argument is essential to Hegel's purpose which is to see the subjective concept against a background of requirements which are posed by the ontological Concept." CHARLES TAYLOR, HEGEL 308 (1975). This is inaccurate in some respects. First, the particulars *are* produced out of the concept, and even the Understanding takes the predicate to *really represent* the subject. Second, that concepts are useless except as used in judgment – this is Kant's conclusion, not Hegel's. *See* IMMANUEL KANT, CRITIQUE OF PURE REASON A695-7/B724-5 (Paul Guyer & Allen W. Wood trans., 1990). Kant limits concepts to the subject, but Hegel intends for the Concept to be the *only* thing. It is, however, probably right that Hegel wants to isolate the subjective concept from the background requirements of the ontological Concept – in the sense that the subject has renounced the Notion and must find it again through the dialectical process.

[17] *E.g.*, RICHARD RORTY, CONSEQUENCES OF PRAGMATISM 205 (1982).

statement has meaning only in so far as it declares that the movement of thought reproduces the movement of being and brings it to its true form."[18]

Freedom. "With the Notion . . . we have entered the realm of freedom." (582) In chapter 18, the Notion was established as "the unity of the *two substances* standing in [reciprocal] relation." (581) In this unity the extremes are free. The extremes enjoy a "self-transparent clarity." (582) The mutual opacity of the substances standing in causal relationship has vanished. Now each extreme is united with its other. "[T]his is *substance raised to the freedom of the Notion*." (582)

Freedom connotes freedom from otherness – Being-for-self as such. Being was the realm of immediacy proper. But Essence likewise partook of idealized immediacy. It had its "*illusory being* in another." (596) In contrast, though originally self-subsistent, Substance has now freely passed into its other, so that the Notion is "immediately a *positedness*." (582) That is to say, Notion is a "simple identity," (582) but equally it contains relation.

As simple identity, Notion *negates* determinateness. This "equality with itself" (582) or "pure identical self-relation" (600) is the Universal. It stands for the proposition that what is different is really the same. But "this identity has equally the determination of negativity." (582) If this negativity is itself negatively determined, the Universal is Individual. In other words, the Universal particularizes itself. "By particularizing itself, the genuine *universal* constitutes its own individuality."[19] Each of these – Universal and Individual – is independently the totality. The Particular, however, is by its nature not *overtly* the totality (though implicitly each part is also the whole).[20] Accordingly, the Universal and Individual are "the free *illusion* . . . of a duality which . . . appears as a complete opposition, yet an opposition which is so entirely *illusory* that in thinking and enunciating the one, the other also is immediately thought and enunciated." (582) This is "the very Notion of the Notion" (596) – that it is Universal *and* Individual. In this guise, "being-in-and-for-self has attained a true and adequate reality." (596) Put in other terms, the Universal particularized is the thinker and his

---

18 MARCUSE, REASON, *supra* note 3, at 64.

19 BURBIDGE, *supra* note 13, at 115.

20 The Particular differentiates itself from *something* and does not purport to be whole. This comports with the point that Dialectical Reason is the critique of the Understanding, *not* separately a definition of the absolute. Only the Understanding and Speculative Reason purport to define the absolute. *Supra* at 92-3.

thoughts. The two together constitute the Individual who actively thinks passive thoughts.[21]

To this definition of Notion Hegel compares "notion" in ordinary parlance. Ordinary meaning, Hegel admits, has its authority, and, though Hegel's theory of Notion is immanently derived, it must also be recognizable to ordinary usage. Unfortunately, "it is not so easy to discover what others have said about the nature of the Notion. For in the main they do not concern themselves at all with the question presupposing that everyone who uses the word automatically knows what it means." (583) Furthermore, "notion" has fallen on hard times.

> Just as it was the fashion for a while to say everything bad about the imagination, and then the memory, so in philosophy it became the habit . . . to heap every kind of slander on the Notion, on what is supreme in thought, while the incomprehensible and non-comprehension are, on the contrary, regarded as the pinnacle of science and morality. (583)

Much later, Hegel returns to the relation of common parlance to philosophical discourse:

> Philosophy has the right to select from the language of common life which is made for the world of pictorial thinking, such expressions as *seem to approximate* to the determinations of the Notion. There cannot be any question of *demonstrating* for a word selected from the language of common life that in common life, too, one associates with it the same Notion for which philosophy employs it; for common life has no Notions, but only pictorial thoughts and general ideas, and to recognize the Notion in what is else a mere general idea is philosophy itself. It must suffice therefore if pictorial thinking, in the use of its expressions that are employed for philosophical determinations, has before it some vague idea of their distinctive meaning; just as it may be the case that in these expressions one recognizes nuances of pictorial thought that are more closely related to the correlating Notions. (708)

Hegel's position is that ordinary users of language *would*, if they thought about it, come to see the speculative content of the words they use.[22]

---

[21] BURBIDGE, *supra* note 13, at 158.

[22] On the relation of philosophical usage to common parlance, John McCumber writes: "Hegel thus recognizes that there are irreducible gaps between the System and what it is to comprehend; and, as his language here suggests, in such cases the System assumes a normative dimension over against representational language." JOHN MCCUMBER, THE COMPANY OF WORDS: HEGEL, LANGUAGE AND SYSTEMATIC PHILOSOPHY 322 (1993). While the normative element is present, Hegel would certainly deny that Logic's function is to comprehend the common usage of terms. This is to deny

Kant. The Subjective Logic commences with an introductory essay, "The Notion in General." Here, Hegel provides a lengthy commentary on Kant, who receives provisional credit for exalting the role of subjectivity in the constitution of objectivity, though ultimately without following through on the critique.

In ordinary parlance, I *have* notions, just as I have a coat, a complexion, etc. So conceived, however, the I is "not the genuine ground and the determinant of its property." (584) Kant, to his credit, went beyond this impoverished concept of the I: "It is one of the profoundest and truest insights to be found in the Critique of Pure Reason that the *unity* which constitutes the nature of the *Notion* is recognized as the *original synthetic* unity of *apperception*, as unity of the *I think* or of self-consciousness." (584)[23] This has always been a difficult part of Kantian philosophy, Hegel says, because it requires that we go beyond the representation of a relation that the *I* has to its properties.

According to Kant, an object is "that in the concept of which the manifold in a given intuition is *united*."[24] The unification of the manifold into a thing, however, "demands a *unity of consciousness* in the synthesis of them." (584) For Kant, "the contents of our experience have no objectivity, but as brought together by the 'I', and brought together under the concepts, they achieve objectivity."[25] The unity of consciousness, then, "constitutes the connection of the representations with the object and therewith their *objective validity*." (584) The unity of the object within consciousness *is* the Understanding itself, and so consciousness is *not just* a thing that understands. It is the very condition for the possibility of things in general. "[I]t is *only* as it is in thought that the object is truly *in and for itself* . . . Thus we are justified by a cardinal principle of the Kantian philosophy in referring to the

---

that Hegel's is an onto-logic.

[23] W.H. Walsh, *Kant as Seen by Hegel*, in HEGEL'S CRITIQUE OF KANT 206, 210 (Stephen Priest ed., 1987) ("the Kantian unity of apperception is the germ of Hegel's doctrine of Spirit. The unity of apperception might be said at a pinch to subdue or appropriate the manifold of sense by forcing the latter to enter into relations with itself; Hegelian spirit similarly appropriates and subdues whatever presents itself as its opposite . . ."). Michael Rosen, however, argues that Hegel reads too much of his own philosophy into Kant and that Kant's view of the subject is much more passive than Hegel represents. ROSEN, CRITICISM, *supra* note 8, at 115-21.

[24] CRITIQUE OF PURE REASON, *supra* note 16, at B137. This is very similar to Hegel's definition of the "thing." Figure 34(a).

[25] TAYLOR, *supra* note 16, at 297.

nature of the *I* in order to learn what the *Notion* [of a thing] is." (585)

Nevertheless, Hegel complains, Kant radically separates subjectivity from reality. Empirical stuff exists on its own account. The Notion is "declared to be something merely *formal* which, since it abstracts from the content, does not contain truth." (586) For Kant, "the Notion is not the independent factor, not the essential and true element of the prior given material; on the contrary, it is the material that is regarded as the absolute reality, which cannot be extracted from the Notion." (587)[26]

In contrast, Hegel thinks that reality is "not the material given by intuition and representation." (587)[27] Any such view of reality, Hegel suggests, precludes philosophy and even religion. "[F]or how can there be any need for religion, how can religion have any meaning, if the fleeting and superficial phenomena of the world of sensuous particulars are still regarded as the truth?" (588)

If "all manifoldness" (588) is made immune from the Notion, and if the Notion is capable only of "the form of abstract universality or the empty identity of reflection," (588-9) then, Hegel asks, how can *genus* be accounted for? Genus is more than mere abstract universality. It is a specific determinateness in its species. "If one would but reflect attentively on the meaning of this fact, one would see that *differentiation* must be regarded as an equally essential moment of the Notion." (589)[28] Kant thought so and reflected the point in

> the extremely important thought that there are synthetic judgements *a priori* [*i.e.*, non-empirical judgments]. This original synthesis of apperception is one of the most profound principles for speculative development; it contains the beginning of a true apprehension of the nature of the Notion and is completely opposed to that empty identity or abstract universality which is not within itself a synthesis. (589)

To expand upon this point somewhat, Kant's *a priori* synthetic judgments produce the conditions for the possibility of experience.[29] These judgments refer to the categories of the understanding. The categories suffuse the objective things that intuition beholds. They are

---

[26] Hegel thought nature logically implies spirit, making him, for Errol Harris, a kind of proto-Darwinist. The truth of the being of nature, then, is that consciousness must emerge from it. For this reason, "Hegel is as much a realist as, and effectively more so, than any other philosopher." HARRIS, *supra* note 8, at 218.

[27] *See* TAYLOR, *supra* note 16, at 297 ("Kant would have received [this twist] with horror").

[28] This is aimed in Spinoza's direction.

[29] CRITIQUE OF PURE REASON, *supra* note 16, at A157/B196.

therefore not mere abstract universals but contain distinction within themselves.

But Kant insufficiently developed the thought. He never got beyond the "psychological reflex of the Notion and has reverted once more to the assertion that the Notion is permanently conditioned by a manifold of intuition." (589)

> It will always stand out as a marvel how the Kantian philosophy recognized the relation of thought to sensuous reality, beyond which it did not advance, as only a relative relation of mere Appearance, and perfectly well recognized . . . a higher unity of both . . . , and yet stopped short at this relative relation and the assertion that the Notion is . . . utterly separate from reality – thus asserting as *truth* what it declared to be finite cognition, and denouncing as an unjustified extravagance and a figment of thought what it recognized as *truth*. (592)

Notion (*i.e.*, subjectivity) without intuition is declared by Kant to be devoid of content, even if non-empirical judgments *a priori* are possible. Even the phrase "synthesis," Hegel complains, "recalls the conception of the *external* unity and a *mere combination* of entities that are *intrinsically separate*." (589) Yet being negative – without content – Kantian subjectivity "surely does contain determinateness and difference within itself." (589) That is to say, since the Kantian subject is entirely negative, it refers to, depends on, and therefore has some positive content against which it compares itself. Furthermore, since all difference and distinction stems from the Kantian subject (and since the Notion is subject), "the Notion is the ground and source of all finite determinateness and manifoldness." (589)

The merely formal role that Kant accords to subjectivity is confirmed in Kant's definition of reason. In reason, "one ought to have expected the Notion to lose the conditionedness in which it still appears at the stage of understanding and to attain to perfect truth." (589) Yet this never occurs. Rather, the relation of reason to the categories of the understanding (*i.e.*, the non-empirical judgments) is said to be dialectical, and the result of dialectic is "the *infinite nothing* – just that and nothing more." (589-90)[30] Accordingly, Kant did not permit reason to produce objective insights. This was "declared to be an abuse." (590) Reason was only regulative. We are licensed to use the notions of reason, but they are never more than hypotheses. "[T]o

---

[30] *See* CRITIQUE OF PURE REASON, *supra* note 16, at 297 ("There was only one way to bring [the antinomies] to conclusion, by declaring both contradictory statements to be false").

ascribe absolute truth to them would be the height of caprice and foolhardiness, for they – *do not occur in any experience*." (590) The products of reason, for Kant, are not true "because they lack the spatial and temporal material of the sensuous world." (590) Yet this is contradictory, as Kant proclaims experience to be an insufficient criterion for the truth.[31]

What is the relation of the Notion to the truth? For Kant, truth is the agreement of cognition with its object.[32] Yet when thinking appropriates an object, the object is altered. It is "changed from something sensuous to something thought." (590) The essential object is left unaffected, and this object-beyond-thought is, for Kant, the truth – an inaccessible truth that we can never know. All we ever know is appearance. Hence, Kant's cognitions are *always* inadequate to their object and never the truth.

On the contrary, Hegel has already shown that Appearance is sublated in the Notion. "[T]hrough the Notion the object is reduced to its non-contingent essential nature." (591) For Hegel, Appearance is not devoid of Essence, but is a manifestation of it. Essence in its "completely liberated manifestation" (591) is the Notion itself. "Abstract thinking, therefore, is not to be regarded as a mere setting aside of the sensuous material, the reality of which is not thereby impaired; rather is it the sublating and reduction of that material as mere *phenomenal appearance* to the *essential*, which is manifested only in the *Notion*." (588) For Hegel, Appearance is Actual only when it erases itself and dissolves itself in Notion. Notion *is* what is left over after Appearance actualizes itself (by erasing itself).

The Notion will bear the usual three shapes of the Understanding, Dialectical and Speculative Reason. At first, Notion is "*only* something *inner*." (596) It equally ought to be something *outer*. In its first stage, Notion is immediate, "and in this guise its moments have the form of immediate, *fixed determinations*." (597) This is the Understanding's account of the Notion. According to the Understanding, Notion is "an *external* form [which] cannot count as a being-in-and-for-self." This version of the Notion is merely "*posited* or *subjective*." (597) What Formal Notion must do is to lose the separatedness between the moments.

In this first stage, the Understanding proposes that Notion is simple.

---

[31] IMMANUEL KANT, CRITIQUE OF JUDGMENT 74 (J.H. Bernhard trans., 1951).

[32] *See* CRITIQUE OF PURE REASON, *supra* note 16, at 48, 460.

Its moments "are immediately the totality of the Notion and are simply the *Notion as such*." (599) Dialectical Reason will assert the diversity of Formal Notion and its moments. Unity is seen as externally imposed. The connection between these self-subsistent moments is Judgment. Eventually, the connection will become *necessary*. Judgment becomes Syllogism (*i.e.*, inference). At this point, the middle term becomes equal to the extremes. When three terms share an identity, Notion becomes Objective.

Objective Notion is the second part of the Subjective Logic. Here, "*formal* Notion makes *itself* its subject matter and in this way is rid of the relation of subjectivity and externality to the object." (597) Objective Notion is "real" – *i.e.*, dialectical. In Objectivity, Notion emerges from its inwardness and passes over into determinate being. But still, Objective Notion suffers from *moments*; "its distinct moments are objective existences in which [Notion] is itself again only the *inner*." (597)

Objective Notion must give itself the form of subjectivity, but not the non-objective subjectivity from which Formal Notion suffers. When it obtains this form, Notion will be Free Notion, which unifies Formal and Objective Notion. When it is free *and* objective, Notion is Idea – "the agreement of the Notion with reality." (614)

A. The Universal Notion

In the large scheme of things, the Notion is a grand middle term – a negation of the negation, or "the infinite unity of the negativity with itself." (601) The "*pure relation*" (601) of the Notion to itself is Universality. If Notion is itself, its other, and the unity of itself and other, Universality is Notion *itself*, "the manifestation *of the identical*." (603)[33]

Universal Notion is abstract. To obtain it, we must omit the

[33] Hegel describes the Universal, Particular and Individual as concrete versions of abstract Identity, Difference and Ground. EL §164. But if Universality is simple, is it not inexplicable? "[F]or an explanation must concern itself with definitions and distinctions and must apply predicates to its object." (601) To *explain* the Universal would be to introduce distinctions into and thereby distort the Universal. Yet the Universal *is* explicable. Though simple self-relation (the Notion *itself*), "it contains *within itself* difference and determinateness in the highest degree." (601) Pure Being may have been inexplicable in the above sense. *Its* Notion was to vanish into its opposite. The Universal "possesses *within itself* the *richest content*." (602)

Particular and the Individual. These *negate* the abstract Universal, and, since we are considering the Understanding's proposition that the Notion is abstractly Universal, we must negate *these*. So the abstract Universal is still, by this observation, a negation of the negation. It is "infected with a *negation*." (829)[34] Such an observation, however, is strictly "for us." The Notion must further develop before it manifests itself as a negation of the negation.

The Universal stands for the "soul . . . of the concrete which it indwells, unimpeded and equal to itself in the manifoldness and diversity of the concrete. It is not dragged into the process of becoming, but *continues* itself through that process undisturbed and possesses the power of unalterable, undying self-preservation." (602) Determination is no Limitation for the Universal, which diffuses into its own (non-)beyond. In Being, identity-with-self existed within Limitation. Such identity-with-self was the Notion only implicitly. Because the Notion was only implicit, "the qualitative determination as such was lost in its other and had for its truth a determination *distinct* from itself." (602) In the Determinations of Reflection, the Universal was *show* (or Illusory Being). But such a show depended upon otherness. As correlative, a Determination of Reflection was self-related but also "a *positive relating* of itself to its other in which it *manifests itself*." (603) Each showed itself in the other, and so each was reciprocally determined. This reciprocity "has the form of an external act." (603)

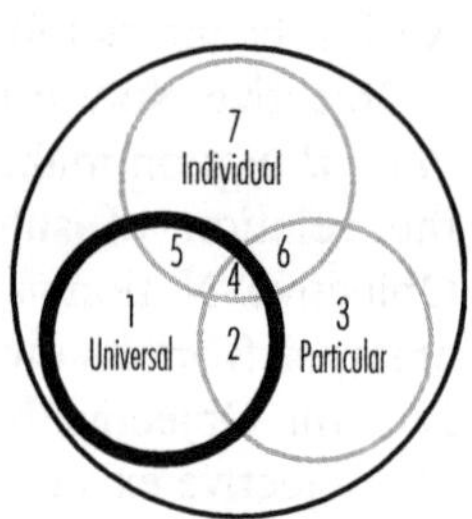

Figure 53(a)
The Universal Notion

In contrast, the Universal is now "posited as the *essential being* of its determination, as the latter's *own positive nature*." (603) That is to say, the Universal is the Substance (*i.e.*, subsisting manifestation) of its own determinations. Substance, it will be recalled, was the unity of Contingency and Necessity. Contingency stood for the groundedness of the Actual in the happenstance of external conditions.[35] Now, "what was a *contingency* for substance, is the Notion's own self-*mediation*." (603) In the Universal, the relation of self to itself is "the *manifested* relation." (603) Accordingly, the Universal is not "the abyss of formless

---

[34] *See* Winfield, *supra* note 11, at 61 ("Far from having a separate existence . . . the abstract universal cannot have its own identity unless it stands in relation to both particularity and individuality").

[35] *Supra* at 402-7.

substance" (603) nor merely inner. Notion is its own origin – "the shaper and creator" (603) of its own self. It is the manifestation of its principle – "the manifestation *of the identical*." (603)

The Universal is said to be "*free* power . . . *free love* and *boundless blessedness*." (603)[36] That Notion is free power was established in Figure 48(a), where we learned that Substance *is* self-manifestation. It must go forth into Accident, from which it is alienated. Now, when it goes forth into its other, the Universal Notion "is itself and takes its other within its embrace, but without *doing violence* to it." (603) In short, the Universal does unto others as it does unto itself, "not by force but by quietly being present in it."[37] In becoming other, it returns to itself. These are indeed the hallmarks of love.

Love implies otherness, however, and we are only at the stage of the Universal Notion – the Notion as itself (and not yet Notion as its other or Notion as the unity of the two). In truth, "we cannot speak of the universal apart from determinateness which to be more precise is particularity and universality." (603) As the absolute is now before us, there is no other to the Notion, even in the initial stage of Universal Notion. Rather, Notion contains all moments within it. "The determinateness [of the Notion] is not introduced from the outside." (603) What the Notion must do is to develop those moments until the moments and the whole *completely* coincide.

Abstraction. When the Universal isolates itself from its other moments, it ceases to be itself. Rather than Universal, it reveals itself to be Particular, determinate, and abstract. The Particular as such does not appear to be a unity of itself, its other and the unity of both; "particularity is not present as a totality." (608) Notion is "*outside itself*." (608) As an abstract, the Universal "is, indeed, the Notion, yet it is without the Notion; it is the Notion that is not posited as such." (609)[38]

---

[36] This recalls the words of Juliet: "My bounty is as boundless as the sea, My love as deep; the more I give to thee, The more I have, for both are infinite." WILLIAM SHAKESPEARE, ROMEO AND JULIET, act 2 scene 2.

[37] BURBIDGE, *supra* note 13, at 113.

[38] Yet Particularization is something the Universal does to *itself*. "[I]n a first move, universality has to be asserted in its negativity, as exclusive of all particular content – that is to say, not as an all-encompassing container, but as the destructive force which undermines every particular content . . . the true Hegelian 'concrete universality' is the very movement of negativity which splits universality *from within*, reducing it to one of the particular elements, one of its own species. It is only at this moment, when universality, as it were, loses the distance of an abstract container, and *enters its own*

When people speak of notions, they usually mean an abstract universal. The Understanding is the faculty of such Notions. The Understanding takes itself to be outside Substance, "and just because it is outside it, a contingent understanding – in which and for which substance is present in various attributes and modes." (609)[39]

Yet abstraction is not as empty as usually thought, Hegel suggests. Abstraction to the point of indeterminateness is, after all, a determinateness, just as *nothing* is and always has been *something*. The Understanding should not be lightly esteemed because it abstracts. The Understanding *fixes* propositions. It proposes abstract universals. But these abstract universals also contain the genuine Universal, and for this very reason the fixities of the Understanding do not stay fixed. Accordingly, "we must recognize the infinite force of the understanding in splitting the concrete into abstract determinatenesses and plumbing the depth of [notional] difference." (610) The Understanding is "alone the power that effects their transition." (610)

More precisely, the fixity of the Understanding presupposes Limit. Limit implies relation to an other. Limited, finite things *ought* to pass away – to travel past their limit. But because these fixities are the genuine Universal, "they are freed from the relation-to-other and have become *imperishable*." (610) To be sure, the abstract universal of the Understanding has the form (but not the content) of the genuine Universal. The abstract universal *will* perish, because its "content is at variance with the form." (610)

The Understanding (or mere intuition) presupposes a material world which has "an indifferent, *sundered* existence in space and time; but surely this absence of unity in the manifold . . . ought not to be counted to it for merit and superiority over intellectual [*i.e.*, Notional] existence." (610) The fixities of the Understanding are mutable, and this points to the Universal. Yet, unless the mechanics of True Infinity are understood, dissolution of one abstract universal simply brings another into view – a Spurious Infinity of abstractions.

The Understanding is praised for according to logical moments "a rigidity of *being* such as they do not possess in the qualitative sphere and in the sphere of reflection." (611) The Understanding is likewise given credit because it "*spiritually impregnates*" (*begeistet*) these isolated moments, such that "they acquire the capability to dissolve themselves

---

frame, that it becomes truly *concrete*." ŽIŽEK, *supra* note 12, at 87.

[39] Hegel refers to Spinoza here. *Supra* at 400.

and to pass over into their opposite." (611) Accordingly, "[t]he highest maturity, the highest stage, which anything can attain is that in which its downfall begins." (611) The dissolution of the finite, Hegel suggests, is the core idea of the genuine Universal.[40] The finite moments of the Understanding are therefore actually a unity of themselves and genuine Universality.

In the end, Hegel suggests, it is a mistake to separate the Understanding from reason (as Kant does). If the Notion is regarded as irrational – *i.e.*, if reason dissolves into antinomies – then reason has failed "to recognize itself in the Notion." (612) Notion is the very condition of reason; "it is form spiritually impregnated, in which the finite, through the universality in which it relates itself to itself, spontaneously catches fire, posits itself as dialectical and thereby is the *beginning* of the manifestation of reason." (612)

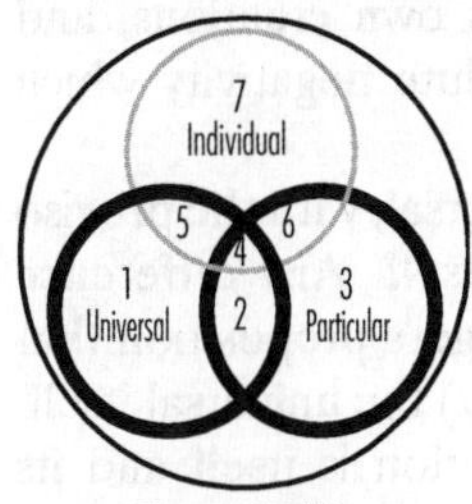

Figure 53(b)
Particular Notion

B. The Particular Notion

Many philosophers argue for the existence of universals, but few bother to argue that there are particulars.[41]

"It is the 'fate' of universality to 'lose' itself in its individuations, to 'fall' into them."[42] So Dialectical Reason proposes that the Universal Notion, as isolated from its other moments, is Particular. If the Notion is (a) itself, (b) its other, and (c) the unity of the two, and if the Universal Notion stood for (a) the self-identical Notion, the Particular Notion stands for (a) itself *and* (b) its other. Particularity is the dialectical, determinate moment of Notion.[43] "Particularization is differentiation." (701) But it is no "determinateness" limited by a beyond. Notion is not limited. Particularity is not truly "other" to Universal. The very substance of Particularity is Universality. These are the same thing. Just as genus is not altered in species, so the Universal is not altered in its Particulars. The Particulars may differ

---

[40] In accordance with this thought, Žižek suggests that the self-sacrifice of the Universal is the core of Christianity itself. ŽIŽEK, *supra* note 12, at 17.

[41] TERRY PINKARD, HEGEL'S DIALECTIC 31-2 (1988).

[42] MARCUSE, ONTOLOGY, *supra* note 11, at 124.

[43] BURBIDGE, *supra* note 13, at 115 ("That which renders a concept determinate is its particularity").

from each other, but they all partake of (and exhibit) the same Universality. Particularity therefore "comprises an undifferentiated instance" of Universality.[44] "*Being in general implies being in particular*."[45]

Determinateness (Particularity in notional parlance) is entirely contained within the Notion at all stages. Reflection is now "the total reflection, the *twofold illusory being* [semblance, appearance] which on the one hand has an illusory reference *outwards* . . . , and on the other hand has an illusory reference *inwards* . . ." (604) Reflection always involves an other; "from this standpoint, the universal possesses a *particularity* which has its resolution in a higher universal." (604) As a "relative universal," the Notion does not really go out into an other but only returns to itself. Hence reflection outwards *is* reflection inwards. "The determinateness . . . is *bent back into itself* out of the externality." (604) For this very reason, Notion is free. No true "other" imposes itself on the Notion. Its differentiations are its own creations, and hence the Notion is "*creative power* as the absolute negativity which relates itself to its own self." (605)

The Particular is the outward show of the Universal, with the proviso that the Universal is as much "other" as it is itself. Any difference belongs solely to the Universal. This leads to Hegel's proposition that there are only two species – species and genus: "(*a*) the universal itself, and (*b*) the particular. The universal as the Notion is itself and its opposite, and this again is the universal itself as its posited determinateness; it embraces its opposite and in it is in union with itself." (606) One of the members of the set is the set itself. This important idea goes to the structure of the Notion as (a) itself, (b) its other, and (c) the unity of itself and other. Genus is (c); it must be seen as a moment no better than the other moments.

This is an idea that delights the Lacanians. It is a joke for Lacan to announce, "I have three brothers, Paul, Ernst, and myself."[46] According to Žižek, this Hegelian trope of genus-as-species stands for hysteria[47] (and Lacan names Hegel "the most sublime of hysterics.)"[48] Hysteria stands for the empty subject demanding to know from the

---

[44] Winfield, *supra* note 11, at 62.

[45] BUTLER, *supra* note 2, at 211.

[46] SLAVOJ ŽIŽEK, FOR THEY KNOW NOT WHAT THEY DO: ENJOYMENT AS A POLITICAL FACTOR 43 (1991).

[47] *Id.* at 44.

[48] JACQUES LACAN, LE SÉMINAIRE DE JACQUES LACAN, LIVRE XVII: L'ENVERS DE LA PSYCHANALYSE 38 (Jacques-Alain Miller ed. 1991).

symbolic realm what his place in the system is, for the subject in Lacanian theory is precisely a universal nothing without inherent content. The hysteric does not feel at home in the realm of the particulars. In that realm, the universal discovers that it is "not All;" it cannot swallow enough particulars to make itself the whole, a disability that is constitutive of subjectivity itself.[49] On the logic of the Hegelian Universal, then, there is always a remainder when the Universal particularizes itself. "There is always an empty place occupied by the surplus element which is the set itself in the form of the empty set."[50] This remainder is precisely the Individual, Hegel's middle term between the Universal and Particular. This means that the split is on the side of the Universal and is indeed constitutive of it. Totalities, then, are always over-determined; there is always something else in addition to the aggregate of particulars – a negative presence which in fact opposes the particulars. For those who still take Hegel to be a totalitarian, this trope about genus and species proves that "there is universality only in so far as there is a gap."[51]

For Hegel, the only true classification of Particulars is the opposition of the Particular to yet another Particular – the Universal, which is on the same level as the Particulars. The ghostly particular that organizes the set – what Lacan would call the Master Signifier – is "*immediate* indeterminate universality; this very indeterminateness constitutes its determinateness or makes it a particular." (606)[52]

Returning to Figure 53(b), Hegel suggests that, if [1] and [3] are both species, then the Universal is just as Particular as the Particular is. Each is a Particular only against its other – the Universal. Thus,

---

[49] ŽIŽEK, KNOW NOT, *supra* note 47, at 43.

[50] *Id.* at 44.

[51] SLAVOJ ŽIŽEK, THE TICKLISH SUBJECT: THE ABSENT CENTRE OF POLITICAL ONTOLOGY 103 (1999).

[52] Of course, in nature, genera often have many species. "This is the impotence of nature, that it cannot adhere to and exhibit the strictness of the Notion and runs wild in this blind irrational multiplicity. We can *wonder* at nature's manifold genera and species and the endless diversity of her formations, for *wonderment* is *unreasoning* and its object the irrational." (607) As per chapter 2, nature is "the self-externality of the Notion . . . , free to indulge itself in . . . variety, just as spirit, too, even though it possesses the Notion in the shape of the Notion, engages in pictorial thinking and runs riot in its endless variety." (608) The variety of species "must not be esteemed as anything more than the capricious fancies of spirit in its representations." (608) Nature's irrationality also produces the genetically aberrant individual – *e.g.*, the acephalous human. Hegel discusses the logical significance of this as an obstacle for Definition. *Infra* at 589.

whereas in Figure 53(a), the Universal was only one of the sides, in Figure 53(b), the Universal is *doubly* one of the sides, since both sides are Particulars. But "if we speak of *two opposed sides*, we must supplement this by saying that it is not merely *together* that they constitute the particular – as if they were *alike* in being particulars only for external reflection." (607) Rather, the point is that each side has a determinateness over against the other side, and this determinateness is in fact *one* determinateness. In the Universal of Figure 53(a) this is simple. In the Particular of Figure 53(b), it is not simple.

Difference is now shown in its truth. It is a *unity* within the Universal. In Being, difference meant limit by an other. In Essence, difference was relative – Essence related itself to an other. Earlier stages, Determinate Being, Something, or the correlate pairs of whole and parts, cause and effect, etc., are, on their own merely thought-determinations; "but they are grasped as determinate *Notions* when each is recognized in unity with its other." (607) Whole and parts, or cause and effect – these were not particulars relatively to each other. Their unity did not achieve Universality. At these earlier stages, difference "has not yet the form of being *one* determinateness." (607) What must be realized is that Whole and Parts or Cause and Effect are but one simple Notion – not two.

In principle, then, the determinateness of the two Particulars is one. This unitary determinateness [2] is itself a moment of the totality. Against this simple moment the Notion differentiates itself, and through this opposition the Notion "gives itself the form of one of its ideal moments, that of *being*; as a *determinate* Notion, it has a *determinate* being in general." (608)

Have we gone back to the beginning, like a humiliated loser in Parcheesi? Hegel assures us not. Notional Being "no longer has the meaning of mere *immediacy*, but of universality, of an immediacy that is identical with itself through absolute mediation, an immediacy that equally contains within itself the other moment, namely, essential being or reflection." (608) In other words, Notion puts forth its being in the world and is truly reflected in that being. The Notion is itself *and* its other – its being in the world.

To summarize, difference is now an essential moment of the Notion, yet not all the implications of this moment have been drawn out yet. If we have examined the Universal *in itself* and the Universal as its other (or Particularity), we have yet to examine the Universal as the *unity* of itself and other. This last moment will be the self-related moment of the Notion, where determinateness as absolute negativity is "posited *for itself*." (612) Individuality is "the third moment of the Notion, in so far as we hold on to its *opposition* to the two other moments." (612) Ironically, Hegel hints, Individuality is "the absolute return of the Notion into itself, and at the same time [is] the posited loss of itself." (612)

"[I]f one insists on *counting* them," (612) there are three determinate Notions – the Universal, the Particular, and the Individual. But enumeration, Hegel warns, is inadequate to the Notion. Number entails Unit,[53] and Unit implies an isolation that is inappropriate to the advanced state of the Notion. Numerical and spatial relation "are the last and worst medium which could be employed" in discussing the Notion. (618)

Enumeration suggests "that we *find* such species *already to hand* and they present themselves *empirically*. In this way, we obtain an *empirical logic* – an odd science this, an *irrational* cognition of the *rational*." (613) Hegel thinks Kant is guilty of this technique. Kant "*borrows* the categories, as so-called root notions, for the *transcendental logic*, from the subjective logic in which they were adopted empirically." (613) Presumably this refers to Kant's alignment of the categories to the logical functions of judgment.[54] It should be acknowledged, however,

---

[53] Figure 13(c).

[54] CRITIQUE OF PURE REASON, *supra* note 16, at 202, 230. Hegel's criticism is answered in KLAUS REICH, THE COMPLETENESS OF KANT'S TABLE OF JUDGMENTS (Jane Kneller & Michael Losonsky trans. 1992). Reich's response to Hegel, however, is a complex argument that turns on the absolute simplicity and indivisibility of the 'I' – a proposition that Hegel would certainly oppose. *See id.* at 31-2. According to Lewis White Beck, in the forward to this book:

> The Metaphysical Deduction of the Categories – the very name is an afterthought introduced only in the second edition [of the *Critique of Pure Reason*] and used only for the nonce by Kant – is one of the least esteemed parts of the *Critique*. Several eminent commentators have passed over it in polite silence, as if embarrassed by Kant's fatuity, and those who enjoy lording it over him are almost unanimous in their conviction that not only is its premise ungrounded, its argument incorrect, and its conclusion false, but also that, even if it were conclusive and correct, it would contribute nothing that is not better provided in other parts of the *Critique*. Such objections were current even in Kant's own day; they were repeated by Hegel, and are commonplaces of Kant criticism today.

Id. at xiii. Beck states that Kant's table of the form of judgments was "the heritage of Aristotelian logic". *Id; see also* ROBERT PIPPIN, KANT'S THEORY OF FORM: AN ESSAY ON THE *CRITIQUE OF PURE REASON* 91 (1982) (undertaking to reinterpret Kant in a more charitable way).

that Hegel's own chapter on judgment basically follows Kant's table of the logical functions of judgment.[55] Undoubtedly, if Kant is accused of empirically *finding* this table, Hegel would insist for himself that he has *derived* it.[56] Yet, as we shall see, the tetrachotomy of this chapter is an unexplained mystery in the *SL*.

Hegel takes the opportunity to denounce attempts to reduce logic to "symbolic" form, as such a practice amounts to "enumeration." Some of his remarks could be taken as a reproach to the pictographic system I have developed to explicate Hegel's Logic. "Now when Notions are so taken that they correspond to such signs, they cease to be Notions. Their determinations are not inert entities like numbers or lines . . . [t]hey are living movements; the distinguished determinateness of the one side is immediately internal to the other side too." (617) I trust readers have learned to view the drawings in this work as pedagogic aides, not as "signs."

C. The Individual

> Not until Hegel, and perhaps not since Hegel, has any concerted effort been made to conceive how universality is intrinsically connected to individuality, thereby enabling the concept to surmount the limitations that would condemn philosophy to futility. Despite the growing mountain of discussion of Hegel's work, his contribution on this score has largely been ignored. This is partly due to a lack of appreciation of the systematic program of the *Logic* and partly due to a failure to get beyond the Logics of Being and of Essence and attend to the crowning arguments of the Logic of the Concept.[57]

If Notion is the unity of (a) itself, (b) its other, and (c) the unity of itself and other, it is time to investigate (c) the unity of Universal and Particular. In Individuality, "the *inseparability* of the Notion's determinations is *posited*." (620) If the Particular was "self-related determinateness," Individuality is "the *reflection* of the Notion out of its determinateness *into itself*." (618) Otherness (Particularity) is made other again (Individuality); the Notion reinstates itself as self-identical.

---

charitable way).

[55] *Infra* at 461. For Kant's table of logical forms of judgment, see CRITIQUE OF PURE REASON, *supra* note 16, at 56.

[56] *See* JEAN HYPPOLITE, LOGIC AND EXISTENCE 135 (Leonard Lawlor and Amit Sen trans., 1997) ("Hegel takes up Kant's reflection on the forms of judgment, but he makes explicit their simultaneous subjective and objective sense").

[57] RICHARD DIEN WINFIELD, AUTONOMY AND NORMATIVITY 44 (2001).

But this self-identity is very – even absolutely – negative.[58] It is so negative that it is *abstract*, which means that Individuality is destined to violate the very idea of the Notion.[59] Its return to self is therefore "the absolute, original *partition of itself*, or, in other words, it is posited as *judgement*." (622) Division of the Individual implies an existence from which the notional Individual is alienated.

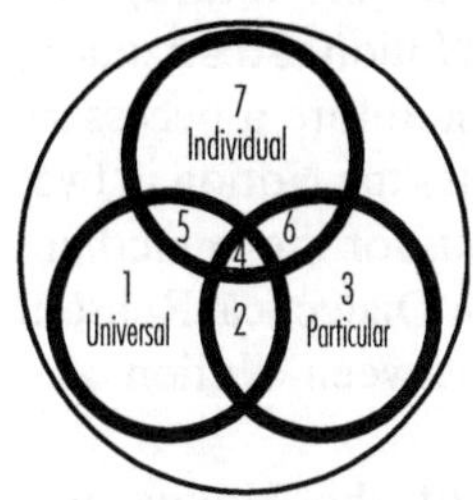

Individual Notion

When the Universal was Particular, negativity had a twofold semblance. First, it was internal to the Universal [1]. Second, negativity was outward [2, 3], and then the Particular was *determinate*. The return of the negative into the Individual is likewise twofold. First, the return is notional. Because Universality and Particularity are already the Notion, these do not pass over into an other. These are already Individual, and Individuality is the truth of Universality and Particularity. Secondly, the return occurs (illegitimately though necessarily) through abstraction, "which lets drop the particular and rises to the *higher* and the *highest genus*." (619) Abstraction, "a *sundering* of the concrete and an *isolating* of its determinations," (619) denies Individuality "and remains destitute of the Notion. Life, spirit, God – the pure Notion itself, are beyond the grasp of abstraction, because it deprives its products of singularity, of the principle of individuality and personality, and so arrives at nothing else but universalities devoid of life, spirit, colour and filling." (619) Yet even though abstraction [7] "strays from the highway of the Notion and forsakes the truth," (619) and despises true Individuality, its abstract universals are nevertheless covertly Individual. Through abstraction, single properties are isolated; properties that genuinely belong to the thing observed. Nevertheless, Individuality in the abstract Universal suffers from a division between *form* and *content*. Such an Individuality is therefore concrete [4, 5, 6] – the opposite of the

---

58 In the *EL*, Hegel states that Individuality is a Universal "stated expressly as a negative identity with itself. Individuality, however, is not to be understood to mean the immediate or natural individual . . . for that special phase of individuality does not appear till we come to the judgement. Every . . . 'moment' of the notion is itself the whole notion . . . but the individual . . . is the notion expressly put as a totality." EL §163.

59 As Hegel will say in the *EL*: "The individual by itself does not correspond to its notion. It is this limitation . . . which constitutes the finitude and the ruin of the individual." EL § 213.

simplex it is supposed to be. "What it is is always more than itself."[60]

Given his poor opinion of abstraction, why does Hegel emphasize abstract universality here as a coequal to immanent return? Because the "abstract" mode of return stands for the Understanding itself. By including it as a genuine-but-one-sided mode of return, the Understanding is made into a moment of the Notion. Abstraction, which will turn out to be the Individual itself, is therefore a necessary moment, but an inadequate one. Abstraction divides the Notion in two, so that, just as the opening chapter of Notion stands for the immediate Understanding, the Judgment chapter will stand for Dialectical Reason. Syllogism will stand for the speculative unity between Notion and Judgment.

In the foregoing discussion, each moment of the Notion was "confounded in the very attempt to isolate and fix it. Only *mere representational thinking*, for which abstraction has isolated [these moments], is capable of holding the universal, particular and individual apart." (620) Only then is it possible to *count* the notional moments. Quantity, in which Being is completely external to the concept, "is nowhere less appropriate than here." (620) Nevertheless, it is the pose of Individuality to be abstracted from the other moments. In spite of this pose, Individuality is *not* distinct in the other moments. Individuality, then, has two moments. It is abstract *and* it is concrete. Accordingly, though Individuality has the positive aspect of reestablishing the Notion, it "is not only the return of the Notion into itself, but immediately its loss." (621) Abstraction is the soul of Individuality. By its logic, abstraction is immanent from the thing on which it operates. Through abstraction, the Universal and Particular *are* Individuals. Individuation *is* differentiation. It is *fixed* difference. Only through abstracted Individuality can the Particular be determined against other Particulars. In short, Individuality is "*posited abstraction*." (621)

To put this in other terms, there is a *Far Side* cartoon showing innumerable identical penguins. One of them is singing the old standard, "I Got To Be Me." The joke of it is that the individual penguin is an individual only through the sheer insistence of distinguishing itself from all the other penguins with which it is really identical. This useless insistence of the penguin is the abstraction on

---

60 THEODOR W. ADORNO, HEGEL: THREE STUDIES 81 (1999).

which Individuality depends.

Individuality represents the ideal of immediacy within the Notion. Accordingly, it is "the immediate identity of the negative with itself" and a "*a being-for-self.*" (621) Recall that Being-for-self expelled itself from itself and became for other. Something similar now happens at a more advanced level. Just as Being-for-self became One, "the individual is a qualitative *one* or a *this.*" (621) As One, it is the "repulsion of itself from *itself*, whereby the many *other* ones are presupposed." (621)[61] In other words, there can never be *one* Individual. There must always be many. Individuality then becomes a negative relation with presupposed others. Common sense reduces Universality to a merely common element of all the Ones. Such a view is one-sided. "When one understands by the universal, what is *common* to several individuals, one is starting from the *indifferent* subsistence of these individuals and confounding the immediacy of *being* with the determination of the Notion." (621) The Universal as common element is "[t]he lowest conception one can have of the Universal." (621)

Abstract indexicality (*i.e.*, "this") was a key moment early in the *Phenomenology*. Now the Individual, taken one-sidedly, is a "this," separate and apart from other Individuals. "This" more appropriately belongs in the sphere of reflection. That is to say, indexicality ("this") implies a pointer who implicitly announces, "I am not *that.*" The Individual, however, no longer repulses all its Being, as Being-for-self did. Repulsion is now abstraction – "the reflecting *mediation* which attaches to the this in such wise that the this is a *posited* immediacy *pointed out* by someone external to it." (622) "This" is immediate, but it is only "this" if it is pointed out – by another Individual. Abstraction is covertly the Notion. External pointing is always self-pointing. The Individual is a this – "the immediate restored out of mediation; but it does not have the mediation outside it – it is itself a repelling separation, *posited abstraction*, yet in its very act of separating, it is a positive relation." (622)

The Individual's act is self-abstraction. It posits its moments as self-subsistent and reflected-into-self. These moments *are*; Notion has sundered itself. "[T]his sundering is reflection as such, the *illusory being* [or appearance] *of the one in the other.*" (622) The moments stand in essential relation – meaning they are Actualities.

Individuals, therefore, are not merely inertly present to one another;

---

61 Figure 9(c).

"such plurality belongs to being." (622) Individuality, "in positing itself as determinate, posits itself not in an external difference but in the difference of the Notion. It therefore excludes the *universal* from itself." (622) Yet the Universal is a moment of Individuality. Individuality, then, depends upon a false consciousness – a radical freedom from otherness.

In the Individual, the Notion has lost itself for a moment. It is no longer the posited unity of the parts. The parts are taken as subsistent in and for themselves. In Individuality, the Notion works a partition of itself, and Notion divided from itself – into subject and object – is the realm of Judgment – "*the relation of determinate Notions*." (616)

20 Judgment

In German, judgment is *Urteil* – "original partition." Consistent with this etymology,[1] Judgment stands for the self-division of Notion, which has sundered itself into two moments – a subjective abstraction [7] and a notional moment [4, 5, 6]. Simultaneously it stands for the conjunction or re-membering of the parts resulting from self-division.[2]

Judgment can be expressed as [7] = [4, 5, 6]; [7] = [4, 5, 6]. The appendage of the inequality to the equality is pursuant to Hegel's early instruction: "if the content is speculative, the *non-identical* aspect of subject and predicate is also an essential moment, but in the judgement this is not expressed . . . . To help express the speculative truth, the deficiency is made good . . . by adding the contrary proposition." (90-1) So conceived, Judgment contains the moments of *distinction* and *relation* – of *reference* and *thought*. The interplay between these two moments is the "heart of the matter" in Judgment.[3]

In Judgment, Notion judges its own self.[4] Self-judging means Notion

---

[1] *See* EL § 86 ("The etymological meaning of the Judgement (*Urteil*) in German goes deeper, as it were declaring the unity of the notion to be primary, and its distinction to be the original partition. And that is what the Judgement really is.").

[2] JOHN W. BURBIDGE, REAL PROCESS: HOW LOGIC AND CHEMISTRY COMBINE IN HEGEL'S PHILOSOPHY OF NATURE 136 (1996).

[3] JOHN W. BURBIDGE, ON HEGEL'S LOGIC: FRAGMENTS OF A COMMENTARY 154 (1981).

[4] For this reason, Judgment is a *reference* (to something immediate and non-notional) and a *self*-reference, since the immediate "other" is the Notion itself. *Id*. at 125.

giving itself an external reality. Judgment is "the omnipotence of the notion" (662) – the tool by which the Notion reestablishes reality *as its own*, after abstract objectivism imploded upon itself in the first two-thirds of the Logic.

Judgment constitutes the first installment on the promise of *intellectual intuition*. Intellectual intuition[5] stands for the ability of God to think objects into existence – divine creation. When God creates a being by *thinking* it, there is nothing extraneous in the object for which God is not responsible. For this reason, an intellectual intuition amounts to "the direct apprehension of things as they are."[6] For Hegel, "judgments no longer function as the most prominent forms of *know-ledge*."[7] Knowledge is on the side of thinking, not being. Rather, Judgment expresses the *synthesis* of thought and being.[8] For this reason, "the *Logic* presents a theology of judgment, not a formal logic of propositions . . . ."[9] "God, sundering himself as Father and Son, is a judgement. All things are a judgement."[10]

In Judgment, as everyone notices, Hegel breaks the trichotomy of immediacy, mediatedness and the unity of immediacy and mediatedness. Now there will be an immediate Judgment, *two* mediated Judgments, and one notional Judgment. Why *two* mediated Judgments? In the *SL*, Hegel does not allude to the change, but in the *EL*, Hegel explains:

> the different species of judgement derive their features from the universal forms of the logical idea itself. If we follow this clue, it will supply us with three chief kinds of judgement parallel to the stages of Being, Essence, and Notion. The second of these kinds, as required by the character of Essence, which is the stage of differentiation, must be doubled . . . [W]hen the Notion, which is the unity of Being and Essence in a comprehensive thought, unfolds . . . it must reproduce these two stages in a transformation proper to the notion . . . [11]

---

5 This is Kant's term. IMMANUEL KANT, CRITIQUE OF PURE REASON B307 (Paul Guyer & Allen W. Wood trans., 1990).

6 STANLEY ROSEN, G.W.F. HEGEL: AN INTRODUCTION TO THE SCIENCE OF WISDOM 267 (1974).

7 HERBERT MARCUSE, HEGEL'S ONTOLOGY AND THE THEORY OF HISTORICITY 29 (Seyla Benhabib trans. 1987).

8 *Id.*

9 CLARK BUTLER, HEGEL'S LOGIC: BETWEEN DIALECTIC AND HISTORY 230 (1996).

10 G.R.G. MURE, THE PHILOSOPHY OF HEGEL 136 (1965).

11 EL §171.

It is necessary, then, to examine Judgment from *both* sides of mediation, since Notion fully occupies each side.

Later, Hegel will speculate that method is arguably tetrachotomous, not triune; the negative moment is both a correlative negation and also an immediate negation, both of which must be accounted for:

> If one insists on *counting*, this *second* immediate is, in the course of the method as a whole, the *third* term to the first immediate and the mediated. It is also, however, the third term to the first or formal negative and to absolute negativity or the second negative; now as the first negative is already the second term, the term reckoned as *third* can also be reckoned as *fourth*, and instead of a *triplicity*, the abstract form may be taken as a *quadruplicity*; in this way, the negative or the difference is counted as a *duality*. (836)

Hegel does not limit the above remark to Judgment. Perhaps, throughout the Subjective Logic, where the Notion reestablishes its own reality, there is *always* quadruplicity, since mediation (*i.e.*, negativity) is always both a mediation and an immediacy. If so, then the question arises why *only* the Judgment chapter and, we should add, the first third of Syllogism[12] are overtly tetradic in form.

Suspiciously, Hegel's path through Judgment corresponds with Kant's table of the logical functions of judgment from the *Critique of Pure Reason*. According to that table:

I *Quantity of judgments*	II *Quality*	III *Relation*	IV *Modality*
Universal	Affirmative	Categorical	Problematical
Particular	Negative	Hypothetical	Assertorical
Singular	Infinite	Disjunctive	Apodeictical

Kant's Table of Logical Functions in Judgment[13]

---

12 *Infra* at 495-8.

13 CRITIQUE OF PURE REASON, *supra* note 5, at A70/B95.

All of Hegel's judgments can be found on Kant's table, though Hegel rearranges the order considerably. Qualitative judgments precede quantitative judgments, consistent with the general priority of Quality over Quantity. Hegel also renames the major headings. Instead of quantity-quality-relation-modality, there is Existence-Reflection-Necessity-Notion. Finally, Hegel rearranges the order in which the quantitative and modal judgments are presented.

Except for these rearrangements, Hegel follows Kant's table of the logical functions of judgment. "In formal logic these are quite externally connected, mere forms of the understanding's reflection indifferent to their content. Hegel tries to make these dry bones live . . . ."[14] Yet, in chapter 7, Hegel did not hesitate to criticize Kant's table of categories for its tetrachotomy. There, Hegel claimed that the third category (relation) was merely inserted. Modality was the true third, and Hegel equated modality with Measure.[15] Now, however, relation (Hegel's Judgments of Necessity) is not merely inserted. It is certainly odd that Hegel should criticize the quadrupartite Table of Categories while basically following the related Table of the Logical Functions of Judgment.[16] This led Marcuse to remark:

> Although Hegel convincingly demonstrates that what is meant and treated as judgment by ordinary linguistic usage aims at the same ontological content as discovered by him, the treatment of judgment in the formal logic is not fitted into this framework. Insofar as Hegel attempts to do so and insists on the traditional "table of judgments," he confuses and obscures the great aspects of his own doctrine.[17]

---

[14] MURE, PHILOSOPHY, *supra* note 10, at 134.

[15] *Supra* at 201-4.

[16] John W. Burbidge, *Hegel's Logic*, in HANDBOOK OF THE HISTORY OF LOGIC 131, 133 (2004) ("There seemed to be something contingent and positivistic about working from a simple table of judgements that had emerged from the history of logic to determine what are the basic categories of the understanding"); RICHARD DIEN WINFIELD, AUTONOMY AND NORMATIVITY 59 (2001) ("Kant is taken to task for metaphysically stipulating the character of the transcendental structure by conceiving it as a noumenal self determined through such unfounded devices as a metaphysical deduction of the categories, which simply adopts, with certain unargued modifications, the typology of judgment of received tradition"). For Kant, the logical function of judgment is the act of the understanding in synthesizing the manifold into one object. CRITIQUE OF PURE REASON, *supra* note 5, at B143. What judgment does is to bring the manifold under one of the categories. *Id*. at 83, 161.

[17] MARCUSE, ONTOLOGY, *supra* note 7, at 127. On 19th century attempts to "reform" Hegel's theory of Judgment, see GIACOMO RINALDI, A HISTORY AND INTERPRETATION OF THE LOGIC OF HEGEL 274-5 n.9 (1992).

Slavoj Žižek, in contrast, stoutly defends Hegel's analysis: "Let is immediately show our cards: the three judgments actually acquire a fourth because 'Substance is Subject'; in other words, the 'lack of identity' between subject and predicate is posited as such in the fourth judgement (that of the Notion)."[18]

I join Žižek in defending Hegel's tetrachotomy of judgment. Why are there four judgments? This can best be understood by examining the grammar of the statement: "the notion is itself, its other, and the unity of itself and other." This can be restated: "The notion is the universal, particular and individual." This may be further reduced to: $A = \{A, B, C\}$, with A standing on both sides of the formula as the universal in its *abstract* and *concrete* forms.[19] Already it is possible to count to four, since A can be counted twice. First, A is abstract and by itself. A is the *lack of identity* between itself and the Notion. Second, A is notional.

In $A = \{A, B, C\}$, A is subject and $\{A, B, C\}$ is predicate. Judgment, "the separation-within-connection of [subject] and [predicate],"[20] proceeds as follows. (1) At first, A is everything; the predicate has no influence over it (Judgment of Existence). (2) Since A is diverse, A is *nothing*. The predicate $\{A, B, C\}$ is *everything* (Judgment of Reflection). (3) In the Judgment of Reflection, A said, "I am not the predicate $\{A, B, C\}$," thereby proving it *is* $\{A, B, C\}$. A is thus restored to a concrete Universality in which A both *is* $\{A, B, C\}$ and is *not* $\{A, B, C\}$ (Judgment of Necessity). This third Judgment equates with Absolute Necessity and Substantiality.[21] Substantiality is not the Notion, however. "Substance is not subject so long as its differentiations are mere accidents, contents adding nothing to the identity of substance, which, for its part, can provide no determinate principle for its own modifications."[22] (4) A knows that it is the author of its own reality – its non-notional accidents and its authentic selfhood (Judgment of the Notion and transition into Syllogism).

In Judgment, the Notion restores for itself a reality that had been canceled in Actuality. To achieve this, all of the Objective Logic is

---

[18] SLAVOJ ŽIŽEK, FOR THEY KNOW NOT WHAT THEY DO: ENJOYMENT AS A POLITICAL FACTOR 179 (1991).

[19] This can be even further reduced to [7] = [[4, 5, 6]], in terms of Figure 53(c), provided [7] ≠ [[4, 5, 6]] is also added.

[20] ROSEN, *supra* note 6, at 65.

[21] ŽIŽEK, KNOW NOT, *supra* note 18, at 192.

[22] Richard Dien Winfield, *From Concept to Judgement: Rethinking Hegel's Overcoming of Formal Logic*, 50 DIALOGUE 53, 57 (2001).

rehearsed for the benefit of the subject. The Judgment of Existence corresponds to the first step – the *realm of Being*. Two versions of mediated Judgments – Reflective Judgment and the Judgment of Necessity – will correspond to Essence. Judgment of the Notion is the culmination of the chapter. At this point subjective Notion establishes itself as objective.[23]

A. The Judgment of Existence (Inherence)

Inside the Individual is both notional and abstract Universality. Unable to digest the abstract Universal, the Individual coughs it up.[24] *A*, the subject, is seen as self-sufficient and independent of the predicate – an immediate "*abstract individual* which *simply is*." (630) This stubborn immediacy means that Judgments of Existence are not true Judgments. They are one-sided propositions. This regressive move must be overcome to reestablish reflective and notional Judgments.

Why does Hegel insert this regressive moment? For one thing, this is what abstractive Understanding demands.[25] Recall that Hegel wrote similar anachronisms into chapter 10, when he discussed the opposition between the Essential and Inessential, and likewise in chapter 12, when he discussed Absolute Ground, where Ground yielded the Grounded, but not vice versa. Indeed, the very appearance of Pure Being was a regression from Absolute Knowing (the last step of the Logic) to immediacy (the antepenultimate step). All of these were regressive abstractions introduced by the Understanding. These regressions energized the process. So, once again, Hegel deals with Judgment of Existence as the common sense view of judgment:

---

[23] The first and third steps in Hegel's method have always been propositions about the nature of the absolute. Clark Butler, however, suggests that "no judgment is by itself such a definition." BUTLER *supra* note 9, at 228. This must be questioned. The *Notion* is the absolute. The Notion is judging its own self and so every proposition about it (as amended by Speculative Reason) must be viewed as definitions of the absolute.

[24] In psychoanalytic terms, the abstract Universal is traumatic. According to Lacan, trauma is "the object that cannot be swallowed, as it were, which remains stuck in the gullet of the signifier." JACQUES LACAN, THE FOUR FUNDAMENTAL CONCEPTS OF PSYCHO-ANALYSIS 270 (1977).

[25] BURBIDGE, LOGIC, *supra* note 3, at 126 ("the *individual* is thought of as immediate *per se* as a pure something, external to the reflective procedures of thinking. When judgement relates these two, then, it takes the *individual* as primary – the subject – and it expresses the fact that the *universal* has been abstracted from it by a judgement in which the abstracted predicate is said to inhere in the concrete individual.").

> From this *subjective* standpoint, then, subject and predicate are considered to be complete, each on its own account, apart from the other: the subject as an object that would exist even if it did not possess this predicate; the predicate as a universal determination that would exist even if it did not belong to this subject. From this standpoint, the act of judgement involves the reflection, whether this or that predicate which is in someone's *head* can and should be *attached* to the *object* which exists on its own account *outside*. (625)

Because of this one-sidedness, the Judgment of Existence implies "the perishableness of individual things" (632) *and* their subsistence in the Notion (which is imperishable). That which comes forth from the Judgment of Existence is subject to alteration and to a return into notional Universality. This, however, is only "for us" at this point.

At first, subject is merely *combined* by external reflection with predicate, "so that, if this combination did not take place, each on its own would still remain what it is." (625)[26] Yet, properly, the predicate *should* belong to the subject. The copula ("is") implies as much.

When diverse words are conjoined, we have mere proposition. The ability to form judgments such as "the rose is red," Hegel comments, "will hardly count as evidence of great powers of judgement." (657) Judgment should be more than this. Judgment and proposition share the form of $A = B$, but this does not mean Judgments are propositions. Indeed, since $A = B$ smacks of proposition, Hegel would have us avoid it. (632) Instead, the Judgment of Existence should bear the form "the subject is the predicate." Even common sense concedes that Judgment requires the predicate to be related to the subject – a Universal must be related to a Particular or Individual. If a statement enunciates something non-universal about a subject, then we have mere proposition. Judgments have a *performative* function in determining the truth of the subject. Judgments purport to be complete.[27] They settle controversies that proposition leaves open. Hegel suggests that "My friend N. is dead" is only a proposition, unless this matter is in controversy. "[I]t would be a judgement only if there were a question whether he was really dead or only in a state of catalepsy." (626) A Judgment establishes a proposition as the definitive truth – "the

---

[26] As Richard Winfield emphasizes, the first three Judgments represent, abstract quality, class and genus. Winfield, *Concept*, *supra* note 22, at 61. Since the Judgment of Existence is merely abstract quality, the subject remains what it is even though *one abstract predicate* fades away.

[27] JOHN MCCUMBER, THE COMPANY OF WORDS: HEGEL, LANGUAGE AND SYSTEMATIC PHILOSOPHY 37-8 (1993)

agreement of the Notion and reality." (631) In Judgment, Hegel's friend N. is definitely predicated in death.[28]

Judgment's first form is simply "*subject is predicate*." (The copula is, for now, invisible.)[29] The subject is taken as determinate and self-identical. But the Understanding makes too much of the supposedly determinate subject. What is the subject? This is "first enunciated by the predicate, which contains *being* in the sense of the notion." (624) In other words, the predicate will tell the Understanding what the subject is.

In Judgment generally, "we want to see *one and the same* object double." (630) First, we want before us an actual Individual. Then we want to know the "essential identity" of it – through the predicate. When the predicate is determined, the Individual is raised to Universality, or, equally, the Universal is Individualized into actuality.

True Judgment is supposed to represent the agreement of the Notion and reality. But the Judgment of Existence is immediate and static. No reflection or movement appears in it. So far, the subject is taken as primary; the predicate lacks self-subsistence. The predicate only *is* if actualized in the subject. There are three kinds of this Judgment: (a) Positive, (b) Negative, and (c) Infinite Judgment.

(a) The Positive Judgment

In the Positive Judgment, "*the individual is universal*." (632) The subject is assumed to be an abstract, determinate Individual. The predicate is an abstract Universal. Mediation between subject and

---

[28] CHARLES TAYLOR, HEGEL 311 (1975) ("what seems to underlie [Judgment] is the attempt to reach a standard of really adequate thought of the object"). Justus Hartnack misinterprets the point here. According to Hartnack, Hegelian judgment is a "sentence [that] is used to eliminate possible doubt or to underline or establish that which the sentence says is, in fact, the case . . . It must be admitted that Hegel is by no means clear regarding this second criterion, and his commentators reflect this lack of clarity." JUSTUS HARTNACK, AN INTRODUCTION TO HEGEL'S LOGIC 94 (Lars Aagaard-Mogensen trans., 1998). In fact, the point is not empirical rhetorical use of a sentence but the real potence of performance. Judgment is self-validating. A verdict (as Hartnack sees) is an example. It is true by the very performance of it.

[29] Ultimately, the copula is as much Individual as the extremes, "for in it the self-subsistent extremes are sublated as in their negative unity." (629) In Judgment of Existence, however, this unity is not yet posited. "[T]he copula is present as the still indeterminate relation of *being* as such." (629) If the unity were "determinate and pregnant," (630) we would be in the realm of Syllogism.

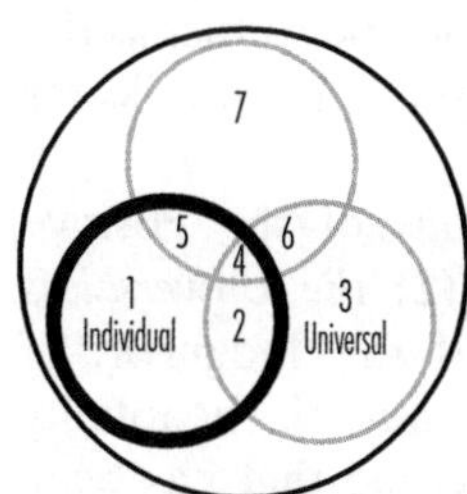

Figure 54(a)
Positive Judgment

predicate is only presupposed. Because this Judgment contains no mediation (the copula being invisible), Hegel names it the Positive Judgment.

Positive Judgment's immediacy is rather illegitimate at this stage of the Logic. As Hegel points out, "In the sphere of the Notion there can be no other *immediacy* than one in which mediation is *essentially* and *explicitly* a moment and which has come to be only through the sublating of that mediation." (631)

Because the subject in "the Individual is Universal" is abstract, it is nothing – "simply a point of reference."[30] It is only the point to which the Universal predicates adhere. Only the predicate "persists in thought and is common to a number of individuals. On this basis it could be considered to be primary – the subject."[31] Dialectical Reason therefore asserts the opposite proposition from that of the Understanding. For Dialectical Reason, "*the universal is individual*." (633)

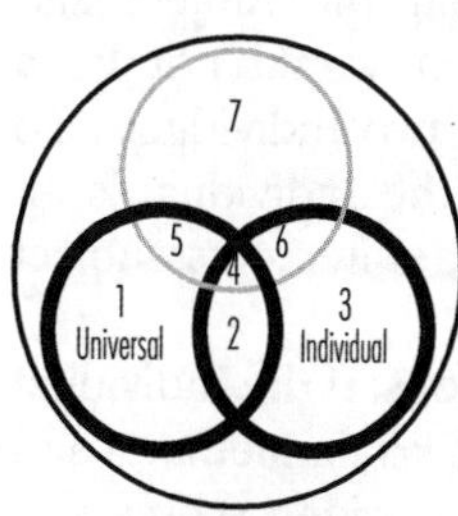

Figure 54(b)
Positive Judgment Reversed

Dialectical Reason sees that subject and predicate *reciprocally* determine each other. Two results follow: (a) The subject "*simply is*" (633) as an immediacy. It is Individual; the predicate is Universal. But, since the subject is determined by the predicate, the subject too is Universal – a concrete Universal.[32] This means that the subject is a complex entity with *many qualities*. (b) The predicate is determined in the subject – not on its own. Yet, as an immediacy, the predicate is an Individual – an abstract Universal. It "contains only *one moment* of the subject's totality to the exclusion of the others." (633) Predicates are as much Individual as the subject is.

---

[30] BURBIDGE, LOGIC, *supra* note 3, at 127.

[31] *Id.*

[32] A "concrete Universal," a phrase Hegel uses heavily in this chapter, is the particularized expression of a universal by an Individual. Deborah Chaffin, *The Logic of Contingency*, in HEGEL RECONSIDERED: BEYOND METAPHYSICS AND THE AUTHORITARIAN STATE 146 (H. Tristram Engelhardt, Jr., & Terry Pinkard eds., 1994). In the Introduction, Hegel identifies the concrete Universal with Speculative Reason. (28)

Any predicate can be made into the subject of a Judgment. Just as the properties in the thing became self-subsistent Matters,[33] the predicates of the Universal subject are Individualizable.

Hegel has, by now, put forth two formulations of the Positive Judgment: (1) *the Individual is Universal*; and (2) *the Universal is Individual*. The first, Hegel says, is the *form* of the Judgment of Existence. The second is its *content*. The subject's *content* is the totality of all predicates. But a *given* predicate is merely one that has been singled out by an external reflection for determination.

The above two formulations must be kept separate, for the moment. If they are united, so that subject and predicate are each Individual and Universal, then each of the extremes would be *Particular*. Indeed, this is their inner determination. Yet, if this were asserted straight out, we would no longer have Positive Judgment, but mere tautology. Subject and predicate must remain in opposition, if their "moment" is to be recognized. We cannot, for now, say that the subject and predicate are *both* Universals. Such a statement would not be a Judgment but merely the sequential assertion of two Individuals. To say, "The Universal is Universal" is also to say "the Individual is an Individual" and "the Particular is Particular." In such statements, subject and predicate cannot be distinguished.

Both (1) and (2), as immediacies, are contradictions. If the Individual is Universal (form), the Individual posits itself as immediate and therefore *not* as Universal; "its predicate is of wider scope and therefore does not correspond to it." (635) In terms of Figure 54(a), the predicate [3] is an immediacy *beyond* Universality [1]. Since Universality is predicate, the predicate [3] is wider than the subject [1, 2] and does not correspond to it.[34] In Mure's phrase, the predicate is a *what* outrunning a *that*.[35]

The same is true for "the Universal is Individual" (content). In Figure 54(b), the subject [1, 2] is "a concrete that is infinitely determined." (635) In other words, the Universal is a Spurious Infinity of individual

---

[33] *Supra* at 354-7.

[34] Subject and predicate "outflank each other." MURE, PHILOSOPHY, *supra* note 10, at 134; *see also* TAYLOR, *supra* note 28, at 311 ("To the extent that judgement can capture the ontological basis of things . . . it must be inter alia a judgement of identity, one in which the terms it links are in an important sense identical. This we plainly do not have in judgements of quality like 'the rose is red.' Hence they still suffer from incommensurability.").

[35] G.R.G. MURE, A STUDY OF HEGEL'S LOGIC 206 (1950).

qualities. As such, the Universal is never fully present. "Such a subject therefore is, on the contrary, *not* a *single* property such as its predicate enunciates." (636) The rose *is* fragrant, but it is a lot more than just fragrant.[36] Fragrance isolated (at the expense of other qualities) is notionless. It exhibits "the opposition of *being* and *reflection* or the *in-itself*." (627) Reflection is what underwrites *subsistence*.

In short, the Positive Judgment, in content and form, does injustice to the Universal. Contrary to its form, it really announces that the subject is *not* the predicate. This is Positive Judgment's speculative result. "[I]ts form in general . . . is incapable of holding within its grasp speculative determinations and truth. The direct supplement to it, the *negative* judgment, would at least have to be added as well." (834)

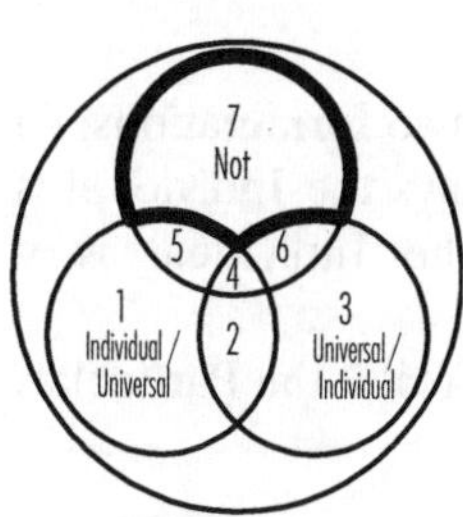

Figure 54(c)
Negative Judgment

Because the Positive Judgment is in contradiction, we pass to the Negative Judgment. The rose is *not* so fragrant after all.

(b) The Negative Judgment

For those who claim that judgments are true whenever they do not formally contradict themselves, Hegel has already shown that the Positive Judgment *inherently* contradicts itself.[37] Its form is inadequate to its content.[38]

Being contradictory, Positive Judgment "has its truth in the negative judgement." (636) The Understanding interprets the Negative Judgment as asserting that the Individual is *not*-Universal. This follows because Positive Judgment puts forth the

---

[36] Otherwise, Burbidge asks, how could the subject be distinguished from the predicate? BURBIDGE, LOGIC, *supra* note 3, at 127. The problem is that the copula is inadequate to express the relation between subject and predicate. *Id.* at 128.

[37] Nor should truth be reserved for the correspondence of a proposition to outside reality. "[W]hoever gives the name of *truth* to the *correctness* of an *intuition* or *perception*, or to the agreement of the *picture-thought* with the object, at any rate has no expression left for that which is the subject matter and aim of philosophy." (636) The truth of Judgment is the *relation* it establishes between subject and predicate. "[A]ll *other content* that appears in a judgement (the *sun* is *round*, *Cicero was a great orator in Rome*, it is day *now*, etc.) does not concern the judgement as such." (636)

[38] BURBIDGE, LOGIC, *supra* note 3, at 132; *see* G.W.F. HEGEL, THE JENA SYSTEM, 1804-5: LOGIC AND METAPHYSICS 91 (John W. Burbidge & George di Giovanni trans. 1986) ("The immediate display of the judgment 'B is A' – that A, the predicate, is something determinate and subsumed under the subject B . . . is the positing of A as not-A.").

subject as an immediacy. An immediate subject cannot be Universal; Universality – "absolutely fluid continuity" (639) – must effortlessly continue into its other. Sticking to its guns,[39] the Understanding now expresses the *non-continuity* of the subject into the predicate. But this does not mean that the Negative Judgment is mere mistake. It too is part of the process. Later, we shall see that the Negative Judgment of *Idea* is the genetically defective Individual. Because Idea makes Negative Judgments, empirical observation proves inadequate for notional Cognition.[40] What we observe may be *non-notional*.

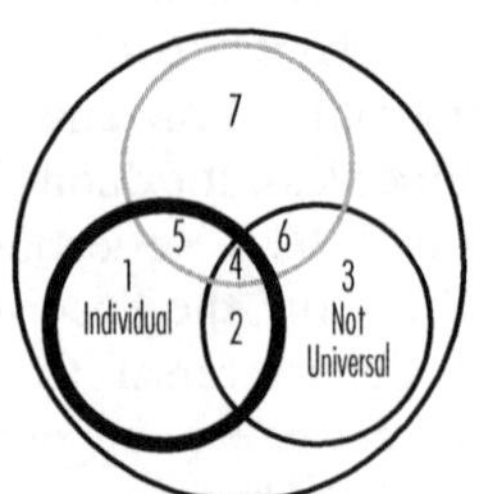

Figure 55(a)
Negative Judgment as Not Universal

Positive Judgment, in its dialectical phase, had two formulations; so does Negative Judgment. If the Understanding says the Individual is *not*-Universal. Dialectical Reason says that the Individual is a Particular.

As established in Chapter 19, the abstract Universal *is* the Particular. Dialectical Reason remembers this. It points out that, if the predicate is only an *abstract* not-Universal, it is perforce a Particular. According to Hegel, "this predicate, just because it is a predicate, or because it stands in relation to a universal subject, is something wider than a mere indi-viduality, and the *universal* [*i.e.*, predicate] is therefore likewise *in the first instance a parti-cular*." (637)[41] In different words, nothing is, after all, something, and the Negative Judgment must necessarily have its positive version.[42] Judgment implies that "something is to be

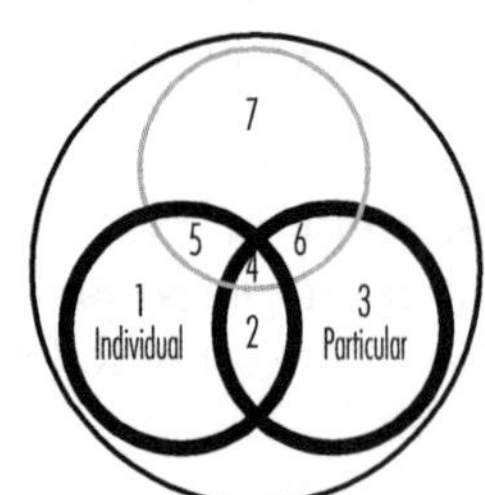

Figure 55(b)
Negative Judgment Reversed

---

[39] Here I disagree with Burbidge, who thinks that the Negative Judgment does not deny the copula. BURBIDGE, LOGIC, *supra* note 3, at 130. According to the Understanding, this is *precisely* what the Negative Judgment does.

[40] *Infra* at 589.

[41] In terms of Figure 55(b), [1] was Individual and [3] was Particular. The Particular is pictographically "wider" than the Individual.

[42] BURBIDGE, LOGIC, *supra* note 3, at 130 ("a thought 'not' inevitably introduces a transition to something positive . . . ").

predicated of the individual subject. Therefore the abstract isolation is not maintained . . . ."[43]

Even though "the Individual is a Particular" is expressed in positive form, it is no mere Positive Judgment: Positive Judgment had immediate abstractions for its extremes. In contrast, Particularity is a mediated term. Negative Judgment *negates* the immediacy of the Positive Judgment and presupposes a *mediated relation* of the two Judgments. Accordingly, the Negative Judgment continues itself into the Positive Judgment and also stands for the relation between the two extremes.[44]

In the dialectic version of Negative Judgment, subject and predicate are back in relation; they are genuinely Universal. What Negative Judgment negates is abstraction. The distinction between subject or predicate nevertheless persists. What then does it mean, then, to judge that a rose is not red? The Negative Judgment merely negates the *given* predicate – red. Red is thus separated from the Universality that belongs to the predicate. The rose, however, continues to have a predicate – a color. All we know is that this color is not red. In its preservation of predication, the Negative Judgment is positive after all.

Negative Judgment, however, is flawed. It concedes that the Individual is *a* Particular, but which? In order to determine what the rose *is*, Negative Judgment leaves us with the need to investigate *all* predicates of the rose. Negative Judgment, disappointingly, represents "merely the moment of alteration of the accidents – or, in the sphere of existence, of the isolated properties of the concrete." (640) Predicates there must be – infinite in number – but what are they precisely? So far, this can be known only positively – not immanently. Negative Judgment has criticized Positive Judgment for its positivity but has not succeeded in sublating positivity.[45]

This is not the only defect. Perhaps the Individual is Particular – a positive assertion. "But the individual is also *not* a particular, for particularity is of wider extent than individuality." (640) In other words, the predicate in Figure 55(b) is a mediating Particular [2] but it is also an immediate not-Universal [3]. As in Positive Judgment, predicate does

---

43 *Id.* at 130.

44 JEAN HYPPOLITE, LOGIC AND EXISTENCE 125 (Leonard Lawlor & Amit Sen trans., 1997) ("the heterology of experience has become a tautology by transforming itself into a unity of opposite terms, by grasping difference as self-difference").

45 For this reason, "the rose is not red" is a proper Negative Judgment, but so is "the red rose is not *just* red." BUTLER *supra* note 9, at 220.

not correspond to subject, to the extent the predicate is not-Universal.

From this perspective, we must concede that the Individual is *not* Particular. The Negative Judgment's negativity is therefore aimed, not at an other, but at *itself*. But this is what Individuality is – the negation of the Particular. Individuality (a second negation) is *restored*.[46] Speculative Reason therefore infers from the Negative Judgment that the Individual is an Individual – an *isolated* Individual.[47] With this derivation accomplished, Judgment once again mediates itself, according to its notional heritage. The relation of subject and predicate purified of all positivity is the Infinite Judgment.

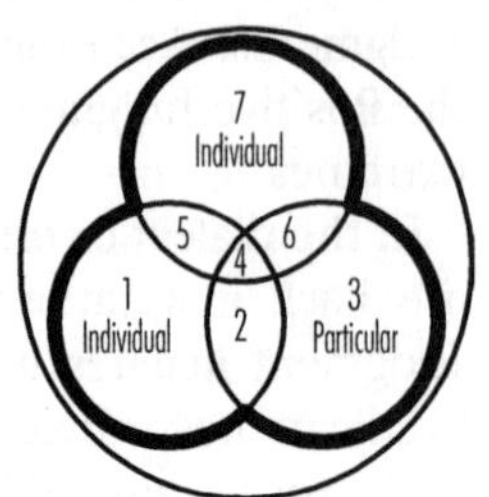

Figure 55(c)
Infinite Judgment

What is posited in the Negative Judgment? A widening of the predicate. In the Positive Judgment, the predicate was too narrow for the subject. In Figure 54(a), [3], taken as an immediacy, did not subsume the subject, as it was supposed to. Now the predicate has "*widened* itself in the negative judgement [from abstract Universality] into *particularity*." (641) Now [3] subsumes [2] and [1]. Furthermore, in negating the immediacy of the Positive Judgment, the Negative Judgment "is no less the *purification* of the universality contained in the predicate." (641) Recalling that the subject is the Universal (on the law of sublation), by virtue of its self-widening, the predicate is now also Universal. This restoration of the Universal in the predicate, however, is merely for us. Universality, invisible in Figure 55(c), must posit itself in the course of Infinite Judgment.

Both Positive and Negative Judgment depend on external reflection. Both express the predicate in positivized form. But Negative Judgment has undergone a transition from external *relation* (the Individual is not Universal) to *determination* (the Individual *is* Particular). The transition from a *non-relation* to *determination* means that the not-Universal is the Particular. And finally, since all we know from the predicate is what the subject is *not*, the predicate is "*completely indeterminate* . . . . Thus the mere *not-white* would be just as much red, yellow, blue, etc., as

---

46 BURBIDGE, LOGIC, *supra* note 3, at 131 ("the double negation implies that what is predicated of the individual subject is neither an abstract universal, nor the particular universal mentioned in the predicate, but instead the individuality that inherently qualifies [as] the subject").

47 *Id*.

black." (638) Only external reflection can tell what the predicate really is. The indeterminacy of the predicate hearkens back to the realm of Being, where "the meaningless *nothing* becomes the limit." (639)

Nevertheless, just as Particularity mediated between Universality and Individuality in chapter 19, so Negative Judgment, by which predicate becomes Particular, mediates between Positive Judgment and Infinite Judgment. The result – Infinite Judgment – will stand for the proposition "The Individual is Individual." Predicate, which has advanced from Universal to Particular, is about to become Individual. All the moments of the Notion will be actualized in the predicate when we are done with the Infinite Judgment.

(c) The Infinite Judgment

Dialectic Negative Judgment has negated the immediacy imposed by the Understanding, but has not entirely escaped it. In effect, Dialectical Reason interprets Negative Judgment as announcing, "I am not an immediacy; I am the Particularity of the subject." Speculative Reason now points out that Dialectical Reason is contradictory. By announcing that *it* is not an immediacy, Negative Judgment proves that it *is* an immediacy. Negative Judgment is merely reflective – an immediacy coupled with a positedness. Reflection at this point, however, is regressive. For this reason, "[t]he negative judgement is as little a true judgement as the positive." (641) In the Negative Judgment "there still remain[s] a *positive relation* of the subject to the predicate." (641)

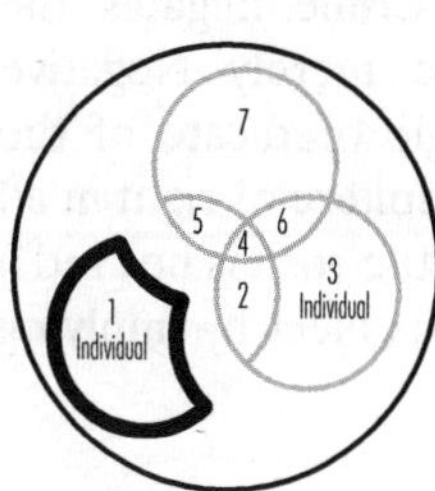

Figure 56(a)
Negative Infinite Judgment (Crime)

This residuum of positivity must be renounced, so that Notion can recapture its self-sovereignty. When positivity is finally defeated, "the *whole extent* of the predicate is negated and there is no longer any positive relation between it and the subject." (641) The relation of subject and predicate, purified of all positivity, is the Infinite Judgment.[48] In the Infinite Judgment, we have "the

[48] This is reflected in Hegel's early essay, *The Spirit of Christianity and Its Fate*, in G.W.F. HEGEL, EARLY THEOLOGICAL WRITINGS 224-5 (T.M. Knox trans., 1948). There Hegel writes of the necessity and the impossibility of the subject setting aside the positivity of the law and of the subject's inability to escape the punishment the law demands.

reflection of the judgement of existence into itself." (640)

The Understanding now interprets the Infinite Judgment as negative, so that there is *no* positive connection between subject and predicate.

The Negative Infinite Judgment is nonsense – a Judgment where the entire form of Judgment is set aside. "It is supposed to be a *judgement* and consequently to contain a relation of subject and predicate; yet *at the same time* such a relation is supposed *not* to be in it." (642) The Negative Infinite Judgment asserts that the subject is not a predicate – but absurdly so. Some examples: Spirit is not red. The rose is not an elephant. The understanding is not a table. In these Judgments, "determinations are negatively connected as subject and predicate, one of which not only does not include the determinateness of the other but does not even contain its universal sphere." (642) These Judgments, correct but absurd, are not Judgments at all, because they cannot help the Notion reestablish a stable reality for itself.[49]

Subject and predicate now have a radically incommensurate *qualitative* relation. This was implicit in the earlier forms of judgment, where subject and predicate had positive difference. Now there is nothing *but* qualitative difference.

Crime. The Negative Infinite Judgment is an interesting moment in the *SL* because Hegel equates it with crime. Crime negates the Universal sphere. Civil wrongs (*i.e.*, torts) are merely Negative Judgments. A civil defendant negates some single predicate of the plaintiff, but, in doing so, recognizes the universal sphere of right in all other instances – just as the Negative Judgment ("the rose is not red") negated red but affirmed the Universality of the subject by implying

---

[49] Why is it necessary to offer such examples as "spirit is a table" in the name of Infinite Judgment? According to Burbidge, The Infinite Judgment must bear the form of a judgment ("the subject is predicate") while "express[ing] the fact that there is no relation at all between subject and predicate. But if there is no relation at all, the act of judging itself is absurd since it is supposed to couple the two . . . To couple them so as to indicate a lack of relation may produce a correct expression, but one that is so insipid that it abandons the rationale for judging altogether." BURBIDGE, LOGIC, *supra* note 3, at 132 (footnote omitted). Hartnack errs in focusing on the truth value of absurd statements, not on the relation absurdity presupposes between subject and predicate. According to Hartnack, "It is difficult to agree with [Hegel] when he says that what is absurd and nonsensical could have a truth-value. It seems to be without sense to try to verify that a spirit is not colored." HARTNACK, *supra* note 28, at 95. Judgment is not about dividing true empirical propositions from false ones. It is about establishing a necessary, objective relation between subject and object, so that the reign of subjectivity can end and that of objectivity can begin.

that the rose has a color. The criminal, however, goes further and denies any validity to the Universal sphere of right. More precisely, what is denied is the entitlement of positive law to determine the rights of the other.

Hegel scandalously remarks, "This infinite judgement does indeed possess *correctness*, since it is an actual deed." (642) Is this some sort of endorsement of crime? Oddly, the answer is yes. The Negative Infinite Judgment stands for the fact that the Notion is *beyond* positive law. The Notion (*i.e.*, subjectivity) is criminal, in the eye of the positive lawyer, but such criminality is a necessary moment in the freedom of the subject. Nevertheless, Hegel is not endorsing psychopathic criminality. Subjectivity must still proceed onward from its freedom from positive law and reestablish its own reality *in* a positive law with which it has a genuine unity. When the law reflects the freedom of the subject, then the subject is "at home" in law and society. Mere "positive" law is an obstacle to the freedom of the Hegelian subject.

But why is the Negative Infinite Judgment a *deed*? I think Hegel means that it is an act of the subject – and subjects must act or, to be more precisely, legislate. The criminal is a *legislator* in Hegel's logic.[50]

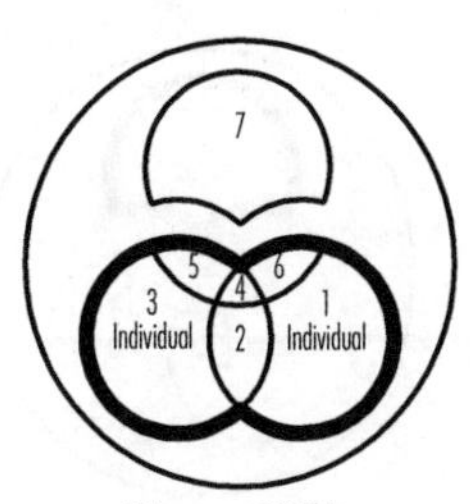

Figure 56(b)
Positive Infinite Judgment

The Negative Infinite Judgment, like its predecessors, is not notional; "in the negatively infinite judgement the difference [between subject and predicate] is, so to speak, *too great* for it to remain a Judgment; the subject and predicate have no positive relation whatever to each other." (643)[51] Dialectical Reason intervenes to remind criminal Understanding that positivity is a necessary moment in the development of

[50] In the *EL*, Hegel says that death is also the Negative Infinite Judgment, whereas disease is merely the Negative Judgment. "In disease, merely this or that function of life is checked or negatived: in death . . . body and soul part, i.e. subject and predicate utterly diverge." EL § 173 Addition.

[51] Mure complains, "Hegel should not . . . have suggested that crime and disease, because they assert the failure of a man to conform to his notion, have no truth at all as Judgement." MURE, LOGIC, *supra* note 35, at 179. But if Judgment represents the performative investiture of notionality into outward manifestation, then neither crime nor sickness can serve to manifest mankind's notionality in the outward universe. Nevertheless, the Negative Infinite Judgment still has its place in the logical progression and so it has some truth. It simply doesn't have truth as a performative *Judgment*.

Judgment. Dialectical Reason asserts what the positive moment of the Negative Judgment also asserted – that predication is generally necessary.[52] The subject (Individual) *is* the predicate (Individual). Accordingly, the positive moment of the Infinite Judgment is "the *reflection of individuality* into itself, whereby it is posited for the first time as a *determinate determinateness*." (642)

Though both assert the necessity of the predicate, the Positive Infinite Judgment is an advance over the Negative Judgment. In the Positive Infinite Judgment, "[t]he individual is hereby *posited* as continuing itself *into its predicate*." (642) Of course, the Positive Judgment started with the proposition, "The Individual is Universal." But *that* individual was the immediate, non-notional, Individual. It was the product of an external reflection – not a positedness.

Now the Individual is notional. And, since the Individual is Universal, "[t]he positive infinite judgement equally runs: *the universal is universal*, and as such is equally posited as the return into itself." (642-3) *Tautology* is "the positive opposite pole of the [negative] infinite judgment . . . ; from "The rose is not an elephant" follows only that "The rose is a rose." The tautology expresses in the positive form only the radical *externality* to the subject of the predicate . . . [T]he only adequate predicate for the subject is the *subject itself*."[53] Yet, Hegel warns, even the Positive Infinite Judgment is no true Judgment. There is identity here, but no difference.[54] "Therefore once again the act of judging collapses."[55]

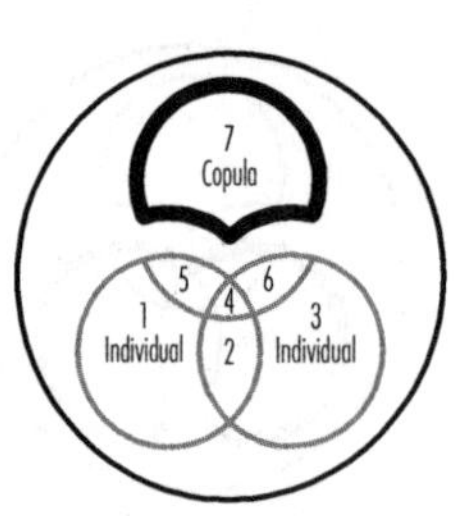

Figure 56(c)
Judgment of Reflection

Speculative Reason ends the lengthy tale of the Positive Judgment. It posits "what the *copula* of the judgement contains, namely, that

---

[52] This is also the conclusion of "law-testing reason" in the *Phenomenology*. SLAVOJ ŽIŽEK, THE PUPPET AND THE DWARF: THE PERVERSE CORE OF CHRISTIANITY 4 (2003).

[53] ŽIŽEK, KNOW NOT, *supra* note 18, at 179.

[54] Žižek complains that, in addition to senseless negation and tautology, there should have been added senseless affirmation: "the rose is an elephant," standing for the inherent lack within subject or predicate that prevents either from becoming a self-identity. *Id*. at 40. But Speculative Reason has pointed out that self-identical entities (which the subject and predicate purport to be) erase themselves and send their being into the copula. The copula itself is sundered, while subject and predicate have failed to complete themselves. Therefore Žižek's amendment is already implied when the copula is presented as the Notion sundered again.

[55] BURBIDGE, LOGIC, *supra* note 3, at 133.

the qualitative extremes are sublated in this their identity." (643) The Judgment of Existence has imploded. Subject and predicate erase themselves and withdraw to the copula.[56] But the copula is no dead unity of the extremes. Since "this unity is the Notion, it is immediately sundered again into its extremes and appears as a judgement, whose terms however are no longer immediate but reflected into themselves." (643) This new *notional* sundering is the Judgment of Reflection.

B. The Judgment of Reflection

In the therapeutic fields of Judgment, Notion slowly reestablishes an obliterated reality. The Judgment of Existence rehearsed the development of Quality. The Judgment of Reflection replays the development of correlative Essence. Whereas the subject previously announced what it *is*, now the subject announces what it is *not*. It concedes that it is *nothing* but its predicates. In the Judgment of Reflection, the *predicate* is subject. Some examples of the Judgment of Reflection: Men are mortal; things are perishable or useful. In such Judgments, the predicate is Universal and the subject is subsumed under the predicate.

Judgment now differs from its earlier form. Universality is no longer abstract. Here, "we first have, strictly speaking, a *determinate content*." (643) That is to say, the subject (content) *is* the predicate (form), or, as Hegel puts it, "the content is the form determination which is reflected into identity as distinct from the form." (643) In other words, the predicate (form) is reflected back into the subject (content); the content is identical to and yet separate from its form. The predicate now expresses "an essential determination, but one which is in a *relationship* or is a *unifying* universality." (643) "The copula . . . begins here to express connexion instead of mere relation."[57]

The Universality on display in the predicate, however, is flawed. No longer abstract, it represents a genuine relation to a subject, but it is still itself an immediacy. That is to say, the predicate (and hence the subject) is a mere Appearance. It genuinely bodies forth from the subject, but neither it nor the subject has being-in-and-for-self. Accordingly, subject and predicate succumb to the law of Appearance.

---

[56] So far, Judgment is a failure. "Either it distinguishes and cannot relate; or it relates and cannot distinguish." *Id.* at 133. Judging must do both of these things.

[57] MURE, LOGIC, *supra* note 35, at 181.

According to this law, they must disappear.[58]

In the Judgment of Existence, all movement was in the predicate. The subject remained unaffected by predication because it was an abstraction – an immediacy. Now the reflective subject does the dancing. The predicate stands pat. Because it is the fixed Universal. As Universal, the predicate applies not only to *this* subject, but to *many* subjects. And "many subjects" implies a generic "subjecthood" – a genus of subjects.[59] The subject therefore multiplies itself – from one Individual to "some" Individuals and finally to *all* Individuals.

(a) The Singular Judgment

The Understanding first interprets the Judgment of Reflection: *this* subject is universal. For example, Gaius is bald. This was the same proposition the Understanding offered in Positive Judgment. But this time subject and predicate are more profoundly understood. The predicate is "*an essential Universal*" (645) – not an abstract immediacy. In Positive Judgment, *the* (not "this") Individual was joined with a not-Universal. By now, however, the predicate is the in-itself [2] of *this* subject. Since the predicate is the in-itself, the subject must now discover itself in its fixed predicates as they come into view. Accordingly, the subject, not the predicate, undergoes alteration. The Understanding sees that the subject is *not* Individual. Rather, the predicate is the Individual.

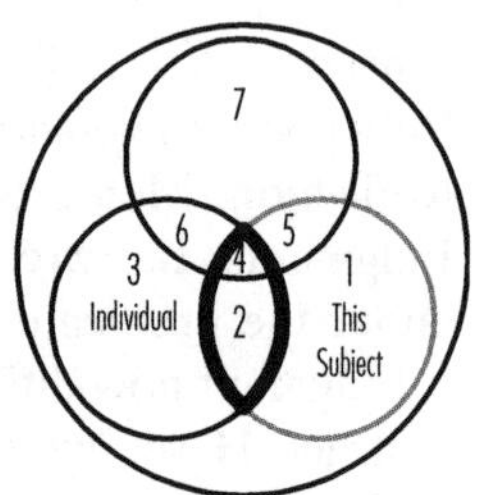

Figure 57(a)
Singular Judgment

[58] Hartnack draws from such examples as "this plant is wholesome" the view that Reflective Judgments "are about the relations the subject has to other objects or persons." HARTNACK, *supra* note 28, at 97. But Judgment is about the Notion's *own judgment of self* – not about which objects are useful. What the Reflective Judgment represents is the subject's assignment of being to its other – in imitation of Reflection generally.

[59] The Judgment of Existence was qualitative. Especially in light of the multiplying subject, shall we now say that the Judgement of Reflection is quantitative? Hegel warns no. Whereas Quality as such was external immediacy, Quantity is mediated, but it is "the *most external determination* belonging to mediation." (644) Whatever Quantity was, it was so by means of outside determination. By now, the subject infers its own (multiplying) content from the predicate.

(b) The Particular Judgment

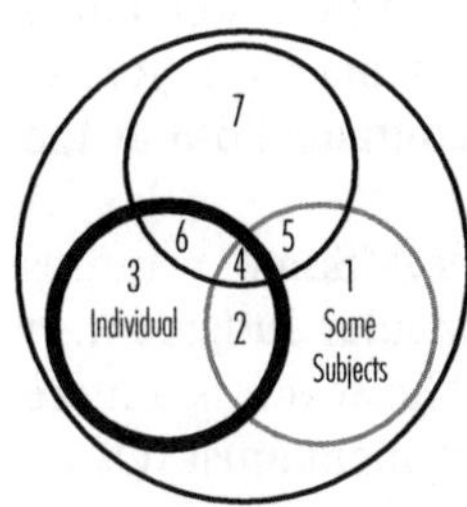

Figure 57(b)
Particular Judgment

The Understanding proposed that *this* subject is Universal, but now Dialectical Reason asserts the opposite – the subject is not-Individual, or, the not-Individual is Universal. Yet we know that the abstract Universal is the Particular. Likewise, the isolated not-Individual is the Particular. Hence, we have the Particular Judgment.

In the Particular Judgment, the subject is not unique but is some subset in the class of subjects.[60] For example, "this thing is useful" separates out "this thing" from things that are *not* useful. The Singular Judgment therefore implicitly refers to a *set* of things. "*This* useful thing" confesses that usefulness is a category broader than *this thing*. Predication must be shared with other things. According to this analysis, the predicate ("useful") stands pat. It is the *true* Individual. The number of subjects to which the Universal applies is multiplied.[61] Useless subjects proliferate.[62] In effect, the Particular Judgment places certain subjects into a class.

At first the Particular Judgment ("*some* men are happy") seems like a Positive Judgment. But Positive Judgment was implicitly Negative Judgment, where connection between subject and predicate is denied.

---

[60] As Winfield emphasizes, Judgment of Reflection generally concerns class membership. Winfield, *Concept*, *supra* note 22, at 60.

[61] Butler declares, "The transition from 'one and only one' entity of a given description to 'some' ('at least two') is clearly not deductive. The transition lies in the introduction of the false assumption that indiscernible entities can be nonidentical, distinguished quantitatively though not qualitatively." BUTLER *supra* note 9, at 221-2. In fact, it is possible to see the many as properly deduced from the one. In Reflective Judgment, the predicate is the Universal. Universal implies *more than one*. Therefore a universal predicate requires a plurality of subjects.

[62] "[A]n ever-wider circle of subjects is subsumed under the predicate as an essential determination which exists in itself." ŽIŽEK, KNOW NOT, *supra* note 18, at 120. John Burbidge makes the Particular Judgment a speculative moment. The Singular Judgment therefore has within it the move of the Understanding ("*This* Individual is Universal") and also the dialectic opposition ("*This* Individual is *not* Universal"). BURBIDGE, LOGIC, *supra* note 3, at 135. I have not followed him in this. I hear the voice of the Particular Judgment to be strictly dialectical – which, strictly speaking, is not inconsistent with, but simpler than, Burbidge's view. Burbidge likewise sends the Particular Judgment through the entire cycle.

Now, however, the Particular Judgment contains *both* a Positive *and* Negative Judgment. To judge that some men are happy is to confess that some are not. "The positive and negative judgements no longer fall apart, but the particular judgement immediately contains both at the same time." (646)

The Particular Judgment, then, trafficks in "some." "Some" requires a more Universal content than the "this" of the Singular Judgment. It inherently refers to genus. The content of "some," however, is a mere empirical content. To this extent, the Particular Judgment must rely on external reflection – a flaw that must be overcome.[63]

In Singular Judgments, "this" reigns supreme, which signals that the subject was nothing but its predicate. But "this" has grown into Particularity – into "some." "Some" implicitly refers to an *all* – the Universal Judgment.

(c) The Universal Judgment

Speculative Reason sees that "this" and "some" implicitly refer to "all." If some men are happy, then some are not. Both these subsets rely upon the genus "man." Universal Judgment adjudicates "all." But it does so from the perspective of external reflection. Universal Judgment is only "a *taking together* of independently existing individuals; it is the *community* of a proposition which only belongs to them in *comparison*. It is this community that is usually the first thing that occurs to subjective, unphilosophical thinking when universality is mentioned." (647) This Judgment represents the common sense view that Universality is something that "*belongs to a number of things*" (647)

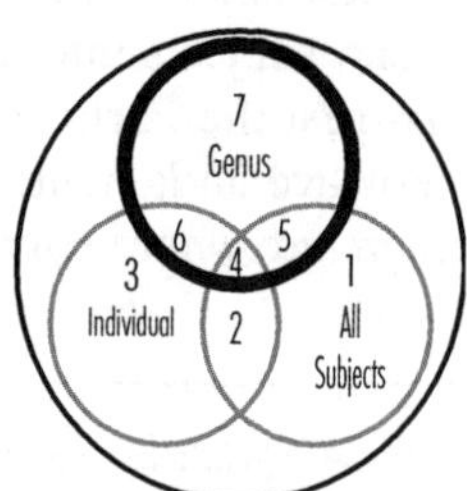

Figure 57(c)
Universal Judgment
(Judgment of Necessity)

But, as philosophy has always known, Universality is not obtained by generalizing from observed subjects. Empirical universality, derived

[63] Richard Dien Winfield, *The Types of Universals and the Forms of Judgment*, in HEGEL'S THEORY OF THE SUBJECT 106 (David Gray Carlson ed., 2005) ("Although extraneous material might be illicitly introduced to further identify which group of individuals belong to the class, particular judgment itself leaves unspecified how the group is defined").

from observing a subset of the class (induction), is "mere *plurality* . . . taken for allness. Plurality, however, no matter how great, remains unalterably mere plurality, and is not allness." (648) Anticipating Karl Popper,[64] Hegel suggests that empirical science is founded on the principle of *falsifiability*: "an empirically universal proposition . . . rests on the tacit agreement that if only no contrary *instance* can be adduced, the *plurality* of cases shall count as *allness*; or, that *subjective* allness, namely, those cases which *have come to our knowledge*, may be taken for an *objective* allness." (648)

Nevertheless, in this false derivation of the Universal from empirical research is "a vague awareness of the true universality of the *Notion*." (648) In inductive reasoning, we witness "the Notion that forces its way beyond the stubborn individuality to which unphilosophical thinking clings and beyond the externality of its reflection, substituting allness *as totality*." (648) Induction is not just subjective nostalgia for objective truth. Universality is immanent to induction. When the scientist hypothesizes about "all men," the genus (man) is, logically speaking, "sundered into individuals." (648) Yet what is intended is that "all men" must become "man;" the set of all subjects must become genus, which now becomes the Individual. At this moment "the *posited* universality has been equated with the *presupposed*." (648)

Hegel conceives of this moment in which "all men" become "man" as the surrender of Individuality by both the subject and predicate to the copula. The *copula* now becomes the self-related and determinate Individual. As such, it is the third determination of Individuality. The first was the Understanding's self-identical Individual in the Judgment of Existence. There the Individual was leftward-leaning in our diagram. The second was the reflective Individual in the Judgment of Reflection – a negation of the Judgment of Existence. There, Individuality was present in the *predicate*, not the subject. But now the Individual is the negation of the negation and, as such, is the Judgment of Necessity. Individuality is now located in the middle term. The result of induction is the inference of a truly objective Universal Individual.[65]

Genus now comes into being – "the universality which is in its own self a concrete." (649) Genus does not inhere only in the subject. It is no mere property. "[I]t contains all the single determinatenesses

---

[64] KARL POPPER, THE LOGIC OF SCIENTIFIC DISCOVERY (1992).

[65] Hegel will define objective Universality as "the *pervasive* gravity that maintains its *identity* [following its] particularization." (724)

dissolved in its substantial solidity." (649) Genus is posited as a negative identity with itself. It is therefore a subject, but no longer one that is merely subsumed in its predicate. "[T]he nature of the judgement of reflection is altogether changed." (649)[66]

Subject and predicate have erased themselves; their being is now in genus or relation. The *copula* is now front and center. "In other words, the subject, in raising itself to universality has, in this determination become equated with the predicate." (650) Subject and predicate are identical *in their self-erasure* – "they have coalesced into the copula." (650)[67] The copula is "the genus or absolute nature of a thing." (650)

This identity will sunder itself again.[68] But what is now revealed is Judgment's inner nature. Subject and predicate enjoy a relation of necessity. Subject and predicate differ only unessentially. "*What belongs to all the individuals of a genus belongs to the genus by its nature*." (650) "All men" becomes "man" in the Judgment of Necessity.[69]

C. The Judgment of Necessity

Reflective Judgment yielded genus, an objective Universality. As

---

[66] One must not, as Michael Inwood does, confuse "genus" with biological incidents. Thus, Inwood claims that Hegel overlooks the fact that genera (*i.e.*, dinosaurs) can become extinct. M.J. INWOOD, HEGEL 435 (1983) Hegel's genus can never become extinct; it is intrinsic to the nature of subject and predicate.

[67] Žižek attributes this Hegelian moment to Lacan: "Lacan's basic premiss is that the leap from the *general* set of 'all men' into the *universal* 'man' is possible only through an exception: the universal (in its difference to the empirical generality) is constituted through the exception; we do not pass from the general set to the universality of One-Notion by way of *adding* something to the set but, on the contrary, by way of *subtracting* something from it, namely the 'unary feature' [*trait unaire*] which totalizes the general set, which makes out of it a universality." ŽIŽEK, KNOW NOT, *supra* note 18, at 40. That is to say, each individual in the set of all men must sacrifice itself if the copula "man" is to come into existence and become the notional individual.

[68] Indeed, this pose in which the Individuals erase themselves to produce a Universal Judgment is the uncritical masculine position, which cannot account for its own position *via à vis* the complete whole it contemplates. SARAH KAY, ŽIŽEK: A CRITICAL INTRODUCTION 40-1 (2003).

[69] Butler suggests that these four judgments stand for description, comparison, analysis and evaluation. BUTLER *supra* note 9, at 229. The claim that Reflective Judgment is "comparison," however, is questionable. True, Reflective Judgment deals with induction, in which a property abstracted from all the individuals is taken as a Universal. But the Universal Judgment is not the product of induction. Rather, it is a logical *deduction*. Abstracting a common property from all men makes sense if and only if there is a genus *man*. This logical conclusion is not the product of comparison.

Judgment replays all the previous steps of the Logic, Hegel suggests that the Judgment of Necessity corresponds to Substantiality, the last part of Essence and postern gate to the Notion. The Judgment of Necessity differs from Substantiality, however. Substantiality was merely inner. Now, substantiality appears "in the form of its Notion." (653) Substance required otherness; it was revealed only in its Accidents. Now, otherness is contained *within* the Judgment of Necessity. "[I]n the judgement of necessity the object appears . . . in its objective universality." (657) In Substantiality, objective Universality was lacking.

As promised in the beginning of this chapter, we come to the third of *four* Judgments. The Judgment of Existence was the realm of immediacy for the Notion. The Judgment of Reflection was the correlative mediated moment. There, the subject was nothing. It depended on predication to supply its content. The predicate was the Individual, not the subject. It would seem that the Judgment of Necessity should therefore be overtly notional. It should present itself, its other, *and* the unity of itself and other.

But this is not so. The notional moment is reserved for the *fourth* Judgment. The Judgment of Necessity is yet another correlative Judgment. For the first time, Hegel breaks the pattern of dividing his chapters into three moments, corresponding to the Understanding, Dialectical Reason and Speculative Reason. Now we are to have *four* moments. One is immediate, two dialectical, the fourth speculative.

What the Judgment of Necessity supplies is a moment of *non*-identity between subject and predicate. The final Judgment of the Notion will represent the knowledge that Notion is the author of both the notional and non-notional moments of subject and predicate.

(a) The Categorical Judgment

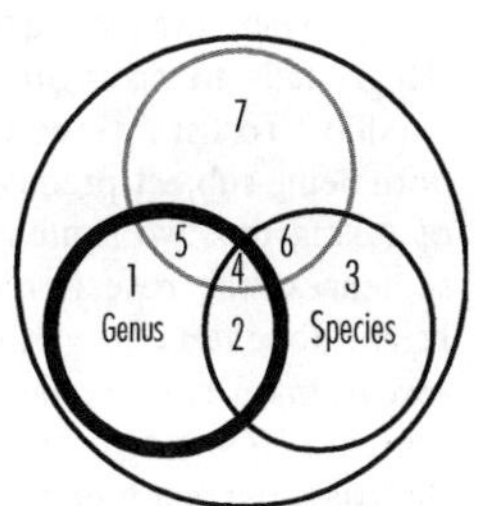

Figure 58(a)
Categorical Judgment

The Understanding proposes that the Judgment of Necessity is the correlation of Genus and Species. It knows that the aggregate of all subjects implies Genus. Genus has being-for-self and so is an objective Universality, but it also has "an external individuality" (653) over against the species. The Individuality of Genus is the "immediate" proposition of the Understanding.

In Categorical Judgment, subject and predicate are substantially identical, but they are also (unessentially) different. Though by now objective, Universality still suffers from "*immediate* particularization." (651) Nevertheless, the Categorical Judgment is an advance over the earlier Judgments. Hegel bids us to distinguish "the rose is red" (Positive Judgment) from the more profound claim that the rose has a vegetable nature. In the lesser Judgments, the predicate (red) is a single contingent content of the subject. Furthermore, not all roses are red. Yet *all* roses *do* have a vegetable nature. In the Judgments of Existence, subject and predicate were not *necessarily* related. Now, in the Categorical Judgment, the copula "has the meaning of *necessity*." (651)[70]

At first, genus is taken as a level higher than the species – a flaw. Genus and species should be on the same level. When genus is simply one of the species, we have *proximate genus* (since, for Hegel, there is no transcendent beyond).[71] For the moment, however, external reflection declares genus to be *higher* than the other species. Determinateness of the Universal is not yet the subject's true principle.

Whether genus has been induced from the species is a contingency. This is the flaw of induction. But Universality must not be so posited. The Categorical Judgment must exhibit the *necessity* of its being.

(b) The Hypothetical Judgment

In Categorical Judgment, the Understanding proposed that genus *is* the species. Dialectical Reason counters that this supposed unity is in fact a *relation* between genus and species. Recalling that genus (Individuality) is *one* of the species of Notion and that these two

---

[70] These are among the remarks Hartnack overlooks in accusing Hegel of confusion: "Hegel fails to distinguish between the "is of predication" and the "is of class membership." To list . . . the two sentences (1) "the rose is red" and (2) "gold is a metal" as both being subject-predicate propositions (and judgments) is clearly mistaken. If instead of taking the two sentences "the rose is red" and "gold is a metal," we take the two sentences "the rose is red" and "red is color" and regard both sentences as subject-predicate sentences, we should be able to infer that the rose is a color – an absurdity that reveals that we have committed a logical error, the error namely of failing to see that the sentence "red is a color" is not a subject-predicate sentence but a sentence stating that the color red is a member of the class of colors." HARTNACK, *supra* note 28, at 94-5. In making this remark, Hartnack completely misses the profound change that has occurred between Judgments of Existence (which are not even true Judgments) and Judgments of Necessity, which pertain to class membership. The last thing Hegel is guilty of is *failing* to note the difference between the "is of predication" and the "is of class membership."

[71] Burbidge calls this "predicated genus," the subject (Genus) necessarily renders itself into an external predicate. BURBIDGE, LOGIC, *supra* note 3, at 140-1.

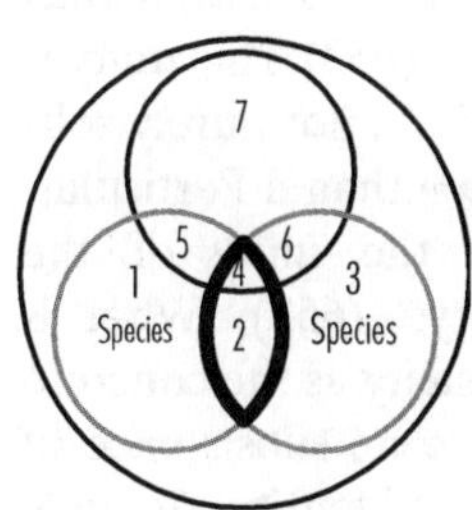

Figure 58(b)
Hypothetical Judgment

concepts are on the same level, Dialectical Reason suggests that the predicate (species) is just as entitled to claim for itself the title of subject (genus) as the subject is. In fact, Dialectical Reason proposes that we don't know which extreme is subject and which is predicate.

The Hypothetical Judgment has the form "If *A*, then *B*." In this form, *A* does not have its own being. It has the being of *B* (and *vice versa*). *A* and *B* are necessarily connected, but whether *A* or *B* is genus remains contingent.

Because *A* and *B* are immediacies, Hypothetical Judgment at first has "the shape of a proposition." (653) The extremes of the Judgment are mere possibilities. The *relation* between them is the main point. Hypothetical Judgment does not establish that *A* or *B* is genus. It only asserts that the being of one is located in the other. As to which, between *A* and *B*, is genus, the jury is still out.[72]

Hypothetical Judgment entails Finitude. In Hypothetical Judgment, each extreme is for-other, not for-itself. But at this advanced stage, a Finite thing does not alter itself and become other. Nor is the Finite thing a mere Appearance that announces itself to be the reflection of another, deeper being. Rather, the relation of self and other is posited as a *necessity*. As the form "if *A* then *B*" indicates, judgments of causality and ground fall under the Hypothetical Judgment, "but here they are no longer relationships of *self-subsistent sides*." (653) Now *A* and *B* "are essentially only moments of one and the same identity." (653)

So far, however, the moments are not yet "individual or particular to universal." (653) The extremes are contingencies. The Hypothetical Judgment is indeterminate in form; we don't know if *A* or *B* is genus. *A* and *B* are "not determined as a relationship of subject to predicate." (653) Yet *A* and *B* are related necessarily, and the unity on display in

---

[72] Errol Harris suggests that Hypothetical and Disjunctive Judgments are both "undoubtedly scientific judgements at the level of understanding . . . " ERROL E. HARRIS, AN INTERPRETATION OF THE LOGIC OF HEGEL 242 (1983). This seems to replace a common sense definition for Hegel's definition. For Hegel, Hypothetical Judgment is dialectical in nature. It asserts only that genus and species are definitely connected, but external reflection must determine which species is genus and which species is merely species.

the Hypothetical Judgment is an actuality. This unity "is *in itself* a *unity of itself* and *its other*, and consequently *universality*." (653) This unity is a true Particular, because it "is a determinate and . . . not purely self-related." (653) But the unity on display is also *more* than a Particular. The immediacies are determinate.[73] Through the unity of the moments, "the particularity is also their totality." (653) "What is therefore truly posited in this judgement is universality as the concrete identity of the Notion, whose determinations have no subsistence of their own but are only particularities posited in that identity. As such, it is the disjunctive judgement." (653)

(c) The Disjunctive Judgment

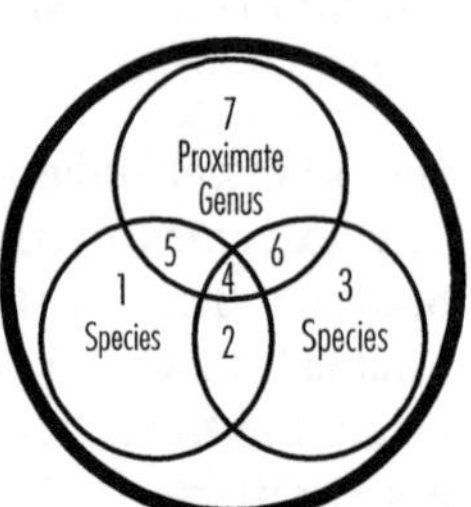

Figure 58(c)
Disjunctive Judgment (Judgment of the Notion)

Disjunctive Judgment is objective Universality "posited in union with its form." (653) It represents the unity of genus and species. So genus (*A*) is both *B* and *C*. "This is the *necessity of the Notion*, in which first the identity of the two extremes is one and same extent, content and universality." (653) But it is equally true that *A* is *either B or C*. Here we have "the *specific difference* of the universal sphere." (654) Genus makes itself into *different* species. Genus is "their *unity* as *determinate* particulars." (654)

Not only identity between genus and species but the *difference* between them is present. And since genus *is* species, genus differentiates itself from itself. Hence the adjective "disjunctive." The fact that genus disjoins itself into Particulars proves that genus is now "the *proximate* genus." (655) A genus is proximate to a species if the species has its specific difference in the essential determinateness of genus.

When genus is taken as higher than species, we have an *empirical* disjunctive judgment, which "lacks necessity." (654) The empirical species are indifferent to being externally subsumed under genus. Any such genus is "not *their* principle." (654) In Categorical Judgment, genus was abstract vis-à-vis the subject – *not* proximate to the subject.

---

[73] Burbidge emphasizes that *A* and *B* in themselves bear the form of Judgments. "They are opposed to each other in such a way that each is in some measure complete in itself; they are clauses." BURBIDGE, LOGIC, *supra* note 3, at 141.

Now genus is proximate.

The identity of the subject, predicate and copula has now been demonstrated "in accordance with the negative unity." (655) These sustain themselves only in their inability to sustain themselves. Their self-erasure is the true, proximate genus. Disjunctive Judgment stands for the idea that, when the individual moments appear, they appear because Notion differentiates itself.[74] Notion is the negative unity of subject, predicate and copula, and when these are distinguished, the Notion itself produces them by distinguishing itself from them. In epistemological terms, the Notion is *thinking* the separate moments of genus and species, and its affirmative thoughts are precisely *not* the Notion-as-thinker. Notion thus alienates itself from itself. Yet, when the Notion reveals its negativity toward subject and predicate, it equally reveals its fundamental connection to them. Thinkers must think. That is what they do. The being of thinkers is in the thoughts. Yet it is equally true that the thinker is *separate* from its thoughts.

The unity is now the notional copula that joins and *disjoins* subject and predicate. The extremes have coalesced there on their own logic. This is the Notion as posited. "[T]he mere judgement of necessity has thereby risen into the *judgement of the Notion*." (657)

To summarize, Disjunctive Judgment (A is both/either B and/or C) has joined and disjoined members for its predicate. But the subject (A) is itself one of the members or species. Universality is now both in the subject *and* the predicate. $A = \{A, B, C\}$. And the subject (A) is likewise a negative unity, separate and apart from the predicate. A does not equal $\{A, B, C\}$. Disjunctive Judgment reveals necessity; what is necessary is that genus must sunder itself into different species. It must be *proximate genus*.

How can genus *cause* the species *and* be indistinguishable from them? The answer is self-erasure. When genus erases itself as an unjustified subjective assumption, genus transfers its being and *becomes* one of the species. Proximate genus is consistent with Hegel's thesis that there is *no unknowable transcendental beyond*. Whatever *is* can be comprehended.

---

[74] BURBIDGE, LOGIC, *supra* note 3, at 148 ("When the *disjunctive judgement* is explicitly integrated with its implicit presuppositions it produces a comprehensive structure of internal relation").

D. The Judgment of the Notion

So far, genus is *really* connected to species. Indeed, it is *one* of the species. The subject now corresponds to *and* is separate from its Universal, objective Notion. The Understanding therefore proposes that empirical species have a connection with the Notion (or genus), leaving open the possibility that "inessential" differences may exist between the species. Species therefore can be judged normatively, based on their "genetic" (*i.e.*, notional) purity.[75]

(a) The Assertoric Judgment

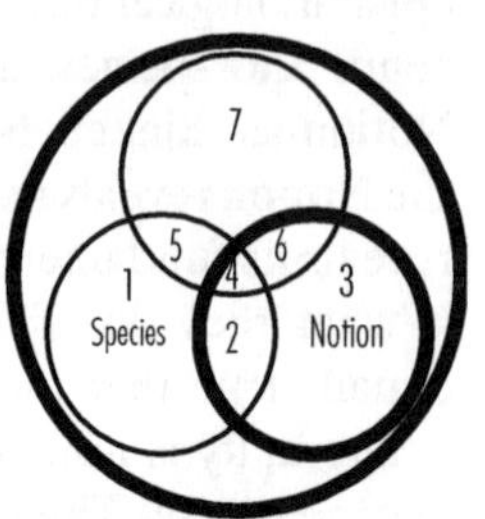

Figure 59(a)
Assertoric Judgment

Assertoric Judgment proclaims: "this house is good,"[76] or "this man is bad." It affirms that there *is* a notion and that the empirical Individual has a *quantitative relation* to it. *That* house is better than *this* house, because it is "closer" to the Notion of house. Admittedly, the empirical house is never perfect; the truly notional house "is an *ought-to-be* to which the reality may or may not be adequate." (657) This is the realm of "*more* or *less* – determinations possessed by a universal in relation to a particularity coming under it." (655)

In the Assertoric Judgment we find "true appreciation." (657) When we say a thing is good or beautiful, the empirical thing compares itself against its Notion. It is not *we* but the subject – the house – that "provides the criterion for its own assessment."[77] The Judgment of the Notion is that the concrete Individual is only an ought-to-be.

Kant called the Judgment of the Notion the judgment of *modality*.

---

[75] Judgment of the Notion vindicates Robert Berman's thesis that Hegelian Individuality most resembles the virtuosic connotation in common usage. Robert Berman, *Ways of Being Singular: The Logic of Individuality*, in HEGEL'S THEORY OF THE SUBJECT, *supra* note 63, at 106. According to Berman Individualism commonly means the virtuosity model ("the ideal city"), inclusivist ("New York, Hoboken, etc., are all cities"), and exclusivist ("Hoboken's no city; New York, now *that's* a city").

[76] *See* David Lamb, *Teleology: Kant and Hegel*, in HEGEL'S CRITIQUE OF KANT 176 (Stephen Priest ed., 1987) ("When reading Hegel one must be like a detective and search for clues, for Hegel does not leave the reader with any familiar objects . . . The house symbolizes the human desire to make the world habitable, to be at home in the world, to be free.") (footnote omitted).

[77] BURBIDGE, LOGIC, *supra* note 3, at 148.

He located modal judgments in an external understanding.[78] According to this view, the problematical judgment is one where affirmation or denial is optional.[79] It is compared to the assertoric (taken as true) and the apodeictic (taken as necessary).[80] Because Kant thought modal judgment to be subjective, his entire theory of Notion was likewise subjective, Hegel says. For Kant, Notion (subjectivity) stands in relation to a dead, external reality. But Notion, as it reemerged from the Disjunctive Judgment, is no such contingency. Earlier Judgments may have been merely subjective, to the extent they relied upon externality. "[T]hese define only schematic possibilities, not specific actualities."[81] The Judgment of the Notion, however, is an *objective* Universality.[82]

In Assertoric Judgment, Notion is posited as the identity of genus and species; "*concretion* of universality and particularization" (658) has been achieved. At first this is a *simple* result. This is Assertoric Judgment's defect. The moments must not be swallowed up in this way. The unity *and* the moments must endure in a true totality: "although objective *universality* has completed itself *in its particularization*, yet the negative unity of the [particularization] merely returns *into [Universality]* and has not yet determined itself to the third moment, that of *individuality*." (658) In other words, the species generated by genus, so far, are only accidents and have no objective worth of their own. From this perspective, the subject is indifferent to its Universal nature; it so far *refuses* to become what it ought to be.

The empirical Individual, Hegel says, is *constituted*. "This constitution is the individuality, which lies beyond the necessary *determination* of the

---

[78] *See* CRITIQUE OF PURE REASON, *supra* note 5, at A/74-5/B100. Hegel's Judgment of the Notion follows Kant's modal judgments in his Table of Logical Functions in Judgment. The modal forms are problematic, assertoric, and apodeictic. *Id.* at A70/B95. Hegel alters the order: assertoric leads, dialectical problematic judgment is second.

[79] CRITIQUE OF PURE REASON, *supra* note 5, at A254/B310.

[80] *Id.* at 57.

[81] BURBIDGE, LOGIC, *supra* note 3, at 148.

[82] Harris complains that "Hegel here gives the modal forms an odd and somewhat arbitrary interpretation as judgements of value." HARRIS, LOGIC, *supra* note 72, at 235-6. But in fact this follows naturally from Disjunctive Judgment, where Speculative Reason sees that one of the Species is notional but not the others. To the extent the Individual is not notional, it is not what it ought to be. There is nothing arbitrary about this progression. Harris goes on to say that, "for Hegel, the criterion of truth is value." *Id.* at 236. This is accurate, if we understand that the closer our judgments are to the notion of things, the closer we are to the truth. Assertoric Judgment, however imperfectly, puts forth this as its criterion of truth.

universal in the disjunctive judgement." (659) Constitution is "the negative *principle* of the genus." (659) That is, if species differ from each other, it is because there is some *inessential* difference, external to the Notion. This idea hearkens back to chapter 2, where Constitution stood for the role of externality in Determination. Its reappearance here shows that, at this late stage of the Logic, Hegel has by no means shut out contingency and chance from the Notion.

In the Assertoric Judgment, the Disjunctive Judgment is sundered into extremes.[83] Unifying Notion, however, is lacking; "verification is a subjective *assurance*." (659) If something is either good or bad, wishing makes it so. Subject ("empirical house") and predicate ("notional house") are related by a third factor – namely the wisher.[84] Obviously, the subjective assurance on which Assertoric Judgment depends "is confronted with equal right by its contradictory." (660) External connection implies that the true connection is still implicit. In the Assertoric Judgment, "the copula is still an immediate, *abstract being*." (660) The immediate Individual does not yet possess a relation to the subject's Notion. Judgment, therefore, is Problematic.[85]

(b) The Problematic Judgment

Problematic Judgment is simply the Assertoric Judgment taken negatively. Assertoric Judgment claimed a relation between concrete Individual and Notion. Notion was taken by the Assertoric Judgment

---

[83] Butler errs in suggesting that Assertoric Judgment "asserts that the absolute in whatever real existence it has satisfies its concept. But the judgment makes this assertion dogmatically, without any ground." BUTLER *supra* note 9, at 226. This overlooks the fact that Assertoric Judgment is an interpretation of Disjunctive Judgment, according to which there are notional and non-notional predicates. Therefore, Assertoric Judgment *never* asserts that a thing satisfies its concept. Quite the opposite is true. The empirical thing inherently *betrays* its concept and therefore is a mere ought-to-be.

[84] Hegel laments, "The Assertory judgement, although rejected by society as out of place when it claims authority on its own showing, has however been made the single and all-essential form of doctrine, even in philosophy, through the influence of the principle of immediate knowledge and faith." EL § 178.

[85] According to Burbidge, the Problematic Judgment constitutes a step of Speculative Reason. The Assertoric Judgment is the Understanding's move. The dialectic move is the observation that, in the Assertoric Judgment, the subject is not self-contained and is therefore incomplete. The Problematic Judgment then mediates these two views – an external reflection must decide whether a judgment of goodness or badness is external or internal. BURBIDGE, LOGIC, *supra* note 3, at 149-50. In contrast, I have portrayed the Problematic Judgment as itself merely a dialectical moment.

as predicate. Dialectical Reason states that, given notionality is the predicate, whether it can be linked to a given subject is contingent; "so far the indeterminateness falls in the copula." (660)[86]

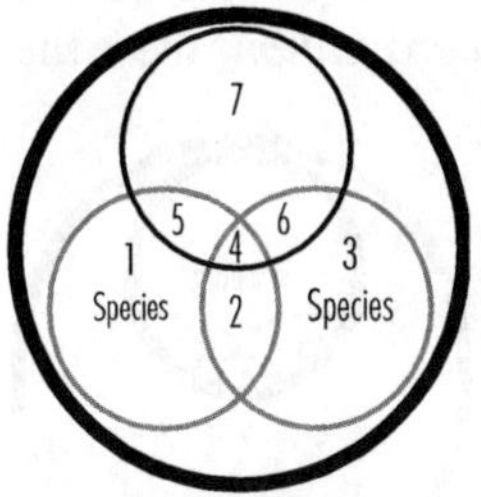

Figure 59(b)
Problematic Judgment

But if Problematic Judgment asserts that the goodness of the house might be unconnected to its Notion (*i.e.*, subjective), it admits that the house might well be notional (*i.e.*, objective). This means the house *itself* will determine what it is. "Thus it contains the *ground* of its *being* or *not being* what it *ought to be*." (661)

The subject is now split between its objective nature (what it ought to be) and what it is – "the particular constitution of its existence." (661) The subject is the ground of its being (or not) what it ought to be. In this sense it is the same as the predicate, which is where Assertoric Judgment placed the Notion. Both extremes are a Universal continuity into its other, a Particular resistance to that continuity, and the unity of these two. In short, each extreme is the whole of Judgment itself, which is the Notion split into its constitutive moments.[87]

(c) The Apodeictic Judgment

Speculative Reason produces the Apodeictic (*i.e.*, certain) Judgment. Perhaps the concrete Individual does or doesn't have a relation with its Notion. One thing is certain, however. *One* of these things is true. Either it is notional or not notional. And, in this certainty, the

---

[86] The critique of the Problematic Judgment – the prior step is really subjective – was also the same critique leveled by the Particular and the Hypothetical Judgments about the prior step. BURBIDGE, LOGIC, *supra* note , at 150. The Particular Judgment was the point that the Singular Judgment, "This man is useful," implies that some men are *not* useful. Usefulness was revealed to be a subjective – not a Universal – quality.

[87] Žižek claims that subjectivity is achieved *only* with the advent of the Judgment of the Notion. Judgment, he writes, is "a matter of the relationship of the object itself to its own Notion – the radical conclusion to be drawn that *there is no Subject without a gap separating the object from its Notion*." ŽIŽEK, KNOW NOT, *supra* note 18, at 131. Yet the gap between the empirical Notion and the notional Notion is already apparent in the Individual, which is both abstract and notional. Therefore one could rightly say that the subject emerges at the *beginning* of the Judgment chapter. One may also complain that it is not just the subject, in Hegel's logic, that is split. *Everything* is split – subject, object, Idea itself.

Individual *is* in communication with its Notion. That is to say, what is notional about things is that they may or may not be notional. Both are equally true. "When the problematic element is thus posited as the problematic of the *thing*, as the thing with its *constitution*, then the judgement itself is no longer problematic, but *apodeictic*." (661)

What then is apodeictic about things?[88] "The thing itself is just this, that its Notion, as the negative of itself, negates its universality and projects itself into the externality of individuality." (661) In the Problematic Judgment, the subject was still a duality. It was subjective and objective.[89] But now the subjective element itself has become problematic. It has lost the immediate determinateness. In short, Hegel has turned skepticism on itself.[90] Skepticism about skepticism is the Apodeictic Judgment.

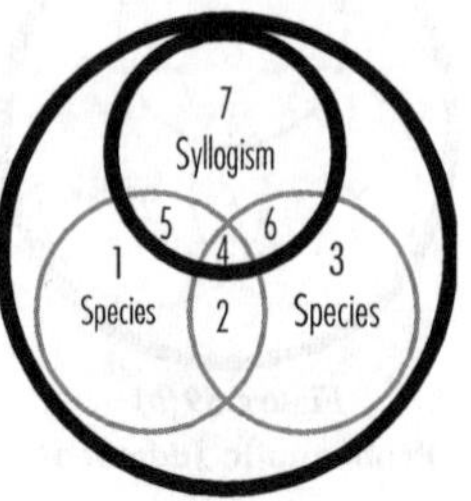

Figure 59(c)
Apodeictic Judgment (Syllogism)

Apodeictic Judgment is "*truly* objective." (662) A thing is now *constituted* as it *ought* to be; the subject now corresponds to its Notion. At this point, the very form of Judgment is suspended. Apodeictic Judgment is "the complete sublation of judgement, because value cannot be merely a predicate. What is good, not *has* but *is* goodness."[91]

Apodeictic Judgment consists of two moments: the objective Universal and the individualized Universal. "Here, therefore, we have

---

[88] Looking forward to Syllogism, Richard Winfield makes the following suggestion. Where *U* = Universal, *P* = Particular, and *I* = Individual, *IPU* is the basic form of Syllogism in chapter 21. This form is already present in the Apodeictic Judgment, which is therefore nascent Syllogism. Richard Dien Winfield, *The System of Syllogism*, in HEGEL'S THEORY OF THE SUBJECT, *supra* note 63, at 127-8. This point can be expressed colloquially as follows. "This house is good" represents the relation of *U* and *P* (or *UP*); the Notion of the house manifests itself in this Particular house. "Perhaps this house is not good" bears the form *PI*; this house is a Particular, separate from what it ought to be – a Universal house. Apodeictic Judgment joins *UP* and *PI* to form the Syllogism *UPI*; whatever the house is, it must be known from its Particulars. *P* therefore mediates the house's connection to its Notion.

[89] Hegel later calls this "the twofold meaning of *subjectivity*" originating in Apodeictic Judgment, "namely the subjectivity of the Notion, and equally of the externality and contingency opposed to the Notion." (709)

[90] BURBIDGE, LOGIC, *supra* note 3, at 153 ("the problematic relation between subject and predicate itself becomes problematic").

[91] MURE, PHILOSOPHY, *supra* note 10, at 136.

the universal which is *itself* and continues itself through *its opposite* and is a universal only as *unity* with its opposite." (662) In short, *A* equals {*A*, *B*, *C*} and *A* does not equal {*A*, *B*, *C*}.

The Apodeictic Judgment has the form, "the house constituted so and so is *good*." (661) But the Apodeictic Judgment is not about empirical houses. Rather, it is the unity of the Assertoric Judgment and the Positive Judgment. Whereas the former *asserts* a comparison between the empirical and notional thing, and whereas the latter asserts doubt of that relation, Speculative Reason is now certain that either there is or is not a relation between empirical thing and its notion. "[T]his is the *absolute judgement on all actuality*," Hegel writes. (662)[92] So much for deconstruction, which maintains that

> Hegel's critique of reflection, and his intensification of it to absolute reflection by elevating the major themes of reflection to the level of the concept or Notion, represents a radical completion of subjectivity, freedom, autonomy, self-certitude and certitude, transcendentality, and so on.[93]

The subject of the Apodeictic Judgment contains constitution and the ought-to-be in immediate unity. But it is still split between what it ought to be and what it is. So far, actuality is in a rather ambiguous situation. But then, we are only finishing the second part of Hegel's Doctrine of Subjectivity. Objectivity is still a chapter away.

Original partition culminates in a return to an absolute relation between the ought-to-be and constitutional being. This relation makes what is actual into a *fact* [*Sache*]. The inner relation of "ought" and "is" is the soul of fact. Since *relation* is the key, the soul of the thing now resides in the copula. "[W]e now have before us the *determinate* and

---

[92] Harris's conclusion is different: "all genuine judgement is evaluative, that is, it grasps its subject in its total relationship to the complete system of the real, and *ipso facto* to the whole experience of the judging subject, or *ego*. That is why we say that it takes a person with great experience to judge soundly." HARRIS, *supra* note 72, at 237. I am unable to follow Harris into the realm of subjective judging through experience. I take Hegel's point to be that there is definitely a notional connection between subject and predicate, though its empirical identification is problematic. The conclusion that those with experience judge better than those without it is a pragmatic point that seems out of place in Hegel's Logic.

[93] RODOLPHE GASCHÉ, THE TAIN OF THE MIRROR: DERRIDA AND THE PHILOSOPHY OF REFLECTION 62 (1986); *see also id*. at 179 ("in Hegel, legislation by totalization is the speculative answer to the aporias of reflection; only by means of a faultless exposition of the system of totality of all determinations of thought could Hegel hope both to overcome the antinomies of reflection . . . ").

fulfilled . . . copula, which formerly consisted in the abstract '*is*', but has now further developed itself into *ground* in general." (662) At first, Being was an immediate determinateness in the subject; now it is *relation* of subject to predicate. Being "has no other *content* than this very *correspondence*, or relation of the subject to the universality." (662)

The form of Judgment has now perished. Subject and predicate have the same content, and "the subject loses its determinateness as against the predicate." (709) The subject points beyond itself and relates itself to the predicate. Even the very act of relating has passed over into the predicate. In fact, relation *is* the content. The copula has rendered itself visible.

Subject and predicate are each the whole Notion. So now is the copula. It relates them but is distinct from them and is their equal in its content. It is "the *copula pregnant with content*." (663) The unity that was lost in the extremes has now been recovered. "Through this *impregnation of the copula the judgement has become syllogism*." (663)[94]

---

[94] "[W]hat is changed by the speculative content in the usual subject-predicate relation of proposition is not only the respective positions of subject and predicate but the very status of the copula in the judgment. The *is* has radically changed meaning: it no longer secures the attribution of predicates to a subject, of Universals to a particular; instead it expresses an identity that is itself both passive and transitive. The copula of the proposition thus becomes the real subject of the speculative proposition. It expresses the Absolute itself – the Absolute that is the totality of the Concept." *Id.* at 48.

21
Syllogism

Syllogism or inference (*Schluss*)[1] is the stage of the *SL* at which the word "rational" begins to appear.[2] Rationality stands for the triune structure of the Notion. "[N]ot only is the syllogism rational, but *everything rational is a syllogism*." (664)[3] "[C]ommon chatter about reason," (664) Hegel complains, neglects to define the term. Perhaps thinking of Kant, Hegel says that "supposedly rational cognition is

---

[1] "It is evident that the term 'syllogism' is the worst possible translation for the German word *Schluss*, which does not signify the well-known scholastic technique for reaching a conclusion, but rather the 'issue,' the 'unification,' the 'reconciliation' of the artificial distinctions of the understanding." EUGÈNE FLEISCHMANN, LA SCIENCE UNIVERSELLE OU LA LOGIQUE DE HEGEL 266 (1968).

[2] Deborah Chaffin, *The Logic of Contingency*, in HEGEL RECONSIDERED: BEYOND METAPHYSICS AND THE AUTHORITARIAN STATE 143, 147 (H. Tristram Engelhardt, Jr., & Terry Pinkard eds., 1994) (rationality "is not one of the categories to be found within the system of categories of the *Logic*, but is rather the title for that which is presented by the theory as a whole.")

[3] "[T]he three figures of the syllogism declare that everything rational is manifested as a triple syllogism . . . [E]ach one of the members takes in turn the place of the extremes, as well as of the mean which reconciles them. Such . . . is the case with the three branches of philosophy: the Logical Idea, Nature, and the Mind. As we first see them, Nature is the middle term which links the others together. Nature . . . unfolds itself into the two extremes of the Logical Idea and Mind. But Mind is Mind only when it is mediated through nature. Then [Mind] is the mean . . . It is Mind which cognizes the Logical Idea in Nature and which thus raises Nature to its essence. In the third place again the Logical Idea becomes the mean; it is the absolute substance both of mind and of nature, the universal and all-pervading principle." EL § 187 Addition.

mostly so busy with its objects that it forgets to cognize reason itself and only distinguishes and characterizes it by the objects that it possesses." (665) Reason is that which recognizes God, freedom, duty, etc. These are Kant's "practical" objects.[4] Left unanswered is, What makes these objects rational? According to Hegel, they are rational because they are triune; their infinitude "is not the empty abstraction from the finite, not the universality that lacks content and determinateness, but the universality that is fulfilled or realized, the Notion that is *determinate* and possesses its determinateness in this true way." (665)

And how does the Notion make itself determinate? "[I]t differentiates itself within itself and is the unity of these fixed and determinate differences." (665) When triune Notion is before us, "reason *rises* above the finite, conditioned, sensuous, call it what you will, and in this negativity is essentially *pregnant with content* [*inhaltsvoll*], for it is the unity of determinate extremes." (665) In Syllogism, Notion is overtly itself, its other, and the unity of self and other.

Syllogism is all about *proof*. In chapter 13, Hegel defined proof as mediated cognition. A proposition that appears as a middle term is a mediated cognition and hence "proved." When a premise is merely given (*i.e.*, "all men are mortal"), proof of *that* premise is demanded. The premise must be proved by becoming a middle term to two other given premises, which in their turn must also be proven.[5] Eventually, the premises of Syllogism must take their turn in the middle. Only then can *all* the premises be proved.

If rationality is the triune form of the Notion, we must account for the fact that Judgment is tetrachotomous, while Syllogism is trichotomous. Comparing the sequences of Judgment and Syllogism, we find:

Judgment	**Syllogism**
Existence	Existence
Reflection	Reflection
Necessity	Necessity
Notion	–

---

[4] IMMANUEL KANT, CRITIQUE OF PURE REASON A798/B826 (Paul Guyer & Allen W. Wood trans., 1990).

[5] CHARLES TAYLOR, HEGEL 314 (1975) ("what is being demanded of the syllogism here is something we do not usually ask of our inferences: not just that the conclusion follow from the premisses, but that these too be grounded in necessity").

Meanwhile, the *initial* Syllogism *of Existence* is *not* triune. It replays the four Judgments:

Judgment	**Syllogism of Existence**
Existence	IPU_E
Reflection	PIU_E
Necessity	IUP_E
Notion	UUU_E

In this table, *I* is Individuality, *P* is Particularity, and *U* is Universality. The subscript *E* stands for "Syllogism of Existence." The subscripts *R* and *N* will denote Syllogism of Reflection and Necessity respectively.

Why is there no *Syllogism* of the Notion? Why does quadruplicity yield to triunity?[6] And why, within triune Syllogism, is the initial Syllogism of Existence tetradic? Hegel does not explain the return of triunity, but he writes that Syllogism is "the restoration of the *Notion* in the *judgement*" (664) Accordingly, in this chapter, I argue that trichotomy returns because the Notion is already comprehended at the beginning of Syllogism. The Judgment of the Notion *is* the Syllogism of Existence. The overlap guarantees that, when, Judgment and Syllogism are considered together, six steps are at stake.[7] The excess in Judgment is swallowed up by the Syllogism of Existence.

A. The Syllogism of Existence

The progress of the four Syllogisms of Existence is as follows: (1) IPU_E, the classic formal Syllogism, is, like the Judgment of Existence, non-notional. Its unity is strictly external to Syllogism. (2) In PIU_E, Syllogism's inability to prove *anything* is the universal predicate; similarly, in the Judgment of Reflection, the subject realized its nothingness. All being was in the external predicate. (3) IUP_E is speculative. It admits that the unity holding Syllogism together is

---

[6] ERROL E. HARRIS, AN INTERPRETATION OF THE LOGIC OF HEGEL 242 (1983) ("The precise answer [for omitting notional syllogism] is hard to come by").

[7] Here is G.R.G. Mure's different answer: "But the puzzle vanishes if we do not look for one-one correspondence, but remember that in the rationality of Syllogism the 'broken-backedness' of the Understanding is mediated and transcended. If we insist on pressing the correspondence we must say, I think, that Syllogism of Necessity 'corresponds to' notional Judgment as well as to Judgement of Necessity." G.R.G. MURE, A STUDY OF HEGEL'S LOGIC 208 (1950).

entirely external to itself. All three terms of Syllogism are seen as fundamentally alike. Difference is externally imposed. At this point, externality – the true unity of Syllogism – is raised to the level of Universality (UUU_E). In fact, UUU_E is not truly a fourth. It is the analytical truth of the prior three steps; UUU_E adds nothing that was not entirely true of IUP_E. Appearances to the contrary, there are only *three* Syllogisms of Existence.

The Understanding begins by "holding rigidly to the *self-subsistence* of the extremes." (665) The middle term or copula is the essential feature – the unity of the extremes. "[T]he *copula pregnant with content*," (663) is precisely where the Judgment of the Notion left off.

At first, the Syllogism of Existence is immediate and formal – not yet concrete. It manifests no internal unity. The extremes are self-identities "that cannot be comprehended, but only indicated."[8] Its overall form is IPU_E.[9] *P* is the middle term "since it unites *immediately* within itself the two moments of individuality and universality." (666)[10]

Following Aristotle, *U* subsumes *P*, and *P* subsumes *I*; the Universal "descends to individuality through particularity." (667) In Syllogism, the *predicate* (*UP*) subsumes and the subject (*PI*) *is* subsumed. *UP* is therefore the major premise and *PI* the minor premise.

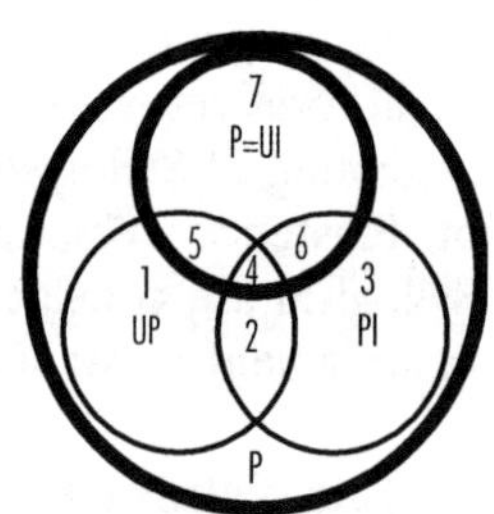

Figure 60(a)
IPU_E

(a) IPU

In IPU_E, the Individual is Universal (and vice versa)[11] through the medium of Particularity. IPU_E's significance is that the abstract individual "emerges by means of particularity into *existence* as into universality, in which it no longer belongs merely to itself but stands in an *external relationship*." (667) Through Particularity,

---

[8] JOHN W. BURBIDGE, HEGEL ON LOGIC AND RELIGION: THE REASONABLENESS OF CHRISTIANITY 132 (1992).

[9] "A *particular* mediates between an *individual* and its category." JOHN W. BURBIDGE, ON HEGEL'S LOGIC: FRAGMENTS OF A COMMENTARY 181 (1981).

[10] Mure suggests that *P* is the middle term because, following the Judgment of the Notion, Notion must manifest itself; Notion is genus, and what genus manifests is Particularity. MURE, LOGIC, *supra* note 7, at 209.

[11] The extremes of each of the following forms can be flipped, so that *IPU* is equally *UPI*, etc. *Id.* at 210 n.1. For example, Hegel will later refer to the second figure of formal syllogism as *UIP*, (690) though he usually writes *PIU*.

the Individual is a *concrete* Universal.

IPU_E is Aristotelian Syllogism. Hegel paraphrases Aristotle as follows: "*When three terms are related to one another in such a manner that one extreme is in the whole of the middle term and this middle term is in the whole of the other extreme, then these two extremes are necessarily united in a conclusion.*" (667-8) The "favorite perfect syllogism" (688) holds:

All men are mortal.
Gaius is a man.
Therefore Gaius is mortal.

To replicate this in the form of IPU_E, Hegel rearranges the terms as follows:

All men are mortal. (*PU*).
Therefore Gaius is mortal. (*P*, or *IU*).
Gaius is a man. (*IP*).

In this Syllogism, *U* inheres in *P*; *P* inheres in *I*; *therefore I* inheres in *U*. The "therefore" belongs to the middle term. It establishes the truth that $P=IU$. In the parlance of symbolic logic, this is the "hypothetical syllogism."[12] Its truths are strictly *conditional* because the premises are conditional.

Two diverse judgments are externally joined to form IPU_E. First is *PU*, where *P* is subject and *U* is predicate. Second is *IP*. Nothing in *PU* demands conjunction with *IP*. Men are *many* things other than mortal; there is no reason why the major and minor premises *must* be brought together. "The *therefore* appears as the conclusion that has taken place in the *subject*, a conclusion deduced from *subjective* insight into the relationship between the two *immediate* premisses." (668)

IP and *PU* are immediate, externally supplied and not themselves proven or mediated by Syllogism. What is expressed between *IP* and *PU* is mere likeness, to which *PU* and *PI* are indifferent. Yet once the two extremes *are* externally conjoined, the "therefore" is no external determination. It is grounded in the nature of the extremes themselves. The copula "therefore" is no empty "is" but is "pregnant with content."

---

[12] IRVING M. COPI, SYMBOLIC LOGIC 34 (5th ed. 1979). A hypothetical syllogism in symbolic logic bears the form: (1) $p \supset q$; (2) $q \supset r$; (3) $r \supset s$. Hegel's Hypothetical Syllogism is what symbolic logic designates as *modus ponens*. *Infra* at 515-6.

(669) IPU_E is not two separate premises and a *diverse* conclusion. The premises may be separate, but the conclusion *follows*.

But as a mere "composition," IPU_E is flawed. In it, the right extreme (*IP*) is an immediate *I*, indifferent to being made part of a Syllogism which reveals one of its *P*'s. *I* has *infinite P*'s that *could* have been revealed. *I* is only *subjectively* brought together with the revealed *P*. Rational thinking cannot proceed by *IPU*. Notional determinations must be *essentially* united. Anything else is "*makeshift*" (669) and "still subjective." (667)[13]

IPU_E is true only if the premises are true. "Accordingly, it is commonly demanded of the premisses that they shall be *proved*, that is, that *they likewise shall be presented as conclusions*." (672) Each premise requires a further Syllogism, made up of two conjoined premises. These in turn demand two new Syllogisms, and "*so on* in a geometrical progression to *infinity*." (673) *I* has an infinite number of middle terms, and each of these middle terms has infinite middle terms. Mediation is, so far, contingent and subjective, "not anything necessary or universal." (674) Spurious Infinity, "an *impotent ought-to-be*," (673) certainly has no place in the domain of the Notion. Because IPU_E yields the Spurious Infinite, "mediation must therefore be effected in another manner." (673)

The truth of IPU_E is that immediate Individuality (*I*) is really the mediator. Gaius is indifferent if external reflection has emphasized his manhood. What really mediates IPU_E is *I* – Gaius himself. Furthermore, *IPU*, the external conjunction of *PU* and *PI*, bids us to "prove" the major (*i.e.*, *PU*) and minor (*PI*) premises. Let us take each in turn. Take *PU*. Here, the excluded mediator is *I*. If we make *I* the middle term, we obtain PIU_E. Similarly, *IP* excludes *U*; if *U* mediates, we have *IUP*. *PIU* next takes the stage.

(b) PIU

In IPU_E, "something [was] united with a qualitative determinateness as a universal, not in and for itself but through a contingency or in an individuality." (674) *I* was a Spurious Infinity of concrete Universals, each revealed in a completely contingent manner. So far *I* was

13 *See* G.W.F. HEGEL, PHENOMENOLOGY OF SPIRIT ¶66 (A.V. Miller trans. 1977) ("in ordinary proof . . . reasons given are themselves in need of further reasons, and so on *ad infinitum*").

"apprehended only in its *externality*." (674) Accordingly, immediacy (*i.e.*, the unproven) is what truly mediates IPU_E. This realization brings *I* into the middle spot between *P* and *U*. Of course, "unprovenness" is precisely what Syllogism is *not* supposed to be.

PIU_E makes the scandal explicit. PIU_E is to be regarded "as a subjective syllogism proceeding in an external reflection." (676) What was supposed to be true is now revealed to be subjective delusion. There is a negative unity – no relation – between *IU*, on the one hand, and *PI* on the other.

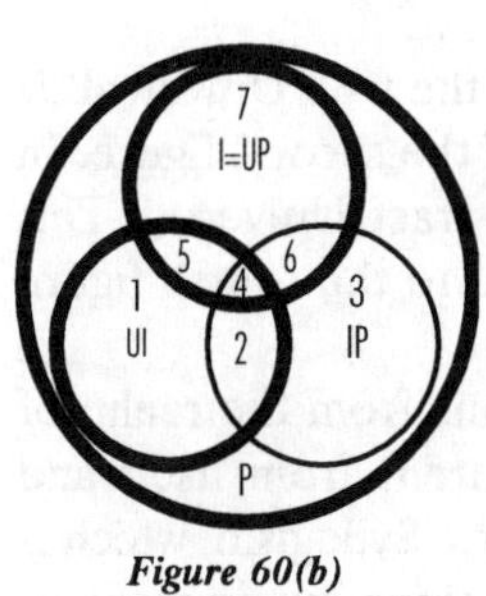

Figure 60(b)
PIU_E

PIU_E contains two judgments, *PI* and *IU*. The second judgment, *IU*=*P*, was IPU_E's result. *IU* is therefore already "proved" (or mediated) by the first Syllogism. In effect, we have learned that *all* *I*'s are *composed*. *PI*, however, remains unproved (*i.e.*, an immediacy). It stands for the proposition that at least one *I* is *not* composed.

Meanwhile, PIU_E and IPU_E have in common *U* as predicate. The subjects *I* and *P* have changed places. The significance of this is that *P* is now "posited in the *determination of the extreme of individuality*," (675) and *I* is likewise posited as Particularity. *I* and *P* are not mere immediacies. On the other hand, they are "not yet posited as concretes." (675) Because *I*=*P*, an outside force is needed to determine which is really *I* and which is *P*.

Neither yet bears a relation to its predicate (*U*). As predicate, *U* is to be taken as the totality of all the particulars *I* has. *U* is genus. Yet *U* can only be revealed in the Syllogism of Existence as *one* of the species that make up the genus.[14] When a species is brought forth as *U*, all the other species (equally *U*) are suppressed. Therefore, when *I* haphazardly reveals itself to be a species of *U*, it equally reveals itself *not* to be *U*, and so *I* "stands in a *negative* relationship to the particular in so far as it is supposed to be its predicate." (675)[15] *P* and *I* are "two qualities that are connected, not in and for themselves, but by means of a contingent individuality." (675) That is to say, the predicate (*U*) is

---

[14] For this reason, PIU_E is "the syllogism of mere *perception* or of contingent existence." (690)

[15] Hegel compares the second figure of *PIU* to the Particular Judgment – which was both positive and negative. In the Particular Judgment, the Singular Judgment ("this thing is useful") was revealed to imply that many things are *not* useful. *Supra* at 479-80.

fixed, but either *I* or *P* is subject. Only external reflection can determine whether the subject is *I* or *P*.

Nevertheless, the transition into PIU_E is "the beginning of the realization of the Notion." (675) Because *P* is isolated and in negative unity with *U*, *P* cannot determine itself. In its indeterminacy, *P* is raised to abstract Universality (*PU*). Put in other terms, PIU_E is mediated only by subjectivity and nothing else. "But if it is the subjectivity of intellectual association that mediates between the terms, then we have identified a type of inference that is neither a determination, nor something individual and unique, but is common to all intellectual operations. This mediating process is *universal* . . . ."[16]

The truth of PIU_E is $P=U$. Particularity is now the true Universal. *U* is now determined to be the true middle term of the second figure. In other words, each of the terms in PIU_E is an abstract Universal. This leads to the third figure, IUP_E, which is identical to the fourth figure UUU_E.

Hegel compares this transition to the transitions from the realm of Being. There, Being-for-self expelled all its content from itself and became Quantity. Something similar now happens. Syllogism, which is supposed to be mediation and proof, is now nothing but immediacy and unproof. All mediation is on the outside. But when such a thing happened in chapter 19 – when isolated Universality became Particularity in Infinite Judgment – Individuality was revealed. As Hegel now puts it, "according to the Notion, individuality unites the particular and universal in so far as it *sublates* the *determinateness* of the particular, and this presents itself as the contingency of the syllogism." (677)

(c) IUP

Unlike its predecessors, IUP_E has no immediate premise. *IU* was the result of the first Syllogism, *PU* the result of the second. Syllogism is now complete. Reciprocal mediation reigns between the first two Syllogisms and this third one.

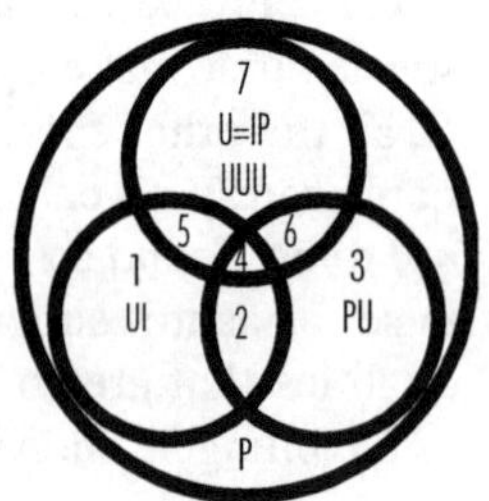

Figure 60(c)
IUP_E (UUU_E)

Each side of IUP_E is proven. Yet the two extremes are still mutually indifferent.

---

[16] BURBIDGE, LOGIC, *supra* note 9, at 166-7.

Universality, which is supposed to be the subsuming predicate is now present on both sides of the third figure. As a result, we cannot tell whether *IU* or *UP* is subject (subsumed) or predicate (subsuming). Outside force must decide. Inference is reduced to mere associational logic.[17]

None of the three Syllogisms is the totality. What totalizes (or mediates) is an outside force. The truth of formal Syllogism is *notional failure*. The terms are determinations of form, not content.

Indifference (abstract Universality) is the true ground of the Syllogism of Existence. IUP_E yields UUU_E – a fourth figure "unknown to Aristotle." (679) *UUU* expresses the equality and merely external unity of the internal parts. In UUU_E, distinguishing between the three terms is "a sheer futility." (679)[18]

Following Mure[19] and Winfield,[20] I do not interpret UUU_E as an independent step in the Logic. It therefore warrants no schematic drawing. Rather, it represents the truth of IUP_E – that nothing internal to Syllogism justifies the identification of any one of them as middle term to the other two.

(d) Mathematical Syllogism

UUU_E represents pure transitivity.[21] This "Mathematical" Syllogism states that if $I=U$, and if $U=P$, then $I=P$. In other words, all the terms are the same. It is impossible to tell which term mediates the other

---

17 *Id.* at 167.

18 Errol Harris draws a different lesson from Mathematical Syllogism: "Things which are equal to the same thing are equal to one another. This, says Hegel, is regarded as an axiom in mathematics, but it is really a logical principle demonstrable through dialectical derivation from the Concept . . . So Hegel demonstrates in an entirely different way what Frege and Russell have attempted to do, that mathematics is deducible in its entirety from pure logic." HARRIS, *supra* note 8, at 245. This, I think, misses the entire point. Hegel's view of Mathematical Syllogism is dark. Mathematics works because Quality is suppressed. The lesson of Mathematical Syllogism is mathematical failure.

19 MURE, LOGIC, *supra* note 9, at 215.

20 Richard Dien Winfield, *The System of Syllogism*, in HEGEL'S THEORY OF THE SUBJECT 132 (David Gray Carlson ed., 2005).

21 Mure writes of *UUU*, "One must confess that this leaves it obscure why . . . Hegel allows it to appear in the dialectical movement." MURE, LOGIC, *supra* note 9, at 216. The answer is that *UUU* represents the inability of Syllogism to generate any result whatever without the aid of external reflection. But since nothing is something, Hegel will find some positive content in nothing in the next few sections.

two. Only external force can identify which of the terms is the middle one. "Here the relationship of inherence or subsumption of the terms is extinguished." (679)

UUU_E represents an *axiom* – "*an absolutely self-evident, primitive proposition*" (680) – that requires no proof. Transitivity is the isolation of Quantity taken in abstraction from Quality. "But for this very reason it is not without presupposition." (680) Transitivity *is* only because Quality is *not*. "The self-evidence of this syllogism, therefore, rests merely on the fact that its thought content is so meagre and abstract." (680)[22]

Hegel also emphasizes that, in a Syllogism, the conclusion is supposed to follow from its premises. But, in the Mathematical Syllogism, the conclusion *contradicts* the premises. The premises – *U*, *I*, and *P* – were immediacies. The Mathematical Syllogism, however, is *nothing but relation*, which contradicts the immediacy of the premises. In short, the Syllogism of Existence is deeply false.

Abstraction is not, however, the final result of the Syllogism of Existence. Abstraction is not notional. Rather, abstraction posits its other, which is what really holds the Syllogisms of Existence together. "Therefore what we truly have before us is not mediation based on a given immediacy, but mediation based on mediation." (681) The other "is not placed through abstraction *outside* the circle but embraced *within* it." (681)

To summarize, across the Syllogism of Existence, the three terms each took a turn in the middle. Qualitative difference between the terms, however, disappeared in UUU_E. Nevertheless, we achieved a positive result – "mediation [*i.e.*, proof] is not effected through an *individual* qualitative determinateness of form, but through the *concrete identity* of the determinations." (681) In other words, the fourth figure (UUU_E) stands for the realization that neither *P*, *I*, nor *U* is properly the middle term. The unity of *all* the terms is the proper middle term – an external force that holds it together. "Mediation has thus determined itself as the indifference of the immediate or abstract form

---

[22] "The syllogistic forms relate abstract concepts that have been isolated through conceptual operations." BURBIDGE, LOGIC, *supra* note 9, at 172. In other words, transitivity works because conceptual operations have isolated quantity from quality. In mathematics, "the process of abstracting is pushed to its limit where all determinate and differentiating characteristics, even that of reference, are excluded, leaving only abstract quantitative identity and the 'axiom' of equality." *Id.*

determinations and as positive *reflection* of one into the other." (681)[23] We have therefore reached the Syllogism of Reflection.

B. The Syllogism of Reflection

Recall the result of Judgment: $I = \{I, P, U\}$; $I \neq \{I, P, U\}$. Four judgments were required because *I* had to be counted twice – as abstract and then as notional Individuality.

The Syllogism of Reflection, where *I* is the middle term, is more advanced than the parallel Judgment of Reflection, which entailed merely an abstract *I*. Syllogism has now dissolved into UUU_E. The subject is therefore *all of Syllogism*. As in the Judgment of Reflection, the Syllogistic version starts with the proposition that the subject is *nothing*. Predicate is everything. But in Syllogism of Reflection, the subject is a *notional* nothing – UUU_E. "It is in this way that the syllogism of reflection is the first to possess *genuine determinateness of form*, in that the middle term is *posited* as the totality of the terms." (687)

(a) The Syllogism of Allness

The first Syllogism of Reflection is Allness. Its form is UPI_R. Here, the subject (U, or UUU_E) is the member of a class. It has external manifestation (*I*) through the medium of *P*. The "particularizing" trait of Syllogism is that each depends on external reflection.

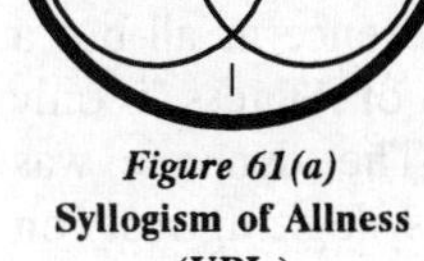

Figure 61(a)
Syllogism of Allness
(UPI_R)

In the Syllogism of Allness, *P* is a notional *P*. UUU_E has erased itself and displaced its Being into *P*. The Particularity of Syllogism is that external reflection decides which member of UUU_E is really *U*, *P*, or *I*. For this reason, Hegel says that the extremes of Syllogism generally are "determinations of the judgement of reflection." (687) That is, they are *Singular* Judgments. External reflection points and says, "*this* part of the Syllogism is *I*, *that* one is *P*, *etc*." Indexicality depends on external

---

[23] "[T]he entire course through the three figures presents the middle term in each of the determinations, and the true result that emerges from it is that the middle is not an individual Notion determination but the totality of them all." (684)

reflection. For this reason, Hegel names *P* (external reflection) as *genus*, which determines the "species."

The Syllogism of Allness counts as "the syllogism of understanding in its perfection." (687) The middle term is no longer "*abstract* particularity but is developed into its moments and is therefore concrete," a state that is "an essential requirement for the Notion." (687) *P* is now $UUU_E=I$. External reflection has become internal to Syllogism. But the Syllogism of Allness has a flaw: "the form of *allness* ... gathers the individual externally into universality. [It] still preserves the individual in the universality as something possessing immediately a separate self-subsistence . . . [S]ingle determinations still form the basis of the universality of reflection that embraces them within itself." (687) Allness is "still not the universality of the Notion but the external universality of reflection." (687)

Dialectical Reason points out that *I* is the true mediator – not *P*. Nothing in the Syllogism of Allness assures us of the truth that *all* Syllogisms depend entirely on external reflection to make them work. A single counter-example destroys the proof.

> All men are mortal
> Gaius is a man.
> Therefore Gaius is mortal.

In this Syllogism, "all men" is a set of empirical Individuals. How do we know that *all* men are mortal? Only external observation, which provides *incidents* of mortality, can be brought to bear. Perhaps the major premise is right and perhaps it is wrong. Nothing in the Syllogism of Allness can establish the truth of the major premise. The conclusion ("therefore Gaius is mortal") is brought to the table by the major premise – not by Syllogism as such. The major premise "presupposes its conclusion." (689) This is "no inference at all but a simple tautology."[24] What we have in the Syllogism of Allness "is only an external, empty *show of syllogizing*." (689) The dynamic was supposed to be objective, but "the essence of this syllogizing rests on subjective *individuality*." (689) Individuals – *subjectively* brought together in a supposed Universal set – are therefore the true middle term of the Syllogism of Allness, which Dialectical Reason takes to be external to Syllogism.

The major premise stands only so long as induction does not falsify

---

[24] BURBIDGE, LOGIC, *supra* note 9, at 174.

it. As a result, the truth of the Syllogism of Allness is induction.

(b) The Syllogism of Induction

The true middle term of the Syllogism of Allness was not *P* but *I*. Hence, the Syllogism of Induction follows the form UIP_R. So far, *I* and *P* are notional, but *U* is abstract. That is to say, both *I* and *P* are "proven" because they have been the middle terms in the first two Syllogisms of Reflection. *U* remains unproven.

The Syllogism of Induction asserts *UP* through the mediation of *I*. For example, in "all men are mortal," mortality is claimed as the predicate – the *Particularity* – of every individual man. The other extreme ("all men") is the universality – but only an abstract *U* subjectively derived. Abstract *U* erases itself and admits that its being resides in the class of individuals that has been subjectively brought together. This erasure in favor of the empirical class proves that $I=[i, i, i\ldots]$ is notional.

The middle term between *U* and *P* – the proof – is the class of all individuals. Figure 61(b) shows a Spurious Infinity as the middle term between a Particular predicate and the claim to Universality. The class of individuals is a Spurious Infinity because one never knows if all individuals have been enumerated. Some unenumerated individual might exist to destroy the truth of the induction.

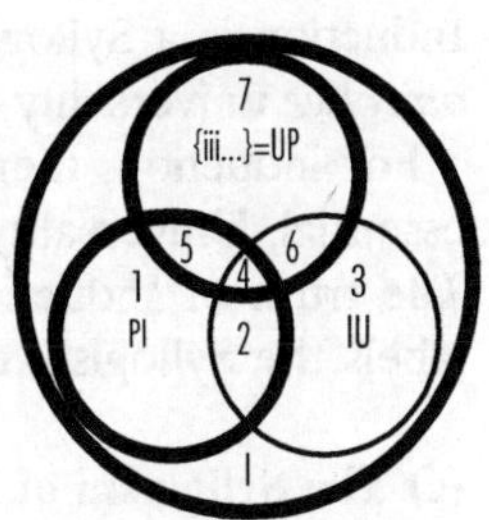

Figure 61(b)
Syllogism of Induction
(UIP_R)

As always, Spurious Infinity is a sign that something is awry. Nevertheless, UIP_R is an advance over UIP_E. Earlier, *I* "was not the subsuming term or predicate." (690) *I* was an immediacy, not the relation of *U* and *P*. Now induction claims perfect unity between *U* and *I*. *UI* (the subject) is coextensive with its predicate (*IP*). The subject ("all men") is comprised by the set of all individual men. The two are taken as the same thing; "the *same* content is posited once in individuality and again in universality." (690) "All men" and "all *these* men" bear a mere formal difference, but substantively they are taken as the same.

Induction from a set of individuals is based on *experience* – "the subjective taking together of the individuals into the genus and of conjoining of the genus with a universal determinateness because this is found in all the individuals." (690) Undoubtedly, the individuals are made into allness by mere external reflection. Universality "remains *a problem*." (691)[25] But induction assigns the role of genus to Spurious Infinity of all individuals.[26] In this sense, induction presupposes its conclusion. Induction is "accepted as valid *although* the perception is admittedly *incomplete*." (691)

"The fundamental character of induction is that it is a syllogism." (691) In it, *I* (as the set of all *i*'s) unites Particulars and proclaims them Universal. Yet the forgathering of *i*'s into *I* is a subjective judgment, which *asserts* (but does not prove) "the immediacy which is *in and for itself*, the *universal* immediacy." (691) Induction takes Universality as essential to its truth.[27] If, per Karl Popper, "individuality is taken as the essential, but universality as only the external determination of the middle term, then the middle term would fall asunder into two unconnected parts and we should not have a syllogism." (691) Induction is a Syllogism only if $I=U$. "[S]uch universality is properly *objective* universality, the *genus*." (691)

For induction, then, universality is "*external but essential*." (691) As essential, Universality is just as much internal to induction as external. The truth of Induction is therefore Universality – IUP_R. This Hegel labels the Syllogism of Analogy.

(c) The Syllogism of Analogy

Analogy is a strange part of the *SL*, with its reference to moon men. Hegel simultaneously denounces and praises analogy as empirically worthless and spiritually necessary.

Induction entails a class of Individuals with the same predicate, which is logically put forth as the Universal. Hence what really mediates induction (Popperian *caveats* notwithstanding) is Universality. Universality of predicates is what the Syllogism of Analogy puts forward.

---

[25] *See* BURBIDGE, LOGIC, *supra* note 9, at 176 ("The process of reflective inference produces only a problematic conclusion").

[26] Winfield suggests that genus is not proper to induction, because genus *determines* the species. Rather, class membership is the issue. A class has no substance of its own and *is* whatever the class members bring to it. Winfield, *Syllogism*, *supra* note 21, at 136.

[27] "That is, it has implicitly formed the demand that only speculative philosophy can satisfy: the demand that universality be concrete, present in and as the experienced other." PETER SIMPSON, HEGEL'S TRANSCENDENTAL INDUCTION, 110 n.9 (1998). "[L]ogical induction has rightly identified the goal of a concept that is one with its instances . . . but lacks the appropriate standpoint for recognizing that identity." *Id.* at 113 n.11.

In analogy, "the universal is seen in the individual case."[28] According to Hegel's definition, "if two objects agree in one or more properties, then a property which one possesses also belongs to the other." (693) Hegel gives a dubious example:

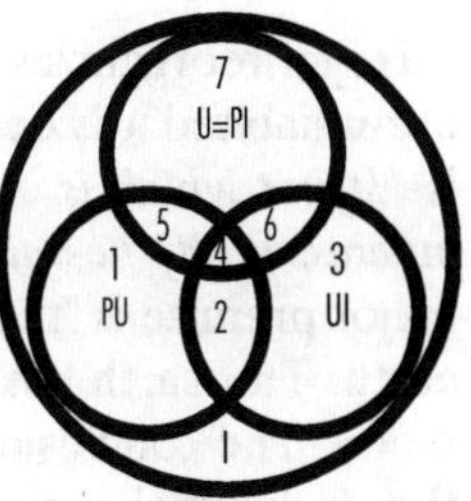

Figure 61(c)
Syllogism of Analogy
(IUP_R)

The *earth* is inhabited [*PU*],
The moon is *an earth* [*UI*],
Therefore the moon is inhabited [*PI*]. (692)

In this example, Analogy degrades reason to "the sphere of mere *representation*." (692) In terms of its content, analogy "should not find a place in logic at all." (692)[29] Analogy's importance, Hegel declares, "itself does not depend on the empirical content." (692) The form of the Syllogism is the main thing. In analogy, Speculative Reason finds that Universality, the implicit middle term in induction, now mediates expressly in the form IUP_R. As mediator, *U* is now *proven* as the very nature of the thing. The thing is a concrete object – an Individual – but *U* is now taken as genuinely *in the thing*.[30] "Here, then, the middle term is an individual but an individual taken in its universal nature." (692)[31]

Analogy is a *relation* between two Individuals, such as the moon and earth. These Individuals share some Universal trait (such as inhabitation). When analogy is based on mere similarity, however, it is not notional.

---

[28] CLARK BUTLER, HEGEL'S LOGIC: BETWEEN DIALECTIC AND HISTORY 249 (1996).

[29] According to Burbidge, the problem with the moon analogy is that "the inference itself cannot establish whether the fact that the earth has inhabitants follows from its essential nature as satellite, or is simply accidental. It is this contingency that frustrates the syllogism and prevents it from symbolizing a necessary inference." BURBIDGE, LOGIC, *supra* note 9, at 178.

[30] For this reason, I disagree with Errol Harris, who finds the point to be that analogy can be "a fruitful stepping-stone to scientific discovery, if used with care and circumspection." HARRIS, *supra* note 6, at 247. The *utility* of analogy is not at stake, but rather the role of *U* in mediating between *P* and *I* which interests Hegel. Admittedly, Hegel does praise the utility of analogy in science, but this is not his speculative point. *See* EL ¶ 190 Addition.

[31] "In this process, reflective thought rises above bare denotation [*i.e.*, assignment of an individual to a class] and assumes that there is an objective ground for conjoining class and determinate characteristics." BURBIDGE, LOGIC, *supra* note 9, at 177.

Hegel reorganizes analogy so that its empirical content ("all earths are inhabited") is demoted to the minor premise. The major premise is "*[t]hat which is subsumed under some other thing in which a third inheres, [and] has also that third inherent in it*" (692) In our case, the major premise is "the moon is an earth." The moon is subsumed by the earth. The earth has a third (inhabitation) and this third inhabits the moon. The conclusion ("therefore the moon is inhabited") shows that the Individual (moon) is continuous with the earth and so is a Universal Individual.

Meanwhile, what was previously formal Syllogism must now appear "as a *determination of content*." (693) That is to say, in the Syllogism of Analogy, Universality *objectively* mediates and therefore is *proven*. This makes Analogy (IUP_R) an advance over IUP_E, which yielded *abstract* Universality.

It may seem, Hegel suggests, that analogy contains "*four terms*, the *quaternio terminorum*." (693) *Quaternio terminorum* is a logical mistake with this form:

A=B
C=D
A=D

In Hegel's example, there are two individuals (earth and moon), a (third) property in common (they are both heavenly bodies). The *quaternio terminorum* is therefore all the other properties of the one individual (including inhabitation) which are now attributed to the second individual. For example:

1. The earth is inhabited (*PI*).
2. The earth is a heavenly body (*IU*).
3. The moon is a heavenly body (*PU*).
4. Therefore the moon is inhabited (*PI*).

If analogy has four terms, how could it be a Syllogism, which has only three? The answer is that Universality is "immediately *also* as the true universality" (693) of the Individuals. The apparent four terms are really only three. Earth and moon *really do share* a Universal – their nature as heavenly bodies. The second and third term are really one single middle term.

Compare this with induction, where the middle term was a set of individuals. Such a mediator was a mere ought-to-be which "ought to be enumerated." (693) Even further back, in the Syllogism of Allness, the middle term was purely external (hence less than an-ought-to-be).

Now, however, "essential universality" (693) mediates. The Individuals share Particulars which are Universals (or so analogy claims). In short, *successful* analogy requires the presence of a *notional* Universal.

Analogy still suffers from externality, which means that it is still a Syllogism of Reflection. That two things share *some* aspect (earth and moon are heavenly bodies) does not prove that they share *all* aspects (such as inhabitation). Only external reflection can decide whether habitation is particular or universal. If "individuality and universality are *immediately* united," (694) then external reflection simply *asserts* that the predicate (habitation) is Universal, not Particular. In such a case, analogies fail as objective proof.

Syllogism, however, is about *mediation*. And mediation requires a positing, not of the immediate being, but of genus. So far, the Universal ("heavenly body") is only implicitly genus; it must become so expressly.

"The moon is inhabited." This was the conclusion (*PI*). But "the earth is inhabited" is also *PI*. Earthly habitation is the major premise brought to the table by external reflection. Since the major premise is the conclusion, the major premise is presupposed, not proved. "Hence this syllogism is . . . the demand for itself to counter the immediacy [*i.e.*, unprovenness] which it contains." (694)

Presupposition here is reflective – contained within the totality. Presupposition has declined since the Syllogism of Existence, where one Syllogism presupposed all other Syllogisms. Each Syllogism was immediate and abstracted from the other. Now presupposition is proven to be a structural part of Analogy. The major premise *is* the conclusion. The Syllogism of Analogy bears the structure of a Determination of Reflection – a unity between immediacy and mediation. Speculatively, an advance has been made. Analogy works when the conclusion is also the major premise. If this occurs, then "mediation [has] coincided with its presupposition." (695)

Hegel insists that analogy is a negation of the negation. How precisely is this so? Recall that the Syllogism of Existence failed to be what it claimed. External reflection (*P*) made it work. Yet *P* involved a foregathering of Individuals in induction. *I*, not *P*, mediated. But *I* mediated only because all *I*'s were universally the same. Every individual Syllogism *[i, i, i . . .]* operated by externality. But *Analogy* is the truth of induction. All Individuals have Universal attributes. "All Syllogisms work by external reflection" is the same as saying that external reflection is *inside* the Syllogisms. Analogy is therefore a negation of the negation. It brings Syllogism's externality *inside*.

U is now proven. It has become the middle term of analogy. When *I* yields to *U*, "the syllogism of reflection has passed over into the *syllogism of necessity*." (695)

C. The Syllogism of Necessity

Syllogism of Existence bore the general form of *IPU*. The true mediating element was external reflection (*P*). In the Syllogism of Reflection (generally, *PIU*), the mediating element was Individuality. *Every* Individual Syllogism is useless to prove *anything*. Now the mediating element is *objective universality* – "universality which contains the entire determinateness of the distinguished extremes." (695)

The Syllogism of Necessity (*IUP*) – the "absolutely *necessary inference*"[32] – is pregnant with content. The middle term is now "not some alien immediate content, but the reflection-into-self of the determinateness of the extremes." (695) The extremes – Individual Syllogisms that prove nothing – have erased themselves and exported their inner identity into the middle term. That which *unites* the extremes with the copula is necessary. That which *differentiates* the extremes is external and unessential.

The Understanding proposes that the nature of Syllogism is the *connection* of the terms. Extremity is portrayed as unnecessary. Dialectical Reason will propose the opposite – that the extremes are everything. Speculative Reason finds merit in both views.

Syllogisms of Necessity follows the pattern of the Judgment of Necessity: Categorical, Hypothetical, Disjunctive.

(a) The Categorical Syllogism

In Categorical Syllogism, "a subject is united with a predicate through *its substance*." (696) Substance hearkens back to Actuality – a proto-Universality. Through its Accidents, Substance actualized itself. But Substance was the statement, "I am *not* the Accidents." Now, the subject *is* its predicates through "the Notion-determination." (696) The subject now says, "I *am* myself, but I am just as much my other, and the unity of myself and other."

Hegel says that the Categorical Syllogism has as its premise the Categorical *Judgment*, which asserts that the genus has its being in the

---

[32] BURBIDGE, LOGIC, *supra* note 9, at 179.

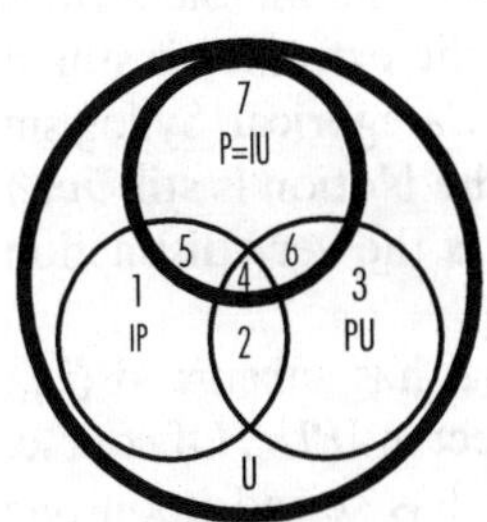

Figure 62(a)
Categorical Syllogism
(IPU_N)

species.[33] In the Syllogism of Analogy, the Universal Individual ($U=IP$) became genus. *Genus* is now the subject, connected to its predicates via objective Universality.

The meta-form of the Syllogism of Necessity is *IUP*, but the Categorical Syllogism nevertheless has the form IPU_N, conforming to the opening moments of the Syllogisms of Existence and Reflection. *P* is the Universal Individual that emerged from Analogy. *U* is to be taken as abstract Universality, or "the accidentality of substance gathered into simple determinateness which however is its essential difference, *specific difference*."(696) In other words, the predicate in the Categorical Syllogism is a set of determinate Universals genuinely set forth by the Individual. Accordingly, Individuality is *actual*.

After the Syllogism of Analogy, the middle term stands for the essential nature of an individual Syllogism. The subject is "no longer contingently united . . . with *any quality* through *any* middle term. [T]he demand for proof, which occurred in the latter and led to the infinite progress, does not arise." (697) So the Categorical Syllogism is no longer entirely subjective. In it, "objectivity begins." (697)

But a dialectical critique is necessary. Categorical Syllogism stands for immediacy (within the context of the Syllogism of Necessity). This immediacy is a fault. As yet, there is imperfect unity between the Individual and its other parts. If *I* is united with *U* in IPU_N (or if species is united with genus), it is connected via Categorical Judgment – a subjective connection. Categorical Syllogism is therefore *both* objective and subjective. It is objective because "the middle term is the pregnant identity of its extremes." (697) That is, the middle term (genus, or *P*) is where self-subsistence of the extremes resides; because of their participation in the middle term, the extremes have "substantial universality." (697)

Yet the extremes are still *distinguishable*. This signals a *subjective* moment. Hegel writes, "the Universality of the middle term is substantial, *positive* identity, but is not equally the *negativity of its extremes*." (697) In other words, the extremes insist on an immediate,

---

33 *Supra* at 484-5.

positive identity against the middle. For this reason the middle term is *not yet* the "negativity of the extremes." Each of the extremes is still "a self-contained universal."[34] The *content* of the Categorical Syllogism is objective, but its form is not. The identity of the Notion is still *inner* – "still *necessity*." (697)[35] What must be negated is the very distinction between the extremes and middle term.

Hegel puts the matter this way. The Universal has subsumed (*i.e.*, eaten) the Individual. This Individual is the subject in IPU_N. Of course, every Individual is the same, yet the Universal has seized upon *one* Individual and has eaten it. Why was *this* Individual seized and not *that* one? Obviously subjective *Judgment* is still at work. But that's not all. The very fact that the Universal *had* to swallow the Individual implies a distinction between Individual and Universal. This distinction is an immediacy and therefore a reproach to notionalism.[36]

It should not be missed that immediacy, once the enemy and the sign of subjectivity, is a *virtue* that Categorical Syllogism (as a whole) lacks. This grander immediacy is "not yet *posited* as that which it is *in itself*." (697) The inferior version of immediacy, however, is still present. It is precisely this immediacy that the extremes must give up to the center.

At this point, the bad immediacy is the presence of an indeterminate number of Individuals. Any given Individual is genuinely subsumed in genus (the middle term), but it is merely contingent that a given Individual is isolated and identified with genus. Furthermore, if the Individual is subsumed, it is also not identical with genus. It has some peculiarities which allow us to distinguish the Individual from the genus; "therefore it also has a specific nature of its own indifferent to the middle term and possessing a content peculiar to itself." (698) In short, Individuals contain non-notional, irrational material. Because of this material, their immediacy (*i.e.*, distinction from its Notion) is contingent. This contingent immediacy must sublate itself, and the fundamental immediacy must express itself.

(b) The Hypothetical Syllogism

Hypothetical *Judgment* was pure, isolated relation. It announced, "if

---

[34] BURBIDGE, LOGIC, *supra* note 9, at 183.

[35] Recall that what was Necessary is that all things are ambiguous with regard to their rationality. See chapter 17.

[36] The Universal must likewise swallow *P*, proving that both extremes in the Syllogism of Necessity – *I* and *P* – bear residua of immediacy.

A, then *B*." Nothing was said about the status of *A* or *B* as genus. Now the Universal Individual of Analogy is on the scene. We can say that *A is genus*. Hypothetical *Syllogism* becomes:

> If *A* is, then *B* is,
> But *A is [genus]*,
> Therefore *B* is. (698)[37]

The relation of *A* and *B* in the major premise bears the form of the Hypothetical Judgment. In the phrase "if *A* is, then *B* is," *A* and *B* are mutually indifferent even if necessarily connected; neither *A* nor *B* can sustain itself, since, at the level of Hypothetical Judgment, we don't yet know whether *A* or *B* exists as genus. *A* and *B* therefore erase themselves and have "*sublated* being or being only in the sphere of Appearance." (699)

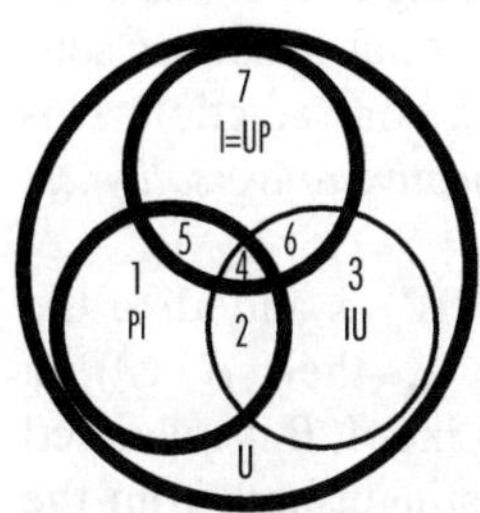

Figure 62(b)
Hypothetical Syllogism
(UIP_N)

Hypothetical Judgment was a dialectic comment on Categorical Judgment, which proclaimed that genus is correlated with species. Hypothetical Judgment added that it is impossible to tell whether the subject is genus or species; only external reflection could assign this determination. One side of Hypothetical Judgment was genus (Universality), the other species (Individuality). Neither *A* nor *B* immanently identifies itself as one or the other. Nevertheless, whichever variable was taken as genus, it stood for Totality of Conditions (*i.e.*, Real Necessity).[38] The other side stood for Actuality. The Totality of Conditions was "the *inner, abstract* side of an actuality." (699) The conditions became Actual only when "*gathered together into an individuality*." (699) The Totality of Conditions, then, was Universal; the Actual is the Individual. One could say that the Totality of Conditions *causes* the Actuality of the thing, but causality, Hegel thinks, is too transitive[39] and does not

---

[37] Logicians would call this form the *modus ponens* (mode that affirms). COPI, *supra* note 13, at 34. Its form is $p \supset q$; p; therefore q.

[38] See chapter 17.

[39] Hegel emphasizes that "the causal relationship has been superseded in the Notion." (715) Causation suggests that one thing originates in another. But in the Notion, everything self-originates. This will be the hallmark of Objectivity. Objectivity constitutes an immediacy, but causation is a mediated (and hence subjective) relationship. *See* Winfield, *Syllogism*, *supra* note 21, at 139.

sufficiently invoke the indifferent existence that A or B enjoys separate and apart from their inherent transitivity.

The *mediating term* of Hypothetical Syllogism is the minor premise – the *being* of A. For this reason, Hypothetical Syllogism bears the form UIP_N. The being of A mediates because of its moment of indifference to B, and because, simultaneously, A sublates itself and sends its being over to B. A (and equally B) can be taken as the Totality of Conditions, or Universality, which translates itself into Actuality. The being that A thus demonstrates is "*being in its Notion*." (700) What A demonstrates is Universality becoming Individual – not in the crude sense of transition, but in the notional sense of self-development, *activity*. The middle term, then, is a contradiction. It is active *and* passive – "the contradiction of the *objective universality* . . . and the *indifferent immediacy*." (700)

When the middle term/minor premise ("but A is") is added to the major premise/Hypothetical Judgment ("if A is, then B is"), a conclusion follows hard upon ("therefore B is"). Like A, B is mediated *and* immediate. The result, however, is to be distinguished from the middle term. The middle term stands for *necessity* – a relation. The result stands for *that which is necessary*. But this difference between necessity and what is necessary is merely "the wholly superficial form of individuality as against universality." (700) The content of result and middle term are the same. Only "*ordinary thinking* [*Vorstellung*]" (700) distinguishes the middle term from the conclusion, or necessity from the necessary. If the two are separated, B wouldn't even be the necessary. The conclusion must therefore be taken as "the identity of the *mediating* and the *mediated*." (700)

Categorical Syllogism – the Understanding's moment – exhibited a positive (*i.e.*, immediate) difference between genus and species. Dialectic Hypothetical Syllogism exhibits a negative unity – a relation [2] that can be distinguished from the extremes. Yet, even so, in Hypothetical Syllogism, the middle term collapses into the extremes and vice versa. Difference between them is formal and subjective. Hypothetical Syllogism therefore stands for the activity of opposition dissolving itself until A and B become empty names for the same thing. Externality has sublated itself and withdrawn into the middle term. The result is Individuality as self-related negativity – "an identity that differentiates itself and gathers itself into itself out of [external] difference." (701)

In Hypothetical Syllogism, the moments still have private, unshared content. This separateness of the moments constitutes mere formality.

Subjectivity/formality holds the mediating factor as distinct and abstract. But now the distinction of mediating and mediated must disappear. What we must see is "[t]hat which is mediated is itself an essential moment of what mediates it." (703) The subjective Individuality of Hypothetical Syllogism yields Disjunctive Syllogism – the last step before subjectivity yields to objectivity.

(c) The Disjunctive Syllogism

Disjunctive Syllogism conjoins Categorical and Hypothetical Syllogism. Categorical Syllogism stood for the affirmative being of the Notion. Here the Universal Individual was subject. Hypothetical Syllogism stood for notional otherness – the negative unity between Notion and its other. Disjunctive Syllogism stands for the unity of affirmative being, otherness, and the unity of being and otherness.

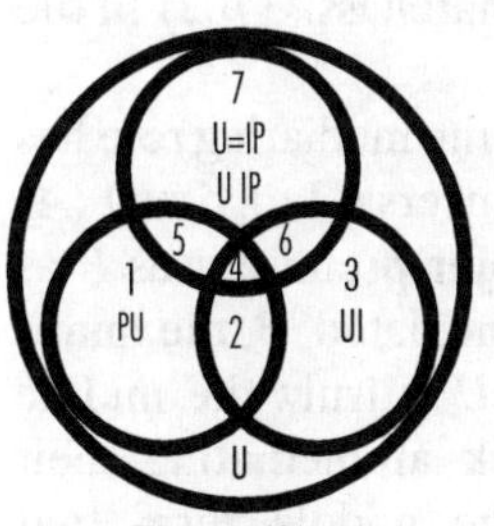

Figure 62(c)
Disjunctive Syllogism
(IUP_N)
(Objectivity)

Disjunctive Syllogism (IUP_N) has for its middle term "the *universality* that is *pregnant with form*." (701) In it, *U* is just as much *I* and *P*, so that Notion, sundered in Judgment, comes together.[40]

In Disjunctive Syllogism, genus (*U*) is coextensive with Species (*I* and *P*): formulaically, *A*=[*B*, *C*, *D* . . .]. *A* represents a unity that *also differentiates itself* within itself.[41] Since it differentiates itself, there is difference between, say *B* and *C*, or between *A* and *B*. Hence, Disjunctive Syllogism is:

---

[40] In modern logic, disjunctive syllogism bears the form *p or q*; *~q*; therefore *p*. COPI, *supra* note 15, at 34.

[41] Taylor draws a different lesson from Disjunctive Syllogism and proclaims it implausible: "What is being sought [is] a necessity of reasoning which requires no postulate, where whatever is given at the beginning must be shown out of the system." TAYLOR, *supra* note 5, at 314. While it may be true that Hegel aims for a groundless philosophical system, it is not fair to say that it is the task of Disjunctive Syllogism to deliver the goods. All that we can say of Disjunctive Syllogism is that Notion differentiates itself from itself within itself. Given that each notional component has served a term in the middle, the Disjunctive Syllogism can be viewed as "proven" and objective.

A is either *B* or *C* or *D*,
But *A* is *B*,
Therefore *A* is neither *C* nor *D*. (701)

Yet it is equally:

A is either *B* or *C* or *D*,
But *A* is neither *C* nor *D*
Therefore, *A* is *B*. (702)

In the above formulations,[42] *A* is subject in all three terms of the Syllogism. In the major premise, *A* is the Universal Individual (genus) that particularizes itself into species. In the minor premise and conclusion *A* is "the exclusive, *individual* determinateness." (702) In the result, *A is* (and is not) the predicate.

Surveying the Syllogistic landscape, notice that the mediating role has rotated. In Categorical Syllogism, a *particular* Universal Individual (*A*) was selected to set forth a predicate. *A*, the major premise, was *P* as such. In Hypothetical Syllogism the "other" (*B*) mediated. *B*, the minor premise, was *I* as such. Now the middle term *U* is truly the middle term. All parts of Syllogism have had a crack at mediating their fellows. Mediation stands for proof – for the middle term that notionally unites the extremes. Throughout Syllogism, mediation has been external to Syllogism. This externality meant that Syllogism was only formal. The worth of Syllogism was subjectively supplied. But now Syllogism mediates itself. That is the significance of each notional moment, *P*, *I*, and *U*, having served as mediator between the other two terms.

Because it exhibits the mediation of *P, I, and U*, Disjunctive Syllogism is "*no longer a syllogism* at all." (702) "The extremes . . . appear only as a positedness which no longer possesses any determinateness peculiar to itself as against the middle term." (702) The content of one moment of the Notion is not privately retained but

---

[42] Taylor's interpretation of these formulations is as follows: "By this criterion even judgments of the kind 'man is a mammal' fail to provide adequate premisses, for . . . while it is not to be questioned that man is a mammal, we could not have this judgement unless man existed." *Id.* at 314-5. This example is inapposite. At stake is the objectivity of subjectivity – not zoological judgment. Categorical Syllogism stood for the *being* of the Notion – understood as an activity. Yet irrational, non-notional materials exist as well – differentiation *from* Notion. Syllogism therefore stands for the self-differentiation and self-objectivization of Notion – a task Taylor's example does not help to elucidate.

entirely shared with the other moments. Disjunctive Syllogism joins together all the moments of Notion in a determinate and simple unity. "[T]he *formalism of the syllogistic process*, and with it the subjectivity of the syllogism and of the Notion in general, has sublated itself." (702-3)

Notional reality does not terminate the *SL*. Recall that the Disjunctive Syllogism produced *notional* elements *and non-notional* elements. The non-notional elements, however, were genuinely Notion's own moments. The non-notional moments now stand over against the notional moments, though in a notional way. The subject has objectified itself, but it also faces a non-notional object. The subject has created a reality from its own resources, but this reality is still a positedness. Indeed, Subjectivity (which is now ending) is a realm of the Understanding. Objectivity (which is now beginning) must therefore have the dual structure just described. Objectivity presupposes a subject-object distinction, which must be overcome. Or, more accurately, subjectivity is now objective, so that there is an object-object distinction. One of these objects is notional but the other is not.

Notion has now exhibited itself as the identity of inwardness and outwardness. The object is outward, but there is still an inward (which is as much object as the object). Since immediacy has become respectable, mediation is now the mark of imperfection. It signifies that the terms of the Notion are not in and for themselves but are for, or are by means of, another. But now mediation itself is sublated. Immediacy of the two objects has been established. Immediacy, of course, is Being. "*[B]eing* is therefore a *fact* . . . that is *in and for itself – objectivity*." (704)

Syllogism v Judgment. Syllogism is triune, Judgment tetrachotomous. Why this should be so remains something of a mystery to Hegelians, but perhaps I can now offer a suggestion.

At first, Judgment and Syllogism followed on the same track. Each had a category corresponding with (1) Existence, (2) Reflection and (3) Necessity. Judgment, however, added the anomalous fourth category of Notion. Recall that (3) the Judgment of Necessity represented Actuality – a state just short of the Notion. And what was Actual and Necessary was that Appearance must disappear. Notion was what remained after Appearance self-erased. Yet Notion itself remained uncertain of itself. This is what the Judgment of the Notion stood for – the proposition that there certainly *is* a Notion, but its exact form is problematic.

Meanwhile, The Syllogism of Existence itself had four categories, which corresponded to the tetrachotomous structure of Judgment. We interpreted UUU_E, however, not to be a separate development but merely an "analysis" of IUP_E. The Syllogism of Existence was therefore triune in form.

I would like to suggest that Syllogism of Existence establishes the objectivity of Judgment. This was accomplished in IUP_E, because, by that point, all three terms took their turn in the middle; each was "proven." What was left in doubt at the end of Judgment was itself placed in doubt. As such it became objective. The one *objective* fact about Syllogism is doubt. Once this Universal was manifested, the minor premise of the Hypothetical Syllogism ("but *A is*") was in play. This, added to the skeptical Syllogism of Reflection, produced the Syllogism of Necessity to give the final "certain" result – an object linked to a subject. Each exhibited all the moments of the Notion and hence each was absolutely self-certain. For this reason, Syllogism was done after three steps. Judgment, however, required four steps, because the certainty in the Judgment of the Necessity was still contested.

In chapter 2, I followed Slavoj Žižek in suggesting that a "silent fourth" was at work throughout the *SL*. In the Objective Logic, this silent fourth was subjectivity itself. That is, Being required subjectivity to "be." Yet this could not be acknowledged officially as of chapter 2. In the Subjective Logic, the *object* is the silent fourth – the disturbing factor that prevents the *SL* from concluding. Notion must now raise this irrational Object to its own level in Idea.

PART VIII
OBJECTIVITY

22 Mechanism

Subjectivity has established its objectivity, but it is still implicated in a subject-object distinction, which must be overcome. The subject, confident that it (not the object) is self-determining,[1] must learn that the external object[2] determines itself just as much as the subject. Indeed, the object *is* the subject.

The object is determined in three ways – as Mechanism, Chemism and Means to Subjective End (*i.e.*, amenability to purpose).[3] Mechanism is the *immediate* moment of dialectic objectivity. It explores what kind of immediacy objectivity enjoys. By now, Logic has trafficked in several versions of immediacy. Crude Being came first. Second, in Essence, Existence was an immediacy to which Essence restored itself – the Ground from which "things" appeared. Third and finally, immediacy was the copula – the relation of subject and predicate.

---

[1] *See* JOHN MCCUMBER, THE COMPANY OF WORDS: HEGEL, LANGUAGE AND SYSTEMATIC PHILOSOPHY 311 (1993) (subjectivity "now considers itself to confront an 'object' other than it – an object which is, because other, precisely *not* a self-determining totality but an 'immediate, unaffected' indeterminate manifold of individual existents") (citation omitted).

[2] At the outset, the object should be taken as the one single, unified object that is simply not the subject. EL § 193, at 256-7. It will soon shatter and fall to pieces, however.

[3] Michael Inwood suggests that this triad is intended to be "a brisk rehearsal, within the sphere of pure thought, of the *Philosophy of Nature*." M.J. INWOOD, HEGEL 336 (1983). On this view, objectivity stands for nature generally. In the *Philosophy of Nature*, however, the relevant triad is mechanics, physics and organics. ERROL E. HARRIS, THE SPIRIT OF HEGEL 148 (1993).

Immediacy now takes the form *A is (and is not) B* – the performativity established in Disjunctive Syllogism. A copula entails extremes. The object therefore "has difference attaching to it: it falls into pieces . . . and each of these individualized parts is also an object . . . "[4] That is, each part is as much the totality as it is the part. "Hence the object is the absolute contradiction between a complete independence of the multiplicity, and the equally complete non-independence of the different pieces."[5]

Notion has now achieved unity with its predicate and is a notional immediacy. As a result, the Notion has determinate being. Yet its determinacy is its flaw. It is still plagued with opposition, which must be overcome before the Logic can end. Long the villain, immediacy is now the hero.

Objectivity's duality can be described as follows. First, a non-notional objectivity stands against the subjectivity of the Notion. Second, there is the Objectivity *of* the Notion – "the *being that is in and for itself*." (709) This duality can be compared to the duality at the end of Notion (chapter 19). At that point, the Individual was abstract *and* notional. Notion had to suffuse itself into its own abstraction – a task performed over the course of Syllogism.[6] Yet the abstract object is unequal to the subject.[7] Now, notional objectivity must suffuse through abstract objectivity before we can traverse the gates of divine Idea.

In Mechanism. the Understanding first proposes that Objectivity is "insensible to difference."[8] The Mechanical Objects are indifferent to each other, and to the extent they are conjoined in relations of mechanical causality, their unity is external. These objects, "if they are altered at all, do not move themselves, but are acted upon."[9]

---

[4] EL § 193, at 257.

[5] *Id.* § 194.

[6] For this reason, one writer suggests that Syllogism stands for *purposive action*, "since Hegel's syllogisms represent a unity of thought and action in a reciprocal relationship between man and nature and between man and man". David Lamb, *Teleology: Kant and Hegel*, in HEGEL'S CRITIQUE OF KANT 177 (Stephen Priest ed., 1987).

[7] Stanley Rosen therefore suggests that Hegel privileges the subject over the object: "it makes no sense to refer to Absolute Objectivity, for then, self-conscious, thinking, and spirituality are excluded from the Absolute at the very outset. The attempt to explain the connection between the subject and the object is already an act of the subject." STANLEY ROSEN, G.W.F. HEGEL: AN INTRODUCTION TO THE SCIENCE OF WISDOM 48 (1974).

[8] EL at § 194.

[9] JOHN W. BURBIDGE, REAL PROCESS: HOW LOGIC AND CHEMISTRY COMBINE IN HEGEL'S PHILOSOPHY OF NATURE 78 (1996)

Mechanism purports to be a non-relation between Objects. Dialectical Reason points out that non-relation is a form of relation. Therefore, the objects cannot keep themselves apart. This is Chemism.

Finally, the repulsion and attraction of objects is brought together; this is the posited *End* or Teleology of Notion. In Teleology, subjective Notion recognizes the object as its own self. Purposiveness, at first external, becomes internal. This is Idea. The very purpose of subject and object is to sacrifice themselves in favor of Idea.

Ontological proof of God. In an essay prior to Mechanism proper, Hegel finally delivers his proof of God – an ontological proof[10] to which he has occasionally alluded.

Hegel's proof of God *is* the transition of Subjectivity into Objectivity at the end of Syllogism (though God as such is to be associated with the Idea at the end of the Logic).[11] What we have learned about subjectivity in the prior chapters is that "the subject only obtains determinateness and content in its predicate." (705) When the subject enjoys a notional unity with its predicates, "there begins . . . *realization* in general." (706)

Objectivity must be conceived as an activity of the Notion expressing itself through its predicates. God renders itself objective in this way. Accordingly, "man was early instructed to recognize God in his *works*." (706)[12] The cognition of God *as activity* "grasps the *Notion* of God in his *being* and being in his Notion." (706)[13]

---

[10] QUENTIN LAUER, ESSAYS IN HEGELIAN DIALECTIC 114 (1977) ("According to Hegel all arguments must ultimately be reduced to the ontological argument and thus share its validity as a description of the human spirit's elevation to God. To understand this would require a complete grasp of the 'System' in its entirety and, above all, a minute understanding of the *Logic*, whose movement constitutes an extended presentation of the ontological argument.").

[11] *See* CHARLES TAYLOR, HEGEL 317 (1975) (Anselm, Descartes and Leibniz "would be horrified to see the kind of 'God' whose existence is here proved, for this existence is inseparable from that of the world as ordered whole, and this is not the God worshipped by Christians").

[12] *Cf.* LAUER, *supra* note 10, at 8 ("The world is other than God, it is 'created' by God; but it is God's self-othering, which is to say that to know God is to know the world, to know the world is to know God, and to know either without the other is to know neither"). Lauer reads the passages just discussed as establishing that, "[f]or Hegel the ultimate reality is not *substance*, as it is for Spinoza, but rather *subject* or Spirit, and its manifestation is spiritual activity." *Id.* at 117.

[13] *Id.* 118 ("Hegel is not . . . much concerned with *whether God exists*; he is very much concerned with *what God does*. What God does, however, is God's self-manifestation (God 'proves' himself), and this self-manifestation is completed in man .

Being can now be revealed for what it is: "the abstract moment of the Notion." (706) Someone who asks "what *is*?" usually asks for existence outside the Notion – outside subjectivity. When the being demanded of God is Existence beyond the Notion, the task of finding God is insuperably difficult. God is not like one hundred thalers, "something to be grasped with the hand . . . , something visible essentially to the outer, not to the inner eye." (707) When abstract being, "temporal and perishable," is accorded the status of truth, when "thought stands opposed to being," God must suffer. (707)

Being's "*truer* and *richer* form" (707) is conceived as *within* the Notion. Such being, when conceived as self-related negativity, is Individuality. Our present position in the Logic is too advanced for an opposition between objectivity, on the one hand, and the Notion, on the other. Therefore, "if the Notion is to be presented as the Notion of God, it is to be apprehended as it is when taken up into the *Idea*." (707) So far, the Notion is in the process of uniting with objectivity, but it is not quite there. Objectivity "is not yet the divine existence." (707) Nevertheless, Hegel claims, objectivity, as presented in the Logic, is "just that much richer and higher than the *being* or *existence* of [Anselm's] ontological proof, as the pure Notion is richer and higher than that metaphysical void of the *sum total of reality*." (707)[14]

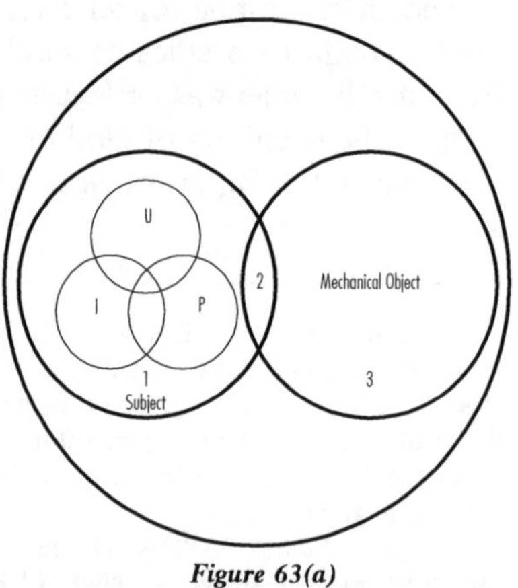

Figure 63(a)
Mechanical Object

A. The Mechanical Object

From the last chapter, the object is "the *syllogism*, whose mediation has been sublated . . . and has therefore become an immediate identity." (711) The Understanding interprets this as the Mechanical Object. The Mechanical Object as immediacy (Leibniz's monad) "does not differentiate itself into *matter* and *form*." (712) Matter might seem to stand for the Universal side of

. . whose thoughts are God's thoughts.").

[14] The "sum total of reality" is the definition of God according to the ontological proof. *Supra* at 59.

the object, and form would seem to be the Individual side. But, by now, any abiding difference between the Universal and Individual is precluded. Nor does the object have properties or accidents, for these would admit of mediation.

A critique at once intrudes upon the Understanding's interpretation of the object. If the Mechanical Object excludes all opposition between itself and its properties, it is indeterminate – it "*contains no relationships*." (712) It is "a vast atom in an infinite void."[15]

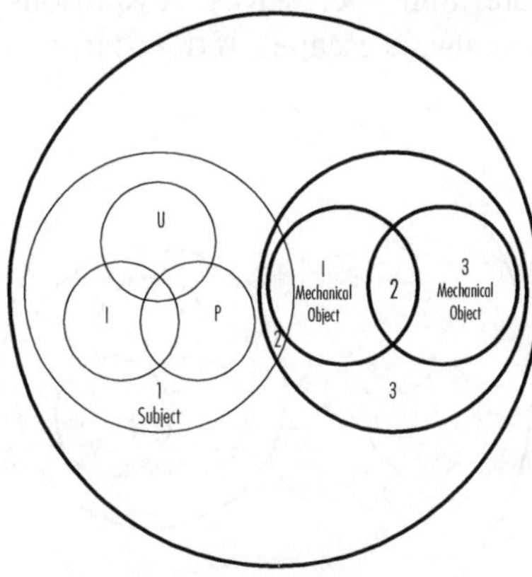

Figure 63(b)
Aggregate of Mechanical Objects

The object *is* the Notion, and as such it has *parts*. Recall that, at this late stage, "being" implies a copula, which implies extremes. But, in Syllogism, each part is as much totality as the totality is. The one object is multiple objects.[16]

The part is the whole, so if parts of *a* whole are perceived, this distinction belongs strictly to external reflection; to this the object itself is indifferent.[17] "[W]hatever relation obtains between the things combined, this relation is one *extraneous* to them that does not concern their nature at all." (711) The object, then, is a mere "*composite* or *aggregate*" (712) – words that, for Hegel, signal that something is wrong.

In composition, the relation [2] between any two Mechanical Objects

---

15 ERROL E. HARRIS, AN INTERPRETATION OF THE LOGIC OF HEGEL 262-3 (1983).

16 *Id.* at 263 ("In the history of philosophy the Parmenidean One proliferated into the atoms of Leukippus and Democritus, each atom being one, indestructible, uncreated and indivisible, like the original Being").

17 These parts are not atoms, however. Hegel has opposed atomism from the start. It will be recalled that atoms attract and repel each other. Having relations of this sort, atoms cannot be objects, in the sense of being totalities. The Leibnizian monad is more like an object than an atom, "since it is a total representation of the world." (712) But the monad is in fact a presupposition of the subject. Its claim to objectivity, Hegel says, comes from its indifference to its own manifoldness. The monad is "merely *implicit* totality," (714) self-enclosed but indifferent to its determinateness. Its "determinateness is not its own, but one that is *posited* by *another* object." (714) At best, the monad exhibits *negative* freedom, whereas objectivity has been brought about by the *positive* freedom of self-development.

is a non-relation – an invention of external reflection. Notion is entirely outside of the Mechanical Objects at this point. In effect, the Mechanical Object has *surrendered its freedom* to the subject.

The immediate Mechanical Object is indeterminate and needs other things to determine it. So far, its determinateness is only that it is not other objects. And if it *needs* other objects to determine itself, those objects need yet other objects to determine themselves. A Spurious Infinity arises in which determinateness always escapes. If this Spurious Infinity is gathered together and called a universe, such a gathering is the achievement of an external will – an external purposiveness.[18]

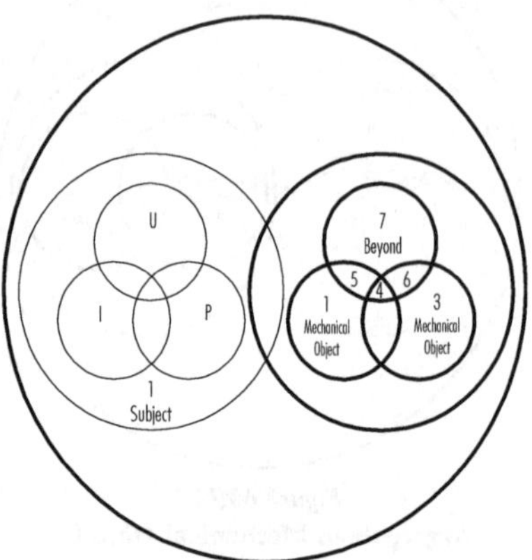

Figure 63(c)
Nature of Mechanical Objects

Speculative Reason observes that, by its nature, the object points beyond itself to other objects for its determination. Objectivity is here revealed to be a *process* of pointing beyond – a pointing toward external purposiveness. The object is supposed to be self-determining, but so far, it is "incommensurable to its own characteristics."[19] In determinism, *self*-determination is always deferred. A determining object can always be located, but this object

[18] The subject, itself an object, is also capable of surrendering its freedom to some other subject-object by thinking mechanically. "A *mechanical style of thinking, a mechanical memory, habit, a mechanical way of acting*, signify that the peculiar pervasion and presence of spirit is lacking in what spirit apprehends or does." (711) Although these things require consciousness, "yet there is lacking in it the freedom of individuality." (711) Such action seems externally imposed, when the actor acts mechanically – when her heart is not in it. Stephen Houlgate finds in this remark proof that Deconstruction has misunderstood Hegel's system. The Derridean critique is that spirit purports to lose itself but has guaranteed its return in advance. Mechanical memory, however, stands for loss, but what returns is not a mechanical repetition of what was lost but is a transformed, different entity. Stephen Houlgate, *Hegel, Derrida, and Restricted Economy: The Case of Mechanical Memory*, 34 J. HIST. PHIL. 79, 88, 93 (1996) ("But this overlooks the fact that spirit's 'return' to itself is actually not a return, not a repetition of itself at a 'higher' level, but a turning into itself, a *coming* to itself . . . in which, through emptying itself of what it has always regarded as meaningful, it comes to be what it has never actually been before").

[19] TAYLOR, *supra* note 11, at 320.

is indifferent to its role. Where, in the deterministic universe, is the ultimate object that serves as first cause? "[D]eterminism is itself indeterminate in the sense that it involves the progression to infinity." (713) It lacks and therefore implies a "final" cause.

Determinism makes weakness its strength. Although it constantly defers the first cause, any object it identifies as *a* cause is indifferent to this status, and equally indifferent to *being* caused. Accordingly, determinism "can halt and be satisfied at any point at will, because the object it has reached in its progress, being a formal totality, is shut up within itself and indifferent to its being determined by another." (713) Explanation is only an empty word in determinism, "since in the other object to which it advances there resides no self-determination." (714)

So far, determinateness has been doubled. It is in the object. It is out of the object. These determinatenesses are identical. Thus, finding that object *A* is what it is because of object *B* is a mere tautology – "an external futile see-saw [*Hin- und Hergehen*]" (714) In fact, there is only one determinateness before us, and it is both in and out of any given object. "[I]ts being doubled expresses . . . externality and nullity of a difference." (714) Hence, objects are now contradictory. They are mutually indifferent – in the double sense of being self-subsistent and being precisely the same. Yet they depend on the other for determinateness. "This contradiction is, therefore, the *negative unity* of a number of objects which, in that unity, simply repel one another: this is the *mechanical process*." (714)

B. The Mechanical Process

The Understanding now proposes that the Mechanical Object is really a process – a movement. The determinateness of the Mechanical Object is not its own. Its being is determined by some other Mechanical Object. The Mechanical Object is therefore a passive mirror reflecting other Mechanical Objects.[20]

Just as the Mechanical Object's unsuccessful immediacy corresponds to crude immediate Being, so Mechanical Process represents the mesne realm of Reflection. Neither of these steps is notional. Mechanical Process reduces the object to reciprocal action. "To shift the reciprocity

---

[20] BURBIDGE, REAL PROCESS, *supra* note 9, at 78 ("When we think of the objective realm *mechanically*, we understand it to be made up of independent objects which, if they are altered at all, do not move themselves, but are acted upon").

of substances on to a *predetermined harmony* means nothing more than to convert it into a *presupposition*, that is, to withdraw it from the Notion." (715)

(a) The Formal Mechanical Process

The Understanding starts out by defining the Formal Mechanical Process as *Communication*. In Figure 64(a), one Mechanical Object communicates determinateness to another. Yet the communicating object does not thereby transform itself into an opposite, as a finite entity would. Rather, the communicator remains what it was.

The communicability of Mechanical Objects is now itself the object. It depends on a third – an intelligence that unifies two Mechanical Objects via a Communication. The large circle around the objective portion of Figure 66(a) can be conceived as this intelligence, which holds fixed the two objects and communication between them.

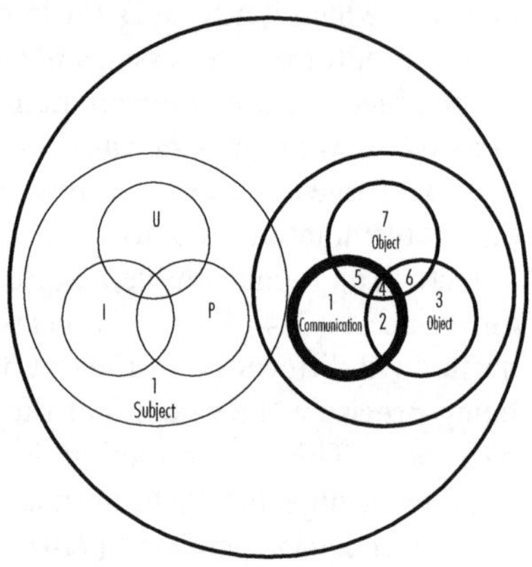

Figure 64(a)
Formal Mechanical Process

Communicability is immaterial. Immaterial objectivity comprehends "[l]aws, morals, rational conceptions in general . . . which penetrate individuals in an unconscious manner and exert their influence on them." (716) Communication, however, does not strictly mean communication between humans. It comprehends, *inter alia*, the communication of "motion, heat, magnetism, electricity and the like." (716) These are often represented as "stuffs or matters," but in truth these communications are "*imponderable* agents" (716-7) that lack materiality.[21]

---

[21] "In saying this Hegel is far in advance of his time. He wrote when these forms of physical phenomena were explained in crassly material terms and scientists spoke of heat and electricity as fluid substances . . . The persistent failure to explain electro-magnetic phenomena mechanistically was just what led at the turn of the century to the abandonment of mechanism in physics with the advent of Planck and Einstein and the theories of quanta and of relativity." HARRIS, LOGIC, *supra* note 15, at 264-5.

The Understanding has posited Universality [7] as the heart of Communication, but Dialectical Reason protests that Universality, when isolated, is Particularity. The Particularity of Communication stands for the proposition that, in their Universality, objects maintain Individuality. Hegel names this self-maintenance *Reaction*. Reaction is not the suspension of communicative action. Rather, Communication requires Reaction. Universal Communication is particularized when the object receives the Communication and stays what it was, even as the Communication remains what *it* is. In the interaction between Action and Reaction, cause gets lost in effect. Meanwhile, the object, indifferent to Universality, finds itself raised to it [7]. As one of many Universals – the other, the Communication, and itself – it is a species in a broader genus. So two actions are ongoing. First, the Communication (a Universal) gets particularized in the object, and the object finds itself raised to Universality, precisely because it is open to Communication.

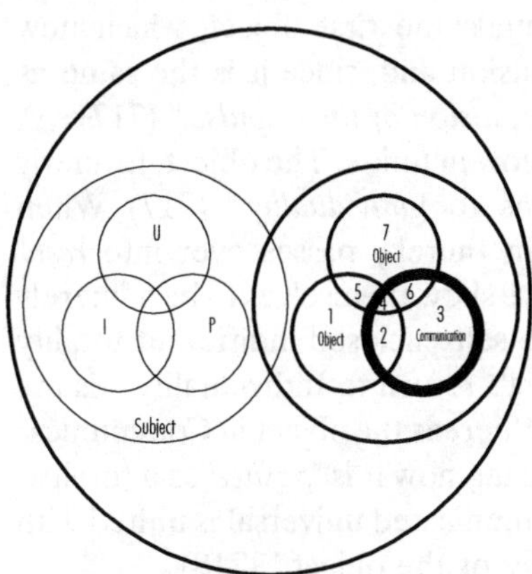

Figure 64(b)
Particularity of Communication (Reaction)

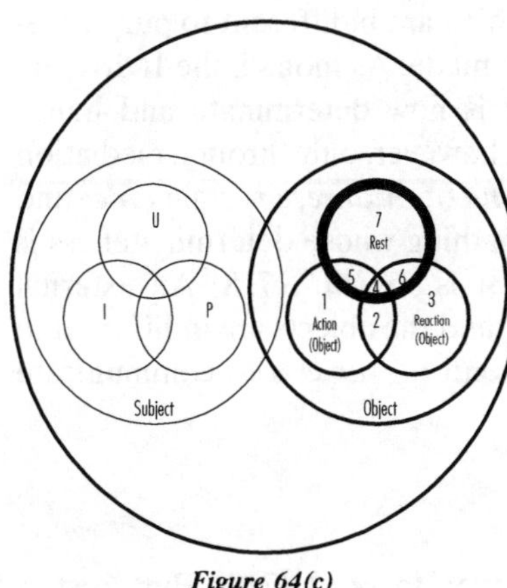

Figure 64(c)
Rest

The way Communication works, Hegel says, is that the passive object takes up the Universal and is now active against the first communicating object. Communication therefore provides the "objective element" (717) to objects. Prior to Communication, the objects are passive monads – open to Communication but indifferent to it. The indifference stands for the failure of self-determination. "To gain the freedom of substance it is not sufficient to represent [the monad] as a totality that is *completely within itself* and has nothing to receive *from without*." (714) The object must overcome passivity to Communication if it is to be truly free. Objectivity is an active principle.

The now-active second object equals the first object, which now becomes passive. Reaction is a repulsion and, since it is the same as action, action itself is "a *reciprocal repulsion of the impulse*." (717)

Universality and Particularity are now in union. The object, formerly a species of the Universal, "returns to *individuality*." (717) When Individuality posits itself, "the action thereby passes over into *rest*." (717-8) Action and Reaction therefore show themselves to be a "merely *superficial*, transient alteration in the self-enclosed indifferent totality of the object." (718) Rest – the object's return to Individuality – is the product of the Mechanical Process. Whereas the object in Communication was *presupposed* to be an Individual, now it is "*posited* as a totality. It is the conclusion in which the communicated universal is united with individuality through the particularity of the object." (718)

But the Individual at Rest is flawed. In it, mediation is sublated. The Individual at Rest is indifferent to having been "determined" by external Communication. There is still a fundamental split between the intelligent purposiveness that comprehends the Mechanical Process and the objects involved in the process, which are indifferent to purposiveness. Nevertheless, progress has been made. As monad, the Individual was indeterminate. As a product, it is now determinate and hence really an object. It becomes an object, however, only through mediation by an other. It is therefore "a *compound* or *mixture*, a certain *order* and *arrangement* of parts, in general, something whose determinateness is not a self-determination but one that is *posited*." (718) An external intelligence establishes the aggregate, and the objects are indifferent to the part they play in it. Objects depend on *subjects* to communicate their unity to them.

(b) The Real Mechanical Process

Mechanical Process "has passed over to *rest*." (718) But Rest is external to the active and reactive objects. It can "be regarded as produced by an *external* cause." (718) Mechanical Objects appear to be stable to some external intelligence, but in truth they are in ceaseless turmoil, pointing to a beyond for their quietude. Yet the active objects have *posited* Rest. In Figure 64(c), [5] and [6] – the Mechanical Objects – announce they are *not* the Mechanical Process, an activity that points to some beyond for determinacy. This activity can be viewed as [4].

And [7]=[4] represents the static side of the Process as a "beyond."

In the Mechanical Process, as captured in Rest, one object [5] is distinguishable from another [6]. An external reflection makes any distinction. Opposition, Hegel says, has now been distributed among the objects. The objects "are not merely diverse, but are now *specifically distinguished* as against one another." (719) In other words, in the Mechanical Process, objects are determined externally.

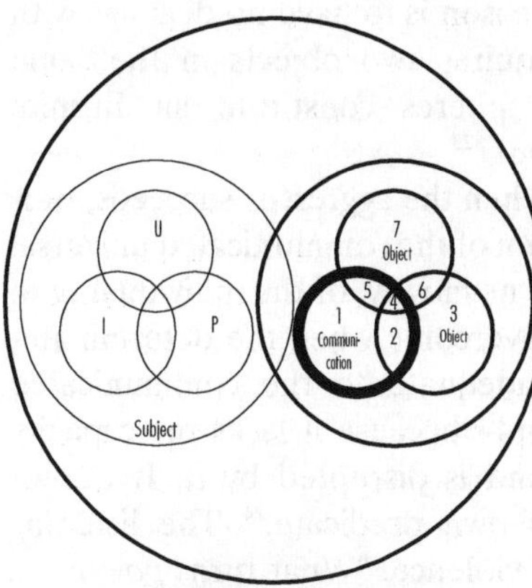

Figure 65(a)
Self-Subsistence in the Face of Communication

Real Mechanical Process is the dialectical segment of Mechanism. Accordingly, the Understanding proposes that the object is what it is because of Communication.[22]

Dialectical Reason asserts that the obverse is true: Communication functions only because it has objects to work on. It depends on the *resistance* of the listening object to the speaking object. "The *weaker* can be seized and penetrated by the *stronger* only in so far as it accepts the latter and constitutes one *sphere* with it." (719) When the listening object goes limp, Communication fails. Hegel gives as an example a musket ball which cannot penetrate a sheet hanging free in the air. The sheet is so weak that the musket ball cannot communicate with it. In human affairs, "the wholly feeble spirit is safer from the strong spirit than one that stands nearer to the strong.

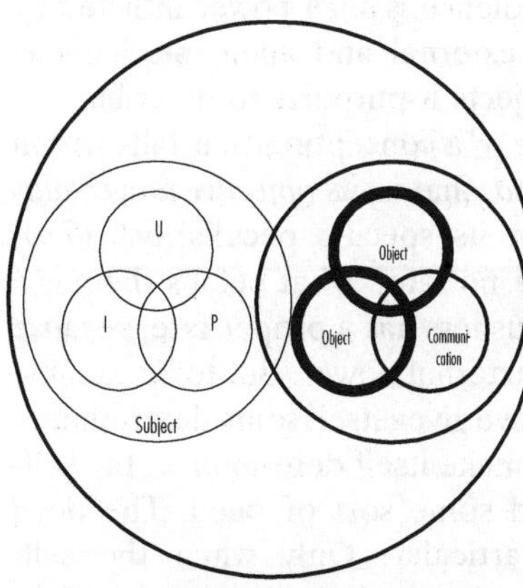

Figure 65(b)
The Non-Self-Subsistence of Communication

[22] Hegel suggests that the Individuality of the objects could be conceived as quantitative – "as a difference of the magnitude of *mass* in the bodies, or as a difference of *intensity*." (719) But this must not be permitted to obscure the point that the objects acting on each other are also "*positively* self-subsistent." (719)

Imagine if you like someone quite dull-witted and ignoble, then on such a person lofty intelligence and nobility can make no impression. The only consistent defence *against* reason is to have no dealings with it at all." (719) Communication requires two objects in the same sphere. Two objects in different spheres constitute an Infinite Judgment – "reason is not an elephant."[23]

Resistance is the precise moment when the aggressor succeeds; "it is the incipient moment of the distribution of the communicated universal and of the positing of the self-related negativity, of the individuality to be established." (720) Resistance is overcome when the determinateness of the "listening" object is inadequate to the communicated universal. The listening object succumbs because it lacks the capacity to absorb what is commu-nicated and is disrupted by it. It cannot integrate the communication as its own predicate.[24] The listening object is, at this point, the victim of violence. "What turns *power* . . . into violence is this, that though power, an objective universality, is *identical* with the *nature* of the object, [power's] determinateness or negativity is not [the listening object's] own *negative reflection* into itself by which it is an individual." (720) Violence is *alien* power inflicted by another object. And, since Rest is external and alien, mechanistic determinism is violence upon the objects it purports to describe.

When violence is objective, it is *fate* – "a conception that falls within mechanism in so far as it is called *blind*, that is, its *objective universality* is not recognized by the subject in its specific peculiarity." (720) Animate beings other than man have no fate; "what befalls them is a contingency." (720) Only self-consciousness has a proper fate, because it can resist and estrange itself from external power. But to be capable of resisting, self-consciousness must have given itself some determinateness which alien fate can disrupt. To make itself determinate, the self-conscious ego must have committed some sort of deed. The deed renders the subject visible and Particular. Only when the self-consciousness is existent is it "open to the communication of its estranged essence." (721)[25] When self-consciousness is estranged from its essence, it enters into a relationship of mechanism between itself and alien power.

---

[23] *Supra* at 474.

[24] The Lacanians would call this disruption "trauma." *See* David Gray Carlson, *The Traumatic Dimension in Law*, 24 CARDOZO L. REV. 2287 (2003).

[25] Here one recalls Hegel's praise of Infinite Judgment (*i.e.*, crime), "since it is an actual deed." (642)

(c) The Product of the Mechanical Process

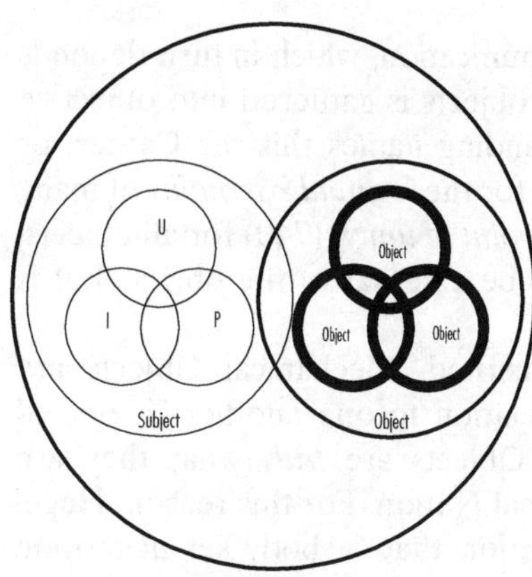

Figure 65(c)
Oneness of the Object

The object at Rest is the product of Communication; determinateness of objects seems posited by external reflection. Rest is "the original formalism of the object" (721) and the negation of the object's *self*-determination. But Real Mechanical Process proves that Communication absolutely requires self-subsistent objects. As a result "mere *semblance of individuality* . . . has been sublated." (721) Genuinely notional Individuality – the unity of the Universal and the abstract Universal (or Particular) – is reinstated. This is the final result of Mechanism's "reflective" segment. The object now depends on Communication and Communication depends on it. The object is this very unity.

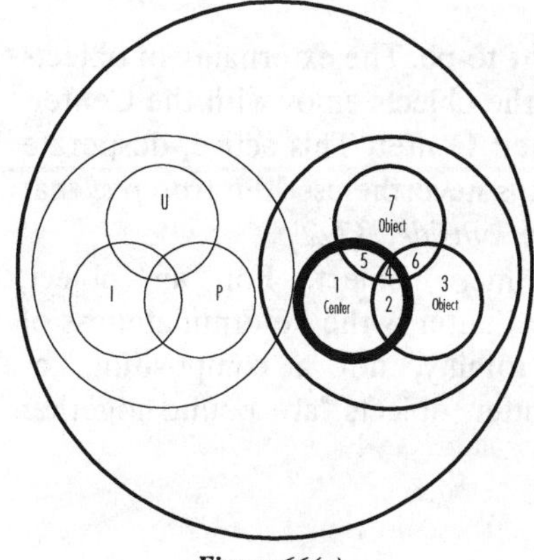

Figure 66(a)
The Center

This unity is not a proper "fate." Rather than facing an alien power, the object encounters its own power and is therefore "a fate immanently determined and rational – a universality that *particularizes itself from within*." (721) Furthermore, the object is established as active difference *and* Rest – a "constant in the unstable particularity of objects." This Hegel identifies as Law – "the truth, and therefore also the foundation, of the mechanical process." (721) We will revisit Law two sections hence.

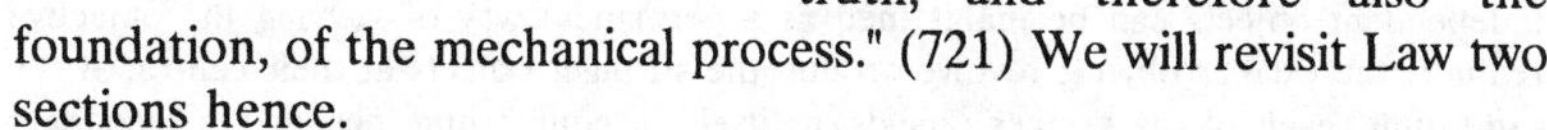

C. Absolute Mechanism

(a) The Center

The object now depends on Communication, which in turn depends on objects. The "empty manifold of objects is gathered into objective individuality." (721-2) The Understanding names this the Center, or "central body." (722) Oddly, it stands for the "*mutual externality* of many objects." The Center is "the *negative point of unity*" (740) for all objects. It *is* the Notion, which appeared to be external to the objects but is now revealed as posited by them.

In so far as this Center is concerned, Mechanical Objects are "unessential single bodies" whose relation to one another "is one of mutual *thrust* and *pressure*." (722) Objects are *truly* what they are because of their relation to a universal Notion. For this reason, Hegel finds empty the Newtonian assumption that "a body set in motion would continue to move in a straight line to infinity if external resistance did not rob it of its motion." (722) External resistance is in truth internal to the object; what is called external resistance is the workings of Centrality itself. The Center is no longer external to the single objects. The single objects are not at Rest in their unity with the notional Center.[26]

This unity, however, is still an ought-to-be. The externality of objects does not correspond with the unity the objects enjoy with the Center. The objects merely strive toward their Center. This active, desperate striving is what Rest has become. It is nevertheless "the true *rest* that is itself *concrete* and not *posited from outside*." (722)

The Center is therefore no mere object. For an object, determinateness is unessential. The Center *is* the determinateness of objects – *explicitly* an objective totality, not a composition, as Mechanical Objects are. In the Center, objects "are bound together into a genuine One." (723)

---

[26] In this respect, I disagree with John Burbidge, who thinks that the dynamic in question is about a hierarchy of self-sufficient objects: "The mechanical perspective of independent objects can be maintained as a permanent way of viewing the objective realm if the weaker objects revolve around the stronger objects at their centre; at the same time, each of the weaker objects, as itself an equilibrium, becomes a secondary centre. A mechanical system of this sort has a persistent pattern, the principles of which can be conceptually identified, and understood as laws." BURBIDGE, REAL PROCESS, *supra* note 9, at 78. Rather, the Center is no material *object* but is the very determinacy of *all* material objects.

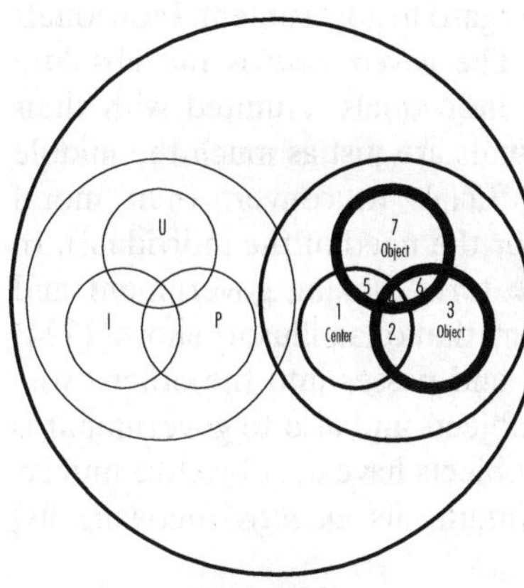

Figure 66(b)
The Extremes

Dialectical Reason complains that the Center in Figure 66(a) has no extremes and so is no Center. It must sunder itself so that the extremes are visible. In Figure 66(b), "the previously non-self-subsistent, self-external objects are . . . by the regress of the Notion determined into individuals." (723) The self-identity of the Center, then, is only an ought-to-be. It is still "infected with *externality*." (723) But in sundering itself in this way, the Center communicates objective Individuality to the extremes. The extremes are now just as central as the Center.

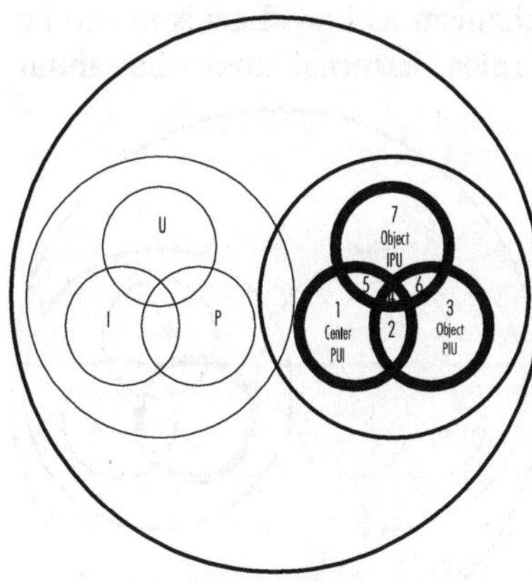

Figure 66(c)
Free Mechanism

Speculative Reason draws from the two preceding steps a trio of syllogisms which are named Free Mechanism. Figure 66(a) is *PUI*. Here, the Center (*U*) gives way to the Individuals who are the true Center of the system. The Center in turn subsumes the more primitive objects whose determinateness is communicated to it and whose significance is external to themselves.

Figure 66(b) is *PIU* (the Syllogism of Reflection). Here the Universal Center subsumes the Individual. But the Individual in turn subsumes those objects that are less than Individuals – the earlier non-self-subsistent objects.

Finally, the non-self-subsistent objects (*P*) become the middle term in a Syllogism of Existence, "in that they are the link between the absolute and the relative central individuality." (723) In *IPU*, the Individuals of Figure 66(b) require externality, and their very relation-to-self is "a *striving* toward an absolute centre." (723) The primitive formal objects are said to be the *gravity* that pulls together the Center and the notional Individual objects.

Hegel draws similar syllogisms with regard to government. Individuals and their needs are the extremes. "The *government* is the absolute centre in which the extreme of the individuals is united with their external existence." (724) But Individuals are just as much the middle term, who activate governmental officials to convert their moral essence into actuality (by providing for the need of the individual). In a third syllogism, *need* is the middle term, linking government and individuals. But this is "formal syllogism, that of an illusory show." (724) Such a syllogism is merely subjective and passes into the other two.

The three syllogisms applicable to objects and also to government is Free Mechanism. "In it the different objects have . . . objective universality, the *pervasive* gravity that maintains its *identity* [following its] *particularization*." (724)

(b) Law

The Understanding sees Free Mechanism as Law. Law is not to be confounded with the imposition of rules. External theorizing about objects is the imposition of order. The theorizing scientist who imposes order establishes *rules*. "Dead mechanism" (725) trafficks in objects that ought to be self-subsistent but are not. "This uniformity is indeed a *rule*, but not a *law*. Only free mechanism has a *law*." (725) As non-self-subsistent, objects have their center outside themselves. This process of pointing to others for their being passes over to Rest and is marked by contingency. This contingency – "*formal uniformity*" (725) – is the external reflection which organizes the objects into mere rules. The Law, then, is that there must be rules.

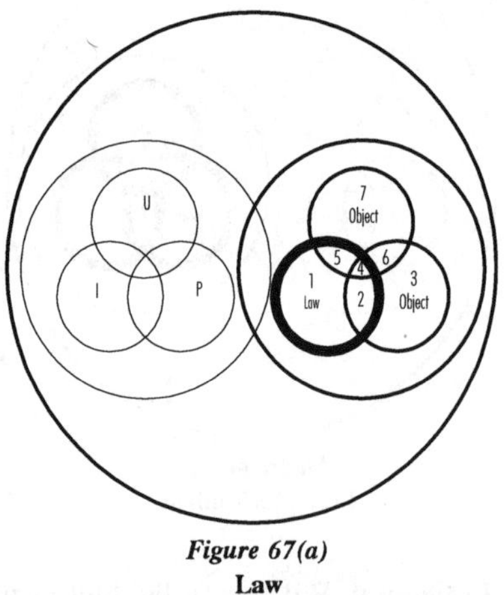

Figure 67(a)
Law

The difference between ideality and External Reality now becomes prominent. This is the dialectic moment of Law. Law must have an external reality to work on. The object has withdrawn into itself and has become Law, but there now arises the opposition of Law – "*simple centrality*" (724) – to the externality governed by Law. Law posits this externality as that which is not in and for itself – the opposite of Law.

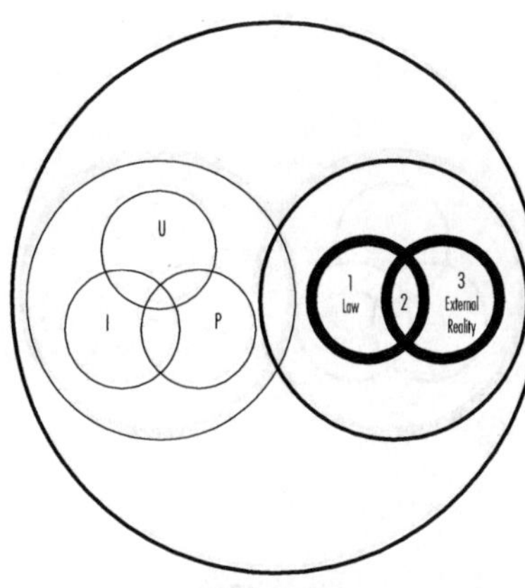

Figure 67(b)
Law and External Reality

External reality ought to exhibit the unity of the Notion. But, so far, external reality only strives for and cannot correspond to this.

Meanwhile, Law's individuality is "*in and for itself the concrete principle of negative unity*." (724) It is a totality. But being negative and concrete, it must exhibit difference. Law is therefore "a unity that sunders itself into the *specific differences of the Notion*." (724) This externality is, however, an internal externality. The totality continues to abide within itself. "[I]t is thus the centre *expanded* within its pure ideality by *difference*." (725) Law therefore reduces objectivity to ideality and renders subjective Individuality into an external objectivity. Law is indeed the very animating principle by which this is accomplished. It is precisely "the spontaneous determination of pure individuality or *of the explicated Notion*." (725)

The ideality of Law is nevertheless to be distinguished from the external reality that is merely a striving. Ideality takes difference up into pure Universality. "This real ideality is the *soul* of the previously developed objective totality, *the absolutely determined identity* of the system." (725)

(c) Transition of Mechanism

The soul of Law is still submerged. The Notion is determinate but inner. Law has not yet confronted its object. When it does, we have reached the level of Chemism. In Chemism, objects include both the self-subsistent Individuals of the totality, and also the more primitive non-Individual objects. Both types of objects face the Law, and Law is immanent in them. Solely in ideal Centrality and its laws do objects possess self-subsistence. The object has repeatedly proved powerless to resist the judgment of the Notion and to maintain itself abstractly. "By virtue of the ideal difference immanent in [the other], its externality is a *determinateness posited by the Notion*." (726)

The Center has fallen asunder. Its unity has passed over to "*objectified opposition*." (726) The external object now strives, not toward the internal object (Law) specifically opposed to it, but to a higher reality. A new centrality is now established as a relation of these negative objectivities in a state of mutual tension. Free Mechanism is now Chemism.[27]

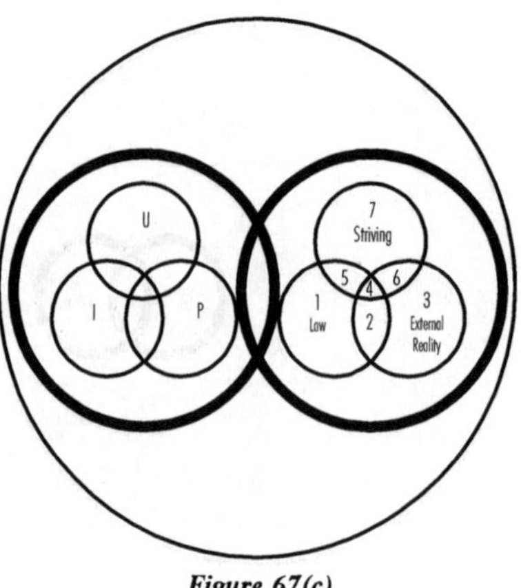

Figure 67(c)
Chemism

What should not be missed in Mechanism is the fact that Mechanical Objects were "indifferent to being determined and . . . equally indifferent to be a determinant." (740) *External* determinedness, posited by Mechanical Objects, has itself become a self-determining *notional* object.[28] This Notion is at first merely the in-itself of the objects. When it becomes for-itself, we will have reached the End – prelude to the Idea.

[27] According to Burbidge, "A mechanical object is complete in itself and indifferent to whatever happens to it. Any movement of change intervenes from outside. In contrast, a chemical object is to be oriented towards another." BURBIDGE, REAL PROCESS, *supra* note 9, at 80. One may question, however, whether indifferent objects are more "complete" than chemical objects.

[28] Hegel emphasizes that the indifference of Mechanical Objects is absolutely essential to the very existence of subjectivity, which needs objects to become subject: "The indifference of the objective world to the determinateness, and consequently to the end, constitutes its external capability of being conformable to the subject." (771)

23
Chemism

In the shortest chapter of the *SL*,[1] we learn that Chemism's "immediate course is simple and is completely determined by presupposition." (727) Figure 67(c) portrays this. There, the Chemical Object strives toward an other object (which is to be viewed as the notional Subject). This other is completely presupposed by the Chemical Object (though, for us, the notional Subject is derived and therefore objective). Hegel admits the name "chemism" is unfortunate. It is not to be taken as referring only to chemistry. It also governs sex, love, friendship and the weather.

The steps in Chemism "are so many stages by which *externality* and *conditionedness* are sublated and from which the Notion emerges as a totality determined in and for itself." (732) This consummates in Teleology, the portal to the Idea.

Chemism's path is, first, formal (merely potential) Neutrality, which Hegel identifies with Particularity. Second is Actualized Neutrality, which represents Individuality. The first two steps entail striving and stasis respectively. The final stage of Chemism is the unity of idealized striving and actual stasis – the Universality of the object. At this point, the externality on which the object depended becomes internalized.

---

[1] John Burbidge thinks that this chapter is not only short but obscure, as "Hegel did not have time to sort out all the details." JOHN W. BURBIDGE, REAL PROCESS: HOW LOGIC AND CHEMISTRY COMBINE IN HEGEL'S PHILOSOPHY OF NATURE 98 (1996)

A. The Chemical Object

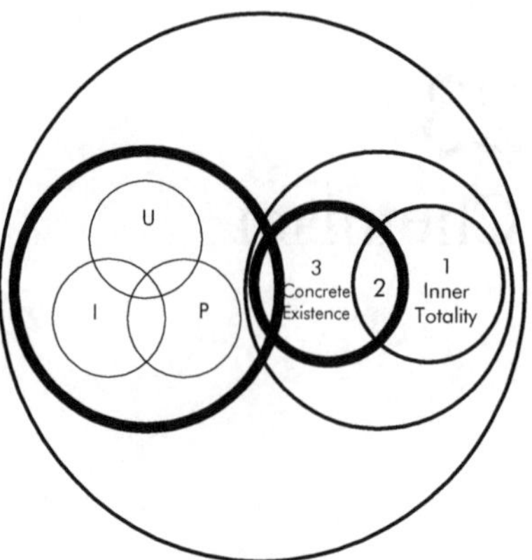

Figure 68(a)
The Chemical Object

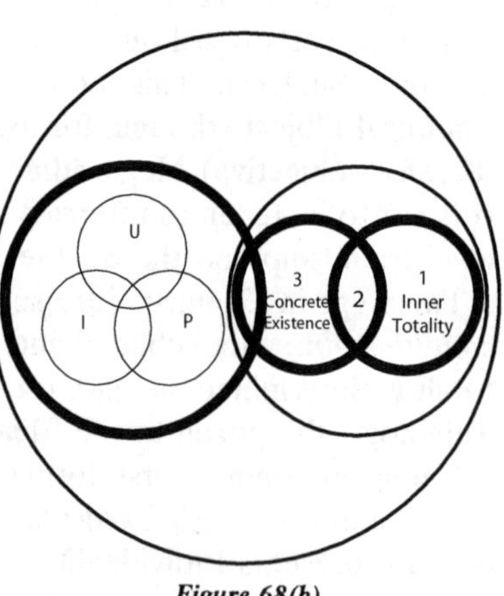

Figure 68(b)
Chemical Process

The Mechanical Object, indifferent to determinateness, was a mere pointing toward some other object as its ground. It was therefore the Mechanical Process. The Chemical Object, however, is determinate. It "exhibits the inherent relationality of essence."[2] Law has communicated determinacy to the object. The Chemical Object is therefore *Particular*, conforming in general to the dialectical position it occupies within the realm of Objectivity.

The Understanding proposes that the Chemical Object determines itself (Law) *and* its other (external reality). What the Chemical Object must do is to sublate its external existence and become "that *real whole* that according to its Notion it is." (727)[3]

The Chemical Object represents a totality that is reflected into itself and out of itself. "[A] chemical object is not comprehensible from itself alone, and the being of one is the being of the other." (728) It is therefore "a *striving* to sublate the determinateness of its existence and to give concrete existence to the objective

---

[2] Stephen Houlgate, *Why Hegel's Concept is not the Essence of Things*, in HEGEL'S THEORY OF THE SUBJECT 20 (David Gray Carlson ed., 2005).

[3] *See* J.N. Findlay, *Hegel and Whitehead on Nature*, in HEGEL AND WHITEHEAD: CONTEMPORARY PERSPECTIVES ON SYSTEMATIC PHILOSOPHY 161 (George R. Lucas, Jr., ed. 1986) (in the chemical process "matter tries to negate its spatio-temporal self-externality").

totality of the Notion." (728) In psychoanalytic terms, it is *desire*.[4]

B. The Chemical Process

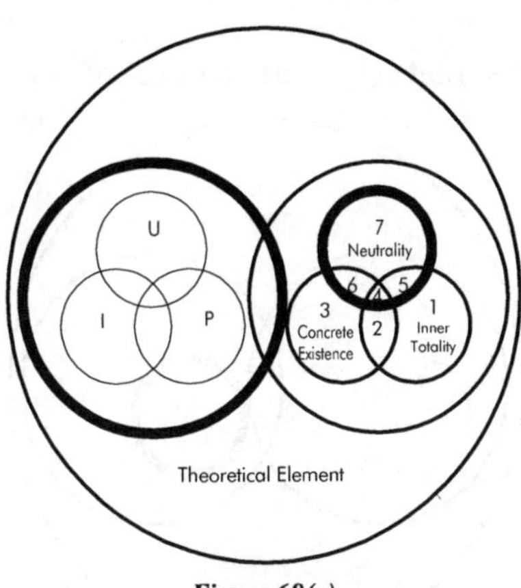

Figure 68(c)
Abstract Neutrality

The Chemical Object lacks self-subsistence. But "it spontaneously tenses itself against this deficiency and initiates the *process* by its self-determining." (728) It is tensed against itself but is just as much tensed against other Chemical Objects. Chemical Objects therefore are in a relation of *affinity*. In this process each object strives to overcome the one-sidedness of the other object and establish its own reality conformable to its Notion – a reality in which both objects will play a part. Each wishes to posit the middle term which is the true implicit nature of each.

Since each object has its being in the other, only external compulsion keeps them apart. But external intervention is needed to assure their transformation – a "*theoretical element*" (728) in which the two objects can communicate. *Water* is the middle term in the material world. *Language* fulfills this role in the spiritual world. When the two objects communicate in this external theoretical element, they neutralize each other. Although Hegel is not clear on the matter, this reference to water or language as that on which the striving objects depend could stand for a reference to the overarching subjectivity within which objectivity plays out. It could be viewed as the ultimate outside circle in Figure 68(c).

In Abstract Neutrality, the relationship of the objects is mere communication – "a quiescent coming-together." (729) In communication, the real differences of objects are reduced to unity. Opposition

---

[4] Chemism is therefore psychoanalytic. According to Lacanian theory, the human subject desires something that supposedly will complete it (the *objet petit a*). The objet petit *a* is some positive thing – a prize, a love object which we *must* have to complete our sense of self. The objet *a*, however, simply masks over a void which is constitutive of the human subject. *See* BRUCE FINK, THE LACANIAN SUBJECT: BETWEEN LANGUAGE AND *JOUISSANCE* 83 (1995).

and tension weaken. The chemical process is extinguished. The contradiction between the Notion and reality is resolved. The extremes of the syllogism have lost their opposition and have ceased to be extremes.

The Understanding now proposes that the true nature of the Chemical Object is Neutral Product. In the Neutral Product, the ingredients can no longer be called objects, because they have lost their tension. "[I]t is an externally applied differentiation that rekindles it; conditioned by an immediate presupposition, it exhausts itself in it." (732)

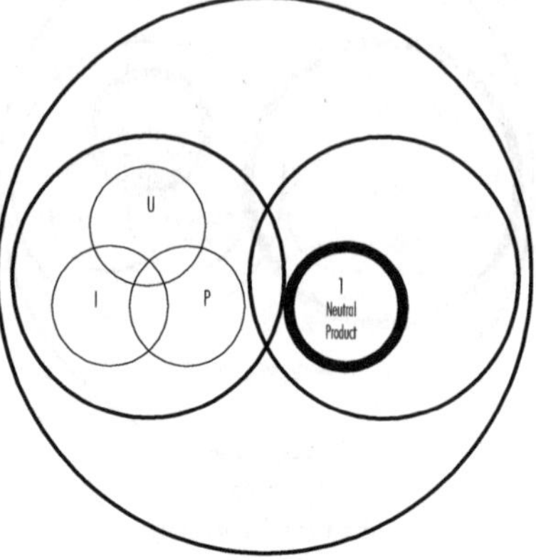

Figure 69(a)
Neutral Product

Dialectical Reason protests that the Neutral Product presupposes pre-neutral Chemical Objects which it has neutralized. It recollects that Neutrality is grounded in the history of desire. The capability of the former objects for tension *and* self-subsistence is therefore preserved. Neutral Product is therefore revealed to be mere formal unity.

Speculative Reason reconciles these two positions. In the Neutral Product, tension is extinguished. But the unity between Neutral Products and their ingredients is essential to the Notion. The two must exist together in a concrete way. Tension is still present, though its place is outside the neutral object. In Figure 69(c), the process of neutralization does not spontaneously rekindle itself. The existence of striving objects is only presupposed, not posited. They are a present memory, but not a presence. Tension exists in an ideal way, alongside the Neutral Product. This ideality implies that the Neutral Product is indeed divisible into the tensed parts that had existed prior

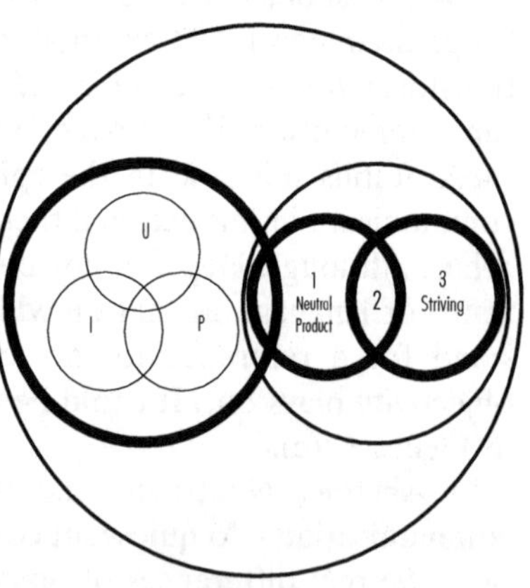

Figure 69(b)
Preservation of Tension

to mutual neutralization. "The neutral body is therefore capable of disintegration."[5]

The middle term that mediates Neutrality and Tension, Hegel says, is a Disjunctive Syllogism. Disjunctive Syllogism, it will be recalled, was Syllogism's finale. In it, the middle term was just as much located in the extremes as in the middle. The Understanding concluded that Disjunctive Syllogism was the Mechanical Object.[6]

By calling the new object a Disjunctive Syllogism, Hegel implies that the object is both unified and disrupted. It is disrupted in the sense that *moments* can still be identified. But the Chemical Objects no longer strive to sublate themselves in neutrality. Rather, the parts are *indifferent* to each other and sustain themselves in unity. An abstract indifferent base exists on one side, against which "the *energizing* principle" (730) stands. The energizing principle thus attains the form of indifferent objectivity.[7]

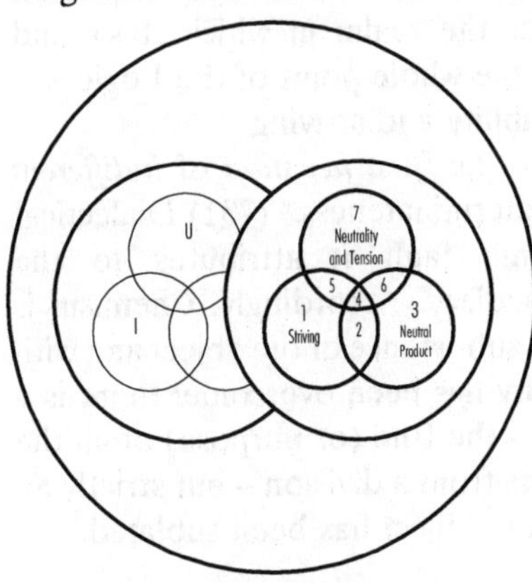

Figure 69(c)
Neutrality and Tension
(End)

The Chemical Object is now exhibited as a negative unity with discernable extremes [4, 5, 6] and as a real unity [7]. To the extent parts of the whole are discernable, they are "liberated from chemical tension." (731) This result counts as the positing of the presupposition with which Chemism began. It will be recalled that the Chemical Object was the pure striving to join with its other. That there *was* an other was merely presupposed. Now the other has been discovered and acknowledged.

---

5 EL § 202, at 266-7.

6 *See* BURBIDGE, *supra* note 1, at 88 (Disjunctive Syllogism is "a comprehensive operation [that] mediates by both distinguishing a concept into disjuncts and recognizing that they exhaust its full description").

7 According to Burbidge, Chemism has three processes: "differentiated objects are combined into a neutral product by way of a neutral medium; a negative activity breaks apart a neutral product into its elements; elements are distributed among objects, thereby differentiating them." BURBIDGE, *supra* note 1, at 161.

C. Transition of Chemism

> Even ordinary chemistry shows examples of chemical alterations in which a body imparts a higher oxidation to one part of its mass and thereby reduces another part to a lower degree of oxidation, in which lower degree alone it can enter into a neutral combination with another different body brought into contact with it, a combination for which it would not have been receptive in that first immediate degree. (731)[8]

Chemism in a sense has returned to its beginning. Striving exists, and neutrality results. But striving survives.[9] Chemism "by this return into its *Notion* sublates itself and has passed over into a higher sphere." (731) Teleology (or End) represents the realm in which stasis and striving coexist side by side. Indeed, the whole point of the Logic was to provide for the coexistence of stability and striving.

Chemism is generally dialectical – the "*first negation* of *indifferent* objectivity and of the *externality* of determinateness." (731) Dialectical Reason always manifests the same fault it attributes to the Understanding – a reliance on immediacy. Accordingly, Chemism is "still infected with the immediate self-subsistence of the object and with externality." (731) But now externality has been overcome; there is a merger of subject and object, which is the End (or purpose) of all the *SL*. End is pre-Idea, which still suffers from a division – but strictly an *internal* division. The externality of the object has been sublated.

---

[8] This describes what chemists call disproportionation. An example: $2HClO_2$ ▸ $HClO+Clo_3H$. BURBIDGE, *supra* note 1, at 235-6 & n.2; *see also id*. at 92 ("Here we do not have one object immediately directed towards another, but intermediate steps are taken with an eye to the whole picture. The totality of the initial ratio (or concept) generates the conditions it needs to establish a real connection with something else, thereby bringing its 'concept' to reality."). Another example postdating Hegel's time involves dielectrism. According to Mure, "the consequent change in electrical charge at the point from which or towards which the shift has occurred serves to initiate chemical reaction with another molecule, and so to produce a fresh compound." G.R.G. MURE, A STUDY OF HEGEL'S LOGIC 244 n.2 (1950).

[9] ERROL E. HARRIS, AN INTERPRETATION OF THE LOGIC OF HEGEL 266 (1983) ("Here we are concerned primarily with the logical relation between simply self-identity and identity in and through difference as the categories of Essence are *aufgehoben*. and exemplified in mechanism and chemism respectively"). Charles Taylor remarks that the Chemism chapter is "pretty heavily indebted to chemical speculations of the time as they were taken up in contemporary philosophies of nature. Hence this chapter is both hard to follow, and unconvincing." CHARLES TAYLOR, HEGEL 321 (1975). Yet what it establishes is what should be very familiar – the unity of stasis and striving, or, to say the same thing, the unity of identity and difference.

24
Teleology

Purposiveness, a great Kantian word,[1] signifies the "future possibility of an object, at which the object is aimed . . . "[2] For Hegel, the future object is Absolute Knowing, which comes about when Notion purges itself of externality. End (*Zweck*) produces itself and for this very reason is purposive. "Where *purposiveness* is discerned," Hegel writes, "an *intelligence* [*Verstand*] is assumed as its author." (734) Having discerned purposiveness, we demand that the "Notion's own free Existence" (734) should be the author of itself.

Teleology is about *final*, not *efficient* or mechanical cause. In efficient cause, externality usurps the place of self-determination. Yet Teleology properly belongs to the *object* (not the subject). At stake in the dialectic between Mechanism and Teleology is "whether the absolute essence of the world is to be conceived as blind natural mechanism or as an intelligence that determines itself in accordance with ends." (734) Fatalism and freedom are in the balance.

While Hegel opts for freedom, this is not to say there is no place in philosophy for mechanistic causation. The truth of Mechanism, however, is more fully expressed in the higher truth of Teleology. End

1 IMMANUEL KANT, CRITIQUE OF JUDGMENT 17 (J.H. Bernhard trans., 1951) ("The agreement of a thing with that constitution of things which is only possible according to purposes is called the *purposiveness* of its form.").

2 Daniel O. Dahlstrom, *Hegel's Appropriation of Kant's Account of Teleology in Nature*, in HEGEL AND THE PHILOSOPHY OF NATURE 168 (Stephen Houlgate ed., 1998).

– Notion in its free Existence – has proven to be the truth of Mechanism and Chemism. Opposed to End is the unfreedom of Notion, "its submergence in externality." (735)

This critique proves that the objective world is capable of error: "Just as the subjective understanding also exhibits errors in itself, so the objective world also exhibits aspects and stages of truth that by themselves are still one-sided, incomplete and only relationship in the sphere of Appearance." (734) Error will constitute the reason why observing reason cannot reliably induce a Universal from given Particulars. Nature is full of non-notional as well as notional materials.[3]

Mechanism and Chemism, then, stand for necessary unfreedom. The Mechanical Object is not self-determining. In Chemism, the Notion either has a one-sided Existence in tension or, as the unity that disjoins the neutral object into tensed extremes, Chemism is dependent on external force and so is external to itself.

End, then, is be found in nature, not in some unknowable beyond.[4] Piety favors linking Teleology with an "*extramundane* intelligence," (735) a bias tending to separate itself from the investigation of nature. A true study of nature aims at immanent knowledge. Yet, Hegel complains, science nevertheless thinks Mechanism, not Teleology, is nature's truth, even though Teleology is the product of immanent development. Yet, in Mechanism, "an essential moment of the totality always lies in something outside it." (735) Mechanism is therefore finite knowledge, always devolving into the bad infinity of cause and effect. So conceived, Mechanism is chemistic, because it strives for a totality it never achieves.

When piety imagines an external God – a Finite End – that serves to unify all objects, it misconceives the notion of Teleology. Content, in such a view, is finite, contradicting what Teleology ought to be, "for end, according to its form, is a totality *infinite within itself*." (736) The *purpose* should be to evolve toward Idea. Mere finite end, however, seems external and therefore unbelievable. In comparison to this,

---

[3] On irrationality's role, see Iain Macdonald, *The Concept and Its Double: Power and Powerlessness in Hegel's Subjective Logic*, in HEGEL'S THEORY OF THE SUBJECT 73 (David Gray Carlson ed. 2005).

[4] *See* CHARLES TAYLOR, HEGEL 321 (1975) ("living things . . . provide the best example of Hegel's category here. For living things have a form which is inherent in them. That is, the form is not imposed by the hazard of outside efficient causes, but is one which they realize themselves as they grow.").

Mechanism does not purport to find any purpose in the objects it considers. When the ego confronts mechanism and Finite End – which is dismissed as an unproved form of Mechanism – it feels infinite freedom. Finite End sets up as absolute "what is trivial and even contemptible in its content," (736) compared to what egotism beholds in a merely mechanistic universe. Finite End "only goes as far as *external purposiveness*." (736) We therefore have only the *form* of purposiveness. Yet, properly, Teleology arises from Mechanism itself.

The Third Antinomy. Kant did great service to philosophy by distinguishing between external and internal purposiveness, Hegel says. Reason was raised by Kant above mere reflective determinations, and Kant was important in opposing freedom and necessity in his third antinomy.[5] According to this antinomy, there is an uncaused thing, or everything is caused. Proof is apagogic: each side is proved by showing its opposite to be impossible. Hegel's contempt for apagogy continues: "The whole round-about method of proof could therefore be spared; the proof consists in nothing but the assertorical affirmation of the two opposed propositions." (738) According to Hegel, Kant bids thinkers to pass from thesis to antithesis according to subjective whim; "this whole standpoint fails to examine the sole question to which philosophic interest demands an answer, namely, which of the two principles possesses truth in and for itself." (739)

Kant knew, of course, that the third antinomy could be solved only dogmatically. Reason therefore licenses but does not require a belief or disbelief in freedom. "They are treated as subalterns rather than as contraries."[6] Hegel, however, insists that the truth of the matter is accessible through reason. And the truth is that each side of the antinomy has its moment of truth.

Hegel does draw a lesson from Kant's discussion of the third antinomy: the unity between the two sides is located in a reflective judgment. For Kant, if only the particular is given, for which the universal must be found, the judgment is reflective. It ascends from the particular to the universal.[7] Reflective judgment points to a middle term between universal reason and subjective intuition. For Hegel, the middle term that subsumes the two sides of the antinomy is Idea.

Properly conceived, End is the concrete Universal, "which possesses

---

[5] *Supra* at 100-2, 423.

[6] HENRY E. ALLISON, KANT'S TRANSCENDENTAL IDEALISM: AN INTERPRETATION AND DEFENSE 38 (1983).

[7] CRITIQUE OF JUDGMENT, *supra* note 1, at 15-6.

in its own self the moment of particularity and externality and is therefore active and the urge to repel itself from itself." (739) That is to say, externality was sublated at the end of Chemism and therefore preserved. This externalizing of externality was a self-externalizing – an actualization of what End is. In short, End is manifestation/externalization of self through the act negating all externality.[8]

End still acknowledges a division between internal and external. It is therefore a judgment – an original partition. But it is no longer a *subjective* judgment. It is *objective*, because the subject of the judgment is already *proven*. The other to such a subject is not merely a predicate but is the subject's own external objectivity.

This judgment is not, however, a Kantian reflective judgment "that considers external objects only according to a unity, *as though* an intelligence had given this unity *for the convenience of our cognitive faculty*." (739) Rather, it is necessary that the subject-object now show its objectivity by shedding its externality through negative activity. The end-relation is therefore more than judgment; "it is the *syllogism* of the self-subsistent free Notion that unites itself with itself through objectivity," (739)

So far, End has proven to be the third to Mechanism and Chemism. It is, however, still in the sphere of objectivity, which is its fault. End – the objectivity of the subject – still confronts an objective world to which it is related.

In Mechanism, Notion was external to Mechanical Objects. Chemism brought Notion into a unity with its other. End is the middle term between the neutrality of Mechanism and the striving in Chemism – the realm in which stasis and striving coexist.

A. Subjective End

End is both the urge to posit externally (Tension, or self-repellant

---

[8] Terry Pinkard finds Teleology deficient, because it is "empirically vacuous." TERRY PINKARD, HEGEL'S DIALECTIC 91 (1988). That is, Hegel does not tell us what the *goal* is. "Either one must extrapolate it from observation of current processes, or it must be revealed to one – most likely through some kind of religious vision." *Id*. In truth, the goal is *known and derived*. The goal is to purge Notion of any dependence on external reflection. Angelica Nuzzo, *The End of Hegel's Logic: Absolute Idea as Absolute Method*, in HEGEL'S THEORY OF THE SUBJECT, *supra* note 3, at 87. For Pinkard, teleology can only be a *subjective* state. PINKARD, *supra*, at 92-3. But this overlooks the Ought – the imperative that finite *objects* must logically cease to be. That is their *purpose*.

negativity) and immunity from transition (Neutrality).[9] It is an advanced True Infinite – "the unity that repels itself from itself and in so doing maintains itself." (740) This contradiction is precisely "the *rational in its concrete existence.*" (741) Rationality consists in holding objective difference in unity. As rational, Subjective End is a syllogism – a middle term that simultaneously refers to its extremes.

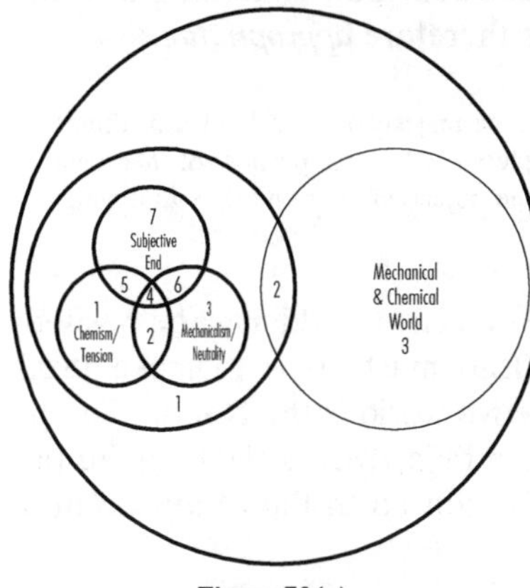

Figure 70(a)
Subjective End

The moments of Notion, however, still exist in mutual indifference; this is Subjective End's defect. But it is an improvement over the self-partition that Judgment was. In the Judgment of Existence, subject and predicate had self-subsistence, but such self-subsistence was mere abstract universality. Now the moments are concrete, objective, and "enclosed within the simple unity of the Notion." (741)

For Subjective (*i.e.*, unrealized) End, self-determination is distinct from external form. Because its determinateness has the form of indifference, it has the shape of presupposition. Subjective End thinks it confronts a mechanical and chemical world. Notion relates itself to this world as if it were given independently of Notion's own work.

Alienated from itself and confronted by an alien object, Subjective End must cancel the objective world and posit the world as its own.[10] Why must it do so? This urge for self-repulsion is simply the workings of the Ought, whereby the negativity of the Finite strives through self-negation to be for-itself by becoming other. For this reason, Subjective End is a new beginning – an urge to develop. (829) Here, at our advanced stage, however, self-negation does not mean Subjective End goes out of existence (like Quality, which went outside itself to become

---

[9] This very immunity means that End is *not* Force expressing itself or Substance manifesting itself in its Accidents. These earlier stages have actuality only in their effects; accordingly, "their activity is transition, against which they do not maintain themselves in freedom." (741)

[10] This absolute opposition to and obliteration of external objectivity (so that freedom can reign) is what Hegel will later call the Good. *Infra* at 589-93.

Quantity). Subjective End stays what it is even as it becomes the objective world it faces.

Unity with the object is End's realization. End is nothing but this urge for self-realization. Teleology is therefore *appropriation*:

> To appropriate is at bottom only to manifest the majesty of my will towards things, by demonstrating that they are not self-complete and have no purpose of their own. This is brought about by my instilling into the object another end than that which it primarily had.[11]

Yet, if this unity is to be realized, the objective world must be posited, not presupposed. What Subjective End must do is to make itself Particular by revealing that the objective world *is* the Notion. So far, the content of the Notion is still When objectivity is shown to be the Notion's self-expression, objectivity is reduced to the *Means* (*Mittel*), End's self-expression.

B. Means

For Subjective End to express itself, internality must posit externality. Subjective End *communicates* when it subsumes the Means. This presupposes a difference between End and its expression (*i.e.*, the objective world). The End-Means distinction is therefore the first negation in which Subjective End erases itself and renders itself external. But, having posited Means, Subjective End attacks it, like a bird that sees its reflection in a mirror. End does not recognize itself as Means.

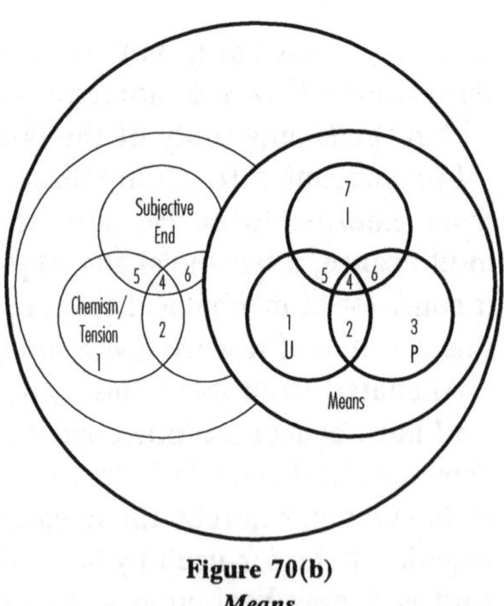

Figure 70(b)
Means

End is the soul of Means, and Means has no power against it. Means is "absolutely penetrable, and receptive of this communication, because it is *in itself* identical with the end." (745) Indeed, Means *strives* towards End like a Chemical Object.

Although Means represents Teleology's dialectic moment, it serves

---

[11] HERBERT MARCUSE, REASON AND REVOLUTION 191 (1999).

as a middle term between Subjective End and Realized End. That is to say, Means is a syllogism, standing for the proposition that End needs externality to be what it must become: "The end unites itself through a means with objectivity." (743) Means at this point "has the shape of an *external* existence indifferent to the end itself and its realization." (743)

Externality, however, is merely a show.

> The absolute Notion possesses mediation within itself in such a manner that its first positing is not a presupposing whose object would have indifferent externality for its fundamental determination; on the contrary, the world as a creation has only the form of such externality, but its fundamental determination is really constituted by its negativity and positedness. (743)

The *world* is Subjective End's expression, which now supposes its creation is external. Notion at this point "divides itself into a positing and a presupposing." (743)

So Means is only a *formal* middle term. It insists upon difference from Subjective End. Yet Means without End is an impossibility. Because it requires End and has its very being there, Means is a "*mechanical object*." (744) It is externally used by Subjective End to make itself Realized End. But Means is more advanced than Mechanical Object. As middle term to Subjective and Realized End, Means reflects the being of these two extremes. Accordingly, "in contrast to the subjective end, the means, as *immediate objectivity*, has a *universality of existence* that the subjective individuality of the end still lacks." (744) Means therefore is a totality that contains End.[12]

C. The Realized End

The activity of Subjective End was directed against the external objectivity. Now Speculative Reason points out that objectivity was the means of Subjective End's own self-realization. The key is that Subjective End's attack on externality turns out to be an attack on itself. The attack is no victory for Subjective End, for that would leave the objective world still an externality, which would simply spur the Subjective End into a bad infinity of attacks: "Were the activity again to consist in merely determining the immediate objectivity, the product

---

[12] *See* TAYLOR, *supra* note 4, at 321 (teleological explanation is "explanation out of totality").

would again be merely a means, and so on to infinity; the outcome would be only a means suitable to end, but not the objectivity of the end itself." (745) Hegel here describes the paradox of consumption as developed in the *Philosophy of Right*.[13] According to this paradox, the autonomous subject is defined as "not the object." It attacks, consumes and proves its independence from the object. But since it is defined as *not the object*, its being is *in* the object. The object must spring back again, if there is to be a subject. The subject must consume again to prove its independence. To break the cycle, the subject needs an object that resists consumption, can "recognize" the subject and can sustain a reciprocal existence over time. In short, the resisting object must *itself* be a subject; the two subjects *contractually* divide the object world between them.[14]

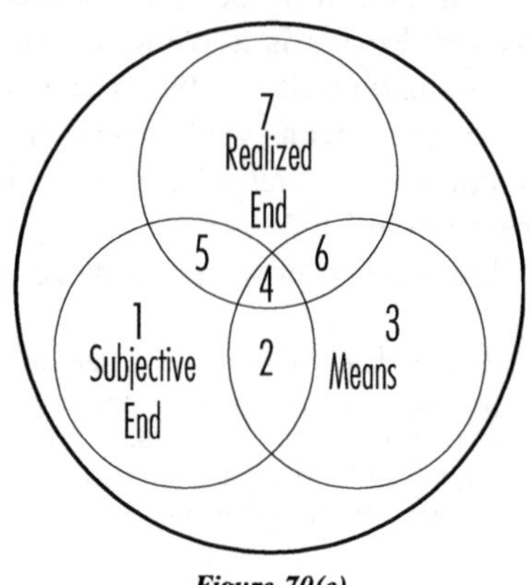

Figure 70(c)
Realized End (Idea)

Something similar happens in Realized End. To avoid a bad infinity, Means must itself be End; "consequently the object must spontaneously conform to the unity of the Notion." (746) Similarly, Subjective End must realize itself as Means to the *other* Subjective End, and the two of them together must form a joint "contractual" reality that is Realized End. For this reason, Hegel emphasizes that material externality "is not an abstract *being* subsisting on its own account over against the Notion; on the contrary, it exists only as a *becoming*." (759) In other words, nature *becomes* Notion by serving as Means to Notion.

The Spurious Infinity of End-Means is said to be the first premise in the syllogism of Teleology – [4, 5, 6] in Figure 70(b). The relation of [4, 5, 6] to Realized End [7] is the second premise – "an *immediate* relation of the middle term [7] to the other extreme [4, 5, 6]." (746) Once again, we have the paradox of an immediate mediatedness. The first premise (End-Means striving, or [4, 5, 6]) is now conceived as an

---

13 GEORG W.F. HEGEL, ELEMENTS OF THE PHILOSOPHY OF RIGHT Addition (Allen W. Wood trans. 1993).

14 *See* David Gray Carlson, *How to Do Things with Hegel*, 78 TEX. L. REV. 1377, 1384-5 (2000).

object within the immediate second relation. Against this object, the middle term [7] has its moment of indifference.

The relation between the two objects ([7] and [4, 5, 6]) is Mechanical and Chemical. Each object is indifferent to its own determination and requires the other to determine it (Mechanical). Each strives toward its other (Chemical). But these processes are now under the dominance of Realized End, taken as a whole. So the relation between Subjective End and external Means is now internalized within Realized End.

The two objects are to be taken as two subjects, each of which initially views the other as means. The attack of Subjective Ends "may be regarded as *violence* . . . in so far as the end appears to be of quite another nature than the object." (746) But in this process, violence is transformed into peace. Realized End mediates the mutual attacks; it is a new object that interposes itself between the fighting objects and "may be regarded as the *cunning of reason*." (746)[15] Notion "puts forward an object as means, allows [Subjective End] to wear itself out in its stead, exposes it to attrition and shields itself behind it from mechanical violence." (747)

In its violent mode, Subjective End is finite, not "rational" in the sense of holding objective difference in unity. The victim (Means) is the middle term between Subjective End and Realized End. Means, which turns the other cheek, is therefore superior to finite End (*i.e.*, external purposiveness). Tools are therefore more advanced than the natural inclinations served by them:

> [T]he *plough* is more honorable than are immediately the enjoyments procured by it and which are ends. The *tool* lasts, while the immediate enjoyments pass away and are forgotten. In his tools man possesses power over external nature, even though in respect of his ends he is, on the contrary subject to it. (747)[16]

Realized End is the truth of the violent Mechanical Process, and in

---

[15] The cunning of reason is "the way in which particular interests and purposes conspire, without the intention of the individual agents, to the realization of a wider and a higher end than they envisage." ERROL E. HARRIS, AN INTERPRETATION OF THE LOGIC OF HEGEL 271 (1983).

[16] It has been suggested that this passage on tools is really about the dignity of labor generally. David Lamb, *Teleology: Kant and Hegel*, in HEGEL'S CRITIQUE OF KANT 173, 175 (Stephen Priest ed., 1987); *see also id.* at 176 ("When reading Hegel one must be like a detective and search for clues . . . [T]he plough, an instrument of labour, represents human destiny. It is the key to the dialectic of history, symbolic of the relationship between man and nature").

such a process Subjective End only meets with itself. The subject is nothing apart from its interaction with the object, and so the subject has its very being *in* the object. The object's externality is mere illusory show. Externality is merely posited by the Notion, which is nothing *but* the activity of externalizing itself.

Hegel has characterized Realized End as the relation of two premises – the bad infinity of End-Means [4, 5, 6] and the middle term [7] that is separate from End-Means. The immediacy and indifference of these relations toward each other implies that Realized End "suffers from the defect of the formal syllogism in general." (749) This defect is that the premises themselves are not conclusions or mediations, but each requires proof on its own.

Consider the first premise – the End-Means relation. Subjective End cannot entirely subsume Means within this relation. Nor can Means subsume Subjective End. Neither can swallow the other. Accordingly, external reflection must interpolate a third term to mediate the two. But this interpolated term is itself Means to the End, and it too requires yet another interpolation, and so on to infinity.

The second premise – the relation of [7] and [4, 5, 6] – suffers from the same fault. Since these have a moment of diversity, they demand proof – a middle term which can only be supplied externally. But this sets up a new demand for a middle term between the middle term and its parts, etc.

> [S]ince the premisses already presuppose the *conclusion* [or missing third term], the conclusion, being based on these merely immediate premisses, can only be imperfect. The conclusion or the *product* of the purposiveness act is nothing but an object determined by an end external to it; *consequently it is the same thing as the means*. (749)

End cannot obtain objectivity by this Means. This proves that Realized End is only Means if so determined by external Subjective End. "Whatever is intended to be used for realizing an end and to be taken essentially as means, is a means which, in accordance with its destiny, is to be destroyed." (750)

There is a theological point here. When taken as an intelligent, purposive Creator who stands apart from the Created, God is reduced to Means – an external object we "use" to explain creation. Means, however, demands further interpolation of a new middle term, and so a God that stands apart from its creation must pass away, like any finite object. Only a self-creating God in unity with all the other creations can endure.

Subjective End, then, presupposes Realized End, which is Subjective End's truth as well as Mean's truth. Subjective End's attack on Means is merely illusory show and already the very sublation of the show. In Realized End, Subjective End "requires to use no violence against the object, no reinforcement against it other than the reinforcing of itself." (751) Within the confines of Realized End, Means is *supposed* to manifest the nullity of its being-in-and-for-self. And this *proves* it has being-in-and-for-self, since, by nullifying itself, it is living up to its very nature. Subjective End therefore must sacrifice itself, thereby proving it is Means to Realized End.[17] This sacrifice is the first sublation – the obliteration of selfish, immediate End. In this sacrifice, Notion is "liberated again into its subjectivity from the immediacy in which it is submerged in the object." (758)

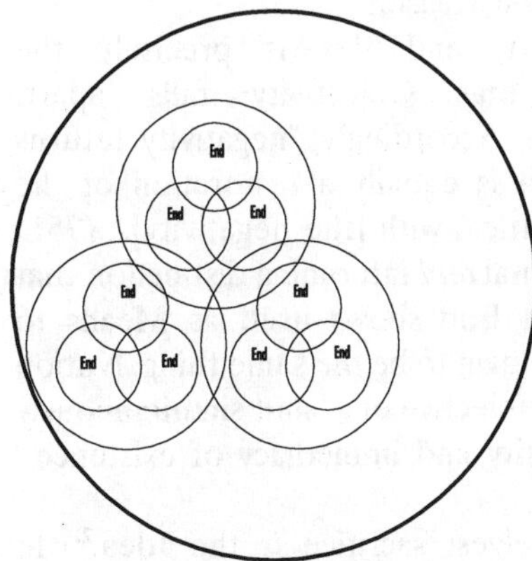

Figure 71(a)
Life (Immediate Idea)

There is a second sublation as well. Realized End is the relation of [7] and [4, 5, 6]. This relation also suffered from immediacy and in need of external proof. That means it is finite and so must pass away. But, in passing away, Realized End does not fall apart. Rather [7] and [4, 5, 6] withdraw into a perfect unity – Immediate Idea, or Life, "the first form in which the substance is conceived as subject."[18] "Life is simply Teleology 'collapsed into immediacy', a system where wholeness and unity is everywhere at work . . . "[19]

Idea, then, is Objectivity as "the total *Notion* that out of its

---

17 Teleology "reiterates the Hegelian idea that the infinite life of the world goes on through and beyond the demise of finite things. It only lives in these finite things, and hence through them, but it perpetually survives their necessary end." TAYLOR, *supra* note 4, at 326. Taylor goes on to say that "at the end of Objectivity we come to a view of the universe as unfolding in fulfillment of an intrinsic purpose." *Id.* at 328. This purpose is described as "a double movement. There is the movement of finite things which go under and succeed each other in an effort to overcome the inconsistency of finitude, to attain the self-coherence of rationality. But there is also the movement of the Idea of rationality itself, which goes out and posits a world of finite things." *Id.* at 329.

18 MARCUSE, REASON, *supra* note 11, at 38.

19 John N. Findlay, *The Hegelian Treatment of Biology and Life*, in HEGEL IN THE SCIENCES 89 (Robert S. Cohen & Marx W. Wartofsky 1984).

determinateness has withdrawn into *identity* with itself." (758) It is portrayed here as the move of the Understanding. It represents the external "proof" – the mediated cognition – that Realized End requires to vindicate itself. Are we then to conclude that Idea is an external reflection?

The answer is yes and no. Figure 71(a) represents the move of the Understanding, but Understanding has now so educated itself that it is *also* the move of Speculative Reason. That is to say, the diverse parts of Realized End now withdraw into Idea. This erasure of diverse parts is precisely what Speculative Reason *is*. Idea, then, represents the unity of the Understanding and Speculative Reason.[20]

In Idea, Objectivity falls apart, and this is precisely the Understanding's proposition – that Objectivity falls apart. Disintegration *is* the objective truth. Accordingly, "negativity returns into itself in such a manner that it is equally a restoration of the objectivity but of an objectivity identical with [the negativity]." (751) This self-identical objectivity is external *and* internal, a distinction that is now sublated. In Idea, Realized End shows itself as Means to reaching Idea. End and Means are shown to be the same thing. Notion is now "the concrete identity of the objective end" and simultaneously "the same identity as abstract identity and immediacy of existence." (752)

End and Means sacrifice themselves; sacrifice *is* the Idea.[21] In sacrifice, Notion determines itself. Its determination is its own indifference to externality and also to subjective internality. Subject and object are now *indifferent*, in the double sense of that word.

Throughout Objectivity, Notion was reciprocal action with itself. Subject presupposed predicate (or object), but the object was the subject all along. The subject maintained itself through negating the object. It lived by repulsion. Indeed, it was nothing *but* this repulsion. But the repulsion is actually a self-repulsion, because the subject was

---

[20] *See* STANLEY ROSEN, G.W.F. HEGEL: AN INTRODUCTION TO THE SCIENCE OF WISDOM 255 (1974) ("there are no subdivisions in the last chapter of the *Logic* because in it dialectic has been transformed into speculation. Dialectic is the process by which understanding is converted into reason.").

[21] Robert Wallace claims that Idea is merely announced, not proved. ROBERT M. WALLACE, HEGEL'S PHILOSOPHY OF REALITY, FREEDOM AND GOD 243 (2005). Wallace excuses Hegel because objects are finites which self-erase and lead to Idea. But this misses the fact that *both subject and object* erase themselves. Subject *is* means to the object, and *vice versa*.

as much object as subject. Hence, Idea is based on negative relation to self.[22] "[O]n this subjectivity alone rests the sublating of the opposition between Notion and reality, and the unity that is truth." (835)

Within Objectivity, the Notion was self-repellant (Mechanical), and a striving toward objectification (Chemical). These presupposed a subject-object standing over against themselves. The Subjective End tried to subjugate this mechanico-chemical world. Here Subjective End thought to meet the object but it only met itself.[23] By subjugating Means, Subjective End proved itself Means to Realized End. Meanwhile, Realized End itself proved defective, and proof of its defect is the whole Idea. In Realized End, "means and mediation are preserved [as] the *last result of the external end-relation*." (753) Sublation of mediation is precisely what Idea is. Idea, then, is "*the totality in its positedness*." (753) It is "therefore essentially this: to be distinct . . . from its *implicit* objectivity, and thereby to possess externality, yet in this external totality to be the totality's self-determining identity." (754) Notion is now Idea, "the unity of *Notion* and *reality*." (758)

---

[22] HERBERT MARCUSE, HEGEL'S ONTOLOGY AND THE THEORY OF HISTORICITY 140 (Seyla Benhabib trans. 1987).

[23] Hegel describes how Ends and Means differ from primitive Cause and Effect. See Figure 50(b). In Cause and Effect, Cause meets itself in Effect, but it doesn't really meet its other. Effect is not thereby elevated to the dignity of Cause. Meanwhile, Cause is slave to external Effect and cannot exist without it. In End and Means, Subjective End meets itself *and its other* in Means. Furthermore, Notion is free in the face of objectivity. Externality is therefore the Notion's own moment – the "form of its immanent differentiation." (748) But otherness is equally honored in Realized End. Realized End is therefore Notion as concrete but abidingly self-identical.

PART IX
IDEA

25
Life

Hegelian Idea is far more invested than "idea" in ordinary parlance – idea as a conception of some possible reality. Such ideas are *possible* but not necessarily *actual*.[1] For Hegel, Idea is the unity of Subject and Object. It is more objective than objectivity itself!

In Idea, subjective Notion contemplates itself as object. For this reason, Hegel, borrowing from Fichte,[2] calls Idea the "subject-object." (758) The object – the subject's own being repulsed in Judgment – now returns to the subject. Accordingly "the Idea fulfills what has been required . . . from the very beginning, namely, the condition that what is in motion remain thoroughly by-itself in this movement and return to itself first through this movement."[3]

---

1 Hegel credits Kant for reclaiming the term "idea" for the actuality of reason. Reason, for Kant, was unconditioned and transcendent *vis-à-vis* phenomena. *See* IMMANUEL KANT, CRITIQUE OF PURE REASON A319-29/B375-86 (Paul Guyer & Allen W. Wood trans., 1990). This meant that ideas had no empirical use. They simply allow for the theorization of perceptions. This is mere *apprehension* (*i.e.*, analytic encounter with alien reality), not *comprehension* (which involves the performative creation of an authentic reality). When comprehension is the standard, Idea is rational, efficacious and unconditioned by an alien objectivity. Kantian ideas are subjective, contingent and valueless. They supposedly transcend phenomena but are really at the same level. They contain "the *untrue being* of the objective world." (756)

2 GIACOMO RINALDI, A HISTORY AND INTERPRETATION OF THE LOGIC OF HEGEL 59 (1992).

3 HERBERT MARCUSE, HEGEL'S ONTOLOGY AND THE THEORY OF HISTORICITY 150 (Seyla Benhabib trans. 1987).

Idea's first stage is Life, wherein there are three stages. First, there is Life, where Notion "pervades its objectivity." (760) This should be interpreted as one *single* meta-Life that confronts unliving objectivity.[4] Life is the urge to negate this objectivity, and so the second stage is Life as active, dialectic *Process*. Life *requires* the object, and the object requires Life. Each sacrifices itself for the other and thereby yields the third stage of Genus Process.[5] Two *equal* Lives face each other longingly, which leads directly to Cognition, the *SL's* penultimate chapter.

A. The Living Individual

Hegel distinguishes strongly between *logical* life and *concrete* life according to the "unphilosophical sciences." (762) In studies such as anthropology or psychology, the Notion "has not yet come to have an objectivity the same as itself." (761) These studies traffick in "given" material – in external actuality. For them, life is the highest stage, representing inorganic nature's withdrawing itself into itself to produce an organic subjectivity. Organic life is therefore Means to spirit. From life arises human consciousness – the phenomenology of spirit.[6]

Logic does not originate in nature. Such an externality would count as a presupposition. Everything about logical Life is derived in the previous steps in the Logic. It stands for thought's *self-movement*. Indeed, Marcuse went so far as to claim that Life is the key to Hegel's ontology – the idea that thought is in motion.[7]

Logical Life is not to be considered an "instrument . . . of a spirit, nor as a moment of the ideal and of beauty." (763) Instrumentality portends a relation to organic reality, while ideal beauty portends the subjective life of human self-consciousness. Logical life is different from body *and* mind. For Logic, Life is *not* the highest stage. Life is only *immediate* Idea. Dialectical Reason holds that Life arises from and

---

[4] "With amazing prescience, Hegel treats the earth as an organic whole, anticipating the Gaia hypothesis only very recently put forward by James Lovelock." ERROL E. HARRIS, THE SPIRIT OF HEGEL 151 (1993).

[5] *See* G.W.F. HEGEL, PHENOMENOLOGY OF SPIRIT (A.V. Miller trans. 1977) ("Life points to something other than itself, viz. to consciousness, for which Life exists as this unity, or as genus").

[6] EL § 187 Addition ("Spirit *is* Spirit only insofar as it is mediated by Nature").

[7] Marcuse (or at least his translator) favors the term *motility* (*Bewegtheit*) of thought. MARCUSE, ONTOLOGY, *supra* note 3, at 181.

stands over against an indifferent object that it cannot yet recognize as its own self. At this point Notion is sundered. At one extreme is Idea [1], the unity of Notion and reality. At the other extreme is objectivity – one that is more advanced than previous versions, where Notion was inner and therefore apparently an external reflection. Now [3] explicitly proceeds from the Notion. What [3] stands for are the *body parts* that Soul animates. The mind-body distinction is the very last moment of opposition of subject and object. The body parts have the form of immediate Being.[8] Objectivity, "having proceeded from the Idea, is immediate being only as the *predicate* of the judgement of the Notion's self-determination." (765)[9]

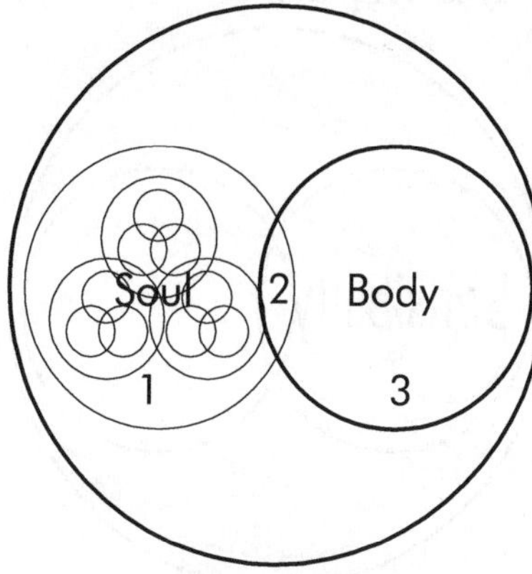

Figure 71(b)
Soul and Body

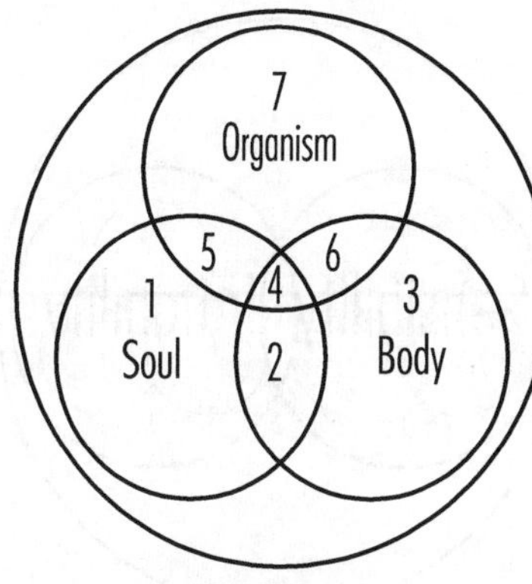

Figure 71(c)
Organism

So far, Objectivity is confronted by Idea as a negative unity, which is the true centrality of Life. Life is "essentially an individual, which relates itself to objectivity as to an *other*, to a non-living nature." (764) Standing over against its own reality, the Living Individual is Soul, "the initiating, self-moving *principle*." (765) Soul, however, is not *just* an immediacy [1]. It permeates [2, 3]. At the stage of Figure 71(b), however, there is a mind-body split. Idea so far suffers from "the form of immediate *being* which, posited on its own account,

---

[8] Although Being has been shown on the right side of the page, by now the Subject is what is objective. Properly there can be no left or right side of the page any more, so that left or right placement can be viewed as arbitrary.

[9] Marcuse therefore states that, for Hegel, *human* consciousness is *not* Idea. Rather it is a *thing* with properties. MARCUSE, ONTOLOGY, *supra* note 3, at 151-2.

is indifferent to the subject." (765) Such a Universality merely inheres in the subject. Universality is, "as it were, only *lent* to [Objectivity]." (765) The unity between Soul and body is Organism.

Life is now truly notional in structure. The Idea of Life pervades the entire organism. Parts without Life would quickly revert to the dead object world. Life is therefore an *urge* to unity but also implicated in externality.

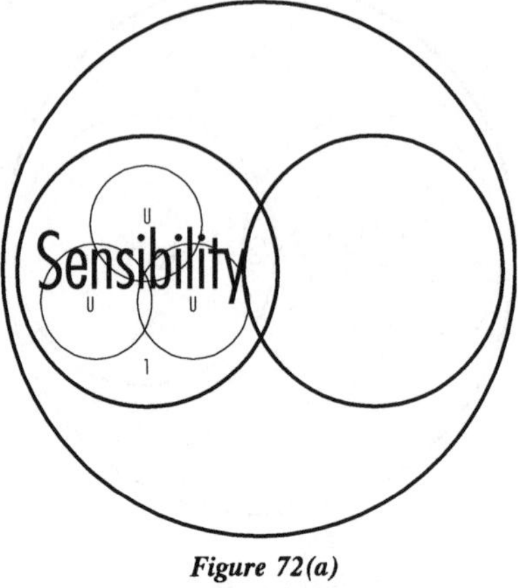

Figure 72(a)
Sensibility

The Understanding's proposition about Organism is that Universality permeates it. The Organism, made up of many body parts, *feels* like a unity. As such the Organism enjoys "the purely internal vibration of vitality, or *sensibility*." (768)

Organism, however, has difference or disunity within it. When difference is posited, the Organism manifests the dialectic moment of *irritability* – the capacity to respond to a stimulus.

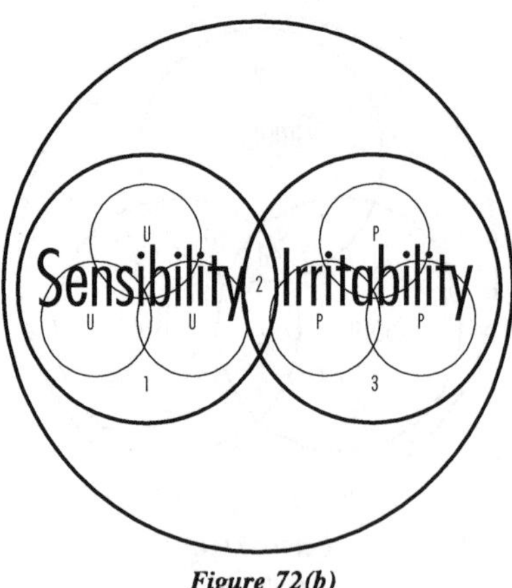

Figure 72(b)
Irritability

Life, taken in isolation, is therefore a Judgment that "detaches itself as an individual subject from objectivity." (764) It "must make differences within itself that are ultimately overcome."[10] In this guise, Life is a "subjective totality" (769) or a "subjective substance" (763) that looks forward to an objective unity not yet manifest. When this positing becomes explicit, Life becomes Particular; "it has thereby sundered itself into the two extremes of the judgement, which

---

[10] PETER SIMPSON, HEGEL'S TRANSCENDENTAL INDUCTION 43 (1998). This implies that Idea has *stages* – even though it is the *truth*. This does not disturb Marcuse. Truth is *process*, constituting the dissolution of the one-sided judgments that Idea makes of itself. MARCUSE, ONTOLOGY, *supra* note 3, at 153.

immediately becomes a syllogism." (764-5)

Upon being irritated, Organism withdraws into itself from external stimuli. But since by now externality is Organism's *own* self, its self-expression is a self-division and self-limitation. Organism splits in multiple parts.

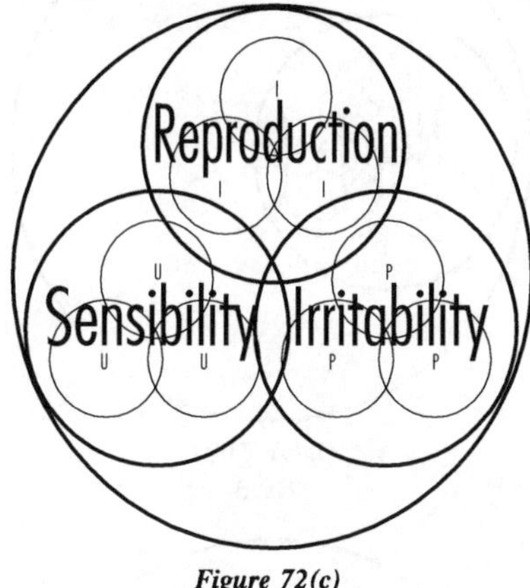

Figure 72(c)
Reproduction

As Particular, Life is a species, alongside other species. How can this be so, when we have before us *one* Life manifesting its being in *one* object (the world)? Recall that the one object is also many objects. The Particular Judgment ("this thing is useful") implied a multiplicity of things (some things must *not* be useful). So Hegel suggests that Life communicates itself in the guise of a variety of distinguishable living things – each a species alongside other species.

Species are diverse, and diverse things pass away. Species therefore imply genus, to which their being is surrendered. Life irritates itself into a self-sacrifice on behalf of genus.

Life is still Individual; Hegel associates Individuality with *Reproduction*. Reproduction should be taken as the replacement of body parts or cells that permit the universal Life to sustain itself. Reproduction is "not to produce offspring, but to '*reproduce*' *what one presently is*: to maintain oneself in existence."[11]

Reproduction is a *process* enclosed within the Individual Life, "which now passes over into a relation to the presupposed objectivity as such." (769) The Individual Life is now the *subjective totality*, facing objectivity. It is now the turn of objectivity to become the same totality that subjectivity is.

B. The Life-Process

The Living Individual reproduces itself and opposes its offspring. Full

[11] Robert M. Wallace, *Hegel's Refutation of Rational Egoism in True Infinity and the Idea*, in HEGEL'S THEORY OF THE SUBJECT 153 (David Gray Carlson ed. 2005).

of self-feeling, the Individual Life has "this *certainty* of the intrinsic *nullity* of the *otherness* confronting it." (770) To prove this certainty, it has the urge to sublate this other.[12] Life preys on Life. Life as genus must feed on its various species. The Understanding therefore proposes that the Individual Life has a Need. As we are in the dialectic portion of Life, Need is twofold. In Need, the Living Individual "posits itself as denied." (770) But in its Need, the Living Individual maintains and distinguishes itself from what it needs.

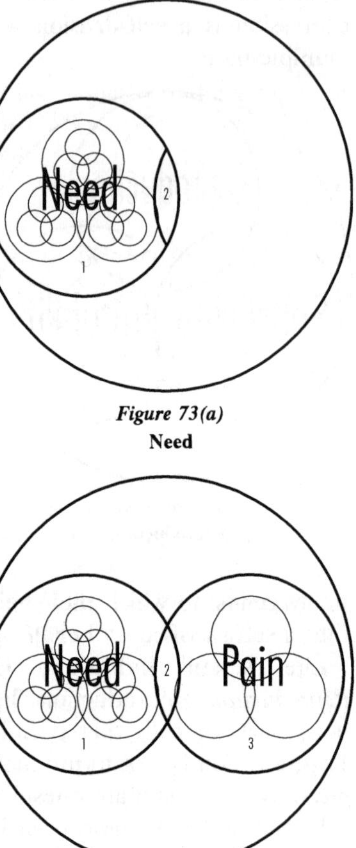

Figure 73(a)
Need

Figure 73(b)
Pain

Individual Life in harmony with the object world is the *good*. Indeed, Idea is by nature good, since it must culminate in harmony. But Individual Life now has a negative moment, so that "the Notion is sundered into an absolute disparity with itself." (770) The disharmony is *Pain* – "the prerogative of living natures." (770) Pain is what Life feels when Life's Need is met by consuming other lives. Pain is Life experiencing self-negation – sensibility to internal disruption. "It is said that contradiction is unthinkable," Hegel remarks, (770) but pain is the *experience* of contradiction. Pain, the "diremption of the living being within itself," (770) is the motive for transition whereby the Individual Life, which

---

[12] STANLEY ROSEN, G.W.F. HEGEL: AN INTRODUCTION TO THE SCIENCE OF WISDOM 240 (1974) (Life is "primarily characterized by desire, and thinking emerges from the process of attempting to satisfy desire"); SIMPSON, *supra* note 10, at 42 ("*life* is that process of overcoming apparent otherness (or, again, unself-conscious desire) which operates prereflectively, or in-itself but not for-itself").

explicitly negates itself, gains an identity with the external world.

The unity of Need and Pain is the Assimilation of the Object (or "eating"). To the extent the Individual Life hungers for objects, the hunger comes from within the Individual Life. The object to be consumed is therefore already inside the Individual Life – pre-eaten, as it were. "That the tension of unsatisfied want is painful is the clearest indication that the wanted object lies within the subject."[13] The object is therefore, in advance, *conformable* to the subject (*i.e.*, edible).

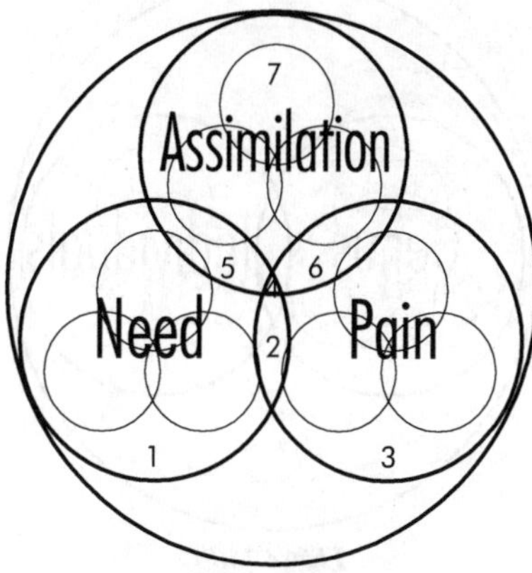

Figure 73(c)
Assimilation of the Object

Assimilation of the Object is violent. It is just as much the dissolution of lives as it is the feeding of the Individual Life. So Dissolution is tied up with reproduction, understood as Life's maintenance.[14]

Figure 74(a)
Genus

C. Genus

Individual Life and the external world were two species. These species are now conjoined in Genus.

Life, standing over against what it has produced, is not yet self-authenticated. So far it is precognitive.[15] It "*just* incarnates itself, without providing any explanation, any account of how this is possible."[16] Cognition begins in Genus, the identity of the Individual Life

---

[13] G.R.G. MURE, A STUDY OF HEGEL'S LOGIC 266 (1950).

[14] *See* John N. Findlay, *The Hegelian Treatment of Biology and Life*, in HEGEL IN THE SCIENCES 87, 99 (Robert S. Cohen & Marx W. Wartofsky 1984) ("for Hegel, the death of the individual points the way to the immortal life of mind . . . ").

[15] MARCUSE, *supra* note 3, at 163.

[16] ERMANNO BENCIVENGA, HEGEL'S DIALECTICAL LOGIC 49 (2002).

and "its previously indifferent otherness." (773) When Genus is at hand, Individual Life "has posited itself *on its own account* as the negative unity of its otherness, as the foundation of itself." (772) In other words, Genus is posited when Individual Lives erase themselves. Self-erasure is what the lives have in common – their negative unity.

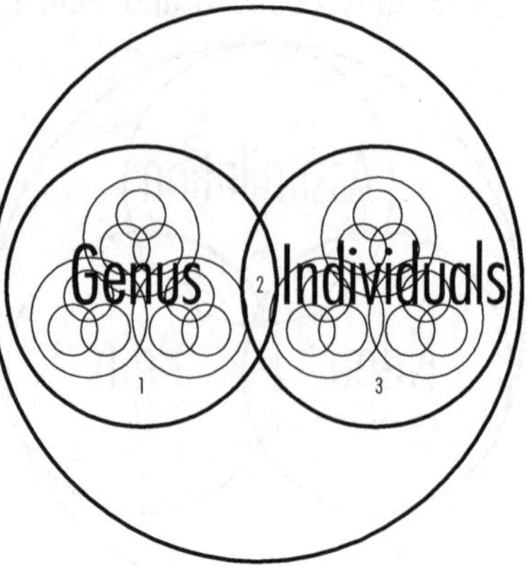

Figure 74(b)
Plurality of Individuals

Genus is not to be taken as zoological taxonomies. "Life is not one genus among others, neither is it one higher than others, but the genus as such."[17] At stake is an increasingly adequate definition of the Absolute. At this late point, the Absolute is Life in general. *All* living things – all thoughts, which are themselves living things – are in the Genus of Life.

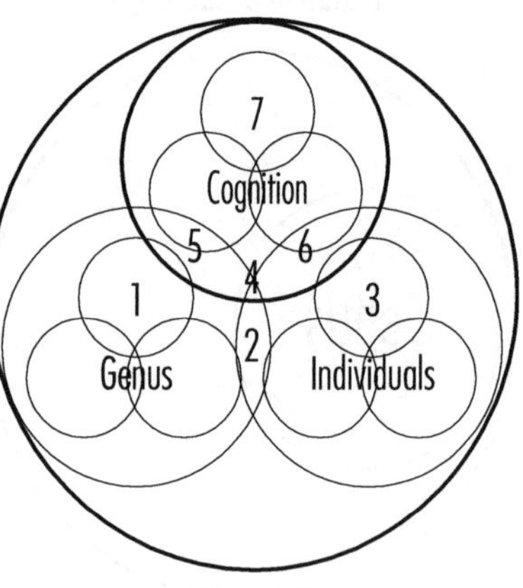

Figure 74(c)
Cognition

In Genus, Life particularizes itself, implying other Lives. There is a duplication of the Individual – "a presupposing of an objectivity that is identical with it, and a relationship of the living being to itself as to another living being." (773)

Now Assimilated, Externality shares in the internal self-feeling of Life. Genus is self-feeling shared perfectly between many Individual Lives. This is a contradiction. If Individual Life is Genus, and if the nature of Individual Life is to sacrifice itself for an other, then Individual Life, as Genus, presupposes there is another Individual Life for whom it *should* sacrifice itself. Accordingly, the Individual Life is for another, not for itself. The Individual does not yet realize that this other is really its own self.

---

17 MARCUSE, ONTOLOGY, *supra* note 3, at 237.

Identity with the other is therefore only implicit. Each Individual is left longing for a feeling of Universality.

The Individuals long to dissolve themselves in Universality. This self-erasure, so that each can know the other, is Cognition.

Hegel states directly that he has in mind Cognition in the biblical sense: "In copulation, the immediacy of the living individuality perishes; the death of this life is the procession of spirit." (774)[18] When Individuals satisfy the tension of their longing and dissolve themselves in Genus, their identity is self-sacrifice. This unity is the Universality of Life – not generated from subjective Notion but from communal Idea. Individual Lives are themselves only the germ of the true Living Individual. This germ is "visible evidence to *ordinary perception* of what the Notion is, and it demonstrates that the *subjective Notion* has *external actuality*." (774) The moment of negative unity and Individuality are posited in this germ, and by it the living species are propagated.[19]

Reproduction is an infinite process, and so, in the Genus process, Idea falls back into bad infinity. But genus has a higher side. In the Reproduction of Individuals, the selfish Individual learns to sacrifice its immediacy. Since Reproduction implies death, the Individual who sublates himself truly comes to know himself as this other Individual who survives.[20] Cognition is therefore both knowledge of the other and knowledge of self.

---

[18] There is also a sense in which death is an obstacle to the spiritual procession. "[I]t is precisely because all life, all living, culminates in death, thus dissolving its specific differences, that it is incapable of developing self-recognition." SIMPSON, *supra* note 10, at 45. But what Simpson is writing about is life's *consumption* of other living objects. When the *other* thing is eaten, it cannot participate in the procession of spirit. When the individual does not eat the other but rather sacrifices itself, then death serves the cause of spiritual progress.

[19] *See* CHARLES TAYLOR, HEGEL 333 (1975) ("the separate individuals strive to unite. But they cannot succeed, or rather they do succeed but only in a third individual, their child. This then steps forward as a new individual, while they, as all particulars, die.").

[20] ROBERT M. WALLACE, HEGEL'S PHILOSOPHY OF REALITY, FREEDOM AND GOD 257-8 (2005).

26
Cognition

> Life is . . . Universality drowned in the Specificity and Individuality which it also needs, whereas Cognition is Universality which has come out of specific-instantial immersion but which still drips with what it has come out of.[1]

Dialectic Cognition is Idea's judgment of itself. It is Idea, but not yet Absolute Idea. Subjectivity has become Universal and objective. But the Universal has particularized itself. Notion now is split between subjective and objective Notion. It is part Idea and part *not* Idea.[2] It is subjective to the extent that its predicate is a dead thing diverse from Life. Death and self-consciousness are thus connected.[3] If I am to perceive myself, I must behold something determinate, limited, finite – outward manifestations separated and alien from me.

If Cognition is subjective, it is not so in the ordinary sense of the human "I."[4] Rather, it is "subjective by reason of its external starting point." (796) Its content is "a *datum* and therefore contingent." (796) It "is still one-sided, possessing the Idea itself only as a sought-for beyond and an unattained goal." (824) It "is a *synthesis of endeavor* and has, but equally has *not*, the Idea in it." (824)[5]

---

[1] John N. Findlay, *The Hegelian Treatment of Biology and Life*, in HEGEL IN THE SCIENCES 87, 90 (Robert S. Cohen & Marx W. Wartofsky 1984).

[2] MARCUSE, ONTOLOGY, *supra* note 3, at 169 (Cognition "views its world as an other . . . thereby misunderstanding the subjectivity of objectivity)".

[3] CHARLES TAYLOR, HEGEL 334 (1975).

[4] MARCUSE, *supra* note 3, at 168.

[5] *See* John W. Burbidge *Cognition and Finite Spirit*, in HEGEL'S THEORY OF THE SUBJECT 177 (David Gray Carlson ed., 2005).

Having sundered itself, subjective Notion now contemplates its other self, and what it contemplates is spirit or self-consciousness, "determinations of the Idea where it has itself for object." (775) Notion now has Determinate Being, but this Determinate Being is strictly a self-difference. Notion distinguishes itself from itself. Spirit, "that which develops and determines itself,"[6] is Notion elevated above Life. "[I]t is from the *Idea of life* that the Idea of spirit has issued." (780)[7]

Hegel equates spirit with *soul*.[8] In previous thought, Hegel says, the metaphysics of spirit or soul involved "determinations of substance, simplicity, immateriality." (775) Ordinary thinking posited the existence of a soul and then searched for the predicates that would agree with the preconception. Such a procedure, Hegel complains, resembles Newtonian physics, "which reduces the world of phenomena to general laws and reflective determinations since it too was based on spirit merely in its *phenomenal* aspect." (775) The metaphysics of the soul was "bound to fall short even of the scientific character of physics." (775-6)

This metaphysic abstracts from empirical selfhood. As Kant emphasized, the smallest empirical element destroys psychology as a science.[9] According to this instinct, nothing is left of psychology except the I, devoid of content. This I, for Kant, is less than a notion. It is "a mere *consciousness* that *accompanies every notion*." (776) "[B]y this 'I', or if you like, *it* (the *thing*) that thinks, nothing further is represented than a transcendent subject of thoughts = *x*, which is cognized only through the thoughts which are its *predicates*." (776)[10] Of the Kantian I, taken in isolation, "we can *never* have the *least conception*." (776)

Kant complains of the "inconvenience" (776) of the I – we must already make use of it in forming a judgment about it. The I, for Kant, is not a single representation but is the form of representation in general. Empirical psychology therefore commits paralogism when it "reifies" (*i.e.*, changes into a phenomenal thing) self-consciousness. The

---

[6] KATHLEEN DOW MAGNUS, HEGEL AND THE SYMBOLIC MEDIATION OF SPIRIT 235 (2001).

[7] This formulation reflects the emergence of mind from nature, in Hegel's Encyclopedia system.

[8] Marcuse calls these passages "among the most brilliant of the entire *Logic* . . ." MARCUSE, ONTOLOGY, *supra* note 3, at 162.

[9] IMMANUEL KANT, CRITIQUE OF PURE REASON A342/B400 (Paul Guyer & Allen W. Wood trans., 1990)

[10] The phrase "thing that thinks" is a Lacanian favorite. SLAVOJ ŽIŽEK, TARRYING WITH THE NEGATIVE: KANT, HEGEL, AND THE CRITIQUE OF IDEOLOGY 125 (1993).

thing that thinks, for Kant, is to be taken as a thing-in-itself.[11] Since the I always occurs in consciousness of some object, empirical psychology unjustifiably infers that the I is a substance, and "further a quantitatively *simple* being, and a *one*, and a something that has a *real existence independently* of the things of time and space." (776-7)

The pre-critical metaphysics of the soul is faulted for starting from *observation* and using external reflection to discover its non-empirical essence. But Kant's criticism of this practice is equally defective. Ignoring the speculative instincts of the Greeks,[12] Kant simply brought Humean skepticism to bear. Since the I could not be known empirically, it must be the unknowable thing-in-itself.

As for the I's inconvenience – we cannot judge the I without using the I – Hegel finds it "ridiculous to call [an inconvenience] this nature of self-consciousness, namely, that the 'I' thinks itself, that the 'I' cannot be thought without its being the 'I' that thinks." (777) This so-called inconvenience is the very nature of self-consciousness and of spirit, each of which makes itself its own object.

If self-consciousness perceives itself, the I is empirically perceptible after all, even if not sensuous. Notion is absolute relation-to-self. Through "a separating judgement, [it] makes itself its own object and is solely this process whereby it makes itself a circle." (777-8)

Kant "barbarously" (778) places the defect in the I because it is the subject which must make itself its own object. But the complaint may be made from the other side. What a defect it is that the subject has no predicate that we can intuit! If objectivity means intuitable in time and space – *i.e.*, sensuous reality – then the I is not objective. But to have risen above sensual reality "is the condition of thinking and of truth." (778) Notion must manifest itself and render itself known.

In ordinary parlance, the I is simple, "not the self-relation that has itself for object." (778) Abstracted in this way, the I is one side of the

---

11 "Paralogisms are a species of unsound syllogism, the especial vice of which consists in employing one and the same word in the two premises with a different meaning." EL § 47 Addition.

12 Gadamer proclaims Hegel "the most radical of the Greeks." HANS-GEORG GADAMER, HEGEL'S DIALECTIC: FIVE HERMENEUTICAL STUDIES 107 (Christopher Smith trans., 1976); *see also* STANLEY ROSEN, G.W.F. HEGEL: AN INTRODUCTION TO THE SCIENCE OF WISDOM 164 (1974) ("But Hegel's Christianity is gnostic or Averroistic, and in that sense, more Greek than the Greeks, to say nothing of Heidegger").

self-relation, with no objectivity, or perhaps an object without subjectivity, "were it not for the inconvenience alluded to, that the thinking subject cannot be eliminated from the I as object." (778) The "inconvenience" is therefore on both sides of the abstract concept of the I. The I uses itself to think itself – Kant's inconvenience. Suppose, however, that the I was merely the subject. It must think *something*, whether it be itself or something else. It therefore *must* have a predicate in actual thoughts. In fact, the I as subject and as object cannot be separated. "[I]t is precisely [this that] Kant wants to stave off in order to retain the mere *general idea*, which does not inwardly differentiate itself and therefore, of course, lacks the Notion." (778)

A notionless conception can indeed oppose itself to the previous metaphysics of the simple soul. But it is just as defectively simple as the metaphysics it opposes, Hegel says. The inconvenience Kant complains of is the very empirical fact that proves the untruth of the I as non-notional thing-in-itself.[13]

Even metaphysics stuck with the fixity of the Understanding aspires to cognize *truth*. Kant's victory over such metaphysics consists of abolishing the very possibility of truth, consigning it to the unknowable thing-in-itself. In defeating metaphysics in this way, Kant

> omits altogether to raise the one question of interest, whether [the I] possesses truth in and for itself. But to cling to phenomena and the mere conceptions given in everyday consciousness is to renounce the Notion and philosophy. Anything rising above this is stigmatized in the Kantian criticism as something high-flown to which reason is in no way entitled. (780)

---

[13] Hegel thinks that Kant's criticism of Moses Mendelssohn is notional, contrary to his other attitudes toward the I. *See* CRITIQUE OF PURE REASON, *supra* note 10, at B413-23. Mendelssohn tried to prove the persistence of the soul by reference to its simplicity. A simple thing, Mendelssohn argued, is incapable of becoming something other. Simplicity served Mendelssohn as the form of general abstraction of the I. Unlike Hegel, Mendelssohn did not suppose that "being" was finite and instantly transformed into non-being. Indeed, soul does persist, but only because it is concrete, not simple. The concrete soul – *i.e.*, the Notion – "cannot therefore pass into that other as though it altered itself in it for the very reason that the *other* to which it is determined is the Notion itself, so that in this transition it only come to itself." (779)

In his criticism, Kant agrees with Mendelssohn that the soul does not have "juxtaposed parts," (779) but soul has *degree*. In Kant's discourse, degree "postulates the possibility of transition into nothing by a *gradual passing away*." (779); *see* CRITIQUE OF PURE REASON, *supra*, at A143/B182-3. What Kant has illegitimately done, Hegel remarks, is to impose on spirit a category of being.

Notion does go beyond notionless phenomena. The justification for this transcendence? Notion has already justified itself, throughout the Logic. Kant himself has portrayed phenomena as untrue. Their untruth necessarily drives the inquiry beyond phenomena.

Cognition's duality. Up to now, all the chapters of the Logic have been triadic, with the exception of Judgment and the opening third of Syllogism, which were tetradic.[14] Tetrachotomy in Judgment was justified because the Notion, in reestablishing its own reality, had to pass through the stages of Being, the *double* stage of Essence, and the final stage of Notion.

Cognition has only two portions – the True and the Good. Reconciliation in Absolute Idea is left for the final chapter. But in fact, Absolute Idea should be understood as third to the True and the Good. Properly speaking, chapter 27 should not be a chapter at all but simply the end of chapter 26.[15] Chapter 27 has *no* explicit subdivisions within it, though, as we shall see, the moves of the Understanding, Dialectical Reason, and Speculative Reason make their final appearance here. In effect, the *true* chapter 27 should be *all* the chapters taken together.

A. The Idea of the True

The fault of Notion at this point is that it faces a presupposed object. This object is merely a determination of the Notion. Notion is therefore still subjective. Notion must be seen as operating within the object. When so seen, Notion will finally conform to the object. It this point, Notion (together with the object) finds *Truth*.

But such a reconciliation is in the future. Idea so far is one extreme in a syllogism. It constitutes a mere subjective reality. For subjective Idea, the object world is a limitation. In fact both extremes of the syllogism are Idea. One extreme is Idea *for itself* and the other is Idea *in itself*.

In Figure 75(a), Idea is certain of itself but confined within itself. It is mere form – abstract Universality. Idea In Itself is equally an

---

[14] Ultimately, I interpreted the Syllogism of Existence to be triadic, since Mathematical Syllogism was simply a restatement of the truth of the third figure of the Syllogism of Existence. *Supra* at 519-20.

[15] ROSEN, *supra* note 13, at 254-5 ("there is no further transition to a higher level but only a development which is at the same time a recollection of what has been accomplished").

immediacy. It is *being*, standing over against thinking. Such an immediacy is Particularity. So far, if this duality has Individuality, it has received it externally. It must bring this externality within itself. What Idea must now do is "to raise its own implicit reality, this formal truth, into real truth." (783)

Figure 75(a)
Idea For Itself and Idea In Itself

Notion is nothing but the urge for self-objectification. But when Notion objectifies itself, it equally sublates itself. Notion is, after all, *subjectivity*. In objectification, Notion assigns its subjective being to the presupposed object. This presupposed object is, of course, its own self.[16] Such an object has a content – Notion's own identity-with-self, in which all opposition has been sublated. For subjective Notion, the object is an Individuality.

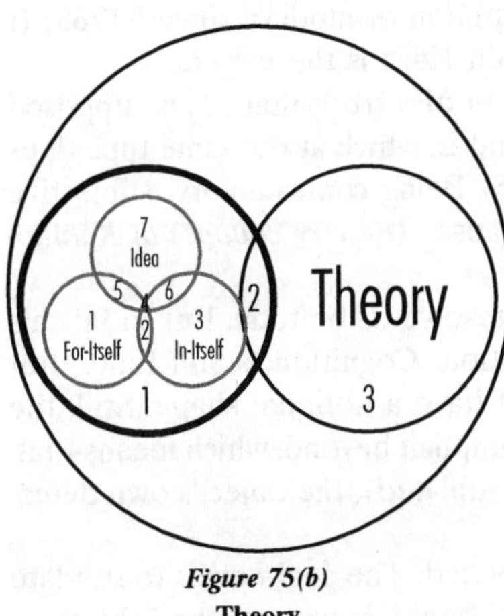

Figure 75(b)
Theory

This urge to posit its own objective Individuality "is the urge therefore to *truth*." (784) Truth is "the agreement of thought with its object." (44) Accordingly, truth is the Idea that has made itself into a reality. It amounts to a *relation* between Notion and its reality – between subject and predicate. Dialectical Reason retorts that, so far, the truth is only *theoretical*. In other words, Notion and its truth are subjective.

When Dialectical Reason names objectivized Idea as subjective Theory, it negates the object world – the

---

16 *See* G.W.F. HEGEL, THE JENA SYSTEM, 1804-5: LOGIC AND METAPHYSICS 182 (John W. Burbidge & George di Giovanni trans. 1986) ("the spiritual is this: that it finds itself in the other of itself. That is why self-equivalent spirit is precisely this very other that spirit finds as itself.").

opposite of what Idea thought it was doing. Figure 75(a) is now revealed to have been only synthesis – "a unity of things that are originally separate and only are externally so conjoined." (784) In this Cognition, the content of the object is merely imposed by the subject. Cognition is still finite. The object has not attained *its* end and has not arrived at *its* truth.

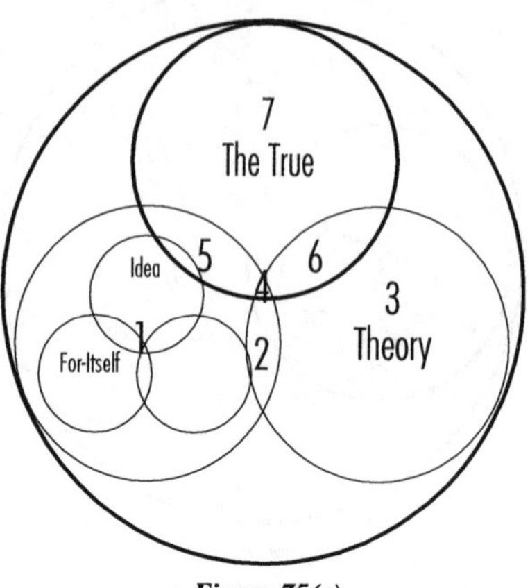

Figure 75(c)
The True

From the theoretical perspective, the object is unknown – a thing-in-itself. "Oddly enough," Hegel remarks, "it is this side of *finitude* that latterly has been clung to, and accepted as the *absolute* relation of cog-nition – as though the finite as such was supposed to be the absolute! . . . [T]he fallacy of taking this untrue relation of cognition as the true relation has become the universal opinion of modern times." (785) It need hardly be added that once again Kant is the target.

Finite cognition is "the contradiction of a truth that . . . is supposed not to be truth – of a cognition of what *is*, which at the same time does not cognize the thing-in-itself." (785) Being contradictory, subjective cognition and the thing-in-itself collapse. *The very collapse of Kantian metaphysics is the True*.

The Truth is that Cognition must resolve its finitude. But so far this resolve is merely an external reflection. Cognition is still finite, not speculative. Objectivity does not yet have a notional shape. Still, the object has been reduced to a merely implicit beyond, which means that, when this beyond is determined (as sublated), the object's own determination will be before us.

The object is already implicitly sublated. The goal now is to sub-late the object expressly. For the moment, however, the object is presupposed as being separate from Idea. The object is essentially in a relationship where Idea is certain of itself and certain that the object is null. So far, Idea is itself and *not* itself. Idea must now realize that it *is* the object. When the object explicitly sublates itself, the Notion explicitly sublates itself as well.

Hegel now recalls the so-called "first premise" of Teleology – the bad infinity wherein End, announcing itself as not Means, proved it *was*

Means to Means.[17] Something similar now occurs with the advent of the True. Idea announces it is not the object, thereby proving it *is* the object: "The determining activity of the Notion upon the object is an immediate *communication* of itself to the object and unresisted *pervasion* of the [object] by the Notion." (786)

But in announcing what it is (and what it is not), "Notion remains in pure identity with itself." (786) This pure identity is an immediacy. Yet it is also a negation and hence not an immediacy. All we have here is Notion negating itself, "restraining itself and making itself passive towards what confronts it." (786) By being passive, Notion hopes the object will show itself for what it is, without distortion. The determination that Notion has just made allows the object to be for itself, "a presupposition that has been merely *found*, as an *apprehension* of a datum." (786)

The Understanding proposes that the True is an objective process in which Idea plays no role. Passive Idea is Analytic Cognition. Confronted with the True (*i.e.*, the collapse of the diverse object), Analytic Cognition merely accepts what is given to it. If the object falls apart, it is none of the Notion's doing. Analytic Cognition is "merely the *apprehension* of what *is*." (794)[18] Its activity is limited to restricting itself and suppressing the obstacle of subjectivity – "an external husk" – (786) in the process of knowledge.

(a) Analytic Cognition

Analysis is the "first premiss" (787) of Cognition. In Analysis, Idea proclaims it is not the object, thereby proving it *is* the object. This first premise does not yet contain mediation, even though Idea by nature is supposed to be perfect communication of its being into the object. As Analysis, Idea "empties itself of its negativity." (787) As completely receptive to the object it analyzes, Analysis adds nothing to the object – or so it pretends. It is therefore a non-relation to the object. Self-identity is the analytical principle, and it denies its transition into the other. But Idea *is* the activity of becoming other. So Analytic Idea excludes itself from itself.

Analysis always proceeds from some *given* subject matter. "[I]t is

---

[17] *Supra* at 554.

[18] "This assumption is not itself analyzed; hence it is equivalent to an *intuition*." ROSEN, *supra* note 13, at 246.

Notionless and undialectical . . . and its progress takes place solely in the determinations of the *material*." (788) It purports to be actual knowledge of the object, but in fact "its products are essentially Notion-determinations . . . *immediately contained* in the subject matter." (787-8) But it is one-sided to suppose that Analysis is *nothing but* subjective (subjective idealism), just as it is one-sided for Analysis to say that it *adds nothing* to the object it encounters (realism). The truth of Analysis is that it is a mediation of these one-sided views. It is "two things in one: a *positing* that no less immediately determines itself as a *presuppo-sing*." (788) The two moments, however, must not be separated.

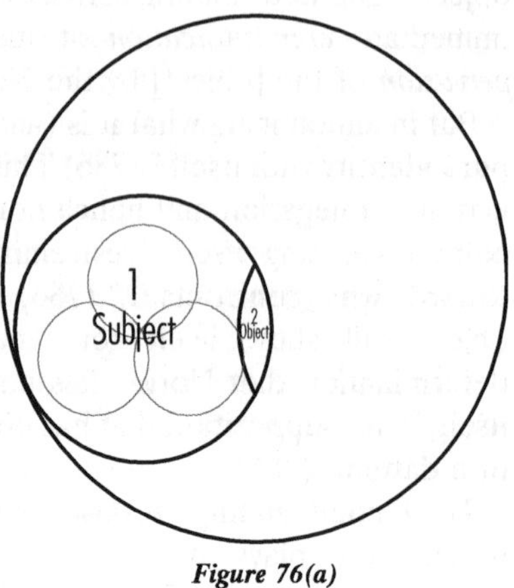

Figure 76(a)
Analysis

The highest point Analysis can reach is the discovery of an abstract essence. But this process of discovery falls into a bad infinity. The discovered essence is merely an appearance, which itself has an essence. A discovered effect has a cause, which itself has a cause. In these activities, Analysis supposedly adds nothing.[19]

Arithmetic. Against Kant, Hegel thinks arithmetic and the "*sciences of discrete magnitude*" (789) (*i.e.*, algebra) are analytical. Analytic cognition starts with some given thing that possesses a contingent manifoldness. Arithmetic and algebra have already been purged of peculiarity and have been rendered abstract. At the end of this abstraction, one is left with "one." If "one" is rendered plural, or if plurality is unified into a sum, this is done externally. "How *numbers* are further combined and separated depends solely on the positing activity of the cognizing subject." (790)

The name of this "one" which external reflection subdivides and rejoins is *magnitude* – the category within which numbers are separated

---

19 Kant's synthetic *a priori* principles are praised as pointing to the unity of self-consciousness. But Kant takes this unity as a given. "Kant spared himself the trouble of demonstrating [the] genuinely synthetic progress – the self-producing Notion," (789) Hegel complains.

and combined. Magnitude is therefore a determinateness that is indifferent to how it is determined. In magnitude there are no immanent determinatenesses. Nothing here can be the stuff of Cognition. All relations located within are contingently arrived at. Nevertheless, any relation so located has a guiding principle – *equality*, "analytic identity." (790) Progress in the science of discrete magnitude "consists in the reduction of the unequal to an ever greater equality." (790) Thus, addition involves combining (potentially) unequal numbers. But multiplication produces the opportunity for powers. Presumably this is progress because the power relation portends quality – not just quantity.[20]

Once a problem is given contingently to a mathematician, further operations between them is "wholly analytic." (790) In fact, it should be recognized that mathematics does not contain theorems – only problems. Analysis "solves a problem but cannot prove a theorem . . . ."[21] As we shall see, however, Hegel reserves for "theorem" the notional form that mathematics cannot possibly comprehend.[22]

Kant declared arithmetic to be synthetic.[23] Hegel disagrees. In analyzing 5+7=12, a plurality (5+7) appears on one side and a unity (12) on the other. But, unless analysis means the tautology of 12=12, analysis must always encounter difference. Just because plurality is reduced to a unity does not mean arithmetic is synthetic. Rather, 5+7 contains the *demand* that 5 and 7 be unified in a single expression. The plus sign (+) constitutes a demand, and the solution is obtained by simply following this demand. In fact, the combination of 5 and 7 is simply counting. And 12 is not different in kind from counting to 5 and then counting 7 more units until 12 is reached.

Synthetic propositions require proof. But 5+7=12 does not. The same process of counting and then breaking off at 5 is used to count seven more units and break off at 12. "It is, therefore, an utterly superfluous bit of scaffolding" (791) to insist on geometry-style proofs to the analytics of arithmetic. "The proof can express nothing but the tautology that the solution is correct because the operation set in the

---

20 *Supra* at 189-92.

21 G.R.G. MURE, THE PHILOSOPHY OF HEGEL 145 (1965); *see also* Antonio Moretto, *Hegel on Greek Mathematics and the Modern Calculus,* in HEGEL AND NEWTONIANISM 149, 154 (Michael John Petry ed., 1993) ("For Hegel, a mathematical definition is a synthesis adopted from outside mathematics itself, whereas a theorem is a synthesis which is internal and necessary to it").

22 *Infra* at 588-9.

23 CRITIQUE OF PURE REASON, *supra* note 10, at B15-17.

problem has been performed." (791-2) That is to say, the problem states "add 5 and 7." The solution simply performs according to this demand.

When power relations are considered, synthesis does occur.[24] Raising x to the power of 2 indicates a qualitative change. x and x^2 exist on different qualitative levels, and qualitative change implies synthesis. That is, X is a line, X^2 is a two-dimensional plane, X^3 is a three-dimensional space. In power relations, "*other* expressions and relationships must be taken as intermediate terms besides those *immediately specified* by the problem or theorem." (792) No longer is the arithmetical expression solved by mere counting. Rather, "analysis becomes synthetic when it comes to deal with *determinations* that are no longer *posited* by the problems themselves." (793)

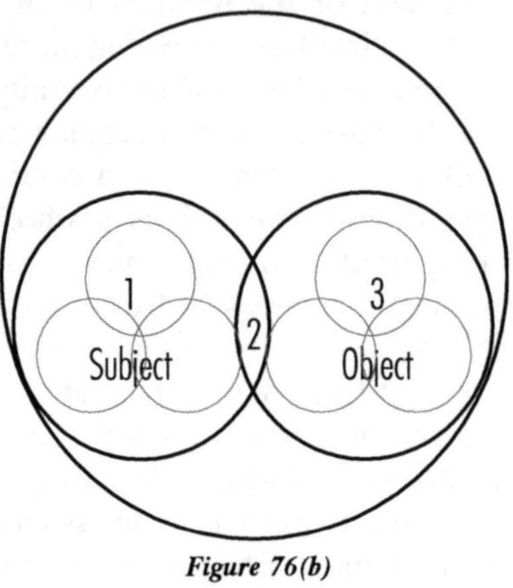

Figure 76(b)
Synthesis

(b) Synthetic Cognition

The transition from analysis to synthesis is the transition from immediacy to mediation – "from abstract identity to difference." (793) Dialectical Reason states that, when Analysis makes determinations within the one object (in arithmetic style), it trafficks in difference, which infers a relation of one thing to an other. That is to say, if the object is divided, then there must be a divider – an external reflection – that made it happen. Analysis is therefore guilty of suppressing this other, which Dialectical Reason now brings to the fore. Even on analytical terms, this suppressed other is an external reflection. The

---

[24] Some examples Hegel gives: $a^n + a^{n-1} \ldots + a = c$. Such a problem is not strictly analytic, because a mathematician must bring something to the table in order to find the solution. The connection of coefficient and root is not pre-expressed in the problem. "The same is true for finding the solution to $x^{m-1}=0$ with the help of the sine." (792) This is surely a misprint. The task is to solve for $x^m = 1$. With the use of imaginary numbers, $x^m = 1$ has m solutions. If $m=3$, then $x^3=1$ had 3 solutions: 1; $(-\frac{1}{2}+\frac{1}{2}i\sqrt{3})$; $(-\frac{1}{2}-\frac{1}{2}i\sqrt{3})$, where $i=\sqrt{-1}$. Each of these solutions is in the form cosA+i(sinA), where A=0°, A=120°, and A=240°.

relation between terms within the object is imposed on it, in so far as the object is concerned. The Notion therefore does not escape from subjectivity in the refuge of Analysis.

If Analysis is *apprehension* (of some self-identical thing), Synthesis is *comprehension* (of the thing in relation to its other). It aims "at grasping the multiplicity of determinations in their unity." (794) Diverse elements are rendered necessarily related in Synthesis. That is to say, the elements are both diverse *and* related.

In Synthesis, Notion posits thoughts (*Begriffsbestimmungen*) and then relates these to its other thoughts. But the relations are immediate unities "and just for that reason, not in the unity by which the Notion exists as subject." (794) These unities belong to the Notion determinations merely implicitly. They appear for the moment to have their unity externally imposed on them,[25] and for this reason Synthesis is still entrenched in finitude.

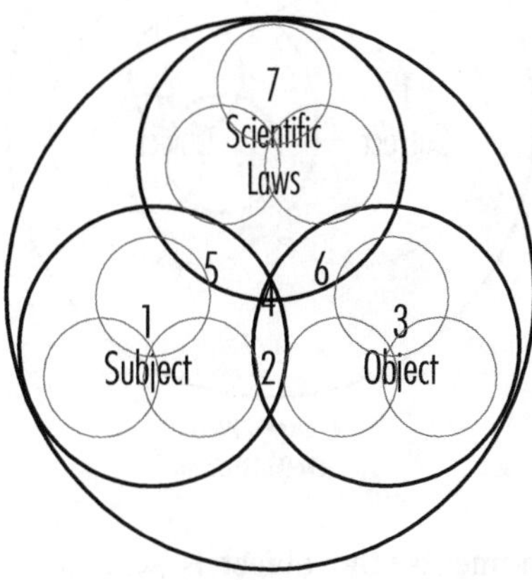

Figure 76(c)
Scientific Laws

Synthetic cognition finds laws to govern the relation between specific Notion determinations, but these laws, not yet notional, are fixed, finite, and subjective. Thought merely "cognizes the ground of phenomena from the *phenomena* themselves." (795) This is the moment of Scientific Laws. For Hegel, science means the *SL*. Accordingly, when Scientific Law reveals itself, it reveals itself in the form of the Notion. The moments of the Universal, Particular and Individual are made manifest.

1. Definition

Objectivity is still given, but now it has the form of the Notion. So the Understanding proposes that the object, subject to Scientific Law, conforms to the law of the Notion; it recognizes within the object the

25 ROSEN, *supra* note 13, at 248 ("There is no internal, dialectical development of the object").

Universal, Particular and Individual. Notion has revealed itself, and, in its empirical appearance, the very Notion of the Individual can be derived.

In the process of Definition, Subjective Notion comes up with an Individual to be defined. Such an Individual is "an *immediate* that is posited *outside* the Notion, since [the Individual] is not yet self-determining." (795) So Cognition is still subjective, as it deals with an external, "given" starting point. The object is not yet seen as identical with the subject.

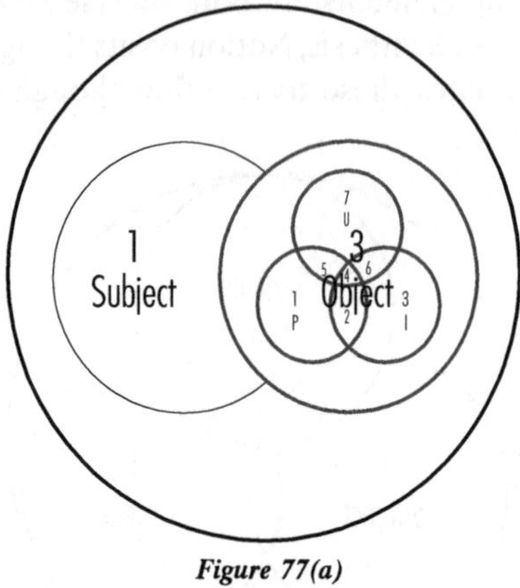

Figure 77(a)
Definition

The "discovered" Individual, however, is placed in some genus and is thereby made Universal. But this Universal contains within it the principle of differentiation of the species – that is, the Universal is proximate genus.[26] By this principle the Universal makes itself Particular. These activities together comprise Definition.

All these moments are recognized when the object is defined. Because it has multiple moments, the object is seen as a manifold. Yet Definition cannot see all these moments at once. Definition must *simplify* what it finds by shedding inessential material. That is to say, Definition concerns itself with the form of the object. It follows from this that Synthesis is contingent knowledge in two senses. First, its content is a datum – an object separate from the subject. Second, whatever quality the subject chooses to focus on in the manifold object is a contingency. It could have focused on some other aspect.

Definition separates the essential and inessential features – the thing-in-itself from its phenomena. Yet, if there is one thing we know by now, the thing-in-itself is not transcendent; it exists at the level of phenomena. Definition has no way of telling which moment is phenomenon and which is thing-in-itself. This is the archetypical problem of Definition, which Synthetic Cognition cannot overcome.

---

[26] *Supra* at 484-5.

Definition is a bad infinity. Any given Particular of the object has a Universal that grounds it. But we can know this Universal only *as* a Particular. If we discover a Universal as ground to a Particular, it is itself a Particular with yet a higher Universal, "and for this again a higher, and so on . . . to infinity." (803) This is Definition's inherent problem. It starts from a given Individual, and with empirical science generally, which does not derive its starting point. Its starting point is always given.[27] Definition is therefore still subjective. In matters of Definition the author is king, "for the end that they are to serve is a determination created out of the subjective resolve." (796)

Hegel carries this point into geometry. Geometrical objects "*are* only what they are *meant* to be." (796) The thought of them is the same as the reality of them. They therefore resemble the products of external purposiveness and the subject matter of arithmetic. Geometric shapes do have some "natural" features, such as continuity, divisibility, and tri-dimensionality – presuppositions in so far as geometry is concerned. Synthetic propositions within geometry entail the "combinations and entanglement" (796) of subjective thoughts. Geometrical logic is non-notional.[28]

Definition concerns itself with taxonomy, where Universality is

---

[27] HERBERT MARCUSE, REASON AND REVOLUTION 72 (1999) ("a real definition cannot be given in one isolated proposition, but must elaborate the real history of the object, for its history alone explains its reality").

[28] Hegel criticizes geometrical proofs for being non-notional and hence not proper proofs. They are not genetic in quality but achieve their ends by exploiting extraneous materials to get the job done. (72) Although geometric proof eventually functions, "on its own account . . . this operation is unintelligent, since the end that directs it is not yet expressed." (812) Accordingly, geometric proof "is a subjective act lacking objectivity." (812) For the point that admixture of empirical elements into reason is the basis of Hegel's critique of geometry, see Moretto, *supra* note 21, at 152-7; Lawrence S. Stepelevich, *Hegel's Geometric Theory*, in HEGEL AND THE PHILOSOPHY OF NATURE (Stephen Houlgate ed., 1998).

Physics too takes a beating. It takes "*forces* or other inner and essence-like forms" which are then "*placed in the forefront* in order that they may provide a general *foundation* that is subsequently *applied to the individual*." (814) One enters into physics, Hegel complains, only if its "presuppositions are *blindly taken for granted*." (815) One commentator finds in these passages "a rather passable description of Newton's method of demonstrative induction. What Hegel described here is exactly what Newton in fact does in his derivation of the universal law of gravity where we find 'Phenomena' and metaphysical 'Rules,' including the reality of gravity itself 'placed in the forefront,' and the explanantia are, in part, deduced from the explenandum." James W. Garrison, *Metaphysics and Scientific Proof: Newton and Hegel*, in HEGEL AND NEWTONIANISM 3, 14 (Michael John Petry ed., 1993).

discovered empirically. Time may vindicate taxonomy. But the selected essence may also prove to be "transitory." (797) In effect, Definition contents itself with marks – determinations in which essentiality may or may not reside. A single external trait is not adequate to the concrete totality of the individual. By way of an example is the observation that only man has an ear lobe. Is the ear lobe, then, the distinctive feature of man? To Synthetic Cognition, It is "quite contingent whether the marks adopted in the definition are pure makeshifts like this, or on the other hand approximate more to the nature of a principle." (798) In any case, Notion cannot be isolated in just one property. Properties are the externality of the thing and are even external to themselves.

Another problem that Definition must face is what today we would call the genetically defective individual. Such an individual proves that there is a difference between Notion and its actualization. Notion needs non-notional nature to secure its external presentation. Yet Notion also encompasses Negative Judgment – the judgment that a predicate is *not* Universal. Bad specimens are part of the process of nature, Hegel implies.[29] The problem genetic defect poses for Definition is that Definition has no real way of knowing whether the particular aspect it chooses for taxonomic purposes is notional or non-notional.

> [T]here is no property against which an instance cannot be brought in which . . . the property taken as its characteristic shows itself immature or stunted . . . Thus for example the essentiality of the brain for physical man is contradicted by the instance of acephalous individuals, the essentiality of the protection of life and property for the state, by the instance of despotic states and tyrannous governments. (799-800)

It cannot suffice for Cognition to assert that the acephalous individual is non-notional; such an assertion implies that Notion is not empirical after all.[30] Definition is "supposed to be the *immediate* Notion, and therefore can only draw on the immediacy of existence for its determinations for objects, and can justify itself only in what it finds already to hand." (800) Definition is therefore a sham because it can never

---

[29] This theme has long been implicit: "But Appearance is the *simply affirmative* manifold variety which wantons in unessential manifoldness; its reflected content, on the other hand, is its manifoldness reduced to *simple difference*." (501-2)

[30] Michael Inwood thinks the acephalous human stands for the proposition that, sometimes, concepts are inherently not erroneous. M.J. INWOOD, HEGEL 369 (1983). This is precisely the *opposite* of Hegel's point: *all* empirical observation is problematic.

name the essential characteristic that reveals the Notion of the object.

2. Division

Definition cannot reliably pluck the flower Notion from the nettle of its outward manifestation, because it may have before it a non-notional flower. Rather, phenomena must be divided into essential and inessential manifestations.

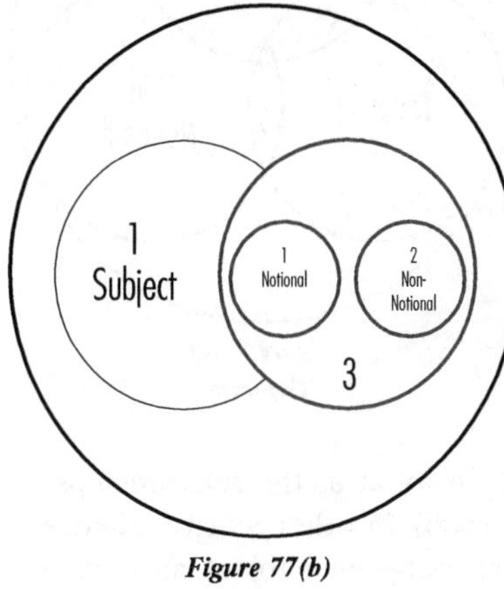

Figure 77(b)
Division

Essential manifestations are the ones that flow from Universality. The Universal must particularize itself, and yet it still partakes of Negative Judgment. Accordingly, we know that some manifestations are Universal, some not. The necessity for division lies in the Universal itself. The Universal is divided within itself.

In Division, the Universal disjoins itself and renders itself into *some* Particulars and some non-notional materials. This is the progress "proper to the Notion" and "the basis of a synthetic science [and] of systematic cognition." (801)

The Universal is *prius* (*das Erste*), the originating principle. In the sphere of Actuality, the concrete *Individual* was the *prius*. But in Cognition, the *prius* must be "something simple, something *abstracted* from the concrete." (801) In this form alone the subject matter has notional form.

Being empirical, the laws that govern division are "formal, empty rules that lead to nothing." (804) So "the business of cognition can only consist, partly, in setting in order the abstract elements discovered in the empirical material, and, partly, in finding the universal determinations of the particularity by comparison." (803-4) As always, comparison (*Vergleichung*) stands for non-notional attributes supplied by external reflection, to which the object is indifferent.

3. Theorem

In Definition, each Particular is taken as Universal. Division isolates Particularity from Universality. Now Cognition moves on to Individuality and Theorem. In Theorem, "the object is cognized in its reality, in the conditions and forms of its real existence." (806)

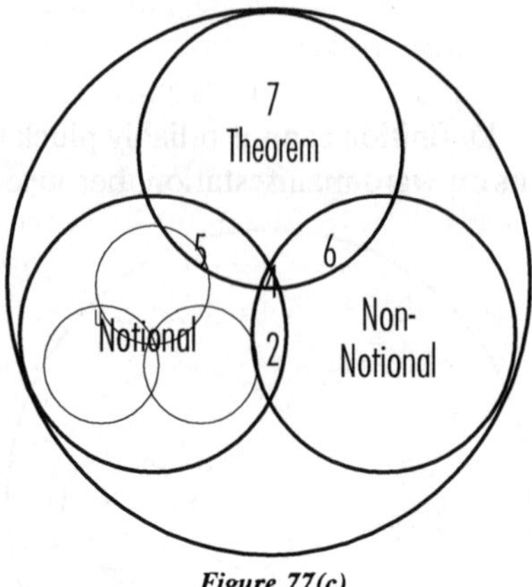

Figure 77(c)
Theorem

Definition contained only one determinateness.[31] Division contained related determinatenesses. Theorem, the unity of these two, represents Idea, "the unity of the Notion and reality." (806) In accord with its dictionary definition, Theorem is *proven*, or mediated, material. It represents all mediation in the universe [4, 5, 6], mediated by a single Individual mind [7].

According to Hegel, the stated definition of Theorem is "the genuinely *synthetic* aspect of an object in so far as the relationships of its determinatenesses are *necessary*." (806) In other words, Theorem states that objects are collaborations between subject and object. Theorem represents *Hegel's* ontology, compared to the True in Figure 75(c), which was the collapse of Kant's epistemology.

In Definition and Division, the synthetic element was added externally. What was given in these stages was assumed to have the form of the Notion, "but, as given, the entire content is merely *presented* . . . , whereas the theorem has to be *demonstrated*." (806) Theorem joins the Notion's subjective creations together and is therefore Idea. Yet Theorem is flawed. It is "still occupied in seeking." (806) The reality it deals with does not expressly proceed from the Notion. It cannot find *itself* in any reality that is merely given to it. Theorem is no better than the earlier cognitions. It has no principle to distinguish the necessary from the unnecessary.

B. The Idea of the Good

In Theorem, the Notion was Individual. It apprehended all the mediations – all the possibilities. It was, in Kantian terms, a transcendental unity of apperception. Yet this intelligence is still

---

[31] JENA LOGIC, *supra* note 17, at 173 (Definition "expresses singularity").

subjective, facing an objectivity wherein Notion cannot recognize itself.[32] The Understanding now proposes that Notion must obliterate all "given" material in which Notion cannot recognize itself.[33] Notion must expressly create its own reality.[34] Only then will Notion be truly free. This mad riot of destruction aimed at anything opposing the Notion is what Hegel calls the Good. The Good, or Practical Idea, represents the Notion's "certainty of its own actuality and of the *non-actuality* of the world." (818) The subject manifests its objectivity in smashing idols. The given materials from which Notion was alienated are now considered a nullity.[35] "All action presupposes a reality 'alien' to the doer . . ."[36] It "treats the world as an empty receptacle for the actualization of its subjective purposes . . . ."[37]

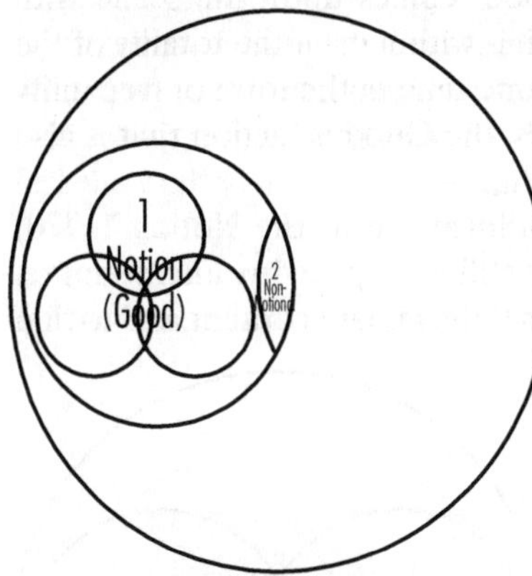

Figure 78(a)
The Good (Practical Idea)

According to the Bible, God created the universe and saw that it was good. But this act of creation is also an act of destruction. The universe is God's manifestation, but it is also a negation of the chaos

---

32 *See* Peter Singer, *Hegel*, in GERMAN PHILOSOPHERS 109, 190 (1997) ("Reality is constituted by mind. At first mind does not realise this. It sees reality as something independent of it, even as something hostile or alien to it.").

33 *See* JENA LOGIC, *supra* note 17, at 168 ("The self-preservation of the I is precisely this removing of what is alien from that circle, so that [the circle] remains only the universal . . . ").

34 Burbidge, *Cognition*, *supra* note 6, at 178 (Good consists of constructing "an object identical with our concepts").

35 According to Harris, the Good is "the unceasing striving to overcome evil, the continuing and unfailing love of one's neighbour, which . . . is an established disposition of mind and will and a persistent on-going activity." ERROL E. HARRIS, AN INTERPRETATION OF THE LOGIC OF HEGEL 286 (1983). This "Sunday school" version is not Hegel's point at all. Rinaldi believes that the true and the good relate to specifically human concerns, not the concerns of spirit. RINALDI, *supra* note 2, at 291. Yet the True is the collapse of Theory; the Good is the obliteration of alienation, very abstract *spiritual* concerns.

36 MARCUSE, ONTOLOGY, *supra* note 3, at 298.

37 *Id*. at 169.

that preceded it. Practical Idea is precisely this same act of creation. It is what Kant would call an *intellectual intuition*, where thought and deed are one.[38] Accordingly, the Good "comes upon the scene with the worth of being absolute, because it is within itself the totality of the Notion, the subjective that is at the same time in the form of free unity and subjectivity." (818) In other words, the Good is "action that is also a form of knowing."[39]

The Good is "objectivity that is conformable to the Notion." (770) Yet it is defective. It is actualized but still a subjectivity. Furthermore, its actuality is an otherness. "[T]his is a determinate content and to that extent [it is] something *finite* and *limited*." (819) Being finite, the various "goods" brought forth by the Notion must pass away. The Notion is caught in the bad infinity of producing goods that cannot sustain themselves.

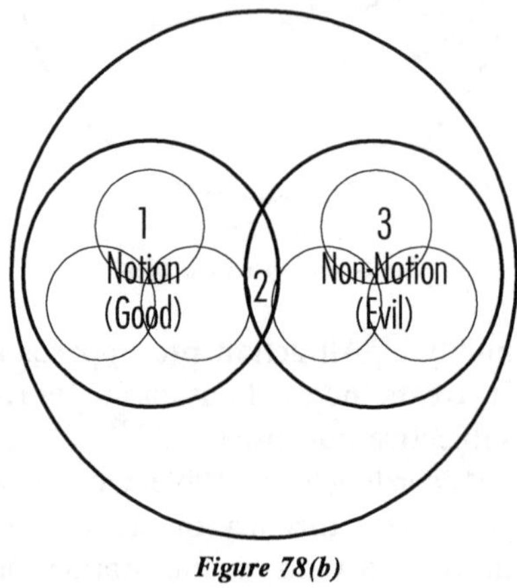

Figure 78(b)
Evil

Dialectical Reason points out that, if the Good is the act of obliterating obstacles to freedom, so that the Idea can be actualized, then the intellectual intuition of Notion must itself be this Good, which must itself obliterate *its* obstacles. The product of the Good has no staying power unless what it produces is also the Good – just as much a progenitor of Goods as Practical Idea is. When the Notion produces Good that

[38] According to Charles Taylor:

> Hegel reproaches Kant for not having cleaved to the notion of an intellectual intuition, which he himself invented. This would be an understanding, which unlike ours did not have to depend on external reception, on being affected from outside, for its contents, but created them with its thought. This archetypical intellect Kant attributed to God; it was quite beyond us. But God's intellect is ultimately revealed to us for Hegel, it only lives in our thought. Hence we can participate in an intellectual intuition. God's thought is ours.

TAYLOR, *supra* note 3, at 301. An intellectual intuition amounts to "the direct apprehension of things as they are . . . " ROSEN, *supra* note 13, at 267.

[39] MARCUSE, ONTOLOGY, *supra* note 3, at 171.

conflicts with the subjective goods of the Notion, the Good finds that it faces obstacles. Hence, the Good of the second individual is Evil for the first.

The good "remains an *ought-to-be*." (820) It aims at freedom but produces only more obstacles. At this late stage, then, Practical Idea faces a topsy-turvy world in which the Good of one is Evil to the other: "There are still two worlds in opposition, one a realm of subjectivity in the pure regions of transparent thought, the other a realm of objectivity in the element of an externally manifold actuality that is an undisclosed realm of darkness." (820)

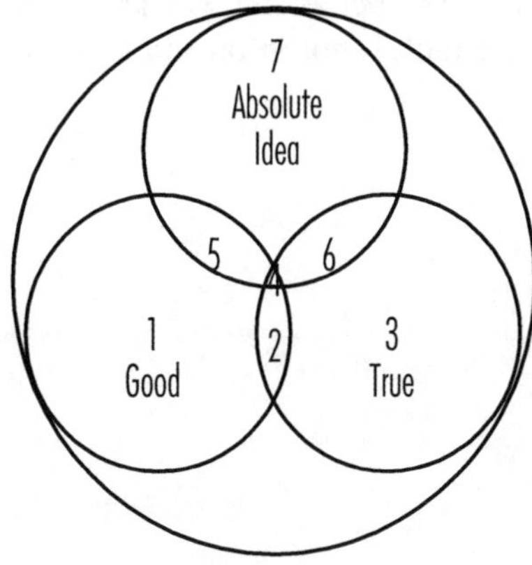

Figure 78(c)
Absolute Idea

Two Ideas now face each other. Yet we also know that these two Ideas are implicitly the *same* Idea. Accordingly, in naming the other Idea Evil, the Good proclaims *itself* evil. And, if Evil is that which impedes the Good, the Good constitutes an obstacle to itself.

Being finite, both Good *and* Evil must self-erase. So Good and Evil replicate the dynamic of Subjective End, which purported to reduce objectivity to Means. But in so doing, it revealed itself to be Means, because Means requires End to be what it is. Both sides required each other.[40] Still, Good is more advanced than external purposiveness. Subjective End was for another, not for itself. The Good is for itself, even as its manifestations are impeded by competing Goods.

Because there are competing Goods, the Good implies otherness – an objectivity – confronting it. What is lacking is knowledge that the Evil otherness is Practical Idea's own self. "*[P]ractical* Idea still lacks the moment of the *theoretical* Idea." (821) In theoretical Idea, subjectivity was certain of itself. Now subjectivity needs to be certain that its *other* is itself. When it realizes this, it will finally cognize itself

40 *See* Brian Lefrow, *God and World in Hegel and Whitehead*, in HEGEL AND WHITEHEAD: CONTEMPORARY PERSPECTIVES ON SYSTEMATIC PHILOSOPHY 262 (George R. Lucas, Jr., ed. 1986) ("This is Hegel's theodicy, and it reinforces the message of God's discreteness from and dependence on the world").

as its other.[41] Such an event requires that subjectivity and objectivity self-erase in favor of their unity.[42]

When this occurs, there is achieved a unity of the Good (thinking or doing) and the True (being, but also self-erasure). The unity of the two is Absolute Idea. On the verge of ending the entire *SL*, Hegel puts self-erasure at the apex. The Absolute Idea is that spirit actualizes itself by *doing*. This is the Good. But the Good is also the True. The True is the collapse of the positivized thing-in-itself. It *is*. What is Good *and* True is when Notion obliterates *itself* as the sole and only obstacle to its freedom.[43] For spirit, the fault is not in the stars but in itself that it is an underling.

---

41 EUGÈNE FLEISCHMANN, LA SCIENCE UNIVERSELLE OU LA LOGIQUE DE HEGEL 19 (1968) (consciousness "is seemingly a fight against the 'object', but finally [it] perceives that it is not in the grip of *[aux prises avec]* something exterior but with itself").

42 The Good self-erases because its attack on the other is an attack on itself. Charles Taylor, however, thinks that the Good fails because it is an unattainable beyond. TAYLOR, *supra* note 3, at 336. This cannot be accepted, because the Good *is* attained in Absolute Idea. The sublation of the Good means preservation as well as cancellation. Taylor also suggests that perhaps two Goods may come into conflict. *Id*. Hegel's point is that they *inevitably* come into conflict.

43 *Cf*. G.W.F. Hegel, *The Spirit of Christianity and Its Fate*, in G.W.F. HEGEL, EARLY THEOLOGICAL WRITINGS 224-5 ("When subjectivity is set against the positive, service's moral neutrality vanishes along with its limited character. Man confronts himself; his character and his deeds become the man himself. He has barriers only where he erects them himself, and his virtues are determinacies which he fixes himself.").

27
Absolute Idea

> The result *is* the process – its perpetual reenactment.[1]

Absolute Idea, the "speculative nucleus"[2] of Hegelianism, is what remains after thinking (Truth) and doing (Good) abolish themselves. The Truth is that self-identical things pass away. The Good is the obliteration of all obstacles to the creation of a reality in which the subject is at home. The *True Good* is the realization that Absolute Idea has only itself as its obstacle. Idea "has given up the knowledge of itself as of something confronting the object of which it is only the annihilation." (69) "Knowing, then, will not be a representation . . . but a presentation . . . and consequently the negation of every and all given presence, be it that of an 'object' or of a subject.'"[3] In short, exposition *is* the subject matter. The two coincide. For this reason,

> Hegel resolutely turns his back on every kind of nostalgia, that is, on every kind of comfort drawn from the image of a given but past sense. But inversely, this is not in order to place his trust in a new given . . . Neither past nor future present, but naked present: that is, stripped down to the point of its coming, in the instability of becoming.[4]

---

[1] EMIL L. FACKENHEIM, THE RELIGIOUS DIMENSION IN HEGEL'S THOUGHT 108 (1967).

[2] GIACOMO RINALDI, A HISTORY AND INTERPRETATION OF THE LOGIC OF HEGEL 8 (1992).

[3] JEAN-LUC NANCY, HEGEL: THE RESTLESSNESS OF THE NEGATIVE 11 (Jason Smith & Steven Miller eds. 1997).

[4] *Id.* at 14.

When this point is established, we have Idea "in this self-determination of *apprehending itself*." (825) "In its most authentic sense, being is comprehended and comprehending being – the concept."[5]

Yet Absolute Idea is not the final step of the Logic. Absolute Idea must develop its moments of immediacy and mediation. When this is accomplished, we reach Absolute Knowing – the phrase that terminates the *Phenomenology* and that initiates the introductory materials as the very last step (and presupposition) of the entire *SL*. Hegel does not use the phrase as such in his final chapter, but he does refer to the "*self-knowing Notion that has itself . . . for its subject matter*." (826) Self-knowing Notion is also generally referred to as Method.[6]

In Absolute Knowing, form and content are united. That is to say, Absolute Idea thinks itself – this thought of itself is its form. But there is nothing beyond this form. Hence, by default, form is also content. The true content of Appearance is its own self.[7] As predicted, it's appearance all the way down. Appearance *is* reality. *Form* is "the soul of all objectivity and all otherwise determined content has its truth in the form alone." (825)

The very use of the word "content" is now outmoded.[8] Content is "the form-determination withdrawn into itself . . . in such a manner that this concrete identity stands opposed to the identity explicated as form." (825) Content, as that term was used in Figure 30(c), "has the shape of an other and a *datum*." (825) Indeed, throughout the *SL*, all

---

[5] HERBERT MARCUSE, HEGEL'S ONTOLOGY AND THE THEORY OF HISTORICITY 129 (Seyla Benhabib trans. 1987).

[6] Hegel distinguishes Method (or free Notion) from merely formal Notion, which is "the *particular* aspect of method." (826) It represents human subjectivity – *our* participation in Absolute Idea. Formal Notion is "knowing's own subjective act, the *instrument* and means" (827) of Method – distinguished from and yet essential to Method. Method, in contrast, is *free* Notion – "the Notion that is determined in and for itself." (823) Free Notion is the middle term of the syllogism of which subject and object are the extremes.

[7] Richard Dien Winfield, *From Concept to Judgement: Rethinking Hegel's Overcoming of Formal Logic*, 50 DIALOGUE 53, 59 (2001) ("the unity of topic and method . . . precludes the difference between knowing and its object on which the representational cognition of consciousness depends") (footnote omitted).

[8] *See* ERMANNO BENCIVENGA, HEGEL'S DIALECTICAL LOGIC 38 (2002) ("There is for [Hegel] nothing *to which* spiritual movement 'happens' (however ineluctably) – spiritual movement is the whole"). Rinaldi puts it this way: abstraction is thought itself. I can abstract from *experience*. But I cannot abstract from abstraction. Since pure thought is before us, there is no further place to go *beyond* thought. RINALDI, *supra* note 2, at 305.

the possible shapes of "content" have been displayed and shown to be untrue.[9] It is now impossible for *any* given object to be some inner essence to which absolute form is merely external and contingent. For this reason, "method identifies its own internal conditions, making no reference to anything external."[10] The point is that method *cannot stand apart from content*. Otherwise, method is dogma, and so are its products. What must occur is a complete merger of substance and procedure – of content and method.

Absolute Idea exhibits all the moments there are – (1) immediacy, (2) mediation and (3) the mediation of immediacy and mediation. First, Absolute Idea is Immediate. I have argued that Figure 79(a) – not Absolute Knowing – is the very first step of the Logic.[11] It stands for the Understanding itself and for immediate Pure Being. This is what the Understanding abstracts in its attempt to express Absolute Idea. Its attempt, however, is a failure. Pure Being *is* Pure Nothing. The name of this collapse is Becoming. "[T]he immediate of the beginning," Hegel writes, "must be *in its own self* deficient and endowed with the *urge* to carry itself further." (829) Such an immediacy is "already *posited* as infected with a *negation*. For this reason too *there is* nothing, whether in *actuality* or *thought*, that is as simple and as abstract as is commonly imagined." (829) In different words, method by its nature

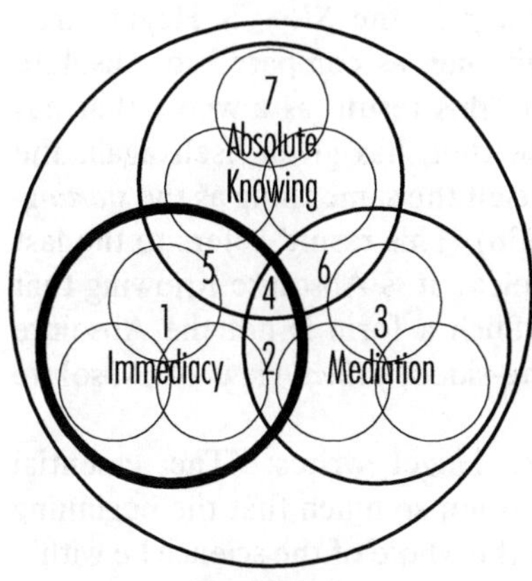

Figure 79(a)
Immediacy

---

[9] In chapter 12 content as such was defined as the process of sublation.

[10] JOHN W. BURBIDGE, ON HEGEL'S LOGIC: FRAGMENTS OF A COMMENTARY 217 (1981). But has not the *SL* been replete with references to that which is external to thought? Indeed, was not nature precisely that which is external to thought? See chapter 2. Burbidge comments, "even though some of those concepts refer to *particularity*, contrast *externality* to *internality*, and emphasize *difference*, their connotation remains strictly intellectual." BURBIDGE, *supra*, at 220. The external is strictly *internal* to thought. For this reason, there is nothing "natural" or unidealized in the *SL*. William Maker, *Hegel's Logic of Freedom*, 2 HEGEL'S THEORY OF THE SUBJECT (David Gray Carlson ed. 2005).

[11] *Supra* at 27-8.

"generates its own incompleteness in the process of its elaboration."[12]

Because immediacy is destined to fail, Logic *must* advance on to a more adequate definition of the absolute. "Hence the advance is not a kind of *superfluity*; this it would be if that with which the beginning is made were in truth already the absolute." (829) In this sense, Absolute Knowing (the last step) is broader and more comprehensive than Immediacy. In effect, Immediacy must *grow into* Absolute Knowing. In effect, *all* of the *SL* is encompassed between Figure 79(a) and 79(c).

Immediacy – the *antepenultimate step* in the *SL* – is Hegel's true beginning. This means that the beginning, as compared to Absolute Knowing, is a *reduction* or *retraction*: "this result, as a whole that has withdrawn into and is *identical* with itself, has given itself again the form of *immediacy*. Hence it is now itself the same thing as the *starting-point* had determined itself to be. (838) "This result" refers to the last step of Absolute Knowing. Nevertheless, it is Absolute Knowing that gives itself the *form* of immediacy. Such a form is not the Absolute Form. Such an immediacy is a one-sided, *failed* view of Absolute Knowing.

In the beginning of the Logic, Hegel writes: "The essential requirement for the science of logic is not so much that the beginning be a pure immediacy, but rather that the whole of the science be within itself a circle in which the first is also the last and the last is also the first." (71) This passage might seem to indicate that the *last* step of the Logic is also the first step. But this remark directly follows a description of spiritual diremption.

> [A]t the *end* of the development [spirit] is known as freely externalizing itself, abandoning itself to the shape of an *immediate being* – opening or unfolding itself . . . into the creation of a world which contains all that fell into the development which preceded that result and which through this reversal of its position relatively to its beginning is transformed into something dependent on the result as principle. (71)

So Absolute Knowing "creates the world" by *reducing* itself to immediacy – an original sin which must of necessity lead to the development of all the forms described throughout the *SL*. "[P]ure being is the unity into which pure knowing withdraws." (72)

But *reduction* of Absolute Knowing to Pure Being is only one way of

[12] BURBIDGE, LOGIC, *supra* note 10, at 225.

viewing the process. Why does this reduction occur? Because there must be a *deficiency* in Absolute Knowing to which the Understanding responds. Pure Being is therefore both a reduction of and an expansion of Absolute Knowing. In short, Absolute Knowing is not Absolute without this necessary, erroneous, one-sided Immediacy.[13] Angelica Nuzzo observes:

> "Being, pure being" with which the logic begins (or has begun) is, in a sense, a more comprehensive concept than that of the absolute idea at the beginning of the last chapter of the logic. And yet the absolute idea also comprehends and at the same time exceeds what has been developed so far as to put itself in the position of uniqueness that allows it to bring the logic to an end.[14]

Absolute Knowing is not the first step of the Logic. Rather, it is *left behind* when the Logic commences, recalling Hegel's earlier dictum that "[w]hat is thus found only *comes to be* through being *left behind*." (402) Like a wise parent begetting a headstrong child, Absolute Knowing, "in its absolute self-assurance and inner poise," (843) stands back from its content, "allowing it to have free play." (73) Childish immediacy – not mediation or the unity of immediacy and mediation – commences the Logic and must grow into Absolute Idea over its course.[15]

Absolute Knowing is a totality, no doubt, but one that includes an absence which the Understanding seeks to plug up with its one-sided proposition. Slavoj Žižek proclaims this

> the ultimate ambiguity if Hegel. According to the standard *doxa*, the telos of the dialectical process is the absolute form that abolishes any material surplus. If, however, this is truly the case with Hegel, how are we to account for the fact that the Result effectively throws us back into the whirlpool, that it is nothing but the totality of the route we had to travel in order to arrive at the Result? In other

---

[13] I therefore disagree with Mure who writes, "In Absolute Idea sublation is perfect, and there is no further onward movement of pure thought save in the sense that the dialectic of the categories is a return of spirit upon itself and may be metaphorically called circular." G.R.G. MURE, A STUDY OF HEGEL'S LOGIC 343 (1950).

[14] Angelica Nuzzo, *The End of Hegel's Logic: Absolute Idea as Absolute Method*, in HEGEL'S THEORY OF THE SUBJECT, *supra* note 10, at 191.

[15] Relevant here is Burbidge's observation that method "is not simply an atemporal logical idea. It equally characterizes the temporal process – the negative dialectic of passing away . . . But these two processes – the one logical, the other temporal – do not stand outside each other, simply sharing a common structure. They are conjoined by a double movement from logic to time and from time to logic." BURBIDGE, LOGIC, *supra* note 10, at 224. In other words, logic enters into history when the Understanding tries (and fails) to understand. The finite immediacies of the Understanding are history itself.

words, is not a kind of leap from "not-yet" to "always-already" constitutive of the Hegelian dialectics: we endeavor to approach the Goal (the absolute devoid of any matter), when, all of a sudden, we establish that all the time we were already there? Is not the crucial shift in a dialectical process the reversal of anticipation – not into its fulfillment, but – into retraction? If, therefore, the fulfillment never occurs in the Present, does this not testify to the irreducible status of *objet a?*[16]

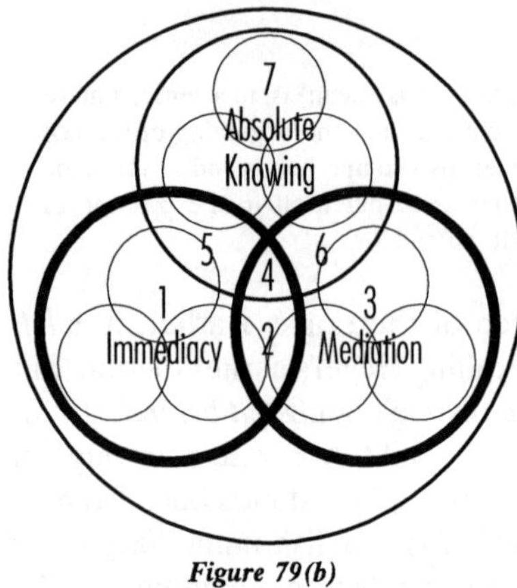

Figure 79(b)
Mediation

Method is, therefore, a totality that is never complete, and this is why the circle always turns.[17] Absolute Knowing requires that there be a one-sided, unspiritual proposition to fill the gap that Method implies.[18]

A simple way to understand this is to consider Absolute Knowing as the negation of the negation. Immediacy is positive proposition. Mediation is the first negation. The negation of the negation cannot merely restore one-sided proposition. In a sense, it is something more – a synthesis of new material. In a sense, it is something less. Something more is needed to describe the absolute than the negation of the negation. There is a hole in the whole, which

---

16 SLAVOJ ŽIŽEK, TARRYING WITH THE NEGATIVE: KANT, HEGEL, AND THE CRITIQUE OF IDEOLOGY 156 (1993). The *objet a* (Lacan's "little other") represents a negativity in the center of subjectivity. The subject desires to fill the void of the *objet a* – an impossible task.

17 *See* Stephen Houlgate, *Hegel's Critique of Foundationalism in the "Doctrine of Essence"*, GERMAN PHILOSOPHY SINCE KANT 27 (Anthony O'Hear ed. 1999) ("The understanding being reached in the *Logic* thus turns out . . . to be an underdetermination of what being is in truth: it tells us merely what being must *first* be understood to be").

18 Is Method analytical or synthetic in quality? Obviously it is both. Nuzzo, *supra* note 14, at 198. Absolute Idea deals only with its own product – not with anything from the outside. It does not "catch . . . at circumstances, examples and comparisons, but [keeps] before it solely the things themselves and brings before consciousness what is immanent in them. The method of absolute cognition is to this extent *analytic*." (830) But within Absolute Idea is difference. Within its scope, its product appears as other, and it relates this other to itself. Such a synthesis, however, is "no longer the same thing as is meant by synthetic in finite cognition; the mere fact of the subject matter's no less analytic determination in general, that the relation is relation within the *Notion*, completely distinguishes it from [finite] synthesis." (831)

the Understanding tries to fill. This hole is none other than [4] – being-within-self. This [4] ends up being a negativity that motivates the neverending circular process of the logic. *It is the silent fourth* that disturbs the unity of Absolute Idea, guaranteeing that the process never comes to rest.[19]

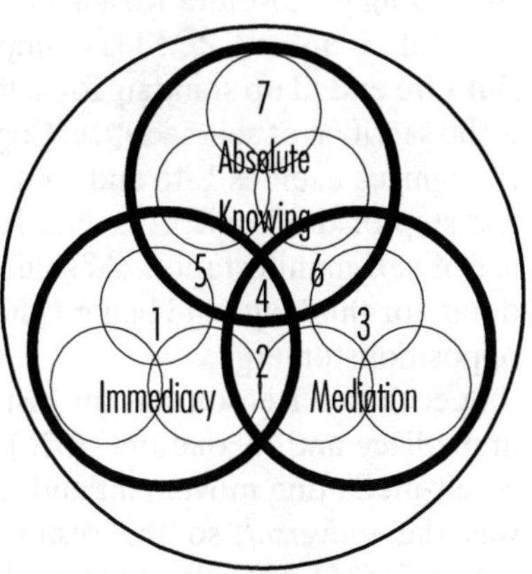

Figure 79(c)
Absolute Knowing
(Method)

But this is to look ahead – or perhaps behind. If Pure Being is incomplete, Absolute Idea contains its necessary supplement. Absolute Idea has something that Pure Being does not – an otherness now seen as indistinguishable from selfhood. In fact, *every* otherness – nature included[20] – is Absolute Idea's own self. Its selfhood therefore comprehends all Mediation. The significance of Mediation is that Absolute Idea is revealed to be an active, dialectic thinker [3] that thinks itself [1]. As such, it has personality:[21]

> The highest, most concentrated point is the *pure personality* which, solely through the absolute dialectic which is its nature, no less *embraces and holds everything within itself*, because it makes itself the supremely free – the simplicity which is the first immediacy and Universality." (841)

---

[19] G.R.G. MURE, THE PHILOSOPHY OF HEGEL 151 (1965) ("In the abstract element of logic, the Idea, which has developed from Pure Being, lacks being as the moment of external reality. This other of pure thought in which the Idea now freely puts itself forth is therefore sheer self-externality, sheer other-being.") (footnotes omitted).

[20] As Hegel puts it earlier, "As this relation, Idea is the *process* of sundering itself into individuality and its inorganic nature, and again of bringing this inorganic nature under the power of the subject and returning to the first simple universality." (759) *See* BURBIDGE, LOGIC, *supra* note 10, at 221 ("[T]hat which is other than thought will not remain impervious to it. For intelligence has already discovered that these limiting characteristics dissolve into a more inclusive perspective.").

[21] Something Hegel declared to be missing in Spinozist substance. *Supra* at 400. According to Clark Butler, the reference to personality invokes the French revolution. "In early nineteenth-century German philosophy no one could invoke a principle of personality without consciously referring to the Kantian notion of the person as a rational end in itself . . . " CLARK BUTLER, HEGEL'S LOGIC: BETWEEN DIALECTIC AND HISTORY 280 (1996).

Personality implies that [1] is Life and [3] is Cognition of Life. Accordingly, Absolute Idea is the return to Life but also the sublation of it. Life is immediate Idea – "impenetrable atomic subjectivity." (824) But Life ended up standing for self-sacrifice, so that Absolute Knowing is the sacrifice of self-sacrifice. Cognition, in contrast, is mediated Idea. It cognizes itself as Life and so it too sacrifices itself. And, in the very last step of the Logic, Absolute Idea returns to immediacy in its final act of self-manifestation. Absolute Knowing is therefore the unity of doing (or thinking) and being – the original unity from which these two oppositions emerge.

Speculative Reason has the last word. Absolute Knowing "is *equally* immediacy and mediation." (836) It is "not a quiescent third, but . . . is self-mediating movement and activity. As that with which we began was the *universal*, so the result is the *individual*, the *concrete*, the *subject*." (836) Absolute Knowing knows itself as a living Individual that must manifest itself in otherness. Absolute Knowing is spirit's own manifestation in the world – *and* spirit's knowledge of its own act. It is a unity of being and doing. In Absolute Knowing, "rational Notion . . . in its reality meets only with itself." (824) Because it creates the world by sending forth the Understanding in its abstraction in order to begin the Logic, Absolute Knowing is "the original unity between subjectivity and objectivity," and "*motility* is also acknowledged thereby as a fundamental character of Being."[22]

Method is Absolute Form's other name. It represents the stage at which there is no transcendental beyond to which self-negating Idea can withdraw. Hegel is keen to emphasize that Method is not simply *given*. As such, it would be external to Logic and hence subjective.[23] Rather, Method has built up itself from itself, and its theme from the beginning has been dissolution of form. "[I]ts entire course, in which all possible shapes of a given content and of objects came up for consideration, has demonstrated their transition and untruth." (826) Method was the movement by which all forms erased themselves. Now, at the close, Method itself is isolated as the core of all there is. It is "*soul and substance*, and anything whatever is comprehended and known in its truth only when it is *completely subjugated to the method*." (826) And since Method is self-erasure, finite thoughts are only *truly*

---

[22] MARCUSE, *supra* note 5, at 4.

[23] JEAN HYPPOLITE, LOGIC AND EXISTENCE 167 (Leonard Lawlor & Amit Sen trans., 1997) (Method "is the opposite of instrumental knowledge or of external reflection, which would be merely subjective").

known when they pass away. Hegel is thus the modern Heraclitus, the weeping philosopher, of whom Hegel said, "there is no proposition of Heraclitus which I have not adopted in my Logic."[24]

Method is to be recognized as "the absolutely infinite force, to which no object, presenting itself as something external, remote from and independent of reason, could offer resistance." (826) In other words, Method requires that the finite must by its own logic pass away; resistance is useless.

The silent fourth. In the second chapter, I alluded to Žižek's suggestion that there is a silent fourth – an external reflection that witnesses the triadic steps of the Logic unfold. There is a difficult passage in the final chapter in which Hegel counts *four* steps in method – the usual three and perhaps the silent fourth. The usual three are immediacy, its negation, and the negation of the negation. The negation of the negation, however, "can also be reckoned as *fourth*." (836) There is added to the traditional three terms an "absolute negativity or the second negative." (836) That is to say, the *first* negative is Negation in Figure 2(b). The second negative is the silent fourth. It is Cognition, which also erases itself in favor of Absolute Idea.

Consistent with this, Hegel suggests that, for finite cognition, Method is not End but Means. To invoke the syllogism of the subject-object distinction, Method (thought in general) is the middle term of subject and object. Through Method, the subject *uses* thought to comprehend objects. Yet thought also divides the subject *from* the object. The extremes of the merely formal syllogism remain diverse. Diverse things, however, self-erase. Self-erasure of the extremes, in turn, is precisely what *True* Cognition is. In True Cognition, the extremes of the syllogism erase themselves and remove themselves to the middle term, which is Method – Notion determined in and for itself. In Method, the silent fourth is dissolved. But it will emerge again in the beginning as the perspective able to discern the difference between what Pure Being was supposed to be and what it was (not) actually.

Logic and nature. The *SL* concludes with some observations that purport to position Logic *vis-à-vis* nature and mind. Absolute Idea, Hegel says, "is the sole subject matter and content of philosophy." (824) "All else is error, confusion, opinion, endeavor, caprice and transitori-

[24] 1 HEGEL'S LECTURES ON THE HISTORY OF PHILOSOPHY 279 (E.S. Haldane & Frances H. Simson trans., 1892).

ness." (824)[25] All things dissolve themselves into Absolute Idea. Absolute Idea, however, likewise negates itself – differentiates itself from itself – thereby producing nature.[26] Nature yields mind (*Geist*),[27] which in turn yields Absolute Idea. In this fashion Hegel previews his *Encyclopedia*, which consists of the *Lesser Logic*, the *Philosophy of Nature* and the *Philosophy of Mind*, in that order. These individual sciences are "[l]inks in this chain . . . each of which has an *antecedent* and a *successor* – or, expressed more accurately, *has* only the *antecedent* and *indicates* its *successor* in its conclusion." (842)[28]

Logic, nature and spirit are "modes" (forms) of Absolute Idea's existence. Art, religion and philosophy are modes of its self-comprehension. But Logic is "the universal mode in which all particular modes are sublated and enfolded." (825) Here Hegel affirms that the

---

[25] Nuzzo holds this passage to be the key to the last chapter. Method is what all prior steps have in common. To the extent anything is added to this, it is an external reflection – a diversity which must erase itself. Method is the only thing left standing, and for this reason the logic can legitimately end with its derivation. Nuzzo, *supra* note 14.

[26] As we saw in chapter 2. According to John Burbidge, "The move from the science of logic to the philosophy of nature has been one of the most difficult aspects of Hegel's whole philosophy. His early colleague, Friedrich Schelling, was to call it an illegitimate leap into another genus." John W. Burbidge, *Hegel's Logic*, in HANDBOOK OF THE HISTORY OF LOGIC 131, 168 (2004). Yet, if the Logic includes its own gap or aporia, why can't we name this very gap *nature*?

[27] Mind stands for *history*, the negation of nature. JOHN F. HOFFMEYER, THE ADVENT OF FREEDOM: THE PRESENCE OF THE FUTURE IN HEGEL'S LOGIC 62 (1994).

[28] Michael Inwood proclaims transition beyond method to be incomprehensible:

> It is clear . . . that something special is supposed to happen at the end of the *Logic*, something of a kind which has not happened within the *Logic*. The fact that logic is a totality, and a circular totality at that, explains why it spills over into another totality, nature. But how does it do that? There is, on the face of it, no reason to suppose that a self-generating, interlocking system of one kind will necessarily "freely release itself" into other such systems. One might be tempted to conclude that Hegel is using the word "totality" ambiguously to mean, firstly, an interlocking, self-contained system and, secondly, an all-embracing system, and that he is wrongly assuming that if the logical idea is a totality in the first sense, then it is a totality in the second sense too.

M.J. INWOOD, HEGEL 379-80 (1983). In fact, if the totality is incomplete, then a supplement is necessarily required. Hegel's insight is that the supplement is not something external to method but is *method itself*. In this passage, Inwood shows an inability to grasp the True Infinite, which becomes something different *and* stays what it is. For this reason, the totality *can* be self-contained *and* embrace otherness, because the other is its own self.

SL is indeed the centerpiece of his entire philosophy. As the *prius*, Logic is "the original *word*, which is an *outwardizing* or *utterance* . . . but an utterance that in being has immediately vanished again as something outer." (825)[29] This outer word, however, "is not yet *otherness*, but is and remains perfectly transparent to itself." (825)[30]

And with such observations, the monumental *SL* draws to a close. But is it true? This we shall assess in our final chapter.

---

[29] ERROL E. HARRIS, THE SPIRIT OF HEGEL 159 (1993) (Hegel "is saying at the end of the Logic that, of necessity, God creates the world ex nihilo"). Hyppolite discourages causal claims. Rather, logic requires nature and *vice versa*. This mutual dependence is underwritten by Hegel's idea that the Universal – the moment of the Logic – already contains the Particular – the moment of Nature. And each of these contains the moment of *Geist*. JEAN HYPPOLITE, GENESIS AND STRUCTURE OF HEGEL'S *PHENOMENOLOGY OF SPIRIT* 602-3 (Samuel Cherniak & John Heckman trans., 1974).

[30] "It is as Hegel says ideally transparent, because it is nothing but thought of thought whereas all the other sciences are thought of some particular matter, which has cognition and not totally transparent content to it." CHARLES TAYLOR, HEGEL 340 (1975)

28
Conclusion

Is the *SL* true? Hegel has shown the question is itself invalid. Truth is the "the agreement of thought with its object." (44) Yet, at the end of the *SL*, thought and object have coincided. The question "is it true?" presupposes the distinction between subject and object and therefore is not a well formed question within Hegel's system. What is *true* in Hegel system is that *both* subject and object self-erase. That is the *Idea*.

The usual (Marxist) objection to Hegel's system is that logic concerns form, not substance. Whatever is going on in Hegel's logic is strictly confined to Hegel's head and does not affect the material world that exists beyond any system of thought.[1] The absence in the *SL* of any reliance on sensuous intuition "awakens the suspicion that the whole Hegelian enterprise is simply a house of dreams – the construct of an ivory tower far removed from the critical tensions of real life."[2] Yet this suspicion is nothing but Kant's dogma of the thing-in-itself, a position that Hegel has completely undercut. In Hegel's analysis, the thing-in-itself beyond thought is diverse and finite. The only truth it has

---

[1] ERMANNO BENCIVENGA, HEGEL'S DIALECTICAL LOGIC 34 (2002) ("To bring up again an obvious reaction that surfaced before, isn't there a radical opposition between anything conceptual at all – not just the traditional concept *table*, say – and this concrete, material table that I am looking at and knocking on, and trying to make sure I don't knock on too hard or I will hurt myself?"). Bencivenga provides an aesthetic interpretation of Hegel. To him, the *Science of Logic* is a narrative, a poem, a subjective exercise.

[2] JOHN W. BURBIDGE, ON HEGEL'S LOGIC: FRAGMENTS OF A COMMENTARY 204 (1981). This is not a sentiment Burbidge agrees with, however.

is that it is a phenomenon, like any other. It dissolves on its own logic, cutting the ground out from any criticism that insists there is a noumenon standing beyond Hegel's logic.

Indeed, the *SL* is all about self-erasure and destruction of finite thoughts. "All . . . possible determinations are now to be systematically derived within the turbulence of continual self-canceling negativity."[3] Even Hegel's derivations dissolve themselves. Dissolution *is* the system.

For this reason, the only way to proclaim the *SL* wrong is to assert something that does not dissolve. But what is that thing? Kant's thing-in-itself? Any such assertion of Kantianism must show *why* the thing-in-itself is immune from sublation. "Declaring [Hegel's] endeavors to be insufficient, or proclaiming them to be arrogant or simply unsuccessful, does not release us from involvement in the very dialectic that he espoused, or the obligation to pursue it to its end."[4] If Hegel is wrong, he is entitled to a demonstration that this is so.

One of the best books on Hegel is Stanley Rosen's contribution, published in 1974,[5] at a time when authors were *expected* to proclaim Hegel's work a failure. And Rosen does not disappoint his readers. Given the high quality and considerable sympathy of Rosen's analysis, I will let him speak generally for all of Hegel's critics.

In my view, Rosen's criticism of Hegel is not well taken. Despite his considerable sympathy for Hegelian themes and his plethora of insights into the nature of Hegel's logic, Rosen falls back on the usual Kantian dogmata in proclaiming Hegel a failure. More specifically, Rosen suggests that any given proposition of the Understanding must be a *successful* description of the logic steps that precede it.[6] If the Understanding asserts *A, B, C . . . P*, "the successful assertion of *P* is guaranteed or certified by the coordinate moment . . . of the development of the Absolute."[7] In other words, the Understanding's move is correct *because* there is only one *possible* proposition it can make, given its place in the logical progression. *P must* follow *O*. *P* is not a *creation* or *performance*, as an intellectual intuition would be. "As Hegel so frequently reminds us, philosophy is a recollection of an already

---

3 HANS-GEORG GADAMER, HEGEL'S DIALECTIC: FIVE HERMENEUTICAL STUDIES 18 (Christopher Smith trans., 1976)

4 ERROL E. HARRIS, THE SPIRIT OF HEGEL 18 (1993).

5 STANLEY ROSEN, G.W.F. HEGEL: AN INTRODUCTION TO THE SCIENCE OF WISDOM (1974).

6 *Id.* at 272.

7 *Id.*

concluded experience."[8] "In sum, *Hegel claims that the actual is brought into being by discourse, and by a discourse which can occur only after the actual presents itself*."[9] The point seems to be that knowledge of the absolute must be an intellectual intuition which *creates*, but all we get from Hegel is the Understanding's intuition which *reports*. Yet what does it report? A noumenal absolute to which it has no access. "So far as I can see, this is a contradiction which has no *Aufhebung*."[10] Hegel's philosophy is therefore "not recollection but *projection* or linguistic constructivism . . . *the eternal is altogether inaccessible:* it conceals itself by the very process which ostensibly reveals it."[11]

This criticism misses a few points. First, the Understanding's proposition *P* is *never* successful; it is *one-sided*. Its failure is why logic progresses. The Understanding's propositions about the absolute are *never* guaranteed. Furthermore, the fate of the Understanding's proposition *is* the system, which is all about self-erasure. And among the things that self-erase is the very assertion of the noumenal beyond on which Rosen's critique is based. Self-destruction is the only thing that truly *is*.

Furthermore, it is not the case that Hegel insists upon the integrity of the various steps of the logic in the order set forth in the *SL*. We have documented how steps were rearranged between the two editions of the *SL*, and how the arrangement in the *EL* does not always match the arrangement in the *SL*. Indeed, Hegel himself says that he does not pretend that the *SL* is incapable of greater completeness. But he knows that his method is the only true one. (54) What Hegel insists upon is the sequence of immediacy, mediatedness and the unity of immediacy and mediatedness. This sequence is iterative; the first third of the *SL* (Being) is comparatively immediate compared to Essence, which is mediated, etc. Within each of these categories are many oscillations that follow the tripartite pattern. The exact *names* assigned to the logical steps Hegel identifies is a matter of judgment and creativity on Hegel's part. For this reason, he rearranged specific steps a bit, consistent with the overall iterative pattern. *Method* is what is true in the *SL*. The empirical *SL* is open to criticism; Hegel would be the first to admit this.

In his criticism, Rosen follows Adorno in denying that the negative

---

8 *Id*. at 273.

9 *Id*.

10 *Id*.

11 *Id*.

is also a positive: "What remains unintelligible is how presence can be explained as a crystallization of absence . . . if form is produced by negative activity, then negative activity cannot be analyzed into formal constituents."[12] But this is just a repetition of the Kantian presupposition of the thing-in-itself that produces forms but is itself not formal or knowable. Hegel's genius is that he does not *privilege* the negative in this way. Being a one-sided positivity, the negative itself is subject to the law of appearance and must disappear. The self-sacrifice of the negative *is* the positivity that Hegel's philosophy preaches. And this is precisely why Rosen's neo-Kantian criticism from noumenal grounds must be rejected.

Rosen also complains that Hegel can account for dissolution of forms but not the *creation* of forms. "What we require is an account of intuition that sees both forms and their oscillations, or determinations and their negations."[13] Yet the only form there is in Hegel's system *is* self-erasure. There *is* no distinction between forms and their "oscillation." For Hegel, these are the same thing, and so he *has* accounted for the creation of forms when he accounts for the dissolution of forms.

Because Hegel supposedly cannot account for positivity, Rosen proclaims "that the Whole is itself less than the Whole; the final stage of the science of wisdom has not yet been achieved."[14] Ironically, this *is* the Whole that Hegel intended – a whole that is *not* whole, and identity that is not an identity. This is the very soul of Speculative Reason itself. As the negation of the negation, it *never* reimposes the one-sided proposition of the Understanding. Something is *always* left out every step of the way. It is for this very reason that the whole is in motion, a neverending circle.

In arguing that all positivities are finite and must pass away, Hegel proves to be a very tough opponent. How can Hegel be criticized except by means of some positivity? Yet any positivity with which Hegel is reproached is a Finite which must, of its own accord, become other and meld with cosmic fluidity of the Hegelian system. What Hegel has given us is a *positive system* of *negativity*. The only thing that endures is self-erasing system.

---

12 *Id.* at 276.
13 *Id.* at 277.
14 *Id.* at 278.

Bibliography

Works by Hegel

ELEMENTS OF THE PHILOSOPHY OF RIGHT (Allen W. Wood trans. (Cambridge: Cambridge University Press 1993).

HEGEL'S LOGIC (William Wallace trans.) (Oxford: Oxford University Press 1975).

HEGEL'S LECTURES ON THE HISTORY OF PHILOSOPHY (E.S. Haldane & Frances H. Simson trans.) (London: Kegan Paul 1892) (three volumes).

HEGEL'S PHILOSOPHY OF MIND (William Wallace & A.V. Miller trans.) (Oxford: Oxford University Press 1971).

HEGEL'S PHILOSOPHY OF NATURE (Michael John Petry trans.) (New York: Humanities Press 1970) (three volumes).

HEGEL'S SCIENCE OF LOGIC (A.V. Miller trans.) (London: George Allen Unwin 1969).

JENA SYSTEM, THE, 1804-5: LOGIC AND METAPHYSICS (John W. Burbidge & George di Giovanni trans.) (Kingston: McGill-Queens University Press 1986).

PHENOMENOLOGY OF SPIRIT, THE (A.V. Miller trans.) (Oxford: Clarendon Press 1977).

PHILOSOPHY OF HISTORY, THE (J. Sibree trans.) (New York: Dover 1991).

DIFFERENCE BETWEEN FICHTE'S AND SCHELLING'S SYSTEM OF PHILOSOPHY, THE (H.S. Harris & Walter Cerf trans.) (Albany: SUNY University Press 1977).

Spirit of Christianity and Its Fate, The, in EARLY THEOLOGICAL WRITINGS (T.M. Knox trans.) (Chicago: University of Chicago Press 1948).

WISSENSCHAFT DER LOGIK (Georg Lasson ed.) (Berlin: Akademie Verlag 1975).

Other Works

ADORNO, THEODOR W., HEGEL: THREE STUDIES (Shierry Weber Nicholsen trans.) (Cambridge: MIT Press 1999).

– NEGATIVE DIALECTICS (E.B. Ashton trans.) (New York: Continuum Publishing Co. 2000).

Allen, Robert van Roden, *Hegelian Beginning and Resolve: A View of the Relationship Between the* Phenomenology *and the* Logic, 13 IDEALISTIC STUDIES 249 (1983).

ALLISON, HENRY E., KANT'S THEORY OF FREEDOM (New Haven: Yale University Press 1990).

– KANT'S TRANSCENDENTAL IDEALISM: AN INTERPRETATION AND DEFENSE (New Haven: Yale University Press 1983).

ALTHAUS, HORST, HEGEL: AN INTELLECTUAL BIOGRAPHY (Michael Tarsh trans.) (Cambridge: Polity Press 2000).

Baur, Michael, *Hegel and the Overcoming of the Understanding*, 22 OWL OF MINERVA 141 (1991).

– *Sublating Kant and the Old Metaphysics: A Reading of the Transition from Being to Essence in Hegel's* Logic, 29 OWL OF MINERVA 139 (1998).

Beck, Lewis White, *Can Kant's Synthetic Judgments Be Made Analytic?*, in KANT: A COLLECTION OF CRITICAL ESSAYS (Robert Paul Wolff ed.) (Notre Dame: University of Notre Dame Press 1967).

BENCIVENGA, ERMANNO, HEGEL'S DIALECTICAL LOGIC (Oxford: Oxford University Press 2002).

BERKOWITZ, ROGER STUART, GIFT OF SCIENCE: LEIBNIZ AND THE MODERN LEGAL TRADITION (Cambridge: Harvard University Press 2005).

BERTHOLD-BOND, DANIEL, HEGEL'S THEORY OF MADNESS (Oxford: Oxford University Press 1995).

Bole, Thomas J., III, *The Cogency of the* Logic's *Argumentation: Securing the Dialectic's Claim to Justify Categories*, in HEGEL RECONSIDERED: BEYOND METAPHYSICS AND THE AUTHORITARIAN STATE (H. Tristram Engelhardt, Jr., & Terry Pinkard eds.) (Dordrecht: Kluwer 1994).

Bonispien, Wolfgang, *Newtonian Atomism and Eighteenth-Century Chemistry*, in HEGEL AND NEWTONIANISM (Michael John Petry ed.) (Dordrecht: Kluwer 1993).

Borzeszkowski, Host-Heino Von, *Hegel's Interpretation of Classical Mechanics*, in HEGEL AND NEWTONIANISM (Michael John Petry ed.) (Dordrecht: Kluwer 1993).

Buchdahl, Gerd, *Hegel on the Interaction Between Science and Philosophy*, in HEGEL AND NEWTONIANISM (Michael John Petry ed.) (Dordrecht Kluwer 1993).

Burbidge, John W., *Chemistry and Hegel's Logic*, in HEGEL AND NEWTONIANISM (Michael John Petry ed.) (Dordrecht Kluwer 1993).

– *Cognition and Finite Spirit*, in HEGEL'S THEORY OF THE SUBJECT (David Gray Carlson ed.) (London: Palgrave McMillan 2005).

– *Hegel's Conception of Logic*, in THE CAMBRIDGE COMPANION TO HEGEL 93 (Frederick C. Beiser ed.) (Cambridge: Cambridge University Press 1993).

– *Hegel's Logic*, in 1 HANDBOOK OF THE HISTORY OF LOGIC (Amsterdam Elsevier/North Holland 2004).

– HEGEL ON LOGIC AND RELIGION: THE REASONABLENESS OF CHRISTIANITY (Albany: SUNY Press 1992).

– ON HEGEL'S LOGIC: FRAGMENTS OF A COMMENTARY (New Jersey: Humanities Press 1981).

– REAL PROCESS: HOW LOGIC AND CHEMISTRY COMBINE IN HEGEL'S PHILOSOPHY OF NATURE (Toronto: University of Toronto Press 1996).

Butler, Clark, *Hegel in an Analytic Mode*, in HEGEL'S THEORY OF THE SUBJECT 170 (David Gray Carlson ed.) (London: Palgrave McMillan 2005).

– HEGEL'S LOGIC: BETWEEN DIALECTIC AND HISTORY (Albany: SUNY Press 1996).

Büttner, Stefan, *Hegel on Galilei's Law of Fall*, in HEGEL AND NEWTONIANISM (Michael John Petry ed.) (Dordrecht Kluwer 1993).

Carlson, David Gray, *Hegel's Theory of Measure*, 25 CARDOZO L. REV. 129 (2003).

– *Hegel's Theory of Quantity*, 23 CARDOZO L. REV. 2027 (2002).

– *How to Do Things with Hegel*, 78 TEX. L. REV. 1377 (2000).

– *Liberal Philosophy's Troubled Relation to the Rule of Law*, 43 U. TORONTO L. J. 257 (1993).

– *On the Margins of Microeconomics*, in DECONSTRUCTION AND THE POSSIBILITY OF JUSTICE (Drucilla Cornell et al eds.) (New York: Routledge 1992).

– *The Antepenultimacy of the Beginning in Hegel's* Science of Logic, in HEGEL'S THEORY OF THE SUBJECT (David Gray Carlson ed.) (London: Palgrave McMillan 2005).

– *The Traumatic Dimension in Law*, 24 CARDOZO L. REV. 2287 (2003).

Chaffin, Deborah, *The Logic of Contingency*, in HEGEL RECONSIDERED: BEYOND METAPHYSICS AND THE AUTHORITARIAN STATE (H. Tristram Engelhardt, Jr., & Terry Pinkard eds.) (Dordrecht: Kluwer 1994).

CHRISTENSEN, DARREL E., THE SEARCH FOR CONCRETENESS (London: Susquehanna University Press 1986).

COLLETTI, LUCIO, MARXISM AND HEGEL (Lawrence Garner trans.) (London: NLB 1973).

COPI, IRVING M., & CARL COHEN, INTRODUCTION TO LOGIC (11th ed.) (Englewood Cliffs, NJ: Prentice Hall 2002).

COPI, IRVING M., SYMBOLIC LOGIC (5th ed. 1979).

Copjec, Joan, *Introduction: Evil in the Time of the Finite World*, in RADICAL EVIL xiv (Joan Copjec ed.) (London: Verso 1996).

Cover, Robert M., *Nomos and Narrative*, 92 HARV. L. REV. 4 (1982).

Dahlstrom, Daniel O., *Hegel's Appropriation of Kant's Account of Teleology in Nature*, in HEGEL AND THE PHILOSOPHY OF NATURE (Stephen Houlgate ed.) (Albany: SUNY Press 1998).

Depré, Olivier, *The Ontological Foundations of Hegel's Dissertation of 1801*, in HEGEL AND THE PHILOSOPHY OF NATURE (Stephen Houlgate ed.) (Albany: SUNY Press 1998).

DERRIDA, JACQUES, POSITIONS (Alan Bass trans.) (London: Athlone Press 1971).

DESMOND, WILLIAM, BEYOND HEGEL AND DIALECTIC: SPECULATION, CULT, AND COMEDY (Albany: SUNY Press 1992).

D'HONDT, JACQUES, HEGEL IN HIS TIME: BERLIN, 1818-1831 (John Burbidge trans.) (Peterborough, Ontario: Broadview Press 1988).

Di Giovanni, George, *The Anti-Spinozism of Hegel: The Transition to Subjective Logic and the End of Classical Metaphysics*, in HEGEL'S THEORY OF THE SUBJECT (David Gray Carlson ed.) (London: Palgrave McMillan 2005).

– *The Category of Contingency in the Hegelian Logic*, in SELECTED ESSAYS ON G.W.F. HEGEL (Lawrence Stepelevich ed.) (Amherst: Prometheus Press 1993).

Dolar, Mladen, *The Cogito as the Subject of the Unconscious*, in SIC 2: COGITO AND THE UNCONSCIOUS (Slavoj Žižek ed.) (Durham: Duke University Press 1998).

Dove, Kenley Royce, *Hegel's "Deduction of the Concept of Science"*, in HEGEL IN THE SCIENCES (Robert S. Cohen & Marx W. Wartofsky eds.) (Dordrecht: Kluwer 1984).

Drees, Martin, *The Logic of Hegel's Philosophy of Nature*, in HEGEL AND NEWTONIANISM (Michael John Petry ed.) (Dordrecht Kluwer 1993).

Engel, S. Morris, *Kant's 'Refutation' of the Ontological Argument*, in Kant: A Collection of Critical Essays (Robert Paul Wolff ed.) (Notre Dame: University of Notre Dame Press 1968).

FACKENHEIM, EMIL L., THE RELIGIOUS DIMENSION IN HEGEL'S THOUGHT (1967).

Ferrini, Cinzia, *Framing Hypotheses: Numbers in Nature and the Logic of Measure in the Development of Hegel's System*, in HEGEL AND THE PHILOSOPHY OF NATURE (Stephen Houlgate ed.) (Albany: SUNY Press 1998).

– *On the Relation Between "Mode" and "Measure" in Hegel's* Science of Logic: *Some Introductory Remarks* 20 OWL OF MINERVA 20 (1988).

Feuerbach, Ludwig, *Towards a Critique of Hegel's Philosophy*, in THE FIERY BROOK: SELECTED WRITINGS OF LUDWIG FEUERBACH (Zawar Hanfi trans.) (New York: Anchor Books 1972).

FINK, BRUCE, THE LACANIAN SUBJECT: BETWEEN LANGUAGE AND *JOUISSANCE* (Princeton: Princeton University Press 1995).

Findlay, John N. , *Hegel and Whitehead on Nature*, in HEGEL AND WHITEHEAD: CONTEMPORARY PERSPECTIVES ON SYSTEMATIC PHILOSOPHY 161 (George R. Lucas, Jr., ed.) (Albany: SUNY Press 1986).

– *The Hegelian Treatment of Biology and Life*, in HEGEL IN THE SCIENCES (Robert S. Cohen & Marx W. Wartofsky) (Dordrecht: Kluwer 1984).

Fleischhacker, Louis, *Hegel on Mathematics and Experimental Science*, in HEGEL AND NEWTONIANISM (Michael John Petry ed.) (Dordrecht Kluwer 1993).

FLEISCHMANN, E.L., LA SCIENCE UNIVERSELLE OU LA LOGIQUE DE HEGEL (Paris: Plon 1968).

FORSTER, MICHAEL N., HEGEL AND SKEPTICISM ((Cambridge: Harvard University Press 1989).

GADAMER, HANS-GEORG, HEGEL'S DIALECTIC: FIVE HERMENEUTICAL STUDIES (Christopher Smith trans.) (Cambridge: Cambridge University Press 1976).

Garrison, James W., *Metaphysics and Scientific Proof: Newton and Hegel*, in HEGEL AND NEWTONIANISM (Michael John Petry ed.) (Dordrecht Kluwer 1993).

GASCHÉ, RODOLPHE, THE TAIN OF THE MIRROR: DERRIDA AND THE PHILOSOPHY OF REFLECTION (Cambridge: Harvard University Press 1986).

GOETHE, JOHANN WOLFGANG VON, ELECTIVE AFFINITIES (R.J. Hillingdale trans.) (London: Penguin 2003).

Goodrich, Peter, *Anti-Teubner: Autopoiesis, Paradox, and the Theory of Law*, 13 SOC. EPIST. 197 (1999).

Greene, Murray, *Hegel and the Problems of Atomism*, 11 INT'L STUD. PHIL. 123 (1979).

Grier, Philip T. *Abstract and Concrete in Hegel's Logic*, in ESSAYS ON HEGEL'S LOGIC (George di Giovanni ed.) (Albany: SUNY Press 1990).

HAAS^SANDREW, HEGEL AND THE PROBLEM OF MULTIPLICITY (Evanston: Northwestern University Press 2000).

HAMPSHIRE, STUART, SPINOZA (New York: Penguin 1951).

HARRIS, ERROL E., AN INTERPRETATION OF THE LOGIC OF HEGEL (Lanham, Md: University Press of America 1983).

– THE SPIRIT OF HEGEL (Atlantic Highlands, NJ: Humanities Press 1993).

Harris, H.S., *General Introduction*, in G.W.F. HEGEL, THE JENA SYSTEM, 1804-5: LOGIC AND METAPHYSICS (John W. Burbidge & George di Giovanni trans.) (Kingston: McGill-Queens University Press 1986).

HART, H.L.A., THE CONCEPT OF LAW (Oxford: Clarendon Press 1961).

HARTNACK, JUSTUS, AN INTRODUCTION TO HEGEL'S LOGIC (Lars Aagaard-Mogensen trans.) (Indianapolis: Hackett Publishing Co. 1998).

Henrich, Dieter, *Anfang und Methode der Logik*, in HEGEL IM CONTEXT (Frankfurt: Suhrkamp 1971).

HOFFMEYER, JOHN F., THE ADVENT OF FREEDOM: THE PRESENCE OF THE FUTURE IN HEGEL'S LOGIC (Madison, NJ: Fairleigh Dickenson University Press 1994).

HOFSTADTER, DOUGLAS R., GÖDEL, ESCHER, BACH: AN ETERNAL GOLDEN BRAID (New York: Basic Books 1979).

Houlgate, Stephen, *Hegel, Derrida, and Restricted Economy: The Case of Mechanical Memory*, 34 J. HIST. PHIL. 79 (1996).

– *Hegel's Critique of Foundationalism in the "Doctrine of Essence"*, GERMAN PHILOSOPHY SINCE KANT 27 (Anthony O'Hear ed.) ((Cambridge: Cambridge University Press 1999).

-THE OPENING OF HEGEL'S LOGIC: FROM BEING TO INFINITY (Purdue University Press 2006).

– *Why Hegel's Concept is not the Essence of Things*, in HEGEL'S THEORY OF THE SUBJECT (David Gray Carlson ed.) (London: Palgrave McMillan 2005).

HYPPOLITE, JEAN, GENESIS AND STRUCTURE OF HEGEL'S *PHENOMENOLOGY OF SPIRIT* (Samuel Cherniak & John Heckman trans.) (Evanston: Northwestern University Press 1974).

– FIGURES DE LA PENSÉE PHILOSOPHIQUE (Paris: Pans 1971).

– LOGIC AND EXISTENCE (Leonard Lawlor and Amit Sen trans.) (Albany: SUNY Press 1997).

INWOOD, M.J., HEGEL (London: Routledge: & Kegan Paul 1983).

Jacobson, Arthur J., *Hegel's Legal Plenum*, in HEGEL AND LEGAL THEORY (Drucilla Cornell et al. eds.) (New York: Routledge 1991).

KANT, IMMANUEL, CRITIQUE OF JUDGMENT (J.H. Bernhard trans.) (London: MacMillan 1951).

– CRITIQUE OF PRACTICAL REASON (T.K. Abbott trans.) (Chicago: University of Chicago Press 1996).

– CRITIQUE OF PURE REASON (Paul Guyer & Allen J. Wood) (Cambridge: Cambridge University Press 1998).

– LOGIC (Robert S. Hartman & Wolfgang Schwarz trans.) (Indianapolis: Bobbs-Merrill 1974).

– RELIGION WITHIN THE BOUNDARIES OF MERE REASON (Allen Wood & George Di Giovanni trans.) (Cambridge: Cambridge University Press 1998).

KAUFMANN, WALTER, HEGEL: A REINTERPRETATION (New York: Atherton Press 1978).

– *The Hegel Myth and Its Method*, in HEGEL: A COLLECTION OF CRITICAL ESSAYS (Alasdair MacIntyre, ed.) (Garden City, NY: Anchor Books 1972).

KAY, SARAH, ŽIŽEK: A CRITICAL INTRODUCTION (Cambridge: Polity Press 2003).

Kisner, Wendell, Erinnerung, Retrait, *Absolute Reflection: Hegel and Derrida*, 26 OWL OF MINERVA 171 (1995).

Knox, T.M., *The Puzzle of Hegel's Aesthetics*, in ART AND LOGIC IN HEGEL'S PHILOSOPHY (Warren Steinkraus & Kenneth I. Schmitz eds.) (Atlantic Highlands, NJ: Humanities Press 1980).

Kosok, Michael, *The Dynamics of Hegelian Dialectics, and Non-Linearity in the Sciences*, in HEGEL IN THE SCIENCES (Robert S. Cohen & Marx W. Wartofsky) ((Dordrecht: Kluwer 1984).

– *The Formalization of Hegel's Dialectical Logic: Its Formal Structure, Logical Interpretation and Intuitive Foundation*, in HEGEL: A COLLECTION OF CRITICAL ESSAYS (Alasdair MacIntyre, ed., 1972) (Garden City, NY: Anchor Books 1972)..

KYBURG, HENRY E., THEORY AND MEASUREMENT (Cambridge: Cambridge University Press 1984).

LACAN, JACQUES, LE SÉMINAIRE DE JACQUES LACAN, LIVRE XVII: L'ENVERS DE LA PSYCHANALYSE (Jacques-Alain Miller ed.) (Paris: Seuil 1991).

– THE FOUR FUNDAMENTAL CONCEPTS OF PSYCHO-ANALYSIS (Alan Sheridan trans.) (New York: Norton 1977).

Lacroix, Alain, *The Mathematical Infinite in Hegel*, 31 PHIL. FORUM 298 (2000).

Lamb, David, *Teleology: Kant and Hegel*, in HEGEL'S CRITIQUE OF KANT (Stephen Priest ed.) (Oxford: Oxford University Press 1987).

LAUER, QUENTIN, ESSAYS IN HEGELIAN DIALECTIC (New York: Fordham University Press 1977).

– HEGEL'S IDEA OF PHILOSOPHY (New York: Fordham University Press 1971).

Lefrow, Brian, *God and World in Hegel and Whitehead*, in HEGEL AND WHITEHEAD: CONTEMPORARY PERSPECTIVES ON SYSTEMATIC PHILOSOPHY (George R. Lucas, Jr.) (Albany: SUNY Press 1986).

Llewelyn, John, *A Point of Almost Absolute Proximity to Hegel*, in DECONSTRUCTION AND PHILOSOPHY: THE TEXTS OF JACQUES DERRIDA (John Sallis ed.) (Chicago: University of Chicago Press 1987).

LOCKE, JOHN, AN ESSAY CONCERNING HUMAN UNDERSTANDING (Oxford: Clarendon Press 1979).

Lucas, Hans-Christian, *Spinoza, Hegel, Whitehead: Substance, Subject and Superject*, in HEGEL AND WHITEHEAD: CONTEMPORARY PERSPECTIVES ON SYSTEMATIC PHILOSOPHY (George R. Lucas, Jr.) (Albany: SUNY Press 1986).

Macdonald, Iain, *The Concept and Its Double: Power and Powerlessness in Hegel's Subjective Logic*, in HEGEL'S THEORY OF THE SUBJECT (David Gray Carlson ed.) (London: Palgrave McMillan 2005).

MAGNUS, KATHLEEN DOW, HEGEL AND THE SYMBOLIC MEDIATION OF SPIRIT (Albany: SUNY Press 2001).

Maker, William, *Beginning*, in ESSAYS ON HEGEL'S LOGIC (George di Giovanni ed.) (Albany: SUNY Press 1990).

– *Hegel's Logic of Freedom*, in HEGEL'S THEORY OF THE SUBJECT (David Gray Carlson ed.) (London: Palgrave McMillan 2005).

– PHILOSOPHY WITHOUT FOUNDATIONS: RETHINKING HEGEL (Albany: SUNY Press 1994).

– *The Very Idea of Nature, or Why Hegel is Not an Idealist*, in HEGEL AND THE PHILOSOPHY OF NATURE (Stephen Houlgate ed.) (Albany: SUNY Press 1998).

MALABOU, CATHERINE, THE FUTURE OF HEGEL: PLASTICITY, TEMPORALITY AND DIALECTIC (Lisabeth During trans.) (New York: Routledge 2005).

Manser, Anthony, *On Becoming*, in HEGEL AND MODERN PHILOSOPHY (David Lamb ed.) (London: Croom Helm, Ltd. 1987).

MARCUSE, HERBERT, HEGEL'S ONTOLOGY AND THE THEORY OF HISTORICITY (Seyla Benhabib trans.) (Cambridge: MIT Press 1987).

– REASON AND REVOLUTION (Atlantic Highlands, NJ: Humanities Press 1999).

MARX, KARL, CAPITAL (Samuel Moore & Edward Aveling trans.) (New York: International Publishers 1967).

MCCUMBER, JOHN, THE COMPANY OF WORDS: HEGEL, LANGUAGE AND SYSTEMATIC PHILOSOPHY (Evanston: Northwestern University Press 1993).

MERLEAU-PONTY, MAURICE, SENSE AND NON-SENSE (Hubert Dreyfus & Patricia Allen Dreyfus trans.) (Evanston: Northwestern University Press 1985).

Miller, Arnold Vincent, *Defending Hegel's Philosophy of Nature*, in HEGEL AND NEWTONIANISM (Michael John Petry ed.) (Dordrecht Kluwer 1993).

Moretto, Antonio, *Hegel on Greek Mathematics and the Modern Calculus*, in HEGEL AND NEWTONIANISM (Michael John Petry ed.) (Dordrecht Kluwer 1993).

MURE, G.R.G., A STUDY OF HEGEL'S LOGIC (Oxford: Oxford University Press 1950).

– THE PHILOSOPHY OF HEGEL (Oxford: Oxford University Press 1965).

NANCY, JEAN-LUC, HEGEL: THE RESTLESSNESS OF THE NEGATIVE (Jason Smith & Steven Miller eds.) (Minneapolis: University of Minnesota Press 1997).

NASH, WALTER, RHETORIC: THE WIT OF PERSUASION (Oxford: Blackwell 1989).

Nuzzo, Angelica, *The End of Hegel's Logic: Absolute Idea as Absolute Method*, in HEGEL'S THEORY OF THE SUBJECT (David Gray Carlson ed.) (London: Palgrave McMillan 2005).

Paolucci, Henry, *Hegel and the Celestial Mechanics of Newton and Einstein*, in HEGEL IN THE SCIENCES 55 (Robert S. Cohen & Marx W. Wartofsky) (Dordrecht: Kluwer 1984).

Pater, Cees de, *Newton and Eighteenth-Century Conceptions of Chemical Affinity*, in HEGEL AND NEWTONIANISM (Michael John Petry ed.) (Dordrecht Kluwer 1993).

Paterson, Alan L.T., *Does Hegel Have Anything to Say to Modern Mathematical Philosophy?* (2002) (unpublished manuscript).

– *The Successor Function and Induction Principle in a Hegelian Philosophy of Mathematics*, 30 IDEALISTIC STUDIES 25 (2002).

Petry, Michael John, *The Significance of Kepler's Laws*, in HEGEL AND NEWTONIANISM (Michael John Petry ed.) (Dordrecht Kluwer 1993).

PINKARD, TERRY, HEGEL: A BIOGRAPHY (Cambridge: Cambridge University Press 2000).

– HEGEL'S DIALECTIC (Evanston: Northwestern University Press 1988).

– *Hegel's Philosophy of Mathematics*, 41 PHIL. & PHENOMENOGICAL RES. 453 (1980-1).

PIPPIN, ROBERT B., HEGEL'S IDEALISM: THE SATISFACTIONS OF SELF-CONSCIOUSNESS (Cambridge: Cambridge University Press 1989).

– KANT'S THEORY OF FORM: AN ESSAY ON THE *CRITIQUE OF PURE REASON* (Cambridge: Cambridge University Press 1982).

PLOTNITSKY, ARKADY, IN THE SHADOW OF HEGEL: COMPLEMENTARITY, HISTORY, AND THE UNCONSCIOUS (Gainesville: University Press of Florida 1993).

POPPER, KARL R., THE LOGIC OF SCIENTIFIC DISCOVERY (New York: Basic Books 1986).

POTTER, MICHAEL, SET THEORY AND ITS PHILOSOPHY (Oxford: Oxford University Press 2004).

– THE OPEN SOCIETY AND ITS ENEMIES (New York: Routledge 1971).

RAWLS, JOHN, A THEORY OF JUSTICE (Cambridge: Harvard University Press 1971).

REICH, KLAUS, THE COMPLETENESS OF KANT'S TABLE OF JUDGMENTS (Jane Kneller & Michael Losonsky trans. 1992).

RINALDI, GIACOMO, A HISTORY AND INTERPRETATION OF THE LOGIC OF HEGEL (Lewiston, NY: Edwin Mellen Press 1992).

Rockmore, Tom, *Foundationalism and Hegelian Logic*, 21 OWL OF MINERVA 40 (1989).

– HEGEL'S CIRCULAR EPISTEMOLOGY (Bloomington: University of Indian Press 1986).

– ON HEGEL'S EPISTEMOLOGY AND CONTEMPORARY PHILOSOPHY (1996).

RORTY, RICHARD, CONSEQUENCES OF PRAGMATISM (Amherst: Prometheus Press 1982).

ROSE, LYNN E., ARISTOTLE'S SYLLOGISTIC (Springfield: Clarence C. Thomas 1968).

ROSEN, MICHAEL, HEGEL'S DIALECTIC AND ITS CRITICISM (Cambridge: Cambridge University Press 1982).

ROSEN, STANLEY, G.W.F. HEGEL: AN INTRODUCTION TO THE SCIENCE OF WISDOM (New Haven: Yale University Press 1974).

Ruschig, Ulrich, *Logic and Chemistry in Hegel's Philosophy*, 7 INT'L J. PHIL. CHEMISTRY 5 (2001).

RUSSELL, BERTRAND, A CRITICAL EXPOSITION OF THE PHILOSOPHY OF LEIBNIZ (New York: Routledge 1992).

– *Introduction*, in A.V. VAILIEV, SPACE, TIME, AND MOTION (New York: Alfred A. Knopf 1924).

– *Logical Positivism*, in LOGIC AND KNOWLEDGE: ESSAYS 1902-1950 (Robert Charles Marsh ed.) (London: MacMillan 1950).

Sedgwick, Sally S., *Hegel's Treatment of Transcendental Apperception in Kant*, 23 OWL OF MINERVA 151 (1992).

Schroeder, Jeanne L. & David Gray Carlson, *Kenneth Starr: Diabolically Evil?*, 88 CAL. L. REV. 653 (2000).

– *The Appearance of Right and the Essence of Wrong*, 25 CARDOZO L. REV. 2481 (2003).

Schroeder, Jeanne L., *Never Jam Today: On the Impossibility of Takings Jurisprudence*, 84 GEO. L.J. 1531 (1996).

– *Pandora's Amphora: The Ambiguity of Gift*, 46 UCLA L. REV. 815 (1999).

– *The Lacanomics of Apples and Oranges: A Speculative Account of the Economic Concept of Commensurabillity*, 15 YALE J. L. & HUMANITIES 347 (2003).

– *The Stumbling Block: Freedom, Rationality and Legal Scholarship*, 44 WM. & MARY L. REV. 263 (2002).

– THE TRIUMPH OF VENUS: THE EROTICS OF THE MARKET (Berkeley: University of California Press 2004).

– THE VESTAL AND THE FASCES: HEGEL, LACAN, PROPERTY, AND THE FEMININE (Berkeley: University of California Press 1998).

Snelders, H.A.M., *The Significance of Hegel's Treatment of Chemical Affinity*, in HEGEL AND NEWTONIANISM (Michael John Petry ed.) , 1993).

SIMPSON, PETER, HEGEL'S TRANSCENDENTAL INDUCTION (Albany: SUNY Press 1998).

Singer, Peter, *Hegel*, in GERMAN PHILOSOPHERS (Oxford: Oxford University Press 1997).

SPINOZA'S SHORT TREATISE ON GOD, MAN, AND HIS WELL-BEING (A. Wolf trans.) (London: Adam & Charles Black 1910).

SPINOZA, CHIEF WORKS OF SPINOZA 370 (R.H.M. Elwes ed.) (New York: Dover 1955).

Stepelevich, Lawrence S., *Hegel's Conception of Space*, 1 NATURE AND SYSTEM 111 (1979).

– *Hegel's Geometric Theory*, in HEGEL AND THE PHILOSOPHY OF NATURE (Stephen Houlgate ed.) (Albany: SUNY Press 1998).

TAYLOR, CHARLES, HEGEL (Cambridge: Cambridge University Press 1975).

Verene, Donald Phillip, *Hegel's Nature*, in HEGEL AND THE PHILOSOPHY OF NATURE (Stephen Houlgate ed.) (Albany: SUNY Press 1998).

Wahsner, Renate, *The Philosophical Background to Hegel's Criticism of Newton*, in HEGEL AND NEWTONIANISM (Michael John Petry ed.) (Dordrecht: Kluwer 1993).

WALLACE, ROBERT M., HEGEL'S PHILOSOPHY OF REALITY, FREEDOM AND GOD (Cambridge: Cambridge University Press 2005).

– *Hegel's Refutation of Rational Egoism in True Infinity and the Idea*, in HEGEL'S THEORY OF THE SUBJECT (David Gray Carlson ed.) (London: Palgrave McMillan 2005).

Walsh, W.H., *Kant as Seen by Hegel*, in HEGEL'S CRITIQUE OF KANT (Stephen Priest ed.) (Oxford: Oxford University Press 1987).

Wartenberg, Thomas E., *Hegel's Idealism: The Logic of Conceptuality*, in THE CAMBRIDGE COMPANION TO HEGEL (Frederick C. Beiser ed. 1993).

WESTPHAL, KENNETH R., HEGEL'S EPISTEMOLOGICAL REALISM: A STUDY OF THE AIM AND METHOD OF HEGEL'S *Phenomenology of Spirit* (Dordrecht: Kluwer 1989).

Willett, Cynthia, *The Shadow of Hegel's* Science of Logic, in ESSAYS ON HEGEL'S LOGIC, in ESSAYS ON HEGEL'S LOGIC (George di Giovanni ed.) (Albany: SUNY Press 1990).

WINFIELD, RICHARD DIEN, AUTONOMY AND NORMATIVITY (Aldershot: Ashgate Publishing Group 2001).

– *From Concept to Judgement: Rethinking Hegel's Overcoming of Formal Logic*, 50 DIALOGUE 53 (2001).

– OVERCOMING FOUNDATIONS: STUDIES IN SYSTEMATIC PHILOSOPHY (New York: Columbia University Press 1989).

– *The System of Syllogism*, in HEGEL'S THEORY OF THE SUBJECT (David Gray Carlson ed.) (London: Palgrave McMillan 2005).

– *The Types of Universals and the Forms of Judgment*, in HEGEL'S THEORY OF THE SUBJECT (2005).

– *The Method of Hegel's* Science of Logic, in ESSAYS ON HEGEL'S LOGIC (George di Giovanni ed.) (Albany: SUNY Press 1990).

Wolf-Gazo, Ernest, *Negation and Contrast: The Origins of Self-Consciousness in Hegel and Whitehead*, in HEGEL AND WHITEHEAD: CONTEMPORARY PERSPECTIVES ON SYSTEMATIC PHILOSOPHY (George R. Lucas, Jr.) (Albany: SUNY Press 1986).

Wolff, Michael, *On Hegel's Doctrine of Contradiction*, 31 OWL OF MINERVA (1999).

WOLFSON, HARRY AUSTRYN, THE PHILOSOPHY OF SPINOZA: UNFOLDING THE LATENT PROCESSES OF HIS REASONING (Cambridge: Harvard University Press 1934).

WOOD, ALLEN W., HEGEL'S ETHICAL THOUGHT (Cambridge: Cambridge University Press 1990).

ŽIŽEK, SLAVOJ, FOR THEY KNOW NOT WHAT THEY DO: ENJOYMENT AS A POLITICAL FACTOR (London: Verso 1991).

– ON BELIEF (2001).

– TARRYING WITH THE NEGATIVE: KANT, HEGEL, AND THE CRITIQUE OF IDEOLOGY (Durham: Duke University Press 1993).

– THE FRAGILE ABSOLUTE – OR, WHY IS THE CHRISTIAN LEGACY WORTH FIGHTING FOR? (London: Verso 2000).

– THE INDIVISIBLE REMAINDER: AN ESSAY ON SCHELLING AND RELATED MATTERS (London: Verso 1996).

– THE METASTASES OF ENJOYMENT: SIX ESSAYS ON WOMAN AND CAUSALITY (London: Verso 1993).

– THE PLAGUE OF FANTASIES (London: Verso 1997).

– THE PUPPET AND THE DWARF: THE PERVERSE CORE OF CHRISTIANITY (Cambridge: MIT Press 2003).

– THE SUBLIME OBJECT OF IDEOLOGY (London: Verso 1991).

– THE TICKLISH SUBJECT: THE ABSENT CENTRE OF POLITICAL ONTOLOGY (London: Verso 1999).

Index

Appendix: The Steps of the Logic

References are to the Figures that illustrate the logical steps and the pages on which they occur